T0207362

Lecture Notes in Computer Science

Lecture Notes in Artificial Intelligence   14273

Founding Editor

Jörg Siekmann

Series Editors

Randy Goebel, *University of Alberta, Edmonton, Canada*
Wolfgang Wahlster, *DFKI, Berlin, Germany*
Zhi-Hua Zhou, *Nanjing University, Nanjing, China*

The series Lecture Notes in Artificial Intelligence (LNAI) was established in 1988 as a topical subseries of LNCS devoted to artificial intelligence.

The series publishes state-of-the-art research results at a high level. As with the LNCS mother series, the mission of the series is to serve the international R & D community by providing an invaluable service, mainly focused on the publication of conference and workshop proceedings and postproceedings.

Huayong Yang · Honghai Liu · Jun Zou ·
Zhouping Yin · Lianqing Liu · Geng Yang ·
Xiaoping Ouyang · Zhiyong Wang
Editors

Intelligent Robotics and Applications

16th International Conference, ICIRA 2023
Hangzhou, China, July 5–7, 2023
Proceedings, Part VII

 Springer

Editors
Huayong Yang
Zhejiang University
Hangzhou, China

Jun Zou (iD)
Zhejiang University
Hangzhou, China

Lianqing Liu (iD)
Shenyang Institute of Automation
Shenyang, Liaoning, China

Xiaoping Ouyang (iD)
Zhejiang University
Hangzhou, China

Honghai Liu (iD)
Harbin Institute of Technology
Shenzhen, China

Zhouping Yin
Huazhong University of Science
and Technology
Wuhan, China

Geng Yang (iD)
Zhejiang University
Hangzhou, China

Zhiyong Wang
Harbin Institute of Technology
Shenzhen, China

ISSN 0302-9743   ISSN 1611-3349 (electronic)
Lecture Notes in Artificial Intelligence
ISBN 978-981-99-6497-0   ISBN 978-981-99-6498-7 (eBook)
https://doi.org/10.1007/978-981-99-6498-7

LNCS Sublibrary: SL7 – Artificial Intelligence

This Springer imprint is published by the registered company Springer Nature Singapore Pte Ltd.
The registered company address is: 152 Beach Road, #21-01/04 Gateway East, Singapore 189721, Singapore

Paper in this product is recyclable.

Preface

With the theme "Smart Robotics for Sustainable Society", the 16th International Conference on Intelligent Robotics and Applications (ICIRA 2023) was held in Hangzhou, China, July 5–7, 2023, and designed to encourage advancement in the field of robotics, automation, mechatronics, and applications. It aimed to promote top-level research and globalize quality research in general, making discussions and presentations more internationally competitive and focusing on the latest outstanding achievements, future trends, and demands.

ICIRA 2023 was organized and hosted by Zhejiang University, co-hosted by Harbin Institute of Technology, Huazhong University of Science and Technology, Chinese Academy of Sciences, and Shanghai Jiao Tong University, co-organized by State Key Laboratory of Fluid Power and Mechatronic Systems, State Key Laboratory of Robotics and System, State Key Laboratory of Digital Manufacturing Equipment and Technology, State Key Laboratory of Mechanical System and Vibration, State Key Laboratory of Robotics, and School of Mechanical Engineering of Zhejiang University. Also, ICIRA 2023 was technically co-sponsored by Springer. On this occasion, ICIRA 2023 was a successful event after the COVID-19 pandemic. It attracted more than 630 submissions, and the Program Committee undertook a rigorous review process for selecting the most deserving research for publication. The Advisory Committee gave advice for the conference program. Also, they help to organize special sections for ICIRA 2023. Finally, a total of 431 papers were selected for publication in 9 volumes of Springer's Lecture Note in Artificial Intelligence. For the review process, single-blind peer review was used. Each review took around 2–3 weeks, and each submission received at least 2 reviews and 1 meta-review.

In ICIRA 2023, 12 distinguished plenary speakers delivered their outstanding research works in various fields of robotics. Participants gave a total of 214 oral presentations and 197 poster presentations, enjoying this excellent opportunity to share their latest research findings. Here, we would like to express our sincere appreciation to all the authors, participants, and distinguished plenary and keynote speakers. Special thanks are also extended to all members of the Organizing Committee, all reviewers for peer-review, all staffs of the conference affairs group, and all volunteers for their diligent work.

July 2023

Huayong Yang
Honghai Liu
Jun Zou
Zhouping Yin
Lianqing Liu
Geng Yang
Xiaoping Ouyang
Zhiyong Wang

Organization

Conference Chair

Huayong Yang   Zhejiang University, China

Honorary Chairs

Youlun Xiong   Huazhong University of Science and Technology, China

Han Ding   Huazhong University of Science and Technology, China

General Chairs

Honghai Liu   Harbin Institute of Technology, China

Jun Zou   Zhejiang University, China

Zhouping Yin   Huazhong University of Science and Technology, China

Lianqing Liu   Chinese Academy of Sciences, China

Program Chairs

Geng Yang   Zhejiang University, China

Li Jiang   Harbin Institute of Technology, China

Guoying Gu   Shanghai Jiao Tong University, China

Xinyu Wu   Chinese Academy of Sciences, China

Award Committee Chair

Yong Lei   Zhejiang University, China

Publication Chairs

Xiaoping Ouyang   Zhejiang University, China
Zhiyong Wang   Harbin Institute of Technology, China

Regional Chairs

Zhiyong Chen   University of Newcastle, Australia
Naoyuki Kubota   Tokyo Metropolitan University, Japan
Zhaojie Ju   University of Portsmouth, UK
Eric Perreault   Northeastern University, USA
Peter Xu   University of Auckland, New Zealand
Simon Yang   University of Guelph, Canada
Houxiang Zhang   Norwegian University of Science and Technology,
                         Norway
Duanling Li   Beijing University of Posts and
                         Telecommunications, China

Advisory Committee

Jorge Angeles   McGill University, Canada
Tamio Arai   University of Tokyo, Japan
Hegao Cai   Harbin Institute of Technology, China
Tianyou Chai   Northeastern University, China
Jiansheng Dai   King's College London, UK
Zongquan Deng   Harbin Institute of Technology, China
Han Ding   Huazhong University of Science and Technology,
                         China
Xilun Ding   Beihang University, China
Baoyan Duan   Xidian University, China
Xisheng Feng   Shenyang Institute of Automation, Chinese
                         Academy of Sciences, China
Toshio Fukuda   Nagoya University, Japan
Jianda Han   Nankai University, China
Qiang Huang   Beijing Institute of Technology, China
Oussama Khatib   Stanford University, USA
Yinan Lai   National Natural Science Foundation of China,
                         China
Jangmyung Lee   Pusan National University, Korea
Zhongqin Lin   Shanghai Jiao Tong University, China

Dou Cui
Hongbin Hu
Shigan Ma
Dahua Qi
Min Lin

Kevin Wa...
Guohua Wa...

Chunhua Wang
Tiexiang Wang

Yuebao Wang

Bogdan M. Wilamowski
Min Xie
Pingchuan Xu
Huayou Yang
Jie Zhao
Wenxing Zhang
Xingming Zhu

Harbin Institute of Technology, China
University of Portsmouth, UK
Kumamoto University, Japan
Smart Robot and Automation Lab, China
Institute of Automation, Chinese Academy of
  Sciences, China
Coventry University, UK
National Natural Science Foundation of China,
  China
Beijing University, China
Shenyang Institute of Automation, Chinese
  Academy of Sciences, China
Shenyang Institute of Automation, Chinese
  Academy of Sciences, China
Auburn University, USA
Nanyang Technological University, Singapore
Chinese University of Hong Kong, China
Chongqing University, China
Harbin Institute of Technology, China
Xi'an Jiaotong University, China
Shanghai Jiao Tong University, China

Contents – Part VII

Marine Robotics and Applications

Multi-robot Systems for Real World Applications

Physical and Neurological Human-Robot Interaction

Visual and Visual-Tactile Perception for Robotics

6D Pose Estimation Method of Metal Parts for Robotic Grasping Based on Semantic-Level Line Matching

Ze'an Liu$^{(\boxtimes)}$, Zhenguo Wu, Bin Pu, Jixiang Tang, and Xuanyin Wang

State Key Laboratory of Fluid Power and Mechatronic Systems, Zhejiang University, Hangzhou, China
12025014@zju.edu.cn

Abstract. The six-dimensional (6D) pose estimation of metal parts is a key technology for robotic grasping in intelligent manufacturing. However, current methods matching edge or geometric features suffer from unstable feature extraction results, which result in low robustness and unsatisfactory accuracy. In this paper, we propose a 6D pose estimation method based on semantic-level line matching. The proposed method uses a line detection network to replace the low-level feature extraction methods and fetch semantic-level line features. After filtered by a segmentation network, the features are utilized to generate object-level line descriptors for representing metal parts. The 2D-3D correspondences are achieved by matching descriptors in a sparse template set. Finally, 6D pose estimation of metal parts is completed by solving the PnP problem. Experimental results show that the proposed method achieves higher accuracy compared with existing methods on the Mono-6D dataset.

Keywords: Pose estimation · Line feature · Metal part · Sparse templates

1 Introduction

Robotic grasping is a fundamental and important ability of robots in intelligent manufacturing [1]. In the industrial field, the object of robotic grasping is usually metal part. Traditional demonstrative robots accomplish grasping tasks through human-preprogrammed procedures, which is difficult for the robots to adapt to changing environments. Thus, it's essential for intelligent robots to perceive metal parts and achieve automatic grasping. The key of automatic grasping is to get the six-dimensional (6D) pose of the metal part i.e., three-dimensional rotation and three-dimensional translation relative to the camera on robot. Vision is the main way for human to identity and observer the world, which can also provide the ability of 6D pose estimation for robots. By recognizing the 6D pose of a metal part via visual sensors, the robot can perceive and process the part in an unfamiliar environment and thus enhancing its adaptability in vary environments.

H. Yang et al. (Eds.): ICIRA 2023, LNAI 14273, pp. 3–13, 2023.
https://doi.org/10.1007/978-981-99-6498-7_1

Depending on the input format, the 6D pose estimation methods can be classified into RGB based methods and RGB-D based methods [1–3]. In the field of industry, most of the metal parts are texture-less objects with strong specular reflection characteristics. Since specular reflection regions lead to serious data loss in the acquired depth images, the RGB-D based methods usually yield poor results for metal parts. By contrast, the RGB based methods only require a single RGB image to estimate the 6D pose, which precludes data loss problem. Therefore, the RGB based methods are more suitable for the application in the actual industrial scenes.

The edge feature [4,5] in an RGB image is an important feature for identifying texture-less metal parts. Some methods [6–8] complete the pose estimation based on edge feature matching. Liu et al. [6] propose Fast Directional Chamfer Matching (FDCM) scheme to compute the minimum directional chamfer distance using edge features. This distance is utilized to match templates, and the pose of the best-matched template is considered as the estimated 6D pose. To further enhance the accuracy of the pose, the Direct Directional Chamfer Optimization method (D^2CO) [7] incorporates an optimization function into the process of FDCM which makes a better result. However, since the number of templates cannot be increased limitlessly, the poses of templates may not cover all conditions, resulting in poor pose estimation accuracy.

To address this issue, several methods based on geometric feature matching [9–11] have been proposed. For instance, Yang's method [11] detect low-level features of both templates and real images. The low-level features are constructed into high-level geometric features for matching to obtain 2D-3D mapping relations. The PnP problem is then solved to achieve pose estimation. This type of method requires only a limited number of templates to maintain the precision in 2D-3D mapping and achieve superior pose estimation results.

These two types of methods fundamentally rely on low-level features. However, the extraction of low-level features is susceptible to fluctuations during environmental changes, such as modifications in lighting conditions, which can influence matching results and result in poor pose estimation accuracy.

In this paper, we propose a method for 6D pose estimation of metal parts with semantic-level line matching. Different from existing methods based on low-level features, the proposed method is based on semantic-level line features. These features refer to objects with a semantic of line segment in the image. Our method identifies semantic-level line features with a line detection network and incorporates a segmentation network to extract object-level line descriptors. By matching the descriptors in a sparse template set, the 2D-3D mapping from the real image to the model of the metal part is realized. The precise 6D pose of the metal part is finally obtained by solving the PnP problem.

2   Method

2.1   Method Framework

As shown in Fig. 1, the entire method flow is mainly composed of detection network, object-level line descriptor extraction, multi-view template generation, descriptor matching and pose estimation. The detection network includes a line detection network and a segmentation network. The line detection network is used to detect semantic-level line features in real image and template images. The segmentation network is utilized to generate the mask of the metal part and refine the line features in the real image. Object-level line descriptor extraction synthesize the semantic-level line features into descriptors. Multi-view template generation extracts object-level line descriptors from template images of different views, resulting in a comprehensive multi-view template. Finally, the multi-view template is matched with the object-level line descriptor of the real image to realize the 2D-2D mapping. Through the relation between the 2D coordinates of the matched template image and the 3D coordinates of the model of metal part, the 2D-3D mapping between the real image and the model is realized. The PnP problem is solved to attain accurate pose estimation.

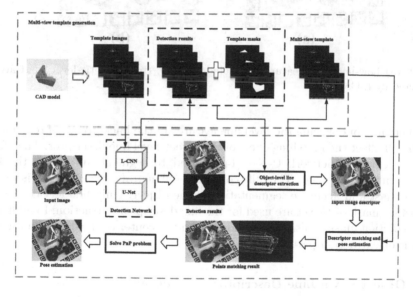

Fig. 1. The overall process of the proposed method.

2.2   Detection Network

The core of the detection network is the line detection network L-CNN [12], which realizes semantic-level line features detection through the uniquely designed feature extraction backbone, junction proposal module, line sample module, and

6   Z. Liu et al.

line verification network. As shown in Fig. 2, semantic-level line feature is similar
with low-level line feature, mainly composed of straight line and two endpoints.
However, the semantic-level line feature implies semantic information of line segment. Compared to the LSD algorithm [13] used in Yang's method [11] and He's
method [10], the L-CNN network can achieve better detection results under illumination changes and complex scenes. At the same time, L-CNN benefits from
the characteristics of semantic-level prediction, and the prediction of line segments is more in line with human cognition in Fig. 2. Thus, the L-CNN can map
real image and template image to the semantic-level line feature space, thereby
eliminating the difference between real and virtual environments and improving
reliability of subsequent pose estimation.

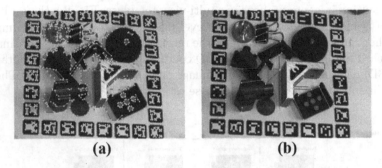

Fig. 2. (a) Low-level line features extracted by LSD. (b) Semantic-level line features
extracted by L-CNN.

There are lots of semantic-level line features in the background of real image,
which will affect the matching effect of the object-level line descriptor. Therefore,
the segmentation network U-Net [14] is used to segment and refine the line
features in the real image. The fully convolutional neural network U-Net is widely
used for fast and accurate segmentation of the object. Only line features in the
prediction mask of U-Net are used for the line descriptor extraction. In addition,
the prediction mask is also utilized to confirm the center of the object in the line
descriptor extraction part.

2.3   Object-Level Line Descriptor Extraction

After the detection and refinement of semantic-level line features are completed,
it becomes essential to utilize a suitable method for describing all line features
in the image to aid in subsequent matching. Inspired by the BOLD operator [5],
we propose an object-level line descriptor to describe each line feature related
to the object. In order to ensure the rotation invariance and scale invariance of
the description, each line feature is described based on its relative angles to its
neighbors as shown in Fig. 3.

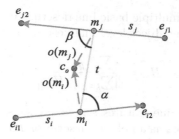

Fig. 3. The relative angles between neighboring line features.

For each pair of line features s_i and s_j, m_i and m_j correspond to the midpoints of the line features, while e_{i1}, e_{i2} and e_{j1}, e_{j2} indicate the two endpoints of s_i and s_j, respectively. To ensure rotation invariance, each line feature must define its direction. According to the mask of object, we can get the maximum bounding box of the object. The vector from the midpoint m_i to the center c_o of the maximum bounding box is denoted as $o(m_i)$. The direction of the line feature can be determined using the following expression:

$$sign\,(s_i) = \frac{(e_{i2} - e_{i1}) \times o(m_i))}{\|\,(e_{i2} - e_{i1}) \times o(m_i)\|} \bullet n \tag{1}$$

where $\bullet$ is the dot product, $\times$ is the cross product. When $sign\,(s_i) = 1$, $s_i = e_{i2} - e_{i1}$, otherwise, $s_i = e_{i1} - e_{i2}$. n is the unit vector to the image plane pointing towards the observer.

We set the vector between m_i and m_j as t, and $t_{ij} = m_j - m_i$, $t_{ji} = m_i - m_j$. The relative angles between t and s_i, s_j can be described as:

$$\alpha = \begin{cases} arccos\left(\frac{s_i \bullet t_{ij}}{\|s_i\|\|t_{ij}\|}\right) & if \;\; \frac{s_i \times t_{ij}}{\|s_i \times t_{ij}\|} \bullet n = 1 \\ 2\pi - arccos\left(\frac{s_i \bullet t_{ij}}{\|s_i\|\|t_{ij}\|}\right) & otherwise \end{cases} \tag{2}$$

$$\beta = \begin{cases} arccos\left(\frac{s_j \bullet t_{ji}}{\|s_j\|\|t_{ji}\|}\right) & if \;\; \frac{s_j \times t_{ji}}{\|s_j \times t_{ji}\|} \bullet n = 1 \\ 2\pi - arccos\left(\frac{s_j \bullet t_{ji}}{\|s_j\|\|t_{ji}\|}\right) & otherwise \end{cases} \tag{3}$$

which yields α and β measurements within the range $[0, 2\pi]$. The line feature s_i and its k nearest neighbor line features generate k pairs of α and β. The angles are quantized to $\frac{2\pi}{\theta}$ bins with a quantization step of θ.

Considering that quantizing α and β generates quantization errors, we adopt a bilinear interpolation approach to allocate weights to quantized α and β. We refer (α, β) to a 2-D coordinate. Each pair of (α, β) generates weights on 4 nearest bins according to the distance between (α, β) and the 4 nearest bins. The weights are accumulated into a 2-D histogram $H_{s_i}^k$ which is a basic line descriptor. In order to enhance the robustness of basic line descriptor, we use different k namely $k_{set} = [k_1, k_2, k_3, \ldots]$ to generate multiple basic line descriptors $H_{s_i}^{k_{set}} =$

$[H_{s_i}^{k_1}, H_{s_i}^{k_2}, H_{s_i}^{k_3}, \ldots]$. The multiple basic line descriptors are accumulated and L2 normalized to generate the object-level line descriptor H_{s_i}.

$$H_{s_i} = \frac{\sum_{k \in k_{set}} H_{s_i}^k}{\left\| \sum_{k \in k_{set}} H_{s_i}^k \right\|_2} \tag{4}$$

For all semantic-level line features $s_{set} = [s_1, s_2, s_3, \ldots]$ in an image I, we combine all line descriptors as an object descriptor $H_I = [H_{s_1}, H_{s_2}, H_{s_3}, \ldots]$.

2.4   Multi-view Template Generation

In order to achieve stable 2D-2D mapping from real image to template image, we need to prepare multiple template images from different perspectives and generate object-level line descriptor for each template image. Considering the rotation invariance and scale invariance of the object-level line descriptor, the number of template images need not be excessive. Thus, we use the Fibonacci grid method as Eq. 5 to generate uniform viewpoints which are distributed over a hemisphere surrounding the model according to Fig. 4.

$$\begin{cases} \phi = \frac{\sqrt{5}-1}{2} \\ z_i = \frac{i}{n} \\ x_i = \sqrt{1 - z_i^2} \bullet \cos(2\pi i \phi) \\ y_i = \sqrt{1 - z_i^2} \bullet \sin(2\pi i \phi) \end{cases} \tag{5}$$

where n is the number of viewpoint, i is the viewpoint index.

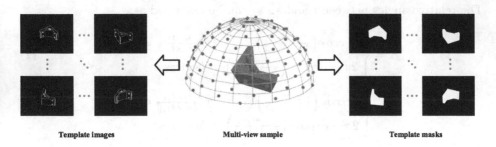

Template images   Multi-view sample   Template masks

Fig. 4. The process of multi-view sample.

In order to weaken the interference of simulated lighting, we utilize the contour image of the model as the template image. The contour image is generated with the method proposed by Ulrich [15]. In the template image, each pixel correspond to a 3D normal vector in model space. If the maximum angle between the 3D normal vector of pixel p and the 3D normal vectors of the eight-neighborhood of pixel p exceeds the threshold, the pixel p is a contour pixel. The final template image only contains the edge of the object.

$$\begin{cases} \delta = 2\sin\left(\frac{\varphi}{2}\right) \\ M_p = \max_{p' \in Nei8(p)} \left(|n\left(p\right) - n\left(p'\right)|\right) \end{cases} \quad (6)$$

where φ is the angle between the normal vectors, δ is the threshold, $n\left(p\right)$ is the 3D normal vector of the pixel p.

In each viewpoint, the template image T_i and mask image M_i are obtained with a special pose of the object as shown in Fig. 4. For the template image T_i in each viewpoint, we directly detect the semantic-level line features through the L-CNN in the detection network part. The results combine the mask image M_i to extract the object descriptor $H_I^{T_i}$. The multi-view template $H_I^{T_{set}}$ is generated from the object descriptors of all template images T_{set}.

2.5 Descriptor Matching and Pose Estimation

We match the object descriptor H_I^R extracted from real image with each object descriptor $H_I^{T_i}$ in the multi-view template $H_I^{T_{set}}$. We use the L2 norm to judge the distance between the two object descriptors, and select the line descriptor $H_{s_k}^{T_i}$ in $H_I^{T_i}$ with the smallest distance from $H_{s_i}^R$ in H_I^R as the matching line descriptor. When the line descriptors are matched, the semantic-level line feature s_i in the real image and s_k in the template image T_i are also matched.

$$H_{s_k}^{T_i} = \operatorname{argmin}_{s_j \in s_{set}^{T_i}} \left\| H_{s_i}^R - H_{s_j}^{T_i} \right\|_2 \quad (7)$$

The distance between each pair of matching line descriptors is recorded. For each template image, take the mean value of distances of all line descriptors as the difference D_{RT_i} between H_I^R and $H_I^{T_i}$.

$$D_{RT_i} = \operatorname{mean}_{s_i \in s_{set}^R} \left\| H_{s_i}^R - H_{s_k}^{T_i} \right\|_2 \quad (8)$$

We calculate the difference value D_{RT_i} for each template and select the first five templates with the smallest D_{RT_i} as candidate templates. Next, we match the endpoints of the corresponding semantic-level line features and complete the 2D-2D mapping from the real image to the template image. We have recorded the depth of each pixel when the template image is generated. The 2D pixel coordinates of the template image can be transformed to 3D coordinates in the model space with the depth and camera intrinsic matrix. Then the 2D-3D mapping from the matched pixels in the real image to the 3D points of the model is completed. Since there are still some wrong matching results, the RANSAC-based EPnP algorithm in OpenCV is used for each candidate template to solve the PnP problem and get the pose estimation. Some outliers are removed by the RANSAC scheme to make the estimation more accuracy. Finally, we select the pose generated by the candidate template with the smallest reprojection error as the final 6D pose T of the metal part.

3 Experiment

3.1 Experiment Setting

In the experiment, all algorithms are completed through OpenGL, OpenCV, and Numpy based on Python3.7. The L-CNN and U-Net of the detection network part are implemented on the public code, using the Pytorch 1.8.1 framework. An RTX-3090 GPU and an Intel Core i7 10700KF 3.8GHz CPU are used for the experiment.

We evaluate the accuracy of our method on the MONO-6D dataset [16], which comprises various metal parts with different poses. For each metal part, there are about 500 images with a resolution of 640×480. Each image contains a complex background, and the metal part is occluded in some images. We divide the dataset into a training set and a test set in an 8:2 ratio. The training set is only used for training U-Net. And we don't train L-CNN instead of using the pretrained weights. The final accuracy results are all evaluated on the test set. In terms of hyperparameters, our method uses 100 templates, and the quantization angle θ for α and β is $\frac{\pi}{12}$.

3.2 Estimation Accuracy

Since these metal parts are all symmetrical objects, we use the ADD-S metric [17] to evaluate the accuracy of pose estimation. In this metric, the model points of metal part are transformed by the estimated pose and the ground-truth pose, and the mean distance of the closet points between the two transformed point sets is calculated. When the mean distance is less than 10% of the model radius, the estimated pose is correct.

We first evaluate the influence of k_{set}. The k_{set} influences the robustness of line descriptor H_{s_i}. We set four k values $[5, 10, 15, 20]$, and take different k_{set} combinations to verify the effect of k_{set}. The result is presented in Table 1. Compare to the basic line descriptor $H_{s_i}^k$ with single k, the line descriptor H_{s_i} with k_{set} yields superior results. This is because the influence of neighboring semantic-level line features are attenuated from near to far. When adding more line features to improve the descriptive ability of the descriptor, the accumulation of multiple $H_{s_i}^k$ maintains the higher influence of the nearest neighboring line features. However, too many line features also influence the uniqueness of the descriptor. Thus, $k_{set} = [5, 10, 15]$ achieves a better result.

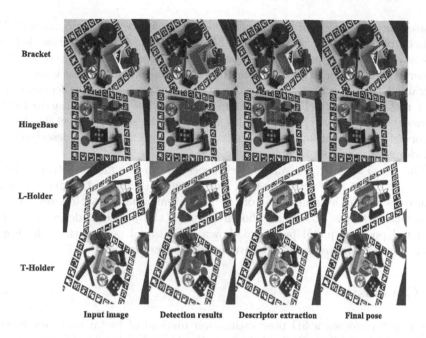

Bracket

HingeBase

L-Holder

T-Holder

Input image   Detection results   Descriptor extraction   Final pose

Fig. 5. The estimation result of the proposed method.

We compared our method with FDCM [6], D²CO [7] and Yang's method [11]. FDCM and D²CO are both based on the edge feature matching. Yang's method

Table 1. ADD-S results of different k_{set} on MONO-6D dataset.

k_{set}	Bracket	HingeBase	L-Holder	T-Holder	Average
[5]	48.51%	19.19%	62.79%	38.74%	42.31%
[10]	17.82%	44.44%	29.07%	28.83%	30.04%
[15]	11.88%	14.14%	31.40%	31.53%	22.24%
[20]	6.93%	22.22%	8.14%	13.51%	12.70%
[5, 10]	70.30%	36.36%	70.93%	63.96%	60.39%
[5, 10, 15]	**73.27%**	**53.54%**	77.91%	**68.47%**	**68.30%**
[5, 10, 15, 20]	71.29%	51.52%	**79.07%**	66.67%	67.13%

Table 2. ADD-S results of different methods on MONO-6D dataset.

Method	Bracket	HingeBase	L-Holder	T-Holder	Average
PDCM	38.75%	56.12%	45.76%	42.32%	45.74%
D²CO	48.76%	64.29%	68.72%	64.23%	61.50%
Yang's method	59.87%	68.75%	62.33%	67.56%	64.63%
Our method	**73.27%**	53.54%	**79.07%**	**68.47%**	**68.59%**

is based on geometric feature matching, which is similar with our method. The final comparison is shown in the Table 2. Compared to the three methods based on low-level feature, our method has more accurate results with Bracket, L-Holder and T-Holder. The unsatisfactory result of HingeBase is caused by the pretrained L-CNN which can only detect less semantic-level line features than other metal parts, which means our method still has the potential to further improve the accuracy. The results also show that the semantic-level line feature is more effective than low-level feature and the object-level line descriptor can provide more reliable matching results.

The Fig. 5 shows the result of each procedure in our method. In the detection results part, the semantic-level line features illustrate the line segments accurately. With the refinement of the mask, only the semantic-level line features related to the object are chosen to extract object-level descriptors. The predicted poses of metal parts are shown in the final pose part of the Fig. 5, which also demonstrates the effectiveness of our method.

4   Conclusion

This paper proposes a 6D pose estimation method of metal parts for robotic grasping. Different from the traditional method based on low-level feature, we use the line detection network to extract semantic-level line feature as the replacement of low-level feature. The line feature combines a segmentation network to extract object-level line descriptor for matching and pose estimation. Compared with the low-level feature, the semantic-level line feature maps the real image and the template image to the semantic-level line feature space, which reduces the difference in matching. Object-level line descriptor is generated for object, which further improves the robustness for matching in complex environments. Experimental results show that the proposed method achieves higher accuracy than the traditional methods on the Mono-6D dataset. In future work, we will consider fusing the line detection network and the segmentation network into one network to improve the efficiency of the whole method.

References

1. Du, G., Wang, K., Lian, S., Zhao, K.: Vision-based robotic grasping from object localization, object pose estimation to grasp estimation for parallel grippers: A review. Artif. Intell. Rev. **54**(3), 1677–1734 (2021). https://doi.org/10.1007/s10462-020-09888-5
2. Zhang, H., Cao, Q.: Detect in RGB, optimize in edge: Accurate 6D pose estimation for texture-less industrial parts. In: 2019 International Conference on Robotics and Automation (ICRA), pp. 3486–3492. IEEE (2019). https://doi.org/10.1109/ICRA.2019.8794330
3. Zhang, X., Jiang, Z., Zhang, H.: Real-time 6d pose estimation from a single RGB image. Image Vis. Comput. **89**, 1–11 (2019). https://doi.org/10.1016/j.imavis.2019.06.013

4. Chan, J., Addison Lee, J., Kemao, Q.: BORDER: an oriented rectangles approach to texture-less object recognition. In: Proceedings of the IEEE Conference on Computer Vision and Pattern Recognition, pp. 2855–2863 (2016). https://doi.org/10.1109/CVPR.2016.312

5. Tombari, F., Franchi, A., Di Stefano, L.: BOLD features to detect texture-less objects. In: Proceedings of the IEEE International Conference on Computer Vision, pp. 1265–1272. IEEE, Sydney, Australia (2013). https://doi.org/10.1109/ICCV.2013.160

6. Liu, M.Y., Tuzel, O., Veeraraghavan, A., Taguchi, Y., Marks, T.K., Chellappa, R.: Fast object localization and pose estimation in heavy clutter for robotic bin picking. Int. J. Robot. Res. **31**(8), 951–973 (2012). https://doi.org/10.1177/0278364911436018

7. Imperoli, M., Pretto, A.: D^{2}CO: fast and robust registration of 3D textureless objects using the directional chamfer distance. In: Nalpantidis, L., Krüger, V., Eklundh, J.-O., Gasteratos, A. (eds.) ICVS 2015. LNCS, vol. 9163, pp. 316–328. Springer, Cham (2015). https://doi.org/10.1007/978-3-319-20904-3_29

8. Wang, Y., Wang, X., Chen, Y.: Multi-surface hydraulic valve block technique hole plug inspection from monocular image. Meas. Sci. Technol. **32**(11), 115016 (2021). https://doi.org/10.1088/1361-6501/ac1460

9. He, Z., Wuxi, F., Zhao, X., Zhang, S., Tan, J.: 6D pose measurement of metal parts based on virtual geometric feature point matching. Meas. Sci. Technol. **32**(12), 125210 (2021). https://doi.org/10.1088/1361-6501/ac2a85

10. He, Z., Jiang, Z., Zhao, X., Zhang, S., Wu, C.: Sparse template-based 6-d pose estimation of metal parts using a monocular camera. IEEE Trans. Industr. Electron. **67**(1), 390–401 (2019). https://doi.org/10.1109/TIE.2019.2897539

11. Yang, X., Li, K., Fan, X., Zhang, H., Cao, H.: A multi-stage 6D object pose estimation method of texture-less objects based on sparse line features. In: 2022 IEEE International Conference on Industrial Engineering and Engineering Management (IEEM), pp. 0221–0225 (2022). https://doi.org/10.1109/IEEM55944.2022.9989794

12. Zhou, Y., Qi, H., Ma, Y.: End-to-end wireframe parsing. In: 2019 IEEE/CVF International Conference on Computer Vision (ICCV), pp. 962–971 (2019). https://doi.org/10.1109/ICCV.2019.00105

13. Von Gioi, R., Jakubowicz, J., Morel, J.M., Randall, G.: LSD: a fast line segment detector with a false detection control. IEEE Trans. Pattern Anal. Mach. Intell. **32**(4), 722–732 (2008). https://doi.org/10.1109/TPAMI.2008.300

14. Ronneberger, O., Fischer, P., Brox, T.: U-net: convolutional networks for biomedical image segmentation. In: Navab, N., Hornegger, J., Wells, W.M., Frangi, A.F. (eds.) MICCAI 2015. LNCS, vol. 9351, pp. 234–241. Springer, Cham (2015). https://doi.org/10.1007/978-3-319-24574-4_28

15. Ulrich, M., Wiedemann, C., Steger, C.: Combining scale-space and similarity-based aspect graphs for fast 3d object recognition. IEEE Trans. Pattern Anal. Mach. Intell. **34**(10), 1902–1914 (2012). https://doi.org/10.1109/TPAMI.2011.266

16. Konishi, Y., Hanzawa, Y., Kawade, M., Hashimoto, M.: Fast 6D pose estimation from a monocular image using hierarchical pose trees. In: Leibe, B., Matas, J., Sebe, N., Welling, M. (eds.) ECCV 2016. LNCS, vol. 9905, pp. 398–413. Springer, Cham (2016). https://doi.org/10.1007/978-3-319-46448-0_24

17. Hinterstoisser, S., et al.: Model based training, detection and pose estimation of texture-less 3d objects in heavily cluttered scenes. In: Lee, K.M., Matsushita, Y., Rehg, J.M., Hu, Z. (eds.) ACCV 2012. LNCS, vol. 7724, pp. 548–562. Springer, Heidelberg (2013). https://doi.org/10.1007/978-3-642-37331-2_42

GelSplitter: Tactile Reconstruction from Near Infrared and Visible Images

Yuankai Lin[1], Yulin Zhou[1], Kaiji Huang[1], Qi Zhong[3], Tao Cheng[2],
Hua Yang[1(✉)], and Zhouping Yin[1]

[1] The State Key Laboratory of Digital Manufacturing Equipment and Technology,
School of Mechanical Science and Engineering, Huazhong University of Science and
Technology, Wuhan 430074, China
huayang@hust.edu.cn
[2] College of Urban Transportation and Logistics, Shenzhen Technology University,
Shenzhen 518118, China
[3] School of Science and Engineering, Tsinghua University, Beijing 100084, China

Abstract. The GelSight-like visual tactile (VT) sensor has gained popularity as a high-resolution tactile sensing technology for robots, capable of measuring touch geometry using a single RGB camera. However, the development of multi-modal perception for VT sensors remains a challenge, limited by the mono camera. In this paper, we propose the GelSplitter, a new framework approach the multi-modal VT sensor with synchronized multi-modal cameras and resemble a more human-like tactile receptor. Furthermore, we focus on 3D tactile reconstruction and implement a compact sensor structure that maintains a comparable size to state-of-the-art VT sensors, even with the addition of a prism and a near infrared (NIR) camera. We also design a photometric fusion stereo neural network (PFSNN), which estimates surface normals of objects and reconstructs touch geometry from both infrared and visible images. Our results demonstrate that the accuracy of RGB and NIR fusion is higher than that of RGB images alone. Additionally, our GelSplitter framework allows for a flexible configuration of different camera sensor combinations, such as RGB and thermal imaging.

Keywords: Visual tactile · Photometric stereo · Multi-modal fusion

1 Introduction

Tactile perception is an essential aspect of robotic interaction with the natural environment [1]. As a direct means for robots to perceive and respond to physical stimuli, it enables them to perform a wide range of tasks and to interact with humans and other objects, such as touch detection [5], force estimation [4], robotic grasping [12] and gait planning [25]. While the human skin can easily translate the geometry of a contacted object into nerve impulses through tactile

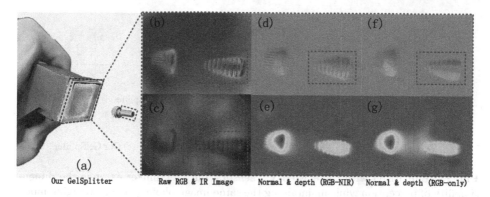

Fig. 1. Comparison with RGB-Only method, our GelSplitter offers a framework for the implementation of multi-modal VT sensors, which can further enhance the performance of tactile reconstruction. (a): Our proposed GelSplitter. (b): A RGB image of our sensor. (c): A corresponding NIR image. (d): The normal map of our PFSNN estimated from the RGB and NIR images. (e): The Depth map reconstructed from the normal map (d). (f): The normal map of the look-up table (LUT) method [28] estimated from the RGB image. (g): The Depth map reconstructed from the normal map (f).

receptors, robots face challenges in achieving the same level of tactile sensitivity, especially in multi-modal tactile perception.

Visual tactile (VT) sensors such as the GelSights [6,22,28] are haptic sensing technology becoming popularity with an emphasis on dense, accurate, and high-resolution measurements, using a single RGB camera to measure touch geometry. However, the RGB-only mode of image sensor restricts the multi-modal perception of VT sensor. RGB and near infrared (NIR) image fusion is a hot topic for image enhancement, using IR images to enhance the RGB image detail and improve measurement accuracy [8,32]. From this perspective, a multi-modal image fusion VT sensor is promoted to enrich the tactile senses of the robot.

In this paper, we present the GelSplitter with RGB-NIR fusion as a solution of the above challenge. This novel design integrates a splitting prism to reconstruct tactile geometry from both NIR and RGB light cameras. Our GelSplitter offer a framework for the implementation of multi-modal VT sensors, which can further enhance the tactile capabilities of robots, as shown in Fig. 1. Additionally, our GelSplitter framework allows for a flexible configuration of different camera sensor combinations, such as RGB and thermal imaging. In summary, our contribution lies in three aspects:

- We propose the GelSplitter, a new framework to design multi-modal VT sensor.
- Based on the framework, we focus on the task of 3D tactile reconstruction and fabricate a compact sensor structure that maintains a comparable size to state-of-the-art VT sensors, even with the addition of a prism and camera.
- A photometric fusion stereo neural network (PFSNN) is implemented to estimate surface normals of objects and reconstructs touch geometry from both

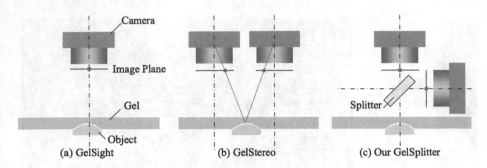

Fig. 2. Comparison with the existed VT sensors, our GelSplitter extends the dimensionality of perception while maintaining the same image plane. (a): The Imaging mode of a typical Geisight-like [28] VT sensor. (b): The Imaging mode of a GelStereo [11] VT sensor. (c): Our imaging mode of GelSplitter maintains the optical centres of the different cameras and align the multi-modal data. In addition, our framework allows for a flexible configuration of different camera sensor combinations, such as RGB and thermal imaging.

infrared and visible images. The common issue of data alignment between the RGB and IR cameras is addressed by incorporating splitting imaging. Our results demonstrate that our method outperforms the RGB-only VT sensation.

The rest of the paper is organized as follows: In Sect. 2, we briefly introduce some related works of VT sensors and multi-modal image fusion. Then, we describe the main design of the GelSplitter and FPSNN in Sect. 3. In order to verify the performance of our proposed method, experimental results are presented in Sect. 4 (Fig. 2).

2   Related Work

2.1   VT Sensor

GelSight [28] is a well-established VT sensor that operates like a pliable mirror, transforming physical contact or pressure distribution on its reflective surface into tactile images that can be captured by a single camera. Building upon the framework of the GelSight, various VT sensors [9,22,23] are designed to meet diverse application requirements, such as [10,16–18]. Inspired by GelSight, DIGIT [13] improves upon past the VT sensors by miniaturizing the form factor to be mountable on multi-fingered hands.

Additionally, there are studies that explore the materials and patterns of reflective surfaces to gather other modal information of touch sensing. For example, FingerVision [27] provides a multi-modal sensation with a completely transparent skin. HaptiTemp [2] uses thermochromic pigments color blue, orange, and black with a threshold of 31 °C, 43 °C, and 50 °C, respectively on the gel material, to enable high-resolution temperature measurements. DelTact [31] adopts an improved dense random color pattern to achieve high accuracy of contact deformation tracking.

The VT sensors mentioned above are based on a single RGB camera. Inspired by binocular stereo vision, GelStereo [6] uses two RGB cameras to achieve tactile geometry measurements. Further, the gelstereo is developed in six-axis force/torque estimation [30] and geometry measurement [7,11].

In current research, one type of camera is commonly used, with a small size and a simplified optical path. The RGB camera solution for binocular stereo vision effectively estimates disparity by triangulation. However, data alignment is a common issue to different kinds of camera images [3], because multi-modal sensors naturally have different extrinsic parameters between modalities, such as lens parameters and relative position. In this paper, two identical imaging windows are fabricated by a splitting prism, which filter RGB component (bandpass filtering at 650 nm wavelength) and IR component (narrowband filtering at 940 nm wavelength).

2.2   Multi-modal Image Fusion

Multi-modal image fusion is a fundamental task for robot perception, healthcare and autonomous driving [21,26]. However, due to high raw data noise, low information utilisation and unaligned multi-modal sensors, it is challenging to achieve a good performance. In these applications, different types of datasets are captured by different sensors such as infrared (IR) and RGB image [32], computed tomography (CT) and positron emission tomograph (PET) scan [19], LIDAR point cloud and RGB image [15].

Typically, the fusion of NIR and RGB images enhances the image performance and complements the missing information in the RGB image. DenseFuse [14] proposes an encoding network that is combined with convolutional layers, a fusion layer, and a dense block to get more useful features from source images. DarkVisionNet [20] extracts clear structure details in deep multiscale feature space rather than raw input space by a deep structure. MIRNet [29] adopts a multi-scale residual block to learn an enriched set of features that combines contextual information from multiple scales, while simultaneously preserving the high-resolution spatial details.

Data alignment is another important content of multi-modal image fusion. Generally, the targets corresponding to multiple sensors are in different coordinate systems, and the data rates of different sensors are diverse. To effectively utilize heterogeneous information and obtain simultaneous target information, it is essential to map the data onto a unified coordinate system with proper time-space alignment [21,24].

Following the above literature, PFSNN is designed for the gelsplitter, completing the missing information of RGB images by NIR image. It generates refined normal vector maps and depth maps. In addition, splitting prisms are embedded to unify the image planes and optical centres of the different cameras and align the multi-modal data.

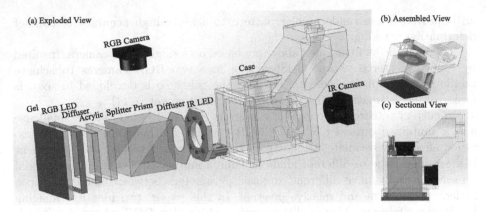

Fig. 3. The design of our GelSplitter, including the exploded view showing inner components, the assembled CAD model, and the Sectional view of the sensor.

3 Design and Fabrication

Our design aims to achieve high-resolution 3D tactile reconstruction while maintaining a compact shape. Figure 3 shows the components and schematic diagram of the sensor design. Following, we describe the design principles and lessons learned for each sensor component.

3.1 Prism and Filters

To capture the NIR image and the RGB image, a splitting prism, band pass filter, narrow band filter and diffuser were prepared. These components ensure that the images are globally illuminated and homogeneous.

The splitting prism is a cube with a side length of 15 mm, as shown in Fig. 4 (a). It has a spectral ratio of 1:1 and a refractive index of 1.5168, creating two identical viewports. Among the six directions of the cube, except for two directions of the cameras and one direction of the gel, the other three directions are painted with black to reduce secondary reflections.

The diffuser in lighting can produce more even global illumination as it distributes light evenly throughout the scene. The octagonal diffuser needs to be optically coupled to the splitting prism to avoid reflection from the air interface, as shown in Fig. 4 (b). "3M Diffuser 3635-70" is used for the sensor.

A 650 nm bandpass filter and 940 nm narrowband filter are used to separate the RGB component from the NIR component. The lens and filter are integrated together, as shown in Fig. 4 (c).

3.2 Lighting

In this paper, five types of colour LEDs are provided for illumination in different directions, including red (Type NCD0603R1, wavelength 615–630 nm),

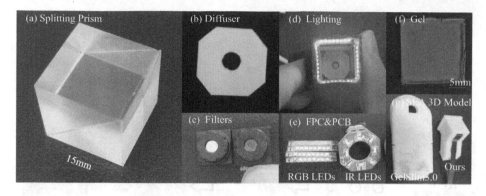

Fig. 4. The inner components and detials of our GelSplitter. (a): The splitting prism. (b): The diffuser. (c): The 650 nm bandpass filter and 940 nm narrowband filter. (d): The lighting. (e): The FPC and PCB to drive LEDs. (f): The Gel with reflective covering. (g): The Silk screen printing plate. (Color figure online)

green (Type NCD0603W1, wavelength 515–530 nm), blue (Type NCD0603B1, wavelength 463–475 nm), white (Type NCD0603W1) and infrared (Type XL-1608IRC940, wavelength 940 nm), as shown in Fig. 4 (d). These LEDs are all in 0603 package size (1.6 × 0.8 mm).

Moreover, in order to represent surface gradient information, LEDs are arranged in two different ways. Firstly, red, green, blue and white LEDs can be arranged in rows, illuminating the four sides of the gel. This allows for a clear representation of surface gradients from different angles. Secondly, infrared LEDs can be arranged in a circular formation above the gel, surrounding the infrared camera. This allows IR light to shine on the shaded areas, supplementing the missing gradient information.

Finally, we designed the FPC and PCB to drive LEDs, as shown in Fig. 4 (e). The LED brightness is configured with a resistor, and its consistency is ensured by a luminance meter.

3.3 Camera

Both NIR and RGB cameras are used the common CMOS sensor OV5640, manufactured by OmniVision Technologies, Inc. The OV5640 supports a wide range of resolution configurations from 320 × 240 to 2592 × 1944, as well as auto exposure control (AEC) and auto white balance (AWB). Following the experimental setting of GelSights [1], our resolution is configured to 640 × 480. AEC and AWE are disabled to obtain the linear response characteristics of the images.

To capture clear images, it is essential to adjust the focal length by rotating the lens and ensure that the depth of field is within the appropriate range. Although ideally, the optical centres of the two cameras are identical. In practice, however, there is a small assembly error that requires fine-grained data alignment.

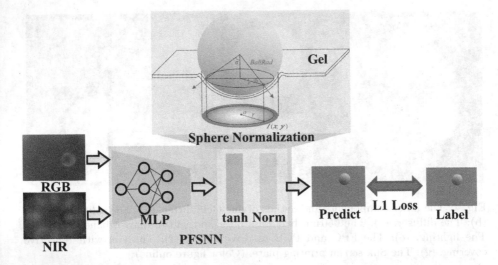

Fig. 5. We propose PFSNN to fuse RGB images and NIR images from GelSplitter, and estimate dense normal maps. PFSNN is composed of multi-layer perceptron (MLP) and sphere normalization, and is supervised by L1 loss function. Furthermore, the fast poisson algorithm [28] can be utilized to solve depth maps based on normal maps.

Both RGB and NIR cameras are calibrated and corrected for aberrations using the Zhang's calibration method implemented in OpenCV. Random sample consistency (RANSAC) regression is used to align the checkerboard corners of the two cameras' images to achieve data alignment.

3.4 Elastomer

Our transparent silicone is coated with diffuse reflective paint. We choose low-cost food grade platinum silicone which operates in a 1:1 ratio. The silicone is poured into a mould and produced as a soft gel mat with a thickness of 1.5 mm. In our experiment, we found that a gel with a Shore hardness of 10A is both pliable enough to avoid breakage and capable of producing observable deformations. To achieve defoaming, it is necessary to maintain an environmental temperature of approximately 10 °C and apply a vacuum pressure of −0.08 MPa.

3.5 SLA 3D Model

We use stereo lithography appearance (SLA) 3D printing to create the case. Compared to fused deposition modelling (FDM) 3D printing of PLA, SLA technology has a higher precision for assemble requirements of the splitting prism. Despite the addition of a prism and a NIR camera, our case still maintains a comparable size to the state-of-the-art VT sensor, GelSlim 3.0 [22], as shown in Fig. 4 (g).

Table 1. Network Architecture of PFSNN.

Layer	Operator	Kernel Size	Input channels	Output Channels
1	Concat	–	4(RGB-NIR)+4(Background)	8
2	Conv2d	1	8	128
3	Relu	–	128	128
4	Conv2d	1	128	64
5	Relu	–	64	64
6	Conv2d	1	64	3
7	Relu	–	3	3
8	Tanh	–	3	3
9	Normalize	–	3	3
10	$x = 0.5x + 0.5$	–	3	3

4 Measuring 3D Geometry

In this section, We introduce PFSNN which fuses RGB images and NIR images from GelSplitter, and estimate dense normal maps. Following, we describe the components and implementation details of PFSNN.

4.1 PFSNN

Network Architecture of the PFSNN is shown in the Table 1. It is composed of multi-layer perceptron (MLP) and sphere normalization. Compared to the look-up table (LUT) method [28], the MLP network is trainable. Through its non-linear fitting capability, the algorithm can combine and integrate information from both RGB and NIR sources.

Sphere Normalization is derived from a physical model of the spherical press distribution and outputs a unit normal vector map, as shown in Fig. 5. It is defined as:

$$n = \frac{tanh(x)}{max(\|tanh(x)\|_2, \epsilon)},\tag{1}$$

where x is the output of the MLP, and ϵ is a small value (10^{-12} in this paper) to avoid division by zero. Furthermore, the fast poisson algorithm [28] can be utilized to solve depth maps based on normal maps. It is defined as:

$$d = Fast\_Poisson(n).\tag{2}$$

Implementation Details. PFSNN requires a small amount of data for training. In this paper, only five images of spherical presses were collected, four for training and one for validation. We test the model with screw caps, screws, hair and fingerprints that the PFSNN never seen before, as shown in Fig. 6.

All of our experiments are executed on a NVIDIA RTX 3070 laptop GPU. Our method is implemented in the PyTorch 2.0 framework, trained with an ADAM optimizer. The batch size is set to 64. The learning rate is set to 0.01 for 20 epochs. There is no use of data enhancement methods.

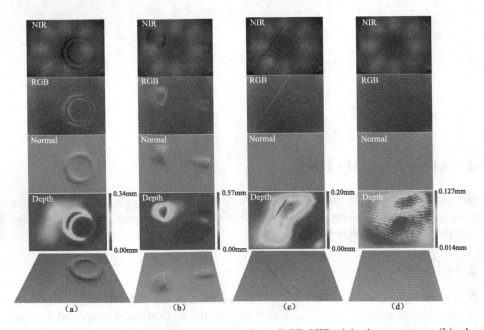

Fig. 6. Result of 3D tactile reconstruction from RGB-NIR. (a): A screw cap. (b): A screw. (c): A hint of hair. (d): A fingerprint. Even though GelSplitter is used to touch these items for the first time, remarkably clear shapes are still able to be reconstructed through the 3D tactile reconstruction process.

Table 2. Experiment Result of PFSNN.

	LUT w/o NIR	LUT w. NIR	PFSNN w/o NIR	PFSNN w. NIR
MAE(°)	9.292	8.731	6.057	5.682

4.2   Result of 3D Tactile Reconstruction

The process of 3D tactile reconstruction can be divided into two main steps. The first step involves calculating the normal map from RGB-NIR. The second step is to apply the fast Poisson solver [28] to integrate the gradients and obtain the depth information. This helps to create a detailed 3D tactile reconstruction, which can be very useful for various applications.

The screw cap, screw, hair, fingerprint is chosen to qualitative testing of resolution and precision, as shown in Fig. 6. In NIR images, the opposite property to RGB images is observed, with higher depth map gradients being darker. This means that our design allows the NIR image to contain information that is complementary to the RGB image and illuminates the shaded parts of the RGB image, as shown in Fig. 6 (a). In addition, our splitting design of imaging allows both the normal vector map and the reconstructed depth map to have a clear texture, as shown in Fig. 6 (b), where the threads of the screw are clearly reconstructed. Hair strands (diameter approx. 0.05 mm–0.1 mm) and fingerprints(diameter approx. 0.01 mm–0.02 mm) are used to test the minimum resolution of the GelSplitter, as shown in Fig. 6 (c) (d).

In addition, our splitter can be easily switched between RGB and RGB-NIR modes and provides a fair comparison of the results, as shown in the Table 2. The LUT method [28] is employed as a baseline to verify the validity of our method. The results show that the addition of NIR reduces the normal error by 0.561° and 0.375° for LUT and PSFNN respectively. Our PFSNN outperforms the LUT, decreasing the error by over 40%.

5   Conclusion

In this paper, we proposed a framework named GelSplitter to implement multimodal VT sensor. Furthermore, we focus on 3D tactile reconstruction and designed a compact sensor structure that maintains a comparable size to state-of-the-art VT sensors, even with the addition of a prism and camera. We also implemented the PFSNN to estimate surface normals of objects and reconstruct touch geometry from both NIR and RGB images. Our experiment results demonstrated the performance of our proposed method.

Acknowledgments. This work was supported by the Guangdong University Engineering Technology Research Center for Precision Components of Intelligent Terminal of Transportation Tools (Project No. 2021GCZX002), and Guangdong HUST Industrial Technology Research Institute, Guangdong Provincial Key Laboratory of Digital Manufacturing Equipment.

References

1. Abad, A.C., Ranasinghe, A.: Visuotactile sensors with emphasis on gelsight sensor: a review. IEEE Sens. J. **20**(14), 7628–7638 (2020). https://doi.org/10.1109/JSEN.2020.2979662
2. Abad, A.C., Reid, D., Ranasinghe, A.: Haptitemp: a next-generation thermosensitive gelsight-like visuotactile sensor. IEEE Sens. J. **22**(3), 2722–2734 (2022). https://doi.org/10.1109/JSEN.2021.3135941
3. Arar, M., Ginger, Y., Danon, D., Bermano, A.H., Cohen-Or, D.: Unsupervised multi-modal image registration via geometry preserving image-to-image translation. In: 2020 IEEE/CVF Conference on Computer Vision and Pattern Recognition (CVPR), pp. 13407–13416 (2020). https://doi.org/10.1109/CVPR42600.2020.01342

4. Bao, L., et al.: Flexible electronic skin for monitoring of grasping state during robotic manipulation. Soft Rob. **10**(2), 336–344 (2023). https://doi.org/10.1089/soro.2022.0014

5. Castaño-Amoros, J., Gil, P., Puente, S.: Touch detection with low-cost visual-based sensor. In: International Conference on Robotics, Computer Vision and Intelligent Systems (2021)

6. Cui, S., Wang, R., Hu, J., Wei, J., Wang, S., Lou, Z.: In-hand object localization using a novel high-resolution visuotactile sensor. IEEE Trans. Industr. Electron. **69**(6), 6015–6025 (2022). https://doi.org/10.1109/TIE.2021.3090697

7. Cui, S., Wang, R., Hu, J., Zhang, C., Chen, L., Wang, S.: Self-supervised contact geometry learning by gelstereo visuotactile sensing. IEEE Trans. Instrum. Meas. **71**, 1–9 (2022). https://doi.org/10.1109/TIM.2021.3136181

8. Deng, X., Dragotti, P.L.: Deep convolutional neural network for multi-modal image restoration and fusion. IEEE Trans. Pattern Anal. Mach. Intell. **43**(10), 3333–3348 (2021). https://doi.org/10.1109/TPAMI.2020.2984244

9. Donlon, E., Dong, S., Liu, M., Li, J., Adelson, E., Rodriguez, A.: Gelslim: a high-resolution, compact, robust, and calibrated tactile-sensing finger. In: 2018 IEEE/RSJ International Conference on Intelligent Robots and Systems (IROS), pp. 1927–1934 (2018). https://doi.org/10.1109/IROS.2018.8593661

10. Fang, B., Long, X., Sun, F., Liu, H., Zhang, S., Fang, C.: Tactile-based fabric defect detection using convolutional neural network with attention mechanism. IEEE Trans. Instrum. Meas. **71**, 1–9 (2022). https://doi.org/10.1109/TIM.2022.3165254

11. Hu, J., et al.: Gelstereo palm: a novel curved visuotactile sensor for 3d geometry sensing. IEEE Trans. Ind. Inf. 1–10 (2023). https://doi.org/10.1109/TII.2023.3241685

12. James, J.W., Lepora, N.F.: Slip detection for grasp stabilization with a multifingered tactile robot hand. IEEE Trans. Rob. **37**(2), 506–519 (2021). https://doi.org/10.1109/TRO.2020.3031245

13. Lambeta, M., et al.: Digit: a novel design for a low-cost compact high-resolution tactile sensor with application to in-hand manipulation. IEEE Robot. Autom. Lett. **5**(3), 3838–3845 (2020). https://doi.org/10.1109/LRA.2020.2977257

14. Li, H., Wu, X.J.: Densefuse: a fusion approach to infrared and visible images. IEEE Trans. Image Process. **28**(5), 2614–2623 (2019). https://doi.org/10.1109/TIP.2018.2887342

15. Lin, Y., Cheng, T., Zhong, Q., Zhou, W., Yang, H.: Dynamic spatial propagation network for depth completion. In: Proceedings of the AAAI Conference on Artificial Intelligence, vol. 36, pp. 1638–1646 (2022)

16. Liu, S.Q., Adelson, E.H.: Gelsight fin ray: incorporating tactile sensing into a soft compliant robotic gripper. In: 2022 IEEE 5th International Conference on Soft Robotics (RoboSoft), pp. 925–931 (2022). https://doi.org/10.1109/RoboSoft54090.2022.9762175

17. Liu, S.Q., Yañez, L.Z., Adelson, E.H.: Gelsight endoflex: a soft endoskeleton hand with continuous high-resolution tactile sensing. In: 2023 IEEE International Conference on Soft Robotics (RoboSoft), pp. 1–6 (2023). https://doi.org/10.1109/RoboSoft55895.2023.10122053

18. Ma, D., Donlon, E., Dong, S., Rodriguez, A.: Dense tactile force estimation using gelslim and inverse fem. In: 2019 International Conference on Robotics and Automation (ICRA), pp. 5418–5424 (2019). https://doi.org/10.1109/ICRA.2019.8794113

19. Ma, J., Xu, H., Jiang, J., Mei, X., Zhang, X.P.: Ddcgan: a dual-discriminator conditional generative adversarial network for multi-resolution image fusion. IEEE Trans. Image Process. **29**, 4980–4995 (2020). https://doi.org/10.1109/TIP.2020.2977573
20. Shuangping, J., Bingbing, Y., Minhao, J., Yi, Z., Jiajun, L., Renhe, J.: Darkvisionnet: low-light imaging via RGB-NIR fusion with deep inconsistency prior. In: Proceedings of the AAAI Conference on Artificial Intelligence, vol. 36, pp. 1104–1112 (2022)
21. Singh, S., et al.: A review of image fusion: methods, applications and performance metrics. Digital Signal Process. **137**, 104020 (2023). https://doi.org/10.1016/j.dsp.2023.104020
22. Taylor, I.H., Dong, S., Rodriguez, A.: Gelslim 3.0: High-resolution measurement of shape, force and slip in a compact tactile-sensing finger. In: 2022 International Conference on Robotics and Automation (ICRA), pp. 10781–10787 (2022). https://doi.org/10.1109/ICRA46639.2022.9811832
23. Wang, S., She, Y., Romero, B., Adelson, E.: Gelsight wedge: measuring high-resolution 3d contact geometry with a compact robot finger. In: 2021 IEEE International Conference on Robotics and Automation (ICRA), pp. 6468–6475 (2021). https://doi.org/10.1109/ICRA48506.2021.9560783
24. Wang, Z., Wu, Y., Niu, Q.: Multi-sensor fusion in automated driving: a survey. IEEE Access **8**, 2847–2868 (2020). https://doi.org/10.1109/ACCESS.2019.2962554
25. Wu, X.A., Huh, T.M., Sabin, A., Suresh, S.A., Cutkosky, M.R.: Tactile sensing and terrain-based gait control for small legged robots. IEEE Trans. Rob. **36**(1), 15–27 (2020). https://doi.org/10.1109/TRO.2019.2935336
26. Xue, T., Wang, W., Ma, J., Liu, W., Pan, Z., Han, M.: Progress and prospects of multimodal fusion methods in physical human-robot interaction: a review. IEEE Sens. J. **20**(18), 10355–10370 (2020). https://doi.org/10.1109/JSEN.2020.2995271
27. Yamaguchi, A., Atkeson, C.G.: Tactile behaviors with the vision-based tactile sensor fingervision. Int. J. Humanoid Rob. **16**(03), 1940002 (2019). https://doi.org/10.1142/S0219843619400024
28. Yuan, W., Dong, S., Adelson, E.H.: Gelsight: high-resolution robot tactile sensors for estimating geometry and force. Sensors **17**(12) (2017). https://www.mdpi.com/1424-8220/17/12/2762
29. Zamir, S.W., et al.: Learning enriched features for fast image restoration and enhancement. IEEE Trans. Pattern Anal. Mach. Intell. **45**(2), 1934–1948 (2023). https://doi.org/10.1109/TPAMI.2022.3167175
30. Zhang, C., Cui, S., Cai, Y., Hu, J., Wang, R., Wang, S.: Learning-based six-axis force/torque estimation using gelstereo fingertip visuotactile sensing. In: 2022 IEEE/RSJ International Conference on Intelligent Robots and Systems (IROS), pp. 3651–3658 (2022). https://doi.org/10.1109/IROS47612.2022.9981100
31. Zhang, G., Du, Y., Yu, H., Wang, M.Y.: Deltact: a vision-based tactile sensor using a dense color pattern. IEEE Robot. Autom. Lett. **7**(4), 10778–10785 (2022). https://doi.org/10.1109/LRA.2022.3196141
32. Zhao, Z., Xu, S., Zhang, C., Liu, J., Zhang, J.: Bayesian fusion for infrared and visible images. Signal Process. **177**, 107734 (2020). https://doi.org/10.1016/j.sigpro.2020.107734

GelFlow: Self-supervised Learning of Optical Flow for Vision-Based Tactile Sensor Displacement Measurement

Zhiyuan Zhang⬤, Hua Yang(✉)⬤, and Zhouping Yin

School of Mechanical Science and Engineering, State Key Laboratory of Digital
Manufacturing Equipment and Technology, Huazhong University of Science and
Technology, Wuhan, China
huayang@hust.edu.cn

Abstract. High-resolution multi-modality information acquired by
vision-based tactile sensors can support more dexterous manipulations
for robot fingers. Optical flow is low-level information directly obtained
by vision-based tactile sensors, which can be transformed into other
modalities like force, geometry and depth. Current vision-tactile sensors
employ optical flow methods from OpenCV to estimate the deformation of markers in gels. However, these methods need to be more precise for accurately measuring the displacement of markers during large
elastic deformation of the gel, as this can significantly impact the accuracy of downstream tasks. This study proposes a self-supervised optical
flow method based deep learning to achieve high accuracy in displacement measurement for vision-based tactile sensors. The proposed
method employs a coarse-to-fine strategy to handle large deformations
by constructing a multi-scale feature pyramid from the input image. To
better deal with the elastic deformation caused by the gel, the Helmholtz
velocity decomposition constraint combined with the elastic deformation
constraint are adopted to address the distortion rate and area change
rate, respectively. A local flow fusion module is designed to smooth
the optical flow, taking into account the prior knowledge of the blurred
effect of gel deformation. We trained the proposed self-supervised network using an open-source dataset and compared it with traditional and
deep learning-based optical flow methods. The results show that the proposed method achieved the highest displacement measurement accuracy,
thereby demonstrating its potential for enabling more precise measurement of downstream tasks using vision-based tactile sensors.

Keywords: Vision-based tactile sensor · Optical flow · Elastic
deformation estimation · Deep learning

1 Introduction

Vision and tactile are crucial sources of information for perceiving and interacting with the world [1]. With computer vision and robotics advancement, vision-
based tactile sensors fusing both modalities are becoming increasingly popular for

H. Yang et al. (Eds.): ICIRA 2023, LNAI 14273, pp. 26–37, 2023.
https://doi.org/10.1007/978-981-99-6498-7_3

enabling intelligent robots to perceive and manipulate delicate objects precisely. A typical visual-tactile sensor hardware comprises three components: a contact module, a camera module, and an illumination module [2]. The contact module requires resilient and optically favorable materials, as its performance directly affects the accuracy of subsequent optical measurements. It is often embedded with a marker layer to visualize the contact material's deformation. The camera and illumination modules can be classified into two main categories based on the measurement principle: a monocular camera system with multi-color illumination systems and multi-camera systems with a monochromatic illumination system. The integration of these three modules allows vision-based tactile sensors to capture and measure various types of information, including force [3], geometry reconstruction [4], sliding detection [5], and object recognition [1].

The displacement of markers in the contact module provides valuable information for measuring additional physical properties, such as the shape of the contacting object, the forces applied, and the roughness of its surface. This information can be analyzed by the robot for downstream tasks. Accurate and dense displacement measurements improve the resolution of other modal information, providing better input for subsequent tasks, thereby enhancing the accuracy of robot perception and manipulation [6]. However, the contact module composed of gel material is characterized by large elastic deformation, which can result in errors in estimating the displacement of existing vision-based tactile sensors using the optical flow algorithm in OpenCV [7]. These inaccuracies in displacement measurements can lead to inaccuracies in the final estimated physical information [8]. Therefore, our motivation is to develop an accurate pixel-level optical flow estimation method to better deal with the deformation properties of the gel materials.

In this study, we introduce a self-supervised learning optical flow approach, named GelFlow, for a more precise measurement of displacement in gel-like materials. Our proposed method offers two novel loss terms, namely the Helmholtz velocity decomposition constraint and elastic deformation constraint, and a practical local flow fusion module to track the movement of gel materials captured by a monocular camera. These contributions improve displacement measurement accuracy and enhance vision-based tactile sensors' capability to estimate physical information. The rest of this paper is organized as follows. Section 2 provides an introduction to previous works related to vision-based tactile sensors and dense displacement processing. In Sect. 3, the structure and individual modules of the proposed GelFlow method are elaborated on and discussed in detail. The comparison results with other optical flow methods and the ablation study are presented in Sect. 4. Finally, the conclusions of this work are discussed in Sect. 5.

2   Related Work

The ability to perceive and model the contact surface's three-dimensional (3D) geometry is a fundamental feature that distinguishes vision-based tactile sensors from conventional tactile sensors. Based on different principles of 3D surface reconstruction, vision-based tactile sensors can be divided into two categories: sensors based on photometric stereo reconstruction and sensors based on multi-view geometry reconstruction. Among the first type of sensors, the GelSight [9] sensor uses an RGB trichromatic light source to illuminate the contact layer and a monocular camera to capture the image. This algorithm enables it to obtain the normal gradient of each pixel, resulting in high accuracy for contact geometry. However, this method requires rigorous structural design and light source calibration. The GelSlim [10] sensor improves GelSight's optical path system by using a mirror-reflective structure so that the camera no longer has to face the contact body, making the entire sensor compact. The DIGIT [11] sensor is low-cost, compact, and provides high-resolution tactile perception, making it more practical for robotic finger manipulation. Unlike the previous flat structure contact layer, DenseTact [12] sensor uses a spherical contact layer, making it more suitable for sensing complex object surfaces. Among the second type of sensors, OmniTact [13] sensor uses multiple micro-cameras to capture multi-directional high-resolution deformation information to obtain accurate and reliable measurement results. GelStereo [14] sensor simplifies the number of cameras required by using binocular cameras to calculate the depth information of the contact surface through the disparity map in left and right views. Tac3D [15] further simplifies the number of cameras by using a monocular camera with a mirror system to achieve a pseudo-binocular imaging effect, achieving the same 3D reconstruction purpose.

In addition to 3D reconstruction, other valuable information, such as force estimation and sliding detection, is also crucial for robot perception. This information is obtained by measuring the deformation of the contact layer and then converting it according to specific criteria. Optical flow is an essential technique for deformation estimation, and accurate optical flow estimation with high resolution can provide more detailed information for more precise and dexterous operations. There are two primary approaches to enhancing the reliability of optical flow estimation: utilizing more precise optical flow algorithms and designing better marker layers. During the early stages of vision-based tactile sensor development, the Lucas-Kanada optical flow method [16] was utilized to track the movement of markers, which could only produce a sparse vector field. Interpolation methods are used for upsampling the sparse field, and significant errors occur during this process [6]. Subsequently, more robust and accurate pixel-level optical flow methods such as Farneback [17] and Dense Inverse Search (DIS) [18] methods were adopted to avoid the interpolation error and improve estimation precision [6]. The conventional marker layer consists of an array of sparse black dot markers, which does not provide rich deformation information. Moreover, a single color pattern lacked robustness in optical flow estimation due to the brightness conservation hypothesis. When using a single color pattern, the similarity of pixels made the optical flow estimation confusing. In order to overcome the limitations mentioned above, researchers have proposed various types of marker layers. [19] added high-density internal markers, which enabled dense optical flow tracking for estimating shear-induced membrane displacement. [6]

replaced the sparse black dot markers with a novel random color pattern, which achieved more accurate and higher resolution two-dimensional (2D) deformation estimation.

In this work, our purpose is to propose a pixel-level optical flow method with high accuracy and robustness. Our method takes advantage of the powerful tools of deep learning, and we hope it can be helpful in deformation estimation and other downstream tasks in vision-based tactile sensors.

3   Method

3.1   Network Architecture

Fig. 1 shows the framework of the GelFlow. First, the encoder module of PWC-Net [20] is adopted to extracted the multi-scale features for the input image pairs I_1 and I_2 and denoted as $F_1^s(I_1)$ and $F_2^s(I_2)$, where the superscript s represents the sth scale of the pyramid. In Optical Flow Estimation Module, apart from basic operators in PWC-Net like Cost Volume Operator, Coarse Flow Estimator and Refined Flow Estimator, we add Local Flow Fusion Module (LFFM) for better gel-like materials deformation estimation. The output flow at the current pyramid scale $V_{1\rightarrow2}^s$ is upsampled by a factor of 2 using bilinear interpolation and then used as the initial flow for the subsequent scale $V_{1\rightarrow2}^{s-1}$. According to the coarse-to-fine strategy, the feature of the second image $F_2^s(I_2)$ are warped [21] using the output flow (denoted by $\tilde{F}_2^s(I_2)$) to reduce the feature distance between the extracted feature of the first image $F_1^s(I_1)$, enabling better handling of large displacement motion. Note that the input flow at the top scale is set to 0, and the final output flow of GelFlow $V_{1\rightarrow2}^0$ is obtained by bilinear upsampling of the output flow by a factor of 4 at the bottom scale. The multi-scale strategy allows for the extraction of richer feature information by convolving the input image at different scales, improving the robustness of optical flow estimation.

3.2   Local Flow Fusion Module

As the cross-linking network structure of the gel material results in its deformation showing overall smoothness [22], thus the generated optical flow field exhibits a blurred effect. Taking advantage of this property, we designed a local optical flow fusion module, and Fig. 2 shows the implementation details of this module. Context features C^s extracted by PWC-Net from each scale are utilized to construct the weight matrix. At each position, the feature vector is dot produced with the feature vectors of its neighboring positions (the number of neighboring positions is determined by the fusion range, usually 3×3 or 5×5) to compute the similarities. The results are then normalized using a softmax function. The weight matrix enables the flow to consider not only the position itself but also its surrounding area, thereby achieving a blurred effect.

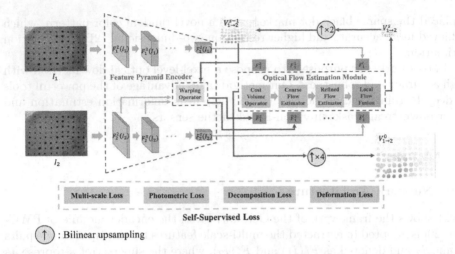

Fig. 1. GelFlow, the proposed architecture for deformation measurement for gel-like materials using coarse-to-fine strategy, local flow fusion module and Self-supervised losses.

3.3   Helmholtz Velocity Decomposition Constraint

The deformation of gel materials is complex due to their elastic properties. Based on the Helmholtz velocity decomposition theorem, compressible motion can be decomposed into four components: translational motion, linear deformation motion, shear deformation motion, and rotational motion, given by

$$\mathbf{u}(\mathbf{x} + \delta\mathbf{x}) = \mathbf{u}(\mathbf{x}) + \mathrm{X}\delta\mathbf{x} + \Theta\delta\mathbf{x} + \mathrm{Z}\delta\mathbf{x}, \tag{1}$$

$$\mathrm{X} = \begin{bmatrix} \varepsilon_{xx} & 0 \\ 0 & \varepsilon_{yy} \end{bmatrix}, \Theta = \begin{bmatrix} 0 & \varepsilon_{xy} \\ \varepsilon_{xy} & 0 \end{bmatrix}, \mathrm{Z} = \begin{bmatrix} 0 & -\omega \\ \omega & 0 \end{bmatrix} \tag{2}$$

where X, Θ and Z denote the linear distortion rate tensor, shear distortion rate tensor, and rotation tensor, respectively; $\varepsilon_{xx} = \partial u/\partial x$ and $\varepsilon_{yy} = \partial v/\partial y$ are the linear distortion rates in the x and y directions, respectively; $\varepsilon_{xy} = (\partial u/\partial y + \partial v/\partial x)/2$ is the shear distortion rate; $\omega = (\partial v/\partial x - \partial u/\partial y)/2$ is the rotational angular rate. By decomposing the flow, we can impose more refined constraints on each component, achieving high-precision flow estimation. Equation 1 can be further transformed as

$$\frac{\mathbf{u}(\mathbf{x} + \delta\mathbf{x}) - \mathbf{u}(\mathbf{x})}{\delta\mathbf{x}} = \mathrm{X} + \Theta + \mathrm{Z}. \tag{3}$$

Thus, the values of linear distortion rate tensor X, shear distortion tensor Θ, and rotational tensor Z are constraint to satisfy the small motions assumption, i.e.

$$\|\mathrm{vec}(\mathrm{X})\|_1 + \lambda_\Theta \|\mathrm{vec}(\Theta)\|_1 + \lambda_\mathrm{Z} \|\mathrm{vec}(\mathrm{Z})\|_1, \tag{4}$$

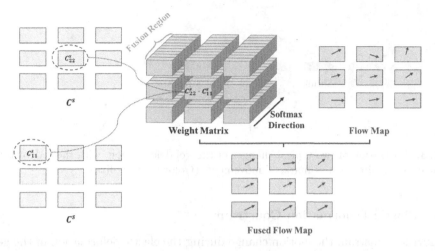

Fig. 2. Structure of Local Flow Fusion Module. The feature vector at each position is dot producted with the feature vectors in the surrounding area. Then, all of the results within the local range are passed through a softmax function and used as weights for weighted fusion with the estimated optical flow. This process results in a locally smooth optical flow field.

where,

$$\|\text{vec}(\text{X})\|_1 = |\varepsilon_{xx}| + |\varepsilon_{yy}|, \tag{5}$$

$$\|\text{vec}(\Theta)\|_1 = 2|\varepsilon_{xy}|, \tag{6}$$

$$\|\text{vec}(\text{Z})\|_1 = 2|\omega|, \tag{7}$$

λ_Θ and λ_Z are coefficients of distortion and rotation tensors, respectively, which values will affect the smooth property of the optical flow; the function $\text{vec}(\cdot)$ is used to convert the input into a vector representation. With the help of the Helmholtz velocity decomposition theorem, the compressible motion can be better estimated [23].

Furthermore, the optical flow estimated on the edge of the image is more precise due to the larger gradient. The deformation of the gel is similar between the edge and other flattened areas. Thus, we adopt an anti-edge-aware weight for the motion smooth term, and the final decomposition loss is written as

$$\mathcal{L}_{dc}^s = \left(1 - e^{-\beta\|\nabla I_1^s\|_1}\right) \left(\|\text{vec}(\text{X})\|_1 + \lambda_\Theta \|\text{vec}(\Theta)\|_1 + \lambda_Z \|\text{vec}(\text{Z})\|_1\right) \tag{8}$$

In Eq. 8, when an edge is detected (indicated by a larger value in $\|\nabla I_1^s\|_1$), the weight $1 - e^{-\beta\|\nabla I_1^s\|_1}$ increases. Consequently, the remaining term in $\mathcal{L}_{dc}^s$ must decrease during the minimization process, which enhances the smoothness between the detected edge and the surrounding area.

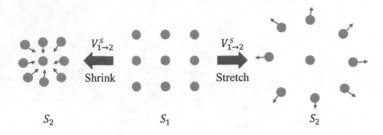

Fig. 3. Illustration of two typical changes of the gel deformation, with the red vectors indicating the direction of markers' movement. (Color figure online)

3.4   Elastic Deformation Constraint

To further constrain the motion change during the elastic deformation of the gel materials, we propose a novel regularization term named the deformation loss term. As shown in Fig. 3, there are two typical deformations in the motion of gel materials, i.e., shrinking and stretching. To enforce spatial consistency in gel motion, we can incorporate a constraint that regulates the change in the area between adjacent pixels before and after deformation. Firstly, the pixel-level area change ratio is estimated between the input image pairs. Then, the estimated motion is smooth over the entire gel materials by constraining the gradient of the ratio. Different from [24], we calculate the deformation ratio separately for the x and y directions:

$$(x^{'} - x_{c}^{'}) = \mathcal{R}_x(x - x_c), \quad x \in \mathcal{N}_{3\times 3}(x_c), \tag{9}$$

$$(y^{'} - y_{c}^{'}) = \mathcal{R}_y(y - y_c), \quad y \in \mathcal{N}_{3\times 3}(y_c), \tag{10}$$

where x' and y' denote the positions x and y warped by the optical flow $V_{1\to 2}$; the subscript c represents the center of the local window; $\mathcal{N}_{3\times 3}$ represents the local window size of 3×3. The final deformation ratio is obtained by multiplying the two ratios together:

$$\mathcal{R} = \mathcal{R}_x \mathcal{R}_y. \tag{11}$$

Finally, the combined anti-edge-aware weight can be utilized to define the deformation loss as follows:

$$\mathcal{L}_{df}^s = (1 - e^{-\beta \|\nabla I_1^s\|_1}) \|\nabla \mathcal{R}\|_1. \tag{12}$$

3.5   Loss Function

The widely used photometric loss function in optical flow tasks is adopted for robust flow estimation, which takes the form:

$$\mathcal{L}_{ph}^s = \alpha \frac{1 - \text{SSIM}(\tilde{I}_1^s, I_1^s)}{2} + (1 - \alpha)\left\|\tilde{I}_1^s - I_1^s\right\|_1, \tag{13}$$

where SSIM denotes the structural similarity index; α represents the balance between SSIM and L_1 distance; $\tilde{I}_1^s$ indicates the warped image I_2^s using the optical flow $V_{1\rightarrow 2}^s$ at scale s. The photometric loss, combined with the proposed decomposition loss and deformation loss, constructs the loss function at each scale. The multi-scale loss is defined as the weighted sum of the losses at each scale, denoted by:

$$\mathcal{L} = \sum_{s=0}^{l-2} \lambda_s \mathcal{L}_{self}^s = \sum_{s=0}^{l-2} \lambda_s (\mathcal{L}_{ph}^s + \lambda_{dc}\mathcal{L}_{dc}^s + \lambda_{df}\mathcal{L}_{df}^s), \tag{14}$$

where l is the number of total scales created by PWC-Net; λ_{dc} and λ_{df} are coefficients that control the balance between each loss; λ_s are parameters that weigh the importance of each scale.

4 Experimental Analysis

4.1 Experiment Setup

The proposed self-supervised learning method does not require labeled training data. Therefore, we extract 1327 image pairs with a resolution of 480×640 pixels from videos captured by [25]. We reserve 8 image pairs with the typical motion of gel deformation (large displacement, shrinking and stretching) for validation and comparison with other optical flow methods. We train the network for 200 epochs on the training dataset, with a batch size of 4 image pairs per epoch. Subsequently, we fine-tune the network for an additional 800 epochs using the validation dataset. The number of pyramid scales, l, is set to 8. The fusion region size of the LFFM is set to 3×3. In the photometric loss term, α is set to 0.85. In the decomposition loss term, β is set to 10, and both λ_Θ and λ_Z are set to 0.01. In the deformation loss term, β is set to 10. In the multi-scale loss term, λ_s is set to 1.0 for each scale, while λ_{dc} and λ_{df} are set to 75 and 0.01, respectively. The images are initially resized to a resolution of 512×640 pixels before being fed into the network. The output optical flows are then resized to the original resolution of the images for validation.

4.2 Evaluation Metrics

Since there are no ground truth labels in the dataset, we need to warp the second images into pseudo-first images using the estimated optical flows and compare the similarity between pseudo-first and authentic-first images. The higher the similarity, the better the estimation. Two widely used metrics for evaluating image similarity are PSNR (Peak Signal-to-Noise Ratio) and SSIM. They are defined as follows:

$$\text{PSNR}(I, \tilde{I}) = 10 \times \log_{10}\left(\frac{(2^n - 1)^2}{\text{MSE}(I, \tilde{I})}\right), \tag{15}$$

$$\text{SSIM}(I, \tilde{I}) = \frac{(2\mu_x\mu_y + c_1)(2\sigma_{xy} + c_2)}{(\mu_x^2 + \mu_y^2 + c_1)(\sigma_x^2 + \sigma_y^2 + c_2)}, \tag{16}$$

where, n represents the bit depth of the pixels; $MSE(I, \tilde{I})$ is the mean square error between the input image I and the warped image $\tilde{I}$; μ_x and μ_y are the means of I and $\tilde{I}$, respectively; σ_x and σ_y are the variances of I and $\tilde{I}$, and σ_{xy} represents their covariance; c_1 and c_2 are constants used to maintain stability. Therefore, we will use these two metrics for comparisons and evaluations in the following subsections.

Table 1. Comparison with traditional and deep learning-based optical flow methods using the validation dataset. '#' represents an image pair. The best and the second-best values within each category are marked as bold and underlined, respectively. The best value among all the methods is marked in red. 'ft' denotes fine-tuning the model on the validation dataset.

	Method	Metric	#1	#2	#3	#4	#5	#6	#7	#8
Traditional	Farneback	PSNR	38.48	35.02	32.57	32.03	31.73	32.31	33.70	32.20
		SSIM	0.96	0.91	0.91	0.89	0.89	0.91	0.91	0.90
	DIS (Ultra-fast)	PSNR	39.64	35.12	32.89	33.23	32.63	32.92	34.93	32.39
		SSIM	0.97	0.92	0.92	0.92	0.92	0.93	0.94	0.91
	DIS (Fast)	PSNR	39.75	35.26	32.89	33.28	32.60	32.97	35.11	32.49
		SSIM	0.97	0.92	0.92	0.92	0.92	0.93	0.94	0.91
	DIS (medium)	PSNR	**40.25**	35.41	33.25	33.86	33.27	33.24	35.41	32.73
		SSIM	**0.97**	**0.92**	0.92	**0.93**	**0.93**	**0.93**	**0.94**	**0.91**
	TV-L1	PSNR	39.98	**35.44**	**33.31**	**33.95**	**33.68**	**33.42**	**35.64**	**32.88**
		SSIM	0.97	0.92	0.92	0.92	0.93	0.93	0.94	0.91
Deep Learning	RAFT	PSNR	37.73	34.83	31.49	31.11	31.17	32.44	34.78	31.57
		SSIM	0.97	0.91	0.91	0.91	0.91	0.92	0.94	0.90
	ARFlow	PSNR	39.76	35.22	32.88	33.44	32.54	33.05	35.30	32.46
		SSIM	0.97	0.92	0.92	0.92	0.92	0.93	0.94	0.91
	SelfFlow	PSNR	40.22	35.31	33.12	33.78	32.99	33.62	35.44	32.65
		SSIM	0.97	0.92	0.92	0.93	0.93	0.93	0.94	0.91
	SelfFlow+ft	PSNR	40.36	35.74	33.35	34.30	33.64	34.22	35.90	33.02
		SSIM	0.97	0.93	0.92	0.93	0.93	0.94	0.95	0.92
	GelFlow	PSNR	40.57	35.90	33.43	34.34	33.65	33.96	35.94	33.11
		SSIM	0.98	0.93	0.93	0.93	0.93	0.94	0.95	0.93
	GelFlow+ft	PSNR	40.76	36.00	33.66	34.71	34.25	35.00	36.13	33.22
		SSIM	0.98	0.93	0.93	0.94	0.94	0.95	0.95	0.93

4.3   Comparisons with Classical Optical Flow Methods

We compared traditional dense optical flow methods (Farneback, DIS, TV-L1) using OpenCV and deep learning-based optical flow methods (RAFT [26], ARFlow [27], and a self-supervised method named SelfFlow using a photometric loss mentioned before with a first-order smoothness loss [28]). The results of the comparison are presented in Table 1. Notably, the self-supervised methods SelfFlow and GelFlow were fine-tuned using the strategy described in Sect. 4.1. The validation dataset showed that TV-L1 and DIS (medium) performed similarly and outperformed other traditional methods. However, the solving strategy of TV-L1 is time-consuming, making it much slower than the optimized DIS method. Consequently, the DIS method is widely used as the dense optical flow estimator in current vision-based tactile sensors.

It is worth mentioning that we directly utilized the pre-trained models of RAFT and ARFlow, testing them on the vision-based tactile dataset. Therefore, their performance may not be satisfactory. On the other hand, SelfFlow and GelFlow were trained on the dataset and further fine-tuned. As a result, they outperformed the existing traditional methods. The excellent performance can be attributed to the strong learning ability of convolutional neural networks and the well-designed loss functions guiding the network output towards the ground truth. Among all the candidate methods, GelFlow achieved the best performance with its proposed flow fusion operation and motion decomposition and deformation loss, which guide the parameters of the network towards global optimization. In conclusion, the comparisons indicate that the proposed GelFlow method is particularly adept at handling gel materials' deformation.

5 Conclusion

In this study, we propose the GelFlow method, which incorporates several novel components to address the challenges posed by gel deformation. Firstly, GelFlow constructs a multi-scale feature pyramid to extract hidden features from the input image pairs and handle large displacements effectively. A local flow fusion module fuses the flow using neighboring flows with appropriate weights. This fusion process achieves a blurred effect, which is crucial for capturing the deformations occurring in gel materials. We propose two novel loss functions to better handle the intricate gel deformations: the velocity decomposition loss and the elastic deformation loss. A photometric loss combined with the proposed two novel motion smoothness losses is used to construct the multi-scale loss to better guide the network from global optimization. Finally, the network is trained in a self-supervised manner, and the comparison result with other optical flow methods indicates that the GelFlow method performs the best due to the superior capacity of the convolutional neural networks to extract valuable features and the strong ability of global optimization.

References

1. Liu, H., Yu, Y., Sun, F., Gu, J.: Visual-tactile fusion for object recognition. IEEE Trans. Autom. Sci. Eng. **14**(2), 996–1008 (2016)
2. Zhang, S., et al.: Hardware technology of vision-based tactile sensor: a review. IEEE Sensors J. **22**, 21410–21427 (2022)
3. Sato, K., Kamiyama, K., Kawakami, N., Tachi, S.: Finger-shaped gelforce: sensor for measuring surface traction fields for robotic hand. IEEE Trans. Haptics **3**(1), 37–47 (2009)
4. Cui, S., Wang, R., Hu, J., Zhang, C., Chen, L., Wang, S.: Self-supervised contact geometry learning by gelstereo visuotactile sensing. IEEE Trans. Instrum. Meas. **71**, 1–9 (2021)

5. James, J.W., Lepora, N.F.: Slip detection for grasp stabilization with a multifingered tactile robot hand. IEEE Trans. Rob. **37**(2), 506–519 (2020)
6. Du, Y., Zhang, G., Zhang, Y., Wang, M.Y.: High-resolution 3-dimensional contact deformation tracking for fingervision sensor with dense random color pattern. IEEE Robot. Autom. Lett. **6**(2), 2147–2154 (2021)
7. Bradski, G.: The opencv library. Dr. Dobb's J. Software Tools Prof. Program. **25**(11), 120–123 (2000)
8. Zhang, G., Du, Y., Yu, H., Wang, M.Y.: Deltact: a vision-based tactile sensor using a dense color pattern. IEEE Robot. Autom. Lett. **7**(4), 10778–10785 (2022)
9. Yuan, W., Dong, S., Adelson, E.H.: Gelsight: high-resolution robot tactile sensors for estimating geometry and force. Sensors **17**(12), 2762 (2017)
10. Donlon, E., Dong, S., Liu, M., Li, J., Adelson, E., Rodriguez, A.: Gelslim: a high-resolution, compact, robust, and calibrated tactile-sensing finger. In: 2018 IEEE/RSJ International Conference on Intelligent Robots and Systems (IROS), pp. 1927–1934. IEEE (2018)
11. Lambeta, M., et al.: Digit: a novel design for a low-cost compact high-resolution tactile sensor with application to in-hand manipulation. IEEE Robot. Autom. Lett. **5**(3), 3838–3845 (2020)
12. Do, W.K., Kennedy, M.: Densetact: optical tactile sensor for dense shape reconstruction. In: 2022 International Conference on Robotics and Automation (ICRA), pp. 6188–6194. IEEE (2022)
13. Padmanabha, A., Ebert, F., Tian, S., Calandra, R., Finn, C., Levine, S.: Omnitact: a multi-directional high-resolution touch sensor. In: 2020 IEEE International Conference on Robotics and Automation (ICRA), pp. 618–624. IEEE (2020)
14. Cui, S., Wang, R., Hu, J., Wei, J., Wang, S., Lou, Z.: In-hand object localization using a novel high-resolution visuotactile sensor. IEEE Trans. Industr. Electron. **69**(6), 6015–6025 (2021)
15. Zhang, L., Wang, Y., Jiang, Y.: Tac3d: a novel vision-based tactile sensor for measuring forces distribution and estimating friction coefficient distribution. arXiv preprint arXiv:2202.06211 (2022)
16. Bouguet, J.Y., et al.: Pyramidal implementation of the affine lucas kanade feature tracker description of the algorithm. Intel Corporation **5**(1–10), 4 (2001)
17. Farnebäck, G.: Two-frame motion estimation based on polynomial expansion. In: Bigun, J., Gustavsson, T. (eds.) SCIA 2003. LNCS, vol. 2749, pp. 363–370. Springer, Heidelberg (2003). https://doi.org/10.1007/3-540-45103-X_50
18. Kroeger, T., Timofte, R., Dai, D., Van Gool, L.: Fast optical flow using dense inverse search. In: Leibe, B., Matas, J., Sebe, N., Welling, M. (eds.) ECCV 2016. LNCS, vol. 9908, pp. 471–488. Springer, Cham (2016). https://doi.org/10.1007/978-3-319-46493-0_29
19. Kuppuswamy, N., Alspach, A., Uttamchandani, A., Creasey, S., Ikeda, T., Tedrake, R.: Soft-bubble grippers for robust and perceptive manipulation. In: 2020 IEEE/RSJ International Conference on Intelligent Robots and Systems (IROS), pp. 9917–9924. IEEE (2020)
20. Sun, D., Yang, X., Liu, M.Y., Kautz, J.: PWC-net: CNNs for optical flow using pyramid, warping, and cost volume. In: Proceedings of the IEEE Conference on Computer Vision and Pattern Recognition, pp. 8934–8943 (2018)
21. Brox, T., Bruhn, A., Papenberg, N., Weickert, J.: High accuracy optical flow estimation based on a theory for warping. In: Pajdla, T., Matas, J. (eds.) ECCV 2004. LNCS, vol. 3024, pp. 25–36. Springer, Heidelberg (2004). https://doi.org/10.1007/978-3-540-24673-2_3

22. Du, Y., Zhang, G., Wang, M.Y.: 3d contact point cloud reconstruction from vision-based tactile flow. IEEE Robot. Autom. Lett. **7**(4), 12177–12184 (2022)
23. Lu, J., Yang, H., Zhang, Q., Yin, Z.: An accurate optical flow estimation of PIV using fluid velocity decomposition. Exp. Fluids **62**, 1–16 (2021)
24. Yang, G., Ramanan, D.: Upgrading optical flow to 3D scene flow through optical expansion. In: Proceedings of the IEEE/CVF Conference on Computer Vision and Pattern Recognition, pp. 1334–1343 (2020)
25. Yang, F., Ma, C., Zhang, J., Zhu, J., Yuan, W., Owens, A.: Touch and go: learning from human-collected vision and touch. In: Thirty-sixth Conference on Neural Information Processing Systems Datasets and Benchmarks Track (2022). https://openreview.net/forum?id=ZZ3FeSSPPblo
26. Teed, Z., Deng, J.: RAFT: recurrent all-pairs field transforms for optical flow. In: Vedaldi, A., Bischof, H., Brox, T., Frahm, J.-M. (eds.) ECCV 2020. LNCS, vol. 12347, pp. 402–419. Springer, Cham (2020). https://doi.org/10.1007/978-3-030-58536-5_24
27. Liu, L., et al.: Learning by analogy: reliable supervision from transformations for unsupervised optical flow estimation. In: IEEE Conference on Computer Vision and Pattern Recognition (CVPR) (2020)
28. Jonschkowski, R., et al.: What matters in unsupervised optical flow. In: Vedaldi, A., Bischof, H., Brox, T., Frahm, J.-M. (eds.) ECCV 2020. LNCS, vol. 12347, pp. 557–572. Springer, Cham (2020). https://doi.org/10.1007/978-3-030-58536-5_33

CLOE: Novelty Detection via Contrastive Learning with Outlier Exposure

Tianyang Liu[1], Quan Liang[1,2], and Hua Yang[2(✉)]

[1] Fujian Provincial Key Laboratory of Big Data Mining and Applications, Fujian University of Technology, Fuzhou 350118, China
2211308071@smail.fjut.edu.cn
[2] School of Mechanical Science and Engineering, State Key Laboratory of Digital Manufacturing Equipment and Technology, Huazhong University of Science and Technology, Wuhan 430074, China
huayang@hust.edu.cn

Abstract. Novelty detection (ND) methods seek to identify anomalies within a specific dataset. Although self-supervised representation learning is commonly used in such applications, inadequate training data may reduce the effectiveness of these methods. It is thus reasonable to use external data to improve these performances. Here, we propose a simple and effective network, CLOE, for image-based novelty detection. Our method includes a pretrained ViT model as a feature extractor and employs the contrastive learning technique to train the dataset with external data. We compare the performance of two types of extra training settings: (1) The augmented data of the original dataset. (2) The fake images obtained from generative models. The demonstrated approach achieves a new state-of-the-art performance in novelty detection, as evidenced by achieving an ROC-AUC of 99.72% on the CIFAR-10 dataset.

Keywords: Novelty detection · Contrastive learning · Outlier exposure

1 Introduction

Novelty detection (ND) [1] involves identifying anomalous samples within a given dataset. This research field has a long-standing history, finds numerous applications in computer vision and holds considerable importance in both scientific research and industrial settings. Here, we address ND tasks with three settings: (i) utilizing a pretrained Vision Transformer (ViT) [2] model as the feature extractor, (ii) employing the method of contrastive learning to enhance the novelty detection capability of the network, and (iii) introducing an outlier exposure dataset as external data for training.

Recently, researchers have discovered that pretrained models enable a network to quickly adapt to optimal settings. The pretrained models typically serve

H. Yang et al. (Eds.): ICIRA 2023, LNAI 14273, pp. 38–47, 2023.
https://doi.org/10.1007/978-981-99-6498-7_4

as the backbone because of their exceptional feature extraction capabilities. Consequently, it is a reasonable approach to seek a backbone with superior feature extraction abilities. The ViT model has proven its superiority in the field of computer vision, particularly when applied to large-scale datasets. As a result, an increasing number of methods now employ the pretrained ViT model instead of the pretrained ResNet model as the feature extractor, leading to promising outcomes.

An important issue in current ND approaches is the reliance on a limited amount of normal training data for representation learning, which can potentially restrict the quality of learned representations [3]. Previous methods have shown that the use of external datasets benefits such applications. Outlier exposure (OE) [4] is a dataset that is employed to simulate anomalies. Various approaches can be used for generating OE, including data augmentation techniques applied to the original dataset, utilization of datasets unrelated to the tested dataset, or generating synthetic datasets using generative models. It is an effective self-supervised method, but it may fail when the samples in the OE dataset resemble anomalies more than normal samples do.

However, the introduction of the OE dataset may misguide the network toward incorrect anomaly detection if the network fails to effectively distinguish between the normal and abnormal features during training. To address these limitations, we incorporate contrastive learning as an approach to optimize the performance of our method. By employing contrastive learning, we seek to enhance the consistency between similar samples while simultaneously increasing the dissimilarity between normal and abnormal images [5].

In this paper, we present a simple yet effective network for novelty detection, called CLOE (contrastive learning with outlier exposure). The main contributions of our work are as follows:

1) We propose a novel network CLOE, which utilizes contrastive learning to compare the features extracted from the normal samples and the outlier exposure. This approach aims to enhance the network's ability to discriminate anomalies.
2) We propose two types of external data settings: (i) augmented data on the original dataset and (ii) an outlier exposure dataset obtained on the original images using the generative model. This OE dataset consists of samples that are similar to the original dataset.
3) Experiments demonstrate the state-of-the-art novelty detection performance of the proposed network (e.g., 99.7% ROC-AUC on CIFAR-10 [6].

2   Related Works

In this section, we provide a review of the relevant literature on one-class ND methods. Numerous effective approaches have been developed to enhance the performance of this task, as can be classified into three categories: utilizing pretrained models, incorporating outlier exposure datasets, and employing contrastive learning.

Pretrained Methods

Several works have used pretrained networks as backbones. In [7], the KNN distance between the test input and the feature set of the training data is employed as the anomaly score. PANDA [3] aims to project the pretrained features into a compact feature space by utilizing the DeepSVDD [8] objective function. In [9], intermediate knowledge from the pretrained network on normal data is distilled into a more compact network. SimpleNet [10] utilizes a pretrained network to extract features from various hierarchies to generate local features.

Outlier Exposure-Based Methods

The main purpose of introducing OE is to augment the training set. Previous studies have demonstrated successful utilization of fake data for ND. The commonly adopted approaches are employing images from other datasets [3] or using synthetic images that may be generated by GANs [11]. Transformaly [12] maps the data to a pretrained feature space and a fine-tuned feature space. FITYMI [13] conducts a comparative analysis of different generative models' FID [14] to illustrate that the quality of generated samples can improve the performance of ND methods.

Contrastive Learning

Contrastive learning differentiates similar samples from others by essential information. AMDIM [15] and SimCLR [5] share the common approach of maximizing similarity between representations from a single image while minimizing similarity with representations from other images. MoCo [16] employs a dynamic dictionary to construct a large and consistent dictionary for effective contrastive unsupervised learning. MSAD [17] introduces a novel loss function to address the challenges of adapting features for anomaly detection and evaluates its significance for adapting features for anomaly detection.

3   Method

In this section, we provide a detailed introduction of our proposed method. Initially, we present the pipeline of our approach, including the training and testing phases in Figs. 1 and 2, respectively. Then, we describe the components of our network, including the fine-tuned feature extractor, the generated outlier exposure and the contrastive loss. Finally, we introduce the anomaly score employed in this paper to discriminate the anomalies.

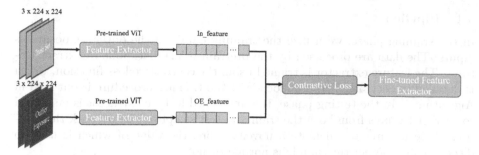

Fig. 1. Training Phase During this phase, the *feature extractor* extracts the features of the training set and outlier exposure separately. The *feature extractor* will be fine-tuned with the contrastive loss.

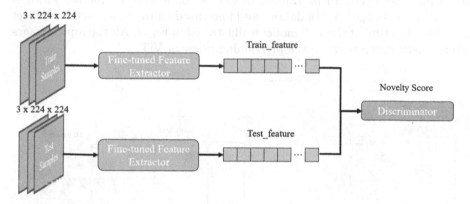

Fig. 2. Testing Phase During this phase, the *fine-tuned feature extractor* extracts the features of both normal and abnormal samples and calculates the novelty score to decide whether the samples are normal or not.

Algorithm 1. CLOE pipeline pseudocode

```
# F: Feature Extractor
# N: Normal Samples
# OE: Outlier Exposure
for i in train_data_size :
    in_f = F(N)
    out_f = F(OE)

    optimizer.no_grad

    loss = contrastive_loss(in_f, out_f)
    loss.backward()
```

3.1 Pipeline

In the training phase, we utilize the training data and the outlier exposure as inputs. The data are processed by the pretrained ViT backbone to extract features. The feature extractor is trained using the contrastive loss function, which is detailed in Sect. 3.4. The pseudocode of the training procedure is outlined in Algorithm 1. In the testing phase, the fine-tuned feature extractor is employed to extract features from both the train and test samples. The network then utilizes these features to calculate a novelty score, the value of which is used to discriminate whether the sample is normal or not.

3.2 Fine-Tuned Feature Extractor

We utilize the ViT-B_16 pretrained model as our feature extractor, which is trained on the ImageNet-21k dataset and fine-tuned on the ImageNet-1k dataset [18]. The structure of the ViT model is illustrated in Fig. 3. All the input images are normalized according to the pretraining phase of ViT.

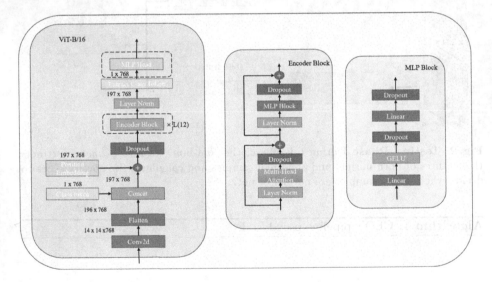

Fig. 3. ViT-B_16 structure The pretrained model contains 12 encoder blocks.

3.3 Generated Outlier Exposure

OE compensates for the lack of anomalous samples in the dataset. In contrast, some methods introduce images from other datasets as external samples, which may result in unpredictable errors. A growing trend in recent studies is the utilization of generative models to obtain synthetic images that closely resemble the original dataset as OE. In our paper, we employ the diffusion model for generating OE due to its ability to produce reasonably high-quality images.

3.4   Contrastive Learning

To ensure that the OE has the intended impact, we incorporate contrastive learning during the training phase. Contrastive learning seeks to minimize the distance between features of normal samples while maximizing the distance between normal and abnormal samples during inference. This technique is defined as

$$d(f(x), f(x^+)) << d(f(x), f(x^-)) \tag{1}$$

where x means the input test images, x^+ means the normal images and x^- means the abnormal images. The contrastive loss function is defined by

$$\mathcal{L}(x_i, x_{oe}) = -\log\left(\frac{\exp(\text{sim}(\frac{\phi(x_i)}{\|\phi(x_i)\|}, \frac{\phi(x_{oe})}{\|\phi(x_{oe})\|})/\tau)}{\sum_1^B \mathbf{1}_{[i \neq m]} \cdot \exp(sim(\frac{\phi(x_i)}{\|\phi(x_i)\|}, \frac{\phi(x_{oe})}{\|\phi(x_{oe})\|})/\tau)}\right) \tag{2}$$

where ϕ means the feature extractor, τ means the temperature coefficient, sim means the calculation of similarity, and B means the size of the batch.

3.5   Anomaly Scoring

During the testing phase, we compute the kNN distances between the features of the target image x and the tested image y to obtain novelty score. The anomaly score tends to be small for comparisons between normal samples, and becomes larger for comparisons involving normal and abnormal samples. By comparing the anomaly score $s(x)$ to a predefined threshold, we can determine whether the tested image is normal or not. The anomaly score is defined as:

$$s(x) = \sum_{\phi(y) \in N_{test}} (1 - dist(\phi(x), \phi(y))) \tag{3}$$

where $\phi(x)$ means the extracted features and $dist$ is the kNN distance.

4   Experiments

In this section, we present the dataset we used to evaluate the proposed method, the implementation details of the experiments, the benchmark settings and the experimental results.

4.1   Datasets

To better compare with previous work, we evaluate our method on the CIFAR-10 dataset. This dataset contains 50K training images and 10K test images with a scale of 32×32 in 10 categories. Typical images are illustrated in Fig. 4.

airplane

automobile

bird

cat

deer

dog

frog

horse

ship

truck

Fig. 4. The CIFAR-10 dataset A representative image for each class in the dataset.

4.2   Implementation Details

This section introduces the configuration implementation details of the experiments in this paper: Pytorch version (1.8.1), system (Ubuntu 20.04), CUDA Toolkit version (11.7.1), CPU (Intel Xeon(R) Gold 6130 CPU@2.10 GHz), memory (256 GB), GPU (NVIDIA RTX 3090), optimizer type (SGD), batch size (20), learning rate (0.001), and temperature coefficient τ (0.25).

4.3   Evaluation Metrics

One-class Novelty Detection Benchmark. To quantitatively analyze our method against others, we evaluate CLOE under the one-class ND settings. In this case, we choose one specific category as normal while considering all other categories as anomalies. During the training phase, the model is trained using the normal samples and OE images. In the testing phase, we evaluate all samples from the test set, classifying any samples not belonging to the normal class as anomalous.

4.4   Experiment Results

To verify the performance of our method, we compare it with the established SOTA methods with and without the OE setting. In the standard setting (without OE), we apply data augmentation techniques to the original training set to generate additional external data. We compare methods such as DeepSVDD [8], MHRot [19], DROC [20], CSI [21], PANDA [3], MSAD [17] and CLIP [22]. On the other hand, under the OE setting, we introduce the generated images as the OE dataset and evaluate the performance with PANDA-OE [3], FITYMI [13] and CLIP-OE [22].

Table 1. CIFAR-10 novelty detection performance (mean ROC-AUC%). Bold denotes the best results.

Category	DSVDD	MHRot	DROC	CSI	PANDA	MSAD	CLIP	Ours
Airplane	61.7	77.5	90.9	89.9	97.4	97.0	**99.4**	99.2
Automobile	65.9	96.9	98.9	99.1	98.4	98.7	**99.4**	99.3
Bird	50.8	87.3	88.1	93.1	93.9	94.8	97.4	**99.5**
Cat	59.1	80.9	83.1	86.4	90.6	94.3	**97.0**	96.1
Deer	60.9	92.7	89.9	93.9	97.5	96.9	**98.1**	95.8
Dog	65.7	90.2	90.3	93.2	94.4	97.2	97.4	**98.9**
Frog	67.7	90.9	93.5	95.1	97.4	98.2	98.1	**98.3**
Horse	67.3	96.5	98.2	98.7	97.5	98.3	**99.0**	98.9
Ship	75.9	95.2	96.5	97.9	97.6	98.5	99.7	99.7
Truck	73.1	93.3	95.2	95.5	97.4	98.3	99.3	**99.5**
Mean	64.8	90.1	92.5	94.3	96.2	97.2	**98.5**	98.5

As shown in Table 1, our method achieves the present SOTA performance with a simple network architecture. The scores presented in the table represent the average AUROC scores across all classes within each dataset. When compared to the previous method, our approach demonstrates significant improvements in ROC-AUC, specifically a 2.1% enhancement in the bird category and a 1.5% improvement in the dog category.

Table 2 indicates that the proposed method outperforms all the current SOTA methods, achieving an impressive ROC-AUC of 99.7%. In some categories, the improvement introduced by CLOE is especially notable. For example, CLOE achieves exceptional performance in the frog category with an ROC-AUC of 100.0% and improved by 0.6% on the cat category.

Table 2. CIFAR-10 with OE novelty detection performance (mean ROC-AUC%). Bold denotes the best results.

Category	PANDA-OE	FITYMI	CLIP-OE	Ours
Airplane	97.4	99.2	99.7	**99.8**
Automobile	98.4	99.4	**99.8**	99.7
Bird	93.9	99.2	99.2	**99.5**
Cat	90.6	98.1	98.8	**99.4**
Deer	97.5	99.5	99.6	99.6
Dog	94.4	98.1	**99.2**	98.9
Frog	97.4	99.8	99.9	**100**
Horse	97.5	99.5	99.8	**99.9**
Ship	97.6	99.2	99.8	99.8
Truck	97.4	98.8	99.9	99.9
Mean	96.2	99.1	99.6	**99.7**

5 Conclusions

This paper presents a novel network CLOE for the one-class novelty detection task. CLOE leverages a pretrained ViT model as the feature extractor and incorporates contrastive learning during the training phase. The network's anomaly detection capabilities are enhanced by utilizing an outlier exposure dataset. The experiments conducted on the CIFAR-10 dataset verified the state-of-the-art performance of our network. In the future, we plan to conduct extensive experiments on multiple datasets to validate the generalizability and robustness of our approach.

References

1. Salehi, M., Mirzaei, H., Hendrycks, D., Li, Y., Rohban, M.H., Sabokrou, M.: A unified survey on anomaly, novelty, open-set, and out-of-distribution detection: solutions and future challenges. arXiv preprint arXiv:2110.14051 (2021)
2. Dosovitskiy, A., et al.: An image is worth 16×16 words: transformers for image recognition at scale (2021)
3. Reiss, T., Cohen, N., Bergman, L., Hoshen, Y.: Panda: adapting pretrained features for anomaly detection and segmentation. In: 2021 IEEE/CVF Conference on Computer Vision and Pattern Recognition (CVPR), pp. 2805–2813. IEEE (2021)
4. Hendrycks, D., Mazeika, M., Dietterich, T.: Deep anomaly detection with outlier exposure (2018)
5. Chen, T., Kornblith, S., Norouzi, M., Hinton, G.: A simple framework for contrastive learning of visual representations. In: International conference on machine learning, pp. 1597–1607. PMLR (2020)
6. Krizhevsky, A., Hinton, G., et al.: Learning multiple layers of features from tiny images (2009)

7. Bergman, L., Cohen, N., Hoshen, Y.: Deep nearest neighbor anomaly detection. arXiv preprint arXiv:2002.10445 (2020)
8. Ruff, L., Vandermeulen, R.A., Görnitz, N., Deecke, L., Kloft, M.: Deep one-class classification. In: International Conference on Machine Learning (2018)
9. Salehi, M., Sadjadi, N., Baselizadeh, S., Rohban, M.H., Rabiee, H.R.: Multiresolution knowledge distillation for anomaly detection. In: Proceedings of the IEEE/CVF Conference on Computer Vision and Pattern Recognition, pp. 14902–14912 (2021)
10. Liu, Z., Zhou, Y., Xu, Y., Wang, Z.: SimpleNet: a simple network for image anomaly detection and localization. arXiv preprint arXiv:2303.15140 (2023)
11. Murase, H., Fukumizu, K.: ALGAN: anomaly detection by generating pseudo anomalous data via latent variables. IEEE Access 10, 44259–44270 (2022)
12. Cohen, M.J., Avidan, S.: Transformaly-two (feature spaces) are better than one. In: Proceedings of the IEEE/CVF Conference on Computer Vision and Pattern Recognition, pp. 4060–4069 (2022)
13. Mirzaei, H., et al.: Fake it until you make it: towards accurate near-distribution novelty detection. In: NeurIPS ML Safety Workshop
14. Heusel, M., Ramsauer, H., Unterthiner, T., Nessler, B., Hochreiter, S.: GANs trained by a two time-scale update rule converge to a local nash equilibrium. In: Advances in Neural Information Processing Systems, vol. 30 (2017)
15. Hjelm, R.D., et al.: Learning deep representations by mutual information estimation and maximization. arXiv preprint arXiv:1808.06670 (2018)
16. He, K., Fan, H., Wu, Y., Xie, S., Girshick, R.: Momentum contrast for unsupervised visual representation learning. In: Proceedings of the IEEE/CVF Conference on Computer Vision and Pattern Recognition, pp. 9729–9738 (2020)
17. Reiss, T., Hoshen, Y.: Mean-shifted contrastive loss for anomaly detection. arXiv preprint arXiv:2106.03844 (2021)
18. Ridnik, T., Ben-Baruch, E., Noy, A., Zelnik-Manor, L.: ImageNet-21k pretraining for the masses. arXiv preprint arXiv:2104.10972 (2021)
19. Hendrycks, D., Mazeika, M., Kadavath, S., Song, D.: Using self-supervised learning can improve model robustness and uncertainty. In: Advances in Neural Information Processing Systems, vol. 32 (2019)
20. Sohn, K., Li, C.L., Yoon, J., Jin, M., Pfister, T.: Learning and evaluating representations for deep one-class classification. arXiv preprint arXiv:2011.02578 (2020)
21. Tack, J., Mo, S., Jeong, J., Shin, J.: CSI: novelty detection via contrastive learning on distributionally shifted instances. Adv. Neural. Inf. Process. Syst. 33, 11839–11852 (2020)
22. Liznerski, P., Ruff, L., Vandermeulen, R.A., Franks, B.J., Müller, K.R., Kloft, M.: Exposing outlier exposure: what can be learned from few, one, and zero outlier images. arXiv preprint arXiv:2205.11474 (2022)

Detection and Positioning of Workpiece Grinding Area in Dark Scenes with Large Exposure

Zhentao Guo[1], Guiyu Zhao[1], Jinyue Bian[1], and Hongbin Ma[1,2(✉)]

[1] School of Automation, Beijing Institute of Technology, Beijing 100081, People's Republic of China
mathmhb@139.com
[2] State Key Laboratory of Intelligent Control and Decision of Complex Systems, Beijing 100081, People's Republic of China

Abstract. Workpiece grinding is a crucial process in the smart manufacturing chain. In order to meet the requirements of industrial precision and relieve heavy work, researchers have developed a vision-based grinding robot. However, the problem of workpiece grinding area detection and positioning is difficult to be solved in dark scenes with large exposure. This paper proposes a method that fuses technologies such as processing of the image, coordinate and point cloud, which can accurately detect and locate the workpiece grinding area. Firstly, A method based on YOLOv7 and improved image preprocessing is used to detect labels of the grinding area. Secondly, A model for the prediction of the coordinates based on multiple linear regression was used to predict the coordinates of missing labels for the same grinding area. Finally, Data processing of the point cloud and transformation of the system of coordinates are used to achieve the acquisition of the coordinates of positioning vertices in the grinding area and conversion from the camera coordinate system to the world coordinate system. We used several sets of data for evaluation in our experiments, and the experimental results show that our proposed method can effectively detect the workpiece grinding area. At the same time, our method can also predict the coordinates of missing labels, which provides a more stable and reliable guarantee for industrial production.

Keywords: Bad scene · Target detection · Image pre-processing · Multiple linear regression · Point cloud

1 Introduction

Vision-based grinding robots can free people from heavy workloads, improve efficiency and quality, and reduce the randomness of risks caused by human operations. However, since complex industrial grinding scenes are generally performed in darker scenes, the depth camera needs to take large exposures to capture the workpiece clearly. This operation leads to poor image quality and affects the

H. Yang et al. (Eds.): ICIRA 2023, LNAI 14273, pp. 48–59, 2023.
https://doi.org/10.1007/978-981-99-6498-7_5

labels detection of the grinding area. Therefore, the detection and positioning of workpiece grinding area in this scenario is challenging problems.

In recent years, many researchers have done a lot of research on industrial robots. Grinding robots with high accuracy and stability have been developed [1–3]. Ding Y [4] implemented a 3D reconstruction of the grinding surface using sensing technology and identified the defects using an artificial neural network approach. The method was validated to eventually achieve 98% accuracy, but it is more dependent on hardware devices such as sensors. Baeten J et al. [5] used a combination of force control techniques and 3D visualization techniques to grind spatial contours by tracking cutting forces. The accuracy of this method can't be guaranteed. Rastegarpanah A et al. [6] proposed an end-to-end framework for the prediction of paths from images when the parameters of the polished path are unknown. None of the above methods have been experimented in complex environments such as actual dark scenes, and their effectiveness can't be verified.

In addition to the development of grinding technology, the task of target detection and techniques of positioning in dark scenes have also been rapidly developed. Wang, J [7] proposed an improved end-to-end YOLOv3 network in dark conditions. Compared with the conventional YOLOv3 target detection model, the algorithm improves the average accuracy from 53.23% to 59.79% in the low-light target detection task. However, the network structure improved by the algorithm has low applicability and universality. Sasagawa, Y [8] proposed a YOLO-in-the-Dark model for merging multiple models. The network of this method is more complex and time-consuming. In addition, there are more practical methods such as hyperspectral image target detection [9], a multi-exposure fusion framework for enhanced low-light images [10], and borrowing illumination estimation techniques to estimate exposure maps [11]. However, all these methods are only designed from a single aspect of the scheme and do not have robustness. These methods are either only designed for a specific scene or improve the detection rate by changing the lighting conditions. Their accuracy is relatively low.

In this paper, we propose a method that fuses technologies such as processing of the image, coordinate and point cloud, which can accurately detect and locate grinding area. Firstly, A method based on YOLOv7 and improved image preprocessing is used to detect labels of the grinding area, which greatly improves the detection accuracy of the labels. Secondly, A model for prediction of the coordinates based on multiple linear regression [12] was used to predict the coordinates of missing labels for the same grinding area, which improves the robustness of the detection of the grinding area. Finally, Data processing of point cloud and transformation of the system of coordinates [13] are used to achieve the acquisition of the coordinates of positioning vertices in the grinding area and conversion from camera coordinate system to world coordinate system. This solution effectively improves the detection and positioning of workpiece grinding area in dark scenes with large exposure, which is conducive to improving the efficiency and quality consistency of the grinding robot grinding.

The main contributions of this paper are as follows:

- A algorithm that fuses pre-processing of image and target detection is used to detect labels of grinding area in dark scenes with large exposures.

- Multiple linear regression is used to predict the coordinates of missing labels in the same grinding area innovatively.
- A method of positioning of grinding area based on data processing of point cloud and transformation of the system of coordinates is introduced.
- Through multiple sets of experiments, our method can improve the accuracy and robustness of the detection and positioning of workpiece grinding area.

2   Methods

2.1   Problem Statement

The grinding tasks in factories are mostly performed in dark scenes, in which case the detection and positioning of workpiece grinding area becomes a difficult problem. The point cloud of the workpiece $\mathbf{P} = \{\mathbf{p}_1, \mathbf{p}_2, ..., \mathbf{p}_n\}, \mathbf{p}_i \in \mathbb{R}^3$ can be processed by target detection and prediction coordinates.

In order to allow the robot arm with the grinding head mounted to be accurately positioned to the grinding area, a transformation matrix can be used to achieve this conversion. $\mathbf{R}$ and $\mathbf{t}$ are the rotation matrix and translation vector from the system of camera coordinates to the system of world coordinates, so the transformed point cloud $\mathbf{P}_w$ can be expressed as:

$$\mathbf{P}_w = \begin{bmatrix} \mathbf{R} & \mathbf{t} \\ \mathbf{0^T} & 1 \end{bmatrix} \mathbf{P}_c \tag{1}$$

The research framework of this paper is divided into four modules: target detection algorithm, pre-processing of images, prediction of the coordinates of missing labels, and data of point cloud processing. Input data are RGB images and depth images. Our goal is to obtain the coordinates of the grinding area in the system of world coordinates, and our general scheme is shown in Fig 1.

2.2   Target Detection Algorithm

Areas in a factory that needs to be ground are often artificially labeled. In complex industrial scenarios, the selection of an efficient algorithm is necessary for prior work. YOLOv7 [17] is the latest YOLO structure of the YOLO series and surpasses all known target detectors in both speed and accuracy. In the research task of this paper, the performance of YOLOv7 is higher than that of other algorithms.

2.3   Pre-processing of Images in Dark Scenes with Large Exposures

False and missing detections are mostly found in dark scenes with large exposures, so pre-processing of image is needed to improve the accuracy and robustness of subsequent target detection and positioning. This section proposes several improved data pre-processing algorithms of images that can effectively identify labels and reduce the interference of large exposures. Uniformly, the pixel value of the input image is denoted by I_{in} and the pixel value of the output image is denoted by I_{out} in the following. Their pixel values range from 0 to 255.

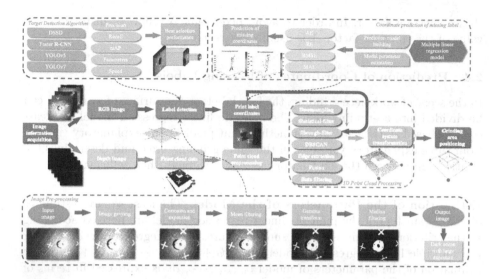

Fig. 1. In the target detection algorithm, YOLOv7 is used as the main algorithm for subsequent labels detection. In the pre-processing of image, Images in dark scenes with large exposure are processed by pre-processing of images. In the prediction of the coordinates of missing labels, A multiple linear regression was used to predict the coordinates of missing labels. Its accuracy was evaluated. In the processing of point cloud, the coordinates of the positioning vertices in the grinding area are obtained after processing of point cloud and coordinate system transformation.

Improved Mean Filtering. Adaptive neighborhood size and pixel weights are introduced into traditional mean filtering. It suppresses noise on the environment or lens under the condition that the detailed features are preserved as much as possible. It is defined as follows:

$$I_{out}(x,y) = \frac{\sum_{(i,j)\in S_{xy}} G(i,j) \cdot I_{in}(i,j)}{\sum_{(i,j)\in S_{xy}} G(i,j)} \qquad (2)$$

where S_{xy} is a neighborhood set centered on pixel (x,y), $G(i,j)$ denotes the weight of pixel (i,j).

Improved Gamma Transform. Adaptive gamma and pixel weights are introduced and they can correct the correction of images after mean filtering and enhance the contrast of labels and non-grinding area with high grayscale values [18]. It is defined as follows:

$$I_{out}(x,y) = A \cdot \left[\sum_{(i,j)\in S_{xy}} W(i,j) \cdot I_{in}(i,j)^{\gamma(i,j)} \right]^{\frac{1}{\sum_{(i,j)\in S_{xy}} W(i,j)}} \qquad (3)$$

where S_{xy} is the pixel value of (x,y) is the centered neighborhood set, $W(i,j)$ denotes the weight of pixel (i,j), $G(i,j)$ denotes the gamma of pixel (i,j) value,

A is a constant factor. In order to avoid pixel value overflow or distortion, the value of the constant factor A is usually between 0 and 1.

2.4 Prediction of Coordinates of Missing Labels

In the scene of workpiece grinding, the four labels on the surface of workpiece can be divided into a grinding area. The multiple linear regression model is a least squares-based statistical analysis method that predicts one explanatory variable from three explanatory variables in the same grinding area, and determines the relationship between the explanatory variables through the coefficients.

Estimation of the Parameters of the Model. The least-squares estimates of the parameters of the multiple linear regression model are derived according to the criterion of minimizing the sum of squares of the regression residuals. For the multiple linear regression model $Y = \beta_0 + \beta_1 z_1 + \cdots + \beta_k z_k + \varepsilon$, if the estimation of the parameters of model $\beta_0 , \beta_1 , \cdots , \beta_k$ is expressed in terms of $b_0 , b_1 , \cdots , b_k$, then the sample regression equation is $\hat{Y} = b_0 + b_1 z_1 + \cdots + b_k z_k$ and the following sum of squared regression residuals can be deduced:

$$V = \sum \varepsilon^2 = \sum [Y \cdot (bz)]^2 \tag{4}$$

among them

$$\varepsilon = \begin{bmatrix} \varepsilon_1 \\ \varepsilon_2 \\ \vdots \\ \varepsilon_n \end{bmatrix}, Y = \begin{bmatrix} Y_1 \\ Y_2 \\ \vdots \\ Y_i \end{bmatrix}, b = \begin{bmatrix} b_0 \\ b_1 \\ \vdots \\ b_k \end{bmatrix}, z = [1, z_{1i}, \dots, z_{ki}] \tag{5}$$

When the first-order partial derivatives of V with respect to $b_0 , b_1 , \cdots , b_k$ are all equal to 0, V has the minimum value. By collation, the resulting system of regular equations is:

$$\begin{cases} b_0 = \overline{Y} - b\overline{z} \\ S_0 = bS \end{cases} \tag{6}$$

among them

$$b = \begin{bmatrix} b_1 \\ b_2 \\ \vdots \\ b_K \end{bmatrix}, \overline{z} = \begin{bmatrix} \overline{z_1} \\ \overline{z_2} \\ \vdots \\ \overline{z_k} \end{bmatrix}, S = \begin{bmatrix} S_{11} & S_{12} & \cdots & S_{1K} \\ S_{21} & S_{22} & \cdots & S_{2K} \\ \vdots & \vdots & & \vdots \\ S_{K1} & S_{K2} & \cdots & S_{KK} \end{bmatrix} \tag{7}$$

where the regular equation has $K + 1$ equations and the unknowns $K + 1$ are also one. As long as the coefficient matrix is non-singular and satisfies the explanatory variable matrix Z column full rank $R(Z) = k$. There are $R(Z'Z) = k$, $Z'Z$ is invertible. The only set of solutions that can be solved for $b_0 , b_1 , \cdots , b_k$ is the least squares estimates of $\beta_0 , \beta_1 , \cdots , \beta_k$.

2.5 Positioning of Grinding Area

Data Processing of Point Cloud. First, the previously obtained 2D pixel coordinates of the four labels of the grinding area are converted to data of point cloud in the system of camera coordinates

$$\begin{bmatrix} x_c \\ y_c \\ z_c \end{bmatrix} = K^{-1} \begin{bmatrix} u \\ v \\ 1 \end{bmatrix} d(u,v) \tag{8}$$

where K^{-1} is the inverse matrix of the camera's internal reference matrix and x_c, y_c, z_c is the 3D coordinate of the pixel in the system of camera coordinates.

Then mitigating data of point cloud by constructing a 3D voxel grid for downsampling. Removal of outliers or noise is necessary due to camera and peripheral noise effects. Specifically, for each point, the statistical information of the points within a certain range around it is calculated, and then based on this information, it is decided whether the point is retained or how to adjust its attribute values [19].

The following straight-pass filtering is used to remove data of point cloud outside the 3D coordinates of the four labels, which can make the data in the grinding area cleaner

$$\mathbf{P}_{filtered} = \{\mathbf{p} \in \mathbf{P} | x_{min} \leq \mathbf{p}_x \leq x_{max}, y_{min} \leq \mathbf{p}_y \leq y_{max}, z_{min} \leq \mathbf{p}_z \leq z_{max}\} \tag{9}$$

where $\mathbf{p}_x$, $\mathbf{p}_y$, and $\mathbf{p}_z$ denote the x, y, and z coordinates of point $\mathbf{p}$ respectively. $\mathbf{P}_{filtered}$ consists of all points $\mathbf{p}$ in the input point cloud $\mathbf{P}$ that satisfy the x, y and z coordinates within the limits.

Since there is a height difference between the grinding area and the surface of the workpiece, a density-based clustering algorithm is used to classify the data of point cloud into classes of different heights.

For the two clusters of the top of the grinding area and the surface of the workpiece, the subsequent edge extraction is performed separately. A starting point $\mathbf{P}_0$ in the same clusters is selected, and the nearest point $\mathbf{P}_j$ from the point $\mathbf{P}_0$ is selected, whose coordinates in the system of polar coordinates of $\mathbf{P}_0$ are as follows:

$$\theta_j = \arctan(\frac{y_j - y_0}{x_j - x_0})$$
$$\phi_j = \arccos(\frac{z_j - z_0}{\sqrt{(x_j - x_0)^2 + (y_j - y_0)^2 + (z_j - z_0)^2}}) \tag{10}$$

where θ_j is the polar angle of the nearest point $\mathbf{P}_j$ from $\mathbf{P}_0$ and ϕ_j is the polar diameter of that point.

The distance and angular difference between $\mathbf{P}_j$ and $\mathbf{P}_0$ can be obtained by calculating:

$$d = \sqrt{(x_j - x_0)^2 + (y_j - y_0)^2 + (z_j - z_0)^2}$$
$$\Delta\theta = | \theta_j - \theta_0 | \tag{11}$$
$$\Delta\phi = | \phi_j - \phi_0 |$$

where d is the distance between two points, $\Delta\theta$ is the absolute value difference of the polar angle between two points, and $\Delta\phi$ is the absolute value difference of the polar diameter between two points.

If any point $\mathbf{P}_i$ satisfies the following conditions, it is added to the set of edge points:

$$\begin{aligned} \Delta\theta &> \theta_{thres} \\ \Delta\phi &> \phi_{thres} \\ d &< d_{thres} \end{aligned} \tag{12}$$

where θ_{thres} and ϕ_{thres} are set thresholds that control the sensitivity of edge points, and d_{thres} is a distance threshold that controls the density of edge points.

The data of point cloud after edge extraction can be used to obtain the 3D coordinates of the eight positioning vertices of the grinding area in the system of camera coordinates by simple data filtering.

Transformation of the Coordinate System. The points in the system of camera coordinates need to be converted to system of world coordinates in order to more accurately determine the position and orientation of the workpiece in the 3D industrial scene. The external parameter matrix of the camera is $[\mathbf{R}|\,\mathbf{t}]$, where $\mathbf{R}$ is a $3 * 3$ rotation matrix and $\mathbf{t}$ is a $3 * 1$ translation vector, which denotes the position and orientation of the camera. We can obtain the following coordinates $\mathbf{P}_w$ in the system of world coordinates

$$\mathbf{P}_w = \begin{bmatrix} X \\ Y \\ Z \\ 1 \end{bmatrix} = [\mathbf{R}|\,\mathbf{t}]\,\mathbf{P}_c . \tag{13}$$

where $[\mathbf{R}|\,\mathbf{t}]$ is the external parameter matrix.

3   Experiment

The image data are collected at the factory site, and a total of 2680 valid images were collected. We divide the training set, validation set, and test set according to 8:1:1.

The computer system we used is ubuntu 20.04, the graphics card is NVIDIA RTX 3090, and the image acquisition device is a Mech-Eye Pro S camera.

3.1   Comparison with Other Target Detection Algorithms

For four target detection algorithms, we use the Pytorch [20] framework to train the network models, and use the Adam optimizer to optimize the trained network models. The input data size is 640*640, the total number of iterations is 200 epochs, the network depth and network width are set according to different algorithms with different parameters, and automatic anchor points are selected. In this section, P(Precision), R(Recall), mAP(mean Average Precision) and S(Speed) are used to evaluate the detection performance of the model.

$$P = \frac{TP}{TP + FP}, R = \frac{TP}{TP + FN}, mAP = \sum \frac{\int_0^1 P(R)dR}{N} \tag{14}$$

where TP is the number of positive samples predicted to be positive; FP is the number of negative samples predicted to be positive; FN is the number of positive samples predicted to be negative.

As shown in Fig. 2, the results indicate that YOLOv7-X outperforms other algorithms in detection accuracy, with an mAP of 78.8%. Meanwhile, the algorithm still shows a good performance available in the speed of inference.

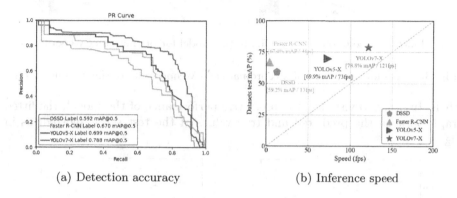

(a) Detection accuracy   (b) Inference speed

Fig. 2. Comparison of target detection algorithms

The comparison of detection accuracy and related performance of different target detection algorithms is shown in Table 1. It can be seen that YOLOv7 has the highest scores of recall and precision and inference speed is the fastest.

Table 1. Comparison detection accuracy and related performance of four target detection algorithms

Model	Precision(%)	Recall(%)	mAP(%)	Parameters(MB)	Speed(FPS)
DSSD [14]	62.5	51.3	59.2	97.15	13
Faster R-CNN [15]	70.6	58.4	67.0	147.48	4
YOLOv5-X [16]	67.7	64.5	69.9	21.23	73
YOLOv7-X [17]	**77.6**	**76.2**	**78.8**	37.06	**121**

3.2 Predicted Results of Missing Labels

Multiple linear regression is used to predict the coordinates of missing labels in the same grinding area. For each missing labels, two separate models are built for prediction, one for predicting the x coordinate and the other for predicting the y coordinate. We collected 250 sets of coordinates of labels in the same area for training the model and the training set and test set are divided according to 8:2.

The visualized four-dimensional data of the model for prediction is shown in Fig. 3, where the colors denote the prediction of the coordinates of missing

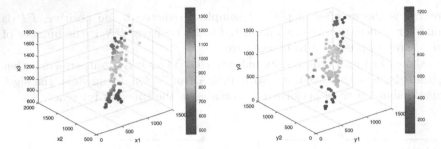

(a) Model for prediction of x-coordinate (b) Model for prediction of y-coordinate

Fig. 3. Model for prediction of x-coordinate and y-coordinate of the missing labels

labels. In order to visualize the predictive performance of the model, the fitted graph between the predicted and true values of the test set is plotted, as in Fig. 4.

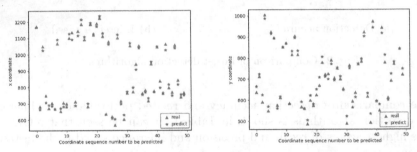

(a) Results of prediction of x-coordinate (b) Results of prediction of y-coordinate

Fig. 4. Comparison of test results of models for prediction

3.3 Positioning of Workpiece Grinding Area

The workpiece depth images are converted to data of point cloud, as in Fig. 5 (a). Then downsampling and statistical filtering is performed, as in Fig. 5 (b) and (c). Positioning of the grinding area by straight-pass filtering is performed preliminary, as in Fig. 5 (d). Then clustering, edge extraction, and fusion of point cloud are used to improve the efficiency and accuracy of data processing of point cloud, as in Fig. 5 (e). Finally, the key data are selected to obtain the eight locating vertices in the grinding area shown in Fig. 5 (f).

Through the transformation of the system of coordinates, the 3D coordinates of the eight positioning vertices of the grinding area in the customs system of world coordinates are obtained, as shown in Table 2.

3.4 Ablation Study

To better evaluate the effectiveness of pre-processing of images in our method, the effect of label detection in the workpiece grinding area before and after pre-

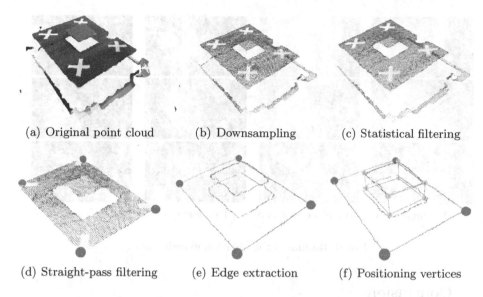

(a) Original point cloud   (b) Downsampling   (c) Statistical filtering

(d) Straight-pass filtering   (e) Edge extraction   (f) Positioning vertices

Fig. 5. Psitioning process of the grinding area

Table 2. Conversion of the coordinates of locating vertex of grinding area

Point	System of camera coordinates	System of world coordinates
1	$[-0.050, 0.049, -0.416]^{\top}$	$[-0.066, 0.049, -0.416]^{\top}$
2	$[0.055, 0.049, -0.419]^{\top}$	$[0.039, 0.048, -0.410]^{\top}$
3	$[0.055, -0.047, -0.419]^{\top}$	$[0.039, -0.048, -0.419]^{\top}$
4	$[-0.050, -0.047, -0.410]^{\top}$	$[-0.066, -0.047, -0.410]^{\top}$
5	$[-0.050, 0.049, -0.366]^{\top}$	$[-0.066, 0.049, -0.366]^{\top}$
6	$[0.055, 0.049, -0.377]^{\top}$	$[0.039, 0.049, -0.377]^{\top}$
7	$[0.055, -0.047, -0.371]^{\top}$	$[0.039, -0.047, -0.371]^{\top}$
8	$[-0.050, -0.047, -0.366]^{\top}$	$[-0.065, -0.047, -0.366]^{\top}$

processing of images is compared. Specifically, the original data in Fig. 6 (a) and the data after pre-processing of images in Fig. 6 (b) are respectively input into the model for detection. The detection results are shown in Fig. 6 (c) and Fig. 6 (d) respectively. It can be seen that the preprocessing of images improves the robustness and accuracy of labels detection.

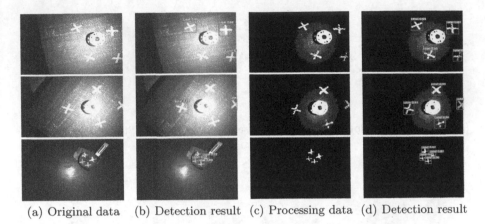

(a) Original data (b) Detection result (c) Processing data (d) Detection result

Fig. 6. Results of the ablation experiments

4 Conclusion

This paper implements the detection and positioning of workpiece grinding areas in dark scenes with large exposures. Specifically, better-performing YOLOv7 is used to detect the labels, while pre-processing of images in dark scenes with large exposure is used to reduce false and missing detections of labels. Then a multiple linear regression is used to predict the coordinates of missing labels innovatively. Finally, the workpiece depth images are converted into data of point cloud. The data processing of point cloud and transformation of the system of coordinates is used to accurately locate the grinding area.

The experimental results show that our proposed method has high accuracy of detection and positioning in dark scenes with large exposures, while effectively avoiding the problems of markings and detections of missing. Through the analysis of the experimental results, we found that the model for the prediction of the coordinates of missing labels and the algorithm of positioning both played an important role in the improvement of the accuracy of positioning. In conclusion, the method proposed in this paper provides a new solution for the detection and positioning of workpiece grinding areas in dark scenes with large exposures, which has practical application value and promotion significance.

Acknowledgments. This work was partially funded by the National Key Research and Development Plan of China (No. 2018AAA0101000) and the National Natural Science Foundation of China under grant 62076028.

References

1. Zhao, X., Lu, H., Yu, W., Tao, B., Ding, H.: Vision-based mobile robotic grinding for large-scale workpiece and its accuracy analysis. IEEE/ASME Transactions on Mechatronics (2022)

2. Chen, C., Cai, Z., Chen, T., Li, Z., Yang, F., Liang, X.: A vision-based calibration method for aero-engine blade-robotic grinding system. Int. J. Adv. Manufact. Technol. **125**, 2195–2209 (2023)
3. Ge, J., et al.: An efficient system based on model segmentation for weld seam grinding robot. Int. J. Adv. Manufact. Technol. **121**(11–12), 7627–7641 (2022)
4. Ding, Y., et al.: Calibration method of laser displacement sensor based on binocular vision. J. Zhejiang Univ. Eng. Sci. **55**(9), 1634–1642 (2021)
5. Baeten, J., Bruyninckx, H., De Schutter, J.: Integrated vision/force robotic servoing in the task frame formalism. Int. J. Robot. Res. **22**(10–11), 941–954 (2003)
6. Rastegarpanah, A., Hathaway, J., Stolkin, R.: Vision-guided MPC for robotic path following using learned memory-augmented model. Front. Robot. AI **8**, 688275 (2021)
7. Wang, J.: An improved YOLO algorithm for object detection in all day scenarios. In: Qiu, H., Zhang, C., Fei, Z., Qiu, M., Kung, S.-Y. (eds.) KSEM 2021. LNCS (LNAI), vol. 12817, pp. 475–486. Springer, Cham (2021). https://doi.org/10.1007/978-3-030-82153-1_39
8. Sasagawa, Y., Nagahara, H.: YOLO in the dark - domain adaptation method for merging multiple models. In: Vedaldi, A., Bischof, H., Brox, T., Frahm, J.-M. (eds.) ECCV 2020. LNCS, vol. 12366, pp. 345–359. Springer, Cham (2020). https://doi.org/10.1007/978-3-030-58589-1_21
9. Zhou, J., Kwan, C., Ayhan, B.: Improved target detection for hyperspectral images using hybrid in-scene calibration. J. Appl. Remote Sens. **11**(3), 035010–035010 (2017)
10. Ying, Z., Li, G., Gao, W.: A bio-inspired multi-exposure fusion framework for low-light image enhancement. arXiv preprint arXiv:1711.00591 (2017)
11. Ying, Z., Li, G., Ren, Y., Wang, R., Wang, W.: A new low-light image enhancement algorithm using camera response model. In: Proceedings of the IEEE International Conference on Computer Vision Workshops, pp. 3015–3022 (2017)
12. Uyanık, G.K., Güler, N.: A study on multiple linear regression analysis. Procedia. Soc. Behav. Sci. **106**, 234–240 (2013)
13. Bian, J., Wang, X., Liao, Z., Ma, H.: Accurate positioning for refueling plug with coarse-to-fine registration and pose correction. In: 2022 China Automation Congress (CAC), pp. 2433–2438. IEEE (2022)
14. Fu, C.Y., Liu, W., Ranga, A., Tyagi, A., Berg, A.C.: DSSD: deconvolutional single shot detector. arXiv preprint arXiv:1701.06659 (2017)
15. Ren, S., He, K., Girshick, R., Sun, J.: Faster R-CNN: towards real-time object detection with region proposal networks. In: Advances in Neural Information Processing Systems, vol. 28 (2015)
16. Jocher, G.: YOLOv5 release v6.1 (2022). https://github.com/ultralytics/yolov5/releases/tag/v6.1. Accessed 29 Apr 2023
17. Wang, C.Y., Bochkovskiy, A., Liao, H.Y.M.: YOLOv7: trainable bag-of-freebies sets new state-of-the-art for real-time object detectors. arXiv preprint arXiv:2207.02696 (2022)
18. Qi, M., et al.: Multi-region nonuniform brightness correction algorithm based on l-channel gamma transform. Secur. Commun. Networks **2022**, 2675950 (2022)
19. Zhao, G., Ma, H., Jin, Y.: A method for robust object recognition and pose estimation of rigid body based on point cloud. In: Liu, H., et al. (eds.) Intelligent Robotics and Applications. ICIRA 2022. Lecture Notes in Computer Science, vol. 13458 pp. 468–480. Springer, Cham (2022). https://doi.org/10.1007/978-3-031-13841-6_43
20. Paszke, A., et al.: PyTorch: an imperative style, high-performance deep learning library. In: Advances in Neural Information Processing Systems, vol. 32 (2019)

Hardware-Free Event Cameras Temporal Synchronization Based on Event Density Alignment

Wenxuan Li[1] 🔟, Yan Dong[1] 🔟, Shaoqiang Qiu[1] 🔟, and Bin Han[1,2]($\boxtimes$)

[1] State Key Laboratory of Intelligent Manufacturing Equipment and Technology, Huazhong University of Science and Technology, Hubei, Wuhan 430074, China
binhan@hust.edu.cn
[2] Guangdong Intelligent Robotics Institute, Dongguan 523106, China

Abstract. Event cameras are a novel type of sensor designed for capturing the dynamic changes of a scene. Due to factors such as trigger and transmission delays, a time offset exists in the data collected by multiple event cameras, leading to inaccurate information fusion. Thus, the collected data needs to be synchronized to overcome any potential time offset issue. Hardware synchronization methods require additional circuits, while certain models of event cameras (e.g., CeleX5) do not support hardware synchronization. Therefore, this paper proposes a hardware-free event camera synchronization method. This method determines differences between start times by minimizing the dissimilarity of the event density distributions of different event cameras and synchronizes the data by adjusting timestamps. The experiments demonstrate that the method's synchronization error is less than 10 ms under various senses with multiple models of event cameras.

Keywords: Event camera · Time synchronization · Multi-sensor system · Online time calibration

1 Introduction

Event cameras are a type of neuromorphic sensor. Unlike traditional cameras that capture images at a fixed frame rate, event cameras can capture real-time changes in illumination. As a dynamic vision sensor, each pixel of an event camera can independently detect logarithmic relative lighting changes. Upon the lighting change of a pixel exceeding the set threshold, the event camera outputs event data [1–3]. Event cameras have several advantages, including no frame rate or minimum output time interval limitation, extremely low latency, and microsecond-level time resolution. They are suitable for processing high-speed-moving scenes, e.g., racing cars and drones. Multiple event cameras can be applied to expand the visual field or acquire multi-view perspectives for a more comprehensive understanding of the environment.

This work is supported in part by the Guangdong Innovative and Entrepreneurial Research Team Program (2019ZT08Z780), in part by Dongguan Introduction Program of Leading Innovative and Entrepreneurial Talents (20181220), in part by the Natural Science Foundation of Hubei Province of China (2022CFB239), in part by the State Key Laboratory of Intelligent Manufacturing Equipment and Technology.

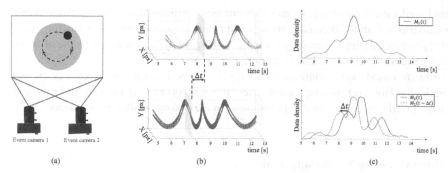

Fig. 1. An illustration of event stream alignment. (a) Two event cameras capture a rotating circle at varying angular velocities simultaneously. (b) The original event stream data of the two cameras, where Δt is the difference between the start times of the two cameras. (c) Δt is calculated by aligning the distributions of event densities $M(t)$.

Synchronization is necessary to ensure the accuracy and reliability of data in a multiple event camera system. As a result of trigger and transmission delays, start time differences between cameras lead to the time offset issues. Hardware synchronization is a commonly used approach to solve the problem. For instance, the DAVIS 240/346 camera created by iniVation[1] requires a stable reference voltage of 3.3V or 5V to generate special event trigger signals for synchronization, while Prophesee's products[2] rely on a 5V reference voltage. The increasing number of sensors results in a corresponding increase in hardware complexity which, in turn, negatively impacts the portability of the method. In addition, certain models of event cameras, such as CeleX5 from CelexPixel[3], do not support external synchronization. Therefore, a hardware-free synchronization method can achieve synchronization of multiple cameras of different models without the need for external circuits.

This paper proposes a novel hardware-free method to achieve synchronization among multiple event cameras by aligning their event density distributions. The method calculates the start time differences by minimizing the dissimilarity between the event density distributions of different cameras (see Fig. 1) and adjusts the timestamps accordingly. The proposed method achieves high accuracy in both indoor and outdoor environments, and can address the synchronization issue of various event cameras of different models.

2 Related Work

2.1 Hardware Synchronization

Certain models of event cameras support hardware synchronization. The hardware synchronization method commonly employs an external circuit platform to solve the time deviation problem. Calabrese et al. [4] synchronized the internal timestamps of the cameras by using a 3.5 mm cable with a 10 kHz clock to connect the cameras. Zou et al.

---

[1] https://inivation.com/

[2] https://www.prophesee.ai/

[3] https://www.omnivision-group.com/technology/

[5] employed a specialized synchronization circuit to initiate the data acquisition of two event cameras and an RGB camera at the same time and prevent any time-shifting. Gao et al. [6] produced a trigger signal by using the onboard external oscillator as the primary clock and the STM32F407 microprocessor.

Hardware-based synchronization is typically performed manually or semi-automatically. However, in cases where the dataset involves long periods and multiple unsynchronized sensors, manual synchronization may prove challenging or impractical [8].

2.2 Hardware-Free Synchronization

Rueckauer et al. [7] utilized the DAVIS camera's integrated IMU to acquire more precise timestamps. The synchronization is accomplished via the motion pose detected by the IMU, yielding synchronization accuracy down to the microsecond level. Osadcuks et al. [8] proposed a clock-based synchronization method for data acquisition sensor array architecture to obtain microsecond-level synchronization with minimal hardware additions to the PIC32 microcontroller. Hu et al. [9] and Binas et al. [10] used computer time to approximately calibrate different sensors, and the errors generated thereby can be ignored due to the data transfer rate of only 10 Hz. Zhu et al. [11] maximized the correlation between the DAVIS camera's integrated IMU and the VI sensor gyroscope angular velocity to calculate time offset. Post-processing can also achieve alignment if there is no synchronization during data acquisition. For instance, Censi et al. [12] suggested matching changes in image intensity with DVS event rates to identify temporal deviations between various data streams. However, these approaches are only applicable to synchronizing event cameras with other sensors and cannot accomplish synchronization among multiple event cameras.

Our method avoids the hardware complexity and compatibility issues associated with hardware synchronization, as well as the issue of some event cameras not supporting it. By calculating the differences between the start times of multiple event cameras through software, our method effectively addresses time deviation issues among multiple event cameras.

3 Methodology

3.1 Problem Description

To distinguish the "time" in different sensors and the real world, we denote the time by:

$$t_{time\ source}^{reference\ timeline}$$

which represents the time t is from *time source* and described in *reference timeline*. We assume two event cameras are used; thus, the *time source* and *reference timeline* can be 1, 2 and w which represent the camera starting first, the camera starting later and the real world, respectively.

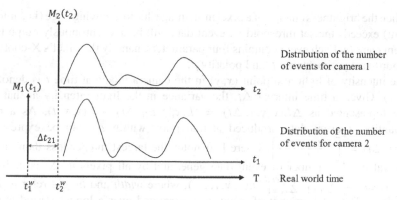

Fig. 2. An illustration of the different "time" in two event cameras and the real world. t_1 and t_2 are the running times for camera 1 and camera 2, and T stands for world time. t_1^w and t_2^w are the start times for the two cameras. Owing to trigger and transmission delays, the event cameras do not start at the same moment, causing a misalignment in time between the cameras. The time offset is what we need to obtain to help adjust and synchronize camera timestamps to ensure temporal consistency across the camera streams. $M_1(t_1)$, $M_2(t_2)$ are defined in Sect. 3.2.

Specifically, as shown in Fig. 2, the start times for the two cameras are denoted as t_1^w and t_2^w. The running times for camera 1 and camera 2 are represented as t_1^1 and t_2^2, respectively. The time interval between camera 1 and camera 2 can be defined as $\Delta t_{21} = t_2^w - t_1^w$.

We can determine the relationship between the running times of camera 1 and camera 2 using the equation $t_1^1 = t_2^2 + \Delta t_{21}$, i.e., $\Delta t_{21} = t_1^1 - t_2^2$. This is valid for all world times t_w^w, where $t_w^w = t_1^w + t_1^1 = t_2^w + t_2^2$. If the *camera index* is the same as the *reference timeline*, the superscript is omitted for simplification. We emphasize that the proposed method can handle different numbers of event cameras, while in this section we only use two cameras for derivation.

3.2 Synchronization Algorithm

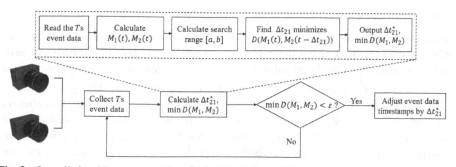

Fig. 3. Overall algorithm process. We calculate Δt_{21} through T s event data. If the $\min D(M_1, M_2)$ is less than the threshold ε, then we adjust the event data timestamps.

When the brightness change of a pixel in an image due to a moving edge (i.e., intensity gradient) exceeds the set threshold C, event data will be asynchronously outputted by the event camera. Each event contains four parameters, namely the pixel's X-coordinate x, Y-coordinate y, timestamp t, and polarity p.

The intensity of light at a point (x, y) in the camera image at time t is denoted as $L(x, y, t)$. Given a time interval Δt, the variance in the light intensity at that point can be represented as $\Delta L(x, y, t, \Delta t) = L(x, y, t + \Delta t) - L(x, y, t)$. As a result, the quantity of event data produced at that point within Δt can be expressed as $n(x, y, t, \Delta t) = \left[\frac{\Delta L(x,y,t,\Delta t)}{C} \right]$, where [] denotes the largest integer less than or equal to that value. The number of event data generated by all pixels in Δt is defined as $N(x, y, t, \Delta t) = \sum_{x=1}^{width} \sum_{y=1}^{height} n(x, y, t, \Delta t)$, where $width$ and $height$ refer to image dimensions. The total amount of event data generated over a longer period is represented as $\tilde{N} = \sum_t N$. Assuming a uniform light source throughout the scene, and when Δt is extremely small, any modifications in brightness within the image can be attributed solely to motion, allowing for an approximation [13]:

$$\Delta L \approx -\nabla L \bullet v \Delta t \tag{1}$$

which means the variance in light intensity ΔL can be attributed to a brightness gradient on the image plane denoted by $\nabla L(x, y, t) = (\partial_x L, \partial_y L)$, moving at a velocity of $v(x, y, t)$.

Assuming that the average gradient of the entire camera pixel image is represented by $\widetilde{\nabla L}$ and that it satisfies the condition $\sum_{x=1}^{width} \sum_{y=1}^{height} \nabla L = R \, \widetilde{\nabla L}$. Similarly, the average velocity of the pixels $\tilde{v}$ should satisfy $\sum_{x=1}^{width} \sum_{y=1}^{height} v = R \, \tilde{v}$, which leads to $\sum_{x=1}^{width} \sum_{y=1}^{height} \nabla L \bullet v \Delta t = R^2 \, \widetilde{\nabla L} \bullet \tilde{v}$. R denotes the total number of pixels present on the camera's image plane, i.e., $R = width \times height$. Consequently, the normalized event density indicating the quantity of events over a unit of time ($\tau = 1$ ms) can be defined as follows:

$$M(t) = \frac{N(x, y, t, \tau)}{\tilde{N}} = \frac{R^2}{\tilde{N}} \left[\frac{\widetilde{\nabla L} \bullet \tilde{v}}{C} \right], t = k\tau, k = 0, 1, 2 \dots \tag{2}$$

Two event cameras generally capture the same scene and have a similar average gradient. Thus, we assume $\widetilde{\nabla L}_1 (t_1) = \widetilde{\nabla L}_2 (t_2)$ for our deduction (This assumption may not be satisfied all the time but the experiments in Sect. 4.1 show that it does not have an obvious effect on synchronization results). If two cameras move together with a same speed (i.e., $\tilde{v}_1 (t_1) = \tilde{v}_2 (t_2)$) at any time, we have $M_1(t_1) = M_2(t_2)$ resulting in $M_1(t_w - t_1^w) = M_2(t_w - t_1^w - \Delta t_{21})$. Shifting a function left or right does not alter its shape, which leads to $M_1(t_w) = M_2(t_w - \Delta t_{21})$. In order to find the time difference between the start times of the two cameras, we need to find Δt_{21}, that minimizes the dissimilarity of the event density distributions of both cameras. That is, at any given time t_w, we seek $M_1(t_w) = M_2(t_w - \Delta t_{21})$. This problem is formulated as:

$$\Delta t_{21}^* = \underset{\Delta t_{21}}{argmin} D(M_1(t_w), M_2(t_w - \Delta t_{21})) \tag{3}$$

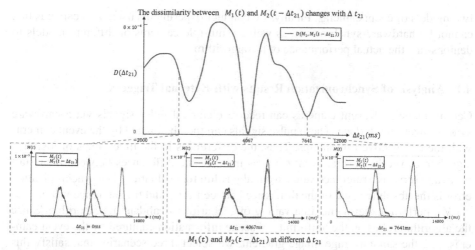

Fig. 4. An illustration of the Δt_{21} traversal process. The upper figure represents the change of the dissimilarity between the two event density distributions over Δt_{21}, and the lower part is the event density distribution image corresponding to three Δt_{21} we select. When $\Delta t_{21} = 4067$, the dissimilarity reaches the minimum value, which is the required Δt_{21}^*.

The function $D(M_1, M_2)$ quantifies the dissimilarity between M_1 and M_2 by utilizing the mean squared error, which is:

$$D(M_1(t_w), M_2(t_w - \Delta t_{21})) = \sum_{t_w} (M_1(t_w) - M_2(t_w - \Delta t_{21}))^2 \tag{4}$$

The initial T s of event data is used to determine the start time difference Δt_{21} of the cameras. If $\min D(M_1, M_2)$ exceeds a threshold ε during this period, the subsequent T s of event data will be used for further calculation until $\min D(M_1, M_2)$ less than ε is obtained. T is set to be 10 and ε is set to be 0.0001 in our method. The timestamps of all outputs are adjusted by subtracting Δt_{21} to compensate for the varying start times of the event cameras. The complete algorithm process is illustrated in Fig. 3.

As shown in Fig. 4, we traverse the Δt_{21} and calculate the square of the difference of two functions with varying Δt_{21} to minimize the dissimilarity. We set the search range to $[a, b]$. To determine a and b, we calculate the difference between the corresponding percentiles of the two functions. In particular, we determine the timestamps Q_1 and Q_2 by calculating the pth percentiles of $M_1(t)$ and $M_2(t)$, respectively. Then we set $a = Q_2^p - Q_1^p - 2|Q_1^p - Q_2^p|, b = Q_2^p - Q_1^p + 2|Q_1^p - Q_2^p|$. Binary percentiles are used in this paper. Next, the range should be searched for the minimum value of $D(M_1, M_2)$ to determine the corresponding value of Δt_{21}.

4   Experiment

This section begins by verifying the theoretical validity and accuracy of the proposed algorithm through experiments conducted under conditions that satisfy the algorithm's assumptions. Then, we test the algorithm in indoor and outdoor environments with two models of event cameras. Finally, we conduct experiments using two cameras that cannot be hardware-synchronized as well as multiple cameras of different models to demonstrate the actual performance of the algorithm.

4.1 Analysis of Synchronization Results with External Triggers

Certain models of event cameras can receive electrical pulse signals via a hardware synchronization interface. These pulse signals can then be logged by the event cameras with their respective timestamps. Thus, the differences in the timestamps of identical signals received by several event cameras indicate the differences between their start times and serve as a reference value in our algorithm for evaluation. The synchronization error is the absolute value of the difference between Δt_{21}^* and the reference value.

We perform experiments in a variety of scenarios to validate the algorithm. Since the algorithm relies on the uniformity of scene information captured by the event cameras, i.e., the same average image gradient, we select three scenarios that satisfy this assumption. Two DAVIS 346 cameras are used to conduct the experiments. The three scenarios are as follows: 1) recording human motion with stationary cameras, 2) capturing a pre-existing dataset displayed on a computer screen with stationary cameras, and 3) moving cameras to record a calibration chessboard. In scenario 1, a person performs a hand-raising motion at a distance of 2 m from the cameras. For scenario 2, we select the dynamic_6dof sequence (dynamic six-degree-of-freedom motion) from Event Camera Dataset [14]. We export the data at a rate of 120 images per second due to the low frame rate of the original data and capture it using the event cameras. In scenario 3, we connect the cameras rigidly and move them at a speed of 10 cm/s to record the calibration chessboard in front of a white wall. In each scenario, the object is captured within the consolidated field of view of the cameras, both of which are placed as close together as possible and facing the same direction to ensure consistency in the recorded scenes. We repeat each experiment 10 times, and each data sequence lasts 30 s. We calculate the average, maximum, and standard deviation of synchronization errors for each experiment. The results are presented in Table 1.

Table 1. Synchronization errors in scenarios that satisfy the algorithm assumptions (units: ms)

Scenes	Average	Maximum	Standard Deviation
Waving people (Fig. 5(a))	2.27	2.34	0.06
Computer screen (Fig. 5(b))	1.69	2.95	0.72
Chessboard (Fig. 5(c))	1.39	1.96	0.42

Experiments in a variety of indoor and outdoor environments are conducted to test the performance of the algorithm with both camera and human motion. Furthermore, we evaluate the algorithm's accuracy of different models of cameras, employing a DAVIS 346 camera and a Prophesee EVK1 Gen4 camera. In addition, we investigate the impact of camera parallel distances (20 cm and 60 cm) in different indoor and outdoor scenarios,

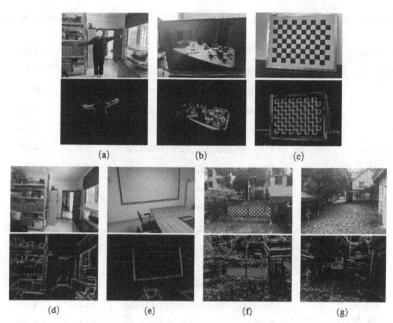

Fig. 5. Images of experimental scenes and corresponding event cameras' output. (a) people waving; (b) video on a computer screen; (c) chessboard in front of a white wall; (d) room with more objects; (e) room with fewer objects; (f) outdoor scene with near objects; (g) outdoor scene with far objects. For image (a-c), the gradient captured by the two cameras is the same, while image (d g) represents a more general scene.

with the camera either moving (at a speed of 10 cm/s) or capturing human motion (in which the person raises one or both hands from a distance of 2 m). These experiments aim to confirm the algorithm's effectiveness across common indoor and outdoor settings. It is worth noting that the assumption in Sect. 3 of equal average image gradient does not hold in these experiments. Table 2 presents the experimental settings and the corresponding results.

We experiment in extreme scenarios that involve placing two cameras in reverse directions and low-light conditions. When the cameras are in reverse directions, the scenes recorded by each camera are entirely different. However, despite the different captured scenes, our algorithm can still align the event data because it requires the event density distributions instead of solely the captured images. Due to the camera's motion, events can still be obtained, resulting in similar event density distributions. Under low light conditions, the average illumination intensity is at 30 lx, while for the above indoor and outdoor environments, the average illumination intensity is 300 lx, and 10000 lx respectively. Since the event camera detects changes in illumination rather than relying on absolute illumination values, the event camera can still obtain events effectively. This is demonstrated by the results in Table 3.

Table 2. Synchronization errors of a DAVIS 346 and a Prophesee EVK1 Gen4 (units: ms)

Seq	Scenes	Descriptions	Average	Maximum
1	Indoor 1 (Fig. 5(d))	Moving camera, 20cm baseline	2.76	6.56
2		Moving camera, 60cm baseline	2.78	6.32
3		Dynamic people, 20cm baseline	3.06	7.32
4		Dynamic people, 60cm baseline	3.47	6.54
5	Indoor 2	Moving camera, 20cm baseline	2.52	4.75
6	(Fig. 5(e))	Moving camera, 60cm baseline	3.43	7.51
7		Dynamic people, 20cm baseline	3.15	6.58
8		Dynamic people, 60cm baseline	3.63	6.88
9	Outdoor 1	Moving camera, 20cm baseline	1.79	5.15
10	(Fig. 5(f))	Moving camera, 60cm baseline	1.88	5.63
11		Dynamic people, 20cm baseline	2.03	5.36
12		Dynamic people, 60cm baseline	3.88	7.91
13	Outdoor 2	Moving camera, 20cm baseline	2.47	4.40
14	(Fig. 5(g))	Moving camera, 60cm baseline	3.14	6.92
15		Dynamic people, 20cm baseline	2.37	4.14
16		Dynamic people, 60cm baseline	3.23	4.69

Table 3. Synchronization errors in extreme environments (units: ms)

Sensors	Conditions	Average	Maximum
DAVIS-DAVIS	Cameras reverse placement	3.46	7.72
	Low light intensity	3.27	5.35
DAVIS-Prophesee	Cameras reverse placement	4.29	9.42
	Low light intensity	4.57	8.25

The results indicate that the algorithm has small overall synchronization errors as the maximum average error under non-extreme conditions is 6.92 ms. Cameras placed at a certain distance under the same motion condition have greater synchronization errors compared to closely placed cameras. Generally, the algorithm performs better in outdoor environments compared to indoor environments. The results obtained from the reverse experiment and the dim lighting experiment have larger synchronization errors, however, they are still within acceptable limits. Hence, the algorithm is effective under all these scenes.

4.2   Analysis of Synchronization Results without External Triggers

The experiments are carried out involving CeleX5 cameras. The absence of hardware synchronization support in the cameras makes it impossible to verify synchronization outcomes and accuracy through mathematical means. A qualitative approach is employed instead to show the accuracy. The experimental setup involves an animated digital timer exhibiting minutes, seconds, and milliseconds separately displayed on a computer screen. Using Fig. 6 as an illustration, the computer screen is captured collectively by the event cameras. The computer screen refreshes at a rate of 120 Hz which means that the screen changes approximately every 8.4 ms.

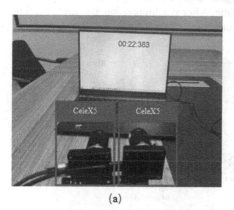 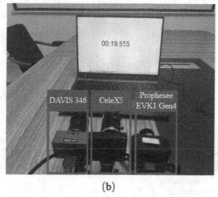

(a)   (b)

Fig. 6. An illustration of the experimental device. Event cameras capture the computer screen at the same time. (a) two CeleX5 cameras. (b) DAVIS 346, CeleX5, and Prophesee EVK1 Gen4 camera.

As shown in Fig. 6(a), the experiment uses software to simultaneously activate the two CeleX5 cameras and the timer. The output event data timestamps of the two cameras are plotted at the cameras' running time of 3 s. The event frame [5] drawing period is set at 8 ms. The results are shown in Fig. 7. The first camera displays the time of 00:06:753, indicating that the camera actually starts when the timer is at 3.753 s due to the delay. The time displayed by the second camera is 00:04:348, stating that the second camera starts to collect data 1.348 s after the timer starts. The synchronization of the two cameras using the algorithm produces outputted images that both show a time of 00:06:753. We state that it does not mean that the algorithm achieves 1 ms accuracy here, but the error is less than the timer refreshing cycle, i.e., 8.4 ms.

Then, we conduct a similar experiment using a DAVIS 346 camera, a CeleX5 camera, and a Prophesee EVK1 Gen4 camera to validate the synchronization of multiple cameras of different models, as shown in Fig. 6(b). The results are shown in Fig. 8, which also proves that the synchronization error of the algorithm is within 8.4 ms.

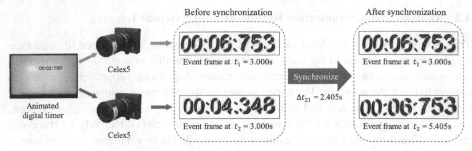

Fig. 7. Experimental results of two CeleX5 cameras. We draw the event frames of two event cameras with a running time of 3.000 s, and the digital difference displayed in the image can be used to represent the difference between the start time. After synchronization, the displayed time was the same, proving that the synchronization error was less than 8.4 ms.

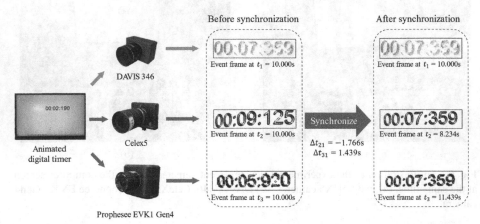

Fig. 8. Experimental results of a DAVIS 346 camera, a CeleX5 camera, and a Prophesee EVK1 Gen4 camera.

5   Conclusion

In this paper, we present a hardware-free time synchronizing method to synchronize different event cameras in a multi-camera system. The proposed method calculates the event density distributions of each event camera and estimates their start delays by minimizing the dissimilarity between the distributions. Experiments show that synchronization errors are within 10 ms in indoor, outdoor, and even challenging scenes. The method can handle the problem of synchronizing any event cameras regardless of models and numbers.

References

1. Lichtsteiner, P., Posch, C., Delbruck, T.: A 128 × 128 120 dB 15 μs latency asynchronous temporal contrast vision sensor. IEEE J. Solid-State Circuits **43**, 566–576 (2008). https://doi. org/10.1109/JSSC.2007.914337

2. Berner, R., Brandli, C., Yang, M., Liu, S., Delbruck, T.: A 240 × 180 10 mw 12 μs latency sparse-output vision sensor for mobile applications. In: Symposium on VLSI Circuits. IEEE Press, New York (2013)
3. Lichtsteiner, P., Delbruck, T.: A 64 × 64 AER logarithmic temporal derivative silicon retina. In: Research in Microelectronics and Electronics, pp. 202–205. IEEE Press, New York (2005). https://doi.org/10.1109/RME.2005.1542972
4. Calabrese, E., et al.: DHP19: dynamic vision sensor 3D human pose dataset. In: Proceedings of the IEEE/CVF Conference on Computer Vision and Pattern Recognition Workshops. IEEE Press, New York (2019). https://doi.org/10.1109/CVPRW.2019.00217
5. Zou, Y., Zheng, Y., Takatani, T., Fu, Y.: Learning to reconstruct high speed and high dynamic range videos from events. In: Proceedings of the IEEE/CVF Conference on Computer Vision and Pattern Recognition, pp. 2024–2033. IEEE Press, New York (2021). https://doi.org/10.1109/CVPR46437.2021.00206
6. Gao, L., et al.: VECtor: a versatile event-centric benchmark for multi-sensor SLAM. IEEE Robot. Autom. Lett. **7**, 8217–8224 (2022). https://doi.org/10.1109/LRA.2022.3186770
7. Rueckauer, B., Delbruck, T.: Evaluation of event-based algorithms for optical flow with ground-truth from inertial measurement sensor. Front. Neurosci. **10**, 176 (2016). https://doi.org/10.3389/fnins.2016.00176
8. Osadcuks, V., Pudzs, M., Zujevs, A., Pecka, A., Ardavs, A.: Clock-based time synchronization for an event-based camera dataset acquisition platform. In: IEEE International Conference on Robotics and Automation, pp. 4695–4701. IEEE Press, New York (2020). https://doi.org/10.1109/ICRA40945.2020.9197303
9. Hu, Y., Binas, J., Neil, D., Liu, S.C., Delbruck, T.: DDD20 end-to-end event camera driving dataset: fusing frames and events with deep learning for improved steering prediction. In: IEEE 23rd International Conference on Intelligent Transportation Systems, pp. 1–6. IEEE Press, New York (2020). https://doi.org/10.1109/ITSC45102.2020.9294515
10. Binas, J., Neil, D., Liu, S.C., Delbruck, T.: DDD17: end-to-end DAVIS driving dataset. arXiv preprint arXiv:1711.01458 (2017)
11. Zhu, A.Z., Thakur, D., Özaslan, T., Pfrommer, B., Kumar, V., Daniilidis, K.: The multivehicle stereo event camera dataset: an event camera dataset for 3D perception. IEEE Robot. Autom. Lett. **3**, 2032–2039 (2018). https://doi.org/10.1109/LRA.2018.2800793
12. Censi, A., Scaramuzza, D.: Low-latency event-based visual Odometry. In: IEEE International Conference on Robotics and Automation. 703–710 (2014). https://doi.org/10.1109/ICRA.2014.6906931
13. Gallego, G., et al.: Event-based vision: a survey. IEEE Trans. Pattern Anal. Mach. Intell. **44**, 154–180 (2020). https://doi.org/10.1109/TPAMI.2020.3008413
14. Mueggler, E., Rebecq, H., Gallego, G., Delbruck T., Scaramuzza D.: The event-camera dataset and simulator: event-based data for pose estimation, visual odometry, and SLAM. Int. J. Robot. Res. **36**, 142–149 (2017). https://doi.org/10.1177/0278364917691115

A Structure-Responsive CNN-Based Approach for Loop Closure Detection in Appearance-Changing Environments

Kangyu Li[1,2](✉) 📵, Xifeng Wang[2], Yangqing He[1], and Lijuan Ji[3]

[1] China Academy of Machinery Science and Technology, Beijing 100044, China
liky@mtd.com.cn
[2] Machinery Technology Development Co., Ltd., Beijing 100037, China
[3] Yanqihu Fundamental Manufacturing Technology Research Institute (Beijing) Co., Ltd., Beijing 101407, China

Abstract. Loop Closure Detection (LCD) is an essential technique for improving the localization accuracy of mobile robot. Despite the efficacy of convolutional neural networks (CNNs) in extracting features, they often overlook the structural information that remains stable even when the environment changes. In this paper, we introduce a novel approach, called Structural-Response Network (SRNet), to enhance appearance invariance. Based upon the multi-frequency feature separation paradigm, our method decomposes high-frequency components and integrates them to construct bi-frequency feature maps. This integration serves as a valuable addition to capturing fine-grained and structural information. The effectiveness of SRNet is demonstrated through both offline experiments on benchmark datasets and online experiments carried out in a manufacturing workshop.

Keywords: Loop closure detection · Simultaneous Localization and Mapping · Robot localization · Robotics

1 Introduction

Visual Simultaneous Localization and Mapping (vSLAM) [1] is an common employed robotics technique used to estimate camera poses and generate maps simultaneously. However, the odometry is susceptible to drift due to the accumulated errors and sensor noise. Loop closure detection (LCD) has been shown to be an effective solution for addressing this issue [2,3]. Specifically, LCD focuses on ascertaining whether the current location has been previously visited. If confirmed, it establishes bounded constraints for pose estimation to correct the errors, whereas a negative result prompts robot to store the current place.

LCD is a daunting task, as variations in viewpoint, illumination, weather or dynamic objects can cause significant environmental differences. These factors can lead to alterations in the visual information, such as brightness and content. Therefore, it is crucial to extract features that are both discriminative and

H. Yang et al. (Eds.): ICIRA 2023, LNAI 14273, pp. 72–83, 2023.
https://doi.org/10.1007/978-981-99-6498-7_7

invariant. Qin et al. [4] report that a stable feature of objects is their structural aspect, which tends to remain consistent despite changes in appearance. This concept motivates us to leverage structural information to enhance the appearance invariance of descriptors.

Handcrafted-feature-based descriptors, despite their emphasis on structural information, often lack robustness in discriminating between different instances. In recent years, convolutional neural networks (CNNs) have become the primary choice for feature representation. Several CNN-based approaches [5–8] have been proposed, resulting in remarkable performance improvements in the LCD task. However, CNN-based descriptors also exhibit certain limitations. Classical CNNs excel in extracting abstract and conceptual features but often overlook structural information. Such features containing rich semantic information may not be optimal for distinguishing visually similar scenes that are not from the same place [9,10], an issue known as perceptual aliasing. This problem stems from the presence of similar visual elements in images taken at different locations, such as the sky and ground (or ceiling and floor indoors).

In this work, we propose a LCD approach that not only generates compact and robust feature representations using CNN but also effectively utilizes structural information to enhance invariance to appearance changes. This capability relies on effectively separating the spatial frequency components of the image. Different frequencies in an image reveal various properties such as fine details and structures at high frequencies, and brightness and shadows variations at low frequencies. The proposed structure-responsive network (SRNet) builds on a feature separation paradigm called Octave Convolution (OctConv) [11], which offers a solution for handling input feature maps with different spatial resolutions. The key difference between OctConv and this work is that our emphasis lies on capturing fine-grained and structural details within high-frequency information. Specifically, our contributions can be summarized as follows:

- We propose a novel structural-response convolution (SRConv), which is designed to overcome the limitations of vanilla convolutions in capturing structural information. SRConv achieves this by integrating high-frequency residuals into bi-frequency feature maps.
- We develop a lightweight structural-response network (SRNet), which seamlessly integrating SRConv with depthwise separable convolution (DSC) to generate global image descriptors.
- Evaluations on benchmark datasets validate the competitive performance of the proposed method. Notably, its practicality is demonstrated through successful online LCD experiments using a mobile robot in the manufacturing workshop.

2   Related Work

Early appearance-based LCD methods employed Bag of Visual Words (BoVW) [12] model or Vector of Locally Aggregated Descriptors (VLAD) [13] to aggregate the local descriptors. FAB-MAP [3] and its enhanced version [14] stand as successful cases that leverages SURF [15] to achieve robust loop closure detection. ORB descriptor is highly efficient computationally, yet maintains good rotation and scale invariance, making it a popular choice for LCD tasks [16,17]. Global descriptors can yield better performance in capturing comprehensive information, resulting in greater robustness and adaptability to appearance changes. HOG [18] and Gist [19] are widely-used global descriptors in LCD tasks. Their compact representation makes it easy to measure the similarity of two images.

Handcrafted feature-based methods, although straightforward to implement, often exhibit reduced performance when dealing with environmental variations. Comparatively, CNN-based methods offer greater advantages in terms of robustness and generalization. Several pre-trained CNN models [9,20] or novel architectures [4,21,22] have been introduced since the pioneering work of Chen et al. [23]. Radenović et al. [24] proposed a novel pooling technique called generalized mean (GeM) pooling, which has demonstrated significant improvement in performance. An impressive work is the end-to-end holistic descriptor NetVLAD [5], which employs differentiable generalized VLAD layers to produce powerful image representations. The success of NetVLAD has led to the emergence of various variants [25,26].

3   Method

3.1   Spatial Frequency Content Separation

As shown in Fig. 1, we employ the Fast Fourier Transform (FFT) algorithm [27] to convert an image from the spatial domain to the frequency domain and separate its spatial frequency content into two components: a low-frequency component (LFC) that represents slowly varying intensity patterns, and a high-frequency component (HFC) that highlights the rapidly changing details. Although high-frequency information being commonly considered as undesirable noise or artifacts that should be eliminated, it holds significant value in the LCD task as it contributes crucial structural information to enhance abstract CNN-based descriptors.

The pooling layer is a fundamental component in CNNs and commonly employs average-pooling or max-pooling techniques. The primary role pooling layer is to reduce the spatial dimensions while retaining vital information and keeping invariance to translations and distortions. This process generates smooth feature maps, denoted as appearance-responsive features (ARF) in this study. Additionally, we can observe the pooling layer can function as a Low-pass Filter (see Fig. 1), even though it lacks a defined cutoff frequency. Compared with FFT algorithm, one advantage of employing pooling is that it doesn't require adding extra modules to the CNN architecture, thereby avoiding any additional computational overhead. Specifically, pooling operation acts as a spatial frequency content separator to filter out the structural component of scene objects. Max-pooling, in particular, yields a more perceptible result. We term this particular component as the structure-responsive residual (SRR). Overall, SRR can effectively captures the high-frequency information such as rapidly changing edges and structural details. Finally, the input feature map can be decomposed into ARF and SRR components based on their frequency content.

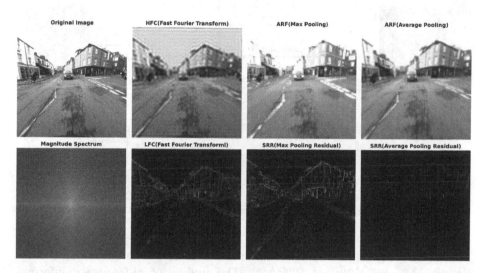

Fig. 1. Spatial frequency content separation based on three different techniques: Fast Fourier Transform (FFT), max-pooling and average-pooling

3.2   Structure-Responsive Convolution

For the vanilla convolution, high-frequency information contained in the SRR is typically filtered out after each pooling operation, resulting in the feature maps that is abundant in semantic information but lacks crucial structural details. To improve the invariance of scene representations, we propose a novel Structure-Responsive Convolution (SRConv) to explicitly incorporate structural information. SRConv is a bi-frequency architecture that extracts the structure-aware SRR component from targeted channels' feature maps and integrate it into non-targeted channels' feature maps. The implementation details of SRConv are provided below, while Fig. 2 showcases the architecture.

Let $X \in \mathbb{R}^{c \times h \times w}$ denote the input feature map of a convolutional layer, where c, h and w represent the number of channels, height and width, respectively. Along the channel dimension, X can be artificially factorized into two sub-tensors, $X^A \in \mathbb{R}^{(1-\alpha)c \times h \times w}$ and $X^B \in \mathbb{R}^{\alpha c \times h \times w}$, where $\alpha \in [0, 1]$ specifies the decomposition ratio and α is set to 0.5 in this paper. As outlined in Sect. 3.1, performing max-pooling on the sub-tensor X^B can yield a smooth low-frequency component $X^{ARF} \in \mathbb{R}^{\alpha c \times \frac{h}{2} \times \frac{w}{2}}$. Subsequently, we resize the tensor X^B to the same resolution as X^{ARF} and then perform pixel-wise subtraction between the corresponding pixels of the two tensors. This process produces the fine-grained high-frequency component $X^{SRR} \in \mathbb{R}^{\alpha c \times \frac{h}{2} \times \frac{w}{2}}$. Hence, we can further factorize the input tensor X into $X = \{X^A, (X^{ARF}, X^{SRR})\}$.

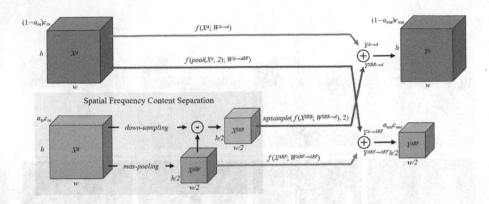

Fig. 2. Design details of the Structure-Responsive Convolution (SRConv).

Let $Y = \{Y^A, Y^{ARF}\}$ be the separated output tensor, where $Y^A \in \mathbb{R}^{(1-\alpha)c \times h \times w}$ and $Y^{ARF} \in \mathbb{R}^{\alpha c \times h \times w}$. The update of bi-frequency information is achieved by computing the sum of feature maps from different resolutions. Formally, The outputs can be obtained by $Y^A = Y^{A \to A} + Y^{SRR \to A}$ and $Y^{ARF} = Y^{ARF \to ARF} + Y^{A \to ARF}$, where the notation "$\to$" to denote the convolutional update. Similar to OctConv, the convolution kernel of SRConv can be divided into four parts $W = [(W^{A \to A}, W^{A \to ARF}), (W^{SRR \to A}, W^{ARF \to ARF})]$. Therefore, the outputs Y^A and Y^{ARF} at location (p, q) can be computed by

$$
\begin{aligned}
Y_{p,q}^A &= Y_{p,q}^{A \to A} + Y_{p,q}^{SRR \to A} \\
&= \sum_{i,j \in \mathcal{N}_k} W_{i+\frac{k-1}{2}, j+\frac{k-1}{2}}^{A \to A}{}^T X_{p+i, q+j}^A \\
&\quad + \sum_{i,j \in \mathcal{N}_k} W_{i+\frac{k-1}{2}, j+\frac{k-1}{2}}^{SRR \to A}{}^T X_{(\lfloor \frac{p}{2} \rfloor + i),(\lfloor \frac{q}{2} \rfloor + j)}^{SRR}
\end{aligned}
\tag{1}
$$

$$
\begin{aligned}
Y_{p,q}^{ARF} &= Y_{p,q}^{ARF \to ARF} + Y_{p,q}^{A \to ARF} \\
&= \sum_{i,j \in \mathcal{N}_k} W_{i+\frac{k-1}{2}, j+\frac{k-1}{2}}^{ARF \to ARF}{}^T X_{p+i, q+j}^{ARF} \\
&\quad + \sum_{i,j \in \mathcal{N}_k} W_{i+\frac{k-1}{2}, j+\frac{k-1}{2}}^{A \to ARF}{}^T X_{(2*p+0.5+i),(2*q+0.5+j)}^A
\end{aligned}
\tag{2}
$$

where the symbol $\lfloor \cdot \rfloor$ denotes floor function. In practical implementations, we use bilinear interpolation $upsample(X, 2)$ to get up-sampling results in Eq. 1. As the index $\{(2*p+0.5+i), (2*q+0.5+j)\}$ is not an integer, we employ average-pooling $pool\,(X,2)$ to get a approximate result. Now, the output tensor $Y = \{Y^A, Y^{ARF}\}$ can be rewrited as

$$
\begin{aligned}
Y^A &= f\left(X^A; W^{A\to A}\right) + upsample\left(f\left(X^{SRR}; W^{SRR\to A}\right),2\right) \\
Y^{ARF} &= f\left(X^{ARF}; W^{ARF\to ARF}\right) + f\left(pool\left(X^A,2\right); W^{A\to ARF}\right)
\end{aligned} \tag{3}
$$

where $f\,(\cdot)$ denotes a vanilla convolution.

3.3   Network Architecture

To enhance the applicability of the robot with limited resources, the proposed Structure-Responsive Network (SRNet) adopt MobileNet [28] as the baseline architecture, but replace the vanilla convolution within the depthwise separable convolution (DSC) with SRConv. According to [9], mid-level features exhibit optimal robustness against appearance changes. Therefore, we discard sequential processing after down-sampling feature maps to dimensions (14, 14, 512). Nevertheless, we preserve the last average-pooling layer and fully connected layer to regulate the dimensionality of the output. Finally, an input image i can be represented as a 500-dimensional descriptor $V_i \in \mathbb{R}^{500}$.

Triplet architecture, a common form of metric learning, has been proven effective in CNN models specifically designed for LCD [5,7]. The idea behind this method is that images captured at the same locations should display maximum similarity compared to images obtained from different locations. We utilized the Google Street View Time Machine dataset built by Arandjelović et al. [5] for training. In our modification, each query image q is accompanied by a positive sample q^+ and a set of negatives $\{q_i^-\}$. To learn the image representation $g(x) \in \mathbb{R}^d$, the triplet ranking loss can be expressed as

$$
L = \sum_{i}^{k} max\left(0,\ \|g(q) - g(q^+)\|_2^2 - \|g(q) - g(q_i^-)\|_2^2 + m\right) \tag{4}
$$

where k is the number of negatives. The value m defines a minimum margin, and L is set to zero in cases where the distance between q and q^- is greater by a margin than the distance between the q and q^+.

4   Experimental Results

In this section, we presents the offline and online experiments to assess the effectiveness of the proposed approach. We utilize a quantitative evaluation to compare SRNet with other approaches. To provide qualitative insight, we also utilize the similarity matrix to visualize the LCD results. Moreover, We discuss the online detection results obtained from a mobile robot operating in a manufacturing workshop.

4.1 Offline Loop Closure

The dataset used in the offline experiments can be categorized into two categories: 1) the first type of dataset is captured at the same places but under different conditions, making it an ideal basis for evaluating place matching performance. We use **ESSEX3IN1** and **SPEDTest** datasets in our experiment. Images with same index numbers represent the same location, and the ground truth tolerances are both strictly set as frame-to-frame; 2) the second type of dataset is obtained by capturing a single trajectory with repeated paths, maintaining continuity between adjacent images. It contains a substantial number of closed loops, closely resembling real-world situations. Our experiments employ the **New College** and **City Center** datasets.

Place Matching Performance. With a focus on perceptual aliasing challenges, the ESSEX3IN1 dataset composed of highly confusing images captured in indoor, outdoor, and natural environments. The SPEDTest dataset was collected across various seasons and illumination conditions, resulting in significant variations in appearance. Comparisons performed against several approaches, including Patch-NetVLAD [26], NetVLAD [5], OctConv [11] and MobileNetv3 [29]. We employ precision-recall (PR) curves, the area under the PR curve (AUC) and recall rate at 100% precision (R_{P100}) as evaluation metrics. The comparison results of PR curves are shown in Fig. 3, the AUC and R_{P100} are presented in Table 1.

As shown in Fig. 3, SRNet exhibits outstanding performance on both benchmark datasets, particularly showcasing state-of-the-art AUC values on the SPEDTest dataset. This demonstrates that SRNet outperforms other approaches in terms of invariance and robustness when dealing with appearance changes. For ESSEX3IN1 dataset, Patch-NetVLAD achieves the best place matching performance owing to its effective utilization of geometric information. Following closely behind, SRNet showcases commendable performance. It should be noted that SRNet demonstrates a significant improvement over OctConv in addressing the issue of perceptual aliasing. This difference in performance can be attributed to the fact that SRNet incorporates high-frequency SRR component into bi-frequency features. This highlights the significance of integrating stable structural information.

R_{P100} is another commonly used metric for evaluating place matching performance in cases where exceptional (even 100% in some cases) precision is required. Referring to the ESSEX3IN1's experimental results provided in Table 1, we can see that all methods are significantly impacted by the perceptual aliasing issue, with none of them achieving satisfactory results on the R_{P100} metric. For the SPEDTest dataset known for its drastic variations in appearance, SRNet showed strong performance, achieving a competitive score of 0.33 R_{P100}, which was nearly double that of the second-ranked OctConv (0.19).

Loop Closure Performance. Figure 4(a) illustrates the navigation route of the robot while gathering the City Center and New College datasets, clearly

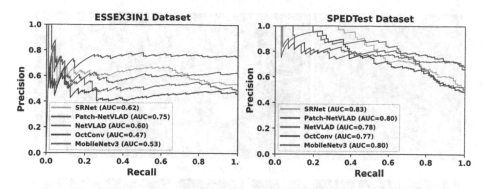

Fig. 3. Here are the comparison results of PR curves.

Table 1. The values of AUC and recall rate at 100% precision (R_{P100}) are listed here.

Approaches	ESSEX3IN1		SPEDTest	
	AUC	R_{P100}	AUC	R_{P100}
SRNet	0.62	0.01	0.83	0.33
Patch-NetVLAD	0.75	0.03	0.80	0.09
NetVLAD	0.60	0	0.78	0.04
OctConv	0.47	0.01	0.77	0.19
MobileNetv3	0.52	0.01	0.80	0.03

indicating a substantial number of closed loops in these trajectories. The loop closures can also be observed in the visualization of similarity matrix. In the similarity matrix images, the diagonal stripes represent the similarity between the images and themselves, while the off-diagonal stripes represent the potential closed loops.

As shown in Fig. 4(b) and (c), the similarity matrix of each dataset is visually represented with two figures. The left figure displays the closed-loop ground truth information, while the right figure illustrates the similarity matrix computed using the proposed SRNet. SRNet efficiently detects most closed loops, as demonstrated by the comparison of similarity matrices. While some missed detections may occur, it is not essential to identify every single closed loop in real-world applications. Notably, this experiment did not involve any posterior, yet it has been demonstrated that the geometric or temporal verification checks can enhance the precision [3,12,16,17].

4.2 Online Loop Closure

To further evaluate the practicability of the proposed method, we conducted online LCD experiments in a manufacturing workshop, a typical operational environment for mobile robots. The robot travels along three routes, indoor, outdoor, and a hybrid route that covers both. Figure 5 shows example images

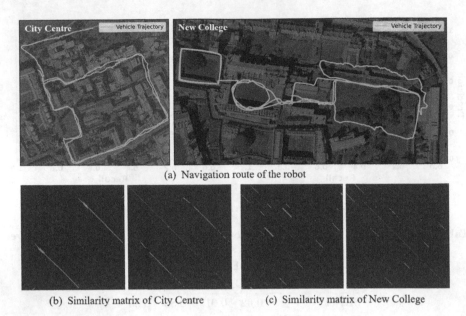

(a) Navigation route of the robot

(b) Similarity matrix of City Centre   (c) Similarity matrix of New College

Fig. 4. (a) Robot's navigation route overlaid on the aerial image, and (b, c) show the similarity matrice images. For (b) and (c), on the left is the Ground Truth Matrix and the right is SRNet-Computed Similarity Matrix.

of manufacturing workshop. Detecting loop closures in this environment is challenging due to dim lighting, numerous dynamic objects, and the similar layout resulting in indistinguishable appearances.

Fig. 5. The example images of the manufacturing workshop.

Figure 6 displays the online detection results from both 3D and 2D perspectives. From the 2D perspective, it is clear that the detected closed loops cover almost all revisited places. Note that the LCD operates at a frequency of one per second, so it is reasonable to observe periodic gaps. Furthermore, the 3D perspective confirms that the matched places are indeed the true positive results. These collective results demonstrate the practicality of the proposed method.

The primary objective of loop closure detection is to improve localization accuracy. To achieve this, we further utilized SRNet's detection results to perform optimization in the backend. Figure 7 presents the results of pose graph optimization. For each experimental case, we present the preliminary trajectory before optimization and the optimized corrected trajectory. Obviously, the accumulated error of

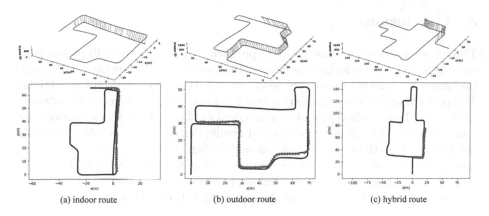

(a) indoor route   (b) outdoor route   (c) hybrid route

Fig. 6. Online experiment results: black line shows the navigation route, while the red dot and connecting line indicate the matched places. (Color figure online)

the optimized trajectory is significantly reduced, particularly in indoor and outdoor cases where numerous misaligned robot trajectories were successfully corrected. Overall, the proposed SRNet can help improve the accuracy estimated robot trajectory and ensure the creation of a globally consistent map.

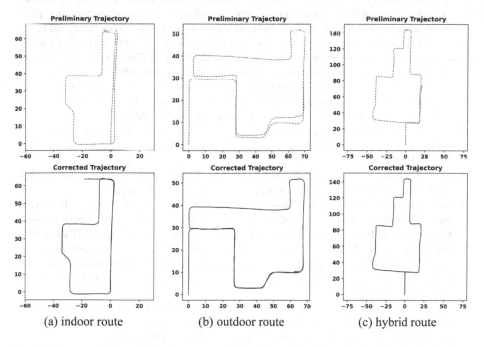

(a) indoor route   (b) outdoor route   (c) hybrid route

Fig. 7. The comparison between pre-optimization and post-optimization trajectories.

5   Conclusions

This paper introduces a novel LCD approach called Structural-Response Network (SRNet), which focuses on leveraging structural information within high-frequency components to enhance descriptor invariance for scene representations. The performance of the proposed approach is assessed using benchmark datasets, while special emphasis is given to its practical applicability in real scenarios with a mobile robot. Promising experimental results demonstrate the effectiveness of the proposed method, particularly in addressing extreme appearance changes and perceptual aliasing. In future work, we plan to utilize SRConv to extend various network architectures and conduct a thorough analysis of performance variances associated with varying choices of the ratio α and kernel size.

References

1. Fuentes-Pacheco, J., Ruiz-Ascencio, J., Rendón-Mancha, J.M.: Visual simultaneous localization and mapping: a survey. Artif. Intell. Rev. **43**, 55–81 (2015)
2. Lowry, S., et al.: Visual place recognition: a survey. IEEE Trans. Rob. **32**(1), 1–19 (2015)
3. Cummins, M., Newman, P.: Fab-map: probabilistic localization and mapping in the space of appearance. Int. J. Robot. Res. **27**(6), 647–665 (2008)
4. Qin, C., Zhang, Y., Liu, Y., Zhu, D., Coleman, S.A., Kerr, D.: Structure-aware feature disentanglement with knowledge transfer for appearance-changing place recognition. IEEE Trans. Neural Networks Learn. Syst. **34**, 1278–1290 (2021)
5. Arandjelovic, R., Gronat, P., Torii, A., Pajdla, T., Sivic, J.: NetVLAD: CNN architecture for weakly supervised place recognition. In: Proceedings of the IEEE Conference on Computer Vision and Pattern Recognition, pp. 5297–5307 (2016)
6. Lopez-Antequera, M., Gomez-Ojeda, R., Petkov, N., Gonzalez-Jimenez, J.: Appearance-invariant place recognition by discriminatively training a convolutional neural network. Pattern Recogn. Lett. **92**, 89–95 (2017)
7. Xin, Z., et al.: Localizing discriminative visual landmarks for place recognition. In: 2019 International Conference on Robotics and Automation (ICRA), pp. 5979–5985. IEEE (2019)
8. Gao, X., Zhang, T.: Unsupervised learning to detect loops using deep neural networks for visual slam system. Auton. Robot. **41**(1), 1–18 (2017)
9. Sünderhauf, N., Shirazi, S., Dayoub, F., Upcroft, B., Milford, M.: On the performance of convnet features for place recognition. In: 2015 IEEE/RSJ International Conference on Intelligent Robots and Systems (IROS), pp. 4297–4304. IEEE (2015)
10. Schubert, S., Neubert, P., Protzel, P.: Unsupervised learning methods for visual place recognition in discretely and continuously changing environments. In: 2020 IEEE International Conference on Robotics and Automation (ICRA), pp. 4372–4378. IEEE (2020)
11. Chen, Y., et al.: Drop an octave: reducing spatial redundancy in convolutional neural networks with octave convolution. In: Proceedings of the IEEE/CVF International Conference on Computer Vision, pp. 3435–3444 (2019)
12. Gálvez-López, D., Tardos, J.D.: Bags of binary words for fast place recognition in image sequences. IEEE Trans. Rob. **28**(5), 1188–1197 (2012)

13. Jégou, H., Douze, M., Schmid, C., Pérez, P.: Aggregating local descriptors into a compact image representation. In: 2010 IEEE Computer Society Conference on Computer Vision and Pattern Recognition, pp. 3304–3311. IEEE (2010)
14. Cummins, M., Newman, P.: Appearance-only slam at large scale with fab-map 2.0. Int. J. Robot. Res. **30**(9), 1100–1123 (2011)
15. Bay, H., Tuytelaars, T., Van Gool, L.: SURF: speeded up robust features. In: Leonardis, A., Bischof, H., Pinz, A. (eds.) ECCV 2006. LNCS, vol. 3951, pp. 404–417. Springer, Heidelberg (2006). https://doi.org/10.1007/11744023_32
16. Mur-Artal, R., Tardós, J.D.: ORB-SLAM2: an open-source SLAM system for monocular, stereo, and RGB-D cameras. IEEE Trans. Rob. **33**(5), 1255–1262 (2017)
17. Campos, C., Elvira, R., Rodríguez, J.J.G., Montiel, J.M., Tardós, J.D.: ORB-SLAM3: an accurate open-source library for visual, visual-inertial, and multimap SLAM. IEEE Trans. Rob. **37**(6), 1874–1890 (2021)
18. Dalal, N., Triggs, B.: Histograms of oriented gradients for human detection. In: 2005 IEEE Computer Society Conference on Computer Vision and Pattern Recognition (CVPR 2005), vol. 1, pp. 886–893. IEEE (2005)
19. Oliva, A., Torralba, A.: Building the gist of a scene: the role of global image features in recognition. Prog. Brain Res. **155**, 23–36 (2006)
20. Hou, Y., Zhang, H., Zhou, S.: Convolutional neural network-based image representation for visual loop closure detection. In: 2015 IEEE International Conference on Information and Automation, pp. 2238–2245. IEEE (2015)
21. Li, K., Wang, X., Shi, L., Geng, N.: CoCALC: a self-supervised visual place recognition approach combining appearance and geometric information. IEEE Access **11**, 17207–17217 (2023)
22. Merrill, N., Huang, G.: CALC2. 0: Combining appearance, semantic and geometric information for robust and efficient visual loop closure. In: 2019 IEEE/RSJ International Conference on Intelligent Robots and Systems (IROS), pp. 4554–4561. IEEE (2019)
23. Chen, Z., Lam, O., Jacobson, A., Milford, M.: Convolutional neural network-based place recognition. arXiv preprint arXiv:1411.1509 (2014)
24. Radenović, F., Tolias, G., Chum, O.: Fine-tuning CNN image retrieval with no human annotation. IEEE Trans. Pattern Anal. Mach. Intell. **41**(7), 1655–1668 (2018)
25. Sarlin, P.E., Debraine, F., Dymczyk, M., Siegwart, R., Cadena, C.: Leveraging deep visual descriptors for hierarchical efficient localization. In: Conference on Robot Learning, pp. 456–465. PMLR (2018)
26. Hausler, S., Garg, S., Xu, M., Milford, M., Fischer, T.: Patch-NetVLAD: multi-scale fusion of locally-global descriptors for place recognition. In: Proceedings of the IEEE/CVF Conference on Computer Vision and Pattern Recognition, pp. 14141–14152 (2021)
27. Nussbaumer, H.J., Nussbaumer, H.J.: The fast Fourier transform. Springer (1981)
28. Howard, A.G., et al.: MobileNets: efficient convolutional neural networks for mobile vision applications. arXiv preprint arXiv:1704.04861 (2017)
29. Howard, A., et al.: Searching for MobileNetV3. In: Proceedings of the IEEE/CVF International Conference on Computer Vision, pp. 1314–1324 (2019)

Visual Sensor Layout Optimization of a Robotic Mobile Adhesive Removal System for Wind Turbine Blade Based on Simulation

Bo Peng[1], Feifan Zheng[2], Fan Zhang[1], Shilin Ming[1], Yan Li[1], Xutao Deng[1], Zeyu Gong[2(✉)], and Bo Tao[2]

[1] DEC Academy of Science and Technology Co, Ltd., Chengdu 611731, China
[2] Huazhong University of Science and Technology, Wuhan 430074, China
gongzeyu@hust.edu.cn

Abstract. In the manufacturing process of wind turbine blades, residual adhesive may overflow after the mold closing of the blades. The overflowing residual adhesive may cause damage to the inside of the wind turbine blades when the blades are in motion during operation. To address this, an adhesive removal robot capable of identifying and removing residual adhesive was designed. The robot is equipped with a vision system that enables adhesive recognition and guides the adhesive removal mechanism. Given the lack of precedents and the complexity of the robot's functions, it was necessary to streamline the development process and optimize the design scheme of the vision system to reduce costs and shorten development cycles. Therefore, a simulation environment using Gazebo was constructed to evaluate different design schemes for safety and effectiveness, and finally the optimization of the sensor layout scheme was realized.

Keywords: Wind turbine blade · Removing adhesive · Robot simulation · Sensor deployment

1 Introduction

Wind turbine blades consist of a pressure surface shell and a suction surface shell which are bonded together using adhesive in a mold. Adhesive are applied to the shear web, main beam cap, front and back edges. After molding, a lot of residual adhesive will be squeezed out and hung on the bonding area in the front edge and shear web. This residual adhesive can fall off during blade movement, potentially leading to major quality issues such as blade shell damage, lightning protection system damage, and blockage of drainage holes. Therefore, an adhesive removal operation is necessary prior to the wind turbine blade being put into service. The internal space within a wind turbine blade is both narrow and long, with the internal space reducing gradually from the blade root to the tip [1]. The residual adhesive at the tip of wind turbine blades is difficult to remove manually. For this reason, it is necessary to design specialized robots which are capable of entering the narrow tip section to remove the residual adhesive located at the shear web and front edge.

© The Author(s), under exclusive license to Springer Nature Singapore Pte Ltd. 2023
H. Yang et al. (Eds.): ICIRA 2023, LNAI 14273, pp. 84–95, 2023.
https://doi.org/10.1007/978-981-99-6498-7_8

The robot needs to be equipped with ranging sensors to perceive the posture of the vehicle body and guide the motion module to adjust in real time. Meanwhile, visual sensors are equipped to realize the autonomous identification and positioning of residual adhesives and guide the primary mechanism to accurately remove adhesives. Therefore, the design of sensor placement scheme is very important. In the process of robot development, it is usually necessary to test different mechanical structures, sensor selection, deployment position and algorithms, so as to find the best solution suitable for actual tasks [2]. Due to limitations in time, space, and cost, it is not always feasible to conduct experiments in actual test environments. In order to speed up the development progress of robots, simulation methods can be used to conduct safe and cost-effective testing of the robot system under development [3]. During the development of the adhesive removing robot, determining the optimal sensor layout is difficult. A virtual environment is built to simulate the candidate sensor layout schemes, and the optimal sensor layout scheme is designed based on the simulation results.

With the increasing demand for robot applications, engineers have put forward higher requirements for the accuracy, robustness and ease of use of robot simulation software [4]. In practical applications, robots are required to assist humans [5, 6] or interact closely with humans [7, 8]. Therefore, robot simulation software must be able to simulate and test the safety and effectiveness of robots truly and reliably. Many simulation software can be applied to the simulation of adhesive removal robots, including Gazebo [9], Webots [10, 11], RobotDK [12], USARSim [13] and OpenRave [14]. All simulated objects in Gazebo have attributes such as quality and friction, which make them behave realistically when interacting [15]. The Webots kernel is based on the ODE engine [16], which provides realistic dynamic simulation effects, and supports multiple programming languages. RobotDK is mainly used for industrial robots and has a diverse CAD model library, including robots from ABB, KUKA, Yaskawa and other manufacturers. USARSim is a versatile multi-robot simulator, it seamlessly interfaces with the Mobility Open Architecture Simulation and Tools framework (MOAST) [17], which allows users to quickly validate new algorithms by rewriting individual modules. OpenRave is mainly used to simulate kinematic and geometric information related to manipulator motion planning for exploration of mission configuration space. Because Gazebo has a variety of sensor plugins, it can simulate the interaction between the robots and the environment, and seamlessly deploy algorithms to the real robots. Therefore, Gazebo is used to build a wind power blade simulation environment to study the working state of the robot under different sensor layouts, so as to achieve sensor deployment optimization.

This paper can be divided into five parts. In the second part, a general structure scheme and a candidate sensor deployment scheme for the task of removing residual adhesives were designed for the robot. In the third part, a simulation platform was built, and the control of the robot was modeled. In the fourth part, we simulated candidate sensor deployment schemes on the simulation platform and optimized the visual system based on the simulation experimental results. The fifth part is a brief summary of the full text.

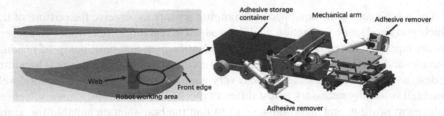

Fig. 1. The cross-section of the wind turbine blade and the structure of the residual adhesive removal robot.

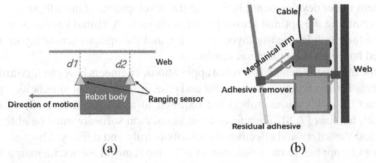

Fig. 2. (a) shows the working mode of the ranging sensor, and (b) shows the residual adhesive removal status of the robot.

2 Design of Residual Adhesive Removal Robot

2.1 The Overall Scheme of Adhesive Removing Robot

According to the working environment and design requirements of the robot, the robot is mainly composed of a motion module, a residual adhesive removal module and a mechanical arm module. The robot was placed at the remote end in advance before the mold closing. After the mold closing was completed, the robot started to autonomously remove residual adhesive. The cross section of wind power blade and the overall structure of the robot are shown in Fig. 1. Since the residual adhesive overflow at the web keeps a certain and invariant distance from the web, the robot maintains line tracking and progresses based on the web during its movement. Two infrared ranging sensors are deployed at the front and rear ends of the robot to provide feedback on the robot's position and posture and adjust the robot's forward carry posture in real time, as shown in Fig. 2(a). On the side near the front edge, due to the changes in the size and shape inside the blade space, the robot needs to be equipped with a mechanical arm that can actively adjust the length and angle, and a residual adhesive removal mechanism is equipped at its end. During the robot movement, adhesive is recognized through visual information, and the length and angle of the mechanical arm are accurately controlled to achieve a good removal of the adhesive on the front edge of wind turbine blades. The overall adhesive removal scheme of the residual adhesive removing robot is shown in Fig. 2(b).

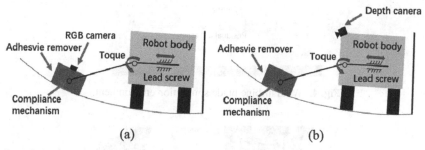

Fig. 3. (a) shows the sensor deployment scheme of Scheme 1, (b) shows the sensor deployment scheme of Scheme 2.

2.2   Candidate Visual Sensor Deployment Scheme

Aiming at the problem that the adhesive position at the front edge will change in real time relative to the robot, it is necessary to deploy a vision sensor to identify the residual adhesive and guide the adhesive removal mechanism at the front edge to remove the adhesive. The general visual guidance system can be divided into eye-in-hand and eye-to-hand structures according to the location of the visual sensor. In the eye-in-hand structural form, the visual sensor is usually fixed on the end effector of the mechanical arm, while in the eye-to-hand structural form, the visual sensor is fixed outside the mechanical arm. Accordingly, we set up two sensor layout schemes.

In scheme 1, the hand-eye structure of eye-in-hand is adopted to deploy the RGB camera on the adhesive removal mechanism, as shown in Fig. 3(a). By identifying the position error of the adhesive centroid position relative to the ideal pixel in the image, a control law was established to guide the adhesive removal mechanism to remove the adhesive. In this scheme, the visual sensor is relatively close to the residual adhesive and the measurement accuracy is high. However, the camera and the residual adhesive removing mechanism move together, and the residual adhesive may be out of the field of view during the movement of the residual adhesive removing mechanism.

In scheme 2, the hand-eye structure of eye-to-hand was adopted to deploy the depth camera on the vehicle body, as shown in Fig. 3(b). The position of the adhesive relative to the robot is calculated by using the RGB image information and depth information of the depth camera. The structural parameters of the mechanical arm are used to carry out the inverse kinematics solution, and the angle of the motor is controlled to make the adhesive removal mechanism at the end of the mechanical arm reach the position of removing adhesive. In this scheme, the visual sensor field of view covers a large area, and the residual adhesive will not leave the field of view due to the movement of the adhesive removal mechanism. However, this deployment scheme will cause the visual sensor to be far away from the residual adhesive, and the visual measurement accuracy is relatively low.

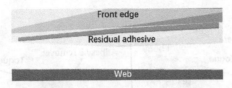

Fig. 4. Wind turbine blade simulation environment.

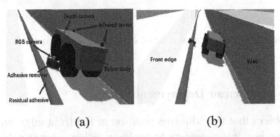

(a)   (b)

Fig. 5. (a) shows the virtual environment inside the wind turbine blade, (b) shows the simulation modeling of the adhesive removing robot.

3   Simulation Environment Construction

3.1   Simulation Environment Construction Based on Gazebo

The simulation environment of robots and blades was modeled by Gazebo, and ROS was used for data transmission and robot control. The purpose of the simulation was to determine the deployment of the vision sensor to direct the removal of adhesive on the front edge side. Therefore, residual adhesive was only placed on the front edge side. Establish SLDPRT format 3D model in Solidworks according to blade and residual adhesive size, then convert into URDF file through sw2urdf plugin to import into Gazebo. To simulate the actual situation of the blade as realistically as possible, the distance and cross-sectional area of the green residual adhesive between the wind turbine blade and the web will vary along the axial direction of the blade, as shown in Fig. 4. For the adhesive removal robot model, xacro is used to write the robot description file, set the size parameters of the robot motion platform, sensor and actuator, import the sensor plugins such as RGB camera, depth camera and ranging sensor, and configure the motor driving parameters of the four-wheel motion platform, thus obtaining the adhesive removing robot model in Gazebo, as shown in Fig. 5.

3.2   Vehicle Pose Control

Since the adhesive removing robot needs to take the web as the benchmark for constant distance line patrol, it is necessary to carry out kinematic modeling on the mobile platform of the robot, and simulate the robot's behavior based on the kinematic model of the mobile platform to verify the performance of the controller. The mobile platform of the adhesive removing robot is a four-wheel differential structure. In the process of robot progress, the linear speed υ and angular speed ω are controlled. The motion model established based on the above conditions is shown in Fig. 6.

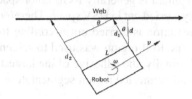

Fig. 6. Kinematic modeling of mobile platform.

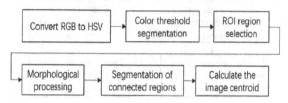

Fig. 7. Adhesive position identification algorithm.

The distance d_1 and d_2 from the robot to the web were obtained by two infrared ranging sensors deployed in front and back of the robot with an interval of L, respectively. The angle θ between the robot and the web is

$$\theta = \arctan\left(\frac{d_2 - d_1}{L}\right) \tag{1}$$

The distance d from the robot to the web is

$$d = \begin{cases} d_1 \cos\theta, & d_1 < d_2 \\ d_2 \cos\theta, & d_1 \geq d_2 \end{cases} \tag{2}$$

In order to enable the robot to move forward with distance d_{target} parallel to the web, the robot is set to move with constant linear velocity υ_c, and the robot angular velocity ω_c is controlled by PID algorithm

$$d_{error} = d - d_{target} \tag{3}$$

$$\theta_{error} = \theta \tag{4}$$

$$\omega_c = K_{p1}d_{error} + \sum K_{i1}d_{errori} + K_{p2}\theta_{error} \tag{5}$$

3.3 Adhesive Recognition Algorithm

Since the adhesive is consistent in color, the adhesive can be identified according to its color characteristics. The recognition algorithm flow is shown in Fig. 7. The visual data directly obtained from the camera is generally RGB color space. In image processing, color segmentation is usually carried out in HSV space. Therefore, conversion is required first, and then image segmentation is carried out according to the threshold to obtain the candidate target mask. The ROI region was used to screen the mask, and the non-target region was excluded. Finally, the adhesive of the largest region was obtained by morphological processing and connected region segmentation.

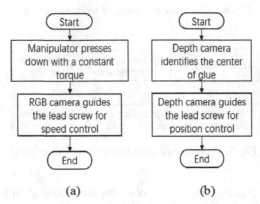

(a)   (b)

Fig. 8. (a) shows the control framework of Scheme 1, (b) shows the control framework of Scheme 2.

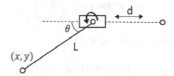

Fig. 9. Simplified two-dimensional planar structure of manipulator.

3.4 Visual Based Control of Adhesive Removal

The mechanical arm for removing residual has three degrees of freedom, including the linear motion freedom driven by a lead screw, the rotational freedom driven by a motor, and the rotational freedom for conforming to the blade surface, as shown in Fig. 3. The movement of the mechanical arm can be guided by the visual data collected by the eye-to-hand depth camera and the eye-in-hand RGB camera. The control framework of the two vision sensor deployment schemes is shown in Fig. 8.

In scheme 1, for the RGB camera, the difference e between the pixel coordinates of the adhesive centroid in the image (u, v) and the set ideal pixel coordinates in the image horizontal coordinate direction is calculated, and the velocity of the prissy joint of the manipulator v_s is calculated according to the following control law

$$v_s = -\lambda e \tag{6}$$

where λ is the amplification factor.

In scheme 2, for the depth camera, the three-dimensional coordinates of the adhesive (X, Y, Z) are calculated based on the adhesive image centroid coordinates (u, v), depth values Z and camera parameters (f_x, f_y, u_0, v_0)

$$X = (u - u_0)\frac{Z}{f_x} \tag{7}$$

$$Y = (v - v_0)\frac{Z}{f_y} \tag{8}$$

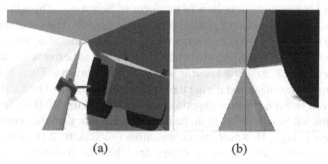

(a)   (b)

Fig. 10. (a) shows the operation of the Scheme 1 adhesive removal robot, (b) shows the images obtained by the RGB camera.

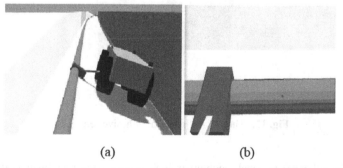

(a)   (b)

Fig. 11. (a) shows the operation of the Scheme 2 adhesive removal robot, and (b) shows the images obtained by the depth camera.

According to the hand-eye conversion matrix of the depth camera and mechanical arm coordinate system, the adhesive position is converted into the mechanical arm coordinate system. Since the mechanical arm only moves on the two-dimensional plane, it can be simplified. When the adhesive position relative to the mechanical arm coordinate system is (x, y), the inverse kinematics solution can be carried out according to the mechanical arm structure parameters shown in Fig. 9, and the movement quantity d of the translation joint can be obtained. The position of the joint is controlled, and the rotational degree of freedom is pressed down with a constant torque.

$$\theta = \arcsin \frac{y}{L} \tag{9}$$

$$d = x - L\cos\theta \tag{10}$$

4 Simulation Comparison and Sensor's Layout Optimization

A robot simulation platform was built in Gazebo to verify the proposed scheme. The robots deploy sensors and controllers in the form of Scheme 1. The adhesive removal effect of the robot in the working process is shown in Fig. 10. The simulation results of Scheme 2 are shown in Fig. 11. To compare the adhesive removal accuracy of different design schemes, the distance error between the center of the adhesive removal mechanism and the center of the adhesive was taken as an indicator, as shown in Fig. 12. The adhesive removal accuracy was measured during the working of the robot. The results are shown in Fig. 13. It can be seen from the experimental results that the RGB camera in scheme 1 is close to the adhesive and has high measurement accuracy, so the removal accuracy of the adhesive is high. However, the depth camera in scheme 2 is far away from the adhesive and can only obtain the image of the side of the adhesive, so the control accuracy is low.

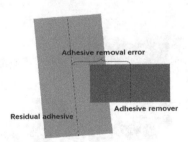

Fig. 12. The error of residual adhesive removal.

When the adhesive removal mechanism is far away from the adhesive, the adhesive in scheme 1 will be out of the RGB camera's field of view, resulting in the RGB camera failing to detect the adhesive and the robot failing to work properly, as shown in Fig. 14. However, the depth camera in scheme 2 can still work normally due to its large field of view, so scheme 2 is more robust and stable than scheme 1.

Therefore, in order to prevent the robot from detaching residual adhesive due to the small field of view of the RGB camera on the eye-in-hand configuration, while ensuring

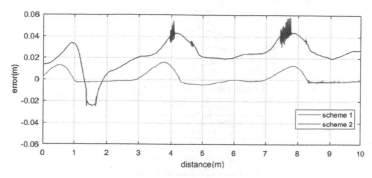

Fig. 13. Adhesive removal accuracy of Scheme 1 and Scheme 2.

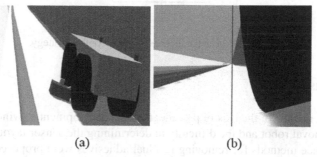

(a)   (b)

Fig. 14. (a) shows the working situation of the robot of Scheme 1, (b) shows the images obtained by the RGB camera.

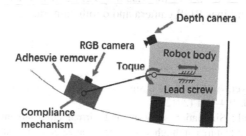

Fig. 15. Sensor deployment scheme.

the accuracy of the removal of the adhesive, a combination of scheme one and scheme two can be used, and the visual sensor deployment is shown in Fig. 15. This scheme uses a depth camera as the global camera to guide the adhesive removal mechanism close to the residual adhesive, and then switches to an RGB camera to guide the adhesive removal mechanism for accurate removal, the control strategy is shown in Fig. 16. The control algorithms for the RGB camera and the depth camera guiding the adhesive removal mechanism in this scheme are consistent with those in scheme 1 and scheme 2, respectively, as shown in Sect. 3.4.

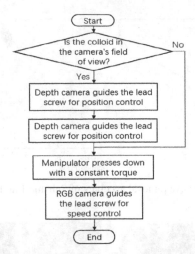

Fig. 16. Residual adhesive removal control strategy.

5 Conclusion

In this paper, in view of the lack of precedents in the development of wind turbine blade adhesive removal robot and the difficulty in determining the sensor layout scheme, two visual guidance methods for removing residual adhesives were proposed, and Gazebo simulator was used to build a virtual environment for wind turbine blade to compare the safety and efficiency of sensor layout schemes. According to the simulation experiment results, we optimized the design of the visual system and ultimately adopted a sensor layout scheme that combines RGB camera and depth camera.

References

1. Cox, K., Echtermeyer, A.: Structural design and analysis of a 10 mw wind turbine blade. Energy Procedia **24**, 194–201 (2012)
2. Shamshiri, R., et al.: Simulation software and virtual environments for acceleration of agricultural robotics: features highlights and performance comparison (2018)
3. Takaya, K., Asai, T., Kroumov, V., Smarandache, F.: Simulation environment for mobile robots testing using ROS and Gazebo. In: 2016 20th International Conference on System Theory, Control and Computing (ICSTCC), pp. 96–101. IEEE, Sinaia (2016)
4. Staranowicz, A., Mariottini, G.L.: A survey and comparison of commercial and open-source robotic simulator software. In: Proceedings of the 4th International Conference on PErvasive Technologies Related to Assistive Environments, pp. 1–8. ACM, Heraklion Crete Greece (2011)
5. Kim, D.-J., Lovelett, R., Behal, A.: An empirical study with simulated ADL tasks using a vision-guided assistive robot arm. In: 2009 IEEE International Conference on Rehabilitation Robotics, pp. 504–509. IEEE, Kyoto, Japan (2009)
6. Hayat, A.A., Parween, R., Elara, M.R., Parsuraman, K., Kandasamy, P.S.: Panthera: design of a reconfigurable pavement sweeping robot. In: 2019 International Conference on Robotics and Automation (ICRA), pp. 7346–7352. IEEE, Montreal, QC, Canada (2019)

7. Taylor, R.H., Stoianovici, D.: Medical robotics in computer-integrated surgery. IEEE Trans. Robot. Autom. **19**(5), 765–781 (2003)

8. Nef, T., Riener, R.: ARM in - design of a novel arm rehabilitation robot. In: 9th International Conference on Rehabilitation Robotics, 2005. ICORR 2005, pp. 57–60. IEEE, Chicago, IL, USA (2005)

9. Qian, W., et al.: Manipulation task simulation using ROS and Gazebo. In: 2014 IEEE International Conference on Robotics and Biomimetics (ROBIO 2014), pp. 2594–2598. IEEE, Bali, Indonesia (2014)

10. Michel, O.: Cyberbotics Ltd. Webots^{TM}: professional mobile robot simulation. Int. J. Adv. Robot. Syst. **1**, 40–43 (2004)

11. Michel, O.: Webots: symbiosis between virtual and real mobile robots. In: Heudin, JC. (eds.) Virtual Worlds. VW 1998. Lecture Notes in Computer Science, vol. 1434, pp. 254-263. Springer, Heidelberg (1998)

12. Chakraborty, C., S., Aithal, P.S.: Forward and Inverse Kinematics Demonstration using RoboDK and C#. Int. J. Appl. Eng. Manag. Lett. **5**, 97–105 (2021)

13. Carpin, S., Lewis, M., Wang, J., Balakirsky, S., Scrapper, C.: USARSim: a robot simulator for research and education. In: Proceedings 2007 IEEE International Conference on Robotics and Automation, pp. 1400–1405. IEEE, Rome, Italy (2007)

14. Diankov, R., Kuffner, J.: OpenRAVE: a planning architecture for autonomous robotics. Robotics Institute, Pittsburgh, PA, Technical report CMU-RI-TR-08-34. P. 79 (2008)

15. Koenig, N.P., Howard, A.: Design and use paradigms for Gazebo, an open-source multi-robot simulator. IROS **4**, 2149–2154 (2004)

16. Hohl, L., Tellez, R., Michel, O., Ijspeert, A.J.: Aibo and Webots: simulation, wireless remote control and controller transfer. Robot. Auton. Syst. **54**, 472–485 (2006)

17. Scrapper, C., Balakirsky, S., Messina, E.: MOAST and USARSim: a combined framework for the development and testing of autonomous systems. Presented at the Defense and Security Symposium, Orlando (Kissimmee), FL May 5 (2006)

Perception, Interaction, and Control
of Wearable Robots

Kinematic and Static Analysis of Flexible Link Tensegrity Robots

Yezheng Kang[1], Jianhuan Chen[1], Lingyu Kong[3], Hao Wang[1,2],
and Genliang Chen[1,2(✉)]

[1] State Key Laboratory of Mechanical Systems and Vibration, Shanghai Jiao Tong
University, Shanghai 200240, China
{yezheng.kang,leungchan}@sjtu.edu.cn
[2] Shanghai Key Laboratory of Digital Manufacturing for Thin-Walled Structures,
Shanghai Jiao Tong University, Shanghai 200240, China
[3] Intelligent Robot Research Center, Hangzhou 311100, China

Abstract. Replacement of rigid bars with slender flexible links in
tensegrity robots improves the kinematic performance of the mechanism,
and broadens its potential applications. Nonetheless, most existing analysis methods for tensegrity robots do not account for the large deformations of flexible links. This paper presents a general modeling and
analysis approach for flexible link tensegrity robots. The interconnection between flexible links and cables is defined using connectivity and
coefficient matrices. The flexible link tensegrity robot is modeled as a
group of hyper-redundant mechanisms constrained by cables, utilizing
the discretization-based method. Subsequently, the analytical model of
flexible link tensegrity robots is formulated as a set of nonlinear algebraic equations. Using this model, the Newton-Raphson algorithm is
employed to identify equilibrium configurations in a variety of given conditions. Finally, a prototype of a planar flexible link tensegrity robot
was constructed, and preliminary experiments were conducted to evaluate the effectiveness of the proposed methods. The experimental results
demonstrate the presented method in this study can achieve precise robot
control.

Keywords: flexible link · tensegrity robot · form-finding · inverse
kinematic analysis

1 Introduction

Currently, the utilization of mobile robots for area exploration that are unreach-
able for humans is of great significance. Although rigid robots exhibit excellent
motion accuracy and speed, their inflexibility and limited adaptability hinder
their overall performance. Moreover, their complex structure renders them vulnerable to damage during movement. On the other hand, soft robots composed
of flexible materials and structures offer excellent compliance, but their rootless

© The Author(s), under exclusive license to Springer Nature Singapore Pte Ltd. 2023
H. Yang et al. (Eds.): ICIRA 2023, LNAI 14273, pp. 99–110, 2023.
https://doi.org/10.1007/978-981-99-6498-7_9

design is challenging. Furthermore, the production and modeling of soft robots are intricate.

Tensegrity robots, which combine the advantages of rigid and soft robots, have been proposed as a solution to these challenges. The tensegrity system comprises both rigid rods and cables, with adjustable lengths to control the overall robot configuration. These robots possess superior characteristics, including high flexibility, large strength-to-mass ratio, high redundancy, and excellent force distribution [1,2]. However, the range of variation in the length of the rigid rods and cables is limited, which results in reduced energy storage capacity and restricted motion performance. Additionally, accurately detecting changes in rod and cable lengths is problematic, making state estimation difficult [3,4]. Furthermore, the interaction between the rigid rods can result in a limited motion range [5]. In order to overcome these challenge, flexible link tensegrity robots have been proposed as an alternative, consisting of flexible links and cables [6–8]. Developing an efficient modeling method for these robots is essential to ensure accurate control and effective application.

The current modeling methods for tensegrity robots can be broadly classified into two categories: kinematical and statical methods [9]. The kinematical approach principally relies on the maximization of the length of rigid rods to achieve the overall stable configuration of the robot, while considering the cable lengths as constant values. An alternative approach is to implement fixed lengths for the rods and minimize the cable lengths to achieve the stable configuration of the robot. Connelly and Terrell [10] analyzed a regular prism tensegrity structure and determined expressions for lengths and poses of members. Pellegrino [11] transformed the equilibrium problem of tensegrity system into a constrained minimization problem where the objective function is the rod lengths, and the constraint is the cable lengths. Motro [12] employed the dynamic relaxation method and kinetic damping technique to solve the equilibrium state of tensegrity structures. On the other hand, statical methods involve establishing the connection between member forces at steady-state configurations. Linkwitz and Schek [13] firstly introduced the force density method, which has been widely utilized in the analysis of various tensegrity mechanisms [14,15]. This approach utilizes force densities as variables and employs a connectivity matrix to express node forces. Based on this model, machine learning are used to produce the force densities of the elements and determine the configuration of tensegrity systems [16,17]. Similarly, Connelly [18] established the energy of tensegrity system by applying forces of rigid rods and cables, and derived the equilibrium condition by computing the minimum energy. Arsenault [19,20] also applied this method for kinematic and static analysis of planar and spatial tensegrity mechanisms. Nonetheless, the primary limitation of the aforementioned methods is that they assume rigid rods and do not consider rods bending, making them unsuitable for the analysis of flexible link tensegrity robots. In addition, research on modeling analysis of flexible tensegrity robots [6,7] has been limited. These methods have only been applied to specific configurations of tensegrity robots with rigid bars and cannot be easily adapted to other configurations of flexible link tensegrity robots.

In this paper, a modeling technique for flexible link tensegrity robots is introduced. The approach involves defining the connection relationship between the cables and flexible links using the connectivity matrix **C** and coefficient matrix **H**. By utilizing a discretization-based method, the tensegrity system is converted into multiple hyper-redundant mechanisms constrained by cables. The system model is then formulated in form of nonlinear algebraic equations. The equilibrium problem is solved using the Newton-Raphson algorithm. The rest of this paper is organized as follows: In Sect. 2, a form finding problem of the flexible link tensegrity robots is formulated. Then, the inverse analysis is presented in Sect. 3. To demonstrate the effectiveness of the proposed method, a prototype is developed and preliminary experiments are conducted in Sect. 4. Finally, conclusions are drawn in Sect. 5.

2 Form-Finding for Flexible Link Tensegrity Robots

In the analysis of flexible link tensegrity robots, form-finding, which determine the stable configuration by specifying cable lengths, flexible link sizes, and their connections, is deemed to be one of the most vital and intricate problems, as it serves as the foundation for designing and controlling the robot. To simplify the analysis, a set of assumptions are made. Firstly, external forces are solely applied to the nodes. Secondly, the members are assumed to be thin and of negligible mass. Thirdly, the cables are assumed to be inextensible. Finally, the connections between the cables and flexible links are approximated as ball joints. As an illustrative example, we consider a planar tensegrity robot with two flexible links and five cables.

2.1 Definition of a Flexible Link Tensegrity Robot

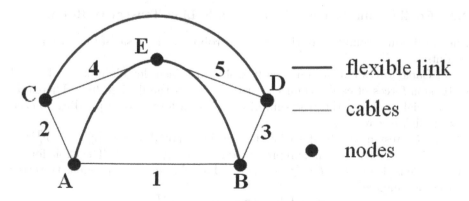

Fig. 1. Planar flexible link tensegrity robot

As illustrated in Fig. 1, the flexible link tensegritiy can be modeled as a graph with five nodes, five cables, and two flexible links. It should be noted that the nodes need not be constrained to the endpoints of the flexible links and can be located at any position along the length of the flexible links. The definition of flexible link tensegrity robots primarily involves the relationship between cables and nodes, as well as between nodes and flexible links.

The connectivity matrix, denoted as $\mathbf{C} \in \mathbb{R}^{s \times n}$, describes the relationship between cables and nodes. The cable i of the matrix connects nodes j and k, $j < k$:

$$\mathbf{C}(a, b) = \begin{cases} 1 & \text{if } a = i, b = j \\ -1 & \text{if } a = i, b = k \\ 0 & \text{else} \end{cases} \tag{1}$$

For example, Fig. 1 is a planar flexible link tensegrity, with a connectivity matrix of

$$\mathbf{C} = \begin{bmatrix} 1 & -1 & 0 & 0 & 0 \\ 1 & 0 & -1 & 0 & 0 \\ 0 & 1 & 0 & -1 & 0 \\ 0 & 0 & 1 & 0 & -1 \\ 0 & 0 & 0 & 1 & -1 \end{bmatrix} \tag{2}$$

Meanwhile, to establish the relationship between nodes and flexible links, a matrix $\mathbf{H}$ is defined as

$$\mathbf{H} = \mathbf{h} \otimes \mathbf{I}_6 \Rightarrow \mathbf{h} = \begin{bmatrix} 1 & 1 & 0 & 0 & 1 \\ 0 & 0 & 1 & 1 & 0 \end{bmatrix} \tag{3}$$

where $\mathbf{I}_6$ is the identity matrix of order 6. Each row of $\mathbf{h}$ corresponds to a flexible link, with the columns representing the nodes. The value at the ith row and j^{th} column of $\mathbf{h}$ is equal to 1 if the jth node lies on the ith flexible link, and 0 otherwise.

2.2 Equilibrium Analysis for a Flexible Link Tensegrity Robot

The equilibrium condition of the proposed robot needs to satisfy following constraints.

1) Cable forces balance on each flexible link: Each flexible link is subjected to tension forces of cables connected to a node on the flexible link. Therefore, it is crucial to ensure that the sum of the tension forces corresponding to each flexible link is zero.

The Cartesian coordinates of nodes can be denoted as $\boldsymbol{r} = [\boldsymbol{r}_a^{\mathrm{T}}, \cdots, \boldsymbol{r}_e^{\mathrm{T}}]^{\mathrm{T}} \in \mathbb{R}^{3 \times 5}$. The cable length can be represented as $\boldsymbol{l}_c = [l_1, \cdots, l_5]^{\mathrm{T}}$. The cable force's magnitude is denoted as $\boldsymbol{f} = [f_1, \cdots, f_5]$. Thus, the robot's force density vector can be obtained as

$$q_i = f_i / l_i \qquad \boldsymbol{q} = [q_1, \cdots, q_5]^{\mathrm{T}} \tag{4}$$

Similar to the equilibrium equations of the force density method [13], the sum of the cable forces acting on each node can be expressed as:

$$\boldsymbol{p}_n = [\boldsymbol{p}_a^T, \cdots, \boldsymbol{p}_e^T]^T = (\mathbf{C} \otimes \mathbf{I}_3)^T \mathrm{diag}(-\boldsymbol{q} \otimes \mathbf{I}_3)(\mathbf{C} \otimes \mathbf{I}_3)\boldsymbol{r} \tag{5}$$

where $\mathbf{I}_3$ is the identity matrix of order 3.

The corresponding force screw can be represented as

$$\boldsymbol{F} = [\boldsymbol{F}_a^T, \cdots, \boldsymbol{F}_e^T]^T = \begin{bmatrix} \boldsymbol{\omega}_a & & \\ & \ddots & \\ & & \boldsymbol{\omega}_e \end{bmatrix} \boldsymbol{p}_n \tag{6}$$

where $\boldsymbol{\omega}_x$ can be represented as

$$\boldsymbol{\omega}_x = \begin{bmatrix} \hat{\boldsymbol{r}}_x \\ \mathbf{I}_3 \end{bmatrix} \in \mathbb{R}^{6 \times 3} \tag{7}$$

Combing the Eqs. 3 and 6, the force balance of flexible links is given by the following equation:

$$\Delta \boldsymbol{F} = \mathbf{H}\boldsymbol{F} = \boldsymbol{0} \tag{8}$$

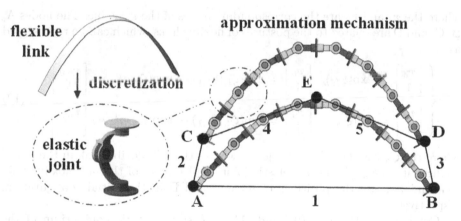

Fig. 2. Approximation mechanism of the flexible link tensegrity robot

2) The balance of load-induced reaction torques/forces in the approximation elastic joints of flexible links: As shown in Fig. 2, a slender flexible link can be converted into a hyper-redundant mechanism with rigid bodies and elastic passive joints, based on our prior works [21,22]. Therefore, the large deformation analysis of a flexible link can be achieved through the kinetostaic analysis of the approximation mechanism. The equilibrium conditions of each approximation mechanism can be represented as

$$\boldsymbol{\tau}_m = \mathbf{K}_m \boldsymbol{\theta}_m - \sum_{j=1}^{N_m} \mathbf{J}_j^T \boldsymbol{F}_j = \boldsymbol{0} \qquad m = 1, 2 \tag{9}$$

where $\mathbf{K}_m$ and $\boldsymbol{\theta}_m$ are the diagonal stiffness matrix and the displacement vector of elastic joints in the mth flexible link, respectively. $\boldsymbol{F}_j$ and $\mathbf{J}_j$ are the wrench and the Jacobian matrix corresponding to the node j, respectively. N_m is the number of nodes on the mth flexible link. Noting that $\mathbf{J}_j$ is dependent on the relative position of the node on the flexible link, which are given by

$$\mathbf{J}_j = \left[\boldsymbol{\xi}_{m,1}, \boldsymbol{\xi}_{m,2}, \cdots, \boldsymbol{\xi}_{m,M}, \boldsymbol{0}, \cdots, \boldsymbol{0} \right]_{6 \times N} \tag{10}$$

Here, $\boldsymbol{\xi}_{m,x}$ is the twist of the xth elastic joint of the mth flexible link in the deformation configuration. M is defined as the number of the elastic joint that is closest to the node j from the base.

3) Cable lengths constraints: To satisfy the inextensibility assumption of the cable, it is necessary to fulfill the cable length constraint. The elastic joints of the flexible links determine the positions of the nodes, making the cable lengths dependent on both the displacement of elastic joints, namely $\boldsymbol{\theta} = [\boldsymbol{\theta}_1^\mathrm{T}, \boldsymbol{\theta}_2^\mathrm{T}]^\mathrm{T}$, and the postures of flexible links, namely $\boldsymbol{\xi}_f = [\boldsymbol{\xi}_{f_1}^\mathrm{T}, \boldsymbol{\xi}_{f_2}^\mathrm{T}]^\mathrm{T}$. These quantities significantly affect the twists of the elastic joints. The geometrical constraints can be represented as

$$\Delta l_i = |\boldsymbol{r}_j - \boldsymbol{r}_k| - l_i = 0 \quad i = 1, \cdots, s \tag{11}$$

where the $\boldsymbol{r}_j$ and $\boldsymbol{r}_k$ are the corresponding nodes of the ith cable. The nodes A, B, C, and D are related to the postures of flexible links, which can be represented as

$$\begin{cases} \begin{bmatrix} \boldsymbol{r}_a \\ 1 \end{bmatrix}] = \exp(\boldsymbol{\xi}_{f_1}), & \begin{bmatrix} \boldsymbol{r}_b \\ 1 \end{bmatrix} = \exp(\boldsymbol{\zeta}_{1,1}\theta_{1,1}) \cdots \exp(\boldsymbol{\zeta}_{1,N}\theta_{1,N}) \begin{bmatrix} \boldsymbol{r}_{b,0} \\ 1 \end{bmatrix} \\[2ex] \begin{bmatrix} \boldsymbol{r}_c \\ 1 \end{bmatrix} = \exp(\boldsymbol{\xi}_{f_2}), & \begin{bmatrix} \boldsymbol{r}_d \\ 1 \end{bmatrix} = \exp(\boldsymbol{\zeta}_{2,1}\theta_{2,1}) \cdots \exp(\boldsymbol{\zeta}_{2,N}\theta_{2,N}) \begin{bmatrix} \boldsymbol{r}_{d,0} \\ 1 \end{bmatrix} \end{cases} \tag{12}$$

where the $\boldsymbol{\zeta}_{m,x}$ is the xth elastic joint twist of the mth flexible link in the initial configuration. $\theta_{m,x}$ is the xth elastic joint displacement of the mth flexible link. $\boldsymbol{r}_{b,0}$ and $\boldsymbol{r}_{d,0}$ are the positions of node B and D in the initial configuration, respectively.

Combine the Eqs. (8), (9), and (11), the system static equilibrium of the flexible link tensegrity robots can be represented in a general form of nonlinear algebraic equations as

$$\boldsymbol{f}(\boldsymbol{q}, \boldsymbol{\xi}_f, \boldsymbol{\theta}) = \begin{bmatrix} \Delta \boldsymbol{F} \\ \boldsymbol{\tau} \\ \Delta \boldsymbol{l} \end{bmatrix} = \boldsymbol{0} \tag{13}$$

where the $\boldsymbol{\tau} = [\boldsymbol{\tau}_1^\mathrm{T}, \cdots, \boldsymbol{\tau}_r^\mathrm{T}]^\mathrm{T}$ and $\Delta \boldsymbol{l} = [\Delta l_1, \cdots, \Delta l_s]^\mathrm{T}$ are the system vector of constraints. By solving these equations, the coordinates of all nodes and shapes of flexible links can be determined. This implies that the geometrical configuration of the flexible links tensegrity robot is obtained, and the form-finding problem is solved. The Newton-Raphson algorithm is employed to solve this form-finding problem. Details about this algorithm are described in the following inverse problem.

3   Inverse Kinematics Problem

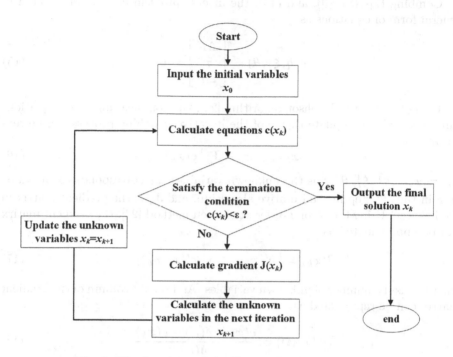

Fig. 3. The flowchart of the Newton-Raphson algorithm

In practical applications, the inverse kinematics problem plays a crucial role in controlling the motion of flexible link tensegrity robots. This problem involves determining the actuators' inputs based on the given robot configuration. In this planar flexible link tensegrity robot, nodes A and B act as the reference nodes, and the robot configuration is established by the coordinates of nodes C and D relative to the reference nodes A and B. In such a case, cables 2, 3, 4, and 5 serve as actuators by controlling the corresponding cable lengths, whereas cable 1 has a fixed length corresponding to the distance between nodes A and B.

For the inverse kinematics, the positions of nodes A, B, C, and D are known. By applying the constraint in Eq. 11, the cable lengths can be directly derived as the actuation inputs. However, since the shapes and relative postures of the flexible links are unknown, a further solution is required.

Based on Eq. (12), the nodes' geometrical constraints are represented as

$$\Delta r = r - r_t = \begin{bmatrix} r_a - r_{a,t} \\ r_b - r_{b,t} \\ r_c - r_{c,t} \\ r_d - r_{d,t} \end{bmatrix} = 0 \tag{14}$$

where the $r_{a,t}$, $r_{b,t}$, $r_{c,t}$, and $r_{d,t}$ represent the desired position of nodes A, B, C, D, respectively, which are provided as inputs for the inverse problem.

Combing Eqs. (8), (9), and (14), the inverse problem can be represented in general form of equations as

$$c(q, \xi_f, \theta) = \begin{bmatrix} \Delta F \\ \tau \\ \Delta r \end{bmatrix} = 0 \tag{15}$$

Using the Newton-Raphson algorithm [23], the nonlinear algebraic equations can be solved. The update theme of the iterative searching process can be represented as

$$x_{k+1} = x_k - J_k^{-1} c(x_k) \tag{16}$$

where $x = [q^T, \xi_f^T, \theta^T]^T$ is the unknown variables. x_k corresponds to the value of x in the kth step in the iterative algorithm, and J_k is the gradient matrix in the kth step. Using the second order Steffensen method [24], the gradient matirx can be approximated as

$$J(x_k) = \begin{bmatrix} c'(x_k(1)) & \cdots & c'(x_k(n_u)) \end{bmatrix} \tag{17}$$

where n_u is the number of unknown variables. And the ith column of the gradient matrix can be represented as

$$c'(x_k(i)) = \frac{c(x_k + \delta(i)) - c(x_k)}{\delta(i)} \tag{18}$$

$\delta(i)$ is the ith row of the equations $c(x_k)$. x_k can be seen as the solution when $c(x_k)$ is less than the predetermined tolerance, namely ϵ. The process for solving the problem is illustrated in Fig. 3.

4   Experimental Validation

4.1   Prototype and Experimental Setup

As depicted in Fig. 4, the prototype was developed using easy-to-implement techniques, consisting of two flexible links and five cables. The flexible links were constructed using ordinary spring steel strips, each having an identical cross-sectional area of 10 mm × 0.4 mm, to provide the necessary large deflection. The elastic and shearing modulus of the spring steel stripes were set to E = 196.5 GPa and G = 80.5 GPa, respectively. 0.5 mm PTFE-coated fiberglass threads were utilized as cables due to their minimal tensile deformation, which could be neglected. The connecting parts, installed on the endpoints and midpoints of the flexible links, were all 3D printed resin components. Micro servo motors were placed at the flexible link endpoints and connected to the cables via pulley wheels. The cable lengths were adjusted by spooling the cables in and out (Fig. 4). All micro servo motors were synchronously controlled by an Arduino

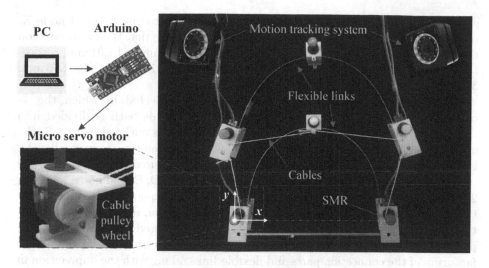

Fig. 4. Experiment setup for the flexible link tensegrity robot

Nano controller, while a personal computer served as the top-level controller and communicated with the Arduino. In addition, the motion tracking system, 'OptiTrack', was employed to capture the robot's real-time configuration via six spherically mounted reflectors (SMRs) affixed to the endpoints and midpoints of the flexible links.

4.2 Positioning Accuracy

To validate the correctness of the proposed method, the positioning accuracy of the developed prototype is evaluated in this section from two perspectives: 1) form-finding problem; and 2) inverse problem.

In the form-finding problem, each active cable length is set to two distinct values: 160 mm and 220 mm for cable 1, 80 mm and 130 mm for cable 2 and 3, and 100 mm and 150 mm for cable 4 and 5. This gives a total of 32 configurations, which are measured to assess the accuracy. For each input group, the corresponding robot configuration can be determined using the approach mentioned in Sect. 2, which is referred to as the nominal configuration. It should noted that the position of nodes A and B were used to construct the base frame, and thus the position error of other nodes was used to evaluate the precision. Specifically, the position errors are calculated as the distance between the nodes in their nominal position and the measured one, which can be represented as

$$\begin{cases} e_c = |\boldsymbol{r}_{c_n} - \boldsymbol{r}_{c_{me}}| \\ e_d = |\boldsymbol{r}_{d_n} - \boldsymbol{r}_{d_{me}}| \\ e_e = |\boldsymbol{r}_{e_n} - \boldsymbol{r}_{e_{me}}| \\ e_f = |\boldsymbol{r}_{f_n} - \boldsymbol{r}_{f_{me}}| \end{cases} \tag{19}$$

where r_{x_n} and $r_{x_{me}}$ represent the nominal and measured positions of node X, respectively. As shown in Fig. 5, the results demonstrate that the mean position error of nodes C, D, E, and F is 1.97 mm,1.60 mm,0.90 mm,and 1.91 mm, respectively. Additionally, the corresponding maximum position errors are 4.66 mm, 3.81 mm, 1.90 mm, and 4.04 mm, respectively.

In the inverse problem, a horizontal path is selected in which the y-coordinates of the nodes C and D are kept fixed. This path is divided into nine points with equal spacing. Utilizing the techniques outlined in Sect. 3, the active cable lengths are derived. Subsequently, the prototype is controlled by inputting these lengths, and the configuration is measured at each point. The results reveal that the mean position errors of nodes C, D, E, and F are 1.84 mm, 2.58 mm, 1.55 mm, and 3.08 mm, respectively. The corresponding maximum position errors are 3.83 mm, 3.22 mm, 2.37 mm, and 3.36 mm, respectively. As mentioned above, several unaccounted factors have contributed to the relatively low positioning accuracy attained. These factors comprise errors during the manufacturing of the connection parts and flexible links, along with the imprecision in motor motion. Therefore, it is believed that further improvements in positioning accuracy can be achieved by utilizing high-precision manufacturing techniques and servo motors in future work.

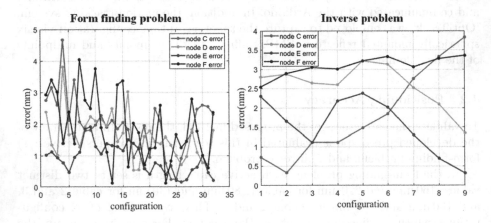

Fig. 5. Positioning accuracy for the planar flexible link tensegrity robot

5   Conclusion

This paper presents a general approach for the kinematic and static analysis of flexible link tensegrity robots. By means of connectivity and coefficient matrices, the connection between cables and flexible links is defined. By utilizing the discretization-based method, a simplified model for the form-finding and inverse problems is obtained, thereby allowing for the utilization of the Newton-Raphson algorithm to determine the equilibrium configuration of the flexible link tensegrity robots. To validate the effectiveness of the proposed method, a planar flexible link tensegrity robot was fabricated as a prototype and experiments on positioning accuracy were conducted. The results demonstrate that the proposed method can accurately predict the configuration of flexible link tensegrity robots. In future work, topics on the stiffness and stability analysis will be further investigated.

Acknowledgement. This research work was supported in part by the National Key R&D program of China under the Grant 2019YFA0709001, and the National Natural Science Foundation of China under the Grant 52022056 and 51875334.

References

1. Liu, Y., Bi, Q., Yue, X., Jiang, W., Yang, B., Li, Y.: A review on tensegrity structures-based robots. Mech. Mach. Theory **168**, 104571 (2022)
2. Shah, D.S., et al.: Tensegrity robotics. Soft Robot. **9**(4), 639–656 (2022)
3. Caluwaerts, K., Bruce, J., Friesen, J.M., SunSpiral, V.: State estimation for tensegrity robots. In: 2016 IEEE International Conference on Robotics and Automation (ICRA), pp. 1860–1865. IEEE (2016)
4. Campanaro, L.: Sensor integration and controller design for a tensegrity-modular robot, Ph. D. thesis, Politecnico di Torino (2018)
5. Pugh, A.: An Introduction to Tensegrity. University of California Press (1976)
6. Fraldi, M., Palumbo, S., Carotenuto, A.R., Cutolo, A., Deseri, L., Pugno, N.: Buckling soft tensegrities: fickle elasticity and configurational switching in living cells. J. Mech. Phys. Solids **124**, 299–324 (2019)
7. Dai, X., Liu, Y., Wang, W., Song, R., Li, Y., Zhao, J.: Design and experimental validation of a worm-like tensegrity robot for in-pipe locomotion. J. Bionic Eng. **20**, 1–15 (2022)
8. Hawkes, E.W., et al.: Engineered jumpers overcome biological limits via work multiplication. Nature **604**(7907), 657–661 (2022)
9. Tibert, A.G., Pellegrino, S.: Review of form-finding methods for tensegrity structures. Int. J. Space Struct. **18**(4), 209–223 (2003)
10. Connelly, R., Terrell, M.: Globally rigid symmetric tensegrities. Structural Topology 1995 núm 21 (1995)
11. Pellegrino, S.: Mechanics of kinematically indeterminate structures, Ph. D. thesis, University of Cambridge (1986)
12. Motro, R.: Forms and forces in tensegrity systems. In: Proceedings of Third International Conference on Space Structures, 1984. Elsevier (1984)
13. Linkwitz, K., Schek, H.J.: Einige bemerkungen zur berechnung von vorgespannten seilnetzkonstruktionen. Ingenieur-archiv **40**, 145–158 (1971)
14. Friesen, J., Pogue, A., Bewley, T., de Oliveira, M., Skelton, R., Sunspiral, V.: DuCTT: a tensegrity robot for exploring duct systems. In: 2014 IEEE International Conference on Robotics and Automation (ICRA), pp. 4222–4228. IEEE (2014)
15. Sabelhaus, A.P., et al.: Inverse statics optimization for compound tensegrity robots. IEEE Robot. Autom. Lett. **5**(3), 3982–3989 (2020)
16. Dong, W., Stafford, P.J., Ruiz-Teran, A.M.: Inverse form-finding for tensegrity structures. Comput. Struct. **215**, 27–42 (2019)
17. Lee, S., Lieu, Q.X., Vo, T.P., Lee, J.: Deep neural networks for form-finding of tensegrity structures. Mathematics **10**(11), 1822 (2022)

110   Y. Kang et al.

18. Connelly, R.: Handbook of Convex Geometry (1993)
19. Arsenault, M., Gosselin, C.M.: Kinematic, static and dynamic analysis of a planar 2-DOF tensegrity mechanism. Mech. Mach. Theory 41(9), 1072–1089 (2006)
20. Arsenault, M., Gosselin, C.M.: Kinematic and static analysis of a three-degree-of-freedom spatial modular tensegrity mechanism. Int. J. Robot. Res. 27(8), 951–966 (2008)
21. Chen, G., Zhang, Z., Wang, H.: A general approach to the large deflection problems of spatial flexible rods using principal axes decomposition of compliance matrices. J. Mech. Robot. 10(3), 031012 (2018)
22. Chen, G., Kang, Y., Liang, Z., Zhang, Z., Wang, H.: Kinetostatics modeling and analysis of parallel continuum manipulators. Mech. Mach. Theory 163, 104380 (2021)
23. Lindstrom, M.J., Bates, D.M.: Newton-Raphson and EM algorithms for linear mixed-effects models for repeated-measures data. J. Am. Stat. Assoc. 83(404), 1014–1022 (1988)
24. Lee, W., Johnson, Riess, R.D.: Numerical Analysis. Addison-Wesley, Reading, MA (1977)

An Autoencoder-Based Feature Extraction Method Applied to the Detection of Lateral Walking Gait Phase

Lijun Yang[1,2] , Kui Xiang[1] , Muye Pang[1] , Mingxiang Luo[2] , Meng Yin[2] , Wenju Li[2] , and Wujing Cao[2(✉)]

[1] School of Automation, Wuhan University of Technology, Wuhan 430070, China
[2] Guangdong Provincial Key Lab of Robotics and Intelligent System, Shenzhen Institute of Advanced Technology, Chinese Academy of Sciences, Shenzhen 518005, China
wj.cao@siat.ac.cn

Abstract. The traditional method of extracting time-domain features is subjective and cumbersome. An autoencoder-based feature extraction method is proposed to overcome these shortcomings. Experiments were conducted to detect gait phases of lateral walking of 10 subjects at various gait cycles (rhythms) and strides, which combined into 9 lateral walking modes. Based on the stacked autoencoder with dropout (AE-dropout), different quantities of features from the original data were extracted. Subsequently, these features were used to detect the phase of lateral walking gait based on decision tree (Tree), k-Nearest Neighbors (KNN), support sector machines (SVM), and artificial neural network (ANN). The results demonstrated that the KNN, SVM, and ANN achieve higher accuracy after using the features extracted by our method for the detection of lateral walking gait phase. Moreover, with the increase of the number of extracted features, the cross-subject accuracy of the four models (AE-dropout + X, X represents Tree, KNN, SVM, and ANN) exhibit similar regularities, which increased first and then decreased. In addition, compared to the method of extracting time-domain features, our method has a smaller standard error of mean (SEM) in cross-subject recognition accuracy for different lateral walking modes. It proves that our method has greater generalization capabilities.

Keywords: Autoencoder · feature extraction · dropout · gait phase · lateral walking · hip exoskeleton

1 Introduction

Hip exoskeleton has been developed for lateral walking, and it is hopeful to overcome the disadvantages of uncontrollable load of traditional elastic band training, as show in Fig. 1 (a) and (b). In order to achieve this goal, it is important to recognize the phase of lateral walking gait. In previous studies [1], the lateral walking gait was segmented into four phases. They are: the narrow double support (NDS, phase 1), the swing of the leading leg (SLL, phase 2), the wide double support (WDS, phase 3), and the swing of trailing leg (STL, phase 4), as show in Fig. 1.

© The Author(s), under exclusive license to Springer Nature Singapore Pte Ltd. 2023
H. Yang et al. (Eds.): ICIRA 2023, LNAI 14273, pp. 111–120, 2023.
https://doi.org/10.1007/978-981-99-6498-7_10

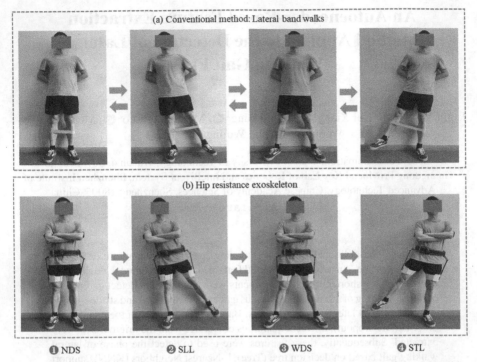

Fig. 1. Lateral walking with hip resistance exoskeleton to replace elastic band, and Lateral walking gait segmentation. (a) Lateral walking with elastic resistance band. (b) Lateral walking with hip resistance exoskeleton.

The traditional method of extracting time-domain features is subjective and cumbersome [2]. To solve this problem, K. Jun et al. proposed an automatic feature extraction method using a recurrent neural network (RNN)-based Autoencoder (AE) [3]. I. Cheheb et al. adopted sparse autoencoders to extract features for recognition under different view angles [4]. Z. Zhang et al. proposed a novel AutoEncoder framework, GaitNet, to explicitly disentangle appearance, canonical and pose features from RGB imagery [5]. A. Elkholy et al. used convolutional autoencoder to learn representative features from the Gait Energy Image (GEI) [6]. J. Kim et al. proposed a feature extraction model based on the Multi-head Convolutional Autoencoder (MCAE) [7]. Q. Wang et al. proposed a sequence-parameter attention based convolutional autoencoder (SPA-CAE) model for feature extraction of Quick Access Recorder (QAR) data [8]. Moreover, the method of extracting features based on autoencoder can also reduce the number and dimension of features [9]. S. Jeon et al. applied a variational autoencoder to map the orientations of the human body segments during a gait cycle to a low-dimensional latent gait vector [10].

Dropout is one of the common methods to prevent overfitting and improve the generalization ability of models [11]. It is often applied in autoencoder to improve the stability and generalization ability of models. K.Chen et al. proposed a stacked autoencoder (SAE) and introduced the dropout trick to prevent over-fitting and accelerate model convergence

[12]. B. Wang et al. set different dropout rates in each layer of Sparse Auto-Encoder to increase the stability and convergence speed of training process [13]. K. Miok et al. presented an approach based on Monte Carlo dropout within (Variational) Autoencoders to improve the imputation error and predictive similarity [14].

In addition, in order to make this hip exoskeleton more adaptable, the recognition results under different walking speed patterns are also worth studying carefully. In the studies of L. Yan [15] and T. Zhen et al. [16], the gait phase detection effect of the improved NN method was explored in different speed modes. H. Sarah et al. collected biomechanical data of amputed-patients walking at 18 speeds [17].

The main contributions of this study are as follows:

(1) Based on the application of lateral walking gait phase recognition, we propose a feature extraction method based on an autoencoder to overcome the shortcomings of traditional feature extraction methods.
(2) After using the features extracted by our method, k-Nearest Neighbors (KNN), support sector machines (SVM), and artificial neural network (ANN) achieve higher accuracy for the detection of lateral walking gait phase.
(3) Compared to the method of extracting time-domain features, our method has a smaller standard error of mean (SEM) in cross-subject recognition accuracy for different lateral walking modes.

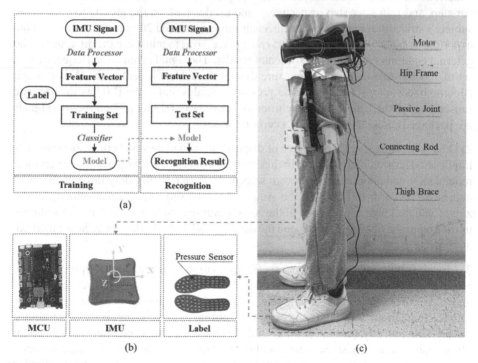

Fig. 2. Experimental equipment and process. (a) Training and testing of recognition model. (b) Data acquisition equipment and control unit. (c) Wearing of hip exoskeleton.

2 Method

2.1 Experimental Equipment and Process

A Self-designed hip exoskeleton was applied for resistance lateral walking in this study, as shown in Fig. 2 (c). It is an exoskeleton of adjustable size that enables active hip abduction and adduction without affecting the wearer's normal walking. Two IMUs (LPMS-B2, Alubi, China) were installed on the front side of the exoskeleton thigh bracket, as shown in Fig. 2 (b). The plantar pressure sensors (RX-ES-48P, RouXi Technology, China) were used as a label for the classification of gait events. The control circuit of hip exoskeleton is a Micro Controller Unit (MCU), which based on 168 MHz Cortex-M4 processor, as shown in Fig. 2 (b).

This experiment was conducted in three phases:

1) Data acquisition phase. Ten adults were recruited as subjects, and they were asked to walk in a straight lateral direction in nine different modes. These patterns consisted of three different stride lengths (40 cm, 50 cm, 60 cm), each containing three different speed patterns (three times formed by the metronome). Two groups were tested for each speed pattern, and each group walked 30 steps laterally. After each experiment, the experimenter needs to return to the origin to prepare for the next experiment. Since the whole experiment was carried out on flat ground, in order to control the speed, we used a metronome to control the subject's step frequency, which was 1.87 s per step, 1.67 s per step, and 1.46 s per step respectively, and used a mark on the ground to control the subject's stride. Before the experiment, each subject received 20 min of training, and the experimental data were collected at the same place, so as to minimize the influence of the external environment on the experimental results. The signal acquisition frequency was set to 200 Hz. Among them, the posture data of the subject is sent to the IMU through Bluetooth technology, and the plantar pressure signal is sent to the IMU by the pressure sensor through the Universal Asynchronous Transceiver (UART). Then the two signals are packaged and sent to the PC in a certain format.

2) Data processing stage. The degree of dispersion, redundancy and correlation are very important data screening indexes. In this study, channel signals with excessive variance, redundancy, and poor correlation were screened out, and finally only three channels of data were retained: roll (that is, the Angle of the z-axis), the angular velocity of the z-axis, and the linear acceleration of the X-axis. Subsequently, the baseline of the data is unified using the filtering method, and the data is standardized using the Z-Score method, as show as in Fig. 3 (a).

3) Model training and recognition stage. Figure 2 (a) shows the generation process of the recognition system. Data from 10 subjects were divided into training set (seven subjects) and testing set (three subjects). This selected data form a training set in the form of vectors (including the data of the subject in nine motion modes), which is used to train the model. Subsequently, the mature model will be converted into a classifier specialized for classification work. These classifiers will be implanted into the corresponding recognition system for recognition experiments. In addition, the data of the test set were divided into 9 test groups according to different lateral walking patterns. These test groups are tested separately using trained models.

2.2 Algorithms

TREE, KNN, SVM, and ANN are widely applied to gait phase recognition. A. Thongsook et al. compared multiple algorithms and demonstrated the excellent performance of C4.5 decision tree [18]. J. Ryu et al. demonstrated that KNN's method is not inferior to the other two methods compared KNN, LDA and QDA in gait phase detection [19]. M. Zago et al. applied the decision tree method to detect gait events with high accuracy used KNN, SVM, and RF methods to recognize gait, and proved the superior performance of RF [20]. L. Shi, et al. compared algorithms such as RF, KNN, SVM, and found that the model constructed by RF can meet the requirements [21]. J. Chen et al. on the human body movement pattern identification based on the SVM algorithm [22]. T. -S. Chen et al. performed gait phase segmentation based on the KNN algorithm [23]. F. Weigand et al. applied ANN to detect and estimate gait phase [24]. The application of these algorithms in the straight gait has obtained good results, which provides a reference for our research on lateral walking gait.

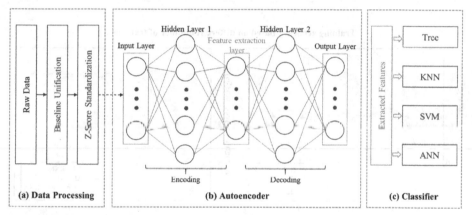

Fig. 3. The structure of the proposed algorithm mode. (a) Data processing process. (b) The specific composition of the autoencoder. (c) Four classification algorithm models.

The structure of the proposed algorithm model is shown in Fig. 3. It mainly consists of a stacked autoencoder (SAE) and four classification algorithms (Tree, KNN, SVM, ANN). The SAE consists of three hidden layers, and each hidden layer is followed by a dropout layer. The output of the hidden layer in the middle is considered the extracted feature, as shown in Fig. 3 (b). The features extracted by SAE are output to a classifier to train four classification models, as shown in Fig. 3 (c). The specific parameter settings of these algorithm models are shown in Table 1. In this article, these parameters are appropriate and not optimal. The environment for the training process of these algorithms is MATLAB 2022.

Table 1. The setting of specific parameters of the algorithms.

Algorithm	Model hyperparameters	Algorithm	Model hyperparameters
AE	Model: Stacked Autoencoder Hidden layer 1 size: 64 Hidden layer 2 size: 64 Activation: Relu	AE-dropout	Model: Stacked Autoencoder Hidden layer 1 size: 128 Hidden layer 2 size: 128 Activation: Relu Dropout: 0.2
Tree	Model: Fine Tree Maximum number of splits: 100 Split criterion: Gini's diversity index	KNN	Model: Fine KNN Number of neighbors: 1 Distance metric: Euclidean Distance weight: Equal
SVM	Model: Fine Gaussian SVM Kernel function: Gaussian Kernel scale: 0.61 Box constraint level: 1	ANN	Model: Neural Network First hidden layer size: 100 Second hidden layer size: 100 Activation: Relu

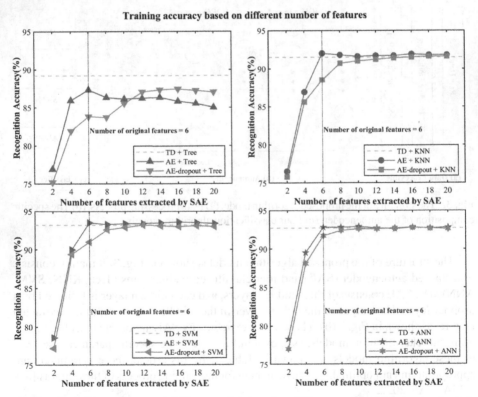

Fig. 4. The training accuracy of different models based on different number of features extracted by SAE.

3 Results

In order to compare the ability of autoencoders to extract features more comprehensively, we set up an experimental group and two control groups. The experimental group used a combined model (AE-dropout + X, X represents four classification algorithms: Tree, KNN, SVM, and ANN) of autoencoder with dropout plus classification algorithm, as shown in Fig. 3. The control group adopted the combined model (TD + X) of time-domain feature (maximum, minimum, mean, standard deviation, root mean square) plus classification algorithm and the combined model (AE + X) of autoencoder plus classification algorithm, respectively. Figure 4 shows that the training accuracy of different models based on different number of features extracted by SAE. From the Fig. 4, it can be seen that as the number of extracted features gradually increases, the training accuracy of AE-dropout + X (X represents four classification algorithms) gradually increases. Moreover, the accuracy of AE-dropout + X is greater than that of AE + X. When the number of extracted features is greater than 12, the accuracy of AE-dropout + X gradually stabilizes (equal to the accuracy of TD + X, except for Tree).

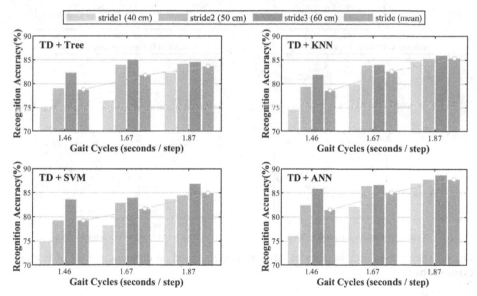

Fig. 5. The cross-subject recognition accuracy of four algorithm models (TD + Tree, TD + KNN, TD + SVM, TD + ANN) in 9 different lateral walking patterns. The horizontal axis represents different gait cycles (the time taken for each step taken).

The three gait cycles in this experiment were formed by the metronome control, and they together with the three stride lengths constituted 9 lateral walking patterns. The first graph of Fig. 5 is the cross-subject recognition accuracy of the TD + Tree, TD + KNN, TD + SVM, and TD + ANN in 9 lateral walking patterns. The horizontal axis represents different gait cycles (the time taken for each step taken). Three gait cycles are 1.46 s/step, 1.67 s/step, and 1.87 s/step. And "stride1 (40 cm)", "stride2 (50 cm)", "stride3 (60 cm)" stands for three stride lengths (40 cm, 50 cm, 60 cm). The "stride (mean)" represents the average recognition accuracy under three different stride sizes. Two laws can be clearly seen from the Fig. 5. One is that when the stride length is the same, the recognition accuracy of the four models gradually increases as the gait cycle increases. The second is that when the gait period is the same, the recognition accuracy of the four models gradually increases as the stride length increases.

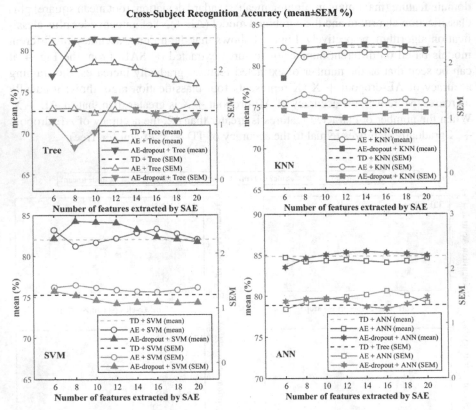

Fig. 6. The cross-subject accuracy of different models based on different number of features extracted by SAE.

Figure 6 shows that the cross-subject accuracy of different models based on different number of features extracted by SAE. As can be seen from the Fig. 6, with the number of features increases, the accuracy of AE-dropout + X increases first and then decreases. When the number of features is between 8 and 14, the AE-dropout + X has greater cross-subject accuracy than TD + X and AE + X. In addition, compared to TD + X and AE + X, AE-dropout + X has a smaller standard error of mean (SEM) in cross-subject recognition accuracy for different lateral walking modes.

4   Conclusion

We propose a feature extraction method based on an autoencoder to overcome the short-comings of traditional feature extraction methods based on the application of lateral walking gait phase recognition. The AE-dropout + KNN, AE-dropout + SVM, and AE-dropout + ANN achieve higher accuracy for the detection of lateral walking gait phase. Compared to the method of extracting time-domain features, our method has a smaller standard error of mean (SEM) in cross-subject recognition accuracy for different lateral walking modes. In addition, the influence of different lateral walking patterns on recognition accuracy is also explored. We found that when the stride length was the same, the shorter the gait cycle, the higher the recognition accuracy. When the gait cycle is the same, the larger the stride, the higher the recognition accuracy.

References

1. Yang, L., Xiang, K., Pang, M., Yin, M., Wu, X., Cao, W.: Inertial sensing for lateral walk-ing gait detection and application in lateral resistance exoskeleton. IEEE Trans. Instrum. Measurement **72**, 1–14 (2023)
2. Sun, L., Zhong, Z., Qu, Z., et al.: PerAE: an effective personalized Autoencoder for ECG-based biometric in augmented reality system. IEEE J. Biomed. Health Inform. **26**(6), 2435–2446 (2022)
3. Jun, K., Lee, D.-W., Lee, K., Lee, S., Kim, M.S.: Feature extraction using an RNN autoencoder for skeleton-based abnormal gait recognition. IEEE Access **8**, 19196–19207 (2020)
4. Cheheb, I., Al-Maadeed, N., Al-Madeed, S., Bouridane, A.: Investigating the use of autoen-coders for gait-based person recognition. In: 2018 NASA/ESA Conference on Adaptive Hardware and Systems (AHS), pp. 148–151. IEEE, Edinburgh, UK (2018)
5. Zhang, Z., Tran, L., Liu, F., Liu, X.: On learning disentangled representations for gait recognition. IEEE Trans. Patt. Anal. Mach. Intell. **44**(1), 345–360 (2022)
6. Elkholy, A., Makihara, Y., Gomaa, W., Rahman Ahad, M.A., Yagi, Y.: Unsupervised GEI-based gait disorders detection from different views. In: 2019 41st Annual International Con-ference of the IEEE Engineering in Medicine and Biology Society (EMBC), pp. 5423–5426. IEEE, Berlin, Germany (2019)
7. Kim, J., Kim, M., Shin, H.: Latent feature separation and extraction with multiple parallel encoders for convolutional autoencoder. In: 2022 IEEE International Conference on Big Data and Smart Computing (BigComp), pp. 263–266. IEEE, Daegu, Korea, Republic of (2022)
8. Wang, Q., Qin, K., Lu, B., Huang, R.: Feature extraction of QAR data via sequence-parameter attention based convolutional autoencoder model. In: 2021 IEEE 3rd International Confer-ence on Civil Aviation Safety and Information Technology (ICCASIT), pp. 352–355. IEEE, Changsha, China (2021)
9. Boe, D., Portnova-Fahreeva, A.A., Sharma, A., Rai, V., Sie, A., Preechayasomboon, P., Rom-bokas, E.: Dimensionality reduction of human gait for prosthetic control. Front. Bioeng. Biotechnol. **9**, n. pag (2021)
10. Jeon, S., Lee, K.M., Koo, S.: anomalous gait feature classification from 3-D motion capture data. IEEE J. Biomed. Health Inform. **26**(2), 696–703 (2022)
11. Zhao, J., Yang, J., Wang, J., Wu, W.: Spiking neural network regularization with fixed and adaptive drop-keep probabilities. IEEE Trans. Neural Netw. Learn. Syst. **33**(8), 4096–4109 (2022)

12. Chen, K., Mao, Z., Zhao, H., Zhang, J.: Valve fault diagnosis of internal combustion engine based on an improved stacked autoencoder. In: 2019 International Conference on Sensing, Diagnostics, Prognostics, and Control (SDPC), pp. 295–300. IEEE, Beijing, China (2019)
13. Wang, B., Ma, B., Xu, K., Zheng, T.: Turn-to-turn short circuit of motor stator fault diagnosis using dropout rate improved deep sparse autoencoder. In: 2018 IEEE 3rd Advanced Information Technology, Electronic and Automation Control Conference (IAEAC), pp. 220–225. IEEE, Chongqing, China (2018)
14. Miok, K., Nguyen-Doan, D., Robnik-Šikonja, M., Zaharie, D.: Multiple imputation for biomedical data using monte carlo dropout autoencoders. In: 2019 E-Health and Bioengineering Conference (EHB), pp. 1–4. IEEE, Iasi, Romania (2019)
15. Yan, L., et al.: Walking gait phase detection based on acceleration signals using voting-weighted integrated neural network. Complex 14, 1–4760297 (2020)
16. Zhen, T., et al.: An acceleration based fusion of multiple spatiotemporal networks for gait phase detection. Int. J. Environ. Res. Public Health 17, n. pag (2020)
17. Sarah, H., et al.: A kinematic and kinetic dataset of 18 above-knee amputees walking at various speeds. Sci. Data 7, n. pag (2020)
18. Thongsook, A., Nunthawarasilp, T., Kraypet, P., Lim, J., Ruangpayoongsak, N.: C4.5 decision tree against neural network on gait phase recognition for lower limp exoskeleton. In: 2019 First International Symposium on Instrumentation, Control, Artificial Intelligence, and Robotics (ICA-SYMP), pp. 69–72. IEEE, Bangkok, Thailand (2019)
19. Ryu, J., Lee, B., Maeng, J., Kim, D.: sEMG-signal and IMU sensor-based gait sub-phase detection and prediction using a user-adaptive classifier. Med. Eng. Phys. 69, 50–57 (2019)
20. Zago, M., Tarabini, M., Spiga, M., Ferrario, C., Bertozzi, F., Sforza, C., Galli, M.: Machine-learning based determination of gait events from foot-mounted inertial units. Sensors 21(3), n. pag (2021)
21. Shi, L., Chao, Q., Xin, D., Liu, G.: Gait recognition via random forests based on wearable inertial measurement unit. J. Ambient Intell. Humanized Comput. 11, 5329–5340 (2020)
22. Chen, J., Zhu, J., Guo, M.: An SVM-based pedestrian gait recognition algorithm using a foot-mounted IMU. In: 2022 IEEE 5th International Conference on Electronics Technology (ICET), pp. 1085–1090. IEEE, Chengdu, China (2022)
23. Chen, T.-S., Lin, T.-Y., Hong, Y.-W.P.: Gait phase segmentation using weighted dynamic time warping and k-nearest neighbors graph embedding. In: ICASSP 2020 - 2020 IEEE International Conference on Acoustics, Speech and Signal Processing (ICASSP), pp. 1180–1184. IEEE, Barcelona, Spain (2020)
24. Weigand, F., Höhl, A., Zeiss, J., Konigorski, U., Grimmer, M.: Continuous locomotion mode recognition and gait phase estimation based on a shank-mounted IMU with artificial neural networks. In: 2022 IEEE/RSJ International Conference on Intelligent Robots and Systems (IROS), pp. 12744–12751. IEEE, Kyoto, Japan (2022)

Sparse Adaptive Channel Estimation Based on Multi-kernel Correntropy

Kun Zhang⬡, Gang Wang⬡, Mingzhu Wei⬡, Chen Xu⬡, and Bei Peng$^{(\boxtimes)}$⬡

University of Electronic Science and Technology of China, Chengdu 611731, China
beipeng@uestc.edu.cn

Abstract. The communication channel estimation between unmanned systems has always been a concern of researchers, especially the channel estimation of broadband wireless communication and underwater acoustic communication. Due to its sparsity, more and more researchers use adaptive filtering algorithms combined with sparse constraints for sparse channel estimation. In this paper, a sparse adaptive filtering algorithm based on correntropy induced metric (CIM) penalty is proposed, and the maximum multi-kernel correntropy criterion (MMKCC) is used to replace the minimum mean square error criterion and the maximum correntropy criteria for robust channel estimation. Specifically, the MMKCC is used to suppress complex impulse noise, and the CIM is used to effectively utilize channel sparsity. The effectiveness of the proposed method is confirmed by computer simulation.

Keywords: Sparse channel estimation · Non-Gaussian noise · Multi-kernel correntropy

1 Introduction

In the past few years, with the breakthrough of AI technology, unmanned systems have shown a trend of clustering, such as unmanned aerial vehicle clusters [1] and underwater unmanned vehicle clusters [2]. Unmanned clusters usually rely on wireless communication technology for a large number of information exchanges. The signal received by the receiving end will invariably be incorrect when the wireless signal is delivered on the real channel due to the unfavorable channel transmission characteristics and the effect of channel noise. The receiver must estimate the channel parameters and adjust the received data in order to recover information from the broadcast data. Therefore, precise channel estimation is a crucial technological difficulty for achieving dependable wireless communication and a crucial research topic for unmanned clustering technology.

This study was founded by the National Natural Science Foundation of China with Grant 51975107, 62076096, and Sichuan Science and Technology Major Project No. 2022ZDZX0039, No.2019ZDZX0020, and Sichuan Science and Technology Program No. 2022YFG0343, No. 23ZDYF0738.

H. Yang et al. (Eds.): ICIRA 2023, LNAI 14273, pp. 121–131, 2023.
https://doi.org/10.1007/978-981-99-6498-7_11

Traditional channel estimation methods are usually based on minimum mean square error (MMSE), maximum likelihood or maximum a posteriori methods. Adaptive filtering algorithms based on the MMSE include recursive least squares (RLS), least mean square (LMS), and normalized minimum mean square (NLMS) methods, which have the ability of online real-time estimation and tracking, so they are widely used in the field of channel estimation. In broadband wireless communication or underwater acoustic communication systems, wireless channels often exhibit sparse structures [3,4], and their important taps are few, and most channels have zero taps. However, traditional LMS and RLS do not take into account the sparse characteristics of the channel, which can lead to skewed results [5]. If the sparsity of a channel can be modeled and exploited, more accurate estimation performance will be obtained and the quality of channel estimation will be improved. Influenced by sparse theories such as the LASSO algorithm and compressed sensing, a sparse adaptive filtering algorithm that adds sparse penalty terms (l_0-norm or l_1-norm) to the cost function came into being. In [6], the zero-attracting LMS (ZA-LMS) algorithm is proposed by introducing the l_1-norm penalty term into the LMS algorithm and modifying the update equation of the parameter vector to be estimated by using the zero attractive term. Compared with the traditional LMS algorithm, it has been proven that the ZA-LMS algorithm can converge faster and reduce the steady-state misalignment mean square error under sparse channel conditions. In [7], the l_1-norm penalty term is further introduced into the RLS algorithm, and the zero-attracting RLS (ZA-RLS) algorithm is proposed.

The above studies are based on the Gaussian noise model. However, in practice, the ambient noise in the workspace of the unmanned system is generally complex, and many noises show significant non-Gaussian characteristics showed significant spike pulses. A large number of significant spike pulses in the time domain means frequent abnormal data and their variance characteristics are manifested as thick probability density function tails. In recent years, robust adaptive filtering in non-Gaussian noise settings has been successfully implemented using the maximum correntropy criterion (MCC) [8]. The MCC is a method to measure the correlation of any two random variables, which can effectively reduce the impact of outliers. Based on the MCC, an LMS-type robust sparse adaptive filtering algorithm combined with the correntropy induced metric (CIM) [9] has been proposed in [10], called CIMMCC. As an approximation form of l_0-norm, the CIM can solve the NP-hard problem caused by l_0-norm minimization. Subsequently, in [11], the maximum mixture correntropy is used to extend the above algorithm, and the CIM-MMCC algorithm is proposed. In [12], an RLS-type algorithm based on the MCC combined with sparse constraints is proposed, called CR-RMC. The constraint term of the algorithm can be set to the l_0-norm or l_1-norm.

In a recent paper [13], Chen et al. presented the theory of multi-kernel correntropy and the maximum multi-kernel correntropy criterion (MMKCC). The MMKCC is more versatile and flexible than the MCC, and it can accommodate more complicated error distributions, such as multi-peak, and skewed distributions. In this paper, the MMKCC is combined with the CIM penalty term, and a sparse adaptive filtering algorithm, called CIM-RMMKCC, is proposed to deal with the complicated channel noise that may appear in channel estimation. And, the performance of the LMS-type algorithm depends heavily on the setting of step size parameter. Compared with the LMS-type algorithm, the RLS-type algorithm including the proposed CIM-RMMKCC has faster convergence speed and more accurate parameter estimation results.

The remaining sections of the paper are organized as follows. The system model for adaptive channel estimation is introduced in the second section. The third section introduces the basic knowledge of CIM and MKC. In the fourth section, the derivation process of the CIM-RMMKCC algorithm is described, and the complete algorithm is summarized. To test the effectiveness of the proposed algorithm for sparse channel estimation under non-zero mean impulsive noise, a simulation experiment is conducted in the fifth part.

2 System Model

Adaptive filters have been widely used in communication fields such as channel estimation, channel equalization, echo cancellation, interference cancellation, and signal prediction because of their simplicity and robustness. In this research, we analyze the channel estimation performance of the adaptive filtering method, and its channel estimation model is shown in Fig. 1. In which, the input signal of the unknown channel is the same as the adaptive filter, and the output signal of the unknown channel is the desired signal. The cost function is constructed by the error between the filter output signal and the desired output signal, and after iteration, the weight vector of the filter is adjusted to continuously approximate the response of the unknown channel, so that the algorithm converges and the channel response value is obtained to achieve channel estimation.

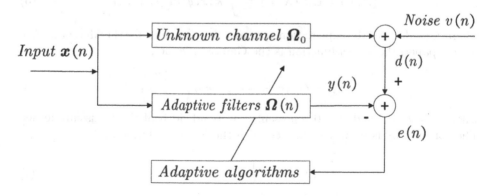

Fig. 1. Channel estimation model.

The system input signal vector is $x(n) = [x_n, x_{n-1}, ..., x_{n-N+1}]^T$. $\Omega_o = [\Omega_{o,1}, \Omega_{o,2}, ..., \Omega_{o,N}]^T$ is the parameter vector of the sparse channel, where N

is the size of the channel memory. $\boldsymbol{\Omega}(n) = [\Omega_n(1), \Omega_n(2), ..., \Omega_n(N)]^T$ is the estimate of the parameter vector at the n-th iteration. The output of the channel is

$$d(n) = \boldsymbol{\Omega}_o^T \boldsymbol{x}(n) + v(n), \tag{1}$$

where $v(n)$ denotes the additive noise. The output of the adaptive filters is

$$y(n) = \boldsymbol{\Omega}^T(n) \boldsymbol{x}(n). \tag{2}$$

The n-th error signal between the adaptive filter output and the channel output is defined as

$$e(n) = d(n) - \boldsymbol{\Omega}^T(n) \boldsymbol{x}(n). \tag{3}$$

It is required to minimize a cost function based on the error signal to get the best estimates of the parameter vectors. Typically, this cost function is expressed as

$$J = E\left(e^2(n)\right). \tag{4}$$

When the cost function J achieves the minimum value, the corresponding $\boldsymbol{\Omega}(n)$ is the optimal estimation vector.

3   CIM and MKC

3.1   Correntropy and CIM

The MKC and CIM are both definitions derived from correntropy, so a brief explanation of correntropy is first given before introducing the MKC and CIM. The correntropy is defined as follows for two random variables, $X = [x_1, x_2, ..., x_N]^T$ and $Y = [y_1, y_2, ..., y_N]^T$, whose joint distribution function is $F_{XY}(x, y)$.

$$V(X, Y) = E\left[k(X, Y)\right] = \int k(x, y) \, dF_{XY}(x, y), \tag{5}$$

where $E(\cdot)$ denotes the expectation operator, $k(\cdot, \cdot)$ stands for the Mercer kernel. In this paper, the kernel function is the Gaussian kernel:

$$k(x, y) = G_\sigma(e) = \frac{1}{\sigma\sqrt{2\pi}} \exp\left(-\frac{e^2}{2\sigma^2}\right), \tag{6}$$

where $e = x - y$, and $\sigma > 0$ represents the bandwidth of the Gaussian kernel. The correntropy is usually estimated with the following formula:

$$\hat{V}(X, Y) = \frac{1}{N} \sum_{i=1}^{N} k(x_i, y_i). \tag{7}$$

CIM is a nonlinear metric based on correntropy [9]. CIM performs better as an approximation to l_0-norm than l_1-norm and l_p-norm, which is defined by

$$CIM(X, Y) = \left(k(0) - \hat{V}(X, Y)\right)^{1/2}, \tag{8}$$

where $k\left(0\right) = 1/\sigma\sqrt{2\pi}$. The l_0-norm of $X = \left[x_1, x_2, ..., x_N\right]^T$ can be approximated by

$$\|X\|_0 \sim CIM^2\left(X, 0\right) = \frac{k\left(0\right)}{N} \sum_{i=1}^{N} \left(1 - \exp\left(-\frac{x_i^2}{2\sigma^2}\right)\right). \tag{9}$$

It has been demonstrated that if $|x_i| > \delta$, where δ is a small positive number, by making $\sigma \to 0$, the results can arbitrarily approach l_0-norm.

3.2   MKC

Correntropy has been effectively used in signal processing as a nonlinear similarity metric. When utilized as a cost function, the kernel function in correntropy often uses the zero-mean Gaussian kernel, which may significantly limit its performance. The multi-kernel correntropy (MKC) is proposed by employing a combination of many Gaussian kernels with varying bandwidths and centers [13] to further increase performance in complicated noise situations. The definition of the MKC is

$$V_{\lambda, c, \sigma}\left(X, Y\right) = E\left[\sum_{i=1}^{m} \lambda_i k_{\sigma_i}\left(X - Y - c_i\right)\right]$$
$$= \iint \left(\sum_{i=1}^{m} \lambda_i k_{\sigma_i}\left(x - y - c_i\right)\right) p_{XY}\left(x, y\right) dx dy, \tag{10}$$

where $c = \left[c_1, c_2, ..., c_m\right]^T$ is the center of the MKC. With the MKC, researchers proposed the maximum multi-kernel correntropy criterion (MMKCC) by maximizing the MKC.

4   CIM-RMMKCC Algorithm

In this section, the MMKCC is introduced into the cost function of adaptive filtering, and combined with the CIM penalty term, a recursive sparse adaptive filtering algorithm is proposed, which is called CIM-RMMKCC.

The cost function of the CIM-RMMKCC combining the CIM and the MMKCC is defined as

$$J\left(\boldsymbol{\Omega}\left(n\right)\right) = \lambda J_{CIM}\left(\boldsymbol{\Omega}\left(n\right)\right) - J_{MMKCC}\left(\boldsymbol{\Omega}\left(n\right)\right), \tag{11}$$

where λ represents the regular term coefficient, which regulates the degree of sparsity penalty.

In the proposed algorithm, the number of kernels of MKC is set to 2, so the cost function of the recursive MMKCC is defined as

$$J_{MMKCC}\left(\boldsymbol{\Omega}\left(n\right)\right) = \sum_{j=1}^{n} \gamma^{n-j}\left[\begin{array}{l}\alpha \exp\left(-\frac{\left(e\left(j\right)-c_1\right)^2}{2\sigma_1^2}\right) + \\ \left(1 - \alpha\right) \exp\left(-\frac{\left(e\left(j\right)-c_2\right)^2}{2\sigma_2^2}\right)\end{array}\right], \tag{12}$$

where α represents the mixing coefficient of MKC, and γ represents the forgetting factor of the recursive algorithm.

The CIM-based sparsity penalty cost function is defined as

$$J_{CIM}\left(\boldsymbol{\Omega}\left(n\right)\right) = \frac{k\left(0\right)}{N}\sum_{i=1}^{N}\left(1 - \exp\left(-\frac{\omega_i^2}{2\sigma_3^2}\right)\right). \tag{13}$$

The derivative of Eq. (12) with respect to $\boldsymbol{\Omega}\left(n\right)$ yields the following equation

$$\frac{\partial J_{MMKCC}\left(n\right)}{\partial \boldsymbol{\Omega}\left(n\right)} = \sum_{j=1}^{n}\gamma^{n-j}\left[\left(\begin{array}{c}\frac{\alpha}{\sigma_1^2}\exp\left(-\frac{\left(e(j)-c_1\right)^2}{2\sigma_1^2}\right)\\+\frac{1-\alpha}{\sigma_2^2}\exp\left(-\frac{\left(e(j)-c_2\right)^2}{2\sigma_2^2}\right)\end{array}\right)d\left(j\right)\boldsymbol{x}\left(j\right)\right]$$
$$-\sum_{j=1}^{n}\gamma^{n-j}\left[\left(\begin{array}{c}\frac{\alpha}{\sigma_1^2}\exp\left(-\frac{\left(e(j)-c_1\right)^2}{2\sigma_1^2}\right)\\+\frac{1-\alpha}{\sigma_2^2}\exp\left(-\frac{\left(e(j)-c_2\right)^2}{2\sigma_2^2}\right)\end{array}\right)\boldsymbol{x}\left(j\right)\boldsymbol{x}^T\left(j\right)\boldsymbol{\Omega}\left(n\right)\right]$$
$$-\sum_{j=1}^{n}\gamma^{n-j}\left[\left(\begin{array}{c}\frac{\alpha c_1}{\sigma_1^2}\exp\left(-\frac{\left(e(j)-c_1\right)^2}{2\sigma_1^2}\right)\\+\frac{(1-\alpha)c_2}{\sigma_2^2}\exp\left(-\frac{\left(e(j)-c_2\right)^2}{2\sigma_2^2}\right)\end{array}\right)\boldsymbol{x}\left(j\right)\right]. \tag{14}$$

Equation (14) can be simplified and expressed as

$$\frac{\partial J_{MMKCC}\left(\boldsymbol{\Omega}\left(n\right)\right)}{\partial \boldsymbol{\Omega}\left(n\right)} = \boldsymbol{\Phi}\left(n\right) - \boldsymbol{\Psi}\left(n\right)\boldsymbol{\Omega}\left(n\right) - \boldsymbol{\Theta}\left(n\right), \tag{15}$$

where

$$\boldsymbol{\Phi}\left(n\right) = \sum_{j=1}^{n}\gamma^{n-j}\left[\left(\begin{array}{c}\frac{\alpha}{\sigma_1^2}\exp\left(-\frac{\left(e(j)-c_1\right)^2}{2\sigma_1^2}\right)\\+\frac{1-\alpha}{\sigma_2^2}\exp\left(-\frac{\left(e(j)-c_2\right)^2}{2\sigma_2^2}\right)\end{array}\right)d\left(j\right)\boldsymbol{x}\left(j\right)\right], \tag{16}$$

$$\boldsymbol{\Psi}\left(n\right) = \sum_{j=1}^{n}\gamma^{n-j}\left[\left(\begin{array}{c}\frac{\alpha}{\sigma_1^2}\exp\left(-\frac{\left(e(j)-c_1\right)^2}{2\sigma_1^2}\right)\\+\frac{1-\alpha}{\sigma_2^2}\exp\left(-\frac{\left(e(j)-c_2\right)^2}{2\sigma_2^2}\right)\end{array}\right)\boldsymbol{x}\left(j\right)\boldsymbol{x}^T\left(j\right)\right], \tag{17}$$

$$\boldsymbol{\Theta}\left(n\right) = \sum_{j=1}^{n}\gamma^{n-j}\left[\left(\begin{array}{c}\frac{\alpha c_1}{\sigma_1^2}\exp\left(-\frac{\left(e(j)-c_1\right)^2}{2\sigma_1^2}\right)\\+\frac{(1-\alpha)c_2}{\sigma_2^2}\exp\left(-\frac{\left(e(j)-c_2\right)^2}{2\sigma_2^2}\right)\end{array}\right)\boldsymbol{x}\left(j\right)\right]. \tag{18}$$

The derivative of Eq. (13) with respect to $\boldsymbol{\Omega}\left(n\right)$ yields the following equation

$$\nabla J_{CIM}\left(n\right) = \frac{\partial J_{CIM}\left(\boldsymbol{\Omega}\left(n\right)\right)}{\partial \boldsymbol{\Omega}\left(n\right)} = \frac{1}{N\sigma_3^3\sqrt{2\pi}}\boldsymbol{\Omega}\left(n\right)\exp\left(-\frac{\boldsymbol{\Omega}^2\left(n\right)}{2\sigma_3^2}\right). \tag{19}$$

According to Eq. (11), Eq. (15) and Eq. (19), the derivative of Eq. (11) can be obtained as

$$\frac{\partial J\left(\boldsymbol{\Omega}\left(n\right)\right)}{\partial \boldsymbol{\Omega}\left(n\right)} = \lambda\nabla J_{CIM}\left(n\right) - \boldsymbol{\Phi}\left(n\right) + \boldsymbol{\Psi}\left(n\right)\boldsymbol{\Omega}\left(n\right) + \boldsymbol{\Theta}\left(n\right). \tag{20}$$

Setting the above equation equal to zero, it can be obtained

$$\boldsymbol{\Omega}(n) = \boldsymbol{P}(n)\boldsymbol{G}(n),\tag{21}$$

where $\boldsymbol{P}(n) = \boldsymbol{\Psi}^{-1}(n)$, $\boldsymbol{G}(n) = \boldsymbol{\Phi}(n) - \boldsymbol{\Theta}(n) - \lambda\nabla J_{CIM}(n)$.

According to the matrix inversion theorem, it can be obtained

$$\boldsymbol{\Psi}^{-1}(n) = \left(\gamma\boldsymbol{\Psi}(n-1) + \eta\boldsymbol{x}(n)\boldsymbol{x}^T(n)\right)^{-1}$$
$$=\gamma^{-1}\boldsymbol{\Psi}^{-1}(n-1) - \frac{\gamma^{-1}\eta\boldsymbol{\Psi}^{-1}(n-1)\boldsymbol{x}(n)\boldsymbol{x}^T(n)\boldsymbol{\Psi}^{-1}(n-1)}{\gamma + \eta\boldsymbol{x}^T(n)\boldsymbol{\Psi}^{-1}(n-1)\boldsymbol{x}(n)},\tag{22}$$

where

$$\eta = \left(\frac{\alpha}{\sigma_1^2}\exp\left(-\frac{(e(n)-c_1)^2}{2\sigma_1^2}\right) + \frac{1-\alpha}{\sigma_2^2}\exp\left(-\frac{(e(n)-c_2)^2}{2\sigma_2^2}\right)\right).\tag{23}$$

Equation(22) can be rewritten as

$$\boldsymbol{P}(n) = \gamma^{-1}\left(\boldsymbol{P}(n-1) - \boldsymbol{k}(n)\boldsymbol{x}^T(n)\boldsymbol{P}(n-1)\right).\tag{24}$$

Here, $\boldsymbol{k}(n)$ has the following form,

$$\boldsymbol{k}(n) = \frac{\eta\boldsymbol{\Psi}^{-1}(n-1)\boldsymbol{x}(n)}{\gamma + \eta\boldsymbol{x}^T(n)\boldsymbol{\Psi}^{-1}(n-1)\boldsymbol{x}(n)}.\tag{25}$$

According to Eq. (24) and Eq. (25), it can be known that

$$\boldsymbol{P}(n)\boldsymbol{x}(n) = \eta^{-1}\boldsymbol{k}(n).\tag{26}$$

Assuming that $\nabla J_{CIM}(n)$ does not vary significantly over one step, then $\boldsymbol{G}(n)$ can be approximated as follows

$$\boldsymbol{G}(n) \approx \gamma\boldsymbol{\Phi}(n-1) + \eta d(n)\boldsymbol{x}(n) - \gamma\boldsymbol{\Theta}(n-1) - \rho\boldsymbol{x}_n - \lambda\nabla J_{CIM}(n-1)$$
$$= \gamma\boldsymbol{G}(n-1) + \eta d(n)\boldsymbol{x}(n) - \rho\boldsymbol{x}(n) - \lambda(1-\gamma)\nabla J_{CIM}(n-1),\tag{27}$$

where

$$\rho = \left(\frac{\alpha c_1}{\sigma_1^2}\exp\left(-\frac{(e(n)-c_1)^2}{2\sigma_1^2}\right) + \frac{(1-\alpha)c_2}{\sigma_2^2}\exp\left(-\frac{(e(n)-c_2)^2}{2\sigma_2^2}\right)\right).\tag{28}$$

Substituting Eq. (26) and Eq. (27) into Eq. (21) yields

$$\boldsymbol{\Omega}(n) = \boldsymbol{\Omega}(n-1) + \boldsymbol{k}(n)(e(n) - \rho) - \lambda(1-\gamma)\boldsymbol{P}(n)\nabla J_{CIM}(n-1).\tag{29}$$

The above is the complete derivation of the CIM-RMMKCC algorithm, and the pseudo-code of the CIM-RMMKCC is summarized within Algorithm 1.

Algorithm 1: CIM-RMMKCC

    Input: sample sequences $d(n), x(n), n = 1, 2, ..., L$
    Output: weight vector $\Omega(n)$
1 **Parameters setting**: select the proper parameters including $\alpha, \gamma, \lambda,$
    $\sigma_1, \sigma_2, \sigma_3, c_1, c_2;$
2 **Initialization**: initialize some parameters including $\Omega(0), P(0)$;
3 **for** $i \leftarrow 1$ **to** L **do**
4 | Calculate the $e(i)$ by Eq.(3);
5 | Calculate the η by Eq.(23);
6 | Calculate the ρ by Eq.(28);
7 | Calculate the $k(i)$ by Eq.(25);
8 | Calculate the $P(i)$ by Eq.(24);
9 | Update the $\Omega(i)$ by Eq.(29).
10 **end**

---

5   Simulation

A simulation experiment is implemented to verify the effectiveness of the proposed CIM-RMMKCC algorithm in this section, and it is compared with some existing sparse channel estimation algorithms(i.e., LMP [14], ZA-LMS, CIM-MCC, CIM-MMCC, l_0-RMC). The time-varying channel parameters to be estimated are configured as follows

$$\Omega_o = \begin{cases} [0, 0, 0, 0, 0, 0, 0, 0, 0, 1, 0, 0, 0, 0, 0, 0, 0, 0, 0, 0] , n \leqslant 3000 \\ [1, 0, 1, 0, 1, 0, 1, 0, 1, 0, 1, 0, 1, 0, 1, 0, 1, 0, 1, 0] , 3000 < n \leqslant 5000 \\ [1, -1, 1, -1, 1, -1, 1, -1, 1, -1, 1, -1, 1, -1, 1, -1, 1, -1] , 5000 < n \end{cases}$$
$$(30)$$

It can be seen that the channel has sparsity within the first 5000 time steps.

In the simulation experiment, the impulsive noise model is considered to be a mixed Gaussian model. The model is defined as

$$mN\left(\mu_1, v_1^2\right) + (1 - m) N\left(\mu_2, v_2^2\right), \tag{31}$$

where $\mu_i \ (i = 1, 2)$ stands for the mean values and $v_i \ (i = 1, 2)$ denotes the variances of the i-th Gaussian distribution.

The mean square deviation (MSD) standard that is defined as Eq. (32), is used to assess the estimated. performance.

$$MSD\left(\Omega(n)\right) = E\left\{\|\Omega_o - \Omega(n)\|^2\right\}. \tag{32}$$

Experiment. The parameters $(\mu_1, v_1, \mu_2, v_2, m)$ of the mixed Gaussian distribution are configured as (0.6,0.01,2,10,0.9). The mixing coefficient of the MKC with different bandwidths in the CIM-RMMKCC is $\alpha = 0.85$. The forgetting factor is $\gamma = 0.99$. The coefficient of the regularization term that controls the CIM penalty is $\lambda = 1$. The bandwidths of the MKC are $\sigma_1 = 1$ and $\sigma_2 = 2$.

In the experiment, the bandwidth of all CIM penalty items is set to 0.01. The centers of MKC are set to $c_1 = 0.6$ and $c_2 = 2$ respectively. The parameter settings of other algorithms are shown in Table 1.

Table 1. Main parameters of each algorithm

Algorithms	Main Parameters					
	μ	γ	σ_1	σ_2	σ_3	λ
LMP(p $=1.2$)	0.01					
ZA-LMS	0.01					0.5
CIM-MCC	0.01		1		0.01	1.77
CIM-MMCC	0.01		2.5	4	0.01	0.7
l_0-RMC		0.995	1			1.5

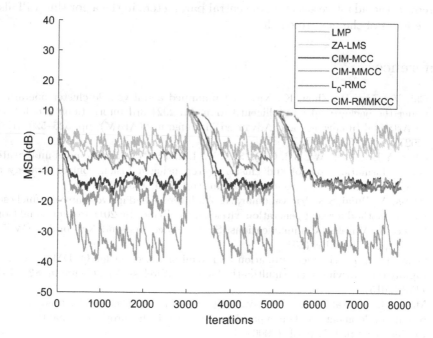

Fig. 2. The performance of each algorithm under non-Gaussian noise.

In Table 1, μ is the step size of the LMS-type algorithms, γ is the forgetting factor of the RLS-type algorithm, and λ is the coefficient of the regularization term for the sparsity restriction. σ_1 and σ_2 are bandwidths of the MCC-type algorithms, σ_3 is the bandwidth of CIM penalty items.

As measured by MSD, the convergence curves are displayed in Fig. 2. As illustrated in Fig. 2, MCC-type estimation algorithms (including CIM-MCC,

CIM-MMCC, l_0-RMC, and CIM-RMMKCC) demonstrate higher convergence accuracy compared to MSE-type algorithms (such as LMP and ZA-LMS) in environments with non-Gaussian noise. The proposed CIM-RMMKCC algorithm in this paper has good estimation accuracy in non-Gaussian noise environment with non-zero mean, demonstrating superior convergence speed and accuracy compared to other algorithms.

6   Conclusion

In this research, a new recursive adaptive filtering method, called CIM-RMMKCC, is developed for sparse channel estimation with non-zero mean impulsive noise. This approach incorporates a CIM-based sparse penalty term into MMKCC. It is confirmed through simulation experiments that the suggested method works as intended.

In the future, we will conduct more analysis on the stability and complexity of the CIM-RMMKCC to adjust the performance and adapt to more environments. Moreover, the adaptive selection of central parameters in the algorithm will also be the focus of the next research.

References

1. Cai, Y., Guo, H., Zhou, K., Xu, L.: Unmanned aerial vehicle cluster operations under the background of intelligentization. In: 2021 3rd International Conference on Artificial Intelligence and Advanced Manufacture (AIAM), pp. 525–529. IEEE (2021)
2. Chen, Y.L., Ma, X.W., Bai, G.Q., Sha, Y., Liu, J.: Multi-autonomous underwater vehicle formation control and cluster search using a fusion control strategy at complex underwater environment. Ocean Eng. **216**, 108048 (2020)
3. Beena, A., Pillai, S.S., Vijayakumar, N.: An improved adaptive sparse channel estimation method for next generation wireless broadband. In: 2018 International Conference on Wireless Communications, Signal Processing and Networking (WiSPNET), pp. 1–5. IEEE (2018)
4. Şenol, H.: Joint channel estimation and symbol detection for OFDM systems in rapidly time-varying sparse multipath channels. Wireless Pers. Commun. **82**, 1161–1178 (2015)
5. Matz, G., Hlawatsch, F.: Time-varying communication channels: fundamentals, recent developments, and open problems. In: 2006 14th European Signal Processing Conference, pp. 1–5. IEEE (2006)
6. Chen, Y., Gu, Y., Hero, A.O.: Sparse LMS for system identification. In: 2009 IEEE International Conference on Acoustics, Speech and Signal Processing, pp. 3125–3128. IEEE (2009)
7. Hong, X., Gao, J., Chen, S.: Zero-attracting recursive least squares algorithms. IEEE Trans. Veh. Technol. **66**(1), 213–221 (2016)
8. Chen, B., Liu, X., Zhao, H., Principe, J.C.: Maximum correntropy Kalman filter. Automatica **76**, 70–77 (2017). https://doi.org/10.1016/j.automatica.2016.10.004

9. Seth, S., Principe, J.C.: Compressed signal reconstruction using the correntropy induced metric. In: 2008 IEEE International Conference on Acoustics, Speech and Signal Processing, pp. 3845–3848 (2008). https://doi.org/10.1109/ICASSP.2008.4518492
10. Ma, W., Qu, H., Gui, G., Xu, L., Zhao, J., Chen, B.: Maximum correntropy criterion based sparse adaptive filtering algorithms for robust channel estimation under non-gaussian environments. J. Franklin Inst. **352**(7), 2708–2727 (2015)
11. Lu, M., Xing, L., Zheng, N., Chen, B.: Robust sparse channel estimation based on maximum mixture correntropy criterion. In: 2020 International Joint Conference on Neural Networks (IJCNN), pp. 1–6. IEEE (2020)
12. Zhang, X., Li, K., Wu, Z., Fu, Y., Zhao, H., Chen, B.: Convex regularized recursive maximum correntropy algorithm. Signal Process. **129**, 12–16 (2016)
13. Chen, B., Xie, Y., Wang, X., Yuan, Z., Ren, P., Qin, J.: Multikernel correntropy for robust learning. IEEE Trans. Cybern. **52**(12), 13500–13511 (2022). https://doi.org/10.1109/TCYB.2021.3110732
14. Weng, B., Barner, K.E.: Nonlinear system identification in impulsive environments. IEEE Trans. Signal Process. **53**(7), 2588–2594 (2005)

Towards Intercontinental Teleoperation: A Cloud-Based Framework for Ultra-Remote Human-Robot Dual-Arm Motion Mapping

Honghao Lv[1], Huiying Zhou[1], Ruohan Wang[1], Haiteng Wu[2], Zhibo Pang[3,4], and Geng Yang[1,2(✉)]

[1] State Key Laboratory of Fluid Power and Mechatronic Systems, School of Mechanical Engineering, Zhejiang University, Hangzhou, China
yanggeng@zju.edu.cn
[2] Zhejiang Key Laboratory of Intelligent Operation and Maintenance Robot, Hangzhou Shenhao Technology, Hangzhou, China
[3] Department of Automation Technology, ABB Corporate Research, Vasteras, Sweden
[4] Department of Intelligent Systems, Royal Institute of Technology (KTH), Stockholm, Sweden

Abstract. Teleoperated robots offer a unique combination of robotic strength and precision, coupled with human judgment and ingenuity, to enhance productivity and safety in complex, unstructured, and hazardous industrial environments. However, teleoperation over ultra-remote distances has posed a significant challenge, with control performance being compromised by the inherent trade-off between distance and latency. This study presents a novel cloud-based human-robot motion mapping framework for ultra-remote teleoperation. An intuitive dual-arm human-robot motion mapping framework based on capturing human motion has been implemented, and private network connectivity is established using the Google Cloud platform for the efficient transfer of control data required for human-robot motion mapping. Moreover, a novel feedforward control framework is proposed to mitigate the negative impact of high network latency on teleoperation control performance. To demonstrate the feasibility of the proposed approach, an intercontinental teleoperation system between China and Sweden was developed, and a series of practical applications were demonstrated by capturing the motion of an operator in Sweden to control the dual-arm robot located over 7800 km away in China. The proposed feedforward control framework for intercontinental teleoperation has the potential utility for improving human-robot interaction performance in ultra-remote teleoperation scenarios with high network latency. More demonstration videos can be found at https://fsie-robotics.com/intercontinental-teleoperation/.

Keywords: Intercontinental Teleoperation · Ultra-Remote · Motion Mapping · Human-robot Interaction · Network Latency

H. Yang et al. (Eds.): ICIRA 2023, LNAI 14273, pp. 132–144, 2023.
https://doi.org/10.1007/978-981-99-6498-7_12

1 Introduction

Teleoperation allows humans to perform manipulation tasks in distant, scaled, hazardous, or otherwise inaccessible environments [1, 2]. By enabling the remote utilization of robotic devices based on the operator intentions, telerobotic systems combine the human intelligence required for unscheduled or flexible tasks with the robotic stable execution ability, resulting in a more intelligent and flexible robot [3]. This arrangement is commonly referred to as human-in-loop operation [4]. A crucial aspect of telerobotic operation involves accurately and reliably obtaining the intentions of the teleoperator and effectively mapping the motion data to control the robotic system [5, 6]. However, in most telerobotic systems, the leader and follower are connected through a communication channel that introduces varying time delays [7]. These delays often lead to instability, overall poor performance, increased coordination errors during task execution, and insufficient transparency [8, 9].

Teleoperation over ultra-remote distances has posed a significant challenge, with control performance being compromised by the inherent trade-off between distance and latency. Lv *et al.* proposed an internal model control (IMC) based latency-aware framework for wireless cloud-fog automation, which is used for handling the time delays and instability-creating elements introduced by wireless communication [10, 11]. Chen *et al.* proposed a novel radial basis function (RBF) neural network-based adaptive robust control design for the bilateral teleoperation system [12]. This work provided a good solution for solving the time-varying delay and uncertainties, but the online and real-time estimation of accurate parameters in environment dynamics with the RBF neural network is quite challenging, which may lead to the performance reduction on the transparency. Many research outputs for solving the time delays and instability-creating elements have been conducted and various controller design methods have been proposed from the perspective of control [13]. However, most of the current studies consider the small delay in milliseconds corresponding to the control loop, which cannot guarantee the performance of robot teleoperation control under the condition of large delay in intercontinental and ultra-remote networks [14, 15].

According to the background described above, we present a novel cloud-based human-robot motion mapping framework for ultra-remote teleoperation. In order to reduce the training cost of teleoperators and capture the motion intuitively, this work uses wearable inertial motion capture techniques to obtain the motion signal of the operator. A preliminary teleoperation experiment was conducted between Vasteras and Stockholm in Sweden at a distance of over 90 km, and the feasibility of the teleoperation scheme was verified, as shown in Fig. 1. On this basis, an intercontinental telerobotic system between China and Sweden over a distance of 7800 km was developed.

The main contributions of this paper are stated below: 1) A novel cloud-based teleoperation architecture is proposed for achieving intercontinental teleoperation; 2) A novel feedforward control framework is proposed to mitigate the negative impact of high network latency on teleoperation control performance, and the comparative experiments under local Ethernet network condition and the intercontinental network condition are conducted. 3) An intercontinental telerobotic system between Sweden and China is implemented and validated.

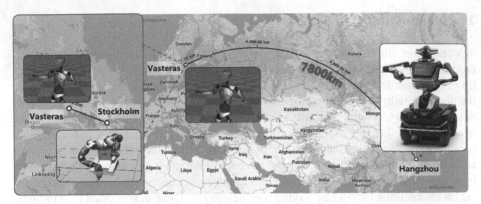

Fig. 1. Overall diagram of the ultra-remote human-robot motion mapping.

The remaining part of this paper is organized as follows. The architecture of the proposed cloud-based framework for ultra-remote teleoperation is introduced in Sect. 2, and the human-motion-based motion mapping strategy for dual-arm motion mapping is described in this Section. Section 3 details the methodology of the feedforward control framework, and the comparative experiments are presented here. The verification and demonstration of an intercontinental telerobotic prototype system are described in Sect. 4. Section 5 concludes the results and limitations of this work.

2   Cloud-Based Framework for Ultra-Remote Teleoperation

In order to achieve intercontinental private network connectivity, traditional personal wireless devices or local network cable connections are not practical and must be provided by the network services offered by cloud providers, such as Amazon Web Services (AWS) [16], Microsoft Azure [17], or Google Cloud Platform (GCP) [18]. Compared to the local network connection, the cloud-based network framework enables efficient resource utilization, simplified management, and improved network performance, while also providing a foundation for deploying and integrating cloud-based applications and services.

2.1   The Architecture of the Intercontinental Communication Link

As described in Fig. 1, this work implements two distance levels of ultra-remote teleoperation, including intercity teleoperation between Vasteras and Stockholm in Sweden (over 90 km), as well as intercontinental teleoperation between China and Sweden (over 7800 km). In order to verify the scalability of the system, two robots with different communication modes are used for Functional verification, as shown in Fig. 2.

For the first telerobotic system achieved based on the YuMi robot, the master side is for capturing the operator's motion data using the motion capture device Perception Neuron 2.0 [19]. And the hand motion poses data, including the position and the orientation, is obtained using the coordinate transformation. Then the human hand pose data is used to map and calculate the desired tool center point (TCP) of the YuMi robot.

Then the track_ik kinematic solver is used to obtain the desired joint configuration [20]. The External Guide Motion (EGM) interface from ABB provides a motion control interface with high frequency (up to 250 Hz) based on the Google Protobuf protocol, which enables real-time human-robot motion mapping. As shown in Fig. 2(a), based on the GCP, a virtualized machine (VM) with an Ubuntu system is implemented as the cloud-based network management server. To build the virtual private network connection, the OpenVPN system is used, which implements techniques to create secure point-to-point or site-to-site connections in routed or bridged configurations and remote access facilities. To validate the control performance of the YuMi robot, on the robot side, the robot side is simulated using the RobotStudio on a Windows PC. The simulated Yumi robot and the human motion generator are set as the clients of OpenVPN. When the EGM motion is activated, the generated joint value queue will be sent using Google Protocol Buffers (Protobuf) based on the UDP protocol. In this case, the communication between the human motion capture part on the Windows 10 system and the Ubuntu 20.04 is connected by a Cloud-based OpenVPN connection.

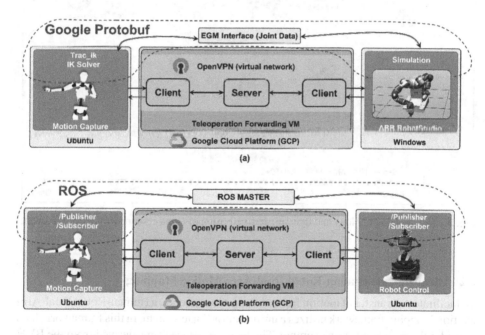

Fig. 2. Communication link for the designed two remote teleoperation systems.

For the second robotic validation case, a real robot platform is used, in which an anthropomorphic dual-arm mobile robot is developed with a pair of collaborative robot arms Jaco2 provided by Kinova Robotics with 6 DoFs. The distributed system of the dual-arm Jaco2 robot is managed via the open-source software Robot Operation System (ROS) [21]. The Jaco2 arm is controlled based on the Kinova-ROS stack provided by Kinova Robotics. Based on the implemented GCP-based OpenVPN virtual private network, the distributed ROS system can be started on multiple machines at remote distances as long as they can connect to the Internet. The ROS master is started at one machine, and the other machine is configured to use the same master, via ROS_MASTER_URI. And all the machines should define their ROS_IP according to their static IP address that is connected to the Internet. Figure 3 illustrates the network topology and the dynamic redistribution of cloud resources of the virtualized network connection from Sweden to China in this work.

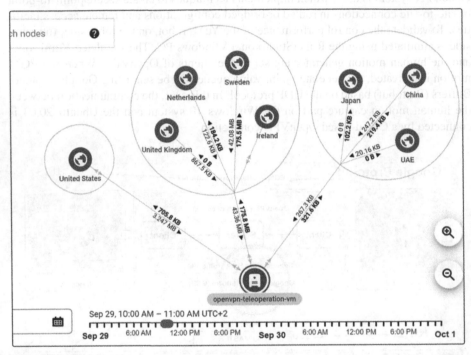

Fig. 3. The network topology and dynamic redistribution of cloud resources GCP for this work.

2.2 Ultra-Remote Human-Robot Dual-Arm Motion Mapping

To facilitate the transfer of motion from an operator to a robot, a Human-Robot Dual-Arm Motion Mapping framework utilizes a unified coordinate system. In this framework, let's consider the right hand as an example. The local reference frame derived from the BVH (Biovision Hierarchy) data stream, representing the operator's hand motion, differs from the local reference frame of the robot. To establish a common reference, we assume a global frame, which aligns its direction with the robot's reference frame. On the robot side, the coordinate frame of the end effector is defined, while the corresponding frame is referred the hand frame on the operator side. The primary objective of the motion transfer process is to determine a sequence of robot gripper poses based on human hand poses. By mapping the operator's hand poses to corresponding robot gripper poses, the motion is effectively transferred from the operator to the robot, allowing for coordinated movements between them.

3 Experiment on the Simulated Robot Motion Platform

To validate the feasibility and the practicality of the built cloud-based framework for ultra-remote teleoperation, the corresponding experiments on the first Simulated YuMi Robot platform are conducted.

3.1 Experiment Design

To investigate the impact of intercontinental networks with high latency on control performance, we conducted comparative motion mapping experiments under two conditions: a baseline scenario using a local Ethernet network and subsequent experiments involving intercontinental connectivity. In each test, human motion data were recorded and played back for a minimum of 60 min. The motion involved swinging the right arm from one side to the other. The human motion data was transmitted at a rate of 125 Hz, and each test lasted for a duration of 4 h to ensure reliable results. Furthermore, comparative experiments were conducted to examine the effects of different control strategies on network congestion from the perspective of the local controller. Both raw and filtered data were utilized under various network conditions to assess their impact. The experimental setup involved a Laptop PC in Sweden running the motion capture software Neuron Axis to generate human motion data. Additionally, a NUC10 PC equipped with ROS (Robot Operating System) was used to simulate the local robot controller. On the Chinese side, another Laptop PC running RobotStudio was employed to simulate the remote YuMi Robot platform. During the teleoperation simulation in RobotStudio, the maximum CPU usage recorded was 18.3%. To ensure time synchronization across multiple computers, we established a network time protocol (NTP) server between the ULT PC and other PCs, including the simulated controller PC and simulated robot platform PC.

3.2 Performance Evaluation

To further quantify the experimental results of the control performance under the network condition with high latency, several key metrics have been carefully chosen and defined for the case study of human motion-based teleoperation on the simulated YuMi robot. The desired joint positions, representing the commands sent from the remote side, are denoted as J_d. On the other hand, the measured joint values, which provide feedback on the actual joint states, are defined as J_r. Both J_d and J_r are time-series signals that are logged alongside the system timestamp, utilizing a sample rate of 500 Hz.

To assess the motion delay in the teleoperation system, the timestamps corresponding to the peaks of J_d and J_r are compared and subtracted. This calculation provides an estimate of the time lag between the desired joint positions and the measured joint values. Furthermore, to evaluate the performance of remote control in the teleoperation setup, the absolute errors between the peak values of J_d and J_r are calculated. These errors referred to as peak amplitude errors, quantify the deviations between the intended joint positions and the actual joint positions during operation.

As shown in Fig. 4, the control performance indicators, including motion delay, peak error, and corresponding network delay, have been recorded. Figure 4 (a) and Fig. 4 (b) represent the experimental record results under local Ethernet connection conditions and intercontinental network connection conditions, respectively. Moreover, the corresponding average motion delay and the peak amplitude error are calculated according to the logged time-series data. For the local network condition, we used the unobtrusive network latency tester (ULT) [22] to obtain the latency, and Ethernet network communication latency is very small, which can be ignored compared to the intercontinental network latency. It is obvious that the intercontinental network introduces hundreds of milliseconds of latency compared to the local Ethernet connection, causing a decrease in the control performance of the remote operation. The average motion delay under the intercontinental network condition is 1.2296 s, which is reasonable compared to the latency of 0.31579 s under the Ethernet connection by adding the extra network latency. For the control performance, the average peak amplitude error is 2.7769° under the intercontinental network condition, which is higher than the baseline condition.

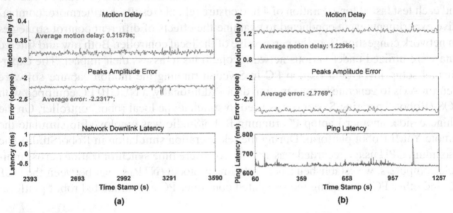

Fig. 4. Comparison results of the experiments on the local Ethernet connection and the GCP-based ultra-remote teleoperation.

3.3 Feedforward Control Framework and the Comparative Results

In order to reduce the impact of network latency on the control performance, a novel feedforward control framework with adding a low-pass filter in the control loop is proposed, as shown in Fig. 5 (a). The figure shows a simplified view of the implemented control system. The proportional controller gain K is used to calculate a velocity correction used to drive the robot position towards the reference position P_{ref}. The time-varying reference position is intended to be used as a feedforward of a desired velocity. After passing through the low-pass filter, the resulting value speed v_r is the resulting velocity, used internally by the robot controller to calculate joint references sent to the low-level servo control. The bandwidth time of the Low-Pass filter can be adjusted to filter the speed contribution of the reference position from the operator side. The control loop can be summarized as the following relation between speed and position in (1), where the P is the current position value feedback from the robot side.

$$v_r = K * (P_{ref} - P) + v_{ref} \qquad (1)$$

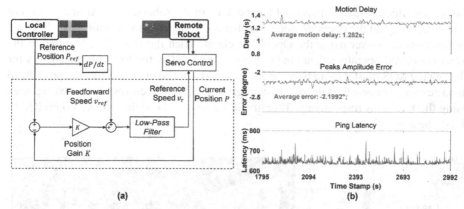

Fig. 5. The ultra-remote feedforward control framework and the improved control performance.

After implementing the proposed feedforward control framework on the intercontinental telerobotic system with high network latency, a series of comparative experimental results were obtained and are presented in Fig. 5 (b). When compared to the initial teleoperation performance under intercontinental network conditions without any rescue methods, as shown in Fig. 4 (b), it is noteworthy that the motion delay remained at a similar level even after the implementation of the feedforward control framework. However, a significant improvement is observed in the average peaks' amplitude error, which has been reduced to 2.1992°. This reduction signifies a 20% decrease in error following the implementation of the proposed feedforward control framework, which is a promising outcome.

4 Verification and Demonstration on a Real Robot

In order to further verify the practicality of our proposed ultra-remote teleoperation, after completing simulation experiments, we conducted functional verification using the designed second physical robot system. At the same time, a series of application demonstrations were designed to further optimize the performance of the ultra-remote telerobotic system.

4.1 Intercontinental Teleoperation System Setup

The first application task for verification is demonstrated in Fig. 6. The intercontinental teleoperation is conducted to finish a dual-arm coordinated assembly task by controlling the robot to insert a cylindrical workpiece into another cylindrical workpiece. On the robot side in China, two cameras are set to monitor the onsite status and give visual feedback to the operator side. One camera is placed directly in front of the robot to monitor the overall motion control status, while the other camera is mounted at the end of the robotic arm to observe the details of assembly operations. The robotic operation sense setting in China is shown as the left part of Fig. 6. The right part of Fig. 6 shows the operator side setting in Sweden. The operator wears the motion capture device and faces the screen which displays the visual feedback from the robotic side. At first, the robot side controller and the operator side controller are connected to the built virtual private network access server using the OpenVPN client. Then the static IP addresses of the robot client and operator client are configured and used as the ROS_IP parameters for sharing the ROS master to transfer the ROS topic data. The operator uses the predefined hand gesture to enable the teleoperation program and grab the corresponding workpieces using the two arms respectively. Then the left arm and the right arm are controlled to finish the assembly task.

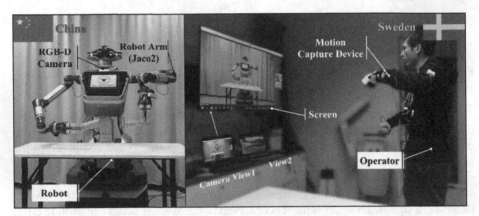

Fig. 6. Ultra-remote teleoperation system setup and the demonstration.

Figure 7 illustrates the task flow of ultra-remote teleoperation. At T = 0 s, the operator readies and enables motion transfer. Then the robot right gripper is guided to approach to the target shaft for a firm grip. With the shaft securely grasped, the robot lifts it to an appropriate height in preparation for the subsequent insertion step. Carefully manipulating the right arm, the operator adjusts the position and orientation of the shaft, ensuring precise insertion into the left-hand target shaft sleeve. By T = 10 s, the operator completes the adjustment and initiates the insertion movement. With coordinated control of both robot arms, the operator successfully finishes the assembly task by T = 13 s. Subsequently, the operator teleoperates the right arm of the robot to retreat to a relaxed state. The entire remote assembly process unfolds seamlessly, highlighting the practicality and feasibility of the ultra-remote teleoperation system from a real-world perspective.

4.2   Vibration Feedback for Safer Teleoperation

To provide intuitive feedback on the robot's operational status to the operator and enhance remote human-robot interaction while ensuring system safety, a vibration feedback subsystem has been developed. This subsystem complements the on-site visual feedback provided by two cameras. Figure 8 illustrates the control setup of the dual-arm robot, where velocity commands are generated based on motion capture data from the operator side. To ensure the robot's safety during its task execution, a self-capacitive sensor-based

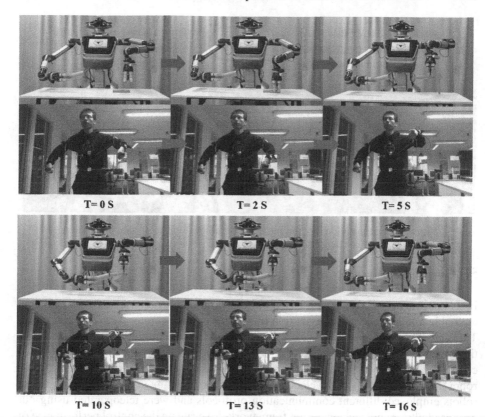

Fig. 7. Flow of the Assembly Task: A operator in Sweden wearing a motion capture device teleoperates a dual-arm robot located in China. The operator guides the robot to perform the intricate task of inserting a shaft into the shaft sleeve.

robot skin is integrated onto the robotic arm. This skin is responsible for detecting the presence of nearby humans or obstacles. When a collision is imminent or an object approaches the robot arm, the skin's state is triggered, activating the attached vibrator. Additionally, to enhance the visibility of the vibration feedback, an LED is connected in parallel with the vibrator. Consequently, the remote operator can observe the vibration states, thereby gaining insight into the on-site robot's motion and collision conditions. The integration of this vibration feedback mechanism allows the operator to perceive the robot's on-site motion and collision states. This information is crucial for the operator to make timely adjustments during teleoperation, ensuring effective control and decision-making.

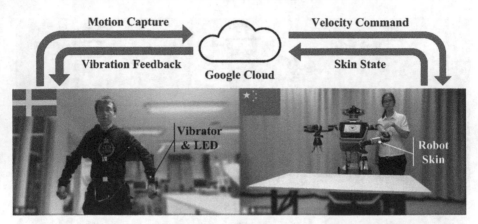

Fig. 8. The schematic vibration feedback data flow for remote safe interaction.

5 Conclusion

In this paper, we present a cloud-based ultra-remote teleoperation framework designed to enable efficient and accurate motion transfer from the operator to a dual-arm robot. This framework operates seamlessly even under real intercontinental network conditions characterized by high latency. To validate the effectiveness of our approach, we conducted teleoperation experiments using two representative dual-arm robots: the YuMi robot from ABB and a self-developed dual-arm robot utilizing the Kinova Jaco2. These robots employed different communication protocols and were teleoperated using our proposed ultra-remote teleoperation framework. To evaluate the control performance of the robots under intercontinental network conditions, we compared it to a baseline established by the control performance under local Ethernet conditions. Our analysis revealed a substantial decrease in control performance due to the high network latency. To mitigate the adverse effects of latency on control performance, we introduced a novel feedforward control framework and seamlessly integrated it into the intercontinental telerobotic system. Notably, the joint position peak amplitude error depicted in Fig. 5 (b) exhibited a significant reduction, indicating the successful implementation of the feedforward control framework and its ability to mitigate the impact of network latency on control performance. From a practical standpoint, the proposed cloud-based ultra-remote teleoperation framework offers significant advantages by eliminating the extensive efforts and costs associated with building and fine-tuning intercontinental control systems.

Acknowledgment. This work was supported in part by the National Natural Science Foundation of China (No. 51975513), the Natural Science Foundation of Zhejiang Province, China (No. LR20E050003), the Major Research Plan of National Natural Science Foundation of China (No. 51890884), the Major Research Plan of Ningbo Innovation 2025. (Grant No. 2020Z022), the Bellwethers Research and Development Plan of Zhejiang Province (No. 2023C01045), and the Swedish Foundation for Strategic Research (SSF) through the project APR20–0023. This work was conducted by Honghao Lv during his tenure as a visiting doctoral student at the Royal Institute of Technology (KTH) in Sweden. Honghao Lv gratefully acknowledges financial support from China Scholarship Council.

References

1. Hirche, S., Buss, M.: Human-oriented control for haptic teleoperation. Proc. IEEE **100**(3), 623–647 (2012)
2. Yang, G., Lv, H., Zhang, Z., Yang, L., Deng, J., You, S., et al.: Keep healthcare workers safe: Application of teleoperated robot in isolation ward for COVID-19 prevention and control. Chin. J. Mech. Eng. **33**(1), 47 (2020)
3. Mahler, J., Matl, M., Satish, V., Danielczuk, M., DeRose, B., McKinley, S., et al.: Learning ambidextrous robot grasping policies. Sci. Robot. **4**(26) (2019)
4. Lv, H., Yang, G., Zhou, H., Huang, X., Yang, H., Pang, Z.: Teleoperation of collaborative robot for remote dementia care in home environments. IEEE J. Transl. Eng. Health. Med. **8**, 1400510 (2020)
5. Lv, H., Kong, D., Pang, G., Wang, B., Yu, Z., Pang, Z., et al.: GuLiM: a hybrid motion mapping technique for teleoperation of medical assistive robot in combating the COVID-19 pandemic. IEEE Trans. Med. Robot. Bio. **4**(1), 106–117 (2022)
6. Parsaei, M.R., Boveiri, H.R., Javidan, R., Khayami, R.: Telesurgery QoS improvement over SDN based on a Type-2 fuzzy system and enhanced cuckoo optimization algorithm. Int. J. Commun. Syst. **33**(11) (2020)
7. Moya, V., Slawiñski, E., Mut, V., Chávez, D., Wagner, B.: Stable bilateral teleoperation control method for biped robots with time-varying delays. J. Rob. **2023**, 3197743 (2023)
8. Lv, H., Pang, Z., Xiao, M., Yang, G.: Hardware-in-the-loop simulation for evaluating communication impacts on the wireless-network-controlled robots. In: Proc. Annu. Conf. IEEE Ind. Electron. Soc., Brussels, Belgium (2022)
9. Aleksy, M., Dai, F., Enayati, N., Rost, P., Pocovi, G.: Utilizing 5G in industrial robotic applications. In: Proceeding of FiCloud (2019)
10. Lyu, H., Bengtsson, A., Nilsson, S., Pang, Z., Isaksson, A., Yang, G.: Latency-aware control for wireless cloud fog automation: framework and case study. TechRxiv (2023). https://doi.org/10.36227/techrxiv.22586044.v2
11. Lv, H., Pang, Z., Bhimavarapu, K., Yang, G.: Impacts of wireless on robot control: the network hardware-in-the-loop simulation framework and real-life comparisons. IEEE Trans. Industr. Inform. **19**(9), 9255–9265 (2023)
12. Chen, Z., Huang, F., Sun, W., Gu, J., Yao, B.: RBF-neural-network-based adaptive robust control for nonlinear bilateral teleoperation manipulators with uncertainty and time delay. IEEE/ASME Trans. Mechatron. **25**(2), 906–918 (2020)
13. Annamraju, S., Pediredla, V.K., Thondiyath, A.: Lyapunov stable teleoperation controllers using passivity analysis. IFAC-PapersOnLine. **53**(1), 435–440 (2020)
14. Baranitha, R., Mohajerpoor, R., Rakkiyappan, R.: Bilateral teleoperation of single-master multislave systems with semi-markovian jump stochastic interval time-varying delayed communication channels. IEEE Trans. Cybern. **51**(1), 247–257 (2021)
15. Handa, A., Wyk, K.V., Yang, W., Liang, J., Chao, Y.W., Wan, Q., et al.: DexPilot: vision-based teleoperation of dexterous robotic hand-arm system. In: Proc. DexPilot: Vision-Based Teleoperation of Dexterous Robotic Hand-Arm System (2020)
16. Mathew, S., Varia, J.: Overview of amazon web services. Amazon Whitepapers **105**, 1–22 (2014)
17. Wilder, B.: Cloud Architecture Patterns: Using Microsoft Azure. O'Reilly Media Inc, US (2012)
18. Bisong, E.: An Overview of Google Cloud Platform Services. Apress, Berkeley, CA (2019)
19. Noitom-Ltd.: Perception neuron. https://noitom.com/perception-neuron-series. Accessed 21 May 2023

20. Beeson, P., Ames, B.: TRAC-IK: an open-source library for improved solving of generic inverse kinematics. In: Proc. IEEE-RAS Int. Conf. Hum. Robot., Seoul, Korea (2015)
21. Quigley, M., Conley, K., Gerkey, B., Faust, J., Foote, T., Leibs, J., et al.: ROS: an open-source Robot Operating System. In: Proc. IEEE Int. Conf. Robot. Autom. workshop, Kobe, Japan (2009)
22. Bhimavarapu, K., Pang, Z., Dobrijevic, O., Wiatr, P.: Unobtrusive, accurate, and live measurements of network latency and reliability for time-critical internet of things. IEEE Internet Things Mag. 5(3), 38–43 (2022)

A Lightweight Ankle Exoskeleton Driven by Series Elastic Actuator

Hao Du, Wei Jiang, Yuepeng Qian, Wenbing Zhuang, Yixuan Guo,
Yuquan Leng, and Chenglong Fu[✉]

Southern University of Science and Technology, Shenzhen 518055, China
fucl@sustech.edu.cn

Abstract. The current research on exoskeleton torque control is relatively extensive, but the performance is suboptimal. Exoskeletons driven by series elastic actuator (SEA) can achieve high force control accuracy through simple position control. However, motor placement at the distal end increases the mass of the body terminal device, which not only increases the moment of inertia of the lower limb but also interferes with the normal movement of the patient, limiting their applicability in assisting the wearer. In this study, to prevent foot drop, we designed a lightweight, unilateral ankle exoskeleton that provides assistance for dorsiflexion via a single motor. By placing the motor and other heavier electronic components at the waist, the inertial load on the human leg is reduced achieving better assistance performance. Torque control assistance for the ankle joint is implemented using modified cascade PI control. When a person walks at a speed of 0.4 m/s, the desired maximum torque is set to 1.5 Nm, and the actual maximum torque is 1.5±0.187 Nm, which is close to the expected value. This demonstrates that the exoskeleton exhibits satisfactory force-tracking performance and can precisely assist individuals with foot drop in their daily walking activities.

Keywords: Ankle exoskeleton · dorsiflexion assistance · series elastic actuator(SEA)

1 Introduction

Stroke, spinal cord injury, brain injury, trauma, and other neurological impairments can lead to ankle joint dysfunction [1]. A subset of patients exhibit foot drop gait due to insufficient dorsiflexion capabilities [2,3]. Individuals with foot drop experience slow walking, limb asymmetry, increased energy consumption, and a higher risk of falling, all of which adversely affect daily mobility. The loss of ambulatory ability diminishes the quality of life, rendering gait rehabilitation indispensable [4].

Although traditional physical therapy has demonstrated effectiveness in gait rehabilitation, manual assistance during rehabilitation training is limited by the experience, number, and physical capabilities of caregivers, and it is unable to

H. Yang et al. (Eds.): ICIRA 2023, LNAI 14273, pp. 145–153, 2023.
https://doi.org/10.1007/978-981-99-6498-7_13

record relevant parameters [5]. Functional electrical stimulation, on the other hand, aims to improve or restore dorsiflexion function by stimulating the associated muscle groups. However, the stimulation intensity must be repeatedly adjusted by the user or initially set to a relatively high value, leading to increased fatigue [6]. Furthermore, ankle-foot orthoses (AFOs) maintain the wearer's lower leg and foot at a fixed angle, restricting normal ankle joint movement during dorsiflexion or plantarflexion and impeding the recovery of ankle joint function [7]. Alternatively, developed wearable lower limb exoskeletons can provide strong support for gait rehabilitation through various assistance strategies [8].

Currently, lower limb wearable exoskeletons for rehabilitation have been extensively researched, with rigid ankle exoskeletons featuring motors and controllers primarily located at the foot's distal end. The increased mass of human terminal devices not only adds to the lower limb's moment of inertia but also interferes with the patient's normal movement [9–11]. Soft exoskeletons place motors or other power sources and controllers closer to the human center of mass at the waist, transmitting power to the ankle joint through Bowden cable sheaths, effectively circumventing the drawbacks of rigid ankle exoskeletons [18]. Position control in soft exoskeletons may generate high interaction torques, disrupting the user's desired movement. Force control is safer and more comfortable, and calculating the stiffness model of a soft exoskeleton to implement force control through position control necessitates the establishment of a complex stiffness model and compensation for frictional effects, resulting in suboptimal consistency of the assistive torque curve. Other researchers have employed torque sensors at the foot's distal end for feedback, realizing closed-loop torque control [13–15]. This approach requires cable tensioning and is highly susceptible to friction, demanding more sophisticated controllers. SEAs utilize series elastic elements (SEEs) to achieve superior force-tracking performance with simple position control [12,16,17,19]. Additionally, the introduced elastic elements decouple the motor reducer's inertia and output. In the event of external interference, such as collisions, they can absorb some of the energy. However, existing ankle exoskeletons designed using SEAs place the motor at the foot's distal end, increasing the weight at the extremity [20,21].

In this paper, a lightweight, unilateral ankle exoskeleton driven by SEA was designed to prevent foot drop and help patients with impaired limbs during walking. This ankle exoskeleton has a reduced distal mass, is quick to wear, and is easily portable. In Sect. 2, we describe the design of the ankle exoskeleton. Section 3 presents the control method. Subsequently, in Sect. 4, we outline the experimental protocol and assistive force. Finally, Sect. 5 concludes the paper.

2   Design of the Ankle Exoskeleton

In order to meet the intrinsic requirements and challenges of pathological gait assistance, several design principles should be established: the range of motion in the sagittal plane of the designed ankle exoskeleton should satisfy the ankle joint's range of motion during normal human walking. The primary goal of the ankle exoskeleton is to cater to the common characteristics of patients with foot drop, namely assisting in dorsiflexion. Therefore, the output torque of the exoskeleton should be designed according to the need for dorsiflexion assistance. Additionally, the ankle exoskeleton system should be as lightweight as possible to reduce the inertia on the human limb and enhance its portability. Other structural elements should be optimized during the design process, and the chosen materials should have the lowest possible density while satisfying strength requirements.

Figure 1 illustrates the design of a lightweight, unilateral ankle exoskeleton. The device consists of a control and actuation module, a Bowden cable transmission, and an ankle assembly. The actuation and control assembly is both lightweight and powerful. The actuator (RoboMaster M3508) can output a peak torque of 5 Nm, and given the deceleration ratio of 2.5 from the actuator end to the foot end, the theoretical output torque to the foot end can reach 12.5 Nm, meeting the required torque for human dorsiflexion. The ankle component can be quickly fastened with straps, and the entire exoskeleton has a weight of 2.2 kg.

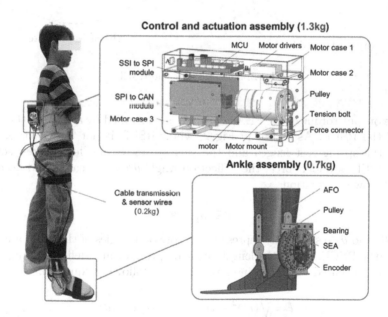

Fig. 1. A prototype of ankle exoskeleton for assisting patients with foot drop in Walking.

The SEE forms a critical component of the entire ankle exoskeleton, where its operating principles, dimensions, and material have significant implications on the torque control performance of the ankle exoskeleton. As depicted in Fig. 2, The ankle exoskeleton SEE designed in this study adopts a rotating configuration, referring to the design principle of the rotating series elastic element

(RSEE) by Qian et al. [22,23], which involves positioning 12 linear springs between an inner ring and an outer ring capable of relative rotation. When the inner ring rotates to a certain angle relative to the outer ring, a corresponding torque is generated between them.

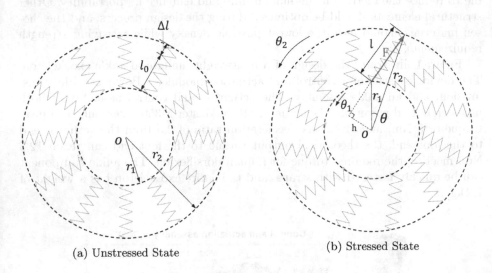

(a) Unstressed State   (b) Stressed State

Fig. 2. Schematic of the RSEE.

The output torque of the SEA is primarily controlled by adjusting the deflection of the RSEE. As shown in Fig. 2, when RSEE is not under force, $l_0, \Delta l$ denote the spring rest length and the spring pre-tension length, respectively. When RSEE is under force, the deflection angle θ can be calculated according to the following equation:

$$\theta = \theta_1 - \theta_2 \tag{1}$$

where θ_1 and θ_2 respectively represent the rotation angles of the inner and outer rings of the RSEE. Then, the length of each spring at any deflection angle l can be calculated based on the cosine law using the following equation:

$$l = \sqrt{(r_1)^2 + (r_2)^2 - 2r_1 r_2 \cos(\theta)} \tag{2}$$

where r_1 is the radius of the connection point of the spring and the inner ring, and r_2 is the radius of the connection point of the spring and the outer ring. Then, the tension of the spring can be calculated according to Hooke's law.

Finally, the output torque of the SEA, that is, the resultant force of all springs, can be calculated by:

$$\tau_e = mkr_1 r_2 \sin(\theta) - \frac{mkl_0 r_1 r_2 \sin(\theta)}{\sqrt{(r_1)^2 + (r_2)^2 - 2r_1 r_2 \cos(\theta)}} \tag{3}$$

where m is the number of springs, k is the spring stiffness, and l_0 is the remaining length of the spring.

3   Control Method

3.1   Gait Phase Estimation

For patients suffering from foot drop, the primary objective is to facilitate dorsiflexion, specifically from the initial to the final phase of the swing. An Inertial Measurement Unit (IMU) installed on the foot can be used to detect the moment when the toe leaves the ground. The gait cycle is defined as the period between two consecutive instances of toe-off (TO). We consider the moment of TO as 0% of the gait, so the calculation of the gait percentage is as follows:

$$P_{gait} = \frac{t - t_{TO}(i)}{t_{TO}(i) - t_{TO}(i-1)} \cdot 100\% \tag{4}$$

where $t_{TO}(i)$ is the time of the i_{th} TO, $t_{TO}(i-1)$ is the time of the $i-1_{th}$ TO. Given that the dorsiflexion moment around the ankle joint occurs between 0–55% of the gait cycle, we implement the dorsiflexion assist mode during this phase, and utilize the zero-torque mode at all other times.

3.2   Modified Cascade PI Control

The overall control system is shown in Fig. 3. The goal of the control system is to provide accurate assistive torque to the ankle by controlling the deflection angle of the inner and outer rings of the elastic element, so as to prevent the foot from dropping during the patient's walking.

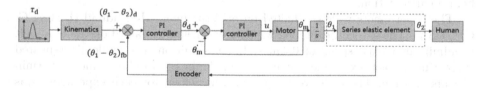

Fig. 3. Modified cascade PI control. With online kinematic computation, the torque control is converted into position control.

Calculate the inverse solution of the expected torque curve τ_d by Newton's method through formula 3 to obtain the expected deflection angle $(\theta_1 - \theta_2)_d$.

Construct function according to formula 3:

$$\tau(\theta) = mkr_1r_2 \sin(\theta) - \frac{mkl_0r_1r_2 \sin(\theta)}{\sqrt{(r_1)^2 + (r_2)^2 - 2r_1r_2 \cos(\theta)}} - \tau_d \tag{5}$$

For the desired τ_d, Taylor expands τ at θ_0 to get

$$\tau(\theta) = \tau(\theta_0) + \tau'(\theta_0)(\theta - \theta_0) + \frac{\tau''(\xi)}{2}(\theta - \theta_0)^2 \tag{6}$$

where $\xi \in (0, \theta_0)$, so if $|\theta - \theta_0|$ is small enough, higher-order terms can be discarded, and we get declination θ:

$$\theta = \theta_0 - \frac{\tau(\theta_0)}{\tau'(\theta_0)} \tag{7}$$

Then for the i_{th} iteration we have

$$\theta_i = \theta_{i-1} - \frac{\tau(\theta_{i-1})}{\tau'(\theta_{i-1})} \tag{8}$$

Finally, the control law of the series elastic drive is obtained as

$$u = \left(K_{vp} + \frac{K_{vi}}{s} \right) \left[\left(K_{pp} + \frac{K_{pi}}{s} \right) ((\theta_1 - \theta_2)_d - (\theta_1 - \theta_2)_{fb}) \right] \tag{9}$$

where K_{vp} is the proportional gain of the speed loop, K_{vi} is the integral term of the speed loop, K_{pp} is the proportional gain of the position loop, K_{pi} is the integral term of the position loop, s is a complex variable.

4   Experiment and Results

4.1   Experimental Protocol

Multiple trials were conducted on a human subject (age 24, weight 67 kg, height 1.81 m). The experiment was approved by Review Board of Southern University of Science and Technology, and all subjects provided written informed consent before participation.

The experiments were conducted on an instrumented treadmill (BERTEC, OH, USA). The subject, equipped with an exoskeleton, walked on the dual-belt treadmill at a fixed speed of 0.4 m/s. Each condition was randomly repeated three times. Each experiment consisted of 4 min of standing time and 6 min of walking time. The assistive torque tracking effect for each experiment was measured to evaluate the effectiveness of the exoskeleton assistance.

4.2   Assistance Force

The actual assistive torque during the walking process is presented in Fig. 4. We set the desired torque curve applied to the ankle joint as the blue line, and the actual torque as the orange line. For the required torque curve, we set the starting point at the moment of TO as 0% and end at 55% of the gait cycle. The maximum expected torque at 30% is 1.5 Nm. The results indicate that the exoskeleton exhibits excellent tracking performance. The maximum actual torque is 1.5 ± 0.187 Nm, which is close to the expected value.

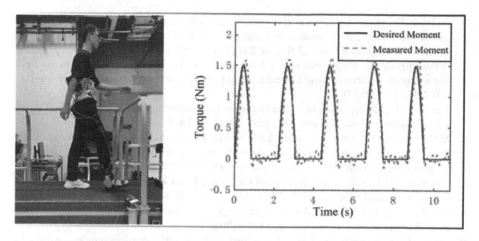

Fig. 4. Results of the torque curve tracking experiment.

5 Conclusion

In this study, a lightweight, unilateral ankle exoskeleton driven by a SEA was designed and tested. The SEA, utilizing a SEE, can achieve superior force-tracking performance with simple position control. We positioned the motor and other electronic components near the body's center of mass at the waist, significantly reducing the mass of the exoskeleton at the wearer's distal end, minimizing the inertial impact on the human limbs, and enhancing its portability. During the dorsiflexion stage of patient's gait, the control strategy employed modified cascade PI controls. When the individual walked at a speed of 0.4 m/s, the maximum desired torque was set at 1.5 Nm. The results demonstrated that the exoskeleton has excellent force-tracking performance and can accurately assist individuals suffering from foot drop in their daily walking.

Acknowledgement. This work was supported in part by the National Natural Science Foundation of China [Grant U1913205, 52175272], in part by the Science, Technology, and Innovation Commission of Shenzhen Municipality [Grant: ZDSYS20200811143601004, JCYJ20220530114809021], and in part by the Stable Support Plan Program of Shenzhen Natural Science Fund under Grant 20200925174640002.

References

1. Winter, D.A.: Biomechanics and Motor Control of Human Gait: Normal, Elderly and Pathological, 2nd edn. University of Waterloo Press, Waterloo (1991)
2. Kluding, P.M., Dunning, K., O'Dell, M.W., et al.: Foot drop stimulation versus ankle foot orthosis after stroke: 30-week outcomes. Stroke **44**(6), 1660–1669 (2013)

3. Stein, R.B., et al.: Long-term therapeutic and orthotic effects of a foot drop stimulator on walking performance in progressive and nonprogressive neurological disorders. Neurorehabil. Neural Repair **24**(2), 152–167 (2010)
4. Wiszomirska, I., Błażkiewicz, M., Kaczmarczyk, K.: Effect of drop foot on spatiotemporal, kinematic, and kinetic parameters during gait. Appl. Bionics Biomech. **2017**(1), 1–6 (2017)
5. Alnajjar, F., Zaier, R., et al.: Trends and technologies in rehabilitation of foot drop: a systematic review. Expert Rev. Med. Devices **18**(1), 31–46 (2021)
6. Miller, L., McFadyen, A., Lord, A.C., et al.: Functional electrical stimulation for foot drop in multiple sclerosis: a systematic review and meta-analysis of the effect on gait speed. Arch. Phys. Med. Rehabil. **98**(7), 1435–1452 (2017)
7. Corcoran, P.J.: Effects of plastic and metal leg braces on speed and energy cost of hemiparetic ambulation. Arch. Phys. Med. Rehabil. **51**, 69–77 (1970)
8. Baud, R., et al.: Review of control strategiesfor lower-limb exoskeletons to assist gait. J. Neuroeng. Rehabil. **18**(1), 1–34 (2021)
9. Ferris, D.P., Czerniecki, J.M., Hannaford, B.: An ankle-foot orthosis powered by artificial pneumatic muscles. J. Appl. Biomech. **21**(2), 189–197 (2005)
10. Shorter, K.A., Kogler, G.F., Loth, E., et al.: A portable powered ankle-foot orthosis for rehabilitation. J. Rehabil. Res. Dev. **48**(4), 1–34 (2011)
11. Font-Llagunes, J.M., Lugrís, U., Clos, D., et al.: Design, control, and pilot study of a lightweight and modular robotic exoskeleton for walking assistance after spinal cord injury. J. Mech. Robot. **12**(3), 031008 (2020)
12. Ma, L., Leng, Y., Jiang, W., et al.: Design an underactuated soft exoskeleton to sequentially provide knee extension and ankle plantarflexion assistance. IEEE Robot. Autom. Lett. **7**(1), 271–278 (2021)
13. Gasparri, G.M., et al.: Verification of a robotic ankle exoskeleton control scheme for gait assistance in individuals with cerebral palsy. In: 2018 IEEE/RSJ International Conference on Intelligent Robots and Systems (IROS), pp. 4673–4678 (2018)
14. Gasparri, G.M., Luque, J., Lerner, Z.F.: Proportional joint-moment control for instantaneously adaptive ankle exoskeleton assistance. IEEE Trans. Neural Syst. Rehabil. Eng. **27**(4), 751–759 (2019)
15. Bishe, S.S.P.A., Nguyen, T., Fang, Y., Lerner, Z.F.: Adaptive ankle exoskeleton control: validation across diverse walking conditions. IEEE Trans. Med. Robot. Bionics **3**(3), 801–812 (2021)
16. Pratt, G.A., Williamson, M.M.: Series elastic actuators. In: Proceedings 1995 IEEE/RSJ International Conference on Intelligent Robots and Systems. Human Robot Interaction and Cooperative Robots, vol. 1, pp. 399–406 (1995)
17. Kong, K., Bae, J., Tomizuka, M.: A compact rotary series elastic actuator for human assistive systems. IEEE/ASME Trans. Mechatron. **17**(2), 288–297 (2011)
18. Guo, Y., Song, B., et al.: A calibration method of non-contact R-test for error measurement of industrial robots. Measurement **173**, 108365 (2021)
19. Kim, S., Bae, J.: Force-mode control of rotary series elastic actuators in a lower extremity exoskeleton using model-inverse time delay control. IEEE/ASME Trans. Mechatron. **22**(3), 1392–1400 (2017)
20. Hwang, S., et al.: Development of an active ankle foot orthosis for the prevention of foot drop and toe drag. In: 2006 International Conference on Biomedical and Pharmaceutical Engineering, pp. 418–423 (2006)
21. Ward, J., et al.: Stroke survivor gait adaptation and performance after training on a powered ankle foot orthosis. In: 2010 IEEE International Conference on Robotics and Automation, pp. 211–216 (2010)

22. Qian, Y., Han, S., Wang, Y., Fu, C.: Toward improving actuation transparency and safety of a hip exoskeleton with a novel nonlinear series elastic actuator. IEEE/ASME Trans. Mechatron. **28**(1), 417–428 (2022)
23. Qian, Y., Han, S., et al.: Design, modeling, and control of a reconfigurable rotary series elastic actuator with nonlinear stiffness for assistive robots. Mechatronics **86**, 102872 (2022)

Simulation Analysis of Synchronous Walking Control for Centaur System

Qigao Cheng[1], Haoyun Yan[2], Kui Xiang[1], Jing Luo[1], Muye Pang[1(✉)],

Yuquan Leng[2(✉)], and Chenglong Fu[2(✉)]

[1] Wuhan University of Technology, Wuhan 430070, China
pangmuye@whut.edu.cn
[2] Southern University of Science and Technology, Shenzhen 518055, China

Abstract. Carrying heavy loads while walking is a physically demanding activity that often results in fatigue and even injury. Therefore, to alleviate this extra burden, wearable exoskeleton robots have been widely researched. Conventional exoskeleton robots typically employ a fixed gait frequency during walking, which can restrict the wearer's mobility and lead to challenges such as the inability to coordinate obstacle-crossing movements. This paper proposes a centaur robot system based on a synchronized walking control scheme. Based on the combination of human lower limbs with the torso of a quadrupedal animal, we design a system with a pair of animal hind legs and a wearable torso. Furthermore, the system exhibits remarkable flexibility and adaptability. In this paper, we validate the feasibility of the synchronous walking control scheme for the centaur robot through WEBOTS, and demonstrate its outstanding performance in human-robot collaboration. In the simulation environment, the control deviation of the posture angles is within 0.1 rad, and the synchronization deviation rate of the walking is maintained within 0.05 s, achieving favorable control effectiveness. The control scheme enables the centaur system to achieve stride frequency synchronization with the wearer during locomotion, while ensuring the maintenance of stable load-carrying capacity.

Keywords: Supernumerary robotic limbs · Human walking · Human-robot collaboration

1 Introduction

In human activities, there are many scenarios that require carrying weight while walking, such as mountain climbers who need carry as many essential items such as food and medicine as possible in their backpacks, firefighters who carry heavy rescue equipment during rescue missions, and soldiers who expend a lot of energy carrying firearms and ammunition during military operations. Thus, how to minimize the energy consumption of the human body during weight-bearing activities has become a crucial issue. Until now, there have been many solutions proposed to address this issue, such as suspended backpacks [1–6] which separate the backpacks from the wearer's back and allows it to vibrate up and down to keep the wearer's center of mass at a relatively constant

© The Author(s), under exclusive license to Springer Nature Singapore Pte Ltd. 2023
H. Yang et al. (Eds.): ICIRA 2023, LNAI 14273, pp. 154–163, 2023.
https://doi.org/10.1007/978-981-99-6498-7_14

height during movement, this approach can effectively reduce problems such as muscle soreness and improve the load-carrying capacity. In addition, there is the BLEEX lower limb exoskeleton [7] developed by the University of California, Berkeley. It achieves its main load-bearing ability through two humanoid metal bionic legs outside the wearer's legs, relying on which it can support most of the load and reduce the wearer's weight. Exoskeleton robots have significant effects in enhancing the wearer's strength because they need to maintain consistency with the wearer's body movements. However, external limb robots can greatly improve the wearer's load-bearing capacity by relying on the structure that is independent of the wearer's limbs.

Traditional exoskeleton robots typically use fixed gait cycles and walking speeds in their control schemes, which cannot adapt to the gait differences of different wearers, leading to problems such as Inability to coordinate gait. Traditional exoskeletons usually have fixed gait cycles and walking speeds during walking, making it difficult to adapt to the gait differences of individual wearers, resulting in gait incoordination. Incongruity between the motion of a robotic exoskeleton and that of the wear can cause various issues, such as a lack of fluidity and flexibility, difficulty in coordinating obstacle-crossing, and limited movement in diverse terrains. In addition, the overall motion of the robot system may not be aesthetically pleasing. Therefore, how to achieve synchronized motion between the exoskeleton robot and the wearer is one of the important issues that need to be addressed in the current exoskeleton robot technology.

This paper proposes an innovative control scheme for the centaur robot [8] based on synchronized walking. This control scheme allows the centaur robot to follow the wearer's gait frequency and walking speed by adaptively adjusting its own gait cycle and walking speed. This system employs the motion controller based on model predictive control [9], which has high real-time performance and adaptability, and can precisely control the robot's motion. By modeling the robot's motion as a single rigid robot, the real-time optimization of the robot's walking was achieved. Moreover, this system can make gait adjustments based on the input of human motion information, while maintaining the stability of the centaur robot's posture.

The structure of this paper consists of Chap. 2, which describes the system overview of the centaur robot; Chap. 3, which presents the control architecture of the centaur robot; Chap. 4, which discusses the synchronized simulation verification results of the centaur robot; and Chap. 5, which provides a conclusion of this paper.

2 System Overview

2.1 Structure Description

The centaur robot, as a novel type of exoskeleton robot, aims to achieve synergistic motion with human under load, improving human's physical ability and load-bearing capacity. The robot is required not only to achieve self-balancing ability but also to meet the needs of human wearing. Through interaction with human, the centaur robot can follow human motion, providing external support and load-sharing for human to achieve the goal of human-robot collaboration. The mechanical structure mainly consists of a backboard, a spinal structure, and two mechanical legs as Fig. 1 show.

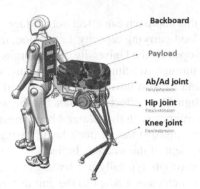

Backboard

Payload

Ab/Ad joint
Flex/extension

Hip joint
Flex/extension

Knee joint
Flex/extension

Fig. 1. The schematic diagram of the mechanical structure of the centaur robot

1) Backboard structure: The backboard structure is worn by the human wearer and is connected to the main body of the centaur structure, the spinal structure. The backboard is made of soft straps and carbon fiber board, which not only increase the wearer's comfort but also reduce the overall weight of the centaur robot. The backboard structure can provide external support for the wearer and can also be used to evaluate the load-carrying capacity of the centaur robot through this structure.

2) Spinal structure: The spinal structure of the centaur robot resembles that of the vertebral column in real quadrupeds. It serves to establish a linkage between the human wearer and the robot legs, while also functioning as a load-bearing component. In accordance with the principles of lightweight design, the central part of the spinal structure is composed of two layers of sandwiched panels, with the hollowed-out section accommodating the robot's electronic control and power supply units.

3) Robotic legs: The two three-degrees-of-freedom robot legs of the centaur robot are installed on the spinal structure, each consisting of three mechanical joints that enable the centaur robot to move like a real horse. These joints are driven by electric motors, which enables the robot legs to move freely and action coordinately.

2.2 Simplified Model

To simplify the computation, the leg mass of the robot is ignored, the mass distribution changes caused by the swing of the robot's legs are neglected, and the entire robot system is modeled as a single rigid body. The single rigid body model with ground reaction force is shown in Fig. 2.

The translational dynamics equation of the centaur robot was established based on Newton's second law and the translational acceleration of the rigid body can be obtained through the equation. Additionally, the rotational dynamics equation was established based on the angular momentum theorem:

Fig. 2. Single rigid body model of centaur robot

$$m\ddot{p} = f_1 + f_2 + f_H - mg \tag{1}$$

$$\frac{d}{dt}(Iw) = r_1 \times f_1 + r_2 \times f_2 + r_H \times f_H \tag{2}$$

$$\dot{R} = [w] \times R \tag{3}$$

In the centaur body, the time derivative of the angular momentum of the single rigid body located at the center of mass equals the sum of all external forces acting on the body and the resulting torque at the center of mass. The control input consists of $u = [f_1; f_2] \subset R^6$, where $f_n = [f_{nx}; f_{ny}; f_{nz}]$ represents the force acting on leg $n = 0, 1$. We selected the state variables as $[\theta; p_z; \omega; \dot{p}_z]$ and the control input as u. Using the world frame, the simplified dynamic equation can be expressed as:

$$\frac{d}{dt}\begin{bmatrix}\theta\\p_z\\\omega\\\dot{p}_z\end{bmatrix} = A_{8\times8}\begin{bmatrix}\theta\\p_z\\\omega\\\dot{p}_z\end{bmatrix} + B_{8\times6}\,u + C_{8\times1} \tag{4}$$

$$A = \begin{bmatrix} 0_{3\times3} & 0_{3\times1} & R_{3\times3} & 0_{3\times1} \\ 0_{1\times3} & 0_{1\times1} & 0_{1\times3} & 1_{1\times1} \\ 0_{3\times3} & 0_{3\times1} & 0_{3\times3} & 0_{3\times1} \\ 0_{1\times3} & 0_{1\times1} & 0_{1\times3} & 0_{1\times1} \end{bmatrix} \tag{5}$$

$$B = \begin{bmatrix} 0_{3\times3} & 0_{3\times3} \\ 0_{3\times3} & 0_{3\times3} \\ I^{-1}[r_1] & I^{-1}[r_1] \end{bmatrix}, C = \begin{bmatrix} 0_{3\times1} \\ 0_{1\times1} \\ I^{-1}[r_H \times f_H] \\ \frac{f_{HZ}}{m} - g \end{bmatrix} \tag{6}$$

3 Control Architecture

If a Centaur robot can adjust its gait by following the wearer's gait information, it can achieve the goal of coordinated movement with the wearer in crossing obstacles or complex terrain. We input the wearer's gait information into the centaur robot's gait scheduler and use model predictive control to control the contact leg during the gait cycle. The overall control diagram is shown in the Fig. 3.

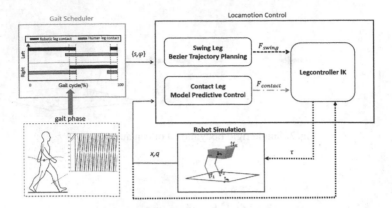

Fig. 3. The gait information recorded during human movement(from a open-source dataset [10]) is input into the centaur robot gait scheduler. In the gait scheduler, the yellow line represents the Centaur's contact phase, and the green line represents the wearer's contact phase, when the wearer's right leg is in the contact phase, the centaur robot's left leg is set to the contact phase. Due to the time delay caused by sensors and algorithmic calculations, the wearer's gait information is often ahead of the centaur robot's. The gait scheduler inputs the gait information of the current control period into the controller, which controls the swing leg and the contact leg of the centaur robot.

3.1   Swing Leg Control

During the swing phase of the ith leg of the centaur robot, equation(7) calculates the final drop point within a gait cycle. Here, P_0 represents the position of the foot end when it first enters the swing period, while P_h represents the projection of the hip joint position on the ground. Furthermore, p_f represents the final foot drop point, $T_{c\phi}$ is the time the leg will spend on the ground. Equation(8) can be used to calculate a swing leg trajectory using the method of Bezier interpolation, where t represents the phase change of swing leg, which ranges from 0 to 1.

$$P_{f,i} = P_{h,i} + \frac{T_{c\phi}}{2}\dot{p}_c \tag{7}$$

$$P_{t,i} = P_{h,i} + t^3(P_{f,i} - P_{h,i}) + 3t^2(1-t)(P_{f,i} - P_{h,i}) \tag{8}$$

3.2   Contact Leg Control

Due to the underactuated nature of centaur robots during locomotion, predictive control is essential in its gait control. Furthermore, the motion of centaur robots is highly nonlinear and uncertain, and can be affected by environmental factors such as irregular terrain and collisions with external objects. Traditional control methods may not be sufficient to meet the stability and performance requirements of the robot. Therefore, model predictive control is chosen for the contact phase control of centaur robot. A formulation of the MPC problem with finite horizon k can be written in the following form:

$$\min \sum_{i=0}^{k-1} ||x[i+1] - x^{ref}[i+1]||Q + ||u||R \tag{9}$$

$$s.t. Dynamics : x[i+1] = \hat{A}[i]x[i] + \hat{B}[i]u[i] \tag{10}$$

$$u_{swing} = 0 \tag{11}$$

The goal of problem is to bring the state x close to the reference and minimize the control input u. To achieve this, the objectives are weighted using diagonal matrices Q and R. The equation describes the condition where the swing leg exerts zero contact forces. The translation of the proposed model predictive control(MPC) problem into a Quadratic Programming(QP) form, which allows for efficient solving, can be found in various related and previous studies [8].

3.3   Gait Scheduling

The gait synchronization method between the centaur robot and the wearer is achieved through the control diagram shown in the Fig. 4. This method is based on three events, which enable the switching between swing phase and contact phase of the centaur robot to follow the wearer's gait. The three events will be sequentially described in detail:

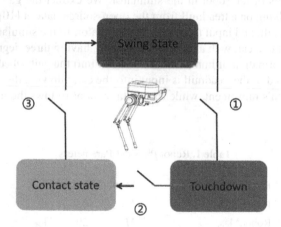

Fig. 4. To achieve the synchronization strategy, which means aligning the $i^{th}(0,1)$ leg of the wearer with the $j^{th}(1,0)$ leg of the robot in the same phase at the same moment. This task is achieved through the detection of three events.

① The event of the robot's swing leg making contact with the ground. The contact event of the robotic leg serves as an indicator of when the robot's swing leg has touchdown. This event is determined based on the knee joint current of the robot's swing leg. When the absolute value of the knee joint current reaches a peak, it is determined that the contact event of the robot's swing leg has occurred.

② The event of heel strike in the human gait information. The transition of the current swing leg of the centaur robot into the contact phase is determined by the heel strike event of the human's gait information. When the human's heel trike event is detected, the corresponding leg of the centaur robot that is currently in the swing phase is switched to the contact phase. The heel strike information of the human is obtained from the "gcLeft" and "gcRight" data in the open-source dataset. These datasets record the gait phase information of a person walking on a treadmill. Heel strike was determined from the motion capture data as the point of zero linear velocity of the heel marker.

③ The event of toe off in the human gait information. The transition of the robotic leg from the contact phase to the swing phase is triggered by the toe off event. This event signifies the initiation of leg swing in the human's gait, and consequently the robot's leg which is in the contact phase is switched to the swing phase.

4 Result

In this section, we will present highlighted results for validation of our proposed control framework. We validate our proposed approach in webots [11]. Table 1 presents several physical parameters of the robot in the simulator. We extract the gait phase information of human walking on a treadmill from the open-source dataset [10], along with the speed of the treadmill, and input them into the simulator. In the simulation, the centaur robot is connected to a car, with a joint between them having three degrees of freedom. The gait phase information of human walking is fed into the gait scheduler of the centaur, while the speed of the treadmill is input into the car, allowing the car to follow the speed of the human's movement, while the centaur robot follows the motion of the car as Fig. 5 show.

Table 1. Robot Physical Parameters

Parameter	Symbol	Value	Units
Robot High	h	0.9	m
Robot Mass	M	20	kg
Robot Inertia (body frame)	$I_{b,xx}$	0.1242	kg.m^2
	$I_{b,yy}$	0.5126	kg.m^2
	$I_{b,yy}$	0.4448	kg.m^2
thigh Link Length	l_{thigh}	0.58	m
knee Link Length	l_{knee}	0.52	m

To verify the function of the gait control method, the walking test of the centaur robot is carried out. As Fig. 6 show, by the coordination of the hip joint, the knee joint, and the ab/ad joint, each robotic leg can follow the human's gait as well as maintain stability in its own posture. In Fig. 6, when the human gait phase reaches 100%, it indicates the occurrence of the heel strike event during walking. The dots in the figure represent the robot leg in the swing phase making contact with the ground.

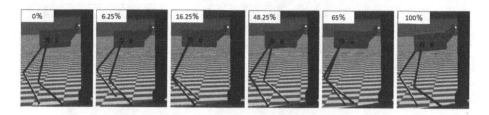

Fig. 5. A complete gait cycle of the centaur robot's locomotion.

Fig. 7 shows the variation of the three Euler angles(roll, pitch, yaw) of the centaur robot as it follows the human walking. From this, it can be found that the robot maintains stable pose during synchronized walking.

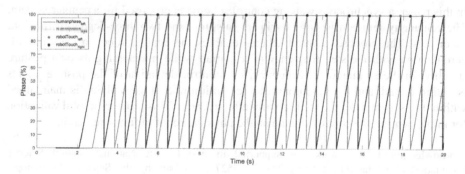

Fig. 6. Illustration of the contact point of the centaur robot and the human motion phase.

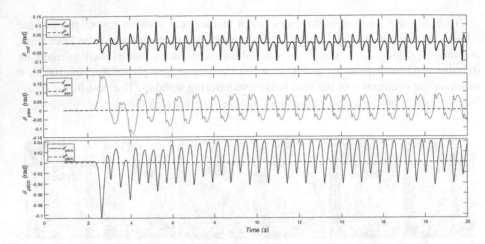

Fig. 7. The variations of the three Euler angles(roll, pitch, yaw) of the centaur robot during its walking motion. θ^r is the real value, and the θ^d is the desird value.

5 Conclusion

In this paper, a synchronous walking control scheme is proposed for a centaur system. The centaur system consists of a backpack, a spine, and two three-degree-of-freedom robot legs. The proposed control scheme enables the centaur robot to walk in synchronization with the step frequency of a human while maintaining its own posture stability. In the simulation environment, the control deviation of the posture angles is within 0.1rad, and the synchronization deviation rate of the walking is maintained within 0.05 s, achieving favorable control effectiveness. This provides a solid validation for implementing the control scheme on the physical robot in future research.

Acknowledgment. This work was supported in part by the National Natural Science Foundation of China [Grant U1913205, 52175272], in part by the Science, Technology, and Innovation Commission of Shenzhen Municipality [Grant: ZDSYS20200811143601004, JCYJ20220530114809021], and in part by the Stable Support Plan Program of Shenzhen Natural Science Fund under Grant 20200925174640002.

References

1. Leng, Y., Lin, X., Yang, L., Zhang, K., Chen, X., Fu, C.: A model for estimating the leg mechanical work required to walk with an elastically suspended backpack. IEEE Trans. Hum.-Mach. Syst. **52**(6), 1303–1312 (2022). https://doi.org/10.1109/THMS.2021.3137012
2. Yang, L., Xu, Y., Zhang, K., Chen, K., Fu, C.: Allowing the load to swing reduces the mechanical energy of the stance leg and improves the lateral stability of human walking. IEEE Trans. Neural Syst. Rehabil. Eng. **29**, 429–441 (2021). https://doi.org/10.1109/TNSRE.2021.3055624

3. Leng, Y., Lin, X., Lu, Z., Song, A., Yu, Z., Fu, C.: A model to predict ground reaction force for elastically-suspended backpacks. Gait Posture **82**, 118–125 (2020)
4. Yang, L., Zhang, J., Xu, Y., Chen, K., Fu, C.: Energy performance analysis of a suspended backpack with an optimally controlled variable damper for human load carriage. Mech. Mach. Theory **146**, 103738 (2020)
5. Wu, Y., Chen, K., Fu, C.: Effects of load connection form on efficiency and kinetics of biped walking. ASME J. Mech. Robot. **8**(6), 061015 (2016). https://doi.org/10.1115/1.4034464
6. Yang, L., Xiong, C., Hao, M., Leng, Y., Chen, K., Fu, C.: Energetic response of human walking with loads using suspended backpacks. IEEE/ASME Trans. Mechatron. **27**(5), 2973–2984 (2022). https://doi.org/10.1109/TMECH.2021.3127714
7. Zoss, A.B., Kazerooni, H., Chu, A.: Biomechanical design of the Berkeley lower extremity exoskeleton (BLEEX). IEEE/ASME Trans. Mechatron. **11**(2), 128–138 (2006). https://doi.org/10.1109/TMECH.2006.871087
8. Di Carlo, J., Wensing, P.M., Katz, B., Bledt, G., Kim, S.: Dynamic locomotion in the MIT cheetah 3 through convex model-predictive control. In: 2018 IEEE/RSJ International Conference on Intelligent Robots and Systems (IROS), Madrid, Spain, pp. 1–9 (2018). https://doi.org/10.1109/IROS.2018.8594448
9. Yang, P., et al.: A centaur system for assisting human walking with load carriage. In: 2022 IEEE/RSJ International Conference on Intelligent Robots and Systems (IROS), Kyoto, Japan, pp. 5242–5248 (2022). https://doi.org/10.1109/IROS47612.2022.9981394
10. Camargo, J., Ramanathan, A., Flanagan, W., Young, A.: A comprehensive, open-source dataset of lower limb biomechanics in multiple conditions of stairs, ramps, and level-ground ambulation and transitions. J. Biomech. **119**, 110320 (2021). https://doi.org/10.1016/j.jbiomech.2021.110320. Epub 2021 Feb 20. PMID: 33677231
11. Magyar, B., Forhecz, Z., Korondi, P.: Developing an efficient mobile robot control algorithm in the Webots simulation environment. In: IEEE International Conference on Industrial Technology, Maribor, Slovenia, 2003, vol. 1, pp. 179–184 (2003). https://doi.org/10.1109/ICIT.2003.1290264

Kinematics Analysis of the Wearable Waist Rehabilitation Robot

Kaicheng Qi[1,2,3], Kefei Fu[1,2,3], Jun Wei[1,2,3(✉)], Chenglei Lui[1,2,3], Jingke Song[1,2,3], and Jianjun Zhang[1,2,3]

[1] School of Mechanical Engineering, Hebei University of Technology, Tianjin 300401, China
jun.wei@hebut.edu.cn

[2] Intelligent Rehabilitation Device and Detection Technology Engineering Research Center of the Ministry of Education, Tianjin 300130, China

[3] Key Laboratory of Robot Perception and Human–Machine Fusion, Hebei Province, Tianjin 300130, China

Abstract. Patients with lumbar injuries are becoming more common and there is a shortage of intelligent rehabilitation equipment. A wearable lumbar rehabilitation robot for the treatment of low back pain disease is designed to help patients recover their lumbar motion. Firstly, the motion characteristics of the human lumbar spine and its range of motion is determined, and based on the size and range of motion of the human lumbar spine, the configuration design of the lumbar rehabilitation robot is proposed, and a 2-PUU/2-PUS parallel mechanism with three rotations and one translation is proposed; then the degree of freedom(DoF) analysis is carried out based on the screw theory; Finally, the kinematic inverse solution analysis is performed based on the Euler transformation and the geometrical characteristics of this parallel mechanism respectively, and validated based on the established virtual prototype model, and the results show that the mechanism motion characteristics meet the requirements of lumbar rehabilitation.

Keywords: Lumbar Spine Rehabilitation · Parallel Mechanism · Screw Theory · Kinematics

1 Introduction

With the development of society and changes in the pace of life and work, patients with low back pain are becoming more common and the patient group is becoming increasingly juvenile [1]. In terms of treatment, conservative treatment is often used clinically in addition to pharmacological and surgical treatment, which has an active role in the treatment and prevention of low back pain disease [2, 3]. Conservative therapy is mainly aimed at patients suffering from milder lumbar diseases can be rehabilitated by physicians with massage, cupping, acupuncture, traction, etc. Due to the fact that many patients with low back pain are not suitable for surgical treatment, conservative treatment of patients with low back pain plays an important role in clinical practice, but conservative treatment methods mostly rely on the medical level of physicians, which

H. Yang et al. (Eds.): ICIRA 2023, LNAI 14273, pp. 164–175, 2023.
https://doi.org/10.1007/978-981-99-6498-7_15

is uneven, with few experienced physicians and expensive treatment [4]. Therefore, researchers have proposed various lumbar rehabilitation robots to assist in the treatment of lumbar spine disorders.

The lumbar rehabilitation mechanism is mainly divided into traction bed type and wearable type, and the traction bed type such as Mikan V. et al. [5] and Wolf S G et al. [6] developed a lumbar rehabilitation mechanism that can perform traction in the prone position and can adapt to the rehabilitation needs of various lumbar spine diseases. Other scholars have proposed wearable lumbar traction robots to assist patients with lumbar traction therapy. Y. Sun et al. [7] developed a wearable lumbar rehabilitation robot with a biologically fused configuration design, which uses a six-degree-of-freedom parallel mechanism to form a human-machine system after wearing with the human lumbar spine to assist patients with lumbar assistance and rehabilitation training. X. Guo et al. [8] uses a 3-RPR parallel mechanism to achieve three DoF of horizontal, vertical, and rotational motion of the moving platform relative to the fixed platform in the coronal plane. Scoliosis is relieved or corrected by changing the position of the thorax relative to the pelvis in the coronal plane [9-10].

In sum, the existing traction bed is relatively large, the bio-fusion type will produce a large human-machine interaction force on the human body, and the three-degree-of-freedom rotation mechanism lacks the rehabilitation action of traction. Therefore, in this study, a robotic mechanism that meets the rehabilitation characteristics of the lumbar spine was designed from the motion characteristics and rehabilitation mechanism of the lumbar spine, and its kinematic analysis and validation are performed.

The paper is organized as follows: In Sect. 2, the physiological characteristics of the human lumbar spine are used as the basis for the lumbar spine rehabilitation robot configuration design. In Sect. 3, the kinematic position analysis of the 2-PUU/2-PUS parallel mechanism lumbar rehabilitation robot mechanism is performed, and then the correctness of the kinematic position analysis is verified based on the established virtual prototype. The Sect. 4 is the conclusion.

2 Motion Characteristics of Human Lumbar Spine and Rehabilitation Robot Configuration Design

2.1 Motion Characteristics of the Lumbar Spine

The motion of the human lumbar spine originates from the special characteristics of the intervertebral lumbar discectomy, which makes the lumbar spine have three directions of rotation, which are forward flexion and backward extension motion around the frontal axis, lateral flexion motion around the sagittal axis, and rotational motion around the vertical axis. as shown in Fig. 1.

The range of motion of the anthropometric range of motion in the standing position in healthy humans is greatest in forward flexion, about 90°, and in back extension, lateral flexion and rotation, about 30°. The range of motion will be reduced in patients with low back injuries [11].

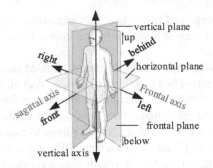

Fig. 1. Human fundamentals and reference axis

Traditional conservative treatment mainly consists of one-on-one massage by physicians. The most common and effective rehabilitation techniques in traditional massage are: pulling, posterior extension wrenching, oblique wrenching, and rotational reset. The rehabilitation robot can break them down into four basic movements: pulling, forward flexion and backward extension, lateral flexion and rotation.

2.2 Lumbar Spine Rehabilitation Robot Configuration Design

Configuration Design. The lumbar rehabilitation robot is a rehabilitation medical equipment, and its design should meet the motion characteristics of lumbar spine rehabilitation, it should also ensure that the rehabilitation process is safe and reliable and avoid harm to the lumbar spine. The lumbar spine motion model can be equated to the spherical joint (S) [12], and according to the features of the lumbar spine motion model, a rehabilitation robot mechanism was proposed.

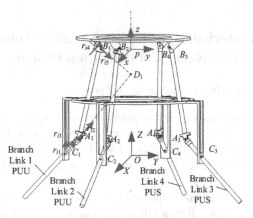

Fig. 2. 2-PUU/2-PUS parallel mechanism

The wearable lumbar rehabilitation robot mechanism proposed in this paper is a 2-PUU/2-PUS parallel mechanism, as shown in Fig. 2, which has four DoF of 3R1T, and it consists of a fixed platform, a moving platform, two PUU branch chains and two PUS branches, and each UPU branch includes one prismatic joint (P-joint) and two Universal joint (U-joints). Each PUS branch includes one P-joint and one U-joint and one spherical joint (S-joint). For the convenience of description, the U-joint connected to the P-joint below in the PUU branch chain is called the lower U-joint, and the U-joint connected to the moving platform above is called the upper U-joint. In its PUU branch link, the axis of the P-joint is called r_{i1}, and the two R-joints of the lower U-joint are called the first R-joint r_{i2} and the second R-joint r_{i3}, respectively; the two rotating subs of the upper U sub are called the third R-joint r_{i4} and the fourth R-joint r_{i5}, in addition, the 2-PUU/2-PUS parallel mechanism has the following geometric features: the axis of r_{i2} coincides with the axis of r_{i1}; the axis of r_{i3} is parallel to the axis of r_{i4}, and parallel to the fixed platform and the moving platform in the initial position; the r_{i1} axis of the two PUU branch links (branch link 1 and branch link 2) intersects with the r_{i5} axis in the initial position at the point D_i.

point C_i indicates the intersection of the axis of the moving sub of the i ($i = 1 \sim 4$) branch links of the 2-PUU/2-PUS parallel mechanism with the fixed platform, In Fig. 1; A_i indicates the center point of the lower U-joint in the i ($i = 1 \sim 4$) branch links; B_i indicates the center point of the upper U-joint in the i ($i = 1 \sim 2$) branch chain and the center point of the S-joint in the i ($i = 3 \sim 4$) branch links. The origin O of the fixed coordinate system $O\text{-}XYZ$ is located at the center of the plane formed by C_i points on the fixed platform, and the origin p of the moving platform $p\text{-}xyz$ is located at the center of the plane formed by B_i points on the moving platform.

DoF Analysis. The DoF analysis of the 2-PUU/2-PUS parallel mechanism is performed in accordance with the screw theory. Firstly, u brunching coordinate system $D_i\text{-}x_iy_iz_i$ is established, where D_i is the intersection point of r_{i1} and r_{i5} axes, z_i direction is the direction of r_{i1} axis, x_i direction is the direction of r_{i3} axis, and y_i direction is determined by the right-hand rule. The motion screw system of the PUU branch link of the 2-PUU/2-PUS parallel mechanism is shown in Fig. 3.

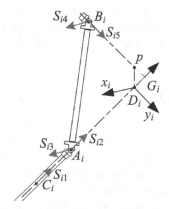

Fig. 3. The screw coordinate system of the PUU branch chain

Based on the screw theory, the motion screw system of the PUU branch link is as follows:

$$S_{i1} = (0; \ S_{i1})^T$$
$$S_{i2} = (S_{oA_i}; \ 0)^T$$
$$S_{i3} = (S_{i3}; \ r_{A_i} \times S_{i3})^T \qquad (1)$$
$$S_{i4} = (S_{i4}; \ r_{B_i} \times S_{i4})^T$$
$$S_{i5} = (S_{pB_i}; \ 0)^T$$

The screw system of the i-th branch link is obtained by solving the reverse screw according to the PUU branch chain motion screw system established by Eq. (1)

$$S_{c,i} = \{S_i\}^r = (S_{i4}; \ r_{G_i} \times S_{i4})^T \qquad (2)$$

From the inverse screw of Eq. (2), it can be seen that in the initial state, the screws system of the two PUU branches are two constrained force along the S_{i3} ($i = 1 \sim 2$) direction. The two PUS branch chain are 6DoF branched links do not produce constrained force or constrained couples. Therefore, the 2-PUU/2-PUS parallel mechanism has four DoF 3R1T, where the direction of 1T (translation) is always perpendicular to both restraining forces at the same time, that is, the direction of translation coincides with the common vertical line of the two constrained force.

3   Kinematic Analysis and Verification

Kinematic analysis is the relationship between the moving platform and the four driving branch chains that can be obtained, and is a prerequisite for analyzing the workspace, Jacobi matrix, and mechanical properties of the lumbar spine rehabilitation mechanism. Kinematic analysis is performed for the 2-PUU/2-PUS parallel mechanism, and the analysis of the mechanism is to solve the position relationship between the input and output components of the mechanism. In this Section, the kinematic inverse solution of the mechanism is solved by the traditional Euler transformation method and the geometric method based on the geometric properties of the 2-PUU/2-PUS parallel mechanism, respectively.

3.1   Inverse Kinematic Analysis Based on Euler Transformation

The coordinate systems O-XYZ and p-xyz are established in the fixed and moving platform of the 2-PUU/2-PUS parallel mechanism,as shown in Fig. 2, and the origin O of the fixed coordinate system is located at the center of the fixed platform circle in the plane formed by C_i, the Z-axis direction is perpendicular to the fixed platform upward, the X-axis points to the C_2 point, and the Y-axis is determined by the right-hand rule; the origin p of the moving coordinate system is located at the center of the moving platform circle in the plane formed by B_i, The z-axis direction is perpendicular to the moving platform upward, the x-axis points to point B_2, and the y-axis is determined by the right-hand rule. The driving joints is the moving joints on four branch links, which are realized by using electric actuators. The length of $C_iA_i(i = 1 \sim 4)$ is taken as the input variable, which is noted as l_1, l_2, l_3, l_4, and the position of the moving platform of the 2-PUU/2-PUS parallel mechanism is the output variable, which is the rotation angle of the moving platform around the X, Y, and Z axes, which is noted as α, β and γ, Since the moving platform has only one translation DoF, the x, y and z are coupled with each other, and any one of these variables can be represented by the other two variables.

In Eq. (4), c (*) = cos (*), s (*) = sin (*). The coordinates B_{i0} of the point B_i in the motion coordinate system and the coordinates of the point C_i in the fixed coordinate system are known, then the coordinates B_i of the point B_i in the fixed system are

$$B_i = R \cdot B_{i0} + P (i = 1 \sim 4) \tag{3}$$

where

$$R = Rotx(\alpha)Rotx(\beta)Rotx(\gamma)$$

$$= \begin{pmatrix} 1 & 0 & 0 \\ 0 & c\alpha & -s\alpha \\ 0 & s\alpha & c\alpha \end{pmatrix} \begin{pmatrix} c\beta & 0 & s\beta \\ 0 & 1 & 0 \\ -s\beta & 0 & c\beta \end{pmatrix} \begin{pmatrix} c\gamma & -s\gamma & 0 \\ s\gamma & c\gamma & 0 \\ 0 & 0 & 1 \end{pmatrix}$$

$$= \begin{pmatrix} c\beta c\gamma & -c\beta s\gamma & s\beta \\ c\alpha s\gamma + c\gamma s\alpha s\beta & c\alpha c\gamma - s\alpha s\beta s\gamma & -c\beta s\alpha \\ s\alpha s\gamma - c\alpha c\gamma s\beta & c\gamma s\alpha + c\alpha s\beta s\gamma & c\alpha c\beta \end{pmatrix} \tag{4}$$

$$P = \begin{pmatrix} x \\ y \\ z \end{pmatrix} \tag{5}$$

Because the point A_i is on the C_iA_i line and the length of the A_iB_i linkage is a fixed value d, therefore

$$C_iA_i = l_i \cdot S_{i1} + C_i \tag{6}$$

$$|A_iB_i| = d \tag{7}$$

where l_i is the length of C_iA_i, from(6)(7) linkage can be obtained l_i and A_i coordinates, but at this time A_i contains α, β, γ, x, y, z six parameter variables, and the body has four DoF, so it is required to eliminate two variables, this paper according to two PUU branch links, the x and y variables are eliminated according to the geometric property that S_{i4} is always perpendicular to A_iB_i ($i = 1 \sim 2$).

Firstly, the coordinate representation of the S_{i50} vector at the initial test position in the moving coordinate system is known, and the coordinate representation of S_{i5} in the fixed coordinate system can be obtained according to the rotation transformation matrix

$$S_{i5} = R \cdot S_{i50} \tag{8}$$

By S_{i5}, S_{i1} is always perpendicular to S_{i4}, so

$$S_{i4} = S_{i5} \times S_{i1} \tag{9}$$

Then according to the Eqs. (8,9)

$$S_{i4} \cdot A_i B_i = 0 \qquad (10)$$

The relationship between the moving platform position parameters represented by α, β, γ and z with the input quantities is obtained, which means that the kinematic position inverse solution of the 2-PUU/2-PUS parallel mechanism is obtained. Although the kinematic inverse solution of this parallel mechanism is obtained by the Euler transformation method, the result of the calculation is too complicated, so it is difficult to use the result of the kinematic inverse solution in the following analysis of the workspace, Jacobian matrix, mechanical properties, and so on, therefore, we consider the kinematic inverse solution method that can make the result simpler, and introduce the geometric solution of the 2-PUU/2-PUS parallel mechanism as follows.

3.2 Geometric Method of Inverse Kinematic Analysis

The 2-PUU/2-PUS parallel mechanism proposed in this paper has the following geometric characteristics, as shown in Fig. 4. The P-joint on four branch links on the fixed platform intersects at a point O, and the second rotational joint of U-joint on two PUU branch links on the moving platform intersects at a point p. The initial position is that the point O coincides with the point p. If point O always coincides with point p in the movement of the mechanism, the mechanism has the motion characteristics of 3 DOFs with continuous centering rotation around point O (p), and if point O is separated from point p during the movement of the mechanism, the mechanism has the motion characteristics of 3 rotations and 1 translation of 4 DOF, precisely because of this special geometric characteristic, the mechanism can carry out the pulling, posterior extension wrenching, oblique wrenching, rotational reset and other actions required for lumbar spine rehabilitation.

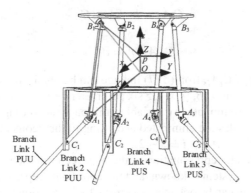

Fig. 4. Coordinate system for solving geometry

The fixed coordinate system and the moving coordinate system O-XYZ, p-xyz are established first. The point O of the fixed coordinate system is the intersection point of the translation joint of the four branched links, the direction of Y-axis is parallel to the direction of C_1C_3 and the direction of C_1C_3, the direction of Z-axis is perpendicular to the plane of the fixed platform and the direction is upward, and the X-axis is determined by the right-hand rule. The origin of the moving coordinate system p is at the intersection point of the second R-joint of the U-joint on the two PUU branch links, and the motion coordinate system overlaps with the fixed coordinate system under the initial position.

The coordinates of B_{i0} under the motion coordinate system are known from the geometric conditions. From the rotation transformation matrix R in Sect. 3.1, the coordinates of the motion coordinate system origin P under the fixed coordinate system origin O are $P = [x, y, z]^\mathsf{T}$, then the coordinates of B_i under the fixed coordinate system are

$$B_i = R \cdot B_{i0} + OP(i = 1 \sim 4) \tag{11}$$

Then the OB_i vector is known, because the OC_i vector is known, so it is easy to derive the angle between the two vectors OB_i and $OC_i, \angle B_i OC_i$, and because the length of A_iB_i is a constant d, so the length of OA_i can be found in the triangle$\angle B_iOC_i$ by the cosine theorem, that is

$$|OA_i|^2 + |OB_i|^2 - |A_iB_i|^2 = 2 \cdot |OA_i| \cdot |OB_i| \cdot \cos \angle B_iOC_i \tag{12}$$

The length of OA_i can be obtained from Eq. (12), because the length of OC_i is a constant, and then the length of C_iA_i can be obtained, and then the redundant variables x and y can be eliminated from Eqs. (8)(9)(10). Thereby obtaining the relationship between C_iA_i and α, β, γ, z, which is the geometric method inverse solution and verified with the results of the kinematic inverse solution based on Euler transformation, and the results are the same with them.

3.3 Kinematic Inverse Solution Validation

In this paper, with the simulation software RecurDyn and mathematical software MATLAB, the 2-PUU/2-PUS lumbar rehabilitation robot mechanism is made to perform four basic motions of lumbar pulling, forward flexion and back extension, lateral flexion and rotation, and the simulation values are analyzed with the theoretical values to verify the correctness of the kinematic inverse solution of the lumbar rehabilitation robot, and the verification process is as follows.

Firstly, given the parameters of this mechanism, $l_{A1B1} = l_{A2B2} = l_{A3B3} = l_{A4B4} = 450$ mm, $l_{OC1} = l_{OC2} = l_{OC3} = l_{OC4} = 370$ mm, $\angle OC_1A_1 = \angle OC_1A_1 = \angle OC_1A_1 = \angle OC_1A_1 = 40°$, The angle between the axis of the second revolute joint of the upper U sub of the two PUU branch chains and the moving platform is $45°$. The 3D model is drawn according to the mechanism scale parameters and imported into RecurDyn software to establish the virtual prototype model as Fig. 5. Secondly, constraints and drives are added in the RecurDyn virtual prototype to make the kinematic simulation analysis of the moving platform according to four basic motions of traction, forward flexion and backward extension, lateral flexion and rotation in lumbar rehabilitation, and set the motion time as 1s and step size as 0.01s to obtain the motion curve of the moving platform and the corresponding drive displacement curve. Finally, the kinematic equations of the moving platform are brought into the inverse kinematic solution and compared and verified with the help of MATLAB software.

Fig. 5. Virtual prototype model

Lateral Flexion Motion Around Y-axis. The moving platform motion inputs are $\alpha = 0$, $\beta = 10°\sin(2\pi t)$, $\gamma = 0$, $z = 524.27$ mm, and the generated curve is shown in Fig. 6.

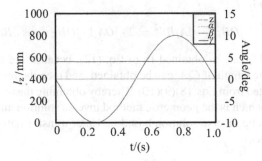

Fig. 6. Motion curve of moving platform (lateral flexion)

The displacement of the drive measured in RecurDyn is shown in Fig. 7 (a), and the corresponding drive displacement is obtained by the input parameters above into the kinematic inverse solution in MATLAB, as shown in Fig. 7 (b).

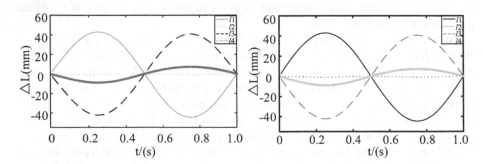

Fig. 7. (a) Simulation displacement curve; (b) Theoretical displacement curves

As can be seen in Fig. 7, the values and motion rules of the l_1, l_2, and l_3 theoretical displacement curves and the l_1, l_2, and l_3 simulation displacement curves are consistent, which proves that the kinematic inverse solution of the 2-PUU/2-PUS lumbar rehabilitation robot mechanism is correct. The motion rules is consistent with the lateral flexion motion rules, and it is also verified that this rehabilitation mechanism can perform the lateral flexion motion to meet the rehabilitation demand. Since this mechanism performs three kinds of motions: forward flexion and backward extension, lateral flexion and rotation, which are similar driving motions, the displacement curves for the two kinds of motions: forward flexion and backward extension and rotation are not shown again.

Pulling Motion Along Z-axis. The moving platform motion inputs are $\alpha = 0$, $\beta = 0$, $\gamma = 0$, $z = 524.27 + 10\sin(2\pi t)$, and the generated curve is shown in Fig. 8.

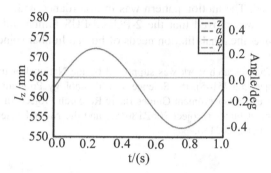

Fig. 8. Motion curve of moving platform (pulling motion)

The displacement of the drive measured in RecurDyn is shown in Fig. 9 (a), and the corresponding drive displacement is obtained by bringing the input parameters above into the kinematic inverse solution in MATLAB, as shown in Fig. 9(b).

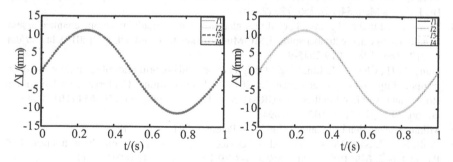

Fig. 9. (a) Simulation displacement curve; (b) Theoretical displacement curves

From Fig. 9, it can be seen that the theoretical displacement curves of l_1, l_2, and l_3 and the simulated displacement curves of l_1, l_2, and l_3 are consistent in value and motion pattern, which again proves that the kinematic inverse solution of the 2-PUU/2-PUS lumbar rehabilitation robot mechanism is correct and consistent with the pulling motion pattern, thus verifying that the rehabilitation mechanism can perform pulling motion to meet the rehabilitation needs.

4 Conclusion

In this paper, firstly, by analyzing the range of motion and rehabilitation mechanism of human lumbar spine, a configuration of a wearable lumbar spine rehabilitation robot was proposed, and its DoF and special position relationship of the mechanism were verified to meet the demand of human lumbar spine rehabilitation. Secondly, the kinematic position inverse solution based on Euler transformation and based on the geometric properties of the mechanism were carried out respectively, and the two inversed kinematics solutions can be verified with each other. Finally, the simulated values measured by establishing a virtual prototype in RecurDyn and the theoretical values calculated in MATLAB were compared and verified. The motion pattern was in accordance with the human lumbar spine motion, and it was proved that the 2-PUU/2-PUS lumbar rehabilitation robot mechanism could meet the rehabilitation needs of human lumbar spine.

Acknowledgment. This research work was supported by the National Natural Science Foundation of China (Project 52075145), the Science and Technology Program of Hebei (Project 20281805Z) and the Central Government Guides Basic Research Projects of Local Science and Technology Development Funds (Project 206Z1801G) and the Natural Science Foundation of Hebei Grant Numbers E2022202130.

References

1. Jan, H., Mark, J., Alice, K., et al.: What low back pain is and why we need to pay attention. Lancet **391**(10137), 2356–2367 (2018)
2. Huang, R., Ning, J., Chuter, V., et al.: Exercise alone and exercise combined with education both prevent episodes of low back pain and related absenteeism: systematic review and network meta-analysis of Randomised Controlled Trials (RCTS) aimed at preventing back pain. Br. J. Sports Med. **54**(13), 766–770 (2020)
3. Tadano, S., Tanabe, H., Arai, S., et al.: Lumbar mechanical traction: a biomechanical assessment of change at the lumbar spine. BMC Musculoskelet. Disord. **20**, 155 (2019). https://doi.org/10.1186/s12891-019-2545-9
4. Hung, Y.-H., Chen, P.-J., Lin, W.-Z.: Design factors and opportunities of rehabilitation robots in upper-limb training after stroke. In: 2017 14th International Conference on Ubiquitous Robots and Ambient Intelligence (URAI), Jeju, Korea (South), pp. 650–654 (2017). https://doi.org/10.1109/URAI.2017.7992694
5. Mikan, V.: Traction bed construction: U.S. Patent 3, 821, 953[P]. 1974–7–2
6. Wolf, S.G., Lossing, W.W.: Method and device for producing variable spinal traction: U.S. Patent 4, 602, 619. 1986-7-29https://doi.org/10.1007/978-1-349-08685-6_17
7. Sun, Y., Wang, H., Tian, Y.: The design and synchronous control of a new lower back exoskeleton. In: 2018 37th Chinese Control Conference (CCC), Wuhan, China, pp. 3949-3954 (2018). https://doi.org/10.23919/ChiCC.2018.8482960
8. Guo, X., Zhou, Z., Mai, J., Wang, Q.: Kinematic and kinetic analysis of 3-RPR based robotic lumbar brace. In: 2020 IEEE/ASME International Conference on Advanced Intelligent Mechatronics (AIM), Boston, MA, USA, pp. 1828–1833 (2020). https://doi.org/10.1109/AIM43001.2020.9158807

9. He, H., Li, J., Shen, H.: A New two -chain 2T1R parallel mechanism with zero coupling degree and its position analysis. In: 2021 3rd International Symposium on Robotics & Intelligent Manufacturing Technology (ISRIMT), Changzhou, China, pp. 487-490 (2021). https://doi.org/10.1109/ISRIMT53730.2021.9597109

10. Zhao, T.S., Li, Y.W., Chen, J., Wang, J.C.: A novel Four-DOF parallel manipulator mechanism and its kinematics. In: 2006 IEEE Conference on Robotics, Automation and Mechatronics, Bangkok, Thailand, pp. 1–5 (2006). https://doi.org/10.1109/RAMECH.2006.252672

11. Mullins, B.M.: Nikki Kelsall,Anatomy of the lumbar and sacral plexuses and lower limb peripheral neuropathies, Surgery (Oxford), 41(4), 193–199 (2023), ISSN 0263–9319

12. Sun,Y., Wang, H., Tian, Y.: The design and synchronous control of a new lower back exoskeleton. In: The 37th China Control Conference (2018)

3D Human Pose Estimation in Video for Human-Computer/Robot Interaction

Rongtian Huo[1], Qing Gao[2($\boxtimes$)], Jing Qi[1], and Zhaojie Ju[3]

[1] School of Communication and Information Engineering, Chongqing University of Posts and Telecommunications, Chongqing 400065, China

[2] School of Electronics and Communication Engineering, Shenzhen Campus of Sun Yat-sen University, Shenzhen 518107, China
gaoqing.ieee@gmail.com

[3] School of Computing, University of Portsmouth, Portsmouth PO13HE, UK

Abstract. 3D human pose estimation is widely used in motion capture, human-computer interaction, virtual character driving and other fields. The current 3D human pose estimation has been suffering from depth blurring and self-obscuring problems to be solved. This paper proposes a human pose estimation network in video based on a 2D lifting to 3D approach using transformer and graph convolutional network(GCN), which are widely used in natural language processing. We use transformer to obtain sequence features and use graph convolution to extract features between local joints to get more accurate 3D pose coordinates. In addition, we use the proposed 3D pose estimation network for animated character motion generation and robot motion following and design two systems of human-computer/robot interaction (HCI/HRI) applications. The proposed 3D human pose estimation network is tested on the Human3.6M dataset and outperforms the state-of-the-art models. Both HCI/HRI systems are designed to work quickly and accurately by the proposed 3D human pose estimation method.

Keywords: Human Pose Estimation · Human-Computer Interaction · Human-Robot Interaction · Deep Learning

1 Introduction

In HCI/HRI, machines must rely on various sensors to sense images, sounds, distances, movements, and other information when interacting with humans. However, studies [1] have shown that most communication between humans is non-verbal, with body movement communication accounting for another 55%. The use of body movement information requires motion capture systems, which use various devices to capture the user's motion trajectory and then process the trajectory data to generate animations or drive robot movements. Currently, the most mainstream motion capture systems based on 3D human pose estimation(HPE) are divided into four categories: mechanical, electromagnetic, acoustic, and optical. Each of the four technologies has its advantages and disadvantages. Optical devices are the least constraining for the user, do not require

H. Yang et al. (Eds.): ICIRA 2023, LNAI 14273, pp. 176–187, 2023.
https://doi.org/10.1007/978-981-99-6498-7_16

excessive equipment to be worn, and are the least affected by the environment. For example, the Microsoft-designed Kinect [2] relies on external depth sensors, working in the range of 0.5–4.5m. For users with long distances, stable pose capture is just not achievable. The conditions of use for optical cameras are relatively simple, and there are no strict requirements for hardware environment and distance. The optical motion capture system uses an optical camera to capture RGB images and later uses 3D human pose estimation network to extract joint features and obtain human motion pose. Among them, the performance of the 3D human pose estimation network is critical.

3D human pose estimation predicts the human joint positions in 3D space from images, videos, or other sources. Nowadays, the research on 3D human pose estimation based on monocular cameras mainly focuses on the one-stage and the two-stage human pose estimation method. One-stage method focuses on the end-to-end implementation of 3D human pose estimation, where the network maps directly to human pose coordinates in the case of input RGB images. For example, Li et al. [3] use a Convolutional Neural Network(CNN) to regress 3D coordinates through a joint multitasking framework. The two-stage approach makes use of intermediate estimation. The 2D coordinates are obtained by the currently more effective 2D pose estimation method, and then the 2D coordinates are mapped to 3D pose coordinates. This method is compatible with state-of-the-art 2D pose estimation methods. For example, Martinez et al. [4] design a simple pose detector containing only linear layers that can lift 2D coordinates to 3D. Pavllo et al. [5] capture temporal information on sequences by temporal convolutional neural networks. Zheng et al. [6] propose a purely transformer-based network to estimate 3D pose using the global learning capability of transformer. Wang et al. [7] design a GCN to utilize short-term and long-term motion information. We propose a human pose estimation detector that lifts from 2D to 3D, combining transformer and GCN to obtain 3D joint coordinates.

In this paper, we introduce temporal information to get better results. The global performance of the transformer is used to capture the features of temporal information, and GCN is introduced to focus on the graph topology relationship between joints and capture the graph structure features. After that, two HRI/HCI systems are designed using the proposed network. The HCI system feeds Human body movements from the optical camera into the neural network. Then 3D joint coordinates are obtained to generate virtual character animation. The HRI system uses an optical camera to capture RGB images and later uses a neural network to extract joint coordinates to realize robot motion following.

The contributions of this paper are: (1) The 3D human pose estimation network, Gformer, is proposed. Gformer captures global features using transformer and inter-joint features using GCN. (2) The HCI system is designed to use a combination of optical motion capture technology and neural networks to obtain accurate 3D human pose coordinates, which are bound to the avatar to generate the animation. The HRI system is designed to use body information for human-robot communication. The optical devices obtain human body images, and the neural networks extract joint information to realize robot motion following. (3)

Our proposed 3D human pose estimation network achieves MPJPE of 47.5mm with the Human3.6M dataset, and the proposed HCI/HRI systems can obtain accurate results quickly.

In the rest of the paper, Sect. 2 reviews the related work to 3D human pose estimation, HCI and HRI systems. Section 3 presents the design of the 3D human pose estimation network, Sect. 4 introduces the designs of the HCI/HRI systems. Section 5 explains the results of the experiments on the proposed human pose estimation network, and the HCI/HRI systems. Section 6 gives the conclusion and future work.

2 Related Work

2.1 Human Pose Estimation

Here we summarise the related work on monocular single-person HPE methods. The one-stage method is an end-to-end estimation method that estimates the 3D human pose coordinates directly from RGB images without intermediate estimation. The two-stage method is a method to lift from 2D to 3D. Researchers use the excellent performance of a 2D human pose detector to get 2D pose coordinates using RGB images or video streams as input. They use 2D pose corresponds as an intermediate estimate and use a 3D pose estimator to map 2D coordinates into 3D space to get accurate 3D pose coordinates. Our model follows the approach of lifting from 2D to 3D, so we focus on this aspect of the work in this section.

2D-to-3D Lifting HPE. Compared with the one-stage method, lifting from 2D to 3D has intermediate estimates, where the 2D coordinates are obtained from the intermediate estimates. Tekin et al. [8] design a two-branch framework to estimate human pose using 2D confidence maps and 3D images simultaneously, and propose a trainable fusion method to fuse features and 2D heat maps. Qammaz et al. [9] propose encoding 2D bones into BVH format for rendering 3D poses.

Transformer in 3D HPE. Since the transformer has shown excellent results in NLP, researchers have continued to introduce the transformer into other fields. Zheng et al. [6] propose the first network composed purely of the transformer in the field of 3D human pose estimation. Li et al. [10] propose a multi-hypothesis transformer model to synthesize the generated multi-hypothesis poses into the final 3D pose.

GCN in 3D HPE. The input of the two-stage method is 2D pose coordinates, which have irregular structural representation compared to the image's grid structure. Some researchers expect to introduce GCN to solve these problems. Ge et al. [11] propose a GCN-based method to estimate 3D hand and human pose from monocular RGB images. Zeng et al. [12] construct a dynamic skeleton graph and propose a hierarchical channel compression fusion layer.

2.2   Human-Computer/Robot Interaction

Human-Computer Interaction. In recent years, with the explosion of various 3D movies and animation, people have begun to focus on creating virtual characters. These characters are different from those in traditional animation. They rely on various devices to capture the movements of actors and use this captured information to generate virtual characters. The current mainstream motion capture devices are divided into four types: mechanical, acoustic, electromagnetic, and optical. Mechanical, acoustic, and electromagnetic devices are more bound to the user's actions and vulnerable to the environment. The optical capture system can capture motion by tracking the key points in the human body. The camera captures the human's movements, and computer technology converts the captured movements into the coordinates of key points. The optical system is not affected by the environment. Actors are also able to do more complex movements in a wider range. Pullen et al. [13] use motion capture data to generate keyframes to create animations. Wei et al. [14] use motion capture techniques to extract skeletal relationships to generate animations.

Human-Robot Interaction. Initially, some researchers [15] use Bayes' theorem to infer the real meaning of the user's operation. Gao et al. [16] designed a parallel network to distinguish between left and right hands and the network is employed for HRI based on hand gestures. Koppula et al. [17] control the assistive robot to by predicting the user's activities. Gao et al. [18] propose a network of fused feature maps for gesture recognition and apply it to space HRI. Cheng et al. [19] recognize human intent by capturing human gesture information and then driving robot movements from the acquired user intent. Gao et al. [20] use multimodal data to identify gesture features in HRI.

3   3D Human Pose Estimation Network

3.1   Detailed Architecture of the Proposed Network

As shown in Fig. 1, we propose a 3D human pose estimation network by lifting from 2D to 3D, taking 2D sequence frames as input, and finally outputting 3D human pose coordinates. The spatial transformer block (STB) extracts inter-joint features, and the temporal transformer block (TTB) extracts temporal features.

Spatial Transformer Block. We introduce a new transformer structure [21]. As shown in Fig. 1, the 2D coordinates are input to STB, which captures the features between joints. First, the ChebGconv layer, which replaces the Embedding layer, is used to upscale the input 2D coordinate extraction features. Then the LayerNorm layer is used to normalize them, and the self-attention between joints is input to the self-attention layer to learn the relationship between joints in each frame. Then, the feedforward network of MLP is replaced by Lam-Gconv

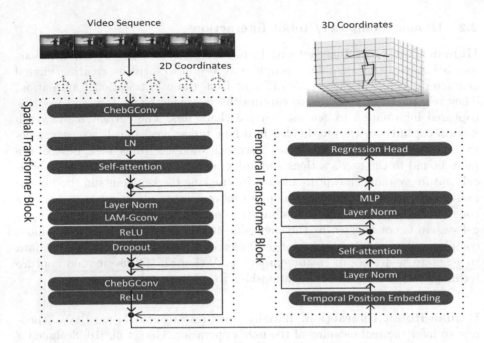

Fig. 1. Overview of the proposed Network.

[22] to refine further and extract the graph structure information between joints. Finally, the GCN structure is used again in the ChebGConv layer to extract the joint features.

Temporal Transformer Block. Our network architecture in this block differs from STB, still using MLP as a feedforward network. The purpose of this part is to learn the relationship between frame sequences. So the high-dimensional feature input temporal position embedding of frame sequences is encoded. After that, global learning is performed for the relationship between frame sequences using the self-attention mechanism. The self-attention layer can focus on the temporal correlation between the overall input sequences.

Regression Head. The input is a series of video frames; the output is the predicted center frame. The center frame is obtained by a weighted average of the features in a series of feature sequences.

3.2   Loss Function

We use mean per joint position error (MPJPE) as the loss function to supervise the training network. The purpose of the loss function is to minimize the errors between the predictions and the ground truth. The loss function equation is shown below:

$$L = \frac{1}{J} \sum\nolimits_{i=1}^{J} \| \mathrm{p}_i - \widehat{p}_i \|_2 \tag{1}$$

where J is the number of joints, $\widehat{p}_i$ and p_i are the ground truth and estimated 3D positions of ith joint in the current pose respectively.

4   Human-Computer/Robot Interaction System

4.1   Human-Computer Interaction System

Figure 2 illustrates the HCI system using an optical motion capture device. The actor's movements are captured by an optical camera, and the images are processed into 2D pose coordinates and fed into the network. An avatar is designed by Unity. The communication between the local system and Unity is established using socket to transfer the 3D pose coordinates from the network P(h) to Unity P(u): P(h)->P(u). The mapping equation is shown below:

$$\begin{cases} P(u)_{x,j} = P(u)_{x,j-1} + \lambda \left[P(h)_{x,j} - P(h)_{x,j-1} \right] \\ P(u)_{y,j} = P(u)_{y,j-1} + \lambda \left[P(h)_{y,j} - P(h)_{y,j-1} \right] \\ P(u)_{z,j} = P(u)_{z,j-1} + \lambda \left[P(h)_{z,j} - P(h)_{z,j-1} \right] \end{cases} \tag{2}$$

where $(P(u)_{x,j}, P(u)_{y,j}, P(u)_{z,j})$ is the 3D joint coordinates of the virtual character mapped into Unity at the moment j, and $(P(h)_{x,j}, P(h)_{y,j}, P(h)_{z,j})$) is the 3D coordinates of the human joint estimated by the pose estimation network at the moment j. The vector λ is the scaling factor.

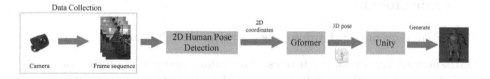

Fig. 2. Overview of the HCI system.

4.2   Human-Robot Interaction System

Figure 3 plots the HRI system. The process includes data acquisition, pose estimation, and robot interaction. The HRI system uses a camera to get the human motion and a pose estimation network to get the 3D coordinates. Finally, the 3D

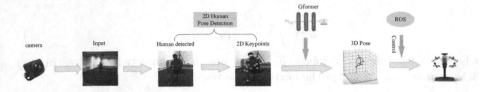

Fig. 3. Overview of the HRI system.

coordinates are transmitted to the robot system, and the ROS system controls the robot to complete HRI. The conventional mapping methods are joint angle mapping and Cartesian space-based mapping. The joint angle-based mapping maps each joint angle to a robot joint through an angle transformation matrix. This method is simple and low latency, but it isn't easy to achieve satisfactory control. Therefore, we still choose Cartesian space-based mapping in this system. The mapping equation is shown as follows:

$$\begin{cases} P(r)_{x,j} = P(r)_{x,j-1} + \eta \left[P(h)_{x,j} - P(h)_{x,j-1} \right] \\ P(r)_{y,j} = P(r)_{y,j-1} + \eta \left[P(h)_{y,j} - P(h)_{y,j-1} \right] \\ P(r)_{z,j} = P(r)_{z,j-1} + \eta \left[P(h)_{z,j} - P(h)_{z,j-1} \right] \end{cases} \quad (3)$$

where $(P(r)_{x,j}, P(r)_{y,j}, P(r)_{z,j})$ is the 3D joint coordinates of the Robot at the moment j, and $(P(h)_{x,j}, P(h)_{y,j}, P(h)_{z,j})$ is the 3D coordinates of the human joint estimated by the pose estimation network at the moment j. The vector η refers to the scaling factor.

5   Experiments

5.1   Experiments on Human Pose Estimation Network

Dataset and Evaluation Metrics. We trained and tested on the commonly used dataset Human3.6M [23]. Human3.6M is an indoor motion dataset containing eleven people performing seventeen movements. Gformer trained on performers S1, S5, S6, S7, and S8 and tested on S9 and S11. We evaluate the effect of the proposed network by MPJPE, which is the average Euclidean distance between all the real joints and the predicted joints in each image frame.

Experiment Implementation. We used Pytorch and Python to implement our proposed network, Gformer. The model was trained and tested on a workstation with two NVIDIA RTX 2080ti GPU, and Adam was chosen as the optimizer. We trained for 80 epochs, with the learning rate set to 5e-5, using the 2D pose coordinates output from the cascaded pyramid network (CPN) as input.

Table 1. MPJPE results of various actions in millimeters on Human3.6M. 2D poses detected by CPN are used as input. The best result is shown in bold.

	Dir	Disc	Eat	Greet	Phone	Photo	Pose	Purch	Sit	SitD	Smoke	Wait	WalkD	Walk	WalkT	Average
Zhao et al. [21]	45.2	50.8	48.0	50.0	54.9	65.0	48.2	47.1	60.2	70.0	51.6	48.7	54.1	39.7	43.1	51.8
Pallo et al. [5]	47.1	50.6	49.0	51.8	53.6	61.4	49.4	47.4	59.3	67.4	52.4	49.5	55.3	39.5	42.7	51.8
Lutz et al. [24]	45.0	48.8	46.6	49.4	53.2	60.1	47.0	46.7	59.6	67.1	51.2	47.1	53.8	39.4	42.4	50.5
Cai et al. [25]	44.6	47.4	45.6	48.8	50.8	59.0	47.2	**43.9**	57.9	**61.9**	49.7	46.6	51.3	37.1	39.4	48.8
Lin et al. [26]	**42.8**	48.6	45.1	48.0	51.0	**56.5**	46.2	44.9	56.5	63.9	49.6	46.2	50.5	37.9	39.5	48.5
Zhai et al. [27]	43.9	47.6	45.5	48.9	50.1	58.0	46.2	44.5	**55.7**	62.9	49.0	45.8	51.8	38.0	39.9	48.5
Gformer	45.13	**46.22**	**43.72**	**46.56**	**50.05**	56.96	**46.11**	44.66	59.41	68.70	**48.40**	**44.74**	50.08	**32.94**	**34.10**	**47.85**

Table 2. The effectiveness of different components. S: Spatial trasformer block, T: Temporal transformer block. The best result is shown in bold

Input length (f)	S	T	MPJPE
81	✓	✗	51.8
81	✗	✓	49.6
81	✓	✓	**47.85**

Comparison with the State-of-the-Art. Table 1 compares our model with other state-of-the-art models, using the data derived from CPN as a 2D attitude detector as model input. We also report the results for fifteen maneuvers. We achieved 47.85mm by MPJPE, which shows that our Gformer is better than the previous method.

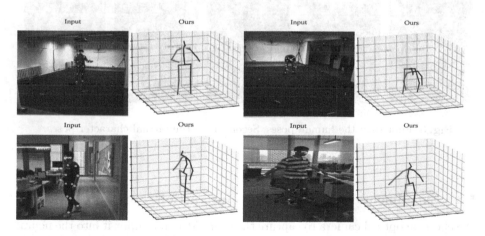

Fig. 4. Qualitative Results.

Impact of Each Component. As shown in Table 2, we conducted ablation experiments for STB and TTB. We set the input frame to 81 frames and the number of layers for STB and TTB to 4. The MPJPE is 51.8mm when only STB is available and 49.6mm when only TTB is available. When STB and TTB are combined, the MPJPE improves to 47.85mm. So it can be seen that each block we introduced has an effect.

Qualitative Results. As shown in Fig. 4, we can see the visualization results of the model. After training on Human3.6M, our model can estimate the 3D pose of the actor accurately and has good results in natural scenes.

5.2   Experiments on Human-Computer Interaction

Due to our proposed two-stage network, the HCI system uses YOLOV3 [28] and ALphapose [29] as a 2D pose detector. The motion video captured by the RGB camera was input to the 2D pose detector. The detector extracted the 2D pose coordinates as the input data of Gformer and outputs the 3D pose. The animation effect generated by the HCI system can be seen in Fig. 5.

Fig. 5. First row: the human poses. Second row: the virtual character poses.

5.3   Experiments on Human-Robot Interaction

We chose an optical camera to capture the user video and input it into the neural network. YOLOV3 first detected the human body. ALphapose detected the 2D pose, and then the 3D pose was detected by Gformer. Then the coordinates were transferred to the robot system to control the robot via the ROS platform. The effect is shown in Fig. 6.

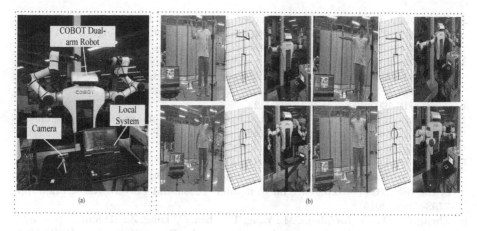

Fig. 6. The experimental equipment and results: (a) The HRI platform. (b) The HRI experiments.

6   Conclusion and Future Work

In this paper, we have proposed a 3D human pose estimation network introducing transformer and GCN. The graph information between each frame of joints is captured using GCN, and sequence features are captured using transformer, and use this network to design an HCI system and an HRI system. The 3D pose estimation network can estimate the human pose well, and the MPJPE achieved 47.85. The two systems designed by the network could also generate virtual character animations and control robots, which can work with high accuracy and speed.

In the future, the speed and accuracy of HCI/HRI will be increasingly required. We will focus on lightweight networks, expecting to improve inference speed while maintaining inference accuracy, which can be better applied in HCI/HRI. In practical applications, there is noise in the captured video data and the results generated by the 2D detector. We will also focus on modeling the input noise to mitigate its effects.

Acknowledgement. This work was supported in part by the National Natural Science Foundation of China (62006204, 52075530), the Guangdong Basic and Applied Basic Research Foundation (2022A1515011431), and Shenzhen Science and Technology Program (RCBS20210609104516043, JSGG20210802154004014). This work is also partially supported by the AiBle project co-financed by the European Regional Development Fund.

References

1. Mandal, F.B.: Nonverbal communication in humans. J. Hum. Behav. Soc. Environ. **24**(4), 417–421 (2014)

2. Fankhauser, P., Bloesch, M., Rodriguez, D., Kaestner, R., Hutter, M., Siegwart, R.: Kinect v2 for mobile robot navigation: evaluation and modeling. In: 2015 International Conference on Advanced Robotics (ICAR), pp. 388–394. IEEE (2015)
3. Li, S., Chan, A.B.: 3D human pose estimation from monocular images with deep convolutional neural network. In: Cremers, D., Reid, I., Saito, H., Yang, M.-H. (eds.) ACCV 2014. LNCS, vol. 9004, pp. 332–347. Springer, Cham (2015). https://doi.org/10.1007/978-3-319-16808-1_23
4. Martinez, J., Hossain, R., Romero, J., Little, J.J.: A simple yet effective baseline for 3D human pose estimation. In: Proceedings of the IEEE International Conference on Computer Vision, pp. 2640–2649 (2017)
5. Pavllo, D., Feichtenhofer, C., Grangier, D., Auli, M.: 3D human pose estimation in video with temporal convolutions and semi-supervised training. In: Proceedings of the IEEE/CVF Conference on Computer Vision and Pattern Recognition, pp. 7753–7762 (2019)
6. Zheng, C., Zhu, S., Mendieta, M., Yang, T., Chen, C., Ding, Z.: 3D human pose estimation with spatial and temporal transformers. In: Proceedings of the IEEE/CVF International Conference on Computer Vision, pp. 11656–11665 (2021)
7. Wang, J., Yan, S., Xiong, Y., Lin, D.: Motion guided 3D pose estimation from videos. In: Vedaldi, A., Bischof, H., Brox, T., Frahm, J.-M. (eds.) ECCV 2020. LNCS, vol. 12358, pp. 764–780. Springer, Cham (2020). https://doi.org/10.1007/978-3-030-58601-0_45
8. Tekin, B., Márquez-Neila, P., Salzmann, M., Fua, P.: Learning to fuse 2D and 3D image cues for monocular body pose estimation. In: Proceedings of the IEEE International Conference on Computer Vision, pp. 3941–3950 (2017)
9. Qammaz, A., Argyros, A.A.: MocapNET: ensemble of SNN encoders for 3D human pose estimation in RGB images. In: BMVC, p. 46 (2019)
10. Li, W., Liu, H., Tang, H., Wang, P., Van Gool, L.: MHFormer: multi-hypothesis transformer for 3D human pose estimation. In: Proceedings of the IEEE/CVF Conference on Computer Vision and Pattern Recognition, pp. 13147–13156 (2022)
11. Ge, L., et al.: 3D hand shape and pose estimation from a single RGB image. In: Proceedings of the IEEE/CVF Conference on Computer Vision and Pattern Recognition, pp. 10833–10842 (2019)
12. Zeng, A., Sun, X., Yang, L., Zhao, N., Liu, M., Xu, Q.: Learning skeletal graph neural networks for hard 3D pose estimation. In: Proceedings of the IEEE/CVF International Conference on Computer Vision, pp. 11436–11445 (2021)
13. Pullen, K., Bregler, C.: Motion capture assisted animation: texturing and synthesis. In: Proceedings of the 29th Annual Conference on Computer Graphics and Interactive Techniques, pp. 501–508 (2002)
14. Wei, Y.: Deep-learning-based motion capture technology in film and television animation production. Secur. Commun. Netw. 2022 (2022)
15. Yu, X., et al.: Bayesian estimation of human impedance and motion intention for human-robot collaboration. IEEE Trans. Cybernet. 51(4), 1822–1834 (2019)
16. Gao, Q., Liu, J., Ju, Z., Zhang, X.: Dual-hand detection for human-robot interaction by a parallel network based on hand detection and body pose estimation. IEEE Trans. Industr. Electron. 66(12), 9663–9672 (2019)
17. Koppula, H.S., Saxena, A.: Anticipating human activities using object affordances for reactive robotic response. IEEE Trans. Pattern Anal. Mach. Intell. 38(1), 14–29 (2015)
18. Gao, Q., Liu, J., Ju, Z.: Robust real-time hand detection and localization for space human-robot interaction based on deep learning. Neurocomputing 390, 198–206 (2020)

19. Cheng, Y., Yi, P., Liu, R., Dong, J., Zhou, D., Zhang, Q.: Human-robot interaction method combining human pose estimation and motion intention recognition. In: 2021 IEEE 24th International Conference on Computer Supported Cooperative Work in Design (CSCWD), pp. 958–963. IEEE (2021)
20. Gao, Q., Liu, J., Ju, Z.: Hand gesture recognition using multimodal data fusion and multiscale parallel convolutional neural network for human-robot interaction. Expert. Syst. **38**(5), e12490 (2021)
21. Zhao, W., Wang, W., Tian, Y.: Graformer: graph-oriented transformer for 3D pose estimation. In: Proceedings of the IEEE/CVF Conference on Computer Vision and Pattern Recognition, pp. 20438–20447 (2022)
22. Kipf, T.N., Welling, M.: Semi-supervised classification with graph convolutional networks. arXiv preprint: arXiv:1609.02907 (2016)
23. Ionescu, C., Papava, D., Olaru, V., Sminchisescu, C.: Human3. 6m: large scale datasets and predictive methods for 3D human sensing in natural environments. IEEE Trans. Pattern Anal. Mach. Intell. **36**(7), 1325–1339 (2013)
24. Lutz, S., Blythman, R., Ghosal, K., Moynihan, M., Simms, C., Smolic, A.: Jointformer: single-frame lifting transformer with error prediction and refinement for 3d human pose estimation. In: 2022 26th International Conference on Pattern Recognition (ICPR), pp. 1156–1163. IEEE (2022)
25. Cai, Y., et al.: Exploiting spatial-temporal relationships for 3D pose estimation via graph convolutional networks. In: Proceedings of the IEEE/CVF International Conference on Computer Vision, pp. 2272–2281 (2019)
26. Lin, H., Chiu, Y., Wu, P.: AMPose: alternately mixed global-local attention model for 3D human pose estimation. In: ICASSP 2023–2023 IEEE International Conference on Acoustics, Speech and Signal Processing (ICASSP), pp. 1–5. IEEE (2023)
27. Zhai, K., Nie, Q., Ouyang, B., Li, X., Yang, S.: HopFIR: hop-wise GraphFormer with intragroup joint refinement for 3D human pose estimation. arXiv preprint: arXiv:2302.14581 (2023)
28. Redmon, J., Farhadi, A.: YOLOV3: an incremental improvement. arXiv preprint: arXiv:1804.02767 (2018)
29. Fang, H.S., et al.: AlphaPose: whole-body regional multi-person pose estimation and tracking in real-time. IEEE Trans. Pattern Anal. Mach. Intell. (2022)

A Real-Time AGV Gesture Control Method Based on Body Part Detection

Yuhang Xu[1], Qing Gao[2(✉)], Xiang Yu[1], and Xin Zhang[3]

[1] School of Communication and Information Engineering, Chongqing University of
Posts and Telecommunications, Chongqing 400065, China
[2] School of Electronics and Communication Engineering, Shenzhen Campus of Sun
Yat-sen University, Shenzhen 518107, China
gaoqing.ieee@gmail.com
[3] State Key Laboratory of Robotics, Shenyang Institute of Automation, Chinese
Academy of Science, Shenyang 110016, China

Abstract. The intelligent control of Automated Guided Vehicles (AGV) has essential research significance and application in logistics loading, unmanned driving, and emergency rescue. As an idealized human-computer interaction method, gesture has tremendous expressive power. Therefore, the gesture-based AGV control method is the mainstream. However, In a complex environment, noise interference can affect the precise and real-time control of AGV. To deal with this problem, a real-time AGV gesture control method based on human body part detection is proposed. We design a simple AGV control method based on human gestures by the relative relationship between human body parts in space. We extend a new branch on the Fully Convolutional One-Stage Object Detection (FCOS), which constrains the detection range of human parts. This method subtly associates the human parts with the human body, which vastly improves the anti-interference capability of gesture recognition. We train the network end-to-end on the COCO Human Parts dataset and achieve a detection accuracy of 35.4% of human parts. In addition, We collect a small dataset for validating the gesture recognition method designed in this paper and achieves an accuracy of 96.1% with a detection speed of 17.23 FPS. Our method achieves precise and convenient control of AGVs.

Keywords: AGV · FCOS · Human part detection · Gesture recognition

1 Introduction

AGV is an automated program-guided transport vehicle [1,2] equipped with optical, radar, vision, and other sensors to achieve positioning and navigation, enabling it to move along a predetermined planning route. However, AGV positioning and navigation require expensive LIDAR, depth cameras, and GPS. In addition, AGV requires a complex map or navigation algorithm design to adapt to the corresponding environment. In order to control AGVs more conveniently, n real-time, and accurately, gesture-based AGV control methods have been proposed in two ways. (1)Wearable device-based gesture AGV control methods [3, 4]: wearable devices integrate sensors such as bending sensors, inertial sensors, and electrode sensors. These sensors are responsible for collecting information on the movement trajectory and gesture of the hand and converting these signals into corresponding control commands. Although this method is fast and accurate, the design process is complex. It requires additional commands calibration and high hardware costs as the basis. (2)Vision-based gesture AGV control methods [5, 6]: with the application of deep learning in computer vision, researchers build CNN networks to classify gestures and convert gesture signals to control the AGV. Such methods are simpler to implement and achieve good performance. However, vision-based methods are often affected by noise, such as illumination and occlusion, which can affect the correct classification of gestures. In addition, can impact the correct control of the AGV.

In order to solve the above existing problems, a real-time AGV gesture control method based on body part detection is proposed. The control of AGV requires stable signals as input, so we design a gesture recognition method for controlling AGV based on the relative position of the left and right hands relative to the face. The human part-based gesture recognition methods are more sample and enable real-time and accurate control of the AGV. In addition, to balance the accuracy and speed of human part detection, we use the anchor-free network FCOS as the basic framework for human part detection and extend a new branch based on it. In the new branch, we focus on the body part based on the human bounding boxes. We combine the gesture recognition and body part detection methods proposed in this paper. The gesture commands from operators and unrelated individuals can be effectively distinguished, improving the AGV control's anti-interference.

To summarize, this paper makes the following contributions:(1) We extend a new benchmark based on FCOS, and the new branch regresses and classifies the human body parts within each human bounding box. The method correlates the body parts with each person. Combined with the hand gesture control method proposed in this paper, it enables the AGV trolley to distinguish which person the command comes from and avoid the interference of an irrelevant person. (2)We design the gesture recognition method based on the relative position relationship of the left and right hands relative to the face. The method contains eight different hand gestures. (3)We design an experiment to control AGV by different gestures to verify the performance of our method. Through the experiment, the accuracy rate reached 35.4% on the COCO Human Parts dataset, and the gesture control method reached 96.1% recognition rate with FPS of 17.23, achieving correct and convenient control of AGV.

The rest of the paper is structured as follows: Sect. 2 reviews the related research status of human part detection and gesture-based human-robot interaction method Sect. 3 presents the overall network structure of our human part detection method Sect. 4 introduces the vision-based gesture AGV control method. Section 5 explains the results of the experiments on the human part detector, vision-based gesture AGV control method. Section 6 gives a summary of the work.

2 Related Work

2.1 Human Part Detection Method

Anchor-Free and Anchor-Based Detector. CNN-based object detection can be divided into anchor-based and anchor-free methods. The anchor-based [7–9]method requires predefined attributes of bounding boxes, such as size, aspect ratio, and the number of anchor boxes. Then it generates region proposal boxes based on the predefined anchor and performs object classification and bounding box offset regression on these proposals. Although this method achieves substantial detection accuracy, the hyperparameters of the complex anchor constrain the generalization ability. The anchor-free detector [10–12] discards the complex design of predefined anchor hyperparameters and predicts the bounding box based on the centroid. FCOS is an anchor-free detection method analyzed at the pixel level, which uses centroids to predict and classify 4D vectors, representing the distance from the centroid to the bounding box. This type of method combines the advantages of one-stage and two-stage object detection methods, balancing the speed and accuracy of detection. Therefore, this paper uses FCOS as the basic framework for building human part detection methods.

Body Part Detection Method. Cascaded stages design methods are widely used in human parts detection tasks recently such as [13,14], which is based on the principle of designing multi-stage networks to progressively classify and regress the targets. In the first step, simple networks are used to filter out the useless background, and then more complex networks are used for more detailed detection or supervision. However, most of the methods treat the objects as independent objects and ignore the correlation between them. The top-down network structure [15,16] detects objects in a coarse-to-fine way. Acquiring the body's bounding box by CNN and FCN in the first stage, and further classifying and regressing objects on the basis of these boxes. The methods effectively resist background interference and subtly correlate these multi-level targets. We follow this top-down approach to structure and design an effective instance-level human part detection network based on FCOS.

2.2 Human Part Detection Method

Wearable Device-Based Gesture AGV Control Methods. Lee et al. [17]collect human hand sMEG signals by designing a bipolar stretchable electrode array sensing device and recognize human gestures based on these electrical signals. They achieve 97% accuracy in the experiment, which is able to control an unmanned vehicle in real-time. Yu et al. [18]use flexible and inertial sensors on the data glove to collect gesture data. They achieve 100% accuracy in gesture recognition, which can control the AGV accurately in real-time. Although this method has a high gesture recognition accuracy, it is inconvenient to use and requires expensive hardware costs to support it.

Vision-Based Gesture AGV Control Methods. Chua et al. [19]use YOLOv3 to train the collected gesture dataset and achieved 96.68%gesture recognition accuracy. They convert the obtained gesture categories into corresponding control commands, which achieve good results in multimedia human-AGV interaction. Zhang et al. [20] recognize gesture movements by detecting 21 key points on the hand, achieving 93% accuracy in a dataset containing eight types of drone control gestures. However, these methods require more parameters and are susceptible to environmental interference. We need gestures that are stable enough not to be disturbed by environmental factors, and they should contain semantic information that the AGV system can easily understand. Therefore, we follow this vision-based gesture human-AGV interaction method and propose the gesture recognition method based on human body parts.

3   The Network Structure of Human Part Detector

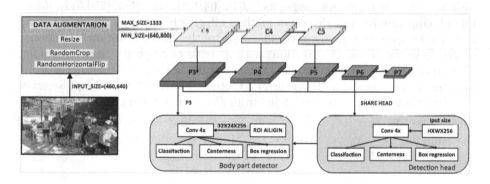

Fig. 1. Architecture of human body part detecor

Fig. 1 shows the overall pipeline of the human body part detection network designed in this paper. We expand on FCOS and explore a lightweight human part detector similar to anchor free. The network consists of an FPN+ feature extraction network, a detection head, and a human part detector. RetinaNet-50 is the backbone to extract feature information of RGB images. Then, the FPN further fuses the features of the extracted features map and outputs six feature layers P3–P7. The detection head is designed for detecting the bounding box of the human instance. The body part detector is designed for further body part detection based on the bounding box of the human instance.

Feature Extracted and Data Augmentation. To enhance the network's robustness and avoid overfitting, a series of data augmentation methods are applied to the input images. The image size in the dataset is (460, 640). In the first step, we set the short edge of the image to an interval (640, 800) and the long edge maximum to 1333. In the second step, we flip the image horizontally and crop it randomly.

Backbone+FPN. We set the RetinaNet-50 as the backbone. First, the RGB image undergoes a series of convolution calculations by backbone to generate several feature maps C3, C4, and C5. Then, the Feature Pyramid Network (FPN) network [21] further fuses the features of the feature map and outputs seven feature layers as P3, P4, P5, P6, P7.P6, and P7 are generated by P5 downsampling. According to each feature layer's receptive field, we set each layer's effective stride to 8,16,32,64,128. The introduction of FPN increases the detection performance of the network for multi-scale objects.

Detection Head. The detection head is an advanced anchor-free structure of Fully Convolutional Networks (FCN). The detection head not only effectively avoids the complex process of setting predefined hyperparameters for the anchor box, but also analyzes objects on a pixel level. As shown in Fig. 1, P3–P7 feature layers share the same detection head. Depending on each feature layer detection task, we set their regression ranges as [0,64], [64,128], [128,256], [256,512], [512,]. Introducing a multi-scale detection method effectively balances the positive and negative samples and improves recall. Importantly, each feature layer generates centroids in the H and W directions with a stride of a specific size. Each point $P_i(x, y)$ on the feature map predicts three outputs: a human classification score, a center-ness score, and a 4D vectors.4D vectors $t^* = (l^*, t^*, r^*, b^*)$ represent the four directions(up, bottom, left, right) from P_i to the bounding box. Noteworthy, The 4D vectors $B_i = (x_0^{(i)}, x_1^{(i)}, y_0^{(i)}, y_1^{(i)})$are calculated from the coordinates of the bounding box $(x_0^{(i)}, y_0^{(i)}$ and $(x_1^{(i)}, y_1^{(i)})$ corresponding to the coordinates of the upper left and lower right corners of the bounding.

$$l^* = x - x_0^{(i)}, t^* = y - y_0^{(i)}$$
$$r^* = x_1^{(i)} - x, b^* = y_1^{(i)} - y_0 \tag{1}$$

Equation (2) shows the loss function of the human bounding box. The types of loss functions for Lcls, Lreg, and Lcenternessare focal loss, bounding box iou loss, and binary cross-entropy loss. Moreover, Lcls, Lreg, and Lcenterness represent the classification for humans offset regression bias, and center-ness outputs.

$$l_{human} = L_{cls} + L_{reg} + L_{centerness} \tag{2}$$

Body Part Detector. As shown in Fig. 1, the body parts detector is designed based on the anchor-free. The size of the human body part is small, so we choose the highest resolution P3 feature layer as input. We use the RoI Align method to project the human bounding box to the P3 feature layer. To further save computational overhead, we reduce the projected features to the size of (32, 24). Four layers of simple 2D convolution compute (32, 24) sized feature maps to extract depth features and perform regression and classification. The loss function of the body parts detector is shown in Eq. (3), which corresponds to the human part's classification, offset regression, and centrality, respectively.

$$l_{\text{part}} = L_{cls} + L_{\text{reg}} + L_{\text{centerness}} \qquad (3)$$

4   Vision-Based Gesture AGV Control Method

4.1   The Overview of AGV Control System

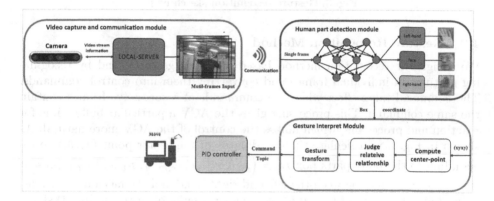

Fig. 2. Architecture of AGV control system

Fig. 2 shows the AGV control system designed in this paper. The system consists of three sub-modules: a video capture and communication module, a human part detection module, and a gesture interpretation module. Video capture and communication module: in order to increase the range of movement of the AGV trolley, we set up a local camera to capture continuous video sequences, including human representation signals. Local-computer send the video stream information to the AGV in a broadcast manner. Body part detection module: extract the continuous video with fixed frequency into a single frame sequence. Then, input the obtained single frame image into the neural network framework designed in this paper for processing. Finally, get the bounding box coordinates of the left and right hands and face. Gesture interpreter module: first, judge the relative position of left and right hands close to the face. Second, convert the relative position relationship into the corresponding gesture command for control. Finally, publish it to the chassis PID controller in the form of a topic to control the AGV.

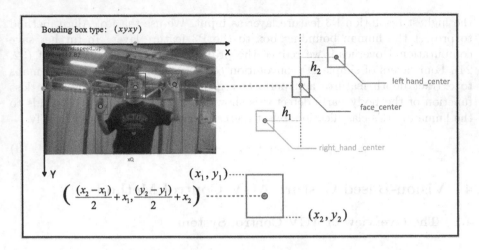

Fig. 3. Gesture recognition sketch map

4.2 Gesture Recognition Method

We design the recognition method based on static gestures, and by recognizing gestures in individual frames and converting them into control commands. The command takes effect when the commands of 5 successive frames contain the same command. This processing gives the AGV a particular buffer time for reaction and processing, which makes the control of the AGV more natural. As shown in Fig. 3, we calculate the coordinates of the center point (x_i, y_i) corresponding to the body parts box $B_i = \left(x_1^{(i)}, x_1^{(i)}, y_1^{(i)}, y_2^{(i)}\right)$. h_1 and h_2 represent the difference values between the left and right hand and the face on the y-axis. So we follow the value of h_1 and h_2 to generate a series of gestures. Eq. (4) shows the formula for (x_i, y_i), Eq. (5) shows the formula for h_1 and h_2.

$$(x_i, y_i) = \left(\frac{(x_2 - x_1)}{2} + x_1, \frac{(y_2 - y_1)}{2} + y_1 \right) \tag{4}$$

$$h_1 = y_{l-hand} - y_{face}, h_2 = y_{r-hand} - y_{face} \tag{5}$$

We believe gestures should have clear semantic information in human-robot interaction, so we design four one-handed gestures and four two-handed gesture commands. As shown in Fig. 4, one-handed gestures indicate AGV movement commands (forward, backward, left, right), and two-handed gestures indicate function commands (accelerate, decelerate, 180° clockwise, stop). Table 1 summarizes the correspondence between gestures and control commands," stop" is the default status. L1, and L2 represent the coordinates of the left and right hand in the y-direction. Moreover, we combine the human part detection and gesture recognition method designed in this paper. We set the human body with the largest proportion in the image as the operator. The AGV only responds to commands issued by the operator but not to commands issued by other unrelated personnel.

Table 1. The correspondence between gesture and the AGV controlling commands.

L1	R1	Corresponding Command
One-hand gesture		
$L_{center-y} > F_{center-y}$	$R_{center-y} = 0$	Move forward
$L_{center-y} = 0$	$R_{center-y} > F_{center-y}$	Move backward
$L_{center-y} < F_{center-y}$	$R_{center-y} = 0$	Move left
$L_{center-y} = 0$	$R_{center-y} < F_{center-y}$	Move right
Two-hand gesture		
$L_{center-y} > F_{center-y}$	$R_{center-y} < F_{center-y}$	Speed up
$L_{center-y} < F_{center-y}$	$R_{center-y} > F_{center-y}$	Slow down
$L_{center-y} > F_{center-y}$	$R_{center-y} > F_{center-y}$	Turn on CW 180°
$L_{center-y} < F_{center-y}$	$R_{center-y} < F_{center-y}$	Stop

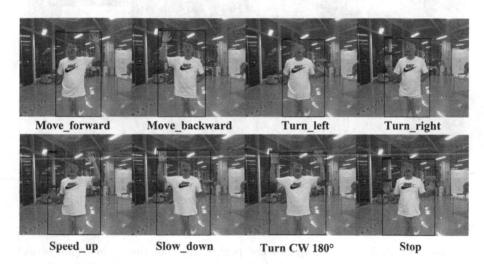

Fig. 4. Different gestures are designed to control the AGV.

5 Experiment

5.1 Experimental Deployment and Dataset

Dataset. We trained the body part detection network end-to-end on the COCO Human Parts dataset [22]. COCO Human Parts contain 268030 person instances and 759420 body parts, averaging 2.83 body parts per human instance.

Experimental Deployment. We built the network and designed the gesture recognition method in the framework of Pytorch and Python. The network performs distributed training on two NVIDIA RTX 2080TI GPUs for 90,000 iterations with 0.9 momentum and 0.0001 weight decay. The total training batch is 8, and the bath per GPU is 4. We set the initial learning rate as 0.004 and decay it by 0.1 at iteration 120000 and 180000 iteration, respectively. In the HRI platform building stage, we chose the AMOV unmanned vehicle as the H-RI object. In order to make the system recognize the gestures better, we arranged the camera to a position about 2m away from the person. Figure 5 shows the human-AGV interaction platform.

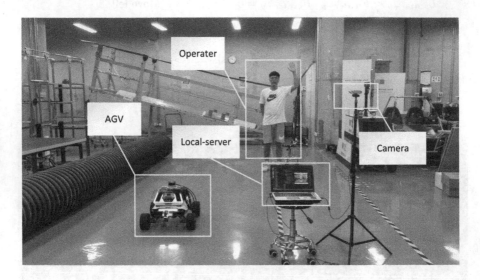

Fig. 5. Human-AGV interaction platform.

5.2   Human-AGV Interaction Platform

As shown in Table 2, we compared the performance of the mainstream object detection network and the network designed in this paper on the COCO Human Part dataset [22]. Our method achieved the best results compared to other mainstream object detection methods in large targets such as persons and small-scale objects such as heads and faces. Therefore, our human part detection method can adapt to multi-scale objects.

Table 2. The accuracy of several methods on the COCO Human Part dataset.

Methods	All categories APs							Per categories APs						
	AP	AP_{50}	AP_{75}	AP_T	AP_S	AP_M	AP_L	person	head	face	r-hand	l-hand	r-foot	l-foot
Faster-C4-R50 [7]	32.0	55.5	32.3	9.9	38.5	54.9	52.4	50.5	47.5	35.5	27.2	24.9	19.2	19.3
RetinaNet-R50 [23]	32.2	54.7	33.3	10.0	39.8	54.5	53.8	49.7	47.1	33.7	28.7	26.7	19.7	20.0
FCOS- R50 [11]	34.1	58.6	34.5	13.1	40.7	55.1	**55.1**	51.1	45.7	**40.0**	29.8	28.1	22.2	21.9
Faster-FPN-R50 [16]	34.8	60.0	**35.4**	14.0	**41.8**	**55.4**	52.0	51.4	48.7	36.7	**31.7**	**29.7**	22.4	22.9
OURS	**35.4**	**63.4**	34.6	**17.4**	41.0	53.1	48.4	**53.8**	**50.8**	40.0	27.6	26.8	**24.5**	**24.7**

5.3 Experiments on Human–AGV Interaction

Experiments On Gesture Recognition Method. In this section of the experiment, we combined the gesture recognition method and the body part detection method. We collected a small validation dataset containing eight gestures with 600 images, with an average of 75 images per gesture. As shown in Table 3, the two methods achieved good gesture recognition accuracy, which has proved the effectiveness of the gesture recognition method we designed. Our method is slightly less accurate than faster rcnn, but much faster than faster rcnn. Our method balanced accuracy and speed, which means it can be applied to a broader range of environments.

Table 3. The correspondence between gesture and the AGV controlling commands.

Methods	One-hand gesture				Two-hand gesture					
	Move forward	Move back-ward	Move left	Move right	Speed up	Slow down	Turn CW 180°	Stop	Total	FPS
Faster-FPN-R50[16]	93.3%	92.0%	100%	100%	99%	95%	100%	96%	96.8%	6.7
OURS	89.3%	90.6%	100%	97.3%	100%	98.6%	96.0%	97.3%	96.1%	17.23

Table 4. The gesture accuracy with interference.

Methods	One-hand gesture				Two hand gesture					
	Move forward	Move back-ward	Move left	Move right	Speed up	Slow down	Turn CW 180	Stop	Total	FPS
FCOS- R50 [11]	77.7%	73%	75%	80%	67%	64%	69%	71.1%	63.8%	16.53
OURS	90.0%	92.0%	98.0%	96.0%	100%	97.7%	100%	100%	96.6%	14.68

Experiments On Gesture Recognition With Interference. We collected a small gesture validation dataset with interference from others, which has 360 images, with an average of 45 images per gesture. Each picture has two people, one is the operator and the other is an unrelated person. As shown in Table 4, the experiments in this section compared the accuracy of the gesture recognition method designed in this paper on different body part detection methods under the interference of others. As shown in Fig. 5, it is difficult for the FCOS-R50-based gesture recognition method to distinguish the correct command under the interference of unrelated persons, while our method can effectively avoid such interference. Because our method correlates body parts with the human body (Fig. 6).

6 Conclusion and Future Work

This paper presented a control method for AGVs based on body part detection. We extended a new branch based on FCOS to detect body parts further,

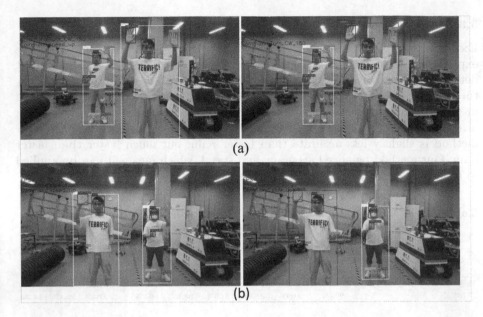

Fig. 6. Gesture command output with interference from unrelated personnel. (a)The output frame is FCOS-R50. (b)The output frame is ours.

balancing the accuracy and speed of detection. We developed a gesture recognition algorithm based on the relative position relationship of human parts and obtained good results. Finally, we designed a human-computer interaction experiment to achieve real-time and accurate control of the AGV. We hope to combine the human part detection method designed in this paper with other gesture recognition algorithms to do more human-computer interaction experiments in the future.

Acknowledgment. This work was supported in part by the National Natural Science Foundation of China (62006204, 62103407), the Guangdong Basic and Applied Basic Research Foundation (2022A1515011431), and Shenzhen Science and Technology Program (RCBS20210609104516043, JSGG20210802154004014).

References

1. Lynch, L., et al.: Automated ground vehicle (AGV) and sensor technologies-a review. In: 2018 12th International Conference on Sensing Technology (ICST). IEEE (2018)
2. Zhou, X., Chen, T., Zhang, Y.: Research on intelligent AGV control system. In: 2018 Chinese Automation Congress (CAC). IEEE (2018)
3. Zhang, Y., et al.: Learning effective spatial-temporal features for sEMG armband-based gesture recognition. IEEE Internet Things J. **7**(8), 6979–6992 (2020)
4. Anwar, S., Sinha, S.K., Vivek, S., Ashank, V.: Hand gesture recognition: a survey. In: Nath, V., Mandal, J.K. (eds.) Nanoelectronics, Circuits and Communication

Systems. LNEE, vol. 511, pp. 365–371. Springer, Singapore (2019). https://doi. org/10.1007/978-981-13-0776-8_33

5. Rautaray, S.S., Agrawal, A.: Vision-based hand gesture recognition for human-computer interaction: a survey. Artif. Intell. Rev. **43**, 1–54 (2015)

6. Mujahid, A., et al.: Real-time hand gesture recognition based on deep learning YOLOv3 model. Appl. Sci. **11**(9), 4164 (2021)

7. Ren, S., et al.: Faster R-CNN: towards real-time object detection with region proposal networks. In: Advances in Neural Information Processing Systems, vol. 28 (2015)

8. Redmon, J., Farhadi, A.: YOLO9000: better, faster, stronger. In: Proceedings of the IEEE Conference on Computer Vision and Pattern Recognition (2017)

9. Redmon, J., Farhadi, A.: YOLOV3: an incremental improvement. arXiv preprint: arXiv:1804.02767 (2018)

10. Law, H., Deng, J.: CornerNet: detecting objects as paired keypoints. In: Ferrari, V., Hebert, M., Sminchisescu, C., Weiss, Y. (eds.) Computer Vision – ECCV 2018. LNCS, vol. 11218, pp. 765–781. Springer, Cham (2018). https://doi.org/10.1007/ 978-3-030-01264-9_45

11. Tian, Z., et al.: FCOS: fully convolutional one-stage object detection. In: 2019 IEEE/CVF International Conference on Computer Vision (ICCV). IEEE (2020)

12. Duan, K., et al.: CenterNet: keypoint triplets for object detection. In: Proceedings of the IEEE/CVF International Conference on Computer Vision (2019)

13. Zhang, K., et al.: Joint face detection and alignment using multitask cascaded convolutional networks. IEEE Sig. Process. Lett. **23**(10), 1499–1503 (2016)

14. Liu, W., et al.: SSD: single shot MultiBox detector. In: Leibe, B., Matas, J., Sebe, N., Welling, M. (eds.) ECCV 2016. LNCS, vol. 9905, pp. 21–37. Springer, Cham (2016). https://doi.org/10.1007/978-3-310-46448-0_2

15. Zhang, S., et al.: AIParsing: anchor-free instance-level human parsing. IEEE Trans. Image Process. **31**, 5599–5612 (2022)

16. He, K., et al.: Mask r-CNN. In: Proceedings of the IEEE International Conference on Computer Vision (2017)

17. Lee, H., et al.: Stretchable array electromyography sensor with graph neural network for static and dynamic gestures recognition system. NPJ Flex. Electron. **7**(1), 20 (2023)

18. Yu, C., et al.: End-side gesture recognition method for UAV control. IEEE Sens. J. **22**(24), 24526–24540 (2022)

19. Chua, S.N.D., et al.: Hand gesture control for human-computer interaction with deep learning. J. Electr. Eng. Technol. **17**(3), 1961–1970 (2022)

20. Alba-Flores, R.: UAVs control using 3D hand keypoint gestures: In: SoutheastCon 2022. IEEE (2022)

21. Lin, T.-Y., et al.: Feature pyramid networks for object detection. In: Proceedings of the IEEE Conference on Computer Vision and Pattern Recognition (2017)

22. Yang, L., et al.: Hier R-CNN: instance-level human parts detection and a new benchmark. IEEE Trans. Image Process. **30**, 39–54 (2020)

23. Lin, T.-Y., et al.: Focal loss for dense object detection. In: Proceedings of the IEEE International Conference on Computer Vision (2017)

Predict Hip Joint Moment Using CNN for Hip Exoskeleton Control

Yuanwen Zhang[1,2], Jingfeng Xiong[1,2], Yuepeng Qian[1,2,3], Xinxing Chen[1,2], Yixuan Guo[1,2], Chenglong Fu[1,2], and Yuquan Leng[1,2(✉)]

[1] Shenzhen Key Laboratory of Biomimetic Robotics and Intelligent Systems, Department of Mechanical and Energy Engineering, Southern University of Science and Technology, Shenzhen 518055, China
lengyq@sustech.edu.cn
[2] Guangdong Provincial Key Laboratory of Human-Augmentation and Rehabilitation Robotics in Universities, Southern University of Science and Technology, Shenzhen 518055, China
[3] National University of Singapore, Singapore 117583, Singapore

Abstract. The assistance of the hip exoskeleton is closely related to hip joint moment, and the corresponding assistance can be generated by hip joint moment directly. However, it is difficult to obtain the hip joint moment directly from the sensor during walking. An effective method is to use deep learning models to predict hip joint moment using hip joint angle information. But there are still many challenges in applying this method to practical control systems. This study designs specific parameters to train a deep neural network for predicting hip joint moments and discusses the effects of the number of convolutional layers (N) and the length of sampling time (SL) on the prediction accuracy and the computation time in a real control system. Experiments show that for $N \leq 5$, using angle information with $SL \leq 1.0\,s$ achieves the highest prediction accuracy. However, for larger values of N ($N > 5$), the optimal SL becomes to be longer, where it increases to $2.0\,s$ and the corresponding RMSE is $0.06260\,Nm/kg$ and $0.05977\,Nm/kg$, respectively. These results indicate the importance of SL for prediction accuracy. Furthermore, a comparative analysis of the computation time with models using different N and SL is performed, and the relationship between computation time and prediction accuracy is discussed. This study provides specific model training parameters and detailed comparative analysis, which facilitates further application of deep learning models on hip exoskeletons.

Keywords: hip exoskeletons · prediction of hip joint moments · neural networks

1 Introduction

Exoskeleton technology has made significant progress in the fields of human augmentation and rehabilitation. For ordinary wearers, exoskeletons can enhance

H. Yang et al. (Eds.): ICIRA 2023, LNAI 14273, pp. 200–209, 2023.
https://doi.org/10.1007/978-981-99-6498-7_18

their strength and endurance, while for individuals with conditions such as stroke, disabilities, and other disease, exoskeletons serve as rehabilitation training tools [9–12]. The magnitude of assistance provided by exoskeletons is closely related to the joint moment of the human body. However, it is challenging to accurately measure and calculate the hip joint moment during real-world applications using conventional wearable sensors.

The field of biomechanical measurement has embraced state of the art methodologies to assess human joint moments, which can be used for hip exoskeleton control. [3–5] explore the application of EMG signal to estimate joint moment or generate exoskeleton assistance. However, this method is limited by the unaccurate measurement due to EMG is sensitive to the skin environment.

Mundt et al. [8] employed optical tracking data to simulate IMU information, which served as input for feedforward and long short-term memory networks, enabling the prediction of joint moments during the lower limb gait process. Molinaro et al. [7] developed a TCN network and utilized 6-axis IMUs positioned on the trunk and thighs, along with a goniometer at the hip joint, to estimate the flexion/extension moment of the hip. Eslamy and Rastgaar [2] developed a nonlinear auto-regressive model with exogenous inputs (NARX) using wavelets and neural networks to estimate sagittal plane ankle, knee, and hip moments during walking using only thigh or shank angles. Nonetheless, these existing methods still presents several challenges to be applied in hip exoskeleton control. One crucial issue pertains to determining parameters that ensure accurate moment prediction and achieve adequate inference speed. This challenge becomes particularly pronounced for real-time exoskeleton wearable devices.

Drawing upon domain-specific knowledge, this study focuses on the application of hip joint moment prediction neural network in the domain of hip exoskeletons. It extensively discusses and analyzes several key parameters that influence the moment prediction in practical control systems. The research encompasses the impact of sampling time length as input for moment prediction networks, as well as the effect of network size on the output accuracy. Moreover, the study explores the relationship between model accuracy and computational time consumption when inference, thereby catering to the utilization of mobile computing devices. The analysis results of these parameters provide better support and serve as valuable references for future research endeavors in the related field.

2 Method

2.1 Hip Joint Model

The motion model of human hip joint can be represented with Fig. 1. Based on the analysis of relevant dynamics [6], it can be approximately represented as Eq. 1.

$$I(\theta) + h(\dot{\theta}) + g(\ddot{\theta}) = \tau \tag{1}$$

As $\dot{\theta}, \ddot{\theta}$ can be derivated by $\theta(t)$ with respect to t, the left side of Eq. 1 can be writen as $f(\theta)$. Therefore, we can get the hip joint flexion/extension moments

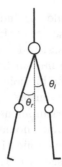

Fig. 1. Hip joint model during human motion, where θ_l and θ_r represent the flexion/extension angles of the left and right legs relative to the vertical line in gravity-aligned direction.

by finding the corresponding relationship between f and θ. However, due to the complexity of the human muscle system, it is very difficult to solve this problem using conventional methods such as physical modeling. To overcome this challenge, deep learning method is used in this research to approximate the function expression of $f(\theta)$.

The key problem now becomes how to optimize the deep learning model, for the model quality is very sensitive to the training input and hyperparameter settings. In the prediction of hip joint moment and its related applications, good training model often require users to select appropriate input data and hyperparameter according to professional knowledge.

2.2   Parameters Selection

Based on the hip joint moment model described above, the calculation of hip joint moment relies on the hip joint angle θ, angular velocity $\dot{\theta}$, and angular acceleration $\ddot{\theta}$. However, considering only these three variables at a single time makes it challenging to accurately obtain the moment τ and leads to control lag. To address this issue, we propose predicting future joint moment by incorporating additional recorded data as input. Figure 2 illustrates the correlation between the hip joint angle over a short period of time and the joint moment in the near future.

The following are the assumptions underlying this study regarding the predictability of hip joint moment for control purposes based on hip joint angles.

(1) Exoskeleton assistance is effective for most regular movements, but it ignores the ineffective assistance during the transition process of movement patterns.
(2) The human body's intrinsic motion independence, which implies that exoskeleton assistance does not introduce changes in motion.

The reason for the existence of Assumption 1 is that external body motion alone is not a sufficient condition for determining human intent. Assumption 2

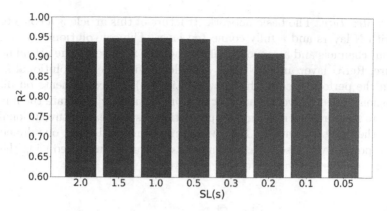

Fig. 2. The R^2 value between the predicted and actual hip joint moment after $0.1\,s$ from now, which uses a deep neural network (N = 4) based on hip joint angles to predict hip joint moment.

is made to ensure that exoskeleton assistance does not directly induce human motion, as this would lead to differences in hip joint angle variations between actual scenarios and the training data.

In order to develop an accurate prediction model, this study investigates the impact of the input data length (sampling time length of hip joint angle, denoted as SL) on the prediction accuracy (RMSE). Additionally, the selection of hyperparameters plays a crucial role in the prediction results. Specifically, we focus on the influence of the number of convolutional layers (N) in this study.

Generally, larger network structures have a higher capacity to learn features but require more computational resources (cost of time, CoT) while most mobile devices used for exoskeleton control often have limited computational power. Therefore, it is crucial to strike a balance between computing resources and prediction accuracy by selecting an appropriate size of network and it's input.

2.3   Net Structure and Train

Dataset and Devices. The dataset utilized in this study was sourced from [1] and consists of participants aged 21 ± 3.4 years with a height of $1.70 \pm 0.07\,m$ and a mass of $68.3 \pm 10.83\,kg$. Mainly using data from treadmill experiments which includes 28 different speeds ranging from 0.5 to $1.85\,m/s$ in $0.05\,m/s$ increments. Prior to analysis, preprocessing was performed to filter out missing moment records and abnormal data values from the dataset. The experimental setup involved the use of computers equipped with an Intel 11 CPU and an NVIDIA RTX3060 for training and inference purposes.

Network Structure. The basic network structure of this article is a convolutional layer with N layers and a fully connected layer. The convolutional layer adopts 32 output channels and a convolutional kernel of 5×1 size. In the actual network structure, ReLU layer and BN layer are added after the convolutional layer to improve the performance of the network Fig. 3(b). In experiments on different convolutional layer networks, in order to more accurately illustrate the impact of changes in network layers on model prediction results, each convolutional layer is set to the same parameters. Before the fully connected layer, one-dimensional adaptive pooling was also added to suppress useless features, reducing the number of parameters in the fully connected layer.

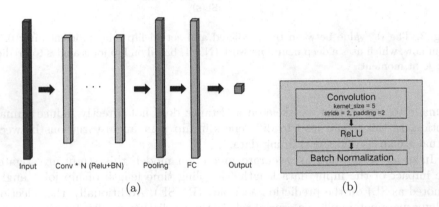

Fig. 3. Illustrations of model structure. (a)Overall network architecture, where N represents the number of convolutional layers. (b) Details of the convolutional layers and the connected layers following them. The convolutional operation has a stride of 2 and a padding of 2.

The primary network architecture employed in this study consists of a convolutional layer with N layers followed by a fully connected layer. Each convolutional layer has 32 output channels and a convolutional kernel of size 5×1. More specifically, ReLU and BN layers are incorporated after the convolutional layer to enhance the network's performance (see Fig. 3(b)).

$$y[i] = \sum_{j=0}^{4} \omega[j] \cdot x[i+j] + b \qquad (2)$$

To accurately examine the influence of changes in convolution layers on model prediction results, each convolutional layer is configured with the same parameters in experiments. Additionally, one-dimensional adaptive pooling is applied before the fully connected layer to suppress irrelevant features and reduce the number of parameters inß the fully connected layer.

Training and Inference. The experiment initially designed training of the network with different SL and N. The specific parameters are indicated in Table 1(as R^2 value for SL = 0.05 s and 0.1 s are relatively small, they will not be further discussed). The dataset used was divided into a training set (70%) and a validation set (30%), and the loss of the training set and the RMSE of the validation set were recorded during the training process.

Table 1. Parameters description.

Parameters	Value
N	1 2 3 4 5 6 7 8
SL	0.2 0.3 0.5 1 1.5 2

After completing the training, the trained model is converted into an inference model, and the inference time of different models is measured as value of CoT.

3   Result

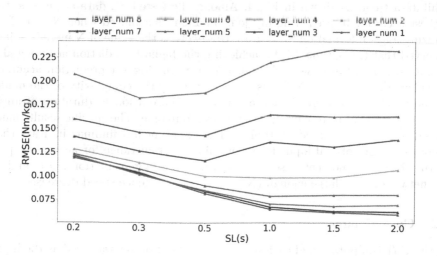

Fig. 4. RMSE curves for different parameters. The curves indicate that a larger N leads to lower RMSE, and the convergence speed decreases when N is greater than 5.

Table 2. Best result for different N among all SL.

Parameter	RMSE	Parameter	RMSE
N = 1, SL = 0.3	0.181937	N = 5, SL = 1.0	0.078839
N = 2, SL = 0.5	0.142831	N = 6, SL = 1.5	0.068497
N = 3, SL = 0.5	0.116296	N = 7, SL = 2.0	0.062600
N = 4, SL = 1.0	0.098193	N = 8, SL = 2.0	0.059768

3.1   Accuracy

After 100 training iterations, the model with the highest accuracy in the validation set (minimum RMSE or maximum R^2) was selected as the result for each
parameter. RMSE and R^2 are used in this research:

$$RMSE = \sqrt{\frac{1}{n} \sum_{i=1}^{n} |y_i - \hat{y}_i|^2} \tag{3}$$

$$R^2 = 1 - \frac{\sum_{i=1}^{n}(y_i - \hat{y}i)^2}{\sum_{i=1}^{n}(y_i - \bar{y})^2} \tag{4}$$

The influence of different SL on the accuracy of hip joint moment prediction
exhibits a trend as shown in Fig. 4. Among the tested SL data sequences, the
highest accuracy in predicting hip joint moment is achieved when N = 1, 2, 3,
utilizing angle information SL = 1.0 s. However, as the value of N increases, it is
observed that the optimal SL for achieving the highest prediction accuracy also
increases. For instance, when N equals 7 or 8, the highest prediction accuracy
is achieved when SL = 2.0 s. This suggests that as the complexity of the model
or the number of features increases, it may require a longer duration of angle
information to accurately predict the desired outcome. The specific results mentioned above are recorded in Table 2. The experimental findings indicate that
there exists an optimal input length within a certain range for accurately predicting hip joint moment based on observing the human motion state, and as
the network size is large enough (N > 5), the convergence speed decreases.

3.2   Cost of Time

In the CoT computation of each model, the validation set was used as the input
data, and the process was repeated 10 times to obtain the average value as the
final result (Eq. 4).

$$CoT = \sum_{i=0}^{9} \frac{T_i}{n} / 10 \tag{5}$$

$$\alpha_{N,SL} = \frac{R^2_{N,SL}}{R^2_{8,2}} \times 100\% \tag{6}$$

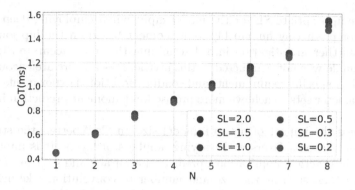

Fig. 5. CoT for different values of N and SL. The results indicate a strong linear relationship between CoT and N, while the relationship with SL is not significant

$$\beta_{N,SL} = \frac{CoT_{N,SL}}{CoT_{8,2}} \times 100\% \tag{7}$$

Figure 5 illustrates the CoT to predict hip joint moment for different values of N and SL. It is evident that as N increases, CoT increases gradually, but SL has few influence on CoT. Therefore, it is crucial to carefully consider the trade-off between computational consumption and accuracy on N. Figure 6 illustrates the ratio (α, β, computed by Eq. 5, 6) of CoT and RMSE with respect to CoT and RMSE under the condition of the highest prediction accuracy (N = 8, SL = 2.0 s) in Table 2.

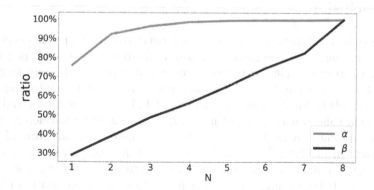

Fig. 6. The variations of α and β with respect to N (under the conditions of SL and N as specified in Table 2), which shows that rate of best R^2 and its CoT for each N comparing to N = 8.

4   Discussion

The study identified a potential optimal range for the input length of network models with different convolutional layers, emphasizing the significance of determining the appropriate SL for the model input when employing deep learning methods for predicting human hip joint moment based on the hip joint angle. However, further investigation into determining the more accurate SL for this specific sample was not conducted in this article. Researchers are encouraged to focus on their specific requirements and conduct additional experiments with different parameter sets to achieve more precise force moment prediction in control systems.

To assess the impact of network model size on CoT better, the study configured convolutional layers with varying numbers of layers. It is important to note that, in practical applications, prediction accuracy and CoT are influenced by more factors, such as the size and number of convolutional kernels, nodes number of other layers. The network structure design in this study aimed to facilitate control over experimental variables and explore the influence of network model size. However, the selection of specific model configurations may require more extensive experiments to strike a better balance between accuracy and computation time consumption across various hyperparameters.

Several important considerations should be highlighted based on the experiment conditions in this research. Firstly, it is crucial to account for the impact of data sampling frequency on the results in practical applications, as in this study it was set at 200 Hz. Secondly, the parameters discussed in this study were specifically related to the prediction model during treadmill walking at different speeds. To apply these parameters in practical work, evaluation of their effectiveness across various scenarios and motion modes may need to be considered.

5   Conclusion

In a controlled environment, deep neural networks have shown effectiveness in estimating human biomechanics. However, further investigation is necessary to apply these predictions to practical control systems. This study proposes a method for determining the training parameters required to apply deep neural network models to hip exoskeletons, aiming at balance the accuracy and cost of computation time consumption of neural network for hip exoskeletons control. Experimental measurements have revealed that there exists an optimal size for input length in predicting hip joint moment with hip joint angle. Furthermore, by analyzing the inference time consumption of the model, the study establishes a relationship between moment prediction accuracy and computation time consumption. This comprehensive consideration serves as a basis for further research on applying this method to control exoskeletons using mobile devices.

Acknowledgement. This work was supported in part by the National Natural Science Foundation of China [Grant52175272, U1913205], in part by the Science, Technology, and Innovation Commission of Shenzhen Municipality [Grant: JCYJ20220530114809021, ZDSYS20200811143601004], and in part by the Stable Support Plan Program of Shenzhen Natural Science Fund under Grant 20200925174640002.

References

1. Camargo, J., Ramanathan, A., Flanagan, W., Young, A.: A comprehensive, open-source dataset of lower limb biomechanics in multiple conditions of stairs, ramps, and level-ground ambulation and transitions. J. Biomech. **119**, 110320 (2021). https://doi.org/10.1016/j.jbiomech.2021.110320
2. Eslamy, M., Rastgaar, M.: Multi-joint leg moment estimation during walking using thigh or shank angles. IEEE Trans. Neural Syst. Rehabil. Eng. **31**, 1108–1118 (2023). https://doi.org/10.1109/TNSRE.2022.3217680
3. Foroutannia, A., Akbarzadeh-T, M.R., Akbarzadeh, A.: A deep learning strategy for EMG-based joint position prediction in hip exoskeleton assistive robots. Biomed. Signal Process. Control **75**, 103557 (2022). https://doi.org/10.1016/j.bspc.2022.103557
4. Gui, K., Liu, H., Zhang, D.: A practical and adaptive method to achieve EMG-based torque estimation for a robotic exoskeleton. IEEE/ASME Trans. Mechatron. **24**(2), 483–494 (2019). https://doi.org/10.1109/TMECH.2019.2893055
5. Gurchiek, R.D., Donahue, N., Fiorentino, N.M., McGinnis, R.S.: Wearables-only analysis of muscle and joint mechanics: an EMG-driven approach. IEEE Trans. Biomed. Eng. **69**(2), 580–589 (2022). https://doi.org/10.1109/TBME.2021.3102009
6. Lim, B., et al.: Delayed output feedback control for gait assistance with a robotic hip exoskeleton. IEEE Trans. Rob. **35**(4), 1055–1062 (2019). https://doi.org/10.1109/TRO.2019.2913318
7. Molinaro, D.D., Kang, I., Camargo, J., Gombolay, M.C., Young, A.J.: Subject-independent, biological hip moment estimation during multimodal overground ambulation using deep learning. IEEE Trans. Med. Robot. Bionics 4(1), 219–229 (2022). https://doi.org/10.1109/TMRB.2022.3144025
8. Mundt, M., et al.: Prediction of lower limb joint angles and moments during gait using artificial neural networks. Med. Biol. Eng. Comput. **58**(1), 211–225 (2020). https://doi.org/10.1007/s11517-019-02061-3
9. Bishe, S.S.P.A., Liebelt, L., Fang, Y., Lerner, Z.F.: A low-profile hip exoskeleton for pathological gait assistance: design and pilot testing. In: 2022 International Conference on Robotics and Automation (ICRA), pp. 5461–5466. IEEE, Philadelphia (2022). https://doi.org/10.1109/ICRA46639.2022.9812300
10. Siviy, C., et al.: Opportunities and challenges in the development of exoskeletons for locomotor assistance. Nat. Biomed. Eng. **7**, 456–472 (2022). https://doi.org/10.1038/s41551-022-00984-1
11. Yang, C., et al.: Current developments of robotic hip exoskeleton toward sensing, decision, and actuation: a review. Wearable Technol. **3**, e15 (2022). https://doi.org/10.1017/wtc.2022.11
12. Young, A.J., Ferris, D.P.: State of the art and future directions for lower limb robotic exoskeletons. IEEE Trans. Neural Syst. Rehabil. Eng. **25**(2), 171–182 (2017). https://doi.org/10.1109/TNSRE.2016.2521160

Marine Robotics and Applications

Study on Design and Performance of a Bionic Fish Driven by Four IPMC Fins

Yujun Ji⬤, Gangqiang Tang, Chun Zhao, Yifan Pan, Denglin Zhu,
and Yanjie Wang$^{(\boxtimes)}$ ⬤

Jiangsu Provincial Key Laboratory of Special Robot Technology, Hohai University,
Changzhou Campus, Changzhou 213022, China
yjwang@hhu.edu.cn

Abstract. Bionic fish, as a combination of fish swimming mechanism and robot technology, provides a new idea for the development of underwater vehicles, and has important research value and application prospect. According to the structure and swimming mechanism of fish pectoral fin, a bionic pectoral fin which can flexibly bend and swing under low voltage is designed by using IPMC material, which has the advantages of simple structure, no noise and low power consumption. At the same time, the bionic fish adopts symmetrical structure design, and uses the mutual force compensation between four IPMC pectoral fins to swim along a fixed trajectory. Experiments show that the swimming speed of IPMC bionic fish can reach 1 mm/s, and keep uniform linear motion, which has the advantages of high flexibility and strong controllability.

Keywords: IPMC · Bionic fish · Swimming gait

1 Introduction

Underwater bionic robot can be used in situations with high maneuverability, and can perform high-risk, long-term and complex underwater operations, such as underwater biological investigation, maritime rescue, seabed exploration and so on. However, traditional underwater bionic robots are mostly driven by motors, which are large in size, complex in structure, limited in application scenarios and poor in flexibility. Therefore, in order to meet the requirements of complex underwater operations, bionic underwater micro-robot driven by intelligent materials came into being because of its compact and efficient mechanism, no noise and strong steering ability. In recent years, piezoelectric actuators, shape memory alloy (SMA) actuators and gel actuators have been applied to bionic underwater micro-robots. [1, 2] These intelligent drivers often need higher driving voltage, which has the disadvantages of power consumption, low security and slow response speed in practical applications. Therefore, the ionic polymer-metal composite material (IPMC) is used as the driving material in this paper, which has the advantages of low driving voltage and fast response, and can avoid the above problems.

Traditional IPMC consists of ion exchange membrane, Nafion (DuPont) membrane with thickness less than 300 μ m and two thin noble metal electrodes deposited on the

H. Yang et al. (Eds.): ICIRA 2023, LNAI 14273, pp. 213–223, 2023.
https://doi.org/10.1007/978-981-99-6498-7_19

membrane surface by chemical and physical means. Under the action of electric field, its internal ions migrate, which leads to the change of its overall structure, resulting in bending, stretching, expansion and other deformation, thus realizing the transformation from electrical energy to mechanical energy [3–7]. It is also called "artificial muscle" because of its similar characteristics with biological muscle. Compared with shape memory alloys actuator, IPMC has the advantages of large bending displacement, silent movement, fast response and long service life. It can produce large deflection displacement and obtain stable deformation under the excitation of AC current of only 1-5V [8–11]. At the same time, IPMC can still work stably in underwater or humid environment. Underwater micro-robot using IPMC actuator has the characteristics of good flexibility, low driving voltage and fast response [12–14]. Therefore, IPMC actuator is widely used in the tail fin of swimming micro robot [15–17]. However, because the displacement of IPMC is greatly affected by the environment, the driving forces on the left and right sides of bionic fish driven by caudal fin are inconsistent, and it is difficult for bionic fish to swim along a fixed trajectory. Therefore, a new type of IPMC bionic fish is designed in this paper. Four IPMC pectoral fins are symmetrically distributed on both sides of the bionic fish, compensating each other and swimming along a fixed trajectory. Compared with IPMC bionic fish driven by caudal fin, it has the advantages of high flexibility and strong controllability.

In this paper, firstly, the layout design and preparation of IPMC pectoral fins are carried out. Secondly, the response frequency and displacement of IPMC are studied, and the voltage frequency and amplitude corresponding to the optimal state of IPMC are found out. Then, the swimming gait of IPMC miniature bionic fish is studied, which lays a foundation for the control of bionic fish. Finally, the prototype experiment shows that the bionic fish can swim in three states, which is ready for the precise control in the future.

2   Design and Fabrication of Bionic Fish

2.1   Design of Bionic Fish

As shown in Fig. 1a, IPMC is used as the pectoral fin driver in this paper to meet the requirements of small size and compact structure of bionic fish. The pectoral fin of the bionic fish is composed of an IPMC sheet and a copper sheet, which are similar to the shape of the pectoral fin. When a voltage is applied at both ends, the IPMC sheet will quickly bend to the cathode and swing with the change of voltage polarity, thus driving the copper sheet to move back and forth. As shown in Fig. 1b, the four identical IPMC pectoral fins are symmetrically distributed on both sides of the bionic fish. The fish is 40 mm in length, 12 mm in height and 18 mm in width at the maximum cross section, and is made of polyester resin material. It consists of an upper cavity and a lower cavity. The lower cavity is filled with water to increase the mass of the lower part of the fish, so that the bionic fish can keep balance in the water. The left side and the right side of the fish body are provided with four clamping grooves for holding IPMC pectoral fins, and wires are connected with the IPMC pectoral fins from the fish body. According to the propulsion principle of median and paired fin (MPF) mode, the swimming of bionic fish is realized by using the propulsion force generated by the backward stroke of IPMC pectoral fin.

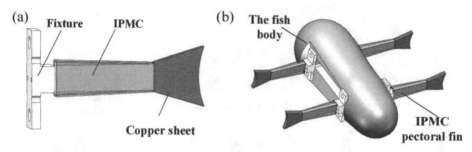

Fig. 1. (a) Biomimetic fin structure. (b) Structure diagram of the bionic fish.

2.2 Fabrication of Bionic Fish

Materials. In this paper, Nafion117 produced from DuPont is used for ion exchange polymer membrane. Palladium ([Pd (NH$_3$)$_4$] Cl$_2$) was purchased from Northwest Non-ferrous Metals Research. Institute, Sodium (NaBH$_4$) was purchased from Shanghai Aladdin Biochemical Technology Co., Ltd. Ammonia water (NH$_3$ · H$_2$O), hydrochloric acid (HCl) and lithium hydroxide (NaOH) were purchased from Sinopharm Chemical Reagent Co., Ltd., and gold water (Au$^+$) was purchased from Taobao, China. All drugs were not treated before use.

Fabrication of IPMC. Firstly, the 3.5 cm x 3.5 cm Nafion117 membrane was put into the fixture, and put into the sandblasting machine for roughening. As shown in Fig. 2a, the air pressure of the sandblasting machine is kept at 0.4MPa, and the distance between the film and the sandblasting port is 10cm, and each side of the film is sandblasted for 30 s. The fixture needs to be moved to the left and right to ensure uniform sandblasting. Secondly, the roughened Nafion117 membrane is put into DI water for ultrasonic cleaning (30 min, 60 °C) to remove the quartz sand remaining in Nafion117 membrane, as shown in Fig. 2b. Then, the Nafion117 membrane is immersed in hydrochloric acid (2 mol /L, 30 min, 99 °C) and DI water (30 min, 99 °C) continuously to purify the membrane. (Fig. 2c, 2d). Thirdly, as shown in Fig. 2e, the pre-treated membrane is placed in an ammonia solution of Pd (NH$_3$)$_4$Cl$_2$ (0.01 mol /L, 50 °C) for 60 min within a water bath thermostatic oscillator (50 °C, 80–90 r / min). After washing with deionized water, the membrane was immersed in NaBH$_4$ solution (0.02 mol / L, pH > 13) for 30 min within a water bath thermostatic oscillator (50 °C, 80–90 r / min). Repeat Impregnation three times. (Fig. 2f). And then the electroplating set-up is composed of titanium anode, DC power supply and cathode array with conductive spring pin, as shown in Fig. 2g. The membrane needs to be trimmed before plating to prevent short circuit on both sides of the IPMC. The solution of Au $^+$ is gold plating solution with mass concentration of 1.2 g / L. Each side is electroplated for 20–30 s under 5V to ensure the uniformity of surface resistance, and the plating is repeated for 5–10 times. Finally, the membrane was immersed in NaOH solution (0.2 mol/L) for 120 min, and finally the membrane was immersed in DI water. (Fig. 2i). All the prepared IPMC samples were cut into 0.5 cm × 2.5 cm strips.

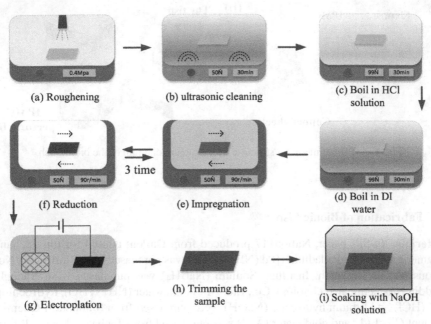

(a) Roughening   (b) ultrasonic cleaning   (c) Boil in HCl solution

(f) Reduction   3 time   (e) Impregnation   (d) Boil in DI water

(g) Electroplation   (h) Trimming the sample   (i) Soaking with NaOH solution

Fig. 2. The detailed fabrication process of IPMC.

Bionic fish assembly. After the preparation steps are completed, we use VHB glue to paste the IPMC sheet and copper sheet together, and install it on both sides of the bionic fish according to the symmetrical structure, as shown in Fig. 3.

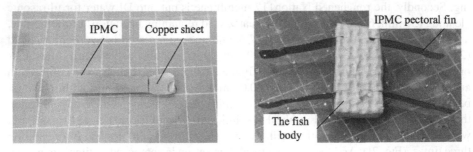

IPMC   Copper sheet   IPMC pectoral fin   The fish body

Fig. 3. Physical diagram of the bionic fish.

3 Driving Voltage of Bionic Fish

According to the kinetic theory, the pectoral fin frequency and oscillation amplitude of the bionic fish determine the swimming speed of the bionic fish. The propulsion efficiency of the fins is related to the vortex pairs generated by the terminal oscillations. Therefore, we need a stable terminal displacement and a suitable frequency to enable the bionic fish to swim quickly and steadily. When the voltage is applied at both sides of the IPMC, cations and bound water molecules migrate to the cathode, which makes water molecules increase on the cathode and cause expansion and bending. When the voltage polarity changes, cations and bound water molecules migrate in the opposite direction, which leads to the reverse bending of IPMC. However, when the frequency of voltage changes too fast and the migration speed of cations and bound water molecules cannot keep up, the deformation of IPMC will decrease. Therefore, we need to determine the voltage frequency corresponding to the maximum response speed of IPMC to obtain the optimal swing speed of IPMC pectoral fin. The experimental set-up is shown in Fig. 4, which is composed of voltage signal generator, signal amplifier, laser displacement sensor, data acquisition card and PC. In the experiment, we clamp one end of IPMC with flat head in the DI water, and make it in cantilever state. Then, we generate various voltage signals with different frequencies and amplitudes through signal generator, and amplify them through signal amplifier, and we use wire to transmit to two ends of IPMC to make IPMC produce bending displacement. Then we use laser displacement sensor to measure the bending displacement of IPMC, and the data is transmitted to PC through the acquisition card. The voltage was 5Vpp to improve the experimental results [18]. The experimental results are shown in Fig. 5. When the voltage frequency is from 0.2 Hz to 3 Hz, the tip displacement of IPMC decreases continuously. Subsequently, the tip displacement of IPMC increases with the increase of voltage frequency. When the voltage frequency is 4.4 Hz, the tip displacement of IPMC reaches the maximum again, forming a resonance peak. The displacement at the end of 1.1 Hz to 5 Hz is stable at about 2mm, indicating that the oscillation frequency range of IPMC fins can be from 1.1 Hz to 5 Hz.

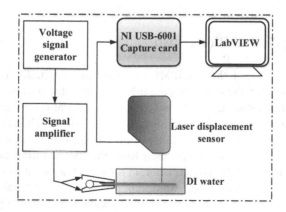

Fig. 4. The experimental set-up.

When the swing frequency of IPMC pectoral fin reaches the maximum, the larger bending deformation will lead to larger propulsion speed. According to previous studies, when the voltage frequency is constant, the bending amplitude of IPMC increases with the increase of voltage amplitude. However, if the voltage amplitude is too high, the water molecules in IPMC will evaporate quickly, and even the IPMC electrode will be broken down, resulting in IPMC failure [11]. Therefore, we need to determine the maximum voltage amplitude of IPMC. The experimental set-up is the same as before. The voltage frequency used in this experiment is 4.4 Hz, and the experimental results are shown in Fig. 5. The tip displacement of IPMC also increases with the increase of voltage amplitude. When the voltage amplitude is 6vpp, the tip displacement of IPMC is twice as much as that of 5vpp. During the experiment, we found that when the voltage amplitude reaches 6vpp, the surface electrode of IPMC will be slightly damaged, and it is difficult for IPMC to work continuously and stably. Therefore, we use the voltage amplitude of 5vpp to ensure that the IPMC works stably and the tip displacement reaches the maximum.

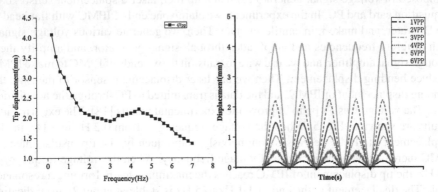

Fig. 5. The tendency of the tip displacement results for the different frequency and amplitude.

4 Swimming Gait of Bionic Fish

When the bionic fish swam, the four IPMC pectoral fins were in different swing states. We call the zero position the state when the IPMC pectoral fin does not bend. When the IPMC pectoral fin generates the backward force, the pectoral fin swings forward to the maximum position, which is called the forward limit position. The pectoral fin swings from the zero position to the forward limit position is called the backward phase, while the pectoral fin returns to the zero position from the forward limit position is called the backward return phase. When the pectoral fin moves backward from the forward to the limit position, it is called the backward limit position. The pectoral fin swings from the zero position to the backward limit position is called the forward phase, while the pectoral fin returns to the zero position from the backward limit position is called the forward return phase. Assuming that the durations of backward phase, backward return phase, forward phase and forward return phase are t_h, t_{h1}, t_q and t_{q1}, respectively, then the backward gait cycle t_H and the forward gait cycle t_Q of the biomimetic fish are:

$$t_H = t_h + t_{h1} \tag{1}$$

$$t_Q = t_q + t_{q1} \tag{2}$$

The bionic fish can swim forward, turn and back up through different gait combinations of four IPMC pectoral fins. The numbers of the IPMC pectoral fins are shown in Fig. 6. The two pectoral fins on the left side of the bionic fish are Leg1 and Leg2, and the two pectoral fins on the right side are Leg3 and Leg4.

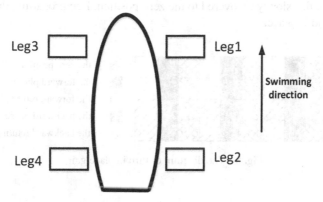

Fig. 6. The numbers of the IPMC pectoral fins.

4.1 Forward Gait

The diagram of the forward gait is shown in Fig. 7. It can be seen that when the bionic fish is swimming forward, the four IPMC pectoral fins are in synchronous motion. At first, Leg1, Leg2, Leg3 and Leg4 are in the zero position, and then the four pectoral fins are subjected to the same voltage at the same time, and the forward phase motion is carried out rapidly. When the four pectoral fins move to the back limit position, the polarity of the voltage is opposite, and the frequency is reduced. The four IPMC pectoral fins carry out the forward return phase slowly. Reciprocating, and the bionic fish swims forward.

4.2 Turn in Place Gait

The diagram of turn in place gait is shown in Fig. 8. It can be seen from the figure that Leg1 and Leg2 are one group, Leg3 and Leg4 are another group when bionic fish are turn in place gait. At first, all four IPMC pectoral fins are at zero position. Then, Leg1 and Leg2 are subjected to the same high frequency voltage at the same time, and Leg3 and Leg4 are subjected to high frequency voltage with opposite polarity. When Leg1

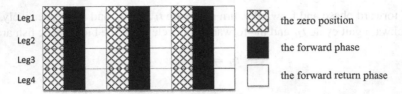

Fig. 7. The diagram of the forward gait.

and Leg2 reach the backward limit position, and Leg3 and Leg4 reach the forward limit position, the positive and negative polarity of voltage applied to each of IPMC pectoral fins are exchanged, and the frequency is reduced. Driven by the applied voltage, the four IPMC pectoral fins slowly recovered to the zero position. Reciprocating, the bionic fish can turn around in place.

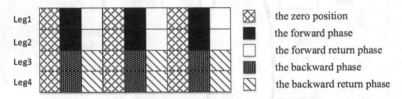

Fig. 8. The diagram of turn in place gait.

4.3 Arc Turning Gait

The arc turning motion of bionic fish means that the forward motion and turning motion of bionic fish are carried out at the same time. The diagram of the arc turning gait is shown in Fig. 9. It can be seen from the figure that when the bionic fish is in the arc turning motion, at first, Leg1, Leg2, Leg3 and Leg4 are at the zero position, and then, Leg1, Leg2 and Leg4 are subjected to the same high-frequency voltage at the same time. Leg3 moves rapidly in the backward phase under the high-frequency voltage with opposite polarity. When Leg1, Leg2 and Leg4 reach the backward limit position, and Leg3 reaches the forward limit position, the positive and negative polarity of the applied voltage are exchanged, and the frequency is reduced, and the four IPMC pectoral fins slowly return to the zero position. Reciprocating, the bionic fish can realize the arc turning motion.

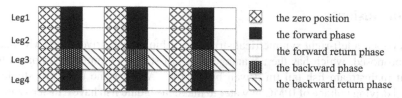

⊠	the zero position
■	the forward phase
☐	the forward return phase
▨	the backward phase
◫	the backward return phase

Fig. 9. The diagram of the arc turning gait.

5 Prototype Experiment

A bionic fish test platform was built to test the swimming performance of IPMC bionic fish in water. Through the platform, we tested the swimming speed and swimming gait of the bionic fish in the water. Due to the limitation of experimental conditions, we have only completed the test of the Forward gait of the bionic fish, while the related test research on the Turn in place gait and Arc turning gait will be in the future. In the experiment, the bionic fish was placed in DI water and connected with a 0.03mm copper wire. The input signal was triangular wave with duty cycle of 75%, voltage frequency of 4.4 Hz and amplitude of 5 Vpp. At the same time, we use copper wire to make the four IPMCs in parallel and keep their driving direction consistent.

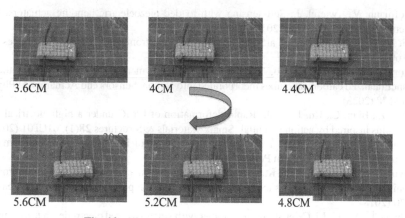

Fig. 10. The actual swimming gait of bionic fish.

The actual swimming gait of bionic fish is shown in Fig. 10. It can be seen from the figure that the bionic fish swam 20 mm in 20 s, the swimming speed reached 1 mm / s, and kept a uniform linear motion, which was consistent with the results of the swimming gait in Sect. 4.2. We can see that the bionic fish driven by pectoral fin of IPMC has certain advantages in path keeping and speed consistency compared with the bionic fish driven by traditional IPMC caudal fin which is hard to control the direction and maintain speed. It lays a foundation for the research on trajectory control of IPMC bionic fish.

6 Conclusions

In this paper, a left-right symmetrical structure of bionic fish driven by IPMC pectoral fin is proposed, which has the advantage of multi-stance swimming compared to the current mainstream fish tail fin driven bionic fish. At the same time, we studied the optimal driving voltage of IPMC in water to make the bionic fish have a faster swimming speed. Through the experiment, when the voltage amplitude is 5 VPP, the fin oscillation frequency ranges from 1.1 Hz to 5 Hz with guaranteed oscillation displacement. Then, the swimming gait of bionic fish was studied, and some experiments were carried out to evaluate the speed of bionic fish in different swimming gait. The experimental results show that the swimming speed of the bionic fish can reach 1 mm / s. It is an important work to optimize the stability of IPMC and establish a more accurate displacement response model in the future research of IPMC bionic fish.

Acknowledgements. This research was supported by the financial support from the National Natural Science Foundation of China (Grant No. 51975184), National Key R&D Program of China (2019YFB1311600). The authors gratefully acknowledge the supports.

References

1. Hofmann, V., Twiefel, J.: Self-sensing with loaded piezoelectric bending actuators. Sens. Actuators, A **263**, 737–743 (2017)
2. Li, T., Li, G., Liang, Y., et al.: Fast-moving soft electronic fish. Science Advances 3(4), e1602045 (2017)
3. Horiuchi, T., Kato, Y., Sugino, T.: Three-layer Ionic Polymer–metal Composite actuator with functionalized carbon nanotubes incorporated into Nafion. Sensors and Actuators A: Physical 114178 (2023)
4. Zhu, Z., Bian, C., Ru, J., et al.: Rapid deformation of IPMC under a high electrical pulse stimulus inspired by action potential. Smart Materials & Structures **28**(1), 01LT01 (2018)
5. Yang, L., Wang, H., Yang, Y.: Modeling and control of ionic polymer metal composite actuators: a review. European Polymer J. 111821 (2023)
6. Byun, J.M., Hwang, T., Kim, K.J.: Formation of a gold nanoparticle layer for the electrodes of ionic polymer–metal composites by electroless deposition process. Applied Surface Science 470 (2018)
7. Chang, L., Yu, L., Li, C., et al.: Ionic polymer with single-layered electrodes: a novel strategy for ionic actuator design. Smart Materials & Structures **27**(10), 105046 (2018)
8. Zhang, H., Lin, Z., Hu, Y., et al.: Low-voltage driven ionic polymer-metal composite actuators: structures, materials, and applications. Advanced Science, 2206135 (2023)
9. Rosset, S., Niklaus, M., Dubois, P., et al.: High-performance electroactive polymer actuators based on ultrathick ionic polymer–metal composites with nanodispersed metal electrodes. ACS Appl. Mater. Interfaces **9**(26), 21998–22005 (2017)
10. Zhao, Y., Xu, B., Zheng, G., et al.: Improving the performance of IPMCs with a gradient in thickness. Smart Materials & Structures **22**(11), 5035 (2013)
11. Lee, S. J., Han, M. J., Kim, S. J., et al.: A new fabrication method for IPMC actuators and application to artificial fingers. Smart Materials & Structures **15**(5), 1217 (2006)
12. Khawwaf, J., Zheng, J., Chai, R., et al.: Adaptive microtracking control for an underwater IPMC actuator using new hyperplane-based sliding mode. IEEE/ASME Trans. Mechatron. **24**(5), 2108–2117 (2019)

13. Shen, Q., Olsen, Z., Stalbaum, T., et al.: Basic design of a biomimetic underwater soft robot with switchable swimming modes and programmable artificial muscles. Smart Materials & Structures **29**(3), 035038 (2020)
14. Cha, Y., Abdolhamidi, S., Porfiri, M.: Energy harvesting from underwater vibration of an annular ionic polymer metal composite. Meccanica **50**, 2675–2690 (2015)
15. Palmre, V., Hubbard, J.J., Fleming, M., et al.: An IPMC-enabled bio-inspired bending/twisting fin for underwater applications. Smart Materials & Structures **22**(1), 014003 (2012)
16. Shen, Q., Wang, T., Kim, K.J.: A biomimetic underwater vehicle actuated by waves with ionic polymer–metal composite soft sensors. Bioinspiration & biomimetics **10**(5), 055007 (2015)
17. Shi, L., Guo, S., Mao, S., et al.: Development of a lobster-inspired underwater microrobot. Int. J. Advanced Robotic Syst. **10**(1), 44 (2013)
18. Chang, L., Yang, Q., Niu, Q., et al.: High-performance ionic polymer–metal composite actuators fabricated with microneedle roughening. Smart Materials & Structures **28**(1), 015007 (2018)

Optimization of Energy Storage for a Miniature Water Jumping Robot

Shihao Zhang[1], Xin Zhang[1], and Jihong Yan[1,2]($\boxtimes$)

[1] State Key Laboratory of Robotics and System, Harbin Institute of Technology,
Harbin 150001, Heilongjiang, China
jhyan@hit.edu.cn

[2] Laboratory for Space Environment and Physical Sciences, Harbin Institute of Technology,
Harbin 150001, Heilongjiang, China

Abstract. The water-jumping robot's energy storage size is the key to improving the jumping performance. Materials with high energy density and large deformability are chosen as robotic energy storage elements, and the storage energy size of water jumping robots can be increased. We design an energy storage mechanism with latex and carbon composite fiber with large deformability and high energy density. The carbon composite fiber deformation was solved the by differential iteration method, and we developed its deformation-force-energy storage model. The energy storage size is increased by optimizing the energy storage elements' dimensional parameters and their installation location. We designed a water jumping robot based on the optimized energy storage mechanism. The optimized robot prototype is manufactured with a weight of 95 g, and the length, width, and height of the robot are 260 mm, 150 mm, and 100 mm, respectively. It has the ability to take off from the water.

Keywords: Energy Storage Mechanism · Water Jumping Robot · Deformation-Force Model

1 Introduction

The miniature water jumping robots have characteristics of superior concealment, water mobility, and obstacle avoidance ability, so they are the hot spot of the water-movement robot. Bongsu et al. [1] designed the first water-jumping robot imitating a water strider, which stored energy by SMA and achieved a water jumping height of 26 mm. Koh J S [2] designed a robot storing energy through a tension spring and releasing it with the TRC mechanism, which can achieve a vertical jumping of 142 mm. Both robots are smaller in scale and weight and are capable of single energy storage and water jumping. Zhao et al. designed the first continuous water jumping robot, which stored energy with a tension spring and was released by an incomplete gear-cam [3]. The estimated energy storage is 0.55 J, and the jumping height and distance are 140 mm and 350 mm, respectively. The robot designed by Jiang et al. store energy by bending and deforming a carbon fiber strip and releasing it with incomplete gears, it can achieve a water jumping height of 142 mm

H. Yang et al. (Eds.): ICIRA 2023, LNAI 14273, pp. 224–236, 2023.
https://doi.org/10.1007/978-981-99-6498-7_20

[4]. Yao et al. designed a robot that can achieve a composite motion of water jumping and gliding, it stores energy via tension and torsion springs and releases energy with incomplete gear. The maximum energy storage is 0.16 J and the water jumping height is 17 mm [5]. Yang et al. designed a continuous water jumping robot via tension and torsion springs, the stored energy is 1.14 J, and the jumping height and distance are 291 mm and 965 mm, respectively [6]. In summary, most of the water jumping robots adopt spring energy storage elements with low energy density, which limits energy storage and jumping performance. The terrestrial-jumping robot can provide a reference for the design of the water-jumping robot in terms of energy storage mechanism. Most of terrestrial jumping robots adopt composite energy storage elements, and latex materials are widely used due to their superelastic properties. Therefore, it has become a research trend for jumping robots to increase energy storage size by selecting high energy density elements [7–12].[1]

The rest of this paper is organized as follows: Section 2 introduces the energy storage and transmission mechanism of the water jumping robot. Section 3 establishes the deformation-force-storage energy model for the latex and carbon composite fiber. In Section 4, the energy storage size is improved by optimizing the installation position and dimensional parameters of latex and carbon composite fibers. In Section 5, the water jumping experiments are carried out. Section 6 concludes this article.

2   Energy Storage and Transmission Mechanism of the Robot

The water jumping robot is designed based on our previous work [6], and the refined structure is shown in Fig. 1. The robot stores energy by the cord, which is connected to the single-sided wire wheel and the slider. The single-side wire wheel is driven by the spline shaft. When the motor is working, the single-side wire wheel compresses the energy storage mechanism by the cord, and the robot starts to store energy. The cam connected with the spline shaft with gears. When it moves to the release position, a single-sided wire wheel is pushed by it along the spline shaft. The cord is released from the single-sided wire wheel. The energy storage mechanism is compressed as Fig. 1, the slider is released along the guide rod mechanism, and the driving leg quickly strikes the water to generate driving force.

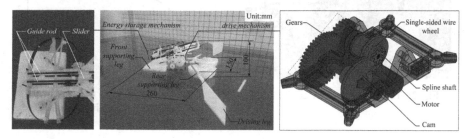

Fig. 1. The water-jumping robot.

[1] Research supported by Equipment Pre-research Application Innovation Project (Geant 62602010202).

3   Modeling of Material Deformation-Force-Energy Storage Properties

Increasing the energy storage size is the key to improving the water jumping performance of the robot, therefore, two high-energy density materials are selected as energy storage elements in this paper: latex and carbon composite fiber. Latex as a super-elastomeric material can generate ten times the deformation, with a low modulus of elasticity and a high energy storage capacity. The carbon composite fiber has a high modulus and it can be used as the support material to increase the energy density. The combination of these two materials can further improve the energy storage size of the robot.

3.1   Latex Deformation - Force - Energy Storage Model

The stress-strain relationship is analyzed to establish the deformation-force-energy storage model. The stress-strain curves were established by the Mooney-Rivlin two-parameter model and calibrated by tensile experiments. The experiment device is shown in Fig. 2. One end of the latex specimen is fixed to the tensile test bench and the other end is attached to the dynamometer. The dynamometer is fixed on the slide Rail and moves with it. The length of the latex is measured by the scale and the force is measured by the dynamometer. The stress-strain relationship was shown in (1), where σ_1 is the latex stress and ε_1 is the latex strain. The measured results and stress-strain curves are shown in Fig. 3. Except for the initial strain (first 10% deformation), the maximum error is 5.17% (at 48% strain).

$$\sigma_1 = 156212\left[1 - \frac{1}{(1 + \varepsilon_1)^3}\right]((1 + \varepsilon_1) + 2.5313) \tag{1}$$

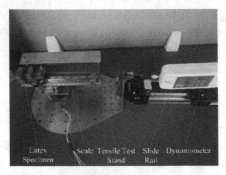

Fig. 2. The tensile test device of latex.

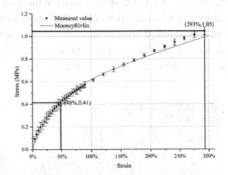

Fig. 3. The comparison of measurement results of latex with the fitting results.

The latex deformation-force-storage relationship can be obtained by integrating Eq. (1).

$$\begin{cases} F = Fl(x, x_0, A_0) = 156212A_0\left(\dfrac{x}{x_0} + 2.5313 - \dfrac{x_0^2}{x^2} - 2.5313\dfrac{x_0^3}{x^3}\right) \\ \\ E = El(x, x_0, V_0) = 156212V_0\left(\dfrac{x^2}{2x_0^2} + \dfrac{x_0}{x} + 2.5313\dfrac{x}{x_0} + 2.5313\dfrac{x_0^2}{2x^2} - 5.29695\right) \end{cases}$$

(2)

3.2 Carbon Composite Fiber Deformation - Force - Energy Storage Model

The carbon composite fiber deformation needs to be solved accurately to establish its deformation-force-energy storage relationship. In the original state, the installation location of carbon composite fibers is symmetrical. Its length is L and spacing is b as shown in Fig. 4. In the compressed state, the height of the carbon composite fiber is h, and the force is F_{hc}. The deformation of carbon composite fibers is symmetrical. So half of its deformation is calculated at first. The carbon composite fiber of $L/2$ is assumed to be modeled as a cantilever beam. And the deformation of this part is solved by the iterative differentiation method.

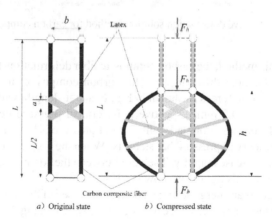

Fig. 4. Carbon composite fiber and latex installation position and deformation.

The deformation is solved as follows. As shown in Fig. 5(a), the $L/2$ length of carbon composite fiber is divided into n pieces. The carbon composite fiber is initially in the state of pressure bar stability, so the vertical pressure will produce unstable deformation. Therefore, the first deformation is calculated under a horizontal force F_0, and it is the initial condition for the iterative calculation. Subsequent deformations are calculated by a vertical force F_c. And the new deformation is calculated on the result of the previous deformation. Until the difference between the two deformation results is less than 0.01 mm. The whole iterative process is shown in Fig. 5 (b). The iterative process is divided into 4 steps. As in Fig. 5(c), in the first step, the reaction force is calculated under the previous deformation. In the second step, the element force is calculated from the reaction force. In the third step, it is first assumed that each element model is calculated as a cantilever beam, and it is built at the end of the previous element. After that, the differential element deformation is calculated, as shown in Fig. 5(d). In the fourth step, the element deformation is transformed into the element coordinates (see Fig. 5(e)). After that, the carbon composite fiber deformation curve can be obtained.

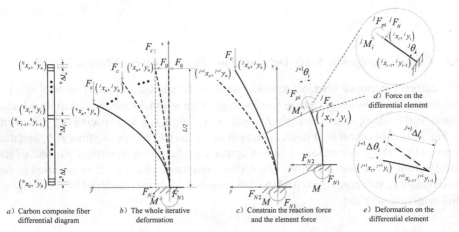

Fig. 5. The iterative deformation solution method for carbon composite fiber.

According to this method, the carbon composite fiber deformation-force relationship can be found by changing different F_c. The carbon composite fiber deformation is calculated under different forces as shown in Fig. 6, and its length, width, and thickness are 90 mm, 4 mm, and 0.5 mm respectively. Its critical pressure Fcr is 5.33 N. The figure shows that the deformation under the critical pressure is basically ignorable. It is consistent with the theory of pressure bar stability. When the pressure is greater than Fcr, the bar deformation increases rapidly. The cure between the force Fc and the distance h can be calculated from this figure, as shown in Fig. 8.

To verify the results, an energy storage module composed of the same carbon composite fiber and a force measurement device is designed as shown in Fig. 7. The measurement device consists of a force-measuring platform, a dynamometer, a rule, a ball screw, and a positioning module. The energy storage module is compressed by the dynamometer, and it moves along the ball screw. The force and compression distance of the energy storage mechanism is measured by the dynamometer and the scale respectively. The measured results and theoretical results are shown in Fig. 8. The maximum error is 6%, which occurs at a compression distance of 11 mm.

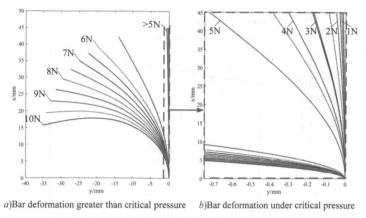

a)Bar deformation greater than critical pressure   b)Bar deformation under critical pressure

Fig. 6. The theory deformation curve of 0.5 mm thick 4 mm wide 90 mm long carbon composite fiber.

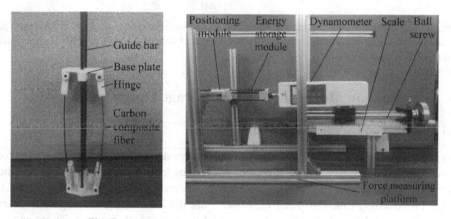

Fig. 7. Energy storage module and measurement device.

The carbon composite fiber energy storage can be obtained by the integral of its element deformation with element force, as Eq. (3).

$$\frac{1}{2}E = \frac{F_c^2 L^3}{24EI} + \frac{F_l^2 a^3 \sin\alpha}{12EI} + \frac{F_c F_l a^3}{12EI} + \frac{F_c F_l \sin\alpha}{12EI}\left[-2a^3 + 3a^2 L\right] - \frac{a F_l^2 \cos^2\alpha}{EA_0}$$

$$(3)$$

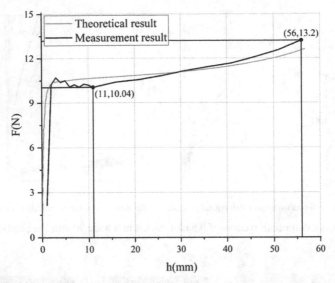

Fig. 8. The measured and theoretical values of force-displacement curves for energy storage elements consisting of carbon composite fibers with a thickness of 0.5 mm, a width of 4 mm, and a length of 90 mm.

4 Combination Model and Energy Storage Optimization

4.1 Installation Location Optimization

As in Fig. 4 the latex is arranged cross-symmetrically on the carbon composite fibers for greater deformation. And a is the distance between the latex installation position and the carbon composite fiber center point. Its coordinates are (x_{ia}, y_{ia}), where $i_a = [2an/L]$, [*] is the rounding function. Then x_0, x, and α are the latex's original length, the latex elongation, and the angle between the force and the horizontal direction. Those can be calculated by Eq. (4).

$$\begin{cases} x_0 = \sqrt{b^2 + 4a^2} \\ x = \sqrt{\left[b + 2(x_n - x_{i_a})\right]^2 + 4y_{i_a}^2} \\ \alpha = \arctan \dfrac{x_{i_a}}{y_n - y_{i_a} + \frac{b}{2}} \end{cases} \quad (4)$$

The relationship between the latex elongation x with installation position a and the compression distance h can be obtained from Eq. (4). As shown in Fig. 9, when b = 30 mm, there were two different trends in the latex elongation x with the compression distance h. The latex elongation increases when a is small. The latex elongation gradually decreases when a is larger. In order to make the latex store energy while the energy storage mechanism is compressed, the installation position a should be small. The relationship between installation positions a and b with the latex maximum deformation is shown in Fig. 10. It can be seen that the latex maximum deformation first decreases and then increases with the growth of a, and it is a negative correlation with b. So the smaller a, and b, the greater the latex maximum deformation, and the greater the energy storage.

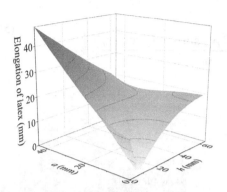

Fig. 9. Relationship between latex length with compression distance h and latex installation position a, at $b = 30$ mm.

Fig. 10. The relationship between the maximum deformation of latex and the installation position a, b.

4.2 Deformation-Force Model of the Combined Energy Storage Mechanism

The carbon composite fibers' deformation is affected by latex. Therefore, the latex force should be added to the model of 3.2 since the second iteration. And the latex force can be calculated by Eq. (2) and Eq. (4). As shown in Fig. 11(a), the latex force and direction will change with the result of iteration, so it needs to be calculated at the beginning of each iteration. The latex force also affects the calculation of the reaction force and element forces, as shown in Fig. 11(b)(c)(d).

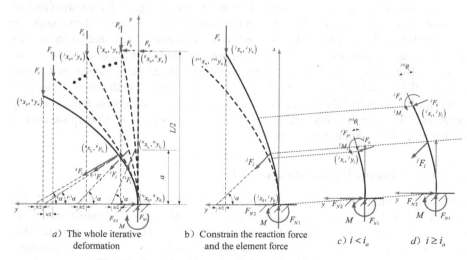

a) The whole iterative deformation

b) Constrain the reaction force and the element force

c) $i < i_a$

d) $i \geq i_a$

Fig. 11. Combined iterative deformation binding solution.

Latex force will also increase the output force of energy storage mechanism as shown in Fig. 12. It is calculated by force balance as shown in Eq. (5).

$$\begin{cases} F_{N1} = F_{hl} + F_l \sin\alpha \\ F_{N2} = F_l \cos\alpha \\ F_{hl} = \dfrac{-F_l x_{i_a} \cos\alpha - F_l y_{i_a} \sin\alpha + F_l \cos\alpha x_n}{y_n} \end{cases} \tag{5}$$

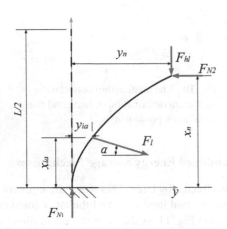

Fig. 12. Latex output force calculation.

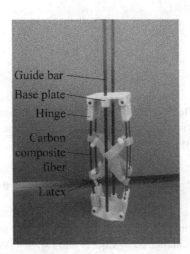

Fig. 13. Compound energy storage mechanism model.

Since then, the deformation-force curve of the composite energy storage mechanism can be calculated. The energy storage mechanism is shown in Fig. 13. It consists of carbon composite fiber and latex, and the length, width, and thickness of the carbon composite fiber are 90 mm, 8 mm, and 0.5 mm, respectively, and the thickness and width of latex are 1.5 mm and 4 mm, respectively. The measurement and theoretical results of output force are shown in Fig. 14. The maximum error occurs when the compression distance is 3 mm. Compared to Fig. 8, with the increase of compression distance h, the latex output force gradually decreases and the carbon composite fiber output force gradually increases. Their output forces can be complementary. It is possible to keep the energy storage mechanism output force at maximum.

4.3 Storage Energy Optimization Analysis

First, the factors influencing latex and carbon composite fiber storage energy are analyzed separately. The latex storage energy is related to its elongation and initial volume as shown in Eq. (2), and their relationship is shown in Fig. 15. The carbon composite fiber energy storage size is calculated by Eq. (3), and it is related to its dimensional parameters. The relationship between carbon composite fiber energy storage with its dimensional parameters is shown in Fig. 16, and compression distance and maximum force are the

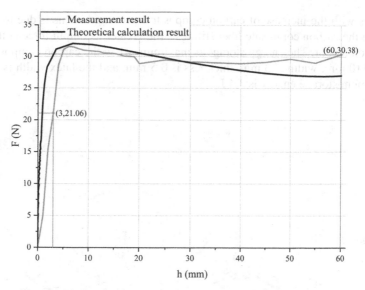

Fig. 14. The comparison of energy storage mechanism output force.

same. It can be seen that the energy storage size increases with width and thickness and decreases with length. That is, the stronger the stiffness of the carbon composite fiber, the greater the energy storage.

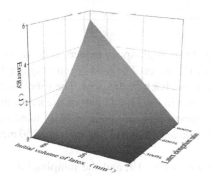

Fig. 15. Latex energy storage with elongation and initial volume change relationship.

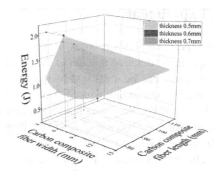

Fig. 16. The relationship between carbon composite fiber energy storage and its size.

The energy storage size of the storage mechanism is influenced by all of the factors above. According to the previous study of the group [6], the maximum output force is set at 30 N, the compression distance is 60 mm. And the effect of different dimensional parameters on energy storage was analyzed, as shown in Fig. 17. It can be seen that the wider the latex the greater the energy storage with the same composite fiber. However, limited by the maximum output force and compression distance, the latex maximum width decreases with the increase of carbon composite fiber width and thickness and it increases with the increase of carbon composite fiber length. This is due to that the greater the the carbon composite fiber stiffness, the greater its output force at the same compression height. The energy storage is maximum when the carbon composite fiber length is 110 mm, width is 3 mm, thickness is 0.5 mm, and the latex width is 12 mm. The maximum storage energy is 3.4 J.

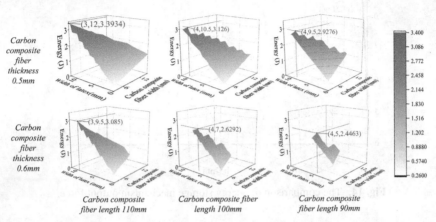

Fig. 17. Relationship between the energy storage size of the energy storage mechanism and the dimensional parameters of the composite fiber and latex.

5 Experiment

The experimental environment is shown in Fig. 18. A high-speed camera was adopted to capture the detailed process of the robot out of the water. The robot's jumping height and distance can be measured by the grid ruler at the back of the pool. The robot body is made by 3D printing with SLA material as shown in Fig. 1, and part of the shafts are made of carbon-composite fiber rods, and the support legs are made of foam material. The weight of the robot is 95 g, and the length, width, and height of the robot are 260 mm, 150 mm, and 100 mm, respectively.

The robot's optimal jumping results is shown in Fig. 19, and the jumping height, distance and pitch angle are 178 mm, 917 mm, and 24.3° respectively.

Fig. 18. The figure of experimental environment

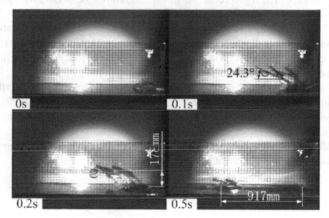

Fig. 19. Robot jumping process.

6 Conclusion

Based on our previous work [6], a water jumping robot was designed, and the energy storage mechanism and the driving mechanism were refined. To optimize the miniature water jumping robot's energy storage size, the high energy density material latex and carbon composite fiber are preferably selected as the energy storage element. And the carbon composite fiber large deformation model is established by the differential iteration method. Then the deformation-force-energy storage model of the energy storage mechanism is established. The maximum energy storage size is 3.4 J, the carbon composite fiber length is 110 mm, the width is 3 mm, and thickness is 0.5 mm, and the latex width is 12 mm. The length, width, and height of the robot are 260 mm, 150 mm, and 100 mm, respectively, and the weight is 95 g. The maximum jumping height distance and pitch angle are 178 mm, 917 mm, and 24.3°, respectively.

References

1. Shin, B., Kim, H., Cho, K.: Towards a Biologically Inspired Small-Scale Water Jumping Robot. IEEE (2008)
2. Koh, J.S., Yang, E., Jung, G.P., et al.: Jumping on water: surface tension-dominated jumping of water striders and robotic insects. BIOMECHANICS. Science **349**(6247), 517–521 (2015)
3. Zhao, J., Zhang, X., Chen, N., et al.: Why superhydrophobicity is crucial for a water-jumping microrobot? experimental and theoretical investigations. ACS Appl. Mater. Interfaces **4**(7), 3706–3711 (2012)
4. Jiang, F., Zhao, J., Kota, A.K., et al.: A miniature water surface jumping robot. IEEE Robotics and Automation Lett. **2**(3), 1272–1279 (2017)
5. Yao, H.W.: A Micro-Compact Surface Jumping and Gliding Robot. Harbin Institute of Technology (2019)
6. Yang, K.: Research on Water Gliding and Jumping Motion of Water Strider-Like Robot. Harbin Institute of Technology (2021)
7. Jung, G., Casarez, C.S., Jung, S., et al.: An Integrated Jumping-Crawling Robot Using Height-Adjustable Jumping Module. IEEE (2016)
8. Jung, G., Casarez, C.S., Lee, J., et al.: JumpRoACH: a trajectory-adjustable integrated jumping-crawling robot. IEEE/ASME Trans. Mechatron. **24**(3), 947–958 (2019)
9. Haldane, D.W., Plecnik, M.M., Yim, J.K., et al.: Robotic vertical jumping agility via series-elastic power modulation. Sci Robot **1**(1) (2016)
10. Hong, C., Tang, D., Quan, Q., et al.: A combined series-elastic actuator & parallel-elastic leg no-latch bio-inspired jumping robot. Mech. Mach. Theory **149**, 103814 (2020)
11. Ma, Y., Wei, Y., Kong, D.: A biologically inspired height-adjustable jumping robot. Appl. Sci. **11**(11), 5167 (2021)
12. Hawkes, E.W., Xiao, C., Peloquin, R., et al.: Engineered jumpers overcome biological limits via work multiplication. Nature **604**(7907), 657–661 (2022)

Design and Research of Flatworm-Inspired Marine Exploration Robot

Wei Su, Qianpeng Wang, Xiao Zhao, Wenrui Liu, and Tao Qin$^{(\boxtimes)}$

School of Mechanical Engineering, Hubei University of Arts and Science,
Xiangyang 441053, China
heu_qt@163.com

Abstract. In response to the practical needs of ocean development, underwater exploration, and marine conservation, a new type of flatworm-inspired marine exploration robot based on the bionics and robotics principles is designed. The robot adopts a double-sided symmetrical arrangement of multiple linkage swing-rod type undulating fins to achieve a sinusoidal motion and propel the robot for underwater bionic swimming. Kinematic models are respectively established for the flatworm-inspired marine exploration robot fish-body and the swing-rod type undulating fin to determine the kinematic parameters of the robot. The motion simulation analysis of the robot fish-body and swing-rod type undulating fin confirms that the robot can swim steadily and the motion models are correctly established. Underwater experiments of the prototype verify that the robot can achieve underwater movement, turning, and other functions, further demonstrating the correctness of the design scheme and theoretical analysis, and providing a new solution for the design of underwater bionic robots.

Keywords: Flatworm-inspired Marine Exploration Robot · Swing guide rod mechanism · Motion analysis · Simulation analysis

1 Introduction

Bionics is a scientific field that involves imitating biological organisms by studying their exceptional characteristics in nature and applying them to technical or artificial systems through analysis and simulation. It is an interdisciplinary and complex discipline characterized by intelligent innovation. Bionics encompasses a wide range of research topics and offers novel insights. In recent years, driven by advancements in modern biological science and robotics, bionic robots that integrate principles of bionics with fundamental disciplines have emerged as a popular multidisciplinary direction, finding extensive applications in fields such as ocean exploration and scientific research [1, 2].

Bionic underwater robots are a specific type of underwater operation robot that takes inspiration from aquatic organisms, mimicking their propulsion patterns or swimming features. These robots possess several advantageous attributes, including low noise, high efficiency, and excellent maneuverability [3]. They hold significant potential for application in ocean development, underwater exploration, marine conservation, and marine security [4]. Based on the location where propulsive force is generated during swimming, the propulsion methods can be broadly classified into two types: the central/paired fin propulsion method (MPF) and the body/caudal fin propulsion method (BCF) [5, 6]. The BCF propulsion method has garnered considerable attention due to its high speed. Conversely, research on the MPF propulsion method has been relatively limited, but it exhibits strong maneuverability and stability, gradually attracting the interest of researchers.

As technology advances, the demands for underwater operations and scientific research tasks continue to rise worldwide. Traditional underwater navigation propulsion methods often rely on propeller-type thrusters, which suffer from drawbacks such as high energy consumption, significant noise, susceptibility to seaweed entanglement, and poor camouflage. Consequently, researchers have extensively studied various types of robotic fish inspired by the propulsion methods of living fish, leveraging their exceptional fluid performance and maneuverability. In recent years, there has been a growing interest in bio-inspired fish utilizing the MPF wave propulsion method. The bio-inspired flatworm robot, designed with a streamlined fish-body, significantly reduces movement resistance in water [7–9]. It employs the MPF wave propulsion method, endowing it with excellent operational capabilities [10, 11]. In comparison to propeller-type thrusters, this approach greatly improves propulsion efficiency and flexibility while reducing energy consumption and noise levels [12, 13]. Moreover, the bio-inspired flatworm robot's controllability can be significantly enhanced through remote control methods, enabling adjustments to its motion direction and speed. By incorporating cameras, sensors, and filtration devices, it can perform functions related to ocean development, underwater exploration, and marine protection.

Drawing on an analysis of existing bio-inspired robot mechanisms and an examination of the body structure and motion characteristics of the flatworm, a bio-inspired flatworm robot featuring a swing rod-driven wave fin was designed. The kinematic model of the robot was established, and the mechanism design was thoroughly studied for its rationality and feasibility through simulation.

2 Overall Design

The overall design scheme of the flatworm-inspired marine exploration robot is illustrated in Fig. 1. It features a symmetrical arrangement structure and primarily consists of a driving motor, a swing-rod-type flapping fin, a fish-body, and a control system. The driving motor, positioned on both sides of the fish-body, is a brushless DC motor responsible for propelling the swing-rod-type flapping fin. Within the fish-body, various components are present, including bionic gills, a camera system, a communication module, and other necessary elements. The control system is located at the tail of the fish-body.

As depicted in Fig. 2, the oscillating rod-type undulating fin is symmetrically positioned on both sides of the fish-body. It comprises a frame, a crankshaft, and an oscillating rod. The crankshaft exhibits a multi-stage regular arrangement featuring a cross-shaped structure, while the oscillating rod can slide and rotate around the axis supported by the frame. Multiple interconnected sets of oscillating rod-type undulating fins emulate

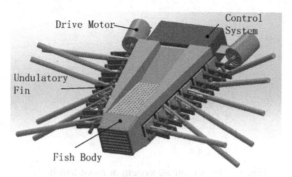

Fig. 1. Flatworm-inspired Marine Exploration Robot overall structure.

the sinusoidal motion of the chaetognath pectoral fins. By rhythmically beating water, these fins generate propulsive force, driving the movement of the robot. Additionally, a biomimetic gill plate is integrated at the front of the fish-body. Utilizing a layered combing structure, it simulates filter feeding to effectively filter and separate marine microplastics.

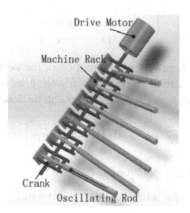

Fig. 2. Swing rod type undulating fin structure.

3   Kinematic Analysis

3.1   Kinematic Modeling of the Robot Fish-Body

Establish the robot fish-body coordinate system O-xyz as shown in Fig. 3 and define the initial position of the origin of the fish-body coordinate system at the center of mass of the fish-body.

Assuming that robot fish-body can only rotate around the z-axis, the coordinate transformation equation is introduced.

$$\begin{cases} \frac{x}{\cos\theta}\cos(\theta + \alpha) = x' \\ \frac{y}{\sin\theta}\sin(\theta + \alpha) = y' \end{cases} \tag{1}$$

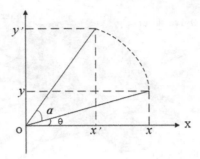

Fig. 3. The coordinate system of robot fish-body

where, α—angular displacement of fish-body around the z-axis motion;

xy—position of a point on the fish-body coordinate system at a certain moment;
$x'y'$—position of a point in the inertial reference system after coordinate transformation at a certain moment.

Simplifying the equation yields:

$$\begin{cases} x' = x\cos\alpha - y\sin\alpha \\ y' = x\sin\alpha - y\cos\alpha \end{cases} \tag{2}$$

In the fish-body coordinate system, the motion of the pectoral fins on both sides is transmitted backward at a certain velocity as a traveling wave[14, 15], and the motion of any point in the y direction on the pectoral fins can be described as:

$$y = A(z)\sin\left(\frac{2\pi x}{\lambda} - 2\pi ft\right) \tag{3}$$

where, x, y—coordinate of any point on the pectoral fin;

$A(z)$—amplitude control factor related to the z-coordinate;
t—motion time;
λ—wave length;
f—wave frequency.

In the fish coordinate system, the traveling wave on the pectoral fin is essentially a simple sine wave controlled by $A(z)$ to determine the amplitude. The sine wave ensures periodic movement of the pectoral fin in the y direction.

As for the movement of any point on the pectoral fin in the z direction of the flatworm-inspired marine exploration robot, it can be described as:

$$z = z_0 + \int_0^t v_z dt \tag{4}$$

where, z—z-coordinate of any point on the pectoral fin;

z_0—initial coordinate;

v_z—velocity of the point in the z-direction;
t—motion time.

The velocity decomposition diagram of any point on the pectoral fin in the y-z plane is shown in Fig. 4, from which it can be seen that:

$$v_z = -v_y \frac{dy}{dz} = -\frac{dy}{dt} \frac{dy}{dz} \tag{5}$$

where, v_y— velocity of the point in the y-direction.

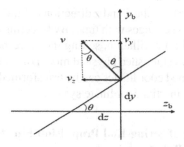

Fig. 4. Velocity decomposition diagram.

In conclusion, Eqs. (3) to (5) form the comprehensive kinematic equation set for the flatworm-inspired marine exploration robot in the fish coordinate system. By determining the position of the center of mass within the fish coordinate system, the inertial coordinate system can be obtained through coordinate transformation.

In the fish coordinate system, assuming that the center of mass of the flatworm-inspired marine exploration robot is located at (x_{c1}, y_{c1}, z_{c1}), the pectoral fin part moves according to the kinematic equation of the flatworm-inspired marine exploration robot in the fish coordinate system. Based on the symmetry of the movement, the x and z coordinates of the center of mass of the pectoral fin part in the fish coordinate system are constant relative to the fish and are designated as (x_{c2}, y_{c2}, z_{c2}), where the values of y_{c2} are:

$$y_{c2} = \frac{\int_{x_a}^{x_b} \int_{z_a}^{z(x)} \left[A(z)sin(\frac{2\pi x}{\lambda} - 2\pi ft)\right] dz dx}{\int_{x_a}^{x_b} \int_{z_a}^{z(x)} dz dx} \tag{6}$$

where, x_a— x-coordinate of the starting position of the pectoral fin along the x-direction;

x_b—x-coordinate of the end position of the pectoral fin along the x-direction;
z_a—z-coordinate of the starting position of the pectoral fin along the z-direction;
$z(x)$—equation of the pectoral fin contour;
$A(z)$—amplitude control equation that changes with z;
t—motion time;
λ—wave length;
f—wave frequency.

Fit the equation of the overall center of mass of the fish-body and pectoral fin in the fish-body coordinate system and establish the equation for the position of the overall center of mass (x_c, y_c, z_c):

$$\begin{cases} x_c = \frac{m_1 x_{c_1} + m_2 x_{c_2}}{m_1 + m_2} \\ y_c = \frac{m_1 y_{c_1} + m_2 y_{c_2}}{m_1 + m_2} \\ z_c = \frac{m_1 z_{c_1} + m_2 z_{c_2}}{m_1 + m_2} \end{cases} \qquad (7)$$

where, m_1— mass of the fish-body;

m_2—mass of the pectoral fin.

In the fish coordinate system, the x and z directions of the overall center of mass are fixed, and only the y direction changes with time. By selecting a suitable frequency f and wavelength for the pectoral fin oscillation, setting the corresponding amplitude control equation $A(z)$, and using the established physical model of the flatworm-inspired marine exploration robot, the obtained coordinates can be transformed to obtain the coordinates of the center of mass in the inertial coordinate system.

3.2 Kinematic Modeling of Swing-Rod Propulsion Fins for Flatworm-inspired Marine Exploration Robot

The schematic diagram of the oscillating guide rod-type undulating fin mechanism is illustrated in Fig. 5, with the xCy coordinate system established as shown. Based on the diagrammatic relationship, the displacement S of point B relative to point C and the angular displacement of the swing rod BC are respectively determined as follows:

$$\begin{cases} S = \sqrt{(l_1 \cos \varphi_1)^2 + (l_4 + l_1 \sin \varphi_1)^2} \\ \varphi_3 = \arccos \frac{l_1 \cos \varphi_1}{S} \end{cases} \qquad (8)$$

where, S—length of oscillating rod BC;

l_1—length of crank AB;

l_4—length of frame AC;

φ_1—angular displacement of crank AB;

φ_3—angular displacement of oscillating rod BC.

The velocity v_r of the slider moving along the swing rod BC and the angular velocity ω_3 of the swing rod BC are respectively given by:

$$\begin{cases} v_r = -l_1 \omega_1 \sin(\varphi_1 - \varphi_3) \\ \omega_3 = \frac{l_1 \omega_1 \cos(\varphi_1 - \varphi_3)}{S} \end{cases} \qquad (9)$$

where, v_r—speed of slider movement;

ω_1—angular velocity of rod AB;

ω_3—angular velocity of oscillating rod BC.

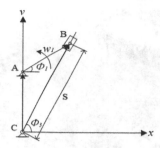

Fig. 5. Mechanism diagram of oscillating guide rod type undulating fin.

The acceleration of the slider moving along the oscillating rod BC a_r and the angular acceleration of the oscillating rod BC are respectively given by:

$$\begin{cases} a_r = S\omega_3^2 - l_1\omega_1^2 \cos(\varphi_1 - \varphi_3) \\ \alpha_3 = \frac{-2v_r\omega_3^2 - l_1\omega_1^2 \sin(\varphi_1 - \varphi_3)}{S} \end{cases} \quad (10)$$

where, a_r—angular velocity of slider;

α_3—angular acceleration of oscillating rod BC.

The rotational speed ω of the planned crank AB is determined by substituting it into the above equations to determine the important motion parameters such as the angular displacement, angular velocity, and angular acceleration of the oscillating rod BC at any instant.

4 Prototype Experiment

To verify the feasibility of the flatworm-inspired marine exploration robot design, an independent robot prototype was designed and manufactured, as depicted in Fig. 6. The robot features a symmetrical structure with multiple sets of interconnected swinging oscillating rod-type flapping fins arranged symmetrically on both sides of the fish-body, equipped with a thin film. The drive motor generates torque, which is transmitted along the crankshaft axis to drive the swinging oscillating rod, resulting in a sinusoidal motion in space. This motion propels the thin film to create a swimming action, enabling the flatworm-inspired marine exploration robot to swim underwater.

The prototype underwent water testing, and different speeds were adjusted via Bluetooth control on a mobile phone to drive the prototype forward and turn, as illustrated in Fig. 7 during the experiment.

Throughout the experiment, the robot's motion was remotely controlled, and the up and down swinging of the flapping fins were clearly observed, along with the motion of the thin film striking the water surface, facilitating forward swimming resembling a sine wave. By adjusting the motor speed, the flatworm-inspired marine exploration robot demonstrated the ability to execute left and right turns, as well as accelerate and decelerate. These results verified the rationality of the robot's structural design, the feasibility of the proposed scheme, and its capability to meet the design and operational requirements.

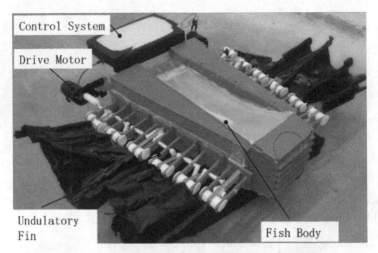

Fig.6. Flatworm-inspired Marine Exploration Robot prototype.

Fig. 7. Flatworm-inspired Marine Exploration Robot underwater experiment.

5   Conclusion

A swing lever type undulating fin mechanism with multiple groups of linkage arranged symmetrically on both sides was designed to achieve sinusoidal water-beating motion, driving the flatworm-inspired marine exploration to swim underwater. It can be applied in various fields such as ocean development, underwater detection, and marine protection. The kinematic model of the flatworm-inspired marine exploration robot body and swing lever type undulating fin mechanism was established, and simulation analysis was carried out to verify the correctness and feasibility of the kinematic modeling. The principle prototype of the flatworm-inspired marine exploration robot was developed, and underwater swimming and turning experiments were carried out to verify the rationality of the robot's structural design and the feasibility of the scheme.

Acknowledgments. This work was supported by Scientific Research Project of Education Department of Hubei Province under Grant No. D20222603, Science and Technology Innovation Team of Hubei University of Arts and Science under Grantr 2022pytd01, Graduate Innovation Project of Hubei University of Arts and Science under Grant YCX202301.

References

1. Wang, Y., Wang, R., Wang, S., Tan, M., Yu, J.: Underwater bioinspired propulsion: from inspection to manipulation. IEEE Trans. Ind. Electron. **67**, 7629–7638 (2020)
2. Wang, R., Wang, S., Wang, Y., Cheng, L., Tan, M.: Development and motion control of biomimetic underwater robots: a survey. IEEE Trans. Syst. Man Cybern, Syst. **52**, 833–844 (2022)
3. Liu, H., Curet, O.: Swimming performance of a bio-inspired robotic vessel with undulating fin propulsion. Bioinspir. Biomim. **13**, 056006 (2018)
4. Zhou, H., Hu, T., Xie, H., Zhang, D., Shen, L.: Computational and experimental study on dynamic behavior of underwater robots propelled by bionic undulating fins. Sci. China Technol. Sci. **53**, 2966–2971 (2010)
5. Scaradozzi, D., Palmieri, G., Costa, D., Pinelli, A.: BCF swimming locomotion for autonomous underwater robots: a review and a novel solution to improve control and efficiency. Ocean Eng. **130**, 437–453 (2017)
6. Liu, Y., Jiang, H.: Optimum curvature characteristics of body/caudal fin locomotion. J. Marine Science and Eng. **17** (2021)
7. Li, G., et al.: Self-powered soft robot in the mariana trench. Nature **591**, 66–71 (2021)
8. Zhou, C., Low, K.H.: Design and locomotion control of a biomimetic underwater vehicle with fin propulsion. IEEE/ASME Trans. Mechatron. **17**, 25–35 (2012)
9. Marcoux, T.M., Korsmeyer, K.E.: Energetics and behavior of coral reef fishes during oscillatory swimming in a simulated wave surge. Journal of Experimental Biology. jeb.191791 (2019)
10. Cai, Y., Chen, L., Bi, S., Li, G., Zhang, H.: Bionic flapping pectoral fin with controllable spatial deformation. J. Bionic Eng. **16**, 916–930 (2019)
11. Rahman, M.M.: Study On Biomimetic Squid-Like Underwater Robots With Two Undulating Side Fins (2013)
12. Yu, J., Wen, L., Ren, Z.: A survey on fabrication, control, and hydrodynamic function of biomimetic robotic fish. Sci. China Technol. Sci. **60**, 1365–1380 (2017)
13. Rahman, M., Sugimori, S., Miki, H., Yamamoto, R., Sanada, Y., Toda, Y.: Braking performance of a biomimetic squid-like underwater robot. J. Bionic Eng. **10**, 265–273 (2013)
14. Wang, S., Wang, Y., Wei, Q., Tan, M., Yu, J.: A bio-inspired robot with undulatory fins and its control methods. IEEE/ASME Trans. Mechatron.Mechatron. **22**, 206–216 (2017)
15. Xing, C., Cao, Y., Cao, Y., Pan, G., Huang, Q.: Asymmetrical oscillating morphology hydrodynamic performance of a novel bionic pectoral fin. JMSE. **10**, 289 (2022)

Coordinated Passive Maneuvering Target Tracking by Multiple Underwater Vehicles Based on Asynchronous Sequential Filtering

Xuechao Cheng, Yuanbo Guo, Jian Gao[✉], Yimin Chen, and Guang Pan

School of Marine Science and Technology, Northwestern Polytechnical University,
Xi'an 710072, China
jiangao@nwpu.edu.cn

Abstract. As a hot topic in the development of marine science, underwater target tracking technology has been playing an important role since its birth. Passive sonar, one of the widely used sensor devices in tracking, collecting data without emitting energy signals, has good concealment. As a sensor carrier with superior performance, autonomous underwater vehicle (AUV) can be used to build an underwater multi-platform collaborative tracking system, to obtain composite observation data and improve tracking performance. In this paper, the problem of cooperative passive tracking of underwater maneuvering targets by multi-AUVs is studied. Aiming at the divergence problem of tracking maneuvering targets by a single AUV, a collaborative tracking system which has multi-AUVs, is formed. In view of the unavoidable asynchronous sampling problem among multi-AUVs, the asynchronous sequential filtering method is derived. In order to solve the prediction model distortion problem, the strong tracking theory is introduced. Therefore, combined with the Unscented-Kalman-Filter, an Asynchronous-Sequential-Strong-Tracking-Filter-Unscented-Kalman-Tracking algorithm (AS-STF-UKT) is proposed. In simulation scenario, it successfully solved the previous problems.

Keywords: Asynchronous Sampling · Strong Tracking Sequential Filter · Unscented Kalman Algorithm · Underwater Multi-AUV Collaboration

1 Introduction

The collaborative passive tracking of the underwater maneuvering target (UMT) is a technology that estimates target motion states. And it plays a significant role

This work is supported partly by the National Key Research and Development Program 2021YFC2803000, and partly by the National Basic Scientific Research Program under Grant JCKY2019207A019.

in marine science fields [1]. It is usually achieved using passive sonar combined with filtering algorithms. And collaboration across multiple platforms will also help. Autonomous underwater vehicle (AUV) is an efficient platform with high flexibility. Carrying passive sonar, AUV can be used as the observation platform of underwater tracking system. UMT generally has the characteristics of high concealment, strong maneuverability, and non-cooperation. Therefore, the single-platform observation data is relatively sparse in time domain. However, the tracking system composed of multi-AUVs, as shown in Fig. 1, can process the observation and estimation data of each platform in the fusion center through underwater acoustic communication. Thus it can make the tracking system more stable and reliable [2].

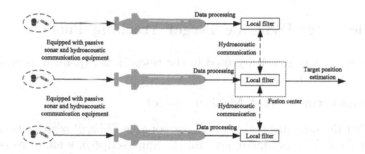

Fig. 1. Underwater multi-AUV tracking system.

As a kind of Bearings-Only Target (BOT) tracking problem [3], the passive observation model is nonlinear. Meanwhile, considering that the movement of UMT is usually highly nonlinear, Recursive-Bayesian-Estimation algorithms are generally used for tracking [4], such as predictive filtering theory [5]. Kalman filter is a typical representative among them [6]. In pursuit of more accurate prediction models, Bar-shalom et al. proposed an Interactive-Multiple-Model (IMM) algorithm that modeled the target motions as random jump system [7], which switches according to a first-order Markov chain [8]. Xin et al. combined particle filter and IMM to propose an underwater target tracking method [9]. Saber et al. proposed distributed tracking based on consensus theory [10], which can realize information collaboration and data fusion through information exchange between sensors.

To sum up, IMM algorithms are usually based on linear systems, and there are few studies about nonlinear azimuth-only tracking systems with weak observability. UKF algorithm, as the leader in dealing with nonlinear problems, can effectively simplify the amount of calculation. In asynchronous sampling problems, issues such as insufficient prior motion information of non-cooperative targets and prediction model parameter mismatch cannot be ignored in practice. Therefore, this paper studies the above-mentioned problems. The main contributions can be summarized as follows.

(1) Aiming at the divergence problem of single-platform tracking, a multi-platform underwater observation system is constructed. Through underwater acoustic communication, multi-source observation data is processed in the fusion center, which improved the sparsity and observation data.

(2) Facing the ubiquitous asynchronous sampling problem, this paper relies on the idea of asynchronous sequential filtering. The time registration work of the fusion center has greatly improved the disorder of the observation data.

(3) When dealing with the problem caused by the prediction model mismatch, this paper draws on strong tracking theory. And furthermore, the Asynchronous-Sequential-Strong-Tracking-Filter-Unscented-Kalman-Tracking (AS-STF-UKT) algorithm is proposed. Simulation results verify its good performance.

2   Underwater Dynamic Target Tracking Theory

In this section, some knowledge used in the research is explained as necessary.

2.1   Maneuvering Target Motion Model

Assume that the sampling period of passive sonar is T; (x, y) represents the coordinates in the OXY coordinate system; the superscript p, v and a respectively represent the position, velocity and acceleration component of the motion state x; F represents the motion state transition matrix; G represents the noise driven matrix; w is the noise of the motion process; and the subscript $k-1$ means the $k-1$ moment; thus, the discrete expression (1) of the target motion model is given.

$$x_k = F_{k-1} x_{k-1} + G_{k-1} w_{k-1} \tag{1}$$

CV Model [11]. Velocity in CV motion can be decomposed, so merely the movement on the x-axis is discussed as an example. The target motion state at the k moment is defined as $x_k = [x_k^p, x_k^v]^T$, then:

$$F = \begin{bmatrix} 1 & T \\ 0 & 1 \end{bmatrix}, G = \begin{bmatrix} T^2/2 \\ T \end{bmatrix} \tag{2}$$

CA Model. CA motion also has decomposability. Taking x coordinate as an example, the target motion state at the k moment is represented as $x_k = [x_k^p, x_k^v, x_k^a]^T$, then:

$$F = \begin{bmatrix} 1 & T & T^2/2 \\ 0 & 1 & T \\ 0 & 0 & 1 \end{bmatrix}, G = \begin{bmatrix} T^2/2 \\ T \\ 1 \end{bmatrix} \tag{3}$$

Constant Turn (CT) Model [12]. Velocity is highly coupled in CT motion, so its motion model should be analyzed as a whole. ω is used to represent the angular velocity, and the target motion state at the k moment is $x_k = [x_k^p, x_k^v, y_k^p, y_k^v]^T$, then:

$$F = \begin{bmatrix} 1 & \frac{\sin\omega T}{\omega} & 0 & -\frac{1-\cos\omega T}{\omega} \\ 0 & \cos\omega T & 0 & -\sin\omega T \\ 0 & \frac{1-\cos\omega T}{\omega} & 1 & \frac{\sin\omega T}{\omega} \\ 0 & \sin\omega T & 0 & \cos\omega T \end{bmatrix}, G = \begin{bmatrix} T^2/2 & 0 \\ T & 0 \\ 0 & T^2/2 \\ 0 & T \end{bmatrix} \tag{4}$$

2.2 Passive Sonar Observation Model

In single-target tracking scenarios, it is usually assumed that the target moves at a constant depth underwater, and the tracking platform is at the same depth. Let T be the period of the passive sonar, $(x(t), y(t))$ and $(x_i(t), y_i(t))$ be the target position and platform position, respectively, and $v(t)$ be measurement noise. Then the measurement equation of passive sonar is given here:

$$z(t) = \arctan \frac{x(t) - x_i(t)}{y(t) - y_i(t)} + v(t), t = 1, ..., kT, k \in Z^+ \tag{5}$$

It can be seen that $(x(t), y(t))$ does not have a unique analytical solution.

2.3 Unscented Kalman Filter

Consider the following discrete nonlinear systems:

$$\begin{cases} x_k = f(x_{k-1}) + w_{k-1} \\ z_k = h(x_k) + v_k \end{cases} \tag{6}$$

The first equation is the prediction model, where f is the state space function; the second equation is the observation model, where h is the nonlinear measurement function, specifically, corresponding to Eq. (5) in this paper. The system is qualified as follows:

(1) w and v are uncorrelated white noise sequences with mean 0, and satisfy:

$$\begin{cases} \text{cov}(w_k, w_j) = Q_k \delta_{kj}, Q_k \geq 0 \\ \text{cov}(v_{k+1}, v_{j+1}) = R_{k+1} \delta_{(k+1)(j+1)}, R_{k+1} > 0 \\ \text{cov}(w_j, v_k) = 0 \end{cases} \tag{7}$$

where δ_{kj} is the Kronecker delta function.

(2) The target initial motion state x_0 obeys Gaussian distribution, and has:

$$\text{cov}(x_0, w_k) = 0, \text{cov}(x_0, v_k) = 0 \tag{8}$$

UKF algorithm is a filtering method based on the Recursive-Bayesian-Estimation idea. The specific implementation process is as follows.

Step 1. Based on the posterior estimate $\hat{x}_{k-1|k-1}$ and posterior error covariance matrix $P_{k-1|k-1}$ at the $k-1$ moment, generate Sigma points:

$$\chi_{k-1|k-1}^s = \begin{cases} \hat{x}_{k-1|k-1}, s = 0 \\ \hat{x}_{k-1|k-1} + \sqrt{(n+\kappa)}L_{k-1|k-1}^s, s = 1, \cdots, n \\ \hat{x}_{k-1|k-1} - \sqrt{(n+\kappa)}L_{k-1|k-1}^s, s = n+1, \cdots, 2n \end{cases} \quad (9)$$

where $\chi_{k-1|k-1}^s$ is the Sigma point s, $L_{k-1|k-1}^s$ represents the s column of the matrix $L_{k-1|k-1}$, and $P_{k-1|k-1} = L_{k-1|k-1}L_{k-1|k-1}{}^T$. Generally let $\kappa = 3 - n$, then the weight of each Sigma point is:

$$W_s = \begin{cases} \frac{\kappa}{n+\kappa}, s = 0 \\ \frac{\kappa}{2(n+\kappa)}, s = 1, \cdots, 2n \end{cases} \quad (10)$$

Step 2. By propagating the Sigma points above, $\hat{x}_{k|k-1}$ and $P_{k|k-1}$ can be obtained as follows:

$$\begin{cases} \hat{x}_{k|k-1} = \sum_{s=0}^{2n} W_s f(\chi_{k-1|k-1}^s) \\ P_{k|k-1} = \sum_{s=0}^{2n} W_s(f(\chi_{k-1|k-1}^s) - \hat{x}_{k|k-1})(f(\chi_{k-1|k-1}^s) - \hat{x}_{k|k-1})^T + Q_{k-1} \end{cases} \quad (11)$$

Predictive measurement $\hat{z}_{k|k-1}$, mutual covariance P_{xz} between state and measurement, and innovation covariance P_{zz} can be obtained by weighted summation:

$$\begin{cases} \hat{z}_{k|k-1} = \sum_{s=0}^{2n} W_s h(\chi_{k|k-1}^s) \\ P_{xz} = \sum_{s=0}^{2n} W_s(\chi_{k|k-1}^s - \hat{x}_{k|k-1})(h(\chi_{k|k-1}^s) - \hat{z}_{k|k-1})^T \\ P_{zz} = \sum_{s=0}^{2n} W_s(h(\chi_{k|k-1}^s) - \hat{z}_{k|k-1})(h(\chi_{k|k-1}^s) - \hat{z}_{k|k-1})^T + R_k \end{cases} \quad (12)$$

Step 3, let Kalman Gain $K_k = P_{xz}P_{zz}^{-1}$, and update the posteriori estimation $\hat{x}_{k|k}$ and posteriori error covariance matrix $P_{k|k}$ at the k moment:

$$\begin{cases} \hat{x}_{k|k} = \hat{x}_{k|k-1} + K_k(z_k - \hat{z}_{k|k-1}) \\ P_{k|k} = P_{k|k-1} - K_k P_{zz} K_k^T \end{cases} \quad (13)$$

3   Multi-AUV UMT Tracking Algorithm

This section uses the UKF algorithm as a blueprint to derive the AS-STF-UKT algorithm in detail.

3.1   Asynchronous Sampling

In the figure below, the target is observed by N AUV platforms with different sampling period. t_k is denoted as the time of data fusion in the fusion center, N_k measurements are collected within the time interval $(t_{k-1}, t_k]$, z_k^i represents the i measurement, and t_k^i is denoted as the arrival time.

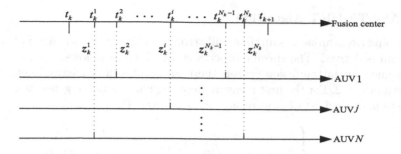

Fig. 2. Measurement timing diagram.

3.2 Strong Tracking Filter

Strong Tracking Filter (STF) is a method to optimize Kalman gain by introducing fading factor. The residual is defined as:

$$\varepsilon_k = z_k - \hat{z}_{k|k-1} \tag{14}$$

The fading factor can be given by the principle of orthogonality:

$$\lambda_k = \max\left(1, \frac{tr(P_k^\varepsilon - \bar{R}_k)}{tr(P_{zz})}\right) \tag{15}$$

among them:

$$\begin{cases} \bar{R}_k = (R_k^{1/2})^T \psi_k^{-1} R_k^{1/2} \\ \psi_k = diag[\psi_{k,j}], \psi_{k,j} = \begin{cases} 1, |\varepsilon_{k,j}| < \gamma \\ \mathrm{sgn}(\varepsilon_{k,j})\gamma/\varepsilon_{k,j}, |\varepsilon_{k,j}| > \gamma \end{cases} \end{cases} \tag{16}$$

where $\varepsilon_{k,j}$ is the j element of ε_k, γ is a constant. P_k^ε is the innovation covariance corresponding to the real measurement, which can be estimated by the follow:

$$P_k^\varepsilon = \begin{cases} \varepsilon_1 \varepsilon_1^T, k = 1 \\ \frac{\xi P_{k-1}^\varepsilon + \varepsilon_k \varepsilon_k^T}{1+\xi}, k > 1 \end{cases} \tag{17}$$

where $0 < \xi \leq 1$ is the forgetting factor, usually 0.95. Therefore, the innovation covariance matrix and mutual covariance matrix become:

$$\begin{cases} P_{k|k-1} = \lambda_k \sum_{s=0}^{2n} W_s(\chi_{k|k-1}^s - \hat{x}_{k|k-1})(\chi_{k|k-1}^s - \hat{x}_{k|k-1})^T \\ P_{xz} = \lambda_k \sum_{s=0}^{2n} W_s(\chi_{k|k-1}^s - \hat{x}_{k|k-1})(h(\chi_{k|k-1}^{1,s}) - \hat{x}_{k|k-1})^T \\ P_{zz} = \lambda_k \sum_{s=0}^{2n} W_s(h(\chi_{k|k-1}^s) - \hat{z}_{k|k-1})(h(\chi_{k|k-1}^s) - \hat{z}_{k|k-1})^T + \bar{R}_k \end{cases} \tag{18}$$

Finally, the Kalman gain is calculated according to $K_k = P_{xz}P_{zz}^{-1}$, and the estimate of the target state is updated as follows.

$$\begin{cases} \hat{x}_{k|k} = \hat{x}_{k|k-1} + K_k \varepsilon_k \\ P_{k|k} = P_{k|k-1} - K_k P_{zz} K_k^T \end{cases} \tag{19}$$

3.3 AS-STF-UKT Algorithm

By combing asynchronous sampling and strong tracking filter, the AS-STF-UKT algorithm is derived. The specific process is described as follows.

Assume that in the fusion center, there are a total of N measurement data, as shown in Fig. 2. For the first measurement, Sigma points are generated by the complete posteriori estimation results $\hat{x}_{k-1|k-1}$ and $P_{k-1|k-1}$.

$$
\chi_{k-1|k-1}^{1,s} = \begin{cases} \hat{x}_{k-1|k-1}, s = 0 \\ \hat{x}_{k-1|k-1} + \sqrt{(n+\kappa)}L_{k-1|k-1}^s, s = 1, \cdots, n \\ \hat{x}_{k-1|k-1} - \sqrt{(n+\kappa)}L_{k-1|k-1}^s, s = n, \cdots, 2n \end{cases} \tag{20}
$$

Propagate these Sigma points, we can get $\hat{x}_{k|k-1}^1$ and $P_{k|k-1}^1$:

$$
\begin{cases} \hat{x}_{k|k-1}^1 = \sum_{s=0}^{2n} W_s f(\chi_{k-1|k-1}^{1,s}) \\ P_{k|k-1}^1 = \sum_{s=0}^{2n} W_s (\chi_{k|k-1}^{1,s} - \hat{x}_{k|k-1}^1)(\chi_{k|k-1}^{1,s} - \hat{x}_{k|k-1}^1)^T + Q_{k-1} \end{cases} \tag{21}
$$

By weighted summation, $\hat{z}_{k|k-1}^1$ can be obtained as follows:

$$
\hat{z}_{k|k-1}^1 = \sum_{s=0}^{2n} W_s h(\chi_{k|k-1}^{1,s}) \tag{22}
$$

Define the residual at this time as:

$$
\varepsilon_k^1 = z_k^1 - \hat{z}_{k|k-1}^1 \tag{23}
$$

According to the strong tracking filter which is described in Sect. 3.2, the fading factor λ_k^1 can be obtained. So the prior error covariance matrix $P_{k|k-1}^1$, mutual covariance P_{xz}^1 between state and measurement, and innovation covariance P_{zz}^1 can be obtained by weighted summation:

$$
\begin{cases} P_{k|k-1}^1 = \lambda_k^1 \sum_{s=0}^{2n} W_s (\chi_{k|k-1}^{1,s} - \hat{x}_{k|k-1}^1)(\chi_{k|k-1}^{1,s} - \hat{x}_{k|k-1}^1)^T \\ P_{xz}^1 = \lambda_k^1 \sum_{s=0}^{2n} W_s (\chi_{k|k-1}^{1,s} - \hat{x}_{k|k-1}^1)(h(\chi_{k|k-1}^{1,s}) - \hat{x}_{k|k-1}^1)^T \\ P_{zz}^1 = \lambda_k^1 \sum_{s=0}^{2n} W_s (h(\chi_{k|k-1}^{1,s}) - \hat{z}_{k|k-1}^1)(h(\chi_{k|k-1}^{1,s}) - \hat{z}_{k|k-1}^1)^T + \bar{R}_k \end{cases} \tag{24}
$$

Then, the Kalman gain is calculated:

$$
K_k^1 = P_{xz}^1 P_{zz}^{1\,-1} \tag{25}
$$

And the incomplete posterior estimation results of the target state is updated as follows:

$$
\begin{cases} \hat{x}_{k|k}^1 = \hat{x}_{k|k-1}^1 + K_k^1 \varepsilon_k^1 \\ P_{k|k}^1 = P_{k|k-1}^1 - K_k^1 P_{zz}^1 K_k^{1T} \end{cases} \tag{26}
$$

When the fusion center receives the second measurement, the results are updated again according to formulas (19) to (24). It should be noted that the state transition matrix of the prediction model is recalculated. Repeat the above steps until the last measurement $z_k^{N_k}$, resulting in a full posteriori estimate at the k moment:

$$\begin{cases} \hat{x}_{k|k} = \hat{x}_k^{N_k} \\ P_{k|k} = P_k^{N_k} \end{cases} \tag{27}$$

4   Simulation Verification

Simulation experiments are designed to verify the AS-STF-UKT algorithm. It is assumed that there are 3 AUV platforms, and their information is shown in Table 1.

Table 1. Platform Properties

Platform	Position	Sampling period
AUV1	$(-50,300)$	$0.5\,\text{s}$
AUV2	$(750,0)$	$1\,\text{s}$
AUV3	$(750,600)$	$1.2\,\text{s}$

For the UMT, the specific motion state is shown in Table 2.

Table 2. Target motion state

Time	Motion
Initial position	$(20,30)$
0–40 s	CV, with $x^v = 10$
40–80 s	CT, with $\omega = 0.075$
80–110 s	CV, with $x^v = -10$
110–150 s	CT, with $\omega = -0.077$
150–165 s	CA, with $x^a = 2$
165–185 s	CA, with $x^a = -0.35$ and $y^a = -1.3$
185–200 s	CV, with $x^v = 2.78$ and $y^v = -27.42$

Assume that the fusion center performs data fusion every 1 s, and the CV model is used as the prediction model. In order to reflect the superior performance of the AS-STF-UKT algorithm, the comparison experiment is designed as follows. For the single AUV2, UKF is adopted, for multi-AUVs, AS-UKT

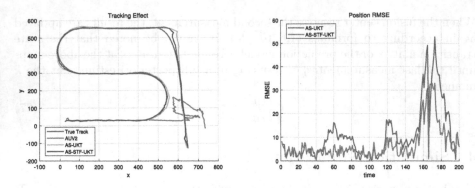

Fig. 3. AS-STF-UKT algorithm simulation effect.

without strong tracking filter and AS-STF-UKT are adopted respectively. Here are the comparison results after 100 Monte Carlo trials (Fig. 3).

From the figure above, the following conclusions could be drawn.

First of all, it can be seen that when the target maneuvers, the tracking by a single AUV is divergent due to the mismatch between the prediction model and the target motion model. Moreover, this divergence is difficult to recover in the follow-up tracking process. This is also in line with our expectations.

Besides, it is worth noting that both AsUKT and AsStfUKT can solve the problem effectively, which is attributed to the introduction of multiple AUV platforms. But, in the face of asynchronous sampling, the position RMSE of the AsStfUKT is overall smaller than that of the AsUKT. Especially in the case of serious distortion of prediction models such as CT and CA motion, and target maneuvering, the estimation of the AS-STF-UKT algorithm is obviously more in line with the real value.

In general, simulation experiments show that the AS-STF-UKT algorithm has strong robustness and can effectively deal with the mismatch of model parameters and asynchronous sampling.

5   Summary

Aiming at the practical application scenario of UMT tracking, this paper studies some specific problems and makes some achievements. The target motion model is naturally unknowable, under this premise, the tracking of single AUV platform is divergent. Therefore, in this paper, multiple AUV platforms are introduced to form a cooperative observation system. In the system, there is also a common problem of asynchronous sampling. So this paper learns from the idea of asynchronous sequential filtering. Meanwhile, prediction model distortions and target maneuvers can also have a large impact on tracking performance. Hence, the strong tracking filter is adopted in this paper. Finally, the AS-STF-UKT algorithm is proposed to deal with these problems, and good results are obtained, which proves that it has stronger robustness and fine performance.

UMT tracking is a complex subject, and many aspects are worth further discussion. In the followup study, the motion of the AUV observation platform, the interaction among AUVs and the target should be fully considered. The algorithm should be improved in a condition more suitable to the reality. In addition, the feasibility of underwater experiment should be seriously considered, and the real performance of the tracking algorithm should be tested in practical applications.

References

1. Ghafoor, H., Noh, Y.: An overview of next-generation underwater target detection and tracking: an integrated underwater architecture. IEEE Access **7**, 98841–98853 (2019)
2. Chen, Z., Xu, W.: Joint passive detection and tracking of underwater acoustic target by beamforming-based bernoulli filter with multiple arrays. Sensors **18**(11), 4022 (2018)
3. Asfia, U., Radhakrishnan, R., Sharma, S.N.: Three-dimensional bearings-only target tracking: comparison of few sigma point Kalman filters. In: Gu, J., Dey, R., Adhikary, N. (eds.) Communication and Control for Robotic Systems. SIST, vol. 229, pp. 273–289. Springer, Singapore (2022). https://doi.org/10.1007/978-981-16-1777-5_17
4. Xie, Y., Song, T.L.: An improved labeled multi-bernoulli filter for bearings-only multi-target tracking. In: 11th Asian Control Conference (ASCC), p. 2060. IEEE (2017)
5. Ebrahimi, M., Ardeshiri, M., et al.: Bearing-only 2D maneuvering target tracking using smart interacting multiple model filter. Digit. Signal Process. **126**, 103497 (2022)
6. Cortes, I., Marin, P., Merwe, J., et al.: Adaptive techniques in scalar tracking loops with direct-state Kalman-filter. In: International Conference on Localization and GNSS, p. 1 (2021)
7. Mazor, E., Averbuch, A., Bar-Shalom, Y., et al.: Interacting multiple model methods in target tracking: a survey. IEEE Trans. Aerosp. Electron. Syst. **34**(1), 103–123 (1998)
8. Li, W., Jia, Y.: Consensus-based distributed multiple model UKF for jump Markov nonlinear systems. IEEE Trans. Autom. Control **57**(1), 227–233 (2011)
9. Xin, W., Xu, M., Wang, H., et al.: Combination of interacting multiple models with the particle filter for three-dimensional target tracking in underwater wireless sensor networks. Math. Probl. Eng. **12**, 939–955 (2012)
10. Olfati-Saber, R., Shamma, J.S.: Consensus filters for sensor networks and distributed sensor fusion. In: IEEE Conference on Decision & Control, p. 6698 (2005)
11. Blair, W.D.: Design of nearly constant velocity track filters for tracking maneuvering targets. In: 11th International Conference on Information Fusion, p. 1. IEEE (2008)
12. Li, X.R., Jilkov, V.P.: Survey of maneuvering target tracking. Part I. Dynamic models. IEEE Trans. Aerosp. Electron. Syst. **39**(4), 1333–1364 (2004)

Robust Tube-Based Model Predictive Control for Marine Ship-Mounted Cranes

Jingzheng Lin[1,2] [iD], Yongchun Fang[1,2(✉)], and Biao Lu[1,2]

[1] Institute of Robotics and Automatic Information Systems (IRAIS), Nankai University, Tianjin, China
ljz970129@mail.nankai.edu.cn, fangyc@nankai.edu.cn
[2] Institute of Intelligence Technology and Robotic Systems, Shenzhen Research Institute of Nankai University, Shenzhen, China

Abstract. Marine ship-mounted cranes are widely used in maritime transportation. For security concern, the payload swing needs to be limited within safe range. However, due to the underactuated nature of the system, the swing angle is hard to be controlled. Worse still, the control problem becomes more challenging when considering the effect of ship-induced disturbances caused by sea waves on the system. Besides, to avoid actuator saturation, the constraints of control input also need to be considered. To this end, in this paper, a robust tube-based model predictive control (TMPC) method, which successfully guarantees the constraints of both input and swing angle, is proposed to achieve satisfactory control performance even under the persistent ship roll perturbation. That is, for the marine ship-mounted crane, a discrete model is first obtained by some elaborate transformation, based on which a tube-based model predictive controller is constructed. To solve the constraint problem of payload swing, which is tough for traditional MPC, some delicate analysis is presented. Specifically, through the coupling relationship between swing angle and trolley acceleration, the swing angle constraint is successfully converted to input constraint. At last, simulation results are presented to illustrate the effectiveness and robustness of the proposed method.

Keywords: Marine ship-mounted cranes · Tube-based model predictive control · Constraints control · Underactuated system

1 Introduction

In recent years, with the increasing demand for ocean development, marine ship-mounted cranes have become indispensable means of maritime transportation.

This work is supported by the National Natural Science Foundation of China under Grant 62203235, 61873132, the Natural Science Foundation of Tianjin under Grant 21JCQNJC00090, the Key Projects of the Joint Fund of the National Natural Science Foundation of China under Grant U22A2050, and the Joint Fund of Guangdong Basic and Applied Basic Research Fund under Grant 2022A1515110046.

H. Yang et al. (Eds.): ICIRA 2023, LNAI 14273, pp. 256–268, 2023.
https://doi.org/10.1007/978-981-99-6498-7_23

Accordingly, how to efficiently and safely control the marine cranes has become a research hotspot. However, marine ship-mounted crane is a typical underactuated system [13], with more degrees of freedoms (DOFs) than their independent available control inputs. For this reason, the control problem of marine ship-mounted crane is very challenging. Unlike land-fixed crane, the marine ship-mounted crane additionally suffers from unfavorable persistent disturbances, such as ship motions, sea winds, and so on, which makes the control problem more difficult. On the other hand, manual operation is very dangerous under the wind and waves in the severe environment, thus the constraints of payload swing angle are vital. Hence, the research on controlling marine ship-mounted cranes safely and efficiently has both theoretical and practical importance.

Recently, land-fixed cranes have attracted extensive attention [10], many elaborately designed control methods have been proposed [9,14]. In contrast, less research is published for the marine ship-mounted cranes [6], due to their more complicated dynamics and persistent disturbances. In [2], by employing Lagrange's method, the marine crane's dynamic model is given, with a nonlinear controller proposed to track the desired trajectories. In [5], a prediction algorithm is proposed for the vertical motion of the ship, and an inversion-based controller is constructed, which considers the dynamic behavior of actuated states. In [7] Lu et.al incorporate the disturbance into the system dynamics, based on which an output feedback controller is designed to achieve satisfactory performance. Other advanced controllers [8,12] are also proposed for marine cranes.

Although the aforementioned results have been obtained for marine cranes, there are still some open problems to be addressed. Specifically, the actuators always have saturation characteristics, besides, for security reasons, it is necessary to limit payload within its working space without violent oscillation. What's more, in many existing works, the model is established under the clear knowledge of the relationship between disturbance and crane system, the control performance will degrade when the model is inaccurate. Fortunately, the above control problems are essentially a constrained optimal control with unknown disturbance and model uncertainty, which can be handled by TMPC strategy. Till now, there have been some works on applying MPC to crane systems. Specifically, [11] proposed a real-time MPC planner which takes the velocity and acceleration constraints into account. In [4], Danijel et.al present an MPC method of gantry/bridge crane, which implements fast transfer for cargos, meanwhile, keeps the payload swing sufficiently small. However, as far as we know, TMPC are rarely used in marine ship-mounted cranes.

Based on the above analysis, a robust tube-based MPC method is proposed for marine ship-mounted crane system, which guarantees satisfactory performance of the system with persistent ship roll disturbance. Specifically, by some mathematical transformation, two discrete models are obtained, namely nominal model and uncertain model, respectively. Based on nominal model, a TMPC designing process is established, whose tightened constraints are obtained by the uncertain model and a robust disturbance invariant. Through adequate mathematical analysis, the constraint of swing angle is successfully converted into the constraint of input, which is hard to solve directly by traditional MPC technique. The performance of the proposed method is illustrated by simulations.

The rest of this paper is arranged as follows: In Sect. 2, the discrete marine ship-mounted crane dynamics are presented, and the control objectives are formulated. Section 3 presents the controller design process, with system constraints fully described and well addressed. In Sect. 4, simulation results are provided to illustrate the performance of the proposed method. The conclusions of this work are summarized in Sect. 5.

2 Problem Statement

2.1 Dynamic Model

The studied marine ship-mounted crane with ship roll disturbance is presented in Fig. 1, where two frames are involved. The $\{Oy_w z_w\}$ represents the world-fixed frame and $\{Oy_s z_s\}$ represents the ship-fixed frame.

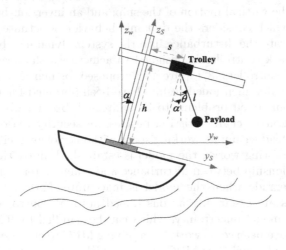

Fig. 1. Schematic illustration of an marine ship-mounted crane.

The dynamic equations of marine ship-mounted cranes can be obtained by utilizing Euler-Lagrange modeling technique[1]:

$$(M + m)\ddot{s} + ml\ddot{\theta}\cos\theta - ml\dot{\theta}^2\sin\theta - F = d_1, \tag{1}$$

$$ml^2\ddot{\theta} + ml\cos\theta\ddot{s} + mgl\sin\theta = d_2. \tag{2}$$

Specifically, the left side of (1) and (2) denote the land-fixed 2-D crane system dynamics, while the main difference is reflected in d_1 and d_2, which denote

---

[1] Ship's roll motion $\alpha(t)$ is supposed to be measurable, while its interference with the ship-mounted crane is unknown.

the α-related ship-induced disturbances [7]. The definitions of parameters and variables involved in (1) and (2) are listed in Table 1, and the following reasonable assumptions are presented:

Assumption 1: The ship-induced disturbances are unknown but bounded in the sense of

$$|d_1| \leq \bar{d}_1, \quad |d_2| \leq \bar{d}_2, \tag{3}$$

where $\bar{d}_1$, $\bar{d}_2$ are positive constants.

Table 1. Parameters/variables of the marine ship-mounted crane.

Parameters/variables	Physical meaning	Units
M	trolley mass	kg
m	payload mass	kg
l	rope length	m
g	gravity acceleration	m/s^2
h	boom height	m
$s(t)$	trolley position	m
$\theta(t)$	payload swing angle	rad
$F(t)$	control input	N
$\alpha(t)$	ship roll motion	rad

2.2   Model Development

According to (1), (2), one has

$$\ddot{s} = \frac{mg\sin\theta\cos\theta + ml\dot{\theta}^2\sin\theta}{\delta} + \frac{F}{\delta} + \frac{d_1}{\delta} - \frac{\cos\theta d_2}{l\delta}, \tag{4}$$

$$\ddot{\theta} = -\frac{\cos\theta}{l}\ddot{s} - \frac{g\sin\theta}{l} + \frac{d_2}{ml^2}, \tag{5}$$

where $\delta = M + m\sin^2\theta$. Considering the system behavior around the equilibrium point $(s, \theta, \dot{s}, \dot{\theta}) = (s_d, 0, 0, 0)$, one can obtain

$$\ddot{s} = \frac{mg\theta}{M} + \frac{F}{M} + \frac{d_1}{\delta} - \frac{\cos\theta d_2}{l\delta}, \tag{6}$$

$$\ddot{\theta} = \left(-\frac{mg}{lM} - \frac{g}{l}\right)\theta - \frac{F}{lM} + \frac{d_2}{ml^2} + \frac{d_2\cos^2\theta}{\delta l^2} - \frac{d_1\cos\theta}{\delta l}. \tag{7}$$

Define the state vector $x = [s, \theta, \dot{s}, \dot{\theta}]$, the system (6), (7) can be written as a state-space equation as

$$\dot{x} = Ax + Bu + \omega, \tag{8}$$

$$y = x, \tag{9}$$

where $u(t) = F(t) \in \mathbb{R}$ represents the system input, $y(t) \in \mathbb{R}^{4 \times 1}$ denotes the system output. The state-space matrices $A \in \mathbb{R}^{4 \times 4}$, $B \in \mathbb{R}^{4 \times 1}$ and $\omega \in \mathbb{R}^{4 \times 1}$ are explicitly defined as

$$A = \begin{bmatrix} 0 & 0 & 1 & 0 \\ 0 & 0 & 0 & 1 \\ 0 & \frac{mg}{M} & 0 & 0 \\ 0 & -\frac{mg}{lM} - \frac{g}{l} & 0 & 0 \end{bmatrix}, \quad B = \begin{bmatrix} 0 \\ 0 \\ \frac{1}{M} \\ -\frac{1}{lM} \end{bmatrix}, \quad \omega = \begin{bmatrix} 0 \\ 0 \\ \omega_1 \\ \omega_2 \end{bmatrix}, \quad (10)$$

where

$$\omega_1 = \frac{d_1}{\delta} - \frac{\cos\theta d_2}{l\delta} \le \bar{\omega}_1 = \frac{\bar{d}_1}{M} + \frac{\bar{d}_2}{lM},$$

$$\omega_2 = \frac{d_2}{ml^2} + \frac{d_2 \cos^2\theta}{\delta l^2} - \frac{d_1 \cos\theta}{\delta l} \le \bar{\omega}_2 = \frac{\bar{d}_2}{Ml^2} + \frac{\bar{d}_1}{Ml} + \frac{\bar{d}_2}{ml^2},$$

with positive constants $\bar{\omega}_1$, $\bar{\omega}_2$ being upper bounds of ω_1 and ω_2. Considering a proper sampling period T, the discrete-time model can be obtained as

$$\begin{aligned} x(k+1) &= A_p x(k) + B_p u(k) + \omega(k), \\ y(k) &= C_p x(k), \ C_p = I_{4 \times 4}, \end{aligned} \quad (11)$$

where $x(k)$ and $y(k)$ denote the system state and the output at time k, $I_{4 \times 4} \in \mathbb{R}^{4 \times 4}$ is the 4×4 identity matrix, discrete system parameter matrices A_p and B_p are calculated as

$$A_p = I_{4 \times 4} + TA, \quad B_p = TB. \quad (12)$$

This paper hereto obtains a linearized discrete-time model, which has been widely used for crane control [15], to simplify the MPC design and reduce computational burden. It is noticed that the system (11) contains the unknown but bounded term ω, thus (11) is called uncertain model, which is subject to state and control input constraints

$$u \in \mathbb{U}, \quad x \in \mathbb{X}, \quad (13)$$

where $\mathbb{U}$, $\mathbb{X}$ are compact sets. According to (3), one has $\omega \in \mathbb{W}$, where $\mathbb{W}$ is compact. Define the nominal system (disturbance-free) corresponding to (11)

$$\bar{x}(k+1) = A_p \bar{x}(k) + B_p \bar{u}(k), \quad \bar{y}(k+1) = C_p \bar{x}(k), \quad (14)$$

where $\bar{x}(k)$ and $\bar{u}(k)$ are the nominal system state and input at time k. The nominal system is also subject to state and control input constraints, which are defined as

$$\bar{u} \in \bar{\mathbb{U}}, \quad \bar{x} \in \bar{\mathbb{X}}. \quad (15)$$

The constraints $\bar{\mathbb{U}}$, $\bar{\mathbb{X}}$ are tighter than the original (defined in (13)), and will be designed later.

2.3   Control Objective

For marine ship-mounted crane system, the control objectives are defined as

1. Steady-state requirements: To position the payload accurately and suppress payload swing in the world-fixed frame, the target position p_d under the world coordinate can be described as

$$p_d = h \sin \alpha + s_d \cos \alpha, \tag{16}$$

where the payload swing angle $\theta_d = \alpha$. Thus, the reference trajectories for the system states can be obtained as

$$s_d = \frac{p_d - h \sin \alpha}{\cos \alpha}, \quad \theta_d = \alpha. \tag{17}$$

2. Safety requirements: Restrain the payload swing angle, i.e., $|\theta| \le \theta_{\max}$, where $\theta_{\max}$ is the maximum allowable swing angle of the payload.
3. Actuator saturation constraint requirements: Restrain the amplitude of the control input, i.e., $|u| \le u_{\max}$, where $u_{\max}$ denotes the maximum allowable control input.

3   Tube-Based MPC and Analysis

In this section, a tube-based MPC method is proposed for the marine ship-mounted cranes affected by ship's roll motion disturbance. The method not only guarantees the constraints of control input, but also considers unactuated states constraints, which are difficult to deal with in underactuated systems. What's more, by introducing the idea of 'tube', the constraints are proved to be effective even in the presence of ship motion disturbance. Before presenting the controller design, the following proposition is provided as preliminary.

3.1   Preliminary

Proposition 1: Let $K \in \mathbb{R}^{1 \times 4}$ denote a feedback component such that $A_K \triangleq A_p + B_p K$ is stable, the minimal disturbance invariant set $\mathbb{Z}$ is calculated as $\mathbb{Z} = \sum_{i=0}^{\infty} A_k^i \mathbb{W}$ [3], with a feedback controller u in the form of $u = \bar{u} + K(x - \bar{x})$, all possible state trajectories can be bounded in 'tube' $\mathbb{Z}$ centered around the nominal trajectory $\bar{x}$, i.e., $x(k+1) \in \bar{x}(k+1) \oplus \mathbb{Z}^2$.

Based on the above preliminary, one can handle the disturbances and model uncertainties in MPC design. Specifically, considering the uncertain model (11), the system states and control input are subject to the polyhedral constraints $(\mathbb{X}, \mathbb{U}) \triangleq \{x \in \mathbb{R}^{4 \times 1}, u \in \mathbb{R} | \Omega x \le x_{\max}, \Lambda u \le u_{\max}\}$. Utilizing the proposition 1, one can simplify the MPC problem of the disturbed uncertain model (11) into the MPC problem of the uncertainty-free nominal model (14). That is, by

---

[2] The detailed proof is in [1].

tightening the constraints of the nominal model using robust set $\mathbb{Z}$, the disturbed states x can be guaranteed within the constraints. The tightened constraints $\bar{\mathbb{X}}$, $\bar{\mathbb{U}}$ are calculated as:

$$\bar{\mathbb{X}} \triangleq \mathbb{X} \ominus \mathbb{Z}, \quad \bar{\mathbb{U}} \triangleq \mathbb{U} \ominus K\mathbb{Z}. \tag{18}$$

As mentioned in proposition 1, the actual input u applied to the real system requires nominal input $\bar{u}$, thus, one needs to solving the constrained optimization problem of the nominal model with the tightened constraints $\bar{\mathbb{X}}$ and $\bar{\mathbb{U}}$.

3.2   MPC Design on Nominal System

Considering the nominal model (14), the difference equation can be obtained as

$$\Delta\bar{x}(k+1) = A_p\Delta\bar{x}(k) + B_p\Delta\bar{u}(k), \ \Delta\bar{y}(k) = C_p\Delta\bar{x}(k), \tag{19}$$

where $\Delta\bar{x}(k)$, $\Delta\bar{u}(k)$, $\Delta\bar{y}(k)$ denote the variation of the state, the input and the output at time k, respectively. Then, the generalized state, as commonly utilized in the design of MPC algorithm, is defined as $x_e(k) = [\Delta\bar{x}(k), \ \bar{y}(k)]^\top$, and the new generalized discrete model can be inferred from (19) as

$$x_e(k+1) = A_e x_e(k) + B_e\Delta u(k), \ \bar{y}(k) = C_e x_e(k), \tag{20}$$

where $A_e \in \mathbb{R}^{8\times8}$, $B_e \in \mathbb{R}^{8\times1}$, $C_e \in \mathbb{R}^{4\times8}$ are derived as

$$A_e = \begin{bmatrix} A_p & 0 \\ C_pA_p & I_{4\times4} \end{bmatrix}, \ B_e = \begin{bmatrix} B_p \\ C_pB_p \end{bmatrix}, \ C_e = \begin{bmatrix} 0 & I_{4\times4} \end{bmatrix}. \tag{21}$$

According to (20), at the sampling time k, the prediction of the system output can be obtained as[3]:

$$Y = Fx_e(k) + \Phi\Delta U, \tag{22}$$

where $Y(k) = [\bar{y}(k+1), \ \bar{y}(k+2), \cdots, \bar{y}(k+N_p)]^\top \in \mathbb{R}^{4N_p\times1}$ denotes the output prediction sequence, $\Delta U(k) = [\Delta\bar{u}(k), \ \Delta\bar{u}(k+1), \cdots, \Delta\bar{u}(k+N_c-1)]^\top \in \mathbb{R}^{N_c\times1}$ denotes the future control input variation sequence, with N_p representing the prediction horizon while N_c being the control horizon, and $N_p \geq N_c$. The detailed expressions of $F \in \mathbb{R}^{4N_p\times8}$, $\Phi \in \mathbb{R}^{4N_p\times N_c}$ are

$$F = \begin{bmatrix} C_eA_e \\ C_eA_e^2 \\ \vdots \\ C_eA_e^{N_p} \end{bmatrix}, \ \Phi = \begin{bmatrix} C_eB_e & 0 & \cdots & 0 \\ C_eA_eB_e & C_eB_e & \cdots & 0 \\ \vdots & \vdots & \ddots & \vdots \\ C_eA_e^{N_p-1}B_e & C_eA_e^{N_p-2}B_e & \cdots & C_eA_e^{N_p-N_c}B_e \end{bmatrix}. \tag{23}$$

According to (17), one can obtain the reference trajectories as

$$\bar{y}_d = [s_d, \ \theta_d, \ \dot{s}_d, \ \dot{\theta}_d]^\top, \tag{24}$$

---

[3] For clarity, $x(k+i)$ denotes the prediction value of x at time $k+i$ based on time k.

where
$$\dot{s}_d = \frac{(p_d \sin\alpha - h)\dot{\alpha}}{\cos^2\alpha}, \quad \dot{\theta} = \dot{\alpha}. \tag{25}$$

Thus, the MPC tracking objective of Y at time k can be presented as

$$Y_d(k) = [\bar{y}_d(k), \ \bar{y}_d(k), \cdots, \ \bar{y}_d(k)]^\top, \tag{26}$$

with $Y_d(k) \in \mathbb{R}^{4N_p \times 1}$. To obtain the optimal input $\bar{u}$, the cost function is correspondingly defined as follows

$$J = (Y - Y_d)^\top Q(Y - Y_d) + \Delta U^\top R \Delta U, \tag{27}$$

where $Q \in \mathbb{R}^{4N_p \times 4N_p}$, $R \in \mathbb{R}^{N_c \times N_c}$ are weighting diagonal matrices. Based on (22), after some simplifications, the cost function (27) is converted into a quadratic programming form

$$\min_{\Delta U} J = \frac{1}{2}\Delta U^\top H \Delta U + f^\top \Delta U, \tag{28}$$

where
$$H = 2(\Phi^\top Q \Phi + R), \quad f = 2\Phi(k)^\top Q^\top \left(Fx_e(k) - Y_d(k)\right). \tag{29}$$

In this way, the optimization problem (28) is transformed into an unconstrained QP problem. By solving (28), one can obtain the change of control input $\Delta\bar{u}(k)$, which is the first element of the control sequence $\Delta U(k)$. Subsequently, the control input of the nominal model can be obtained as $\bar{u}(k) = \Delta\bar{u}(k) + \bar{u}(k-1)$. Accordingly, the actual control input of the uncertain model can also be derived

$$u(k) = \bar{u}(k) + K\left(x(k) - \bar{x}(k)\right). \tag{30}$$

Repeat the above procedures until the control termination condition is met.

3.3   Tightened Constraints

According to (28), one have an unconstrained QP problem of the nominal model, therefore, in this subsection, the tightened constraints are discussed to meet control requirements. As stated in proposition 1, the robust disturbance invariant set $\mathbb{Z}$ can be calculated, based on (18), as long as one define the constraints $\mathbb{X}$ and $\mathbb{U}$ of the uncertain model, the tightened constraints $\bar{\mathbb{X}}$ and $\bar{\mathbb{U}}$ can be obtained by set subtraction.

For the marine ship-mounted crane, the control input usually has an upper bound, which can be described as $|u(k)| \leq u_{\max}$. Then, one converts this actuator saturation constraint into the constraint on ΔU as

$$\Lambda \Delta U \leq \Gamma, \tag{31}$$

where
$$\Lambda = \begin{bmatrix} \overbrace{1 \ \ 0 \cdots 0}^{N_c} \\ -1 \ 0 \cdots 0 \end{bmatrix}, \quad \Gamma = \begin{bmatrix} u_{\max} - u(k-1) \\ u_{\max} + u(k-1) \end{bmatrix}. \tag{32}$$

Similarly, the payload swing angle also has an upper bound described as $|\theta(k)| \leq \theta_{\max}$, which needs to be converted to the inequality constraint on ΔU. However, due to the underactuated characteristics of the system, the following facts exist

$$|\theta(k)| \leq \theta_{\max} \Rightarrow \Omega x(k+1) \leq \Theta \Rightarrow \Omega A_p x(k) + \Omega B_p u(k) + \Omega w(k) \leq \Theta \quad (33)$$

where

$$\Omega = \begin{bmatrix} 0 & 1 & 0 & 0 \\ 0 & -1 & 0 & 0 \end{bmatrix}, \quad \Theta = \begin{bmatrix} \theta_{\max} \\ \theta_{\max} \end{bmatrix}. \quad (34)$$

According to (10), it is obvious that $\Omega B_p = [0 \ 0]^{\top}$, which indicates that the constraint cannot be solved directly. Therefore, it is necessary to find an indirect method to solve (33).

Back to the (5), after som lineariaztion, one can obtain

$$\ddot{\theta} = -\frac{1}{l}\ddot{s} - \frac{g\theta}{l} + \frac{d_2}{ml^2}, \quad (35)$$

define the new vector $\eta = [\theta, \dot{\theta}]^{\top}$, the above equation can be converted into

$$\dot{\eta} = M\eta + N, \quad (36)$$

where

$$M = \begin{bmatrix} 0 & 1 \\ -\frac{g}{l} & 0 \end{bmatrix}, \quad N = \begin{bmatrix} 0 \\ -\frac{\ddot{s}}{l} + \frac{d_2}{ml^2} \end{bmatrix}. \quad (37)$$

The general solution of (36) can be obtained as

$$\eta(t) = \exp(Mt)\eta(0) + \int_0^t \exp[(t-\tau)M]N(\tau)d\tau, \quad (38)$$

where $\exp(Mt)$ and $\eta(0)$ are

$$\exp(Mt) = \begin{bmatrix} \cos(\sqrt{-r}t) & (\sqrt{-r})^{-1}\sin(\sqrt{-r}t) \\ -\sqrt{-r}\sin(\sqrt{-r}t) & \cos(\sqrt{-r}t) \end{bmatrix},$$

$$\eta(0) = [\theta(0), \dot{\theta}(0)]^{\top}, \quad r = -\frac{g}{l}, \quad (39)$$

with $\theta(0)$, $\dot{\theta}(0)$ being the initial values of $\theta(t)$, $\dot{\theta}(t)$, respectively. Based on (37-39), one can obtain

$$\theta = \theta(0)\cos(\sqrt{-r}t) + (\sqrt{-r})^{-1}\sin(\sqrt{-r}t)\dot{\theta}(0) + \zeta$$

$$= \sqrt{\theta^2(0) - r^{-1}\dot{\theta}^2(0)}\sin(\sqrt{-r}t + \phi) + \zeta, \quad (40)$$

where

$$\zeta = \int_0^t \left(-\frac{\ddot{s}}{l} + \frac{d_2}{ml^2}\right)\sin[\sqrt{-r}(t-\tau)](\sqrt{-r})^{-1}d\tau, \quad \phi = \arctan\left(\frac{\theta(0)}{\dot{\theta}(0)}\sqrt{-r}\right). \quad (41)$$

Assume $\ddot{s}$ has the upper bound $|\ddot{s}| \leq a_{max}$, then (40) can be further deduced to

$$|\theta| \leq \sqrt{\theta^2(0) + \frac{l}{g}\dot{\theta}^2(0)} + \frac{1}{gl}a_{max}T + \frac{\bar{d}_s\sqrt{\frac{l}{g}}}{ml^2}T \leq \theta_{max}. \qquad (42)$$

After simplification, a_{max} is selected as

$$a_{max} = \frac{\sqrt{lg}}{T}\left(\theta_{max} - \sqrt{\theta^2(0) + \frac{l}{g}\dot{\theta}^2(0)} - \frac{\bar{d}_s\sqrt{\frac{l}{g}}}{ml^2}T\right). \qquad (43)$$

According to (6), one has

$$-\bar{d}_1 - \frac{\bar{d}_2}{l} \leq -M\ddot{s} + mg\theta + F \leq \bar{d}_1 + \frac{\bar{d}_2}{l}, \qquad (44)$$

combined with $|\ddot{s}| \leq a_{max}$, one can further obtain

$$-\bar{d}_1 - \frac{\bar{d}_2}{l} - mg\theta - Ma_{max} \leq F \leq \bar{d}_1 + \frac{\bar{d}_2}{l} - mg\theta + Ma_{max}. \qquad (45)$$

Then, similar to (31) and (32), one can convert the constraint on payload swing angel (33) to constraint on input.

Till now, by transforming state constraint to input constraint (31), (45), one get uncertain model constraint U. The tightened constraint can be obtained by $\bar{U} = U \ominus KZ \triangleq \{\bar{\Delta}U \in \mathbb{R}|\bar{A}\Delta U \leq \bar{\Gamma}\}$. The resulting QP problem can be formulated as

$$\min_{\Delta U} J = \frac{1}{2}\Delta U^\top H \Delta U + f^\top \Delta U, \qquad (46)$$
$$\text{s.t. } \bar{A}\Delta U \leq \bar{\Gamma},$$

and the actual control input is obtained in (30).

4   Simulation Results

To demonstrate the performance of the method, the simulation results are carried out in MATLAB. The system parameters and disturbances are determined as

$$M = 6.5 \text{ kg}, \quad m = 1.0 \text{ kg}, \quad l = 0.75 \text{ m}, \quad g = 9.8 \text{ m}, \quad h = 0.6 \text{ m},$$
$$\alpha(t) = 3\sin(0.2\pi t)^\circ, \quad s_d = 1.0 \text{ m}, \quad s(0) = 0 \text{ m}, \quad \theta(0) = 0^\circ, \quad N_p = N_c = 20, \quad (47)$$
$$Q = \text{diag}(30, 10, 1, 1), \quad R = 0.05, \quad K = [-23.6, 11.2, -21.17, 2.5].$$

The simulation results with different constraints are illustrated in Fig. 2. The constraints in left subgraph are $|\theta| \leq 10^\circ$ and $-10 \leq u \leq 30$ N, while those in right subgraph are $|\theta| \leq 8^\circ$ and $-10 \leq u \leq 10$ N. One can directly find that, the proposed method ensures the system states track their reference trajectories in

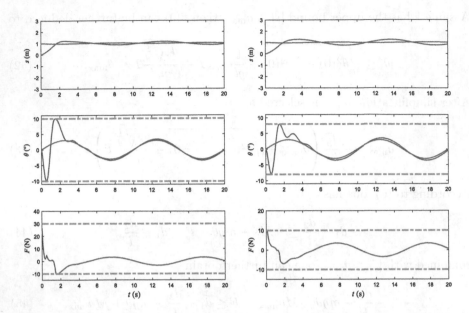

Fig. 2. Simulation results with different swing angle and control input constraints. Blue solid line: proposed method; Red solid line: reference trajectory; Green dotted-dashed line: the swing angle and control input constraints. (Color figure online)

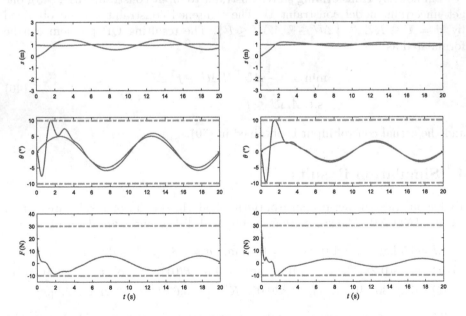

Fig. 3. Simulation results with different disturbance and parameter uncertainty. Blue solid line: proposed method; Red solid line: reference trajectory; Green dotted-dashed line: the swing angle and control input constraints. (Color figure online)

the presence of persistent ship roll motion. Even under different constraints, the method limits the payload swing angle and control input successfully.

To further demonstrate the robustness of the method, simulations with different ship roll motion and parameter uncertainty are implemented, which can be seen in Fig. 3. The left subgraph presents the system state trajectories with ship motion $\alpha(t) = 3\sin(0.2\pi t)°$, and the right subgraph presents the state trajectories under parameter uncertainty ($M = 7$ kg, $m = 0.95$ kg in actual system). The results show that, the proposed method has good robustness under the variable disturbance and uncertainty of system parameters.

5 Conclusion

In this paper, a robust tube-based model predictive control method is presented for marine ship-mounted crane with ship roll motion, which guarantees the constraints effectively on system states and control inputs under the influence of interference. The core contribution lies in that, in the presence of nonvanishing perturbations, this paper utilizes the robustness characteristic of tube-MPC to deal with the constraints. Moreover, elaborately, the constraint of payload swing angle is converted to input constraint, which would have been hard to solve without this approach due to the underactuated nature of the system. The simulation results demonstrate the feasibility of the method and illustrate the satisfactory control performance. In the future, explorations of the efficiency of solving disturbance invariant set and the method applied to higher dimensional models will be discussed.

References

1. Mayne, D.Q., Seron, M.M., Raković, S.V.: Robust model predictive control of constrained linear systems with bounded disturbances. Automatica **41**(2), 219–224 (2005)
2. Fang, Y., Wang, P., Sun, N., Zhang, Y.: Dynamics analysis and nonlinear control of an offshore boom crane. IEEE Trans. Industr. Electron. **61**(1), 414–427 (2014)
3. Ilya Kolmanovsky, E.G.G.: Theory and computation of disturbance invariant sets for discrete-time linear systems. Math. Probl. Eng. **4**, 317–367 (1997)
4. Jolevski, D., Bego, O.: Model predictive control of gantry/bridge crane with anti-sway algorithm. J. Mech. Sci. Technol. **29**(2), 827–834 (2015)
5. Küchler, S., Mahl, T., Neupert, J., Schneider, K., Sawodny, O.: Active control for an offshore crane using prediction of the vessel's motion. IEEE/ASME Trans. Mechatron. **16**(2), 297–309 (2011)
6. Lu, B., Fang, Y., Lin, J., Hao, Y., Cao, H.: Nonlinear antiswing control for offshore boom cranes subject to ship roll and heave disturbances. Autom. Constr. **131**, 103843 (2021)
7. Lu, B., Fang, Y., Sun, N., Wang, X.: Antiswing control of offshore boom cranes with ship roll disturbances. IEEE Trans. Control Syst. Technol. **26**(2), 740–747 (2018)
8. Ngo, Q.H., Hong, K.S.: Sliding-mode antisway control of an offshore container crane. IEEE/ASME Trans. Mechatron. **17**(2), 201–209 (2012)

9. Ramli, L., Mohamed, Z., Efe, M., Lazim, I.M., Jaafar, H.: Efficient swing control of an overhead crane with simultaneous payload hoisting and external disturbances. Mech. Syst. Signal Process. **135**, 106326 (2020)
10. Rams, H., Schöberl, M., Schlacher, K.: Optimal motion planning and energy-based control of a single mast stacker crane. IEEE Trans. Control Syst. Technol. **26**(4), 1449–1457 (2018)
11. Richter, M., Arnold, E., Schneider, K., Eberharter, J.K., Sawodny, O.: Model predictive trajectory planning with fallback-strategy for an active heave compensation system. In: 2014 American Control Conference, pp. 1919–1924 (2014)
12. Yang, T., Sun, N., Chen, H., Fang, Y.: Neural network-based adaptive antiswing control of an underactuated ship-mounted crane with roll motions and input dead zones. IEEE Transactions on Neural Networks and Learning Systems **31**(3), 901–914 (2020)
13. Zhang, A., Lai, X., Wu, M., She, J.: Nonlinear stabilizing control for a class of underactuated mechanical systems with multi degree of freedoms. Nonlinear Dyn. **89**(3), 2241–2253 (2017)
14. Zhang, M., et al.: Adaptive proportional-derivative sliding mode control law with improved transient performance for underactuated overhead crane systems. IEEE/CAA J. Automatica Sin. **5**(3), 683–690 (2018)
15. Zhou, W., Xiaohua, X.: Optimal motion planning for overhead cranes. IET Control Theor. Appl. **8**, 1833–1842 (2014)

Multi-UUV/USV Adaptive Cooperative Search Using Online State Information

Wenjie Li[1], Jian Gao[1(✉)], Yimin Chen[1], Pei Cui[2], Junjun Lv[2],
and Guang Pan[1]

[1] School of Marine Science and Technology, Northwestern Polytechnical University,
Xi'an 710072, China
jiangao@nwpu.edu.cn
[2] Science and Technology on Underwater Test and Control Laboratory, Dalian
116013, China

Abstract. Unmanned Surface Vessel (USV) and Unmanned Underwater Vehicle (UUV) detect the same task plane while located in different planes, and have to avoid obstacles autonomously in cooperative search in unknown environments. This paper proposes an adaptive cooperative search method for a USV/UUV heterogeneous cross-domain swarm based on online state information. Considering the different planes of USV/UUV detection, we establish a USV/UUV detection model with a forward-looking sonar according to the cross-sectional view. In order to guarantee the safety of USV/UUV, an obstacle avoidance algorithm based on predictive guidance is designed. Finally, the task environment is rasterized to establish the state information structure of grids and USV/UUV. On this basis, USV/UUV adaptively plans the search path according to its own motion state. The state information of each grid is updated online until USV/UUV swarm completes the search task. Simulation results show that USV/UUV can accomplish cooperative search safely in an unknown environment. Compared with a UUV homogeneous swarm, the USV/UUV swarm shortens the search time and improves the cooperative search efficiency.

Keywords: USV/UUV · Detection model · Heterogeneous swarm · Cooperative search

1 Introduction

The use of UUV for underwater target search plays an important role in ocean exploration and resource exploitation, which has attracted wide attentions and researches from countries around the world. UUVs can achieve large range and long duration navigation, and has the characteristics of distribution and strong

Supported by the National Key Research and Development Program under Grant of 2021YFC2803000 and the Basic Scientific Research Program under Grant of JCKY2019207A019.

robustness, effectively overcoming the problem of low search efficiency of a single agent [1–4]. Homogeneous unmanned underwater swarms are composed of homogeneous UUV with consistent performance, which has a simple structure and is easy to implement, but has a single function and limited application scope. Compared with homogeneous UUV swarms, heterogeneous USV/UUV swarms combine the advantages of different agents, and have a stronger ability to complete complex tasks [5–7], in which UUV undertakes the main tasks, while USV plays a role in improving navigation accuracy, providing energy, and serving as communication relay. Therefore, constructing heterogeneous swarms for cooperative searching has become a research hotspot.

At present, most heterogeneous ocean exploration systems are based on the research of heterogeneous swarm collaboration between USV and UUV [8,9]. In [10], the cooperative mechanism between USV and UUV fully uses the advantages of fast USV speed, strong UUV concealment, and flexible use. USV can track path via waypoints, and provides energy to UUV. However, the literature did not consider obstacle avoidance issues. [11] proposed a cross-domain adaptive cooperative planning method based on a system composed of one USV and one UUV, constructing a USV cyclic search pattern to guide the UUV to reach the target. Similarly, UUV can improve positioning accuracy by referring to the position of the USV in [12]. In addition, USV serves as a transit station for underwater and above water, independently recycling UUV, playing a role in supplementing energy and transmitting information [13,14]. The USV only serves as an auxiliary equipment and does not perform specific search tasks. Motivated by the literature above, we proposed the method that USV also participates in the search task with UUV, and the USV/UUV can autonomously avoid obstacles in the environment.

The rest of this work is organized as follows. Section 2 establishes the kinematics model and sonar detection model of USV/UUV cooperative search. In Sect. 3, considering the presence of obstacles in unknown environments, a predictive guidance-based obstacle avoidance algorithm is designed. Then, this paper proposes an adaptive online cooperative search algorithm based on online state information. Based on region division, we establish a search model to determine the optimal task grid for USV/UUV at the next moment. Section 4 shows the simulation results, and compares them with the simulation search results of UUVs, and finally we concludes the paper in Sect. 5.

2   USV/UUV Cooperative Search Model

2.1   Establishment of USV/UUV Kinematics Model

This paper only considers the two-dimensional planar cooperative search of USV/UUV at a certain depth. Based on the North-East-Down frame, let the coordinates of USV/UUV in the geographic frame be (x, y), the yaw angle is ψ, and the USV/UUV kinematics model is simplified as:

$$\begin{cases} \dot{x} = u\cos\psi - v\sin\psi \\ \dot{y} = u\sin\psi + v\cos\psi \\ \dot{\psi} = r \end{cases} \tag{1}$$

In the equation, the velocity vectors u and v corresponding to the ox-axis and the oy-axis, respectively. r represents the angular velocity around the Z-axis.

2.2   Establishment of Sonar Detection Model

The USV/UUV swarm uses multi-beam active forward-looking sonar for target detection, with the detection radius $R = 150$ m, the horizontal reconnaissance sector opening angle $\theta = 120°$, and the vertical opening angle $\partial = 15°$. The sonar has 80 beams. The constraint model between the target and the sonar sensor can be simplified as follows:

$$\begin{cases} \sqrt{x_{bt}^2 + y_{bt}^2} \leq R \\ \dfrac{|y_{bt}|}{\sqrt{x_{bt}^2 + y_{bt}^2}} \leq \sin \dfrac{\theta}{2} \end{cases} \tag{2}$$

where (x_{bt}, y_{bt}) represents the position of the target in the body-fixed frame of UUV.

Due to the small vertical opening angle of the sonar, it is necessary to tilt the sonar downwards at a certain angle for the USV, in order to search for underwater targets using a forward-looking sonar when a USV is on the waters surface. The detection area that the sonar can cover varies at different depths. Compared to UUV, the detection ability of USV is reduced.

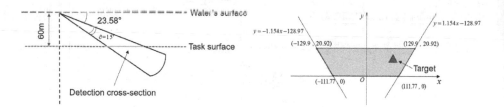

Fig. 1. Side View of USV Sonar Detection

Fig. 2. USV sonar detection model

This paper takes a two-dimensional plane with a detection depth of 60m as an example. Given a sonar depression angle of 23.58, the detection cross-section of the USV is a trapezoid. The side view of the USV sonar cross-section detection is shown in Fig. 1. Establish the USV body-fixed frame as shown in Fig. 2, and transform the position coordinates of the target from the geographic frame to the USV body-fixed frame. The position of the target relative to the USV in the USV body-fixed frame is (x_{bts}, y_{bts}), and the detection model of the USV is:

$$\begin{cases} 0 \leq y_{bts} \leq 20.92 \\ y_{bts} \geq -1.154x_{bts} - 128.97 \\ y_{bts} \geq 1.154x_{bts} - 128.97 \end{cases} \tag{3}$$

3 Cross-Domain Adaptive Cooperative Search Based on Online State Information

Due to the unknown prior information in the task area, the search strategy should have good robustness and adapt to multiple environment as much as possible. This paper adopts a cooperative search method based on online state information for unknown environments, which can safely obtain environmental information through real-time collision avoidance and cover the task area as much as possible. Firstly, we divide the task area into several grids and use different flag bits to distinguish the grid and the search status of USV/UUV. During the search process, the location of the searched targets and obstacles is continuously stored, and the search flag bits of the grid are updated to obtain environmental information of the task area. When USV/UUV detects obstacles, USV/UUV interrupts the search task and prioritizes obstacle avoidance. After obstacle avoidance, USV/UUV continues to perform the target search task. The main process of the search strategy at each moment is shown in Fig. 3.

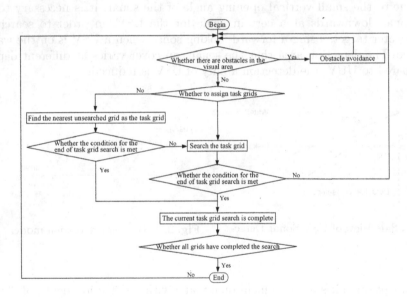

Fig. 3. Target Search Process

3.1 Obstacle Avoidance Algorithm

Under the premise of only considering static convex obstacles, this paper adopts a real-time obstacle avoidance method based on predictive guidance. The USV/UUV only stores the obstacle points within the detection range of the sonar, which are less than or equal to 40 m away from the USV/UUV, and avoids them.

Firstly, we establish obstacle avoidance rules.

$$f\left(d_i\right) = \begin{cases} d_i \leq 30 \\ 30 < d_i \leq 40 \end{cases} \tag{4}$$

$$f\left(\eta_i\right) = \begin{cases} 0 \leq \eta_i \leq 0.5 \\ 0.5 < \eta_i \leq 0.1 \end{cases} \tag{5}$$

where d_i is the distance between obstacles and USV/UUV, and η_i is the propor-tion of obstacles occupying the sonar detection beam. According to the Eqs. (4) and (5), we divide d_i and η_i into two levels based on the urgency of obstacle avoidance separately.

Secondly, we calculate the virtual target point $(x_{\mathrm{vtl}}, y_{\mathrm{vtl}})$ that USV/UUV needs to reach during obstacle avoidance. Taking into account the distance and occupation ratio of obstacles, the calculation of virtual target points can be divided into the following four situations:

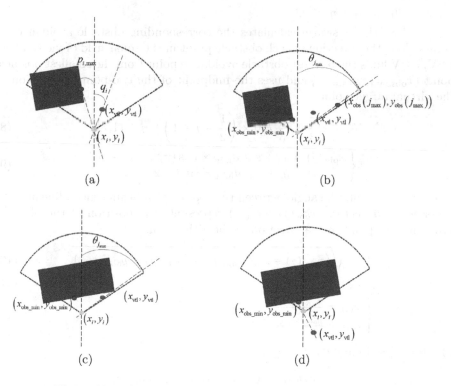

(a)

(b)

(c)

(d)

Fig. 4. Virtual Target Point Location Diagram in Four Cases

(1) $30 < d_i \leq 40$ and $0 \leq \eta_i \leq 0.5$

If the minimum obstacle point is on the left side of the sonar, USV/UUV turns to the right to avoid the obstacle, otherwise turn to the left.

$$\begin{cases} q_i = \frac{P_{i,\max}+\pi/3}{2}, P_{i,\min} < 0 \\ q_i = \frac{P_{i,\max}-\pi/3}{2}, P_{i,\min} > 0 \end{cases} \tag{6}$$

$$\begin{cases} x_{\text{vtl}} = x_i + \varepsilon \times d_{\min} \times \cos{(\pi/2 - \psi_i - q_i)} \\ y_{\text{vtl}} = y_i + \varepsilon \times d_{\min} \times \sin{(\pi/2 - \psi_i - q_i)} \end{cases} \tag{7}$$

where $P_{i,\max}$ represents the angle of the obstacle point farthest from the ith USV/UUV relative to the USV/UUV sonar forward vector, which is negative on its left and positive on its right. The meaning of $P_{i,\min}$ is the opposite. q_i represents the angle of the virtual target point relative to the forward-looking vector of the USV/UUV sonar during obstacle avoidance. (x_i, y_i) represents the position of the ith search subject. $d_{\min}$ indicates the distance to the nearest obstacle point of the USV/UUV. $\mathcal{E}$ represents the distance ratio of obstacle avoidance distance points.

(2) $d_i \leq 30$ and $0 \leq \eta_i \leq 0.5$

The USV/UUV swarm calculates the corresponding obstacle avoidance far points along the direction of each obstacle point in the sonar field of view. Then, USV/UUV finds the farthest obstacle avoidance point from the smallest obstacle point $(x_{\text{obs\_min}}, y_{\text{obs\_min}})$, and uses the midpoint of the two-point connection as the virtual target point.

$$\theta_j = -\frac{\pi}{3} + \frac{2\pi}{3}/80 \times \left(\frac{1}{2} + j - 1\right) \quad j \in (1, 80) \tag{8}$$

$$\begin{cases} x_{\text{obs}}(j) = x_i + \varepsilon \times d_{\min} \times \cos{(\pi/2 - \psi_i - \theta_j)} \\ y_{\text{obs}}(j) = y_i + \varepsilon \times d_{\min} \times \sin{(\pi/2 - \psi_i - \theta_j)} \end{cases} \tag{9}$$

where θ_j represents the angle between the sonar's j'th beam central line and the sonar forward vector, $(x_{\text{obs}}(j), y_{\text{obs}}(j))$ represents the position of the obstacle avoidance far point in the direction of the j'th beam.

$$d_j = \sqrt{\left(x_{\text{obs}}(j) - x_{\text{obs\_ min}}\right)^2 + \left(y_{\text{obs}}(j) - y_{\text{obs\_ min}}\right)^2} \tag{10}$$

$$j_{\max} = \arg\max{(d_j)} \tag{11}$$

$$\begin{cases} x_{\text{vtl}} = \frac{x_{\text{obs}}(j_{\max})+x_{\text{obs\_min}}}{2} \\ y_{\text{vtl}} = \frac{y_{\text{obs}}(j_{\max})+y_{\text{obs\_ min}}}{2} \end{cases} \tag{12}$$

(3) $30 \leq d_i \leq 40$ and $0.5 \leq \eta_i \leq 1$

$$(x_{\text{vtl}}, y_{\text{vtl}}) = (x_{\text{obs}}(j_{\max}), y_{\text{obs}}(j_{\max})) \tag{13}$$

The obstacle avoidance far point farthest from the smallest obstacle point $(x_{\text{obs\_min}}, y_{\text{obs\_min}})$ is selected as the virtual target point.

(4) $d_i \leq 30$ and $0.5 \leq \eta_i \leq 1$

$$\begin{cases} x_{\text{vtl}} = x_i - \varepsilon \times d_{\min} \times \cos{(\pi/2 - \psi_i - q_i)} \\ y_{\text{vt1}} = y_i - \varepsilon \times d_{\min} \times \sin{(\pi/2 - \psi_i - q_i)} \end{cases} \tag{14}$$

USV/UUV selects the virtual target point for obstacle avoidance in the opposite direction of the minimum obstacle point relative to USV/UUV.

Thirdly, obstacle avoidance paths are planned based on predictive guidance method.

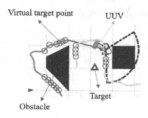

Fig. 5. Obstacle Avoidance Diagram

As shown in Fig. 5, the blue polygon represents the obstacle, the triangle represents the target to be searched, and the dots around the obstacle represent the virtual target points generated during the obstacle avoidance process. It can be seen from the Fig. 5 that USV/UUV can safely avoid obstacles.

3.2 Adaptive Cooperative Search Based on Online State Information

Firstly, the task area is evenly divided into several grids, with the state of the cth grid is $I_c(k) = [f_{\text{lock}}(k), n_{\text{tar}}(k)]$ and the state of the ith search subject is $M_i(k) = [f_{\text{sub}}(k), f_{\text{task}}(k)]$. Among them, $f_{\text{lock}}(k)$ is the search flag bit of the grid, indicating whether the grid has been searched.

$$f_{\text{lock}}(k) = \begin{cases} 0, & \text{Unsearched area} \\ 50, & \text{Area to be searched} \\ 100, & \text{Searched area} \end{cases} \tag{15}$$

$n_{\text{tar}}(k)$ is the target flag of the grid. When there is no target present in the grid, $n_{\text{tar}}(k) = 0$, otherwise, $n_{\text{tar}}(k) = 1$. The task flag bit $f_{\text{sub}}(k)$ for USV/UUV indicates whether there is an assigned task grid for USV/UUV. $f_{\text{sub}}(k) = 0$ indicates that the USV/UUV has not yet been assigned a task grid, and $f_{\text{sub}}(k) = 1$ means that the USV/UUV has already been assigned a task grid. $f_{\text{task}}(k)$ is the achievement flag of USV/UUV. $f_{\text{task}}(k) = 0$ indicates that the search task for the USV/UUV task grid has not yet ended, and $f_{\text{task}}(k) = 1$ represents that the USV/UUV task grid search has ended.

At first, a task grid is assigned to USV/UUV based on the flag bits of each grid, USV/UUV determines the unsearched grid closest to it as the task grid. The search status of the grid is changed to the area to be searched. The grid cannot become the task grid of other search subjects.

$$d_c = \sqrt{(x_i - x_c)^2 + (y_i - y_c)^2}. \tag{16}$$

$$c_{\min} = \arg\min(d_c) \tag{17}$$

Among them, d_c represents the distance between the i'th search subject and the center of the c'th grid. (x_c, y_c) represents the center position of the c'th search area, and c_{min} represents the grid sequence number closest to USV/UUV. In the search task, the speed of USV/UUV remains unchanged. When USV/UUV encountering obstacles, real-time predictive guidance is used to prioritize deceleration and obstacle avoidance. After obstacle avoidance is completed, the original speed is restored.

When the distance between the USV/UUV and the center point of the task grid is within the effective search radius, it is considered that the USV/UUV has completed the search of the task grid. The achievement flag bit of USV/UUV is 1, and the search flag bit of the grid is 100. USV/UUV has completed the search of the grid for this task.

$$f_{\text{task}}(k+1) = \begin{cases} 0, & d_c \geq r_{es} \\ 1, & d_c < r_{es} \end{cases} \tag{18}$$

$$n_{\text{tar}}(k) = \begin{cases} 0, f_{\text{lock}}(k) \neq 100 \\ \begin{cases} 0, & \text{no target} \\ 1, & \text{exist target} \end{cases} f_{\text{lock}}(k) = 100 \end{cases} \tag{19}$$

$$r_{es} \geq \min[a_{1\text{en}}, a_{\text{wi}}] \tag{20}$$

$$\begin{cases} r_{es\_UUV} \leq R_{UUV}. \\ r_{es\_USV} \leq R_{USV} \end{cases} \tag{21}$$

where r_{es} represents the effective search radius of USV/UUV, a_{len} represents the length of the task grid, and a_{wi} represents the width of the task grid. R_{UUV} and R_{USV} represent the maximum detection range of UUV and USV, respectively.

Grids that have already been searched will no longer be searched to avoid resource waste. USV/UUV resets the task flag and achievement flag to 0 to start the next round of search, and continues to search for the nearest unsearchable grid. After determining the next task grid, a Proportion Integral Differential(PID) control method based on line of sight guidance is used to guide the USV/UUV from its current position into the next task grid. During the guidance process, if encountering obstacles, priority should be given to obstacle avoidance. After obstacle avoidance is completed, the task grid should be replanned. When all grid search flags in the task area are set to 100, it is considered that the task area has been searched.

4   Simulation Results

4.1   Simulation Results of USV/UUV Cooperative Search

The task area is an area of 1000 m × 1000 m with a depth of 60 m. UUV searches in the underwater task plane, while USV detects targets from the surface downwards and plays a role in assisting search and communication relay. The initial

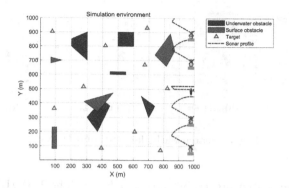

Fig. 6. Distribution Map of USV, UUVs, Targets, and Obstacles

environment of the simulation is shown in Fig. 6, with blue polygons representing underwater obstacles that UUV needs to avoid, and red polygons representing surface obstacles that USV needs to avoid. This paper randomly sets 10 static targets need to be searched, represented by triangle. There are 4 UUVs and 1 USV at equal intervals on the right side of the task area for cooperative search. The blue dotted line represents the sonar detection. When performing search tasks, the speed of UUV is 2.5 m/s, the speed of USV is 4 m/s; and both have a speed of 2 m/s to avoid obstacle. The angular velocity is $\omega_y = \pi/20(\text{rad/s})$. While maintaining good communication between USV and UUV, sonar detection probability and false alarm probability are not considered.

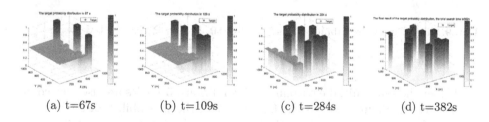

| (a) t=67s | (b) t=109s | (c) t=284s | (d) t=382s |

Fig. 7. Target Probability Graph of USV and UUVs

At the initial stage, the environmental information is unknown, and the probability of each grid having a target is 0.5. During the search process, for every target found, the probability of the grid where the target is located is set to 1. If no targets are detected, the probability of the grid is 0. The red pentagram indicates the searched target position. At the 382nd second, the USV and UUVs completed the search for the task area. Figure 7 shows the process of the probability distribution of targets. The path planning of the USV and each

278   W. Li et al.

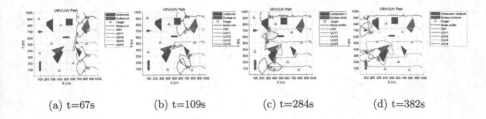

(a) t=67s   (b) t=109s   (c) t=284s   (d) t=382s

Fig. 8. Search Paths for USV and UUVs

UUV during the search process is shown in Fig. 8. The USV/UUV completed the search of the task area safely.

4.2 Simulation Results and Comparative Analysis of UUV Swarm Cooperative Search

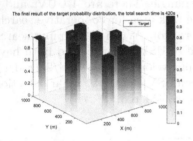

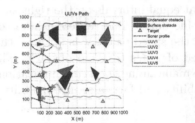

Fig. 9. Final Target Probability Graph   **Fig. 10.** Search Paths of UUV Swarm

Under the same initial environmental conditions, 5 UUVs are used for cooperative search. Figure 9 shows the final result of the probability distribution of targets. The search path is shown in Fig. 10, and the search time is 420 s.
Fig. 11 shows the number of grids searched by the USV/UUV swarm and UUVs at each moment under the same initial environment. At the beginning of the search, the number of grids searched by the two swarms is basically the same. As time goes on, the advantage of fast USV search speed gradually manifests, with more grids being searched by USV/UUV.

$$Cr = \frac{S_S}{S_A} \times 100\% = \frac{S_{SP}}{S_{AP}} \times 100\% \qquad (22)$$

Equation above represents the calculation method for regional coverage. Since the searched area is not a regular polygon, the pixel method is used for calculation. Among them, Cr represents the area coverage, S_S represents the area

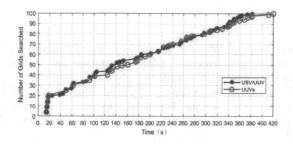

Fig. 11. Number of grids searched at each moment

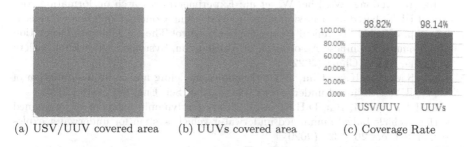

(a) USV/UUV covered area   (b) UUVs covered area   (c) Coverage Rate

Fig. 12. Coverage of cooperative Search in Different Swarms

searched by USV/UUV, and S_A represents the total area of the task area. S_{SP} and S_{AP} are the number of pixels in S_S, S_A.

The green part of Fig. 12 (a), (b) represents the searched area. The histogram in Fig. 12 (c) shows the regional coverage rate of the two swarms. It can be seen that the distributed online search method proposed in this paper basically achieves full coverage of the task area, and the area coverage of USV/UUV cooperative search is slightly higher than that of UUVs. We can conclude that USV has the advantage of fast sailing speed, which can compensate for its poor search ability and play a certain role in assisting search. Compared to homogeneous swarms with only UUV for target search, USV assisted UUV swarms for search shorten search time, greatly improve search efficiency, and improve regional coverage.

5   Conclusion

This paper proposes a USV/UUV cooperative search method which is based on online state information to search for static targets in unknown shallow water environments. An obstacle avoidance algorithm based on predictive guidance is also designed for potential obstacles in the environment. In addition, real-time task grid allocation to USV and UUVs ensures that the final search time of UUVs and USV is basically the same, solving the problem of uneven allocation of search resources when the environment is unknown, improving search efficiency, and making it more adaptable to complex underwater environments.

References

1. Zhenqiang, D., Weiping, W., Hongzhou, C., et al.: Configuration analysis method and geometric interpretation of UUVs cooperative localization based on error ellipse. Ocean Eng. **244**, 110299 (2022)
2. Shaoyuan, N., Hongjian, W., Yingmin, G., et al.: Research on UUVs swarm threat assessment and strategy selection. In: Global Oceans 2020, pp. 1–6. Singapore - U.S. Gulf Coast, Biloxi, MS, USA, (2020). https://doi.org/10.1109/IEEECONF38699. 2020.9389334
3. Anonymous: WHOI ENGINEERS WORK TO ADAPT SWARMING CAPABILITIES FOR LOW-COST UUVs. Ocean News & Technology (2022)
4. Shijie, L., Xudong, W., Zhe, W., et al.: Experimental research on formation control of UUVs based on behavior rules. In: 41st China Control Conference Proceedings, pp. 355–360. Technical Committee on Control Theory, Chinese Association of Automation, Chinese Association of Automation, Systems Engineering Society of China, Anhui, China (2022)
5. Hong, S.M., Ha, K.N., Kim, J.-Y.: Dynamics modeling and motion simulation of USV/UUV with linked underwater cable. J. Mar. Sci. Eng. **8**(5), 318 (2020)
6. Vu, M.T., Van, M, Bui, D.H.P., et al.: Study on dynamic behavior of unmanned surface vehicle-linked unmanned underwater vehicle system for underwater exploration. Sensors **20**, 1329 (2020)
7. William, O.O., Christopher, D.H.: Cross-domain synergy: advancing jointness. Joint Force Quarterly: JFQ **73**, 123–128 (2014)
8. Huixi, X., Chenglin, J.: Review of research on cooperative ocean exploration system based on USV and AUV heterogeneous platforms. J. Univ. Chin. Acad. Sci. **38**(02), 145–159 (2021)
9. Anonymous: Aquabotix Releases Revolutionary SWARMDIVER MICRO USV/UUV. Ocean News & Technology (2018)
10. Hong, S.M., Nam, K.S., Ryu, J.D., et al.: Development and field test of unmanned marine vehicle (USV/UUV) with cable. IEEE Access **8**, 193347–193355 (2020)
11. Ferri, G., Djapic, V.: Adaptive mission planning for cooperative autonomous maritime vehicles. In: 2013 IEEE International Conference on Robotics and Automation, pp. 5586–5592. IEEE, Karlsruhe (2013). https://doi.org/10.1109/ICRA.2013. 6631379
12. Norgren, P., Ludvigsen, M., Ingebretsen, T., et al.: Tracking and remote monitoring of an autonomous underwater vehicle using an unmanned surface vehicle in the Trondheim fjord. In: OCEANS 2015-MTS/IEEE, pp. 1–6. IEEE, Washington (2015). https://doi.org/10.23919/OCEANS.2015.7401975
13. Sarda, E.I., Dhanak, M.R.: A USV-based automated launch and recovery system for AUVs. IEEE J. Oceanic Eng. **42**(1), 37–55 (2017)
14. Wigley, R., Proctor, A., Simpson, B., et al.: Novel AUV launch, recovery new approaches using combined USV-AUV method. Sea Technol. Worldwide Inform. Leader Marine Bus. Sci. Eng. **59**(6), 24–27 (2018)

Design and Analysis of Co-axial Twin-Propeller Trans-media Vehicle

Chihao Du[1], Tao Wang[1], Shuo Liu[1,2,3]($\boxtimes$), Shanmin Zhou[4], Yong Cai[4], and Zijing Yu[1]

[1] Key Laboratory of Ocean Observation-Imaging Testbed of Zhejiang Province, Zhejiang University, Zhoushan 316021, China
shuoliu@zju.edu.cn
[2] Hainan Institute, Zheiiang University, Sanva 572025, China
[3] Ministry of Education, The Engineering Research Center of Oceanic Sensing Technology and Equipment, Zhoushan 316000, China
[4] Ocean Research Center of Zhoushan, Zhejiang University, Zhoushan 316021, China

Abstract. This paper mainly proposes a co-axial twin-propeller trans-media vehicle, based on the concept of water-air hybrid drive. Airborne collapsible counter-rotating twin paddles are arranged in a co-axial pattern on top of the vehicle, and three underwater thrusters with a certain angle to the body of the vehicle are arranged at the end of the vehicle in a circumferentially even distribution. The overall low resistance streamline shape of the vehicle can effectively reduce the drag force of the vehicle when moving on the water surface and improve the maneuverability performance. Combined with the force situation of the vehicle in different environments and movement modes, the mathematical model of the cross-media vehicle is established through multi-rigid body dynamics analysis. The hydrodynamic coefficients are solved by computational fluid software, and simulation tests are conducted in simulink. The results prove the feasibility of the proposed design and method.

Keyword: Co-Axial Twin-Propeller · Trans-Media Vehicle · Dynamical Model · Hydrodynamic Coefficient · Simulation Test

1 Introduction

With the increasing human demand for energy and the depletion of resources on land, the oceans, which account for 71% of the global surface area, are becoming increasingly important. Marine resources need corresponding exploration and detection tools.

Trans-media vehicles require not only the ability to move in the air, but also have the ability to operate underwater and freely cross the water-air interface [1]. The research teams have approached the design of trans-media vehicles from different perspectives, which can be broadly categorized as fixed-wing structures, bionic structures, and rotary-wing structures [2].

North Carolina State University has developed the "EagleRay" fixed-wing trans-media vehicle, which uses batteries as a power source and is equipped with a series of sensors. The prototype of this vehicle has been experimented, can work in the water

© The Author(s), under exclusive license to Springer Nature Singapore Pte Ltd. 2023
H. Yang et al. (Eds.): ICIRA 2023, LNAI 14273, pp. 281–292, 2023.
https://doi.org/10.1007/978-981-99-6498-7_25

and air,can also be carried out across the water and air medium movement [3]. The MIT has developed a principle prototype of an amphibious imitation flying fish and conducted in-depth research on the theory of flying fish swimming, mechanism design implementation, and drive control methods [4]. A hybrid UAV was proposed by Shanghai Jiaotong University [5]. The structure of fixed-wing UAV and underwater glider as well as quadrotor UAV was integrated for design and can work in different mediums to achieve long distance. Rutgers University has developed a rotor trans-media vehicle called Navigator [6], which uses a two-layer co-axial eight-rotor design scheme and a layered hybrid control strategy.

From the existing research results, the current main implementation scheme of trans-media vehicle directly follows the design form of fixed-wing UAVs or multi-rotor UAVs, and each of these two types of trans-media vehicle has unique performance advantages and shortcomings. Fixed-wing trans-media vehicles have lower energy consumption and higher flight speed in the air, but their mobility and maneuverability are not as good as rotary-wing vehicles, and they cannot achieve low-speed flight and aerial hovering. At the same time, fixed-wing trans-media vehicle can only be high-speed state of cross-media movement, that is, a fast dive into the water or a high-speed dash out of the water. Therefore, the fixed-wing trans-media vehicle in the water to avoid violent fluid damping and impact, which is a fixed-wing vehicle in the trans-media process of structural safety, power performance and handling technology has more stringent requirements. In contrast, multi-rotor trans-media vehicles inherit the excellent maneuverability of multi-rotor UAVs, with stable low-speed flight, vertical takeoff and landing, and fixed-point hovering capabilities. However, the larger paddle area of the multi-rotor vehicle generates a larger drag when the vehicle moves underwater. Based on the analysis of the above research progress, this paper proposes a trans-media vehicle structure based on co-axial dual-paddle with vertical takeoff and landing strategy. The structure has good aerial hovering capability and underwater maneuverability, and can ensure the stability of the trans-media process.

2   Design of Structural Principle

2.1   System Design

In order to meet the working requirements of air-sea trans-media vehicles, this study uses a collapsible co-axial twin-propeller mechanism for aerial propulsion and three water propellers for underwater propulsion. For the design of the aerial propulsion mechanism, the common structural schemes of single-paddle, multi-axis multi-paddle and co-axial dual-paddle are compared and analyzed. The single-paddle scheme has a simple drive system and easy maintenance, but it cannot achieve the balance of propeller torque, and the maximum pull force that can be provided under the same disc area is small; the multi-axis multi-paddle scheme can provide a larger pull force and achieve hovering, but its overall disc area is larger, which will generate a larger resistance when the vehicle moves underwater; the co-axial dual-paddle scheme can provide a larger pull force and achieve the balance of torque, and the use of collapsible form can ensure the above advantages while significantly reducing the drag on the underwater movement of the vehicle. The foldable co-axial twin-paddle solution is considered to be the better choice, considering the factors of tension, torque and drag.

The trans-media vehicle mainly includes the main shaft, the paddle system for air, the drive mechanism, the maneuvering mechanism, the flow linear shell, the pressure-resistant watertight chamber, the underwater propulsion system, the flight control system, the surface navigation control system, the communication system, the attitude sensor, and the power supply.

There are positioning holes on the main shaft, and the paddle system, drive mechanism and maneuvering mechanism are mounted on the main shaft in order from top to bottom, and symmetrically distributed.

There are three underwater thrusters, which are fixedly connected to the lower watertight hatch cover through the mounting base, evenly distributed along the circumference, and at a certain angle to the body of the vehicle. The thrust extension line intersects at one point to ensure the multi-degree of freedom movement of the vehicle. Relying on the differential control of the thrust distribution of the three thrusters, the steering and attitude adjustment of the vehicle can be achieved.

The air paddle system is used to provide flight power. The paddle is connected to the paddle hub by the paddle clamp, and the paddle clamp adopts a streamlined structure, and the paddle can be folded axially under the action of gravity to reduce the navigation resistance, and can be fully expanded during flight with the high-speed rotation of the motor. The paddle system designed in this paper adopts the structure of non-variable pitch of upper paddle and variable pitch of lower paddle, the upper paddle only produces rotational motion in the horizontal plane, the vehicle uses semi-differential motion to change the attitude, and the pitch and roll are achieved by changing the angle of orientation of the lower paddle.

The drive mechanism consists of two drive motors, two electronic governors, a fixed support, and a gear drive. Since the motors will be immersed in water during the operation of the vehicle, it is necessary to make reliable waterproof treatment for the motors. The stator winding of the motor is made of conventional enameled wire with additional waterproof paint process as the bottom waterproof protective layer, and then a second waterproof protective layer is added with epoxy resin.

The steering mechanism includes a tilt disk, two waterproof servos, and four connecting rods. The two servos are symmetrically mounted on the center axis by the fixing device, and are fixedly connected to the tilt disc by the connecting rods. The tilt disk is fixedly connected to the lower paddle through the connecting rod. When the flight control system issues a command to make the servo produce different swing angles, the swing of the servo changes the tilt direction of the tilt disk through the transmission of the servo swing arm, the connecting rod and the small ball hinge ball head, so as to realize the free control of the tilt disk plane and make the lower paddle produce a cycle variable pitch when it rotates, and then make the direction of the lift force acting on the lower paddle change to realize the pitch and roll of the vehicle.

The watertight capsule is used to fix and provide a dry and sealed environment for electronic components such as control mechanism, attitude sensors, power supply equipment, communication equipment, etc. The pressure-resistant watertight capsule includes the main cylinder made of POM material, the upper watertight capsule cover, the lower watertight capsule cover and the O-rings. In order to realize the electric power and communication connection between the equipment inside and outside the chamber, and to consider the convenience of installation, maintenance and disassembly of the equipment, three cable feedthroughs are designed on the sealed hatch at each end.

In the control system of the vehicle, two sets of independent controllers work separately. The flight control system uses the universal flight controller (referred to as flight control). The universal flight control system has good compatibility with the vehicle's electrical system, in addition to providing stable and reliable flight and vertical takeoff and landing operations, but also in a simpler way to integrate into the vehicle's entire control logic framework and electric system architecture. The core processor of the underwater motion control system is developed using an STM32 microcontroller board, which manages the power supply of the system, acquires and stores sensor data, and communicates wirelessly with the ground station (Fig. 1).

 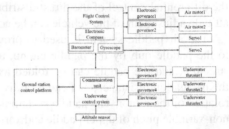

(a) Overall structure diagram   (b) Control system block diagram

deflector 1, upper paddle 2, paddle clamp 3, paddle hub 4, lower paddle 5, streamlined housing 6, upper watertight hatch cover 7, watertight capsule 8, lower watertight hatch cover 9, underwater motor 10, underwater motor mount 11, underwater propeller 12

Fig. 1. Structure diagram of the aircraft and control system block diagram

After creating the trans-media vehicle model, the material density of each component was assigned by SOLIDWORKS software, and the mass properties tool was applied to calculate the model mass, center of gravity, and volumetric moment of inertia. Rhino software is used to delineate the waterline of the vehicle, and the floating center position and buoyancy are solved. The relative position of the center of gravity and the floating center can be adjusted by optimizing the shape size of the pressure-resistant watertight chamber and the mass distribution of the internal components.

2.2   Operation Mode

The smooth trans-media motion is the key link between the surface sailing process and the air flight process. The cross-media vehicle finally chooses vertical takeoff and landing as the standard operation of cross-media motion, and this strategy is mainly due to the following two considerations:

First, the vertical takeoff and landing approach allows for greater takeoff weight for a given maximum output thrust of the propulsion system. Second, the speed and attitude of the vehicle should be well controlled during the water entry process. Therefore, the vertical takeoff and landing method can realize the slow and smooth landing of the vehicle on the water surface.

The main working process of trans-media vehicle is as follows: in air flight mode, the aerial folding dual paddles are rotated at high speed, the paddles open under the action of centrifugal force and generate enough lift, while the dual paddles can offset each other's dynamic torque to keep the balance of the vehicle body, by controlling the rotational speed of the upper and lower paddles, and the action of the servo to achieve different flight states and attitudes of the vehicle in the air. When the vehicle needs to cross the water medium, the vehicle drops to a specified height, shut down the air motor, at this time, the upper and lower paddles are axially folded due to the action of gravity, the vehicle also slowly vertical under the action of gravity into the water; after the vehicle into the water, relying on the end of the three underwater thrusters to provide power, and achieve steering and attitude adjustment. When the vehicle needs to come out of the water medium, the control system combines the feedback data from the attitude sensor and uses PID control to allocate the rotational speed to the underwater thruster, so that the vehicle moves upward for a distance and steadily perpendicular to the water surface. At this time, the air motors are driven, and the air paddles unfold and rotate at high speed under the action of centrifugal force. The underwater thrusters and the air paddles work together to pull the vehicle out of the water, and the underwater thrusters are turned off after exiting the water (Fig. 2).

Fig. 2. Illustration of the motion process of the trans-media vehicle

3 Modeling and Parameter Calculation

3.1 Dynamical Model

Modeling close to realistic motion is the basis for analyzing cross-media vehicle performance and designing motion control algorithms. Vehicle modeling covers both kinematics and dynamics.

An accurate and unambiguous description of the motion of the vehicle in space requires, first of all, the establishment of a unified reference system. Two sets of coordinate systems are usually established with reference to the SNAME specification [7]:

body coordinates and geodesic coordinates, as shown in Fig. 3. The position vector η, velocity vector v and thrust vector τ of the vehicle are shown in Eq. (1).

$$\eta = [x,y,z,\phi,\theta,\psi]^T$$
$$v = [u,v,w,p,q,r]^T$$
$$\tau = [X,Y,Z,K,M,N]^T \tag{1}$$

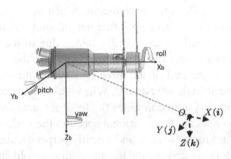

Fig. 3. Schematic diagram of the definition of geodesic and body coordinates for vehicle

The kinematic model of a vehicle describes the transformation of the body's attitude (linear and angular velocities) in the geodesic and airframe coordinate systems, which is determined by the rotation relationship between the two coordinate systems. In most cases, the "ZYX" Eulerian rotation rule is used to study the motion of the vehicle [8]. Therefore, there exists the transformation matrix $J(\Theta)$ such that: $\dot{\eta} = J(\Theta)v$.

where the Euler angles $\Theta = [\phi,\theta,\psi]^T$. $J(\Theta)$ is a function with Euler angles as variables, and the transformation matrix $J(\Theta)$ is defined as:

$$J(\Theta) = \begin{bmatrix} R(\Theta) & 0_{3\times3} \\ 0_{3\times3} & T(\Theta) \end{bmatrix} \tag{2}$$

where $J(\Theta)$ is composed of the linear velocity rotation matrix $R(\Theta)$ and the angular velocity rotation matrix $T(\Theta)$. Set, $c(\cdot) = cos(\cdot)$, $s(\cdot) = sin(\cdot)$, $t(\cdot) = tan(\cdot)$, and $T(\Theta)$ and $R(\Theta)$ are defined as:

$$T(\Theta) = \begin{bmatrix} 1 & s\phi t\theta & c\phi t\theta \\ 0 & c\phi & -s\phi \\ 0 & \frac{s\phi}{c\theta} & \frac{c\phi}{c\theta} \end{bmatrix} \quad R(\Theta) = \begin{bmatrix} c\psi c\theta & -s\psi c\phi + c\psi s\theta s\phi & s\psi s\phi + c\psi c\phi s\theta \\ s\psi c\theta & c\psi c\phi + s\phi s\theta s\psi & -c\psi s\phi + s\theta s\psi c\phi \\ -s\theta & c\theta s\phi & c\theta c\phi \end{bmatrix} \tag{3}$$

The ocean environment is complex, and the forces acting on the vehicle are classified in many ways. As radiation forces and external forces of the ocean environment. Radiation forces include additional mass forces, damping forces, and reversion forces. External forces in the marine environment include wind, wave and current effects. The action of the hydrodynamic forces of the vehicle can be linearly superimposed on the rigid body motion in the form of fractional forces [9].

$$M_{RB}\dot{v} + C_{RB}(v)v = \tau_{env} + \tau_{hydro} + \tau_{pro} \tag{4}$$

From the Fossen hydrodynamic model, the hydrodynamic action τ_{hydro} can be expressed as:

$$\tau_{hydro} = -M_A \dot{v} - C_A(v)v - D(|v|)v - g(\eta) \tag{5}$$

where M_{RB} denotes the inertia matrix generated by the rigid body mass and rotational inertia of the vehicle, $C_{RB}(v)$ denotes the Coriolis force and moment matrix, τ_{env} denotes the external environmental forces and moments, τ_{pro} denotes the thruster thrust and moment output, M_A denotes the additional mass matrix of the vehicle, $C_A(v)$ denotes the additional mass component of the Coriolis force and moment, $g(\eta)$ denotes the vehicle reversion force, $D(|v|)$ denotes the damping matrix, and τ_{hydro} denotes the hydrodynamic force.

The restoring force is also known as the generalized static force, that is, the force that the system will be subjected to no matter what state it is in. In most cases, the position of the buoyant center is higher than the center of mass in the system, and the resulting moment generated by the body is called the reversion moment. The gravitational and buoyant forces on the vehicle under the geodesic coordinates are:

$$f_G^g = [0, 0, G]^T, f_B^g = [0, 0, -B_i]^T \tag{6}$$

During the operation of the vehicle, its buoyancy is highly coupled with the water entry depth and attitude angle. To simplify the calculation, this paper treats the vehicle as a cylinder for equivalence for the time being. The coordinate of the vehicle's center of gravity and floating center under the airframe coordinate system are:

$$r_G^b = [0, 0, 0]^T, r_B^b = \left[x_B, y_B, z_B\right]^T \tag{7}$$

Combined with the coordinate transformation matrix, the return moment array of the vehicle in the airframe coordinate system is:

$$g(\eta) = \begin{bmatrix} f_G^b + f_B^b \\ r_G^b \times f_G^b + r_B^b \times f_B^b \end{bmatrix} = \begin{bmatrix} -(G - B_i)\sin\theta \\ (G - B_i)\cos\theta\sin\phi \\ (G - B_i)\cos\theta\cos\phi \\ -y_B B_i \cos\theta\cos\phi + z_B B_i \cos\theta\sin\theta \\ z_B B_i \sin\theta + x_B B_i \cos\theta\cos\phi \\ -x_B B_i \cos\theta\sin\theta - y_B B_i \sin\theta \end{bmatrix} \tag{8}$$

The additional mass force $M_A \dot{v}$ is the hydrodynamic force from the inertial action of the surrounding liquid to which the vehicle is subjected during the acceleration process. For practical applications of marine vehicles, the role of the elements on the non-diagonal of the additional mass matrix of a low-speed underwater vehicle is generally smaller than the role of the diagonal elements, especially for vehicles with symmetry in the coordinate plane, where the role of the non-diagonal elements is negligible. The additional mass matrix M_A can be simplified as:

$$M_A = -\text{diag}\left\{X_{\dot{u}}, Y_{\dot{v}}, Z_{\dot{w}}, K_{\dot{p}}, M_{\dot{q}}, N_{\dot{r}}\right\} \tag{9}$$

For conventional underwater vehicles with a fixed shape, their M_A can generally be considered as a constant coefficient matrix since they are always fully submerged in water during operation. However, for a trans-media vehicle, the volume changes before and after it crosses the medium, and its additional mass matrix will also change. Therefore, $\Delta M_A(l)$ is introduced in this paper as a correction term for the additional mass matrix that varies continuously with the draft length l.

The damping $D(|v|)$ of a vehicle is a hydrodynamic force that is a function of the vehicle's motion speed and is very difficult to calculate or estimate accurately. It is decomposed into four types in the Fossen model: potential flow damping $D_P(|v|)$, surface friction damping $D_S(|v|)$, emerging wave damping $D_W(|v|)$, and vortex shedding damping $D_M(|v|)$.

In practical control applications, the Fossen model generally assumes that the damping of the vehicle is uncoupled and that damping terms above the second order are neglected. In addition, the Fossen model assumes that the vehicle has good symmetry, so the damping matrix $D(|v|)$ of the vehicle is generally reduced to the sum of linear damping and quadratic damping:

$$D(|v|) = -\text{diag}\{X_u, Y_v, Z_w, K_p, M_q, N_r\}$$
$$- \text{diag}\{X_{u|u|}|u|, Y_{v|v|}|v|, Z_{w|w|}|w|, K_{p|p|}|p|, M_{q|q|}|q|, N_{r|r|}|r|\} \qquad (10)$$

3.2 Calculation of Hydrodynamic Parameters

In this paper, the computational fluid software AQWA is used to numerically solve the additional mass of the vehicle. This study first verifies the rationality and accuracy of using AQWA software to calculate the inertial hydrodynamics of small sizes. The additional mass of a standard sphere is calculated using AQWA software and compared with the empirical formula. From the derivation of the empirical formula, the additional mass of the sphere is $2/3\pi\rho r^3$, and here ρ is selected as 1025 kg/m^3. Firstly, the calculation model is established for the sphere with the radius of 1 m, and the calculation results are shown in Table 1. From the results, it can be seen that the error gradually decreases with the increase of the number of surface elements, which meets the requirements of calculation rationality and accuracy.

Table 1. Additional mass of sphere (radius 1m, density 1025 kg/m^3, depth 10 m)

Direction	Number of nodes	Theoretical value (kg)	Calculated values (kg)	Error
Heave	452	2164	2343	8.3%
Heave	3836	2164	2286	5.6%
Heave	14524	2164	2183	0.9%

The trans-media vehicle model studied in this paper is suitably simplified and imported into AQWA software for solution to calculate the additional mass matrix of the vehicle half submerged in water. It is tabulated as follows:

$$M_{A1} = diag\left\{\left[0.45, 1.68, 2.97, 2.83 \times 10^{-6}, 1.12 \times 10^{-3}, 5.89 \times 10^{-4}\right]\right\} \quad (11)$$

In this paper, the numerical estimation of damping $D(|v|)$ for the trans-media vehicle is performed using Fluent, a fluid calculation software based on the finite element method. First of all, before conducting the computational fluid analysis, the 3D model of the trans-media vehicle is simplified. For the propeller, paddle clamps, paddle hubs and other model details do not play a crucial role in the analysis of damping, rather numerous model details increase the burden of meshing and fluid calculation. Meshing is an important part of Fluent. The number of meshes and the quality of meshes of the analyzed object determine the speed of the fluid calculation process and the accuracy of the calculation results. In this paper, about one million grid cells are used for the analytical calculations of damping. In this paper, the turbulent flow model of the flow field is set to the $k\text{-}\omega SST$ model, which is used to restore the separation process between laminar and turbulent flow (Fig. 4).

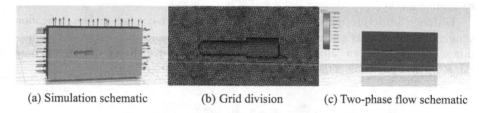

   (a) Simulation schematic   (b) Grid division   (c) Two-phase flow schematic

Fig. 4. Fluent simulation related schematic

For the three translational directions of surge, sway and heave, this paper sets the velocity interval 0.2 m/s and performs five damping simulations at different speeds in each of the three translational directions. In this paper, we set an interval of 1 rad/s and perform five calculations of the damping moment at different rotational velocities in each of the three rotational directions.

For the discrete points of damping force versus sailing speed calculated from the above study, the second-order polynomial function of MATLAB is used to fit the relationship between damping and sailing speed in this paper. The results are shown in the following figure (Fig. 5):

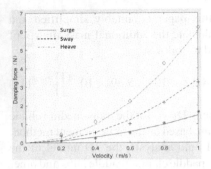
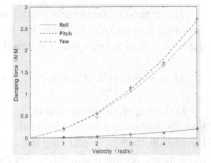

(a) Translational direction fitting results   (b) Rotation direction fitting results

Fig. 5. Damping curve fitting results

4 Surface Navigation Simulation Analysis

In order to verify the validity and accuracy of the above mathematical model of the trans-media vehicle in describing the motion state of the vehicle, this section will use the SIMULINK platform of MATLAB R2021b to numerically simulate the XOZ plane navigation motion.

Different thrusts are applied to the trans-media vehicle to conduct surface navigation simulation experiments and observe the changes of the vehicle pitch angle. The simulation schematic is shown below. The simulation solver is ode4 (Runge-Kutta), the base sampling time is 0.01, and the simulation time is set to 100 s (Fig. 6).

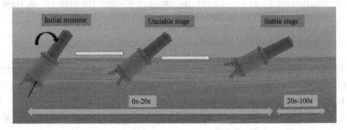

Fig. 6. Diagram of navigation simulation

A force of 4N is applied to each of the two thrusters below, and the simulation results are shown below (Fig. 7):

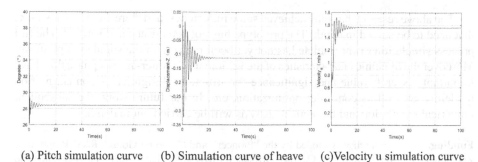

(a) Pitch simulation curve   (b) Simulation curve of heave   (c)Velocity u simulation curve

Fig. 7. Simulation curve of sailing with 4N thrust applied

A force of 2N is applied to each of the two thrusters below, and the simulation results are shown below (Fig. 8):

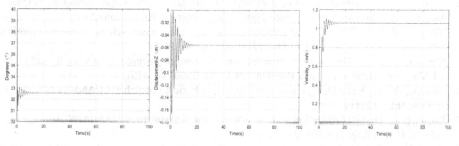

(a) Pitch simulation curve   (b) Simulation curve of heave   (c)Velocity u simulation curve

Fig. 8. Simulation curve of sailing with 2N thrust applied

The simulation results show that, under the premise that the initial angle between the vehicle and the water surface is 40°, with the increase of the applied thrust, the vehicle moves upward, the angle with the water surface decreases, and finally reaches a new equilibrium state, which can effectively improve its surface navigation performance, and the simulation experiments have initially verified the effectiveness of the design method in this paper.

5 Summary

This paper proposes a vertical takeoff and landing strategy, based on the co-axial dual-paddle trans-media vehicle structure. The developed structure has good air hovering ability and underwater maneuverability, and can ensure the repeatability of the trans-media process.In this paper, the system composition of the vehicle and its main operation mode are introduced in detail, the dynamics and kinematics of the vehicle are modeled, the calculation methods related to the hydrodynamic parameters are described, and the XOZ three-degree-of-freedom model is built on the simulink simulation platform for surface navigation simulation experiments.

The above research has only achieved some milestones, and there are still many tasks that need to be solved in depth. The prototype has not been tested and verified. The full process simulation of the vehicle has not yet been realized in the simulation platform. Moreover the dynamic characteristics of the vehicle in the water-air two-phase flow have important research value and significance for structural design, cross-domain motion modeling, as well as controller optimization, etc. In our future work, the subsequent numerical simulation and theoretical analysis will be carried out in depth.

Funding. This research was funded by the "Pioneer" and "Leading Goose" R&D Program of Zhejiang (2023C03124 and 2022C03041), Research Program of Sanya Yazhou Bay Science and Technology City (SKYC2020–01-001), and "the Fundamental Research Funds for the Central Universities" + "226–2023-00049".

References

1. Crouse, G.: Conceptual design of a submersible airplane. 48th AIAA Aerospace Sciences Meeting Including the New Horizons Forum and Aerospace Exposition (2010)
2. Yang, J., et al.: Simulation and experimental research on trans-media vehicle water-entry motion characteristics at low speed. Plos One **12**(5), e0178461 (2017)
3. Stewart, W., et al.: Design and demonstration of a seabird-inspired fixed-wing hybrid UAV-UUV system. Bioinspiration & Biomimetics **13**(5), 056013 (2018)
4. Gao, A., Techet, A.H..: Design considerations for a robotic flying fish. OCEANS'11 MTS/IEEE KONA. IEEE (2011)
5. Lu, D., et al.: Design, fabrication, and characterization of a multimodal hybrid aerial underwater vehicle. Ocean Eng. **219**, 108324 (2021)
6. Zu'bi, H., et al.: Loon Copter: Implementation of a hybrid unmanned aquatic–aerial quadcopter with active buoyancy control. J. Field Robotics **35**, 764778 (2018)
7. SNAME[1950]: Nomenclature for treating the motion of a submerged body througu a fluid. The society of Naval Architects and Marine Engineers, Technical and Research Bulletin, p. 1–15 (1995)
8. Nelson, R.C.: Flight Stability and Automatic Control, vol. 2. WCB/McGraw Hill, New York (1998)
9. Newman, J.N.: Marine Hydrodynamics. The MIT Press. Cambridge, MA (1977)

Design of an Autonomous Underwater Vehicle for Targeted Water Sampling

Shijun Wu, Wenbo Zhang, Xun Wang, and Xiaoyang Fu

School of Mechanical Engineering, Zhejiang University, Hangzhou 310000, Zhejiang, China
22225014@zju.edu.cn

Abstract. In this paper, we introduce an autonomous underwater vehicle for the collection of target water samples. The designed sampling autonomous underwater vehicle (S-AUV) consists of three parts: an electronic control cabin, a sampling cabin and a sensor cabin. The S-AUV can collect up to 8 target water samples during a single cruise. Each sample has a volume of 500 mL and can be taken within 40 s. The excellent sampling ability and control effect of the designed S-AUV are verified by pool test and lake test.

Keywords: AUV · sampling · underwater robotics

1 Introduction

At present, there are many researches on water sampling technology of ocean, river and lakes. On the one hand, water quality can be monitored through water sampling to realize water environment protection; on the other hand, minerals, microorganisms or trace elements in water samples can be analyzed for further scientific research.

There are mainly two ways to sample and monitor the water quality of rivers and lakes. One is that the staff carries portable instruments for sampling analysis, the second is that the staff drives special vehicles carrying instruments to the site for sampling analysis. These methods require a lot of manpower and material resources, and can not achieve real-time monitoring. Modern water quality sampling and monitoring can be realized more intelligently and autonomously by using autonomous surface vehicle (ASV). The new HydroNet ASV [1], developed by ROBOTECH of Italy, is equipped with a sampling system combined with a wheel winch. The sensor and water sampler can be lowered to a maximum depth of 50 m to collect multiple samples, achieving water quality sampling at different depths. The SESAMO catamaran [2] developed at CNR-ISSIA, and the ASV Lizhbeth [3] developed by the Swiss National Science Foundation, also use similar winches to collect water samples at specified depths. For the deep-sea target water sampling, the traditional way is to use the Human Occupied Vehicle (HOV) or the Remoted Operated Vehicle (ROV) to operate the sampling devices for sampling. For example, the "Alvin" HOV and "Jason II" ROV in the United States used various samplers such as "IGT" [4], "POP gun", and "SPE" [5] to sample hydrothermal plumes in the hydrothermal zone of the Pacific and Atlantic mid-ocean ridges. The China's

H. Yang et al. (Eds.): ICIRA 2023, LNAI 14273, pp. 293–303, 2023.
https://doi.org/10.1007/978-981-99-6498-7_26

"Jiaolong" and "Shen Hai Yong Shi" HOV sampled the hydrothermal plume with the "CGT" sampler and "Six shooter" sampler developed by the HOME research team of Zhejiang University [6, 7].

Autonomous Underwater Vehicle (AUV) has strong operation ability and high movement flexibility. In recent years, the research of using AUV with onboard sampling device for target water sampling has been carried out continuously. The "Dorado", a cruising-type AUV developed by Stanford University and the Monterey Bay Aquarium Research Institute, is capable of conducting routine operations in the ocean at a depth of up to 1,500 m [8–10]. It carries 10 "Gulper" water samplers to collect samples and can identify plankton-rich flows in the ocean. The "Gulper" sampler is capable of sucking in about 1.8 L of water samples in less than 2 s. Because the "Dorado" AUV is a traditional cruising-type AUV, it does not have the ability of hover sampling. Researchers in Woods Hole Oceangraphic Institution used a hovering-type AUV called "Sentry" with two "SyPRID" samplers to sample the ocean's plankton water masses [11]. The SyPRID sampler is a high-capacity, high-resolution deep-sea plankton sampling system developed specifically for the "Sentry" AUV. The sampler is mainly composed of an inlet valve, a filter pipe, a net and a pump. After the inlet valve is opened, water samples are extracted by an axial pump. After the water sample passes through the filter tube, the plankton in the water sample is filtered and collected into a net at the bottom of the filter tube. The sampling system is deployed on both sides of the "Sentry" AUV. Although this deployment approach compromises the hydrodynamic performance of the AUV, it makes the sampling system easy to install.

Our goal is to design an autonomous underwater vehicle for sampling target water samples, enabling hover sampling at fixed depth and long-distance cruising. The design AUV is expected to sample multiple points during a single voyage. In this paper, we present the design of a sampling Autonomous Underwater Vehicle(S-AUV), and the results of tests in laboratory pool and lakes.

2 Vehicle Overview

The three-dimensional diagram of the designed S-AUV is shown in Fig. 1. The S-AUV is a hover-capable torpedo shaped AUV. The tail is the electronic control cabin. It is sealed and equipped with electronic equipment, including inertial sensor, GPS navigation module, electronic compass module, power monitoring module, wireless communication module and battery, etc. The head is a permeable sensor compartment. A vertical propeller is installed at the front of the sensor compartment. Water quality sensor, depth sensor and other devices that need to contact water are placed at the rear. The other cabin spaces are filled with buoyancy materials to modify the S-AUV's overall buoyancy such that it floats on the water's surface when submerged and has a buoyancy slightly higher than gravity. The sampler compartment is a permeable cabin equipped with a sampling system. The S-AUV is equipped with four thrusters, two horizontally and two vertically. Two horizontal thrusters at the tail control the advance and retreat motion of S-AUV, and can generate torque to control the yaw motion. The vertical thrusters can independently control the heave motion and the pitching motion of the S-AUV.

There are horizontal rudder blades on both sides of the electronic control cabin, which form the propeller-rudder combination drive system with the horizontal propeller at the tail. When the S-AUV moves horizontally at high speed, the rudder blades cooperate with the horizontal propeller to maintain the stability of the horizontal attitude and maintain the depth of the S-AUV in the vertical direction. Thereby, S-AUV can rely more on rudder pads rather than vertical thrusters for depth control to reducing power consumption and increasing AUV endurance during cruising.

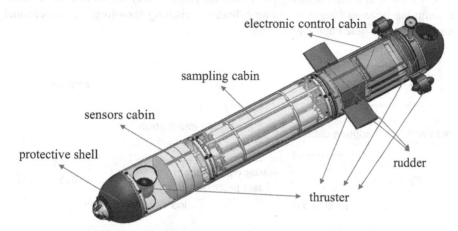

Fig. 1. The three-dimensional diagram of the S-AUV

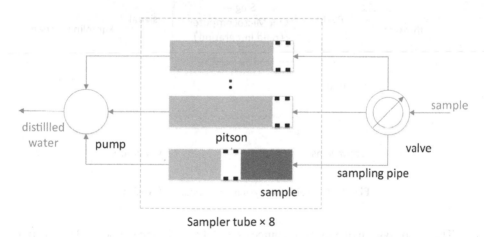

Fig. 2. Schematic illustration of the sampling system

The working principle diagram of the AUV sampling system is shown in Fig. 2. The sampling system is installed in the sampling cabin of the AUV, with eight sampling tubes distributed in a circular pattern around it. The multi-channel rotary valve and suction pump are installed in the middle of the eight sampling tubes. Before sampling, the sampling tube is filled with distilled water. During sampling, the sample is drawn into the cylindrical sampler body from outside of the vehicle fairing. The distilled water occupying the volume behind the piston is expelled through outlets in the rear end cap of the sampler. The dimensions and shape of the sampler constrained by the available space within the S-AUV mid-body, are 20 cm in diameter and 50 cm in length. This resulted in a sampler cylinder with a volume of 500 mL. The length of the sampler body is 435 mm. In order to reduce the weight, volume and power consumption of the sampling system, the pump used is a DC brushless motor submersible pump with working voltage of DC 12–16 V, and the operating power consumption is only 30 W. In order to meet the sampling system of eight sampling cylinders switching sampling, a multi-channel rotary valve is designed and customized.

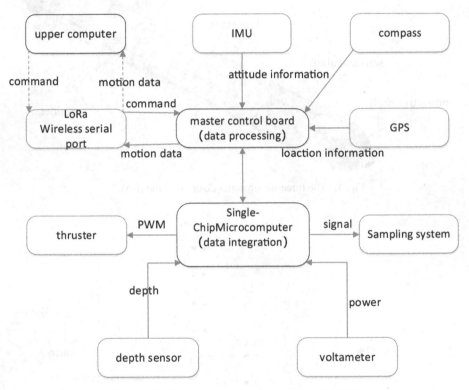

Fig. 3. The hardware system architecture of S-AUV

The sensor system of S-AUV is composed of GPS positioning module, IMU inertial sensor, depth sensor, electronic compass, etc. In the sampling process at fixed depth, depth information can be obtained through the depth sensor in real time. In the process of surface navigation cruise, the position and yaw angle information can be obtained through the GPS module and electronic compass. At the same time, the pitch angle and roll angle are obtained by IMU inertial sensor. The communication module implements real-time wireless communication of AUV through LoRa. The controller and data processing are realized on the master control board and single chip microcomputer. The overall hardware framework of S-AUV is shown in Fig. 3.

The AUV designed in this paper is light and flexible, as shown in Fig. 4. The total length is 1800 mm, the outer diameter of the cabin part is 200 mm, the maximum transverse length is 400 mm, the mass is about 28 kg, the maximum speed can reach 1.5 m/s, and the endurance can reach 3 h. The sampling system is designed as one cabin of the AUV, which greatly improves the hydrodynamic performance of the AUV and is suitable for long-distance cruise. Moreover, the sampling system is convenient to disassemble and to retrieve samples for further analysis.

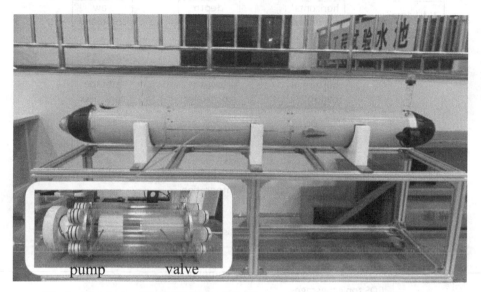

Fig. 4. The photo of S-AUV: the sampling system is equipped in the middle cabin

3   Control Architecture

S-AUV motion control program is designed based on Robotics Operating System (ROS), an open-source robotics platform. The S-AUV designed in this paper has four controllable degrees of freedom. The four degrees of freedom control can be realized by four independent closed-loop controllers, namely, depth control, advance control, pitch control and yaw control (Fig. 5).

In the automatic control, the AUV receives the motion instruction through the LoRa module. The master control board can directly obtain data from sensors such as IMU and GPS or indirectly obtain sensor data integrated with STM32. After the information from sensors such as GPS and IMU is sent to the master control board, it is processed by the sensor integration program and the corresponding information topic is released. The three motion controller programs of horizontal, depth and attitude subscribe the required sensor information and motion instructions, calculate and generate the force and torque in each direction, and publish the corresponding force or torque topic. Then the forces and torques in each direction are integrated and sent to the thrust distribution

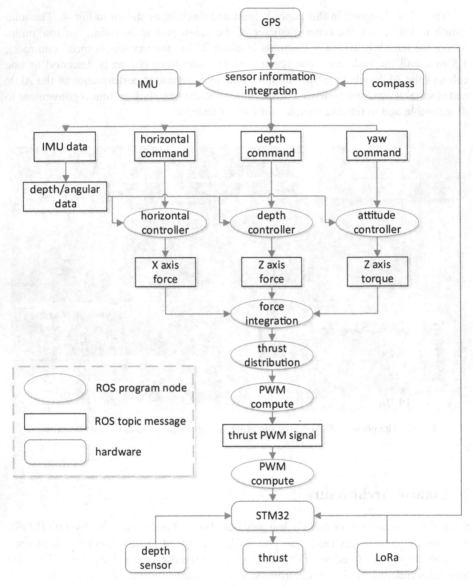

Fig. 5. The control node block diagram of S-AUV

controller. Thrust distribution controller is a universal program, which can generate the corresponding action factor matrix according to different AUV thruster distributions, solve the overall thrust/torque command into the thrust command of each thruster, and publish the thrust topic of the thruster. The PWM computing node calculates the PWM wave control frequency required by each brushless thruster through the thrust-PWM frequency mapping relationship. Then the STM32 board receives PWM information and controls corresponding thruster movement. The block diagram of control node is shown in Fig. 4.

4   Experiments and Results

4.1   Pool Test

The S-AUV has mainly two motion modes: hover and cruise. The kinetic performance of S-AUV was tested in a laboratory pool. The hover control performance of AUV is generally verified through step depth determination experiments. The AUV is controlled to remain in hover at different depths. In this experiment, two different depths of 1m and 1.5m were selected to hover for 60 s, while maintaining a pitch angle of 0°. The test result is shown in Fig. 6. Figure 6 (a) is the depth data and Fig. 6 (b) is the pitch angle data. The red line is the desired depth and pitch, and the blue line is the actual depth and pitch. After the depth switch command is issued, the AUV responds quickly. The depth overshoot shall not exceed 0.2m, and the depth error after stabilization shall not exceed

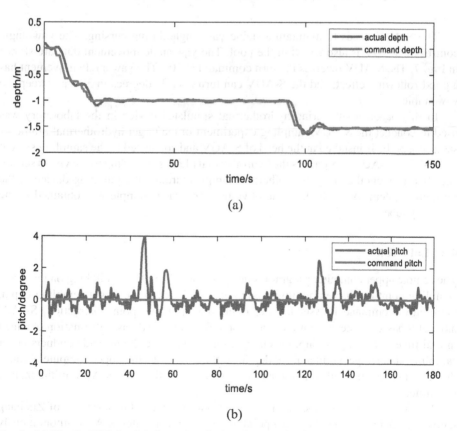

(a)

(b)

Fig. 6. (a) The S-AUV depth information during the step depth determination experiment. (b) The S-AUV pitch information during the step depth determination experiment

0.1m. The pitch angle error of AUV in hovering state is less than ± 3 degree. When switching hovering depth, there may be significant fluctuations in pitch angle because of the movement of the vertical thruster, but the maximum error shall not exceed ± 4 degrees. Experiments have shown that AUV can maintain horizontal hovering state.

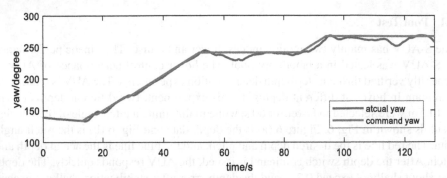

Fig. 7. The actual yaw and command yaw during the yaw control test

The S-AUV needs to maintain a stable yaw angle during cursing. The yaw angle control of S-AUV is also tested in the pool. The yaw angle movement data are shown in Fig. 7. The S-AUV receives the turn command at 10s. The yaw angle movement has a good following effect, and the S-AUV can turn over 90 degrees in 30 s and keep the yaw stable.

In this paper, a submarine hydrothermal simulated device in the laboratory was used to conduct the S-AUV sampling experiment of the target hydrothermal plume. A sampling probe is installed at the head of S-AUV and connected to the sampling system (Fig. 8). The S-AUV approaches the hydrothermal plumes according to the vision sensor, and then extracts the target hydrothermal samples through the pumping device of the sampling system. After the test, the obvious black water sample was obtained in the sampling tube.

4.2 Lake Test

The remote upper computer program is designed based on QT. By clicking on the target sampling point on the remote upper computer, and setting the target sampling depth, the control command is issued. After obtaining the target point instruction, S-AUV navigates based on the current GPS position information and yaw information obtained in real time, achieving autonomous navigation of the target point, and conducts hover sampling of the target point at fixed depth. At the same time, the upper computer obtains the real-time position information and draws motion path of the S-AUV in the map in real time.

The S-AUV navigation sampling test was carried out in Qizhen Lake of Zhejiang University. After clicking the target point on the upper computer, S-AUV autonomously moves to target position, and carried out hover sampling with a fixed depth of 0.5 m for 50 s. The upper computer can display the S-AUV's target sampling sites and motion

Fig. 8. The hydrothermal fluid sampling test in the laboratory pool

trajectory, as shown in Fig. 9. The photo of lake test is shown in Fig. 10. At the end of the sampling, the piston in the sampling tube moves to the other end and the sampling tube is filled with the target water sample. The target water sample can be obtained by opening the sampling compartment of the S-AUV, as shown in Fig. 11.

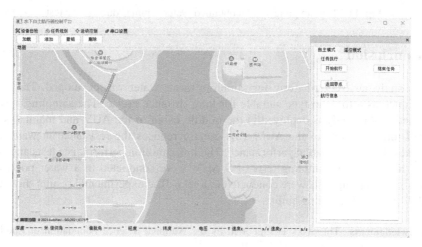

Fig. 9. The picture of remote upper computer interface

Fig. 10. The photo of S-AUV lake test

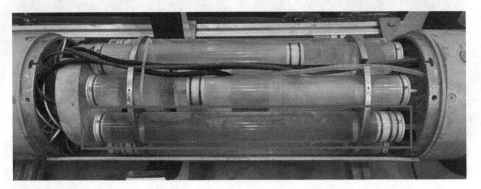

Fig. 11. The sampling system obtained water samples during lake test

5 Conclusion

In this study, an AUV platform for sampling target water was developed. The AUV is designed as a torpedo type suitable for long distance cruise. The sampling system designed in this study is deployed in the middle cabin of the AUV and maintains the overall torpedo shape of the AUV. This greatly reduces the resistance in water and improves the hydrodynamic performance. The basic motion performance tests and simulated hydrothermal sampling tests of S-AUV were conducted in a water pool, and navigation sampling tests were conducted in a lake. The experimental results show that S-AUV has good sampling ability.

Acknowledgments. This work is supported by the National Science Foundation of Zhejiang Province, China (Grant No. LR21E090001).

References

1. Ferri, G., Manzi, A., Fornai, F., et al.: The HydroNet ASV, a small-sized autonomous catamaran for real-time monitoring of water quality: from design to missions at sea. IEEE J. Oceanic Eng. **40**(3), 710–726 (2014)
2. Caccia, M., Bono, R., Bruzzone, G., et al.: Sampling sea surfaces with SESAMO: an Autonomous craft for the study of sea-air interactions. IEEE Robot. Autom. Mag. **12**(3), 95–105 (2005)
3. Hitz, G.: Autonomous inland water monitoring: design and application of a surface vessel. IEEE Robot. Autom. Mag. **19**(1), 62–72 (2012)
4. McNichol, J., Sylva, S.P., Thomas, F., Taylor, C.D., Sievert, S.M., Seewald, J.S.: Assessing microbial processes in deep-sea hydrothermal systems by incubation at in situ temperature and pressure. Deep Sea Res. Part I **115**, 221–232 (2016)
5. Mccollom, T.M., Seewald, J.S., German, C.R.: Investigation of extractable organic compounds in deep sea hydrothermal vent fluids along the mid-atlantic ridge. Geochim. Cosmochim. Acta **156**, 122–144 (2015)
6. Ji, F., Zhou, H., Yang, Q., et al.: Geochemistry of hydrothermal vent fluids and its implications for subsurface processes at the active Longqi hydrothermal field, Southwest Indian Ridge. Deep Sea Research Part I Oceanographic Research Papers, 122 (2017)
7. Wang, S., Wu, S., Du, M., et al.: A new serial sampler for collecting gas-tight samples from seafloor cold seeps and hydrothermal vents. Deep Sea Res. Part I **161**, 103282 (2020)
8. Ryan, J.P., Johnson, S.B., Sherman, A., et al.: Mobile autonomous process sampling within coastal ocean observing systems. Limnol. Oceanogr. Methods **8**(8), 394–402 (2010)
9. Zhang, Y., Ryan, J.P., Bellingham, J.G., et al.: Autonomous detection and sampling of water types and fronts in a coastal upwelling system by an autonomous underwater vehicle. Limnol. Oceanogr. Methods **10**(11), 934–951 (2012)
10. Pennington, J.T., Blum, M., Chavez, F.P.: Seawater sampling by an autonomous underwater vehicle: "Gulper" sample validation for nitrate, chlorophyll, phytoplankton, and primary production. Limnol. Oceanogr. Methods **14**(1), 14–23 (2016)
11. Billings, A., et al.: SyPRID sampler: a large-volume, high-resolution, autonomous, deep-ocean precision plankton sampling system. Deep Sea Res. Part II **137**, 297–306 (2017)

A Novel Motion Planning Algorithm Based on RRT-Connect and Bidirectional Approach for Free-Floating Space Robot

Hongwen Zhang[1], Yongxing Tang[2], and Zhanxia Zhu[2(✉)]

[1] Zhejiang Lab, Hangzhou 310000, Zhejiang, China
[2] School of Astronautics, Northwestern Polytechnical University, Xi'an 710072, Shanxi, China
zhuzhanxia@nwpu.edu.cn

Abstract. This paper investigates the motion planning from initial configuration to goal configuration for Free-Floating Space Robot (FFSR) and suggests a motion planning algorithm named Bidirectional RRT For FFSR (BiD-RRT-For-FFSR). Similar to RRT-Connect, BiD-RRT-For-FFSR constructs a tree from initial configuration and a tree from goal configuration. Local planner for random extension of a tree is proposed for the growth of these two trees, and local planner for bidirectional extension of two trees is developed for the connection of these two trees. Inspired by the projection method, these local planners involve an iteration process and are based on error projection. In each iteration, actions are generated by mapping the configuration error using the pseudo-inverse of Jacobian matrix, which enables the tree to grow towards a desired direction. Unlike projection method for geometric motion planning, these local planners can directly consider differential constraints. Besides, local planner for bidirectional extension adopts the bidirectional approach, which allows the configuration error between two trees to converge.

Keywords: Free-Floating Space Robot · Sampling-Based Motion Planning · Motion Planning under Differential Constraint

1 Introduction

A space robot consists of a base satellite and a manipulator. FFSR [1] disables the position and attitude controllers of the base satellite, providing advantages such as fuel savings, making it widely used in on-orbit services. This paper investigates the motion planning from initial configuration to goal configuration (MP-from-IC-to-GC) for FFSR. Compared to MP-from-IC-to-GC of a fixed-base manipulator, MP-from-IC-to-GC of FFSR is more complex [1]. The fixed-base manipulator's configuration comprises its joint angles, but FFSR's configuration includes both the base attitude angles and the manipulator's joint angles. There exist complex first-order differential constraints between the base attitude angles

© The Author(s), under exclusive license to Springer Nature Singapore Pte Ltd. 2023
H. Yang et al. (Eds.): ICIRA 2023, LNAI 14273, pp. 304–316, 2023.
https://doi.org/10.1007/978-981-99-6498-7_27

and joint angles. Hence, when it comes to planning the motion of FFSR, hierarchical planning cannot be utilized. Instead, one must directly consider differential constraints (motion planning under differential constraints, MP-Under-DC). Besides, due to the requirements of ground communication and solar panel orientation for the base satellite, the disturbance of the base attitude needs to be within a certain range. However, FFSR does not have controller to directly control its orientation, and can only indirectly adjust its orientation through joint movements. This further increases the difficulty of planner design.

There are primarily 3 types of approaches for FFSR's motion planning. **The first type** focuses the steering problem of FFSR, i.e., how to generate a series of actions (i.e. joint angular velocities) to let FFSR move from the initial configuration to the goal configuration. Examples of this type include disturbance map method [2], and bidirectional method [3], etc. However, these methods focus on using joint motions to control the base attitude, but do not consider collisions. **The second type** uses polynomials with unknown coefficients to parameterize FFSR's joint trajectories, and converts FFSR's motion planning into an optimization problem. The fitness function is usually the base attitude disturbance at the final time, and meta-heuristic methods such as particle swarm optimization [4] and genetic algorithm [5] are used to solve the optimization problem. However, it's difficult to control the trajectory's shape with this method, making it difficult to consider collisions. **The third category of methods** is based on methods such as convex optimization [7] and convex quadratic programming [6]. This class of methods is highly efficient, but it suffers from local optima.

Many existing methods for MP-Under-DC are sampling based motion planning method (SBMP). In SBMP, RRT-based methods are well-suited for MP-Under-DC, so we adopt RRT-based methods for FFSR's motion planning. Choosing proper local planners is crucial for RRT-based methods. For **system with simple differential constraint** like locally controllable linear system, the analytical solution to its two-point boundary value problems (BVPs) can be used as local planner [8]. For **system with complex differential constraint**, linearization or approximation can be employed to solve BVPs to get local trajectories. Besides, **local planning scheme without solving BVPs** randomly selects action and time duration, and then performs forward integration [9]. FFSR is a complex system, so there is no analytical solution for its BVPs. Approximately solving FFSR's BVPs requires solving lots of nonlinear optimization problems for a complex system, which is computationally expensive. In addition, local planning schemes without solving BVPs randomly select actions, making it difficult to adjust the base attitude angles related to constraints.

This paper proposes a new method for designing local planners of FFSR. Inspired by the projection method for motion planning problems with task constraints [10], this method involves an iteration process and is based on error projection. In each iteration, actions are generated by mapping the configuration error using the pseudo-inverse of the Jacobian matrix, allowing the local trajectory to grow towards the desired direction. But unlike the projection method, this approach is based on state transition equations and involves integration to consider differential constraints. Based on this local planning method and RRT-

Connect [12], we proposes the BiD-RRT-For-FFSR for MP-from-IC-to-GC of FFSR. BiD-RRT-For-FFSR constructs two trees, one from the initial configuration and the other from the goal configuration. Besides, a local planner for random extension of a tree, as well as local planner for bidirectional expansion of two trees are developed. Considering that the degree of freedom of FFSR's manipulator is less than the dimension of FFSR's configuration space, local planner for bidirectional expansion of two trees adopts the bidirectional approach [3], which enables the configuration error between the two trees to converge.

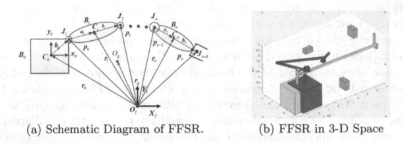

(a) Schematic Diagram of FFSR.   (b) FFSR in 3-D Space

Fig. 1. Schematic Diagram of FFSR and FFSR in 3-D Space.

2 Motion Equations of FFSR and Problem Defination

2.1 Motion Equations of FFSR in Velocity Form

This paper focuses on a single-arm FFSR shown in Fig. 1, which includes $n+1$ rigid bodies: the base satellite (B_0) and n links of the manipulator ($B_1, \cdots, B_n$). It also has n rotating joints ($J_1, \cdots, J_n$) which connect adjacent rigid bodies. We provides some motion equations of FFSR in velocity form that is necessary for this paper, and other motion equations for FFSR can be found in [11]. FFSR is not subject to external forces, thus its momentum is conserved. The momentum of FFSR includes the linear momentum P and angular momentum L:

$$\begin{bmatrix} P \\ L \end{bmatrix} = \begin{bmatrix} M E & M\tilde{r}_{og}^T \\ M\tilde{r}_{og} & H_\omega \end{bmatrix} \begin{bmatrix} v_0 \\ \omega_0 \end{bmatrix} + \begin{bmatrix} J_{T\omega} \\ H_{\omega\psi} \end{bmatrix} \dot{\Theta} = H_b \begin{bmatrix} v_0 \\ \omega_0 \end{bmatrix} + H_m \dot{\Theta} \qquad (1)$$

$\dot{\Theta}$ is the joint angular velocity vector, and definitions for each matrix ($\tilde{r}_{og}$, H_ω, etc.) in Eq. (1) can be found in [11]. Assuming $P = 0$, $L = 0$ in beginning, then the satellite's linear velocities (v_0) and angular velocities (ω_0) can be obtained:

$$\begin{bmatrix} v_0 \\ \omega_0 \end{bmatrix} = -(H_b)^{-1} H_m \dot{\Theta} = J_{b\Theta} \dot{\Theta} = \begin{bmatrix} J_{bv} \\ J_{b\omega} \end{bmatrix} \dot{\Theta} \qquad (2)$$

ω_0 is represented as $^b\omega_0$ in the fixed coordinate system (FCS) of the base satellite, and the relationship between $^b\omega_0$ and first derivative of the base attitude angles ($\dot{\boldsymbol{\Psi}}_0 = [\dot{\alpha}_0, \dot{\beta}_0, \dot{\gamma}_0]^T$) can be expressed as follows [11]:

$$^b\boldsymbol{\omega}_0 = \boldsymbol{N}_0 \begin{bmatrix} \dot{\alpha}_0 & \dot{\beta}_0 & \dot{\gamma}_0 \end{bmatrix}^T \tag{3}$$

of which: $\boldsymbol{N}_0 = \begin{bmatrix} 1 & \tan(\beta_0)*\sin(\alpha_0) & \tan(\beta_0)*\cos(\alpha_0) \\ 0 & \cos(\alpha_0) & -\cos(\alpha_0) \\ 0 & \sin(\alpha_0)/\sin(\beta_0) & \cos(\alpha_0)/\cos(\beta_0) \end{bmatrix}$. Considering Eq. (2)

and Eq. (3), we can get:

$$\dot{\boldsymbol{\Psi}}_0 = \boldsymbol{N}_0^{-1}(^b\boldsymbol{\omega}_0) = \boldsymbol{N}_0^{-1}(^I\boldsymbol{R}_0)^{-1}\boldsymbol{\omega}_0 = \boldsymbol{N}_0^{-1}(^I\boldsymbol{R}_0)^{-1}\boldsymbol{J}_{b\omega}\dot{\boldsymbol{\Theta}} = \boldsymbol{J}_{b\Psi}\dot{\boldsymbol{\Theta}} \tag{4}$$

$^I\boldsymbol{R}_0$ is the attitude transformation matrix from the base's FCS to the inertial coordinate system. Finally, we can obtain the state transition equation of FFSR:

$$\dot{\boldsymbol{q}} = \begin{bmatrix} \dot{\boldsymbol{\Theta}} \\ \dot{\boldsymbol{\Psi}}_0 \end{bmatrix} = \begin{bmatrix} \boldsymbol{E}_{n \times n} \\ \boldsymbol{J}_{b\Psi} \end{bmatrix} \dot{\boldsymbol{\Theta}} = \boldsymbol{J}_{q\Theta}\dot{\boldsymbol{\Theta}} \tag{5}$$

$\boldsymbol{q}$ is the configuration of FFSR. Assuming FFSR's manipulator has 7 joints, i.e., $n = 7$, then $\boldsymbol{E}_{n \times n}$ is an 7×7 identity matrix, and $\boldsymbol{J}_{q\Theta}$ is a 10×7 matrix.

2.2   MP-from-IC-to-GC for FFSR

Given the initial configuration $\boldsymbol{q}^I$ and the target configuration $\boldsymbol{q}^G$, MP-from-IC-to-GC for FFSR requires computing an action(joint angular velocity) trajectory: $\dot{\boldsymbol{\Theta}}(t) \rightarrow U, t \in [0, t_f]$. Based on this action trajectory, a configuration trajectory ($\boldsymbol{q}(t), t \in [0, t_f]$) obtained by integrating Eq. (5) from $\boldsymbol{q}^I$ should satisfy: (1) The configuration at the final time equals to $\boldsymbol{q}^G$: $\boldsymbol{q}(t_f) = \boldsymbol{q}^G$; (2) In free configuration space: $\boldsymbol{q}(t) \in \boldsymbol{C}_{free}$; (3) Within a certain range: $\boldsymbol{q}(t) \in [\boldsymbol{q}^{min}, \boldsymbol{q}^{max}]$, especially the base attitude angles are within a certain range: $\boldsymbol{\Psi}_0 \in [\boldsymbol{\Psi}_0^{min}, \boldsymbol{\Psi}_0^{max}]$.

3   Bi-Directional RRT for Free-Floating Space Robot

We proposes the Bidirectional RRT For FFSR (BiD-RRT-For-FFSR, *Algorithm 1*, abbreviated as *Alg*-1) to slove FFSR's MP-from-IC-to-GC. Like RRT-Connect, *Alg*-1 has a tree from $\boldsymbol{q}^I$ (**Tree**^{I}) and a tree from $\boldsymbol{q}^G$ (**Tree**^{G}). Unlike RRT-Connect, each tree node includes both $\boldsymbol{q}$ and $\dot{\boldsymbol{q}}$. Firstly, **Tree**^{I} is initialized by $\boldsymbol{q}^I$ and $\dot{\boldsymbol{q}}^I$, and **Tree**^{G} is initialized by $\boldsymbol{q}^G$ and $\dot{\boldsymbol{q}}^G$. After initialization, BiD-RRT-For-FFSR runs K loops, and in each loop:

Step A. Use a randomly sampled configuration to guide the extension of **Tree**^{I} or **Tree**^{G} (*Alg*-1, Line 4 or 10).

Step B. If **Tree**^{I} or **Tree**^{G} is successfully extended (*Extend = True, Alg*-1, line 6 or 12) and a new node ($\boldsymbol{q}_{new}^I$ or $\boldsymbol{q}_{new}^G$) is generated, the local planner for bidirectional expansion of two trees (*Alg*-5) is used to simultaneously extend **Tree**^{I} and **Tree**^{G}. This local planner is based on bidirectional approach [3] and includes two types: *BiExtend1()* and *BiExtend2()* (*Alg*-1, line 7 and 13). If

Tree^I is extended in **Step A**, then **Step B** runs *BiExtend1()*, otherwise it runs *BiExtend2()*. When *Extend = False*, proceed to the next loop directly.

Step C. If *Tree^I* and *Tree^G* is connected (*Connect = True*), the algorithm succeeds(*Alg-1*, line 8 or 14). Otherwise, proceed to the next loop.

In **Step A**, *Tree^I* and *Tree^G* are extended alternately. This alternation is achieved by changing the value of *swap*, which can be either 0 or 1. In each loop, *Tree^I* is extended if *swap = 1*, and *Tree^G* is extended if *Swap = 0*. After the random extension, change the value of *Swap* (*Alg* 1, Line 5 or 11).

Algorithm 1: BiD-RRT-For-FFSR

1 *Tree^I*.Init()← $q^I, \dot{q}^I$;   *Tree^G*.Init()← $q^G, \dot{q}^G$;   *swap* = 1 ;
2 **for** $i = 1$ **to** K **do**
3   **if** *swap* = 1 **then**
4      $(Extend, q^I_{new}, \dot{q}^I_{new})$ ← RandomExtend(*Tree^I*) ;
5   *swap* = 0 ;
6   **if** *Extend* **then**
7   *Connect* ← BiExtend1(*Tree^I*,*Tree^G*,$q^I_{new}, \dot{q}^I_{new}$) ;
8   **if** *Connect* **then Break**

9   **else**
10      $(Extend, q^G_{new}, \dot{q}^G_{new})$← RandomExtend(*Tree^G*);
11   *swap* = 1 ;
12   **if** *Extend* **then**
13   *Connect* ← BiExtend2(*Tree^I*,*Tree^G*,$q^G_{new}, \dot{q}^G_{new}$);
14   **if** *Connect* **then Break**

Algorithm 2: RandomExtend(*Tree*)

1 q_s ← RandomConfig(), $q_{ext}, \dot{q}_{ext}$ ←NearestNode(*Tree*, q_s);
2 $q_{now}, \dot{q}_{now}$ ← $q_{ext}, \dot{q}_{ext}$;
3 $i = 0$;
4 **while** *TermiConditions* = *False* **do**
5    $q_{next} = q_{now} + \dot{q}_{now} * \Delta t$;
6   *Collision* ← CollisionCheckModule(q_{next});
7    $\dot{q}_{next}$ ←ActionforRandomExtend($q_{next}, \dot{q}_{now}, q_{sample}$) ;
8   *Tree*.AddNode($q_{next}, \dot{q}_{next}$), $q_{now}, \dot{q}_{now}$ ← $q_{next}, \dot{q}_{next}$;
9    $i = i + 1$
10   *TermiConditions* ←CheckTermiCondition() ;
11 *Extend = True*;   **if** $i < Ite_{min}$ **then** *Extend = False*
12 **return** $(Extend, q_{next}, \dot{q}_{next})$;

3.1 Local Planner for Random Extension of Tree

Alg-2 presents the local planner for the random extension of a tree. Firstly, randomly sample a configuration q_s, and the point closest to q_s on the *Tree* is selected as the node to be extended q_{ext} (*Alg-2*, Line 1). Then, local planning is conducted from q_{ext} towards q_s to generate a collision-free local trajectory that satisfies the constraints (Lines 2~10 of *Alg*-2). Similar to the projection method [10], this local planner involves an iterative process and is based on error projection. In each iteration, it generates actions by mapping the configuration error using the pseudo-inverse of $J_{q\Theta}$ (Eq. (5)), which allows FFSR to gradually move towards q_s. Specifically, each iteration includes the following setps:

Step A. Integrate from the current configuration q_{now} to get the next configuration q_{next} (*Alg*-2, Line 5). It is necessary to determine whether the newly generated q_{next} is in C_{free} (*Alg*-2, Line 6). However, since there may not be a significant gap between q_{next} and q_{now}, it is not necessary to perform collision detection on q_{next} for each iteration. In *Alg*-3, we propose to detect the q_{next} only when the gap between q_{next} and the recently detected configuration ($q_{LastChecked}$) exceeds a predefined threshold (*CheckThreshold*).

Algorithm 3: CollisionCheckModule(q_{next})

---
1   $Collision = False$;
2   **if** $max(q_{next} - q_{LastChecked}) \geq CheckThreshold$ **then**
3      $Collision = $ CollisionCheckAlgorithm(q_{next});
4      $q_{LastChecked} = q_{next}$;
5   **return** $Collision$;

Step B. Generate an action ($\dot{\Theta}_{next}$) that allows FFSR to transit from q_{next} towards q_s and return $\dot{q}_{next}$ (*Alg*-2, Line 7). As shown in *Alg*-4: Firstly, calculate Jacobian matrices $J_{b\Psi}$ and $J_{q\Theta}$ when $q = q_{next}$ (Line 1). Then compute the error $\Delta q = q_s - q_{next}$, and generate a desired action $\dot{\Theta}_d$ that can reduce Δq by using $(J_{q\Theta})^+$ to project Δq. For continuity of actions, $\dot{\Theta}_d$ is not directly used as the actions when $q = q_{next}$ for FFSR. Instead, calculate the acceleration $\ddot{\Theta}_d$ and then integrate it to obtain $\dot{\Theta}_{next}$ (Line 3). Finally, use $J_{b\Psi}$ to multiply $\dot{\Theta}_{next}$ to obtain $\dot{\Psi}_{b.next}$, and return the configuration velocity $\dot{q}_{next}$(Line 4~5).

Algorithm 4: ActionforRandomExtend($q_{next}, \dot{q}_{now}, q_s$)

---
1   $(J_{b\Psi}, J_{q\Theta}) = $ JMatrixCal(q_{next}) ;
2   $\Delta q = q_s - q_{next}$, $\dot{\Theta}_d = (J_{q\Theta})^+ \Delta q$;
3   $\ddot{\Theta}_d = (\dot{\Theta}_d - \dot{\Theta}_{now}) * K$, $\dot{\Theta}_{next} = \dot{\Theta}_{now} + \ddot{\Theta}_d * \Delta t$;
4   $\dot{\Psi}_{b.next} = J_{b\Psi}\dot{\Theta}_{next}$
5   **return** $\dot{q}_{next} = \left[(\dot{\Psi}_{b.next})^T \ (\dot{\Theta}_{next})^T\right]^T$;

Step C. Insert the generated q_{next} and $\dot{q}_{next}$ into the **Tree** and prepare for the next iteration (*Alg*-2, Line 8).

Step D. Determine whether to terminate the iteration (*Alg*-2, Line 10). Iteration should stop when one of the following situations occurs: collision happens, the max number of iteration is reached ($i \geq Ite_{max}$), $q_{now} \notin [q^{min}, q^{max}]$.

    If local planner stops after very few iterations (i.e., $i < Ite_{min}$), the generated local trajectory is of limited significance, and should be abandoned (*Extend* = *False*, *Alg*-2, Line 11). Finally return *Extend*, q_{next} and $\dot{q}_{next}$ (*Alg*-2, Line 12).

3.2 Local Planner for Bidirectional Expansion of Two Trees

We use *BiExtend1()* (*Alg*-1, Line 7) as an example to introduce the local planner for bidirectional expansion of two trees. If **Tree**^{I} is successfully extended and $q_{new}^I, \dot{q}_{new}^I$ are returned, *BiExtend1()* is executed to extend both **Tree**^{I} and **Tree**^{G}. The process of the local planner for bidirectional extension is similar to the process of local planner for the random extension of a tree (*Alg*-2), with the only difference being that the former simultaneously extends two trees.

Algorithm 5: BiExtend1($\textbf{Tree}^I, \textbf{Tree}^G, q_{new}^I, \dot{q}_{new}^I$)

---

1 $(q_{ext}^I, \dot{q}_{ext}^I) \leftarrow (q_{new}^I, \dot{q}_{new}^I),$ $(q_{ext}^G, \dot{q}_{ext}^G) \leftarrow$ NearestNode($\textbf{Tree}^G, q_{new}^I$);

2 $(q_{now}^I, \dot{q}_{now}^I) \leftarrow (q_{ext}^I, \dot{q}_{ext}^I),$ $(q_{now}^G, \dot{q}_{now}^G) \leftarrow (q_{ext}^G, \dot{q}_{ext}^G)$;

3 $i = 0$;

4 **while** *TermiConditions = False* **do**

5      $\quad q_{next}^I \leftarrow q_{now}^I + \dot{q}_{now}^I * \Delta t,$ $q_{next}^G \leftarrow q_{now}^G + \dot{q}_{now}^G * \Delta t$;

6      $\quad (Collision^I, Collision^G) \leftarrow$ CollisionCheckModule(q_{next}^I, q_{next}^G);

7      $\quad (\dot{q}_{next}^I, \dot{q}_{next}^G) \leftarrow$ ActionForBiExtend($q_{next}^I, \dot{q}_{now}^I, q_{next}^G, \dot{q}_{now}^G$) ;

8      $\quad \textbf{Tree}^I$.AddNode($q_{next}^I, \dot{q}_{next}^I$), $\textbf{Tree}^G$.AddNode($q_{next}^G, \dot{q}_{next}^G$);

9      $\quad q_{now}^I, \dot{q}_{now}^I \leftarrow q_{next}^I, \dot{q}_{next}^I,$ $q_{now}^G, \dot{q}_{now}^G \leftarrow q_{next}^G, \dot{q}_{next}^G$;

10     $\quad i = i + 1$

11     $\quad$ *TermiConditions* $\leftarrow$ CheckTermiCondition() ;

12 $Connect = False$;   **if** $\|q_{now}^I - q_{now}^G\| \le \delta$ **then** $Connect = True$ **return** $Connect$;

As depicted in *Alg*-5, firstly, q_{new}^I is selected as the node to be expanded for **Tree**^{I}, i.e. q_{ext}^I, and the node closest to q_{new}^I on **Tree**$_G$ is selected as the node to be expanded for **Tree**^{G}, i.e. q_{ext}^G (*Alg*-5, Line 1). Then, local planning for extensions of **Tree**^{I} and **Tree**^{G} is conducted to generate a local trajectory starting from q_{ext}^I and another local trajectory starting from q_{ext}^G. It should be noted that the local planner attempts to connect the endpoints of these two trajectories. Similar to *Alg*-2, *Alg*-5 involves an iterative process and is based on error projection. The specific steps of each iteration are as follows:

Step A. Integrate from current configuration q_{now}^I to get the next configuration q_{next}^I for **Tree**^{I}, and integrate from current configuration q_{now}^G to obtain the next configuration q_{next}^G for **Tree**^{G} (*Alg*-5, Line 5). Use *Alg*-3 determine whether the newly generated q_{next}^I and q_{next}^G are in C_{free} (*Alg*-5, Line 6).

Step B. Utilize the action generation algorithm for bidirectional expansion (*Alg*-6) to generate $\dot{\Theta}_{next}^I$ for **Tree**^{I} and $\dot{\Theta}_{next}^G$ for **Tree**^{G}. $\dot{\Theta}_{next}^I$ enables FFSR to move from q_{next}^I towards q_{next}^G, while $\dot{\Theta}_{next}^G$ enables FFSR to move from q_{next}^G towards q_{next}^I. **As shown in *Alg*-6:** Firstly, calculate the Jacobian matrices $J_{b\Psi}^I$ and $J_{q\Theta}^I$ when $q = q_{next}^I$, and calculate $J_{b\Psi}^G$ and $J_{q\Theta}^G$ when $q = q_{next}^G$ (*Alg*-6, Line 1). Next, compute the error Δq between q_{next}^I and q_{next}^G (*Alg*-6, Line 2). By combining $J_{q\Theta}^I$ (10×7) and $J_{q\Theta}^G$ (10×7), the Augmented Bidirectional

Jacobian Matrix $\boldsymbol{J}_{AugBi}$ with dimension of 10×14 is obtained [3]:

$$\boldsymbol{J}_{AugBi} = \begin{bmatrix} \boldsymbol{J}_{q\Theta}^{I} & -\boldsymbol{J}_{q\Theta}^{G} \end{bmatrix} \tag{6}$$

Using the pseudo-inverse of $\boldsymbol{J}_{AugBi}$, to map $\Delta\boldsymbol{q}$ to the action space, generating $\dot{\boldsymbol{\Theta}}_{d}^{Bi}$ with dimensions of 1×14 (*Alg*-6, Line 3). The first 7 elements of $\dot{\boldsymbol{\Theta}}_{d}^{Bi}$ are the expected actions for $\boldsymbol{Tree}^{I}$, denoted as $\dot{\boldsymbol{\Theta}}_{d}^{I}$, and the last 7 elements are the expected actions of $\boldsymbol{Tree}^{G}$, denoted as $\dot{\boldsymbol{\Theta}}_{d}^{G}$. When $\boldsymbol{q} = \boldsymbol{q}_{next}^{I}$, $\Delta\boldsymbol{q}$ can be reduced if FFSR moves with actions $\dot{\boldsymbol{\Theta}}_{d}^{I}$; When $\boldsymbol{q} = \boldsymbol{q}_{next}^{G}$, $\Delta\boldsymbol{q}$ also can reduced if FFSR moves with actions $\dot{\boldsymbol{\Theta}}_{d}^{G}$. Similar to *Alg*-4, to ensure continuity of actions, FFSR also does not directly use $\dot{\boldsymbol{\Theta}}_{d}^{I}$ and $\dot{\boldsymbol{\Theta}}_{d}^{G}$ as actions (*Alg*-6, Line 5,6). Use $\boldsymbol{J}_{b\Psi}^{I}$ to multiply $\dot{\boldsymbol{\Theta}}_{next}^{I}$ to obtain $\dot{\boldsymbol{\Psi}}_{b.next}^{I}$, and use $\boldsymbol{J}_{b\Psi}^{G}$ to multiply $\dot{\boldsymbol{\Theta}}_{next}^{G}$ to obtain $\dot{\boldsymbol{\Psi}}_{b.next}^{G}$ (*Alg*-6, Line 7). Finally, return $\dot{\boldsymbol{q}}_{next}^{I}$ and $\dot{\boldsymbol{q}}_{next}^{G}$.

Algorithm 6: ActionForBiExtend($\boldsymbol{q}_{next}^{I}, \dot{\boldsymbol{q}}_{now}^{I}, \boldsymbol{q}_{next}^{G}, \dot{\boldsymbol{q}}_{now}^{G}$)

1   $(\boldsymbol{J}_{b\Psi}^{I}, \boldsymbol{J}_{q\Theta}^{I}) \leftarrow$ JMatrixCal($\boldsymbol{q}_{next}^{I}$), $(\boldsymbol{J}_{b\Psi}^{G}, \boldsymbol{J}_{q\Theta}^{G}) \leftarrow$ JMatrixCal($\boldsymbol{q}_{next}^{G}$);

2   $\Delta\boldsymbol{q} \leftarrow \boldsymbol{q}_{next}^{I} - \boldsymbol{q}_{next}^{G}$;

3   $\boldsymbol{J}_{ExtBi} \leftarrow [\boldsymbol{J}_{q\Theta}^{I}, -\boldsymbol{J}_{q\Theta}^{G}]$, $\dot{\boldsymbol{\Theta}}_{d}^{Bi} \leftarrow (\boldsymbol{J}_{ExtBi})^{+}\Delta\boldsymbol{q}$;

4   $\dot{\boldsymbol{\Theta}}_{d}^{I} \leftarrow \dot{\boldsymbol{\Theta}}_{d}^{Bi}(1:7)$, $\dot{\boldsymbol{\Theta}}_{d}^{G} \leftarrow \dot{\boldsymbol{\Theta}}_{d}^{Bi}(8:14)$;

5   $\ddot{\boldsymbol{\Theta}}_{d}^{I} \leftarrow (\dot{\boldsymbol{\Theta}}_{d}^{I} - \dot{\boldsymbol{\Theta}}_{now}^{I}) * K$, $\dot{\boldsymbol{\Theta}}_{next}^{I} \leftarrow \dot{\boldsymbol{\Theta}}_{now}^{I} + \ddot{\boldsymbol{\Theta}}_{d}^{I} * \Delta t$;

6   $\ddot{\boldsymbol{\Theta}}_{d}^{G} \leftarrow (\dot{\boldsymbol{\Theta}}_{d}^{G} - \dot{\boldsymbol{\Theta}}_{now}^{G}) * K$, $\dot{\boldsymbol{\Theta}}_{next}^{G} \leftarrow \dot{\boldsymbol{\Theta}}_{now}^{G} + \ddot{\boldsymbol{\Theta}}_{d}^{G} * \Delta t$;

7   $\dot{\boldsymbol{\Psi}}_{b.next}^{I} \leftarrow \boldsymbol{J}_{b\Psi}^{I} \dot{\boldsymbol{\Theta}}_{next}^{I}$, $\dot{\boldsymbol{\Psi}}_{b.next}^{G} \leftarrow \boldsymbol{J}_{b\Psi}^{G} \dot{\boldsymbol{\Theta}}_{next}^{G}$;

8   **return** ($\dot{\boldsymbol{q}}_{next}^{I} = [(\dot{\boldsymbol{\Psi}}_{b.next}^{I})^{T}, (\dot{\boldsymbol{\Theta}}_{next}^{I})^{T}]^{T}$,
    $\dot{\boldsymbol{q}}_{next}^{G} = [(\dot{\boldsymbol{\Psi}}_{b.next}^{G})^{T}, (\dot{\boldsymbol{\Theta}}_{next}^{G})^{T}]^{T}$)

Step C. Insert the generated $\boldsymbol{q}_{next}^{I}$ and $\dot{\boldsymbol{q}}_{next}^{I}$ into $\boldsymbol{Tree}^{I}$, and insert the generated $\boldsymbol{q}_{next}^{G}$ and $\dot{\boldsymbol{q}}_{next}^{G}$ into $\boldsymbol{Tree}^{G}$ (*Alg*-5, Line 8). Prepare for the next iteration (*Alg*-5, Line 9).

Step D. Iteration should stop when one of the following situations occurs (*Alg*-5, Line 11): collision happens ($Collision^{I} = True$ or $Collision^{G} = True$), the max number of iteration is reached ($i \geq Ite_{max}$), the configuration parameters are not within the predefined range ($\boldsymbol{q}_{now}^{I} \notin [\boldsymbol{q}^{min}, \boldsymbol{q}^{max}]$, or $\boldsymbol{q}_{now}^{G} \notin [\boldsymbol{q}^{min}, \boldsymbol{q}^{max}]$), $\boldsymbol{Tree}^{I}$ and $\boldsymbol{Tree}^{G}$ are connected ($\|\boldsymbol{q}_{now}^{I} - \boldsymbol{q}_{now}^{G}\| \leq \delta$, where δ is a sufficiently small positive constant).

Since the number of columns of the matrix $\boldsymbol{J}_{AugBi}$ in Eq. (6) is greater than the number of rows, generating actions for the two trees according to Line 3 of *Alg*-6 enables the error $\Delta\boldsymbol{q}$ between $\boldsymbol{Tree}^{I}$ and $\boldsymbol{Tree}^{G}$ to converge [3].

4   Simulation Study

The numerical simulation consists of two parts: **The first part of the simulation** uses the two suggested local planners to solve the local planning problem of FFSR. It should be noted that the purpose of the first part is to verify that the local planner of *Alg*-2 is unable to converge the configuration error, while the local planner of *Alg*-5 is capable of doing so. Therefore, when using *Alg*-2 and *Alg*-5 to solve the local planning problems of the first part, collision detection and iteration terminations are not considered. **The second part of the simulation** is aimed at validating the efficacy of BiD-RRT-For-FFSR for MP-from-IC-to-GC of FFSR.

A FFSR with a base satellite and a 7-joint manipulator has been selected for simulation. Table 1 outlines dynamic parameters of FFSR and the size of each rigid body of FFSR. Table 2 provides the D-H parameters of the manipulator. Each rigid body is treated as a cuboid for simplicity, whose length (L), width (W), and height (H) are shown in Table 1. In addition, there are 3 cuboid obstacles: The center of the 1th is at $(1, 1, 2.8)m$, with size of $0.8m(L)$, $0.4m(W)$, and $0.4m(H)$. The 2th is at $(4, 0, -1)m$, with $0.4m(L)$, $0.8m(W)$, and $0.8m(H)$. The 3th is at $(6, 1.5, 2.5)m$, with $0.4m(L)$, $0.8m(W)$, and $0.8m(H)$.

Table 1. Dynamic and Parameters of FFSR and Size of Rigid Bodies

Rigid Body	mass(kg)	Inertia Matrix ($kg \cdot m^2$)			Size of Rigid Bodies		
		I_{xx}	I_{yy}	I_{zz}	L(m)	W(m)	H(m)
Base	900	6000	12000	8000	1	1	1
Link1	20	20	20	30	0.35	0.16	0.16
Link2	20	20	20	30	0.35	0.16	0.16
Link3	40	1	40	40	4	0.16	0.16
Link4	40	1	40	40	4	0.16	0.16
Link5	20	20	20	30	0.35	0.16	0.16
Link6	20	20	20	30	0.35	0.16	0.16
Link7	40	10	8	4	1.2	0.16	0.16

Table 2. D-H Parameters of the Manipulator

i	1	2	3	4	5	6	7
$a_{i-1}(m)$	0	0	0	4	4	0	0
$\alpha_{i-1}(°)$	0	90	90	0	0	90	90
$d_i(m)$	2.5	0.35	0.35	0	0.35	0.35	1.2
$\theta_i(°)$	600	20	20	40	40	20	20

4.1   Simulations for Local Planning of FFSR

Simulation Example 1 for Local Planning of FFSR. The initial configuration is: $\boldsymbol{\varPsi}_b^I = [0,0,0]°$, $\boldsymbol{\varTheta}^I = [0,0,0,0,0,0,0]°$, and the goal configuration is: $\boldsymbol{\varPsi}_b^G = [0,5,10]°$, $\boldsymbol{\varTheta}^G = [15,20,25,30,35,40,45]°$. The results of *Alg*-2 are shown in Fig. 2 (a) and (b), and the results of *Alg*-5 are shown in Fig. 2 (c) and (d). we can see that *Alg*-2 is unable to converge the configuration error ($\Delta\boldsymbol{q}$), while *Alg*-5 based on the bidirectional method [3] can make the $\Delta\boldsymbol{q}$ converge. This is because in the action generation algorithm of *Alg*-2, i.e., *Alg*-4, the number of rows of the $\boldsymbol{J}_{q\varTheta}$ used to project $\Delta\boldsymbol{q}$ is greater than the number of columns, so *Alg*-2 is unable to converge $\Delta\boldsymbol{q}$. On the other hand, in the action generation algorithm of *Alg*-5, i.e., *Alg*-6, the number of columns of the $\boldsymbol{J}_{ExtBi}$ used to project $\Delta\boldsymbol{q}$ is greater than the number of rows, so *Alg*-5 can make $\Delta\boldsymbol{q}$ converge.

Simulation Example 2 for Local Planning of FFSR. For local planning problem of simulation example 2, $\boldsymbol{\varPsi}_b^I = [0,0,0]°$, $\boldsymbol{\varTheta}^I = [0,0,0,0,0,0,0]°$, and $\boldsymbol{\varPsi}_b^G = [1,1,1]°$, $\boldsymbol{\varTheta}^G = [1,1,1,1,1,1,1]°$. We use *Alg*-2 to solve this local planning

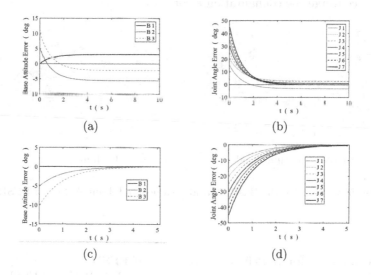

(a)   (b)

(c)   (d)

Fig. 2. Results of Simulation Example 1 for Local Planning of FFSR.

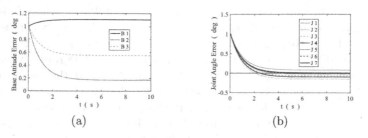

(a)   (b)

Fig. 3. Result of Simulation Example 2 for Local Planning of FFSR.

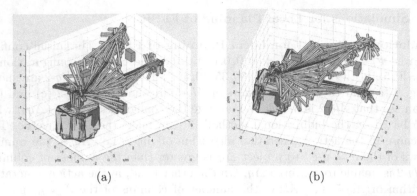

(a)   (b)

Fig. 4. The Motion Trajectory of FFSR from q^I to q^G in 3D Space.

problem, and the simulation results are shown in Fig. 3 (a) and (b). It can be seen that although the error between q^I and q^G is very small, *Alg*-2 is still unable to converge the configuration error.

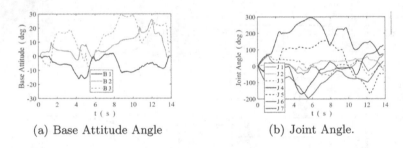

(a) Base Attitude Angle   (b) Joint Angle.

Fig. 5. Changes of the Base Attitude Angles and Joint Angles of FFSR.

4.2   Simulation for MP-from-IC-to-GC of FFSR

This subsection presents the simulation which uses BiD-RRT-For-FFSR to solve MP-from-IC-to-GC of FFSR, and the initial configuration is: $\boldsymbol{\Psi}_0^I = [0, 0, 0]°$, $\boldsymbol{\Theta}^I = [0, 0, 0, 0, 0, 0, 0]°$, and the goal configuration is: $\boldsymbol{\Psi}_0^G = [0.26, -0.64, 2.18]°$, $\boldsymbol{\Theta}^G = [66.73, -14.05, -26.42, 125.69, -46.17, 72.11, 28.76]°$. FFSR in 3-D space is shown in Fig. 1 (b), where the cyan FFSR represents the case when $q = q^I$ and the red FFSR represents the case when $q = q^G$. The range of values for FFSR's base attitude angles is: $|\boldsymbol{\Psi}_0| \leq [30, 30, 30]°$, and the range of values for FFSR's joint angles is: $|\boldsymbol{\Theta}| \leq [300, 300, 300, 300, 300, 300, 300]°$, where $|\boldsymbol{x}|$ represents the absolute value of $\boldsymbol{x}$. After 190 loops of BiD-RRT-For-FFSR, *Tree*^{I} and *Tree*^{G} were successfully connected, and the planning was successful. The motion trajectory of FFSR from q^I to q^G in 3D space is shown in Fig. 4. To more comprehensively display the motion trajectory of FFSR, Fig. 4 is presented from different perspectives. During the motion of FFSR from q^I to q^G, the changes in the base attitude angle and joint angles are shown in Fig. 5. We can see that the values of the base attitude angles and joint angles both meet the requirements.

5 Conclusion

This paper proposes a motion planning algorithm called BiD-RRT-For-FFSR for MP-from-IC-to-GC of FFSR. The overall process of MP-from-IC-to-GC of FFSR is similar to RRT-Connect, but with a difference, which is the introduction of bidirectional extension of two trees. To directly consider the differential constraints of FFSR, we propose a new method for designing local planners. This method involves an iterative process and is based on error projection. In each iteration, actions are generated by mapping the configuration error using the pseudo-inverse of the Jacobian matrix, allowing FFSR to grow towards the desired direction. BiD-RRT-For-FFSR constructs a tree from the initial configuration and a tree from the goal configuration, and includes two types of local planners: a local planner for random extension of a tree, and a local planner for bidirectional extension of two trees. The latter is used for the connection of these two trees and adopts the bidirectional approach to allow the configuration error between the two trees to converge. A FFSR with a base satellite and a 7-joint manipulator was selected for simulation. The simulation results for local planning of FFSR have validated that the local planner for bidirectional extension of two trees can allow the configuration error to converge. The simulation results for MP-from-IC-to-GC of FFSR have validated the effectiveness of the proposed BiD-RRT-For-FFSR.

References

1. Flores-Abad, A., Ma, O., Pham, K., Ulrich, S.: A review of space robotics technologies for on-orbit servicing. Prog. Aerosp. Sci. **68**, 1–26 (2014)
2. Dubowsky, S., Torres, M. A.: Path planning for space manipulators to minimize spacecraft attitude disturbances. In: 1991 IEEE International Conference on Robotics and Automation, Sacramento, CA, USA, pp. 2522–2528. IEEE (1991)
3. Nakamura, Y., Mukherjee, R.: Nonholonomic path planning of space robots via a bidirectional approach. IEEE Trans. Robot. Autom. **7**(4), 500–514 (1991)
4. Liu, X., Baoyin, H., Ma, X.: Optimal path planning of redundant free-floating revolute-jointed space manipulators with seven links. Multibody Syst. Dyn. **29**(1), 41–56 (2013)
5. Wang, M., Luo, J., Fang, J., Yuan, J.: Optimal trajectory planning of free-floating space manipulator using differential evolution algorithm. Adv. Space Res. **61**(6), 1525–1536 (2018)
6. Virgili-Llop, J., Zagaris, C., Zappulla, R., Bradstreet, A., Romano, M.: A convex-programming-based guidance algorithm to capture a tumbling object on orbit using a spacecraft equipped with a robotic manipulator. Int. J. Robot. Res. **38**(1), 40–72 (2019)

7. Misra, G., Bai, X.: Task-constrained trajectory planning of free-floating space-robotic systems using convex optimization. J. Guid. Control. Dyn. **40**(11), 2857–2870 (2017)
8. Webb, D.J., Van Den Berg, J.: Kinodynamic RRT*: asymptotically optimal motion planning for robots with linear dynamics. In: 2013 IEEE International Conference on Robotics and Automation, Karlsruhe, Germany, pp. 5054–5061. IEEE (2013)
9. Li, Y., Littlefield, Z., Bekris, K.E.: Asymptotically optimal sampling-based kinodynamic planning. Int. J. Robot. Res. **35**(5), 528–564 (2016)
10. Berenson, D., Srinivasa, S., Kuffner, J.: Task space regions: a framework for pose-constrained manipulation planning. Int. J. Robot. Res. **30**(12), 1435–1460 (2011)
11. Xu, W., Li, C., Wang, X., Liu, Y., Liang, B., Xu, Y.: Study on non-holonomic cartesian path planning of a free-floating space robotic system. Adv. Robot. **23**(1–2), 113–143 (2009)
12. Kuffner, J.J., LaValle, S.M.: RRT-connect: an efficient approach to single-query path planning. In: Proceedings 2000 IEEE International Conference on Robotics and Automation, San Francisco, CA, USA, pp. 995–1001. IEEE (2000)

A Hybrid Workspace Mapping Method Based on Force Feedback for Underwater Teleoperation Systems

Xubo Yang, Jian Gao$^{(\boxtimes)}$, Haozhe Zhang, Yimin Chen, Jingwei Guo, and Sijia Su

School of Marine Science and Technology, Northwestern Polytechnical University, Xi'an 710072, China
yangxubo@mail.nwpu.edu.cn, jiangao@nwpu.edu.cn

Abstract. Underwater robot teleoperation plays a crucial role in underwater tasks, but underwater teleoperation systems often employ master-slave heterogeneous structures, which undoubtedly introduces more difficulties and challenges for workspace and operation precision. In light of this, this paper proposes a force-feedback-based hybrid workspace mapping method applicable to underwater teleoperation systems. First, we design a force-feedback-based hybrid workspace mapping method and conduct various simulation tests and analyses. The results demonstrate that the method can effectively enhance the spatial breadth and operational accuracy of teleoperation. Subsequently, we construct an underwater teleoperation digital twin platform to implement underwater target grasping tasks, which yield satisfactory results. Moreover, the digital twin platform established in this paper can better mitigate the effects of communication latency and underwater environmental interference on operations, making it more conducive to the implementation of underwater teleoperation tasks and reducing the burden on operators.

Keywords: Underwater teleoperation · Master-slave heterogeneity · Force feedback · Digital twin

1 Introduction

Underwater manipulators, as an indispensable component of underwater work robots, play a crucial role in carrying out tasks such as underwater target search and retrieval, equipment inspection, and maintenance [1–3]. Many underwater tasks require precise operation by the manipulator to be completed. However, given the current state of technology, underwater robots are not yet capable of autonomously handling exceptionally complex tasks, necessitating human intervention for operations. This technology, where humans send commands for remote control, is referred to as teleoperation [4,5]. Generally, teleoperation refers to a system where a master manipulator controls a slave manipulator to perform complex tasks in environments that are difficult for humans to access or harmful to them. It has been widely applied in fields such as space exploration,

H. Yang et al. (Eds.): ICIRA 2023, LNAI 14273, pp. 317–328, 2023.
https://doi.org/10.1007/978-981-99-6498-7_28

counter-terrorism, disaster relief, remote medicine, and deep-sea operations [6–8].

A teleoperation system mainly comprises several modules, including a master hand controller/manipulator, a slave operational manipulator, a slave controller, and a communication link. Due to the constraints of human body structure and the need for direct human operation, the size and structure of master manipulators tend to be relatively uniform. Conversely, slave manipulators often have different structures and forms depending on the application field. For instance, surgical robots require smaller manipulator sizes to ensure surgical precision, while industrial or underwater robots typically utilize larger manipulators.

Teleoperation systems are classified into two types based on the differences in master-slave manipulator structures: master-slave isomorphic teleoperation systems [9] and master-slave heterogeneous teleoperation systems [10,11]. As the name implies, master-slave isomorphism means that the master and slave manipulators have similar structures and sizes, ensuring the same workspace for both. This type of teleoperation can use joint angle mapping methods, allowing the slave manipulator to follow the master manipulator's movements completely. This approach offers higher coordination and immersion. Unlike master-slave isomorphic teleoperation systems, master-slave heterogeneous systems have different workspaces for the master and slave manipulators, rendering joint angle mapping methods inapplicable. Therefore, it is necessary to optimize the mapping of the master-slave workspace to achieve stable operation, inevitably sacrificing some workspace while increasing operational precision and difficulty.

Chaudhury [12] developed a Monte Carlo method for determining the workspace of spatial parallel and hybrid manipulators, which can be challenging for such manipulators with multiple degrees of freedom. Conti [13] proposed a workspace drift control method, which reduced the scaling factor of proportional position mapping and improved teleoperation precision and workspace utilization. A hybrid workspace mapping method was introduced in [14], consisting of joint space mapping, position space mapping, and a transition space between the two. A vision-based underwater manipulator teleoperation method was presented in [15], controlling the master end-effector's pose based on visual information to realize remote manipulator control. A disturbance-based observer was incorporated into the underwater teleoperation bilateral impedance control method, effectively suppressing interference caused by internal model uncertainty [16].

In this paper, a hybrid workspace mapping method based on force feedback is proposed for underwater robot teleoperation systems. This method efficiently integrates the teleoperation breadth and accuracy, catering to complex teleoperation tasks. The contributions of this paper are as follows.

1. We propose a position-velocity hybrid mapping method based on force feedback. Multiple sets of simulation validation demonstrate that the hybrid mapping method with force feedback offers higher operational precision and spatial utilization compared to traditional position mapping methods.
2. We develop a high-fidelity, highly transparent underwater robot digital twin system and design a virtual reality teleoperation scheme to overcome the

adverse effects and challenges posed by remote communication latency and the complex, ever-changing underwater environment on teleoperation.

3. We establish an underwater robot teleoperation experimental environment and apply the proposed method to underwater target grasping tasks. The results show that the force-feedback-based hybrid mapping method effectively improves the efficiency and robustness of teleoperation.

2 Spatial Position Mapping

Spatial position mapping, in essence, involves calculating the position and orientation of the master manipulator's end-effector using its joint angles through forward kinematics. The relative position is then proportionally scaled and transmitted to the slave side. On the slave side, the received data is used to solve the inverse kinematics, determining the corresponding joint angles for the slave manipulator.

Due to the differences in the structures of the master and slave manipulators, an unreasonable mapping ratio may result in the mapped relative position having no solution on the slave side. To address this issue, it is necessary to analyze and solve the workspaces of both master and slave manipulators and determine the optimal mapping ratio. This ensures that the points in the master-slave workspaces are mapped one-to-one and that the slave workspace achieves the best spatial utilization.

The constant proportion position workspace mapping method can be represented as shown in Eq. (1).

$$\begin{cases} P_S = K P_M + \Delta \\ \phi_S = \phi_M \end{cases} \tag{1}$$

where P_S represents the relative position of the slave manipulator's end-effector with respect to its base coordinates, and P_M denotes the relative position of the master hand controller with respect to its base coordinates. The mapping ratio coefficient is represented by $K = \begin{bmatrix} K_x & K_y & K_z \end{bmatrix}$, while the spatial offset is denoted as $\Delta = \begin{bmatrix} X_{offset} & Y_{offset} & Z_{offset} \end{bmatrix}$. Furthermore, ϕ_S refers to the joint angles at the end of the slave manipulator, and ϕ_M indicates the joint angles at the end of the master hand controller.

3 Force-Feedback-Based Hybrid Workspace Mapping

In order to address the issues of low operational precision, low workspace utilization, and high cognitive cost in traditional workspace mapping methods for heterogeneous master-slave teleoperation, this paper proposes a force-feedback-based position-velocity hybrid mapping method. This method involves performing small-scale position mapping within the master workspace and variable-ratio velocity mapping in the outer peripheral space while incorporating force feedback to mitigate deviation caused by velocity mapping. Finally, a transition space is introduced between the position mapping and velocity mapping spaces to resolve edge effects during spatial transitions, as illustrated in Fig. 1.

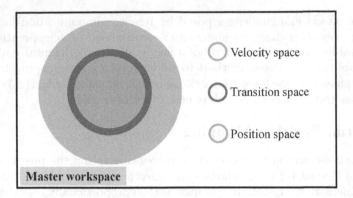

Fig. 1. Master hand controller workspace.

3.1   Position Mapping Method in the Master Workspace

Let the current position of the master hand controller's end-effector be denoted as $\boldsymbol{P}_M = [p_{xm}, p_{ym}, p_{zm}]^T$, the control cycle as T, and the recorded position of the hand controller's end-effector in the previous cycle as $\boldsymbol{P}'_M = [p'_{xm}, p'_{ym}, p'_{zm}]^T$. Then, the displacement of the master hand controller's end-effector $\Delta \boldsymbol{P}_M$ satisfies the relationship shown in Eq. 2.

$$\begin{bmatrix} \Delta p_{xm} \\ \Delta p_{ym} \\ \Delta p_{zm} \end{bmatrix} = \begin{bmatrix} p_{xm} \\ p_{ym} \\ p_{zm} \end{bmatrix} - \begin{bmatrix} p'_{xm} \\ p'_{ym} \\ p'_{zm} \end{bmatrix} \tag{2}$$

According to the calculated end-effector displacement for the current control cycle, we update the end-effector position of the previous cycle $\boldsymbol{P}'_M = \boldsymbol{P}_M$. Taking into account the structural differences between the master and slave devices, as well as the precision requirements for task execution, we set the position mapping ratio coefficient matrix $\boldsymbol{k}_p = [k_{px}, k_{py}, k_{pz}]^T$. The end-effector position offset $\Delta \boldsymbol{P}_S$ for the slave manipulator then satisfies the relationship shown in Eq. 3.

$$\begin{bmatrix} \Delta p_{xs} \\ \Delta p_{ys} \\ \Delta p_{zs} \end{bmatrix} = \begin{bmatrix} k_{px} & 0 & 0 \\ 0 & k_{py} & 0 \\ 0 & 0 & k_{pz} \end{bmatrix} \begin{bmatrix} \Delta p_{xm} \\ \Delta p_{ym} \\ \Delta p_{zm} \end{bmatrix} \tag{3}$$

Based on the information above, the position of the slave manipulator's end-effector $\boldsymbol{P}_S$ can be determined as shown in Eq. 4.

$$\boldsymbol{P}_S = \boldsymbol{P}'_S + \Delta \boldsymbol{P}_S \tag{4}$$

where $\boldsymbol{P}'_S$ represents the end-effector position of the slave manipulator in the previous cycle.

3.2   Force-Feedback-Based Velocity Mapping Method

To limit the mapping ratio of the velocity mapping method, a transition space is introduced at the lower limit of the velocity space. In this paper, both the transition space and the velocity space will be considered together. Let the distance by which the master hand controller's end-effector position exceeds the position mapping space (i.e., the edge offset) be $\boldsymbol{\varepsilon} = [\varepsilon_x, \varepsilon_y, \varepsilon_z]$. Define the width of the transition space as e, the velocity mapping ratio coefficient as $\boldsymbol{k}_v = [k_{vx}, k_{vy}, k_{vz}]^T$, and the transition interval as $\{\boldsymbol{\varepsilon}|0 < \|\boldsymbol{\varepsilon}\| < e\}$, within which no mapping takes place. The maximum and minimum speeds of the slave manipulator's end-effector in the velocity mapping space are denoted as $v_{\max}$ and $v_{\min}$, respectively. The final velocity of the slave manipulator's end-effector $\boldsymbol{v}_s$ can be determined as shown in Eq. 5.

$$
\boldsymbol{v}_s = \begin{cases} 0, 0 < \|\boldsymbol{\varepsilon}\| < e \\ \begin{pmatrix} k_{vx} & 0 & 0 \\ 0 & k_{vy} & 0 \\ 0 & 0 & k_{vz} \end{pmatrix} \begin{pmatrix} \varepsilon_x \\ \varepsilon_y \\ \varepsilon_z \end{pmatrix} (\|\boldsymbol{\varepsilon}\| - e) + \frac{\varepsilon}{\|\varepsilon\|}(\boldsymbol{v}_{\min} \|\boldsymbol{\varepsilon}\| - \boldsymbol{v}_{\min} e), \ e < \|\boldsymbol{\varepsilon}\|, \|\boldsymbol{v}_s\| \leq \boldsymbol{v}_{\max} \\ \frac{\varepsilon}{\|\varepsilon\|-e} \boldsymbol{v}_{\max}, \|\boldsymbol{v}_s\| > \boldsymbol{v}_{\max} \end{cases}
$$

$$(5)$$

where $\|\boldsymbol{\varepsilon}\|$ represents the displacement of the edge offset, and $\|\boldsymbol{v}_s\|$ denotes the magnitude of the slave manipulator's end-effector velocity.

Under velocity mapping, the position offset of the slave manipulator's end-effector $\Delta\boldsymbol{P}_s$ satisfies the relationship shown in Eq. 6.

$$\Delta\boldsymbol{P}_s = \boldsymbol{v}_s T \qquad (6)$$

where T represents the control cycle duration, and the position of the slave manipulator's end-effector $\boldsymbol{P}_s$ follows Eq. 3.

By utilizing a force-feedback device, it is possible to set a counterforce $\boldsymbol{F}_{tele}$ that opposes the direction of $\boldsymbol{\varepsilon}$ and proportional in magnitude. This relationship can be represented as shown in Eq. 7.

$$\boldsymbol{F}_{tele} = -k_F \frac{\varepsilon}{\|\varepsilon\|} \qquad (7)$$

where k_F represents the force feedback coefficient.

4   Experiments

4.1   Simulation Analysis

To verify the reliability and superiority of the position-velocity hybrid mapping method based on force feedback, a comprehensive evaluation and validation will be conducted from multiple perspectives. In this study, the master hand controller used is Geomagic's Touch six-degree-of-freedom (6-DOF) hand controller, which features six DOF joints and three DOF force feedback mechanism, as shown in Fig. 2. J_1, J_2, and J_3 are active joints, and J_4, J_5, and J_6 are passive joints. The slave manipulator used is the HR-301-5-075-103 underwater manipulator by Hai Ren Technology Co., Ltd. This manipulator has four degrees of freedom and one gripper, all equipped with force sensors, as shown in Fig. 3.

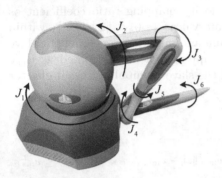

Fig. 2. Touch hand controller.   **Fig. 3.** Slave manipulator.

To ensure a close approximation of the master and slave workspace dimensions, we set the mapping proportionality coefficient K and introduce the spatial position offset Δ to compensate for differences in the master-slave workspace positions. Through multiple simulation corrections, the specific parameter values were calibrated and set as $K_x = 2.1, K_y = 2.6, K_z = 3.1, X_{offset} = 0.13, Y_{offset} = 0, Z_{offset} = 0.25$. As there is no need to consider the structural differences between the master and slave workspaces, it is possible to make each proportionality coefficient satisfy $k_{px} = k_{py} = k_{pz}$ to guarantee the absence of anisotropy in the end-effector velocity of the slave manipulator. The workspace position-velocity hybrid mapping parameters were set to $k_{px} = k_{py} = k_{pz} = 0.7, k_{vx} = k_{vy} = k_{vz} = 1.2, T = 0.1s$, while the force feedback coefficients were established as $k_F = 0.125$.

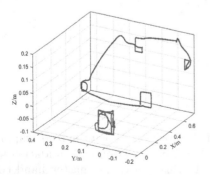

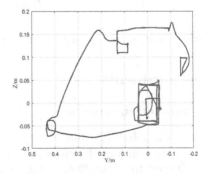

Fig. 4. Hybrid mapping of master-slave end-effector trajectories.

Figure 4 presents the results of the hybrid mapping for master-slave end-effector trajectories. As shown in the figure, the movements of the master device's end-effector occur within a small range, while the slave manipulator's end-effector demonstrates a broader scope of activity. This ensures that precise operations can be conducted within a limited range, such as drawing a rectangle or circle. These findings indicate that the hybrid mapping method effectively satisfies the fundamental control requirements for both master and slave ends.

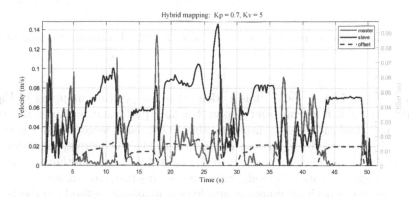

Fig. 5. Hybrid mapping of master-slave end-effector velocities and edge offset.

Figure 5 illustrates the master controller's end-effector velocity values and the slave manipulator's end-effector velocity values during the teleoperation process under hybrid mapping. As seen in the figure, the slave manipulator's end-effector velocity is significantly reduced, primarily remaining below 0.1 m/s. This effectively minimizes instabilities and potential hazards associated with teleoperated slave endpoints. Additionally, due to the mapping proportionality value being less than one, the position mapping exhibits a smaller velocity for the slave end-effector compared to the master end-effector. This ensures the precision of teleoperation. When the master end-effector position exceeds the position mapping space, maintaining a specific position within the velocity mapping space allows for stable velocity mapping. This results in the master end-effector remaining stationary while the slave end-effector can move steadily, guaranteeing that the master controller can manipulate the slave manipulator over an extensive range within a small workspace.

To verify the precision and stability of the position-velocity hybrid mapping method, a two-dimensional planar line segment tracking task was designed. The target tracking line segment was set within a range of 0.2 m in length and 0.08 m in width, composed of nine linear segments. The two-dimensional simulation data was provided by the Touch controller and a four-degree-of-freedom simulated manipulator, specifically from their respective X and Z axes. This allowed the simulation data to be considered as the projection of a three-dimensional task onto the XOZ plane. The simulation results are illustrated in Figs. 6 and 7.

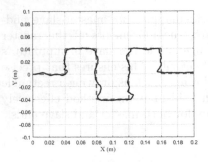

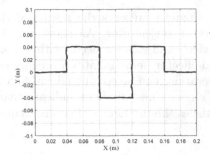

Fig. 6. Position mapping tracking task.   **Fig. 7.** Hybrid mapping tracking task.

As shown in Figs. 6 and 7, it is evident that the position mapping in Fig. 6 exhibits greater fluctuations and poorer tracking performance. Since the two-dimensional simulation is established on the XOZ plane, larger fluctuations are observed during ascending and descending movements. In contrast, Fig. 7 demonstrates that the end-effector position in the hybrid mapping method tracks the target line segment more effectively. Figure 8 presents the error values for the distance between the position mapping and hybrid mapping methods to the target line segment during the task. The hybrid mapping method yields significantly smaller error values than the position mapping method. The average error for position mapping is 1.218 mm, while the average error for hybrid mapping is 0.425 mm, resulting in a precision improvement of 186%.

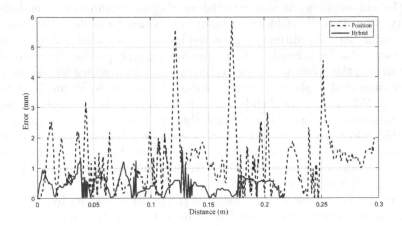

Fig. 8. Error comparison for hybrid and position mapping tracking task.

To compare the impact of force feedback on hybrid mapping teleoperation performance, a simulation task is designed to move a three-dimensional manipulator end-effector target to random points within the slave manipulator's workspace. Figure 9 shows that the hybrid mapping method with force feedback completed the task in 31 s using mainly position mapping and low-speed velocity mapping, with minimal switching frequency between the two modes.

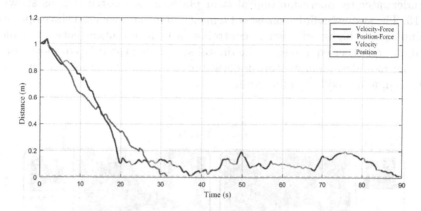

Fig. 9. Distance between manipulator end-effector and target.

Without force feedback, the hybrid mapping method demonstrates faster speed in the first 20 s. This is because effective hints and distinctions for velocity mapping are provided without force feedback, and no larger feedback force is generated at high speeds to indicate prohibition. Therefore, unconstrained velocity mapping can perform better over long distances. However, when approaching the target, the hybrid mapping method without force feedback cannot concentrate on precise and effective control due to the absence of force feedback as the boundary between position mapping space and velocity mapping space. Consequently, there is frequent switching between position mapping and velocity mapping, and the task is finally completed at 90 s.

As observed, the hybrid mapping method with force feedback has a significant advantage over the hybrid mapping method without force feedback. The primary reason lies in the instability of the velocity mapping based on offset distance amplification in the position-velocity hybrid mapping. When the operator cannot intuitively obtain the current mapping state, it is easy to fall into misconceptions, leading to an amplified velocity mapping proportion. In this context, force feedback plays a crucial role in constraining and reminding the operator of the current mapping state. It limits arbitrary switching between position mapping space and velocity mapping space by employing a transitional space. Moreover, the reverse force of the velocity mapping ingeniously indicates the direction of the manipulator end-effector's movement to the operator, reducing their cognitive load. Overall, the hybrid mapping method with force feedback provides better performance, precision, and stability when compared to the method without force feedback.

4.2 Experimental Validation

In order to verify the effectiveness and reliability of the force feedback-based position-velocity hybrid mapping algorithm in actual teleoperation systems, an underwater teleoperation digital twin platform is constructed, as shown in Fig. 10. The system mainly consists of a master hand controller, a slave operation manipulator, a high-performance controller, a high-resolution network camera, a switch, and other equipment. The digital system is primarily composed of the following modules: manipulator, underwater environment, target display, target prediction, and auxiliary interaction.

Fig. 10. Underwater teleoperation digital twin platform.

A grasping task for underwater teleoperation has been designed, and the object grasping and placement are carried out in a virtual twin environment. The spatial mapping algorithm used is the force feedback-based position-velocity hybrid mapping method. The dynamic process of object grasping is shown in Fig. 11.

The trajectory of the manipulator's end-effector and the target object are illustrated in Fig. 12, while the distance curve between them is depicted in Fig. 13. It can be observed that the manipulator achieves the process of grasping the object from a distance of 0.5 m in approximately 10 s. Throughout this procedure, the relative distance between the arm and the target remains stable and continuous, effectively demonstrating the high stability and accuracy inherent to the hybrid mapping approach. Moreover, by employing the twin system for control purposes, the primary focus is on the virtual environment, thereby effectively mitigating potential communication latency and underwater interference impacts on operation. This consequently enhances the implementation of remote underwater manipulation tasks.

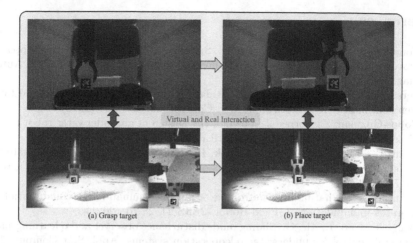

Fig. 11. Dynamic grasping process in underwater teleoperation.

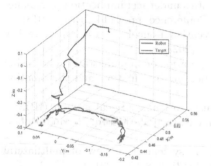

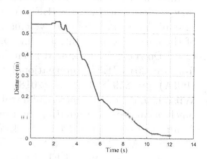

Fig. 12. Trajectory of end-effector and target object.

Fig. 13. Distance between end-effector and target object.

5   Conclusion

Addressing the inconveniences encountered in master-slave heterogeneous tele-operation systems during operation, this paper proposes a hybrid workspace mapping method based on force feedback for underwater robotic teleoperation systems. Through comprehensive simulation analyses and comparisons, this approach demonstrates its capability to efficiently enhance the spatial breadth and operational precision of teleoperation tasks. By constructing an underwater teleoperation digital twin platform, the practical engineering application of this method attains satisfactory results, further validating that the proposed technique can accommodate complex teleoperation tasks. Simultaneously, the established digital twin platform effectively mitigates the impact of communication latency and underwater interference on operations, thereby facilitating the implementation of underwater teleoperation tasks and alleviating the burden on operators.

References

1. Youakim, D., Ridao, P., Palomeras, N., Spadafora, F., Ribas, D., Muzzupappa, M.: Moveit!: autonomous underwater free-floating manipulation. IEEE Robot. Autom. Mag. **24**(3), 41–51 (2017)
2. Zereik, E., Bibuli, M., Mišković, N., Ridao, P., Pascoal, A.: Challenges and future trends in marine robotics. Annu. Rev. Control. **46**, 350–368 (2018)
3. Cobos-Guzman, S., Torres, J., Lozano, R.: Design of an underwater robot manipulator for a telerobotic system. Robotica **31**(6), 945–953 (2013)
4. Shim, H., Jun, B.H., Lee, P.M., Baek, H., Lee, J.: Workspace control system of underwater tele-operated manipulators on an ROV. Ocean Eng. **37**(11–12), 1036–1047 (2010)
5. Brantner, G., Khatib, O.: Controlling ocean one: human-robot collaboration for deep-sea manipulation. J. Field Robot. **3838**(1), 28–51 (2021)
6. Wang, T., Gao, J., Xie, O.: Sliding mode disturbance observer and q learning-based bilateral control for underwater teleoperation systems. Appl. Soft Comput. **130**, 109684 (2022)
7. Jakuba, M.V., et al.: Teleoperation and robotics under ice: implications for planetary exploration. In: 2018 IEEE Aerospace Conference, pp. 1–14. IEEE (2018)
8. Matsui, Y., et al.: Robotic systems in interventional oncology: a narrative review of the current status. Int. J. Clin. Oncol. 1–8 (2023)
9. Codd-Downey, R., Jenkin, M.: Wireless teleoperation of an underwater robot using li-fi. In: 2018 IEEE International Conference on Information and Automation (ICIA), pp. 859–864. IEEE (2018)
10. Wilson, J.T., et al.: Intraocular robotic interventional surgical system (IRISS): mechanical design, evaluation, and master-slave manipulation. Int. J. Med. Robot. Comput. Assist. Surg. **14**(1), e1842 (2018)
11. Shahbazi, M., Atashzar, S.F., Patel, R.V.: A systematic review of multilateral teleoperation systems. IEEE Trans. Haptics **11**(3), 338–356 (2018)
12. Chaudhury, A.N., Ghosal, A.: Determination of workspace volume of parallel manipulators using Monte Carlo method. In: Zeghloul, S., Romdhane, L., Laribi, M.A. (eds.) Computational Kinematics. MMS, vol. 50, pp. 323–330. Springer, Cham (2018). https://doi.org/10.1007/978-3-319-60867-9_37
13. Conti, F., Khatib, O.: Spanning large workspaces using small haptic devices. In: First Joint Eurohaptics Conference and Symposium on Haptic Interfaces for Virtual Environment and Teleoperator Systems. World Haptics Conference, pp. 183–188. IEEE (2005)
14. Chen, Z., Yan, S., Yuan, M., Yao, B., Hu, J.: Modular development of master-slave asymmetric teleoperation systems with a novel workspace mapping algorithm. IEEE Access **6**, 15356–15364 (2018)
15. Zheng, Z., Xie, J., Su, T., Li, X., Ni, Y.: A novel remote control method oriented to underwater maninulators. In: 2021 IEEE International Conference on Mechatronics and Automation (ICMA), pp. 843–848. IEEE (2021)
16. Wang, T., Li, Y., Zhang, J., Zhang, Y.: A novel bilateral impedance controls for underwater tele-operation systems. Appl. Soft Comput. **91**, 106194 (2020)

A Lyapunov-Based Model Predictive Virtual Vehicle Guidance for Path Following Control of Autonomous Marine Vehicles

Boxu Min, Jian Gao[✉], Xi Lu, Zhenchi Zhang, Yimin Chen, and Guang Pan

School of Marine Science and Technology, Northwestern Polytechnical University,
Xi'an 710072, China
jiangao@nwpu.edu.cn

Abstract. This paper proposes a Lyapunov-based model predictive virtual vehicle guidance (LMPC-VV) method for path-following control of autonomous marine vehicles (AMVs). Apart from a guidance virtual vehicle for characterizing waypoints information, an additional virtual vehicle is employed to act as a reference model for path following controllers, whose trajectory is generated online by using the model predictive control (MPC) method. Especially, a contractive constraint is constructed via a backup saturated controller, by which a globally convergent and optimized motion planning considering hard velocities constraints is achieved for AMVs. The feasibility of the designed optimization problem and the closed-loop stability are rigorously proved. Simulation results are further provided to verify the effectiveness of the proposed scheme.

Keywords: Autonomous marine vehicles · Model predictive control · Virtual vehicle guidance

1 Introduction

In the past decade, autonomous marine vehicles including autonomous surface vehicles (ASVs) and autonomous underwater vehicles (AUVs) have attracted a lot of attention due to their increasing abilities in executing complex tasks in ocean environment, including ocean transportation, environmental monitoring, and underwater interventional operations [1–3]. Path-following control is a crucial and foundational technique for AMVs. Many advanced methods have been involved in the design of the path-following controllers [4–6].

Supported by the National Natural Science Foundation of China under Grant of 51979228, the National Basic Scientific Research Program under Grant of JCKY2019207A019, and the Practice and Innovation Funds for Graduates Students of Northwestern Polytechnical University under Grant of PF2023058.

H. Yang et al. (Eds.): ICIRA 2023, LNAI 14273, pp. 329–339, 2023.
https://doi.org/10.1007/978-981-99-6498-7_29

Because of the underactuated characteristic of ASVs and AUVs, a guidance-control hierarchical framework is generally considered [7]. The guidance system provides a reasonable reference signal, while the controller generates control inputs to track the reference signal so as to track the target path. Mainstream guidance principles fall into two categories. The first one is the line-of-sight (LOS) method and its variations. The LOS guidance converts the path-following problem to the tracking of a reference heading angle, that is, the LOS angle [8]. Considering the drift problem when AMVs operating in currents, various improved LOS methods with sideslip angle compensation mechanisms are proposed in [9,10]. A recent review on advance LOS guidance methods can refer to [11]. The other guidance principle is the virtual vehicle based method, which is proposed based on the assumption that any reference path can be generated by a virtual vehicle [12,13]. Then the path-following problem is converted to the tracking of the virtual vehicle. The main drawback of this guidance method lies in that when the AMV is far away from the virtual vehicle (during the initial stage or due to collision avoidance), large control efforts are required and may violate the actuator saturation constraint. An improved strategy addressing this problem is proposed in [13] by employing a dynamic virtual vehicle as a reference model. The dynamic virtual vehicle is located within a certain range from the AMV thus can alleviate the amplitude of the control inputs. However, velocities or actuator constraints can still not be explicitly handled, and optimized tracking performance can not be guaranteed.

Motivated by the observations above, this paper proposes a novel guidance method by incorporating a dynamic virtual vehicle whose trajectory is generated online by using the model predictive control method [14]. It is worth noting that although MPC has been employed in the motion planning or control of AMVs in [15,16], the feasibility and closed-loop stability are not well proved. Inspired by the Lyapunov-based MPC [17,18], a contractive constraint is constructed via a backup saturated controller, by which a globally convergent and optimized motion planning considering hard velocities constraints is achieved. By using the proposed Lyapunov-based model predictive virtual vehicle guidance method, the AMV can achieve optimized path-following performance without violating the input saturation constraint.

2   Problem Formulation

2.1   Modelling of AMVs

According to [20], the kinematic and dynamic models describing the planar motion of an AMV are given as follows:

$$
\begin{aligned}
\dot{x} &= u\cos\psi - v\sin\psi \\
\dot{y} &= u\sin\psi + v\cos\psi, \\
\dot{\psi} &= r
\end{aligned}
\tag{1}
$$

$$\dot{u} = f_u(\boldsymbol{v}) + \frac{1}{m_u}\tau_u$$

$$\dot{v} = f_v(\boldsymbol{v}) \qquad , \qquad (2)$$

$$\dot{r} = f_r(\boldsymbol{v}) + \frac{1}{m_r}\tau_r$$

where $[x, y, \psi]$ is the position and yaw angle of the AMV in the earth fixed frame. $\boldsymbol{v} = [u, v, r]^T$ denotes the surge speed, sway speed, and yaw rate. $[m_u, m_v, m_r]^T$ refers to the inertial parameters including added mass. $f_i(\boldsymbol{v}), i = u, v, r$ represents the hydrodynamic functions.

2.2   Virtual Vehicle Guidance Principle

In the virtual vehicle guidance framework, we assume that any reference path can be generated by a guidance virtual vehicle (GVV) whose dynamic is denoted by

$$\dot{x}_g = u_g \cos \psi_g$$

$$\dot{y}_g = u_g \sin \psi_g \,, \qquad (3)$$

$$\dot{\psi}_g = r_g$$

where $[x_g, y_g, \psi_g]^T$ is the position and yaw angle of the guidance virtual vehicle. u_g and r_g are the surge speed and yaw rate, which are programmed offline according to the specific waypoints information. The procedure on how to obtain the command value of u_g and r_g according to the waypoints information and the manoeuvrability of AMVs is presented in [12] and omitted here for brevity.

The virtual vehicle method converts the path-following problem to the tracking of the guidance virtual vehicle. However, the virtual vehicle is usually programmed without considering any inertia factors. When the AMV deviates a large distance from the virtual vehicle (during initial stage or for obstacle avoidance purpose), large control efforts are required to eliminate tracking errors, which may violate the input saturation constraint. To solve this problem, as shown in Fig. 1, a dynamic virtual vehicle (DVV) can be employed as a reference model between two vehicles.

It is worth remarking that the dynamic virtual vehicle asymptotically converges to the guidance virtual vehicle in [13] without considering velocity constraints and tracking effect. Following that scheme, optimized tracking performance cannot be achieved. In this paper, the trajectory of the dynamic virtual vehicle is generated online by designing its surge speed and yaw rate commands as follows:

$$\dot{x}_d = u_d \cos \psi_d$$

$$\dot{y}_d = u_d \sin \psi_d \,. \qquad (4)$$

$$\dot{\psi}_d = r_d$$

The meanings of the variables in Eq. (4) are similar to those in Eq. (3).

Especially, two requirements should be fulfilled when designing u_d and r_d:

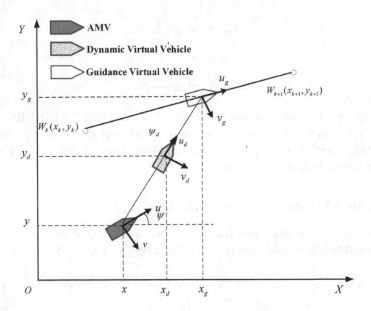

Fig. 1. Virtual vehicle guidance principle

- The dynamic virtual vehicle should globally converge to the guidance virtual vehicle with an optimized tracking performance.
- u_d and r_d should satisfy the velocity constraints, that is

$$|u_d(t)| \le u_{\max} \quad \text{and} \quad |r_d(t)| \le r_{\max}, \quad \forall t \ge 0, \tag{5}$$

where $u_{\max} > \sup_{t \ge 0} |u_g(t)|$ and $r_{\max} > \sup_{t \ge 0} |r_g(t)|$ are positive constants.

3 Lyapunov-Based Model Predictive Virtual Vehicle Guidance

3.1 Guidance Law Design

In this section, a Lyapunov-based model predictive controller is developed to generate command signals, u_d and r_d. As the DVV serves as a reference model, its initial states are the same as the AMV's, that is $x_g(0) = x(0), y_g = y(0), \psi_g(0) = \psi(0)$.

By using a coordinate transformation, the tracking errors between the dynamic virtual vehicle and the guidance virtual vehicle can be described by

$$\begin{bmatrix} x_e \\ y_e \\ \psi_e \end{bmatrix} = \begin{bmatrix} \cos\psi_d & \sin\psi_d & 0 \\ -\sin\psi_d & \cos\psi_d & 0 \\ 0 & 0 & 1 \end{bmatrix} \begin{bmatrix} x_g - x_d \\ y_g - y_d \\ \psi_g - \psi_d \end{bmatrix}. \tag{6}$$

Taking the derivatives of Eq. (6) yields

$$\dot{x}_e = r_d y_e - u_d + u_g \cos \psi_e$$
$$\dot{y}_e = -r_d x_e + u_g \sin \psi_e \qquad . \qquad (7)$$
$$\dot{\psi}_e = r_g - r_d$$

The control objective is then transformed to design u_d and r_d that makes

$$\lim_{t \to \infty} x_e = 0,$$
$$\lim_{t \to \infty} y_e = 0, \qquad (8)$$
$$\lim_{t \to \infty} \psi_e = 2K\pi,$$

where K is some fixed integer.

We define the aggregated error vector as $\boldsymbol{x}_e = [x_e, y_e, \sin(\psi_e/2)]^T$, and the aggregated input vector as $\boldsymbol{u} = [u_d, r_d]^T$. Then by utilizing Eq. (7), there is $\dot{\boldsymbol{x}}_e = \boldsymbol{f}(\boldsymbol{x}_e, \boldsymbol{u})$. Additionally, we denote $\boldsymbol{u}_e = [u_d - u_g, r_d - r_g]^T$. Following the methodology of MPC, we derive the command signals u_d and r_d at each sampling instant by solving a constrained finite-horizon optimization problem and selecting the first component of the solution sequence.

Consider the following finite-horizon cost function

$$J\left(\boldsymbol{x}_e\left(t_k\right), \boldsymbol{u}_e\left(s; t_k\right)\right)$$
$$= \int_{t_k}^{t_k+N} \left[\|\boldsymbol{x}_e\left(s, t_k\right)\|_Q^2 + \|\boldsymbol{u}_e\left(s, t_k\right)\|_R^2\right] ds, \qquad (9)$$

where Q and R are positive-definite weighting matrices. $\boldsymbol{x}_e(s; t_k)$ and $\boldsymbol{u}_e(s; tk)$ are the predicted state and input error sequence vectors. N denotes the prediction horizon. The finite-horizon optimization problem is formulated as follows:

$$\boldsymbol{u}\left(s; t_k\right) = \arg \min_{\boldsymbol{u}} J\left(\boldsymbol{x}_e\left(t_k\right), \boldsymbol{u}_e\left(s; t_k\right)\right) \qquad (10)$$

$$\text{s.t.} \quad \boldsymbol{x}_e\left(t_k, t_k\right) = \boldsymbol{x}_e\left(t_k\right), \qquad (11)$$

$$\boldsymbol{u}\left(s; t_k\right) \in \mathbb{U}, s \in \left[t_k, t_k + N\right], \qquad (12)$$

$$\dot{V}_a\left(\boldsymbol{x}_e\left(t_k\right), \boldsymbol{u}\left(t_k\right)\right) \le \dot{V}_a\left(\boldsymbol{x}_e\left(t_k\right), \pi\left(\boldsymbol{x}_e\left(t_k\right)\right)\right), \qquad (13)$$

$$\dot{\boldsymbol{x}}_e\left(s; t_k\right) = \boldsymbol{f}\left(\boldsymbol{x}_e\left(s; t_k\right), \boldsymbol{u}\left(s; t_k\right)\right), s \in \left[t_k, t_k + N\right], \qquad (14)$$

where, $\pi(\boldsymbol{x}_e) = [u_d^*, r_d^*]$ is an auxiliary control law, given by [19]

$$u_d^* = u_g + \frac{c_1 x_e}{\sqrt{1 + x_e^2 + y_e^2}},$$

$$r_d^* = r_g + \frac{c_2 u_g \left(y_e \cos \frac{\psi_e}{2} - x_e \sin \frac{\psi_e}{2}\right)}{\sqrt{1 + x_e^2 + y_e^2}} + c_3 \sin \frac{\psi_e}{2}, \qquad (15)$$

and $V_a = \frac{c_2}{2}\left(\sqrt{1 + x_e^2 + y_e^2} - 1\right) + 4(1 - \cos(\psi_e/2))$ is the corresponding Lyapunov function. c_1, c_2, and c_3 are positive tuning parameters. $\mathbb{U}$ is a compact and convex set characterized by $u_{\max}$ and $r_{\max}$. Equation (13) is a contractive constraint which guarantees that the derivative of the auxiliary Lyapunov function can be only either smaller or equal to that driven by the auxiliary control law [17, 18].

3.2 Feasibility Analysis

In this section, we prove that the LMPC scheme is recursively feasible, that is, we can find an admissible solution for the optimization problem (10) at each sampling instant.

From (15), it is trivial to check that the auxiliary control law is bounded, and we can ensure $|u_d^*(t)| \leq u_{\max}$ and $|r_d^*(t)| \leq r_{\max}, \forall t \geq 0$ by selecting appropriate c_1, c_2, and c_3. Therefore, a feasible solution can always be found by selecting

$$\tilde{u}\left(s; t_k\right) = \pi\left(\boldsymbol{x}_e(s)\right), s \in [t_k, t_k + N]. \tag{16}$$

Therefore, it is confirmed that the proposed LMPC-VV guidance law is recursively feasible.

3.3 Stability Analysis

The stability result of the auxiliary control law (15) is first summarized in Lemma 1.

Lemma 1 [19]: *Consider the error system (7), and bounds u_{max} and r_{max}. If u_g is uniformly continuous, by using the auxiliary control law (15), the dynamic virtual vehicle can asymptotically and globally converge to the guidance virtual vehicle meanwhile the velocity constraints can be satisfied by tuning parameters.*

Proof. Please refer to [19].

The stability property of the proposed LMPC controller can be directly obtained by applying Lemma 1, and is summarized in Theorem 1.

Theorem 1. *Consider the error system (7), and bounds u_{max} and r_{max}. If u_g is uniformly continuous, and u_d and r_d are determined by solving the constrained model predictive control problem (9)–(14), the dynamic virtual vehicle globally and asymptotically converges to the guidance virtual vehicle. In addition, the stable property still holds when suboptimal solutions are implemented.*

Proof. From the contractive constraint (13), the derivative of the auxiliary Lyapunov function driven by the MPC based command signals u_d and r_d is always less than or equal to that driven by the auxiliary control law. Therefore, the proposed LMPC controller inherits the stability property of the auxiliary control law [17, 18]. Besides, it admits the suboptimal solutions, since the closed-loop system is stable as long as constraint (13) is satisfied [17]. The proof is complete.

4   Path-Following Controller Design

In this section, we design a simple model-based controller to ensure that the AMV can well track the dynamic virtual vehicle, so as to track the reference path. The design process directly follows [13].

First, by using a coordinate transformation, the errors between the AMV and the DVV are defined by

$$\begin{bmatrix} x_{e1} \\ y_{e1} \\ \psi_{e1} \end{bmatrix} = \begin{bmatrix} \cos\psi & \sin\psi & 0 \\ -\sin\psi & \cos\psi & 0 \\ 0 & 0 & 1 \end{bmatrix} \begin{bmatrix} x_d - x \\ y_d - y \\ \psi_d - \psi \end{bmatrix}. \tag{17}$$

Then, to stabilize the tracking errors, virtual control laws are illustrated with

$$\alpha_u = k_1 x_{e1} + u_d \cos\psi_{e1}$$
$$\alpha_{\psi_e} = -\arctan\left(\frac{k_2 y_{e1} - v}{u_{d0}}\right), \tag{18}$$

where

$$u_{d0} = \begin{cases} \sqrt{u_d^2 - (k_2 y_{e1} - v)^2}, & |k_2 y_{e1} - v| \le u_d \\ u_d, & |k_2 y_{e1} - v| > u_d \end{cases}, \tag{19}$$

k_1 and k_2 are positive control gains. To avoid directly calculating the derivatives of the virtual control laws, the dynamic surface control technique [12] is employed here to get:

$$\gamma_i \dot{\beta}_i + \beta_i = \alpha_i, \quad \beta_i(0) = \alpha_i(0), \quad i = u, \psi_{e1} \tag{20}$$

where, γ_i refers to the time constant of the first-order filters. Similarly, the virtual control law and first order filter for r are designed as

$$\alpha_r = -k_3(\beta_{\psi_{e1}} - \psi_{e1}) + r_d - \dot{\beta}_{\psi_{e1}}, \gamma_r \dot{\beta}_r + \beta_r = \alpha_r, \beta_r(0) = \alpha_r(0) \tag{21}$$

Finally, the actual control laws are given by

$$\tau_u = m_u(k_u u_e + \dot{\beta}_u + f_u(v))$$
$$\tau_r = m_r(k_r r_e + \dot{\beta}_r + f_r(v)) \tag{22}$$

By implementing control law (22), all the tracking errors are ultimately bounded. The proof is omitted here for brevity.

5   Simulation Results

In this section, simulations are performed to examine the effectiveness of the proposed guidance law. The control object is selected as the ASV in [20]. In the simulations, the surge speed, yaw rate, and the initial states of the guidance virtual vehicle are denoted by

$$u_g = 3\text{m/s}$$

$$r_g = \begin{cases} 0, 0 < t < 30 \\ 0.05, 30 < t < 60 \\ 0, 60 < t < 90 \\ -0.1, 90 < t < 105 \\ 0, 105 < t < 135 \end{cases} \tag{23}$$

$$[x_g, y_g, \psi_g] = [100\text{m}, 50\text{m}, 0]$$

The parameters in guidance and control laws are selected as

$$N = 7, u_{\max} = 4.5\text{m/s}, r_{\max} = 0.5\text{rad/s}, Q = 1000I, R = 100I$$
$$c_1 = 1.5, c_1 = 0.1, c_3 = 0.3, k_1 = 0.1, k_2 = 0.1, k_3 = 0.1, \tag{24}$$
$$\gamma_u = \gamma_r = \gamma_{\psi_c} = 0.1, k_u = 1.5, k_r = 10.5$$

The initial states of the ASV are $[x, y, \psi] = [60\text{m}, 50\text{m}, 30/57.3\text{rad}]$. The simulation results are demonstrated in Fig. 2, 3, 4 and 5.

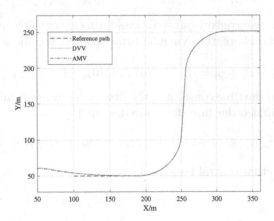

Fig. 2. Path-following control effect of the proposed scheme

From the simulation results, it is shown that the proposed LMPC-VV guidance can provide a reasonable and optimal motion planning when the AMV deviates a large distance from the reference path at the initial stage. Through tracking the DVV, the AMV can approach the reference path with a good transition and steady state performance. Additionally, the velocity constraints can be well guaranteed, and the actuator saturation can be effectively alleviated. The control inputs seem somewhat large. It is reasonable because we set a relatively large command speed ($u_g = 3$ m/s).

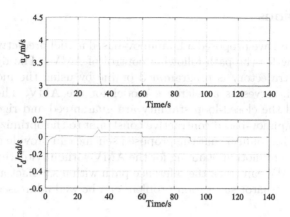

Fig. 3. Surge speed and yaw rate commands of the DVV

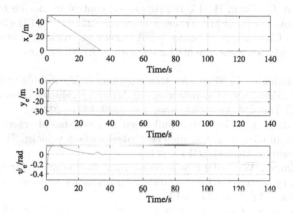

Fig. 4. Tracking errors of the DVV

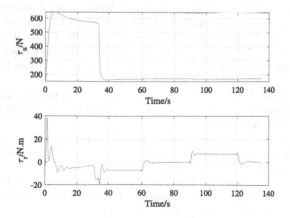

Fig. 5. Control inputs of the AMV

6   Conclusions

In this paper, we have proposed a Lyapunov-based model predictive virtual vehicle guidance law for the path-following control of AMVs. The dynamic virtual vehicle, whose trajectory is programmed online by using the model predictive control method, serves as a reference model for the AMV. The feasibility of the scheme and the closed-loop stability are guaranteed and rigorously proved by adding a Lyapunov-based contractive constraint to the optimization problem. Simulation results confirm that the proposed scheme can provide an optimal and globally convergent motion planning for the AMV without violating velocity constraints. The AMV can track the reference path with a satisfactory performance meanwhile the actuator saturation problem can be well addressed.

References

1. Shi, Y., Shen, C., Fang, H., Li, H.: Advanced control in marine mechatronic systems: a survey. IEEE/ASME Trans. Mechatron. **22**, 1121–1131 (2017)
2. Tijjani, A.S., Chemori, A., Creuze, V.: A survey on tracking control of unmanned underwater vehicles: experiments-based approach. Annu. Rev. Control. **54**, 125–147 (2022)
3. Heshmati-Alamdari, S., Nikou, A., Dimarogonas, D.V.: Robust trajectory tracking control for underactuated autonomous underwater vehicles in uncertain environments. IEEE Trans. Autom. Sci. Eng. **18**, 1288–1301 (2021)
4. Wang, N., Su, S.-F.: Finite-time unknown observer-based interactive trajectory tracking control of asymmetric underactuated surface vehicles. IEEE Trans. Control Syst. Technol. **29**, 794–803 (2021)
5. Qiao, L., Zhang, W.: Adaptive second-order fast nonsingular terminal sliding mode tracking control for fully actuated autonomous underwater vehicles. IEEE J. Oceanic Eng. **44**, 363–385 (2019)
6. Zhang, G., Chu, S., Zhang, W., Liu, C.: Adaptive neural fault-tolerant control for USV with the output-based triggering approach. IEEE Trans. Veh. Technol. **71**, 6948–6957 (2022)
7. Yu, Y., Guo, C., Yu, H.: Finite-time PLOS-based integral sliding-mode adaptive neural path following for unmanned surface vessels with unknown dynamics and disturbances. IEEE Trans. Autom. Sci. Eng. **16**, 1500–1511 (2019)
8. Min, B., Zhang, X.: Concise robust fuzzy nonlinear feedback track keeping control for ships using multi-technique improved LOS guidance. Ocean Eng. **224**, 108734 (2021)
9. Liu, L., Wang, D., Peng, Z., Wang, H.: Predictor-based LOS guidance law for path following of underactuated marine surface vehicles with sideslip compensation. Ocean Eng. **124**, 340–348 (2016)
10. Liu, L., Wang, D., Peng, Z.: ESO-based line-of-sight guidance law for path following of underactuated marine surface vehicles with exact sideslip compensation. IEEE J. Oceanic Eng. **42**, 477–487 (2017)
11. Gu, N., Wang, D., Peng, Z., Wang, J., Han, Q.-L.: Advances in line-of-sight guidance for path following of autonomous marine vehicles: an overview. IEEE Trans. Syst. Man Cybern. Syst. 117 (2022)
12. Zhang, G., Zhang, X.: Concise robust adaptive path-following control of underactuated ships using DSC and MLP. IEEE J. Oceanic Eng. **39**, 685–694 (2014)

13. Zhang, G., Deng, Y., Zhang, W., Huang, C.: Novel DVS guidance and path-following control for underactuated ships in presence of multiple static and moving obstacles. Ocean Eng. **170**, 100–110 (2018)

14. Shi, Y., Zhang, K.: Advanced model predictive control framework for autonomous intelligent mechatronic systems: a tutorial overview and perspectives. Annu. Rev. Control. **52**, 170–196 (2021)

15. Liu, C., Hu, Q., Wang, X., Yin, J.: Event-triggered-based nonlinear model predictive control for trajectory tracking of underactuated ship with multi-obstacle avoidance. Ocean Eng. **253**, 111278 (2022)

16. Kong, S., Sun, J., Qiu, C., Wu, Z., Yu, J.: Extended state observer-based controller with model predictive governor for 3-D trajectory tracking of underactuated underwater vehicles. IEEE Trans. Industr. Inf. **17**, 6114–6124 (2021)

17. Shen, C., Shi, Y., Buckham, B.: Trajectory tracking control of an autonomous underwater vehicle using lyapunov-based model predictive control. IEEE Trans. Industr. Electron. **65**, 5796–5805 (2018)

18. Liu, C., Gao, J., Xu, D.: Lyapunov-based model predictive control for tracking of nonholonomic mobile robots under input constraints. Int. J. Control Autom. Syst. **15**, 2313–2319 (2017)

19. Yu, X., Liu, L., Feng, G.: Trajectory tracking for nonholonomic vehicles with velocity constraints. IFAC-PapersOnLine **48**, 918–923 (2015)

20. Lu, Y., Zhang, G., Sun, Z., Zhang, W.: Adaptive cooperative formation control of autonomous surface vessels with uncertain dynamics and external disturbances. Ocean Eng. **167**, 36–44 (2018)

Overview of Technologies in Marine Robotics

He Shen[1,2(✉)], Jinxin Zeng[1,2], and Yixin Yang[1,2]

[1] School of Marine Science and Technology, Northwestern Polytechnical University,
Xi'an 710072, Shaanxi, China
shenhe@nwpu.edu.cn
[2] Shaanxi Key Laboratory of Underwater Information Technology, Xi'an
710072, Shaanxi, China

Abstract. Marine robotics is a fast-growing and important branch of robotics. Meanwhile, it is highly interdisciplinary and faces special challenges in the marine environment. This paper provides a systematic overview of core technologies in marine robotics. Building upon the operational "sense-think-act" paradigm, we put forward five clusters of technologies, including "sense", "think", "act", "system", and "interactions". These interconnected five clusters of technologies form a framework for readers to have a quick grasp of the technologies in marine robotics. Following this framework, special challenges and recent progress are also presented. Finally, future trends in addressing these special challenges are also brought to readers' attention.

Keywords: Marine Robotics · Technology Clusters · Progress and Challenges · Future Trends

1 Introduction

Ocean covers about two-thirds of the earth and plays an important role in the ecosystem, yet our understanding of the ocean is very limited due to difficulties in access. Marine robots have been are slowly changing this situation. For example, BP has been using a robot fleet consisting of surface and underwater vehicles (e.g., Waveglider, Autonaut, C-worker, Seaglider, Seastick, Microsub, Hugin) to monitor its facility operating conditions [1]. This fleet covers a workspace from the ocean's surface to the seabed. More and more of these robotic systems are used for widely spread domains, such as logistics and transportation, fishery and aquaculture, offshore mining, scientific research, defense, and education. Some typical examples are listed in Fig. 1.

As an important branch of robotics, marine robotics concerns the designing, building, programming, and operating of robots for marine applications. Some commonly used marine robots include floats, surface vessels, sea gliders, remote-operated or autonomous underwater vehicles, and hybrid vehicles. There is no unambiguous way to categorize marine robots. According to their working environment, they are typically grouped into surface, underwater, or hybrid robots. They can also be grouped according to size, function, or autonomy level. Since autonomy separates robots from machines, this paper

© The Author(s), under exclusive license to Springer Nature Singapore Pte Ltd. 2023
H. Yang et al. (Eds.): ICIRA 2023, LNAI 14273, pp. 340–351, 2023.
https://doi.org/10.1007/978-981-99-6498-7_30

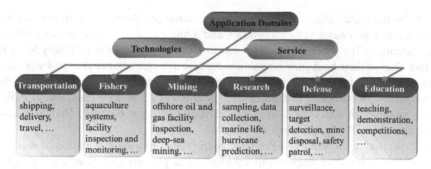

Fig. 1. Typical applications of marine robotics

will focus on autonomous robotic systems. Herein, a very brief history of the development of autonomous marine robotic systems is summarized.

Due to the direct influence of human activities, marine monitoring has always been important for scientific research. Floats are the most commonly used monitoring platforms for data collection to support scientific research, such as the detection of sea level changes, hydrological cycles, climate changes, diagnosis of global ice volume, and improvement in ocean forecasts [2]. With sensors installed, floats can be automated to collect samples and transmit data back in a controlled manner. At the meantime, multiple floats can work together to cover a large spatial area. Since 1998, NOAA's Argo program has been using an array of autonomous floats to obtain temperature and salinity measurements of the upper 2,000 m of the global ocean [3]. By 2020, Argo had become an international collaborative project with 34 countries participating, more than 15,000 floats deployed, and nearly a global coverage.

Autonomous surface vehicles, including autonomous vessels and autonomous sailboats, also have experienced significant progress over the past several decades. Numerous autonomous surface vehicles have been developed for bathymetric mapping. Some literature considers the first autonomous surface vehicle was developed from the MIT Sea Grant program in 1993 [4]. With the integration of sensors for oceanographic data collection, the ACES (Autonomous Coastal Exploration System) was developed in 1997. Following this, many other institutions released their autonomous surface vehicles. Later in 2017, U.S. Navy launched the Unmanned Surface Vehicle Master Plan and initiated the effort of utilizing surface vehicles as a gateway relay interface for underwater acoustic and above-water radio frequency or satellite communications. In 2010, DARPA designed an unmanned vessel for autonomous deployment. Since then, autonomous surface vehicles have experienced very fast growth. A comprehensive review can be found in the literature [5].

Between 1970 and 1990, many concepts and prototypes of autonomous underwater vehicles were developed. Autonomous underwater vehicles enable measurements in inaccessible areas such as deep sea and under-ice environments. Equipped with sensors, these mobile platforms can sample with optimized strategies. The enabling technologies for underwater vehicles share a lot in common with surface vehicles, including autonomy, endurance, and navigation, but some technologies have to be specially designed for underwater applications, such as precise underwater navigation and manipulation, limited by the bandwidth of acoustic communication [6]. Along with the conventional autonomous underwater vehicles, gliders and bioinspired designs have also received much attention. The concept of a glider was first introduced in 1989 by Henry Stommel. Gliders change their buoyance for motion control through volume change by pumping from or to an oil-filed bladder. Attitude control is normally achieved by shifting their internal mass. This working principle is energy efficient yet slow (-25–35 cm/s), making gliders suitable for data collection in long duration but slow motions. Their navigation is corrected by GPS signals when they surface.

Bioinspired underwater vehicles have been receiving a lot of attention as well. The biomimetic designs are proposed to achieve better performance in efficiency, agility, maneuverability, drag reduction, and so on. For example, a penguin-inspired robot with a bionic air lubrication system was developed to reduce drag [7]. Fish-like robots are extensively studied for higher propulsion efficiency and better maneuverability. A comprehensive review of the structural design, actuator, sensor, modeling theory, and control strategy can be found in [8, 9].

The sustainable development of the marine economy has been receiving increasing attention. The advancement in marine robotics is leading us to more efficient solutions for our current business models and bringing more data for us to understand the ocean at a faster pace but at a much lower cost [10]. Meanwhile, emerging technologies enable new abilities of marine robotic systems and further promote new applications. However, marine robotics is still a challenging subfield of robotics due to the unique challenges in the marine environment. These challenges prevent the simple transfer of our success from other domains. Hence, in this paper, we present the current progress, challenges, and trends in marine robotics technologies. It provides readers with a quick grasp of the scope of work in marine robotics. Hopefully, it may inspire more scholars to apply their specialties in other domains to help solve problems faced by the marine robotics community.

The rest of the paper is organized as follows. Section 2 presents the technologies of marine robotics and their classifications. Section 3 explains the special challenges faced by marine robotic systems, as well as the current progress. Section 4 summarizes some future trends. Conclusions are drawn in Sect. 5. Limited by the length of this paper, instead of trying to cover all the new technology progresses published in the literature, this paper focuses on the upper-level knowledge structure and cites other surveys for interested readers to learn more details.

2 Technologies

2.1 Overview

Before talking about the technologies in marine robotics, let us first define a logic framework to illustrate the relationship between application domains, system abilities, and technologies. Three key components drive the development of robotics, including application domains, system abilities, and technologies [11]. The relationship among them is well described in Fig. 2. The application domains set the requirement and further drive the development of system abilities. From the other direction, technologies provide robotic systems capabilities and further enable system abilities. Improved system abilities will, in return, promote new application domains and technologies. Here, application domains are similar to market domains, which define where and how robotic systems are used. System abilities are very loosely defined, and they provide a domain and technology-independent way of characterizing the whole robotic system performance. These abilities include but are not limited to adaptability, perception ability, cognitive ability, decisional autonomy, dependability, interaction ability, manipulation ability, and motion ability.

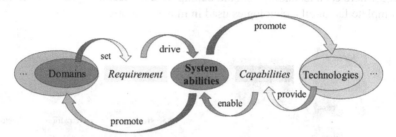

Fig. 2. Logic framework of the relationship between applications domains and technologies

In robotics, the well-known sense-think-act paradigm in Fig. 3 explains the general process of how a robotic system works at a high level. Like all other robotic systems, marine robots rely on various types of sensors to collect environmental information. Then, algorithms are used for reasoning and deciding on actions to take. In completing the tasks, actions are taken according to the decisions using actuators.

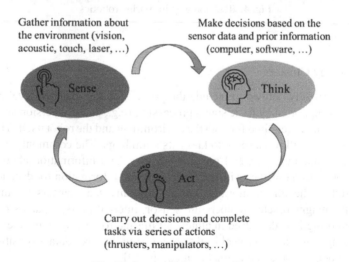

Fig. 3. Sense-think-act paradigm

The sense-think-act paradigm mainly focuses on the cycle of how a robot reacts to sensed information, and it does not reflect the robotic system itself and how the robot interacts with its surroundings. Adding the system and interactions to the three components in the sense-think-act scheme, we can roughly categorize the technologies in marine robotics into interconnected five clusters: sense, think, act, system, and interactions, as shown in Fig. 4. Here, the system refers to the technologies that support a robot's development, such as sensors, actuators, mechanics, electronics, software, and tools. The interactions are mainly in two parts, i.e., human-robot or robot-robot interactions and robot-environment interactions. The interactions will likely involve communications and collaborations. Note that these five clusters of technologies do not exclude each other regarding where each technology should belong, and the technologies listed in Fig. 4 is not a complete list of all technologies used in marine robotics.

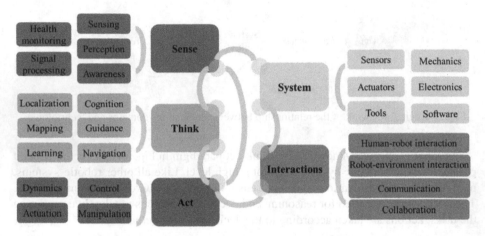

Fig. 4. Technologies in marine robotics

2.2 Technology Clusters

Sense is very broadly defined to include the process of sensing, low-level perception, and awareness supported by basic signal processing (e.g., data conversion and filtering). Sensing is commonly required for both the environment and the robot itself. The environmental information allows a robot to know its soundings. The commonly used sensors include radar, camera, sonar, and pressure sensors. The information about the robot itself is not only used together with the environmental information for decision-making but also used for health monitoring. Some commonly seen sensors for this purpose include IMU, magnetometer, temperature sensor, internal pressure, and strain gauges. Health monitoring is widely used in almost all marine robotic systems to ensure it's in sound working conditions. Typical health monitoring involves data acquisition, feature extraction, modeling, and operational evaluation [12].

   Think defines a cluster of decision-making related technologies, which include cognition (e.g., object recognition), guidance (e.g., planning and optimization), localization and navigation, mapping, learning, etc. Here, most of the technologies used in ground robots can be directly applied to surface vehicles. But the situation is drastically different for the underwater environment, mainly limited by underwater communication. Because of the absence of GPS signals, underwater robots have to rely on onboard sensors for navigation, and the dead reckoning will slowly lose its accuracy due to the well-understood drift problem of IMUs. Some other assistive navigation methods have been proposed, including terrain-matching navigation, geophysical field matching, star navigation, and magnetic field navigation [13]. Integrated navigation systems are often used in real-world applications, which can enhance the navigation system's stability, accuracy, and durability. Due to the low bandwidth of acoustic communication, underwater robots have to rely on their limited computational resources for object recognition. The quality of acoustic images is very low, conventional feature-based image analysis methods do not work well, and it gives artificial intelligence a chance for high performance object recognition. The guidance, navigation, and control follow the framework in Fig. 5. The guidance module tells the robot where to go, navigation finds out where the robot is, and the control module prepares actuation commands to move the robot to desired locations. Guidance and navigation belong to this cluster of technologies, while control will be assigned to the following "Act" cluster.

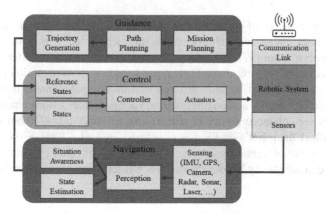

Fig. 5. Organization of a typical guidance, navigation, and control system

Act refers to the process of a robot carrying out the decisions. It brings the robot from its current state to a desired/reference state through a series of actions. The process involves dynamics, modeling, control, and actuation. Some typical examples include motion control, cooling control, and force control. Dynamics is a subdivision of mechanics that is concerned with the response of a system to forces and is composed of kinematics and kinetics. It is used in control system design, analysis, and derivation for model-based control algorithms. An overview of recent advances in the control of marine robotic systems can be found in [14]. From a historical perspective, the development of control theory went through three phases, classic control theory, modern control theory, and intelligent control theory. The definition of intelligent control is still ambiguous, although the general idea is to introduce artificial intelligence for control performance improvement. Some recent studies on the utilization of artificial intelligence in the closed-loop control framework are presented in [15].

System refers to the physical robot and tools used in robot development. The technologies consist of mechanical design (e.g., structure and body, mechanisms, hydrodynamics), mechatronics (e.g., sensors, actuators, embedded systems, power electronics), and integrations (e.g., integration of parts and payload). The commonly used sensors in marine robotic systems include hydrophones for detection, cameras for close inspection, IMU and magnetometer for navigation, pressure sensor for depth measurement, sonar for underwater mapping, radar or lidar for mapping above the water surface, etc. Some examples of actuators used in marine robotics are various types of propellers, control surfaces, and motors in robotic manipulators. Another essential component of the system consists of the tools used for robot development. In mechanical systems, computer aided design and computational fluid dynamics software are used for structure, thermal, and hydrodynamics analysis. There are also many software packages developed for simulations of robot operations. For example, the marine robotics unity simulator was developed to simulate multi-robot in ocean environments [16]. Another simulation tool Stonefish provides advanced simulations for hydrodynamics, underwater sensors, and actuators.

Interaction consists of human-robot interactions, robot-robot interactions, and robot-environment interactions. Human-robot interaction concerns how humans operate or work with a robot [17]. No matter how advanced a robotic system is, it would still be incorrect to blindly eliminate human participation in its operation [18]. Designing robots to better support humans through human-computer interaction has always been a hot topic in robotics, and so does marine robotics. Interactions among robots are also important for enhanced ability in performing complex tasks. Robot-environment interactions affect the robot's performance in finishing tasks. Studies on this topic are mainly on modeling of terrain dynamics for predictions of robot operation and control methods that can adaptively handle the unknown interactions between robots and their environment.

3 Special Challenges and Progress

3.1 Environment

The ocean environment presents a high corrosion environment where the combination of moisture, oxygen, salt, and sodium chloride cause metals to corrode much faster than freshwater. The major types of corrosion for marine robotic systems include general, pitting, crevice, and galvanic corrosion [19]. Many factors, including temperature, velocity, pressure, pH level, dissolved oxygen, salinity, pollutants, etc. influence the corrosion process. There are two principal methods for corrosion prevention, cathodic protection and coating, and they are typically used in conjunction. Another environmental challenge is high pressure for deep-sea operations. Cylindrical, spherical, and conical shells are widely used in high-pressure designs. Sealing is another factor that limits the depth rating of marine robotic systems [20]. Designing and optimizing these structures will require detailed finite element analysis, which can be very time-consuming.

3.2 Energy

Most robotic systems are self-contained in a compact size, and the space for the energy storage device is normally very limited; thereby, energy storage is another challenge for marine robots. There are three main ways to handle the energy constraint: choose high-capacity power sources, lower power consumption by reducing data collection/transmitting/processing, and generate ocean energy from the ocean environment. Among the three methods, power generation is more sustainable and receives a lot of attention [21]. Other than some traditional renewable solar and wind energy [22], the ocean provides additional sources for energy generation, including ocean waves [20], currents, tides [23], and temperature changes. Seatrec has developed a self-contained energy system that can use phase-changing materials to harvest energy from the temperature gradient for floats.

3.3 Communication

Communication is always needed in robotics for information sharing in the form of electromagnetic, free-space optical, or acoustic waves. Above the ocean surface, communication is not significantly different from other robotic systems, given the availability of satellites, radars, and radio frequency communication. But, underwater communication has always been challenging since electromagnetic signals are heavily damped. The commonly used underwater communication methods include acoustic, radio, and optical communications. Acoustic is the most practical way for long-range underwater communication. Meanwhile, acoustic signals, especially shallow-water acoustics, are subject to time-varying multipath, ambient noise, and surface scattering, which may lead to inter-symbol interference and significant Doppler shifts and spreads [24]. Acoustic communication also has a low data rate on the order of kbps, limited to the low carrier frequency ranging from 10 Hz to 1 MHz. Radio and optical communication can only be used for short-range underwater communication. Optical communication is more advantageous in communication range and data rate but requires alignment between the transmitter and receiver [25]. A comparison of the three communication methods is provided in Table 1, and their communication range and data rate are provided in Fig. 6.

3.4 Autonomy

The level of autonomy can be assessed on the three components in the sense-think-act paradigm, including (1) situation awareness, (2) decision making, planning, and control, and (3) external interaction. To enable modular development and upgrade of the functional capabilities of autonomous marine robots, the autonomy architecture is loosely defined in eight high-level functions, including (1) mission management, (2) engineering operations, (3) maneuver operations, (4) processing operations, (5) sensor and effector management, (6) communications operations, (7) support operations, and (8) situational awareness [27]. Limitations to marine autonomy arise from the aforementioned challenges in the environment, energy, and communication. The difficulties further lead to poor capabilities in underwater localization and navigation. Underwater perception is

Table 1. Commonly used wireless communication method in ocean robotics [26]

Method	Advantages	Limitations
Acoustic	• Widely used form for underwater communication • Long range up to 20 km	• Low data rate and large time delay • Transceivers are bulky, costly, and consume high power • Harmful for marine animals
Radio	• Smooth transition through air/water • Immune to water quality/turbulence • Moderate data transfer rate	• Short range (several meters) • Transceivers are bulky and costly • High power consumption
Optical	• High data rate up to Gbps • Very little latency • Transceivers are small and low cost	• Requires alignment throughout the data transmission process • Short range (up to several tens of meters)

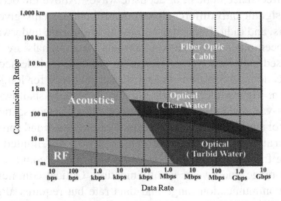

Fig. 6. Comparison of the commonly used communication methods [26]

also challenging since the light won't travel far, which limits the application of visual perception. Meanwhile, the acoustic image database is not well established, and the images have very low resolution, presenting a challenge for developing perception algorithms. Artificial intelligence has been increasingly used for many subfields in autonomy, such as path planning [28], control [29], object recognition [30], and health monitoring. Compared to conventional methods, artificial intelligence methods have the potential to play a great role in these fields. In addition, marine robotics needs to discuss the interlinkages between modeling, control, perception, and planning, which are important for autonomy. The terrain aided navigation is also presented with a great challenge due to the lack of underwater topographic maps and the environment is unstructured without reliable features. Besides, the complex underwater environment and limited communications require a high degree of autonomy to perform the same tasks as vehicles operating in other environments.

4   Future Trends

The main drivers for future marine robotics are the need from new applications and the expectation for better performance. Some examples of new applications are deep-sea mining and under-ice polar exploration. Autonomy, energy, and communication will continue to be the enabling technologies for future marine robotic systems. Autonomy is mainly quantified by the ability to complete the sense-think-act loop. Hence, it requires advancement in many technologies and their integrations. Artificial intelligence is increasingly used in many technologies under these three clusters, such as modeling, perception, navigation, control, and planning. Some special focuses are given to trustworthy artificial intelligence, which has the following essential building blocks: validity and reliability, safety, security and resiliency, accountability and transparency, explainability and interpretability, privacy, and fairness.

Another trend is the long endurance designs, which are achieved from both energy saving and production. The development of new sensors and actuators with a low energy consumption footprint is a research topic in this effort. Compared with the current sensor technology, biological sensors have more advantages regarding low energy consumption and no pollution. Studies on biomimetic propulsion have great potential to achieve higher efficiency and maneuverability than conventional actuators.

Additionally, pursuing higher performance guidance, navigation, and control algorithms never stopped. Optimized path planning can effectively save energy and improve the endurance of marine robotic systems. Algorithms that can adapt to the dynamic environment and cooperate with multiple agents also receive wind attention in the research community. Compared with conventional algorithms, the upcoming new algorithms generally have nonlinear, self-organizing, and self-learning characteristics.

Besides, since communication has been an enabling technology for marine robotic systems, especially underwater robots, a trend in research for faster-speed communications is observed [31]. For networked robotic systems, fast communication is a must-have technology [32]; hence, developing new techniques to improve data rate and maintain underwater communication distance is one of the most important research topics.

Finally, developing high-fidelity models for effective simulations is a trend. A digital twin can help us develop better-performed robotic systems with less requirement for costly experiments. Hardware in the loop simulation platforms will continuously be designed and used for advancing robotic technologies.

5   Conclusions

Marine robotics is fast growing yet challenging subfield of robotics. Aiming to provide readers with a quick grasp of the core technologies and help them understand the relationships among these technologies, we present a technology overview, current progress, challenges, and trends in marine robotics. The relationship among the applications, technologies, and system abilities is explained. Building upon the sense-think-act paradigm, we organized the core technologies into five clusters, including "sense", "think", "act", "system" and "interactions". It provides a framework for researchers to have a quick grasp of the architecture of marine robotic systems. Then, some special challenges marine robotic systems face in the environment, energy, communication, and autonomy are discussed. Finally, the future trends in marine robotics are also briefly mentioned.

References

1. BP, How A New Robot Fleet is Monitoring the Underwater World (2016). https://www. bp.com/en/global/corporate/news-and-insights/reimagining-energy/ocean-monitoring-with-robot-technology.html
2. Albaladejo, C., Soto, F., Torres, R., Sánchez, P., López, J.A.: A low-cost sensor buoy system for monitoring shallow marine environments. Sensors **12**(7), 9613–9634 (2012)
3. Baringer, M., Schmid, C.: The Argo Program: Two Decades of Ocean Observations. https://www.aoml.noaa.gov/two-decades-argo-program/
4. Rowley, J.: Autonomous unmanned surface vehicles: a paradigm shift for harbor security and underwater bathymetric imaging. IEEE Oceans 2018 Charleston Ocean **2018**, 1–6 (2019)
5. Liu, Z., Zhang, Y., Yu, X., Yuan, C.: Unmanned surface vehicles: an overview of developments and challenges. Annu. Rev. Control. **41**, 71–93 (2016)
6. Nicholson, J.W., Healey, A.J.: The present state of autonomous underwater vehicle applications and technologies. Mar. Technol. Soc. J. **42**(1), 44–51 (2008)
7. Pan, J., Zhou, Z., Wang, J., Zhang, P., Yu, J.: Development of a penguin-inspired swimming robot with air lubrication system. IEEE Trans. Industr. Electron. **70**(3), 2780–2789 (2023)
8. Raj, A., Thakur, A.: Fish-inspired robots: design, sensing, actuation, and autonomy—a review of research. Bioinspir. Biomim. **11**(3), 031001 (2016)
9. Li, Y., et al.: A comprehensive review on fish-inspired robots. Int. J. Adv. Rob. Syst. **19**(3), 1–20 (2022)
10. Xiang, J.: Marine Science and Technology in China: a Roadmap to 2050 (2009)
11. Roadmap, M.: Robotics 2020 Multi-annual Roadmap for Robotics in Europe (2016)
12. Sohn, H., Farrar, C.R., Hemez, F., Czarnecki, J.: A review of structural health. Library.Lanl.Gov, pp. 1–7 (2001)
13. Zhang, T., Xia, M., Zhang, J., Zhu, Y., Tong, J.: Review of underwater navigation and positioning technology. GNSS World China **46**(2), 98–103 (2022)
14. Shi, Y., Shen, C., Fang, H., Li, H.: Advanced control in marine mechatronic systems: a survey. IEEE/ASME Trans. Mechatron. **22**(3), 1121–1131 (2017)
15. Schöning, J., Riechmann, A., Pfisterer, H.J.: AI for closed-loop control systems new opportunities for modeling, designing, and tuning control systems. In: ACM International Conference Proceeding Series, vol. 1, no. 1, pp. 318–323 (2022)
16. Loncar, I., et al.: MARUS - a marine robotics simulator. In: IEEE Oceans Conference Record, pp. 1–7, 17–20 October 2022
17. Goodrich, M.A., Schultz, A.C.: Human–robot interaction: a survey. Found. Trends Hum.-Comput. Interact. **1**(3), 203–275 (2007)
18. Han, I.X., Meggers, F., Parascho, S.: Bridging the collectives: a review of collective human-robot construction. Int. J. Archit. Comput. **19**(4), 512–531 (2021)
19. Abbas, M., Shafiee, M.: An overview of maintenance management strategies for corroded steel structures in extreme marine environments. Marine Struct. **71**, 102718 (2020)
20. Ye, Z., Ye, L., Zhu, H.: A FEM analysis method of hyper-elastic contact problem for sealing structure. J. Naval Univ. Eng. **17**, 109–112 (2005)
21. Buckle, J.R., Knox, A., Siviter, J., Montecucco, A.: Autonomous underwater vehicle thermoelectric power generation. J. Electron. Mater. **42**(7), 2214–2220 (2013)
22. Shen, H., Ruiz, A., Li, N.: Fast online reinforcement learning control of small lift-driven vertical axis wind turbines with an active programmable four bar linkage mechanism. Energy **262** (2023)

23. Shi, W., Wang, D., Atlar, M., Guo, B., Seo, K.C.: Optimal design of a thin-wall diffuser for performance improvement of a tidal energy system for an AUV. Ocean Eng. **108**, 1–9 (2015)
24. Zolich, A., et al.: Survey on communication and networks for autonomous marine systems. J. Intell. Rob. Syst. **95**(3–4), 789–813 (2018). https://doi.org/10.1007/s10846-018-0833-5
25. Zhu, S., Chen, X., Liu, X., Zhang, G., Tian, P.: Recent progress in and rerspectives of underwater wireless optical communication. Progress in Quant. Electron. **73**, 100274 (2020)
26. Sajmath, P.K., Ravi, R.V., Majeed, K.K.A.: Underwater wireless optical communication systems: a survey. In: 2020 7th International Conference on Smart Structures and Systems (2020)
27. Rothgeb, M.: Unmanned Maritime Autonomy Architecture (2019)
28. An, D., Mu, Y., Wang, Y., Li, B., Wei, Y.: Intelligent path planning technologies of underwater vehicles: a review. J. Intell. Robot. Syst. Theory Appl. **107**(2) (2023)
29. Christensen, L., de Gea Fernández, J., Hildebrandt, M., Koch, C.E.S., Wehbe, B.: Recent advances in AI for navigation and control of underwater robots. Curr. Robot. Rep. **3**(4), 165–175 (2022)
30. Lorencin, I., Anđelić, N., Mrzljak, V., Car, Z.: Marine objects recognition using convolutional neural networks. Nase More (2019)
31. Zhang, F., et al.: Future trends in marine robotics. IEEE Robot. Autom. Mag. **22**, 14–122 (2015)
32. Ehrich Leonard, N.: Control of networks of underwater vehicles BT - encyclopedia of systems and control. In: Baillieul, J., Samad, T., (eds.) Springer International Publishing, Cham, pp. 351–356 (2021)

Multi-robot Systems for Real World Applications

An MFG Online Path Planning Algorithm Based on Upper and Lower Structure

Jinwei Liu[1,2], Wang Yao[2,3,4(✉)], and Xiao Zhang[1,2,3(✉)]

[1] School of Mathematical Sciences, Beihang University, Beijing 100191, China
[2] Key Laboratory of Mathematics, Information and Behavioral Semantics,
Ministry of Education, Beihang University,
Beijing 100191, China
[3] Zhongguancun Laboratory, Beijing 100094, China
[4] Institute of Artificial Intelligence, Beihang University,
Beijing 100191, China
{liujinwei,yaowang,xiao.zh}@buaa.edu.cn

Abstract. The collision-free path planning problem for multi-agent systems becomes increasingly complex as the number of agents increases. Mean-field game theory has proven effective for solving large-scale problems but is limited by the difficulty of solving higher-dimensional equations, which must fix beginnings and terminations. This paper proposes a new algorithm combining upper and lower layers to achieve online path planning. We utilize the mean field games process as the primary action of the lower layer, while the path planning of the grid method determines the global Markov process of the upper layer. By integrating the mean field games as an act of the global Markov process, we transfer the system's state by considering the environment. Simulation experiments verify the feasibility of this approach, providing a new and effective means for online path planning of large-scale multi-agent systems.

Keywords: Online Path Planning · Multi-agent System · Mean Field Games · Large-Scale Problems

1 Introduction

In large-scale multi-agent path planning methods, the purpose of individuals is to consider constraints such as obstacles, dynamic environments, and limited sensing or communication capabilities and navigate them from their respective starting positions to the desired destination. It has enormous applications in transportation [9], terrain surveying, agricultural applications, commercial performances, and other fields. The purpose is to find collision-free paths while optimizing various performance standards. As the number of agents increases,

Supported by National Key R&D Program of China (2022ZD0116401).

the problem becomes more complex and computationally challenging. In addition, constraints, uncertainty, and dynamic environments further complicate the planning process.

Many researchers have paid attention to the Mean Field Games approach of collision-free algorithms for large-scale multi-agent systems. For instance, [4] analyzes linear McKean-Vlasov forward-backward stochastic differential equations (SDEs) that arise in leader-follower games. The analysis uses mean-field type control and includes terminal state constraints on the state process. [3] considers a discrete-time mean field control model with standard environment states and rigorously establishes approximate optimality as the number of agents grows in the finite agent case and find that a dynamic programming principle holds, resulting in the existence of an optimal stationary policy. [12] presents a mean-field game (MFG) control-based method that ensures collision-free trajectory. Mean Field Games models use forward-backward partial differential equations, including the Fokker-Planck-Kolmogorov (FPK) equation for forward and the Hamilton-Jacobi-Bellman (HJB) equation for backward, to transform the distribution and value function of agents.

Due to the agents' complex state quantities, overcoming the solution of high-dimensional state equations is often necessary. In order to address high-dimensional problems, Chen et al. [1] utilized the Hamiltonian matrix structure of a system of related ordinary differential equations (ODEs) and applied a subspace decomposition method to find the solution. Provided generative adversarial neural network solutions [8, 10], which avoided high-dimensional machine learning approaches. In [12], a numerical solution was proposed for solving multipopulation high-dimensional stochastic MFGs, which showed good performance in solving FPK-HJB equations. However, current approaches rely on the pretraining process, which can only handle a fixed environment with starting and terminal points. When the environment or target changes, these methods may be invalid.

In order to overcome this shortcoming, we proposed combining upper and lower layers by taking the mean field games algorithm as the lower layer to solve the problem of collision-free and using A* as the upper layer to solve the online path planning. In order to better combine, we use the average game method to conduct pre-training "behavioral sets". At the same time, we use the A* algorithm to organize the elements of the behavior set. In this case, the behavior transfer can be regarded as a Markov Process determined by the upper layer.

Our main contributions can be summarized as follows:

- A large-scale multi-agents Mean Field Games path planning algorithm is proposed to solve the disadvantages that other high-dimensional average games cannot be planned.
- A combination of upper and lower layers is proposed. Different path planning algorithms assigning different paths on the upper layer can combine the average field game method of the lower layer for path planning.

– A process of considering the speed changes between the connection between behaviors is proposed to make the path planning trajectory smoother and avoid mutation from speed.

2   Problem Statement

2.1   Mean Field Games

Mean Field Games are a class of mathematical models describing large agent populations. These models use probability distributions to describe the entire system's behavior rather than focusing on individual agents. The goal of Mean Field Games is to find a Nash equilibrium, which is a state in which no agent can improve their outcome by unilaterally changing their behavior. To achieve this equilibrium, the initial distribution of agents, denoted by $\rho_0 \in \mathcal{P}(\mathbb{R}^n)$,(where $P(R_n)$ is the set of all probability distributions on R_n), is used as input to solve a pair of partial differential equations known as the HJB-FPK Coupled equations. By solving these equations, Mean Field Games can identify the Nash equilibrium of the system.

$$- \partial_t\phi - \nu\Delta\phi + H(x, \nabla\phi) = f(x, p) \quad \text{(HJB)}$$
$$\partial_t\rho - \nu\Delta\rho - div(\rho\nabla_p H(x, \nabla\phi)) \quad \text{(FPK)} \quad (1)$$
$$\rho(x, 0) = \rho_0, \quad \phi(x, T) = g(x, \rho(\cdot, T))$$

in which, $\phi : \mathbb{R}^n \times [0, T] \rightarrow \mathbb{R}$ means the value function, guiding the agents to a specific distribution, $H : \mathbb{R}^n \times \mathbb{R}^n \rightarrow \mathbb{R}$ is the Hamiltonian, describing the conditions of the environment, $f : \mathbb{R}^n \times \mathcal{P}(\mathbb{R}^n)$ describes the multi-agent system's interaction to the agent, $\rho(\cdot, t) \in \mathcal{P}(\mathbb{R}^n)$ denotes the distribution at the specific time t, $g : \mathbb{R}^n \times \mathcal{P}(\mathbb{R}^n) \rightarrow \mathbb{R}$ means the terminal condition, guiding the multi-agent to the distribution of termination. Morcover, [6], [10] and [8] give a standard assumption that convexity of H and Monotonous function f and g, under the above conditions, the excitation and uniqueness of Eq. 1 can be guaranteed. [2] gives a more detailed provement.

Applying Mean Field Games (MFGs) to online path planning presents a significant challenge due to the high dimensionality of the MFG solver based on GANs network. The long training times and poor generalization to changing starting and ending points make it difficult to use MFGs for online path planning.

However, given that MFGs are effective for large-scale group systems, it may be possible to apply this feature to individual online path-planning scenarios. By using MFGs as the underlying algorithm for the movement behavior of the group system, we can leverage the large-scale planning benefits of MFGs. To address the limitations of GAN-based solvers, the upper layer of our approach involves using Grid-based algorithms such as the A^* algorithm to handle the actual path planning situation. Markov Decision Processes (MDPs) provide a way to maintain the large-scale characteristics of the MFG algorithm while enabling effective online path planning and avoiding the limitations of GAN-based solvers.

2.2 MFGs and Markov Decision Process

Markov Decision Processes (MDPs) provide a way to maintain the large-scale characteristics of the Mean Field Games (MFG) algorithm while enabling effective online path planning and avoiding the limitations of GAN-based solvers. MDPs have the Markov property, which states that the state of the current moment is only related to the state and action of the previous moment and is independent of the state and action conditions of other moments.

$$p(s_{i+1}|s_i, a_i, \cdots, s_0, a_0) = p(s_{i+1}|s_i, a_i)$$

The conditional probability on the right side of the equation is called the transition probability between states of MDP. Our proposed approach combines the large-scale planning capabilities of the MFG algorithm with the precision of the $A*$ algorithm in online path planning. We use MDP as a bridge between the two algorithms, allowing the lower-layer MFG algorithm to generate a set of movement behaviors based on pre-trained behavioral sets. The upper-layer A^* algorithm handles the path planning based on the current environment and target location. By leveraging the Markov property of MDP, our approach offers an efficient and effective solution for large-scale online path planning in multi-agent systems.

3 Model Establishment

Referring to a single agent's online path planning algorithm, we divide the map into grids for large-scale multi-agent path planning. This simplifies the cluster behavior of a group in complex environments. After the grid is established, the large-scale multi-agent system can use the Mean Field Games (MFGs) method to construct basic actions such as front, rear, left, and right. We also consider the system's starting and ending states and the acceleration and deceleration process in the behavior concentration. Based on these ideas, we propose a large-scale multi-agent control method that combines upper and lower layers.

We propose a large-scale multi-agent control method combining the upper and lower layers based on the above ideas.

We address the problem of large-scale multi-agent path planning with variable terminations. To solve this, we pre-define the action set of Mean Field Games (MFGs) and use it as the lower layer of the algorithm. The upper layer uses basic path planning techniques and Markov Decision Processes (MDPs) as a bridge between the two layers, allowing us to solve the variable endpoint problem in large-scale multi-agent path planning.

In the MFG method between grids, we begin at the center of the starting grid and end at the center of the target grid. Additionally, we set the random parameter μ of the diffusion term, which ensures that the diffusion degree of the multi-agent is positively correlated with the size of the divided grid. We also set the start and end points relative to their positions so that for different adjacent grids, as long as their behavior is the same, they use the same MFG-based control process. This enables us to efficiently and effectively plan paths for large-scale multi-agent systems with variable endpoint scenarios.

The final large-scale multi-agent path planning algorithm can be realized through the established basic behavior and Markov decision process based on MFGs. Its main idea is

- Divide the scene into grids, and the size of the grid is related to the degree of dispersion of the large-scale multi-agent system
- Establish action sets for large-scale multi-agent system transfer between grids by MFGs method
- Establish the upper-layer path planning algorithm and use the Markov decision process to combine the upper and lower-layer algorithms
- Through the Markov decision process, plan the actions of the lower layer so that large-scale multi-agents can implement online path-planning algorithms (Fig. 1)

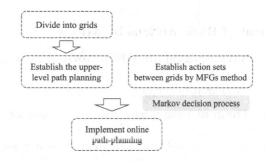

Fig. 1. The Global Logic Framework

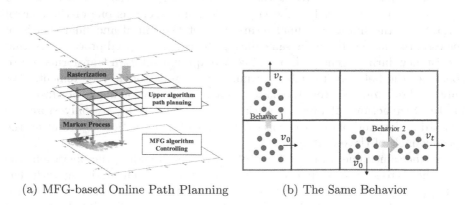

(a) MFG-based Online Path Planning   (b) The Same Behavior

Fig. 2. Algorithms Statement

3.1 Basic Assumptions

The assumptions presented in [12] provides a valuable framework for simplifying the control method of large-scale multi-agent systems. By assuming that each individual has the same status and can accurately locate himself, we can eliminate the need for complex decision-making mechanisms and communication protocols. Furthermore, by limiting the interaction range of each agent to a specific radius, we can reduce the computational complexity of the system and improve its scalability.

To facilitate the movement of agents between grids, we assume that the operating range is large enough to divide the site into uniform grids. This allows us to use the MFG method to control the large-scale group behavior of the agents. The completion time of the path planning is also assumed to be related to the complexity of the path, which includes the length of the path and the situation of obstacles. This assumption is realistic since the speed of agents is relatively fixed and has an upper limit, so the longer and more complex the path, the more time it will take to plan. Overall, these assumptions provide a solid foundation for developing efficient and effective control methods for large-scale multi-agent systems.

3.2   Establishment of Basic Actions by MFGs

Pre-training of Behavior Based on MFG Method. The Hamilton has this form

$$H(x, p, t) = c||p||_2 + f(x, \rho(x, t)) \tag{2}$$

where f is the control term to avoid congestion, c is a constant, representing the maximum speed.

To simplify the number of behaviors, we describe a basic behavior using relative terminal velocity, where "relative" refers to the direction of velocity corresponding to the direction of movement. As shown in Fig. 2(b), we consider Behavior1 and Behavior2 to be the same behavior. To ensure consistency of actions, we use the speed of the large-scale multi-agent as one of the control variables in the initial and final terms. We set the initial and final speeds of the essential actions to be the same during the constant speed process, ensuring consistency during agent path planning. We apply a rotation transformation to construct the behavior to reduce training costs and storage requirements. We only need to train and store the basic behavior and rotation angle. For instance, for the four actions of forward, backward, left, and right, we only store the forward action and obtain the control amount of other actions by rotating the specific angle of the essential action.

At the same time, in the process of starting and ending the operation, the agent needs to start or stop at rest, so its behavior is also inconsistent with that in the process. After pre-training, our multi-agent has a basic action set, which can ensure the movement of individuals between grids and build the essential action. Its implementation method is

$$\inf_{\rho, v} \int_0^T \left\{ \int_\Omega \rho(x, t) L(x, v(x, t)) dx + \mathcal{F}(\rho(\cdot, t)) \right\} dt + \mathcal{G}(\rho(\cdot, T)) \tag{3}$$

$$\text{s.t.} \quad \partial_t \rho - v\Delta\rho + \nabla \cdot (\rho v) = 0, \quad \rho(x, 0) = \rho_0(x),$$

where $L : \mathbb{R}^n \times \mathbb{R}^n \to \mathbb{R}$ is the Lagrangian function corresponding to the Legendre transform of Hamiltonian H, $\mathcal{F}, \mathcal{G} : \mathcal{P}(\mathbb{R}^n) \to \mathbb{R}$ are mean field interaction terms, $\nu : \mathbb{R} \times [0, T] \to \mathbb{R}^n$ is the velocity field, ϕ is the Lagrange multiplier, we can get

$$\sup_{\phi} \inf_{\rho(x,0)=\rho_0(x),v} \int_0^T \left\{ \int_\Omega \rho(x,t) L(x, v(x,t)) \mathrm{d}x + \mathcal{F}(\rho(\cdot,t)) \right\} \mathrm{d}t$$

$$+ \mathcal{G}(\rho(\cdot, T)) - \int_0^T \int_\Omega \phi(x,t)(\partial_t \rho - \nu \Delta \rho + \nabla \cdot (\rho(x,t) v(x,t)) \mathrm{d}x\, \mathrm{d}t. \tag{4}$$

Finally, by integrating parts and finding the minimum value of v, the Hamiltonian can be obtained as

$$H(x, p) = \inf_v \{ -p \cdot v + L(x, v) \}, \tag{5}$$

we can get

$$\inf_{\rho(x,0)=\rho_0(x)} \sup_{\phi} \int_0^T \left\{ \int_\Omega (\partial_t \phi + \nu \Delta \phi - H(x, \nabla \phi)) \rho(x,t) \mathrm{d}x + \mathcal{F}(\rho(\cdot,t)) \right\} \mathrm{d}t$$

$$+ \int_\Omega \phi(x,0) \rho_0(x) \mathrm{d}x - \int_\Omega \phi(x,T) \rho(x,T) \mathrm{d}x + \mathcal{G}(\rho(\cdot, T)). \tag{6}$$

where $\mathcal{F}$ is the process control constraint and $\mathcal{G}$ is the terminal constraint control.

Unlike the general MFG equation, we add the terminal speed contribution to the terminal item $\mathcal{G}$.

We can set the position constraint of the initial term and termination term in the adjacent grid points and determine the speed direction of the previous and next phases so that it can be used as the speed constraint of the initial term and the speed constraint of the termination term. That is

$$z = \mathcal{G}(\rho(\cdot, T)) = \int_\Omega ||x - x_T||_2 \rho(x, T) dx + \int_\Omega ||v - v_T|| \rho(v, T) dv \tag{7}$$

There are two reasons. One is to ensure that the agent can reach the speed set by us when reaching the next grid and ensure the consistency of the action. The other is to ensure that it can also gradually move towards the final speed during the operation process, thus avoiding speed mutation and other problems during the movement process and making the trajectory smoother. We can get the monotonicity of f and g, that is

$$\int_{\mathbb{R}^n} (f(y, \rho_1) - f(y, \rho_2)) d(\rho_1 - \rho_2)(y) > 0 \,\text{for all}\, \rho_1 \neq \rho_2$$

$$\int_{\mathbb{R}^n} (g(y, \rho_1) - g(y, \rho_2)) d(\rho_1 - \rho_2)(y) > 0 \,\text{for all}\, \rho_1 \neq \rho_2 \tag{8}$$

And we have the convexity of H, that is

$$H(x, p + q) - H(x, q) - \frac{\partial H}{\partial p}(x, p) \cdot q = 0 \implies q = 0 \tag{9}$$

We can get the existence and uniqueness of the solution of this system according to [7].

Solving High Dimensions MFGs. By parameterizing the function and solving for it, the GANs-based method can effectively solve high dimensions Mean Field Games. Firstly initializing the neural networks, we can assume

$$
\begin{aligned}
\phi_\omega(s,t) &= (1-t)N_\omega(x,t) + tg(x), \\
G_\theta(z,t) &= (1-t)z + tN_\theta(z,t)
\end{aligned}
\tag{10}
$$

in which z is sampled from the initial distribution ρ_0, $\rho(\cdot,t) = G_\theta(\cdot,t)|_{\rho_0}$ is the forward time item from ρ_0, and $G_\theta(\cdot,t)$ can sample from $\rho(\cdot,t)$. In Eq. 10, ϕ_ω and G_θ are able to satisfy the initial and terminal conditions, and by training the population item G_θ and the individual value function ϕ_ω alternately, we can solve the High Dimensions MFGs [8].

3.3   Markov Decision Process and Basic Behavior

The serial connection of the behaviors trained in advance needs to use the Markov decision process. The critical method of combining the upper and lower layers is to pass the state chain of the global plan to the lower layer to affect the behavior of the lower layer. In this method, the action of the lower layer is determined by two parts, namely, the direction of motion and the direction of terminal velocity. The moving direction of the global path planning in the upper layer determines the moving direction of the large-scale agents in the lower layer. The moving direction of the next stage of the upper-layer global path planning determines the direction of the end velocity. Determined individually if in initial/final state, which is a Markov chain carried out by other systems. The specific algorithm is as Fig. 3.

The path planning speed of the large-scale multi-agent can stay the same. Since the initial and final state of the large-scale multi-agent control of the standard MFG method is static, this may cause speed vibrations during the connection process of different behaviors, resulting in instability in the connection process of the agents. In order to make the agent more stable during operation, it is necessary to set the same speed when the behavior is connected.

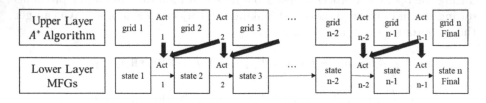

Fig. 3. Combination of upper and lower layers

3.4   Upper Algorithm Path Planning

After determining the relationship between behaviors based on the MFGs method at the bottom layer, the path planned by the top layer method can be used as a reference trajectory. Different path planning algorithms can be applied in specific scenarios to achieve different clustering effects, such as the A^* algorithm, fast random spanning tree algorithm, artificial potential field method, etc. After determining the global path planning of the top layer, the Markov chain of the global state transition is given, and finally, the behavior of the lower layer is determined.

Firstly, the map is rasterized, and the A^* algorithm [5] is used to plan the global path of the map with the grid. Record the globally optimal path to form a Markov state chain. Its main idea is $f(n) = g(n) + h(n)$, where $f(n)$ is the comprehensive priority of node n, then we select the next node to traverse, we always select the node with the highest comprehensive priority (the lowest value). $g(n)$ is the cost of node n from the starting point. $h(n)$ is the estimated cost of node n from the endpoint, which is the heuristic function of the A^* algorithm. A^* algorithm selects the node with the lowest $f(n)$ value (the highest priority) from the priority queue as the next node to be traversed during the operation.

4   Simulation Results

Large-scale multi-agent path planning simulation experiments at the same destination verify the effectiveness and feasibility of this method in different initial and terminal distributions. The following example cannot be implemented using the previous grid-based method because its starting and end points are variable. We also explained the difference ν Value and used an analytical solution to illustrate the accuracy of APAC-Net (Fig. 4).

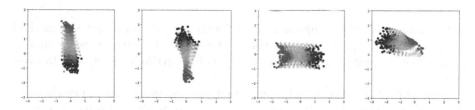

Fig. 4. Basic Actions-Up, Down, Left, Right with different terminal velocity direction

4.1   Pre-training of Behavior Based on MFG Method

We assume that the time between two adjacent grids is $T = 1$. At the same time, we refer to the APAC method [8] and use the neural network method to solve the MFG equation. The neural network has three hidden layers, each with 100 hidden units. The ResNet method is used to solve the two networks. The training process uses ADAM method $\beta = (0.5, 0.9)$, the learning rate of Φ_ω is 4×10^{-4}, the learning rate of G_θ is 1×10^{-4}, the weight attenuation is 10^{-4}, and the HJB penalty parameter is $\lambda = 1$.

4.2 Global Algorithm

Set the grid size to 1×1, and its unit size is the same as the diffusion item. At the same time, set the first key coordinate to $(2, 1)$. After reaching the first endpoint, change the coordinate position to $(-2, -2)$. After the upper layer of planning Fig. 5(a), the result is as shown in Fig. 5(b). Time is expressed in color. Specifically, blue represents the start time, red represents the end time, and the middle color represents the middle time.

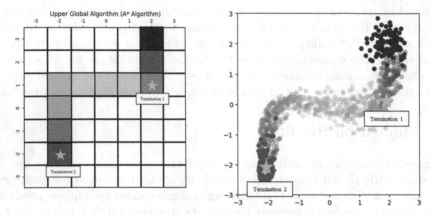

(a) Online Path Planning-Upper Layer   (b) Online Path Planning-Lower Layer

Fig. 5. Simulation Results (Color figure online)

We can see that the group can reach different key points through this method in an organized way, and it does not need to train in advance every time it changes the endpoint like other methods (shch as APAC-Net [8] and Res-Net [11]).

Meanwhile, our study includes simulation experiments to determine the security scope for different intelligence quantities. The results, depicted in Fig. 6a, reveal that our algorithm maintains high stability, achieving a success rate of over 98% even with 1,000 intelligence quantities by Simulation calculating. In addition, Fig. 6b shows that the training process converges quickly, as evidenced by the decreasing Training Total Loss. These findings highlight the effectiveness and efficiency of our algorithm in handling large-quantity agents' path planning and support its potential for practical use.

5 Conclusion

This paper proposes a novel large-scale multi-agent path planning algorithm that addresses the current challenge of achieving real-time performance with mean-field game methods. The algorithm combines the upper and lower layers

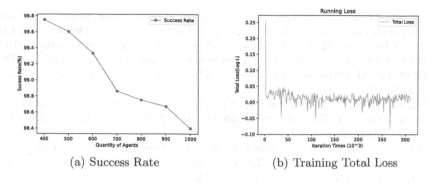

(a) Success Rate   (b) Training Total Loss

Fig. 6. Simulation Results

of planning, utilizing the mean-field game algorithm as the implementation tool for the lower layer to realize the fundamental behavior of the agents. The upper layer uses a standard path planning algorithm to plan the reference path, with the Markov decision process used to combine the upper and lower-layer methods. Introducing a speed constraint into the terminal constraint of the mean field game solves the continuity problem of the upper and lower layer combination, enabling the path planning problem of the variable endpoint of the large-scale multi-agent team to be addressed. Both theoretical derivation and experimental results demonstrate the feasibility of the proposed method for large quantities of agents and its ability to converge to a stable solution. This algorithm provides a promising solution for online, large-scale multi-agent path planning problems. However, because this method uses the Mean Field Games theory, it will reach convergence when participating in the number of individuals $n \to \infty$. Therefore, one of the disadvantages of this algorithm is that it is necessary to limit the number of individuals to be able to try.

References

1. Chen, X., Huang, M.: Linear-quadratic mean field control: the hamiltonian matrix and invariant subspace method. In: 2018 IEEE CONFERENCE ON DECISION AND CONTROL (CDC). pp. 4117–4122. IEEE Conference on Decision and Control, IEEE; Mitsubishi Elect Res Labs; United Technologies Res Ctr; MathWorks; IEEE Control Syst Soc; Soc Ind & Appl Math; Inst Operat Res & Management Sci; Japanese Soc Instrument & Control Engineers; European Control Assoc; Skydio; IEEE CAA Journal Automatica Sinica; Springer; Taylor & Francis; Princeton Univ Press; Elsevier (2018), 57th IEEE Conference on Decision and Control (CDC), Miami Beach, FL, DEC 17–19, 2018
2. Chow, Y.T., Darbon, J., Osher, S., Yin, W.: Algorithm for overcoming the curse of dimensionality for time-dependent non-convex hamilton-jacobi equations arising from optimal control and differential games problems. J. Sci. Comput. **73**(2–3, SI), 617–643 (2017). https://doi.org/10.1007/s10915-017-0436-5

3. Cui, K., Tahir, A., Sinzger, M., Koeppl, H.: Discrete-time mean field control with environment states. In: 2021 60TH IEEE Conference on Decision and Control (CDC), pp. 5239–5246. IEEE Conference on Decision and Control, IEEE; IEEE CSS (2021). 60th IEEE Conference on Decision and Control (CDC), ELECTR NETWORK, DEC 13–17 (2021). https://doi.org/10.1109/CDC45484.2021.9683749

4. Fu, G., Horst, U.: Mean-field leader-follower games with terminal state constraint. SIAM J. Control Optim. 58(4), 2078–2113 (2020). https://doi.org/10.1137/19M1241878

5. Hart, P.E., Nilsson, N.J., Raphael, B.: A formal basis for the heuristic determination of minimum cost paths. IEEE Trans. Syst. Sci. Cybern. 4(2), 100–107 (1968). https://doi.org/10.1109/TSSC.1968.300136

6. Huang, J., Li, X., Wang, T.: Mean-field linear-quadratic-gaussian (LQG) games for stochastic integral systems. IEEE Trans. Autom. Control 61(9), 2670–2675 (2016). https://doi.org/10.1109/TAC.2015.2506620

7. Lasry, J.M., Lions, P.L.: Mean field games. Japan. J. Math. 2(1), 229–260 (2007). https://doi.org/10.1007/s11537-007-0657-8

8. Lin, A.T., Fung, S.W., Li, W., Nurbekyan, L., Osher, S.J.: Alternating the population and control neural networks to solve high-dimensional stochastic mean-field games. Proc. Natl. Acad. Sci. United Atates America 118(31) (2021). https://doi.org/10.1073/pnas.2024713118

9. Resmerita, S., Heymann, M., Meyer, G.: A framework for conflict resolution in air traffic management. In: 42ND IEEE Conference on Decision and Control, vols. 1–6, Proceedings, pp. 2035–2040. IEEE; SIAM; Control Syst Soc; SICE; Informs; Honeywell Lab; Natl Instruments; XEROX; MathWorks (2003), 42nd IEEE Conference on Decision and Control, Maui, HI, DEC 09–12 (2003)

10. Ruthotto, L., Osher, S.J., Li, W., Nurbekyan, L., Fung, S.W.: A machine learning framework for solving high-dimensional mean field game and mean field control problems. Proc. Natl. Acad. Sci. United States America 117(17), 9183–9193 (2020). https://doi.org/10.1073/pnas.1922204117

11. Wang, G., Li, Z., Yao, W., Xia, S.: A multi-population mean-field game approach for large-scale agents cooperative attack-defense evolution in high-dimensional environments. Mathematics 10(21) (2022). https://doi.org/10.3390/math10214075

12. Wang, G., Yao, W., Zhang, X., Li, Z.: A mean-field game control for large-scale swarm formation flight in dense environments. Sensors 22(14) (2022). https://doi.org/10.3390/s22145437

Intelligent Scalable and Fault-Tolerant Coordination Approach for Collective Construction Robots

Mohamed Elbeltagy[1,2], Zhu-Feng Shao[1,2(✉)], Ming Yao[1,2], and Zhaokun Zhang[3]

[1] State Key Laboratory of Tribology, Tsinghua University, Beijing 100084, China
muj19@mails.tsinghua.edu.cn, shaozf@mail.tsinghua.edu.cn
[2] Beijing Key Lab of Precision/Ultra-Precision Manufacturing Equipment and Control,
Tsinghua University, Beijing 100084, China
[3] Pengcheng Laboratory, Shenzhen 518055, China

Abstract. Collective Robotic Construction (CRC) is an emerging field that aims to create autonomous multi-robot systems capable of building or modifying the environment. In this work, a novel coordination algorithm for CRC based on the Multi-Robot Task Allocation (MRTA) approach is proposed and implemented through the MURDOCH architecture. MURDOCH is a resources-centric and auction-based task allocation framework that enables multiple robots to bid on tasks, then select the most capable and well-suited robot for execution. This research extends the MURDOCH algorithm architecture by introducing modifications to enable a group of construction mobile robots to build structures using cube blocks. A mathematical model is established to describe the relationship between the robots and the blocks, as well as construction strategies. The proposed approach is validated with the ROS framework and Gazebo robotic simulator. Simulation demonstrates the implementation of the MURDOCH algorithm for CRC, highlighting the effectiveness of our proposed modifications in building structures.

Keywords: Collective robotics construction · multi-robot systems · Murdoch algorithm · auction-based task allocation

1 Introduction

The rapid increase in global urbanization has led to a rise in demand for affordable housing. Unfortunately, many regions of the world are still facing severe housing shortages due to various reasons such as famine and war, forcing around 60 million families to flee their homes [1]. The Collective Robotic Construction (CRC) is a burgeoning research field inspired by the construction found in nature of some birds and insects, which involves the utilization of autonomous multi-robot systems to build or modify the environment [2] making this field the perfect solution for the previously mentioned case. However, despite the potential benefits of CRC, it still faces several challenges, and previous demonstrations were limited to working with relatively small assemblies, with few robots, and in a controlled environment, thus not ready for real-life applications. Previous research on autonomous collective robot construction relied on simple rules [3] or a single computational unit to control the team of autonomous robots [4, 5]. However, the lack of robot coordination among the individual construction robots limits the system's scalability and reliability, making it prone to construction failure in case of robot errors during task execution.

The significances of the proposed research are as follows:

1. Implementation of a multi-robot coordination algorithm based on the Multi-Robot Task Allocation (MRTA) approach using market-based techniques such as MUR-DOCH [6] for a group of construction robots.
2. Introduction of construction strategies to regulate the construction process.
3. Implement a more reliable and fault-tolerant collective robotics construction system than previous methods.
4. Combining the closed-loop advantage of a centralized system and eliminating its single point of failure [7] as in the distributed systems is significant in implementing a scalable, more reliable, and fault-tolerant collective robotics construction system.

2 Related Work

The process of collective robotics construction (CRC) has been inspired by the construction process of social insects like termites and wasps, who use stigmergy for indirect coordination [2]. M. Allwright et al. have proposed a construction platform called Swarm Robotics Construction System (SRoCS), which uses stigmergy for coordinating the construction process in unknown environments with using onboard sensors for detecting stigmergy construction blocks [8]. The robots circle the construction perimeter to detect stigmergic cues generated by the stigmergy block and facilitate the decentralized coordination of the robots. Similarly, J. Werfel et al. developed the TERMES robotic platform to achieve the collective construction of three-dimensional structures inspired by the behavior of termites [9, 10]. The system uses multiple autonomous mobile robots that use passive building blocks to construct structures in a decentralized manner using decentralized construction algorithms. The proposed system offers significant improvements in the speed and efficiency of construction processes. On the other side, significant challenges must be overcome before these technologies can be widely adopted. For instance, the SRoCS and TERMES platforms have scalability and reliability concerns due to current experiments only involving a limited number of robots and building blocks. The communication and coordination among robots in both systems heavily rely on each other, making them vulnerable to communication failures or interference. Additionally, the stigmergy coordination method used in the SRoCS system can be influenced by environmental factors. Consequently, there is a need for further testing, evaluation, and modifications to the existing platforms to ensure their feasibility and efficiency in collective robotics construction.

The key solution for a more efficient, scalable, and fault-tolerant CRC system can be viewed from the approach of the coordination among construction robots' agents based on task allocation for construction blocks. Different research was carried out in the field of multi-robot task allocation (MRTA). Parker et al. presented the ALLIANCE algorithm, a distributed, behavior-based framework that utilizes mathematically modeled motivations to enable robots to form coalitions for MRTA. The feasibility of the approach is tested on a team of mobile robots performing hazardous waste cleanup. Market-based algorithm MURDOCH is developed as a distributed algorithm used for multi-agent task allocation [13]. MURDOCH introduces the tasks as auctions, agents bid for tasks to ensures efficient allocation by selecting the agent with the lowest bid [6]. Gerkey et al. validated the MURDOCH approach in two different domains: a loosely coupled task allocation with heterogeneous group of robots, and a tightly coupled domain that requires cooperation among robots to cooperatively move a box to a goal location [14]. The MURDOCH algorithm shows an advantage over the ALLIANCE algorithm for being more suited for dynamic environments with a centralized component existing in the form of an auctioneer.

Inspired by the pusher-watcher [14], a novel CRC system adopting the architecture of the MURDOCH algorithm is developed. The system has been implemented on a group of simulated mobile robots that move a predefined construction blocks into designated construction area with construction strategies to ensure an effective and reliable construction process. Integrating MURDOCH algorithm with the CRC system add scalability and fault-tolerance to the system. Additionally, combining the benefits of a closed-loop system while eliminating the disadvantages of a centralized system, such as single point of failure, communication overhead, and delays.

3 System Architecture

The objective of this research is developing a CRC system capable of constructing 2D structures using mobile robots and predefined construction blocks. Each robot is assigned the responsibility of transporting one block to its designated coordinate. To tackle this challenge, we drew inspiration from the coordination behavior of human workers cooperating to construct a building. Like these workers, each robot will transport one brick and install it in a designated part, following a blueprint prepared by engineers. The construction site is monitored by a "watcher", with a crucial role in regulating the construction process including tasks assigning to each robot and monitoring construction robots and block status.

Considering the above requirements, a set of constraints are defined to regulate the construction problem:

- The construction block's width is either equal to or greater than the width of the construction robot $Block_w \geq Robot_W$.
- Each robot is assigned to transport only one block to the designated destination.
- Electro-permanent magnet grippers are equipped on each robot to prevent the displacement of blocks while pushing, and permanent magnets are affixed to the corners of each block to facilitate robot-block docking and self-alignment with other blocks [15].
- The construction site is monitored by the watcher system that utilizes a global positioning system to obtain the coordination of each block.
- The environment is obstacle-free; obstacle avoidance is only considered through the coordination algorithm with low-level obstacle detection on each robot.

3.1 Robot-Block Modeling

Considering the aforementioned constraints, the model describing the robot - block relationship is shown in Fig. 1.

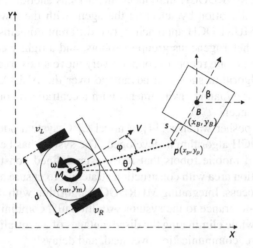

Fig. 1. Robot – block distance and orientation model.

The mobile robot M is required to move towards the designated point P of the block B for efficient docking and transportation. For simplicity, the masses, acceleration and friction are not considered. Point p represents a secure docking distance between the robot and the block. By determining the coordinates of block B (x_B, y_B) and orientation angle β, the coordinates of point p (x_P, y_P) are calculated using the following approach:

$$x_p = x_B - s\cos\beta, \; y_p = y_B = -s\sin\beta \qquad (1)$$

To determine the global position and orientation of the mobile robot M, the linear velocity V and angular velocity ω are calculated are firstly calculated,

$$V = \frac{v_L + v_R}{2}$$
$$\omega = \frac{v_L - v_R}{d} \qquad (2)$$

By the integrating the two elements of Eq. (2) with respect to time, we get the position and orientation of robot M:

$$\int_{t_0}^{t_i} \omega = \varphi$$
$$\int_{t_0}^{t_i} \dot{x} = V\cos\varphi = x_m \qquad (3)$$
$$\int_{t_0}^{t_i} \dot{y} = V\sin\varphi = y_m, i \in \{1, 2, 3, \ldots, n\}$$

Once the position and orientation of robot M and block B are obtained, a proportional controller system is derived leading robot – block's point p distance $r \approx 0$, $\varphi - \theta \approx 0$, and orientation $\beta \approx 0$ converges to zero.

robot – block's point P distance r and angle θ respectively are calculated as follows:

$$r = \sqrt{(x_m - x_p)^2 + (y_m - y_p)^2}$$
$$\theta = \tan^{-1} \frac{(x_m - x_p)}{(y_m - y_p)} \tag{4}$$

The proportional controller satisfying the requirement distance and angle convergence to zero is described as below:

$$V = k_l \times r$$
$$\omega = k_a \times \varphi \tag{5}$$

where k_l, and k_a are linear and angular velocities positive gains. Ultimately, the alignment of the robot M and block B is attained when the difference between the robot's current heading φ and the block's orientation β approaches zero $\varphi - \beta = 0$. This criterion is met through the previously implemented angular velocity proportional controller, which satisfies the alignment requirement.

3.2 Construction Strategies

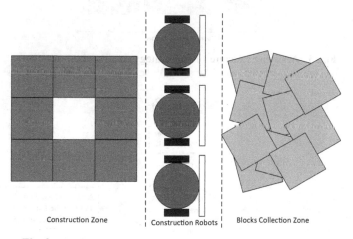

Construction Zone   Construction Robots   Blocks Collection Zone

Fig. 2. An Overview illustration for the system's three sections.

The proposed CRC system is comprised of three main sections: the blocks collection zone, the construction robots, and the construction zone. The blocks collection zone replicates the randomness of real-life construction sites by scattering construction blocks throughout the area. Construction robots are strategically positioned to face the blocks' collection zone, enabling them to effectively retrieve the blocks and transport them to the designated construction zone. The construction zone, as shown in Fig. 2, is located on the left side of the scene and serves as the primary area for construction activities.

Additionally, construction strategies are devised to ensure a dependable and efficient construction process while mitigating collisions and confusion among construction robots. These strategies are discussed below.

Structure slicing.

Structure growth strategy is developed enabling construction robots to build a required structure without collision. Our approach is inspired by K. Sugawara et al.'s work [15]. The growth strategy involves starting with a "seed" block, which serves as the starting point for the construction. The structure is then sliced into columns that grow from left to right and rows that grow from bottom to up, as illustrated in Fig. 3.

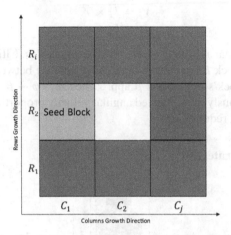

Fig. 3. Applying structure slicing strategy on a required structure.

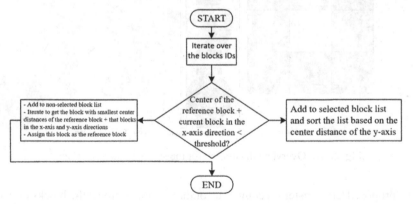

Fig. 4. Block Selection Algorithm Flow Chart

Since the robots cannot reach the blocks placed beyond those in their line of sight, an algorithm has been developed to select blocks that fall within the robot's reachability. It is necessary to have prior knowledge of the ID of one of the robots that are facing the blocks, which serves as a reference point. The threshold value in this context represents the distance between the centers of two blocks when their sides are in contact with each other.

Robot-block collection and construction.

After linking to the chosen blocks, the robots are programmed to move in reverse to prevent alteration in the poses of the remaining unattached blocks then rotate 180 degrees to face the construction area. Upon reaching the designated block space, the robot will align itself in a straight line with the space and place the block, thereby ensuring the stability of the already placed blocks and achieving smooth block placement. The robot-block collection and construction strategies are illustrated in Fig. 4.

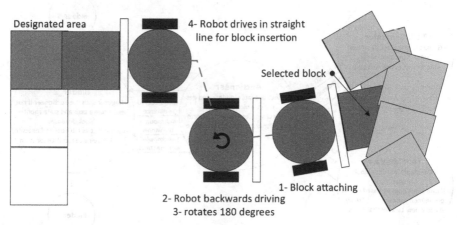

Fig. 5. One construction robot links to the selected construction block then the trajectory in dashed red line to place the block in the designated area.

4   Coordination Algorithm

The core coordination architecture of this developed CRC system is task allocation through the implementation of the MURDOCH algorithm. Each block requires transportation is allocated as a task, which is auctioned off within the system. The capable robots then place their bids on the tasks, and the auctioneer selects the most suitable robot for the job. The bids of task execution can be determined based on various parameters. In our system, we take into account two parameters: the shortest Euclidean distance between the robot and the block $dist(R_M, B_B)$, as well as the battery level of each robot. For a robot M and block B, the profit function is calculated as follows:

$$Fit = \sum \frac{1}{dist(R_M, B_B)} + batt\_level * 100\% \tag{6}$$

The selected robot for the allocated task is also expected to comply with the resource requirements set forth by the MURDOCH algorithm. However, since our system utilizes only homogenous robots that function as construction robots and a monitoring system that serves as a watcher robot, we do not utilize the resource publishing and subscribing mechanism, but only the bid request and response.

Algorithm Implementation.

Our MURDOCH-CRC algorithm is implemented on the ROS framework, drawing inspiration from previous literature [18]. The ROS-implemented system is comprised of four key components: the task generator, task monitor, auctioneer, and bidders. Figure 5 illustrate coordination process for each block. Further elaboration on the functions of each component is be presented below (Fig. 6).

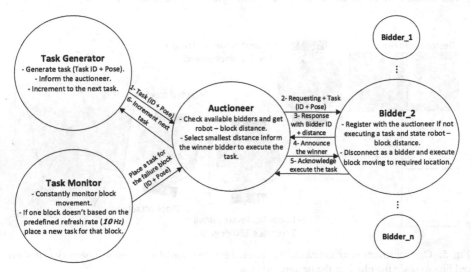

Fig. 6. Task allocation process flow using the coordination algorithm.

The task generator and task monitor.

Each block allocated for transport is assigned a task consisting of three elements (C_j, R_i, β): the column position, row position, and orientation of the designated block's coordination respectively. Each task is assigned a unique ID to facilitate monitoring and status updates. The task generator node component, in conjunction with the ArUco marker detection system, calculates the block's current pose, which is then transmitted to the auctioneer for further processing and auctioning. When a task is completed, the task generator node is updated, and the next block is selected for transport. This process continues until all blocks have been transported to their designated areas.

The task monitor node continually monitors the selected block's position with a refresh rate of 10 Hz. In case there is no change in the position of a selected block while being transported, the monitor node identifies this issue and alerts the auctioneer to allocate a new task for that block.

The auctioneer and the bidder.

The auctioneer is the central component of the CRC coordination algorithm responsible for managing the MURDOCH algorithm and allocating tasks based on the highest bid. Its role is vital in the successful execution of the CRC system. Using the ROS Services protocol [21], the auctioneer sends a request to all available bidders to check their availability for coordinating with the required block. Available bidders respond back with their Euclidean distance to the block and battery level. The auctioneer selects the robot with the highest bid, thereby maximizing the profit of the task, and announces the winning bidder. On the other hand, each robot is assigned one bidder to represent it in communication with the auctioneer. Once a winning bidder is selected by the auctioneer, the bidder must send an acknowledgment to the auctioneer, disconnect from the system to avoid participating in subsequent auctioning rounds, and request the assigned robot to begin executing the task.

5 Experimental Validation

Simulation experiments are carried to verify the main contribution of our CRC system including the system's scalability, and fault-tolerance. Several tests are conducted using the open-source 3D robotics Gazebo simulator which is capable of simulating various sensors and actuators to provide a realistic representation of robot behavior [19]. In our simulation environment, a group of non-holonomic differential steering Turtlebot3 robots was used as construction robots. These robots are equipped with various sensors such as encoders, a 360-degree laser range finder, an RGB-D camera, and an IMU. The Turtlebot3 platform is highly modular and customizable, making it an ideal choice for our research [20]. The construction blocks used in the simulation were white boxes measuring $0.22 \times 0.22 \times 0.11$ m, and each box was equipped with a unique ArUco marker tag for global positioning using a ceiling positioning camera.

The experiments were divided into three sets with 5 trials for each set. The first and second set are to verify the scalability of the system and the third set is to verify the fault tolerance. The CRC system is programed to construct a simple structure of five blocks to form a wall.

In the first experimental set, two Turtlebot3 robots are utilized to transport selected Four construction blocks to their designated locations. First and second experimental scalability test are recorded in this footage[1]. The coordination system is aware of the position of the seed block and, based on user requirements for constructing a wall, the CRC-MURDOCH algorithm assigns tasks to each robot. The developed construction strategies regulate the process, thus eliminating the need for complex trajectory planning for the robots. The average time elapsed over five trials is 3 min and 30 s. In the second set of experiments, three robots are introduced to perform the same construction process. The average time taken this time is 2 min and 10 s which is an evident for our proposed system scalability. As more robots are introduced, the construction process takes less time to complete. The ROS node communication diagram for our CRC coordination system is shown in Fig. 7.

The main nodes for the MURDOCH coordination algorithm are the/auctioneer, and/bidder_n. Each robot has /robot_move_n node embedding the robot-block model described in Sect. 3 with the developed construction strategies discussed in Sect. 4. The

---

[1] https://youtu.be/mLQztvbeyDk.

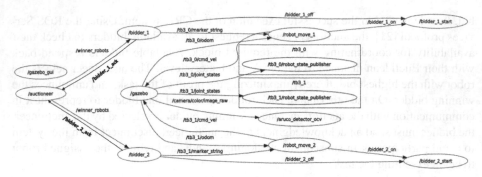

Fig. 7. The second experimental set ROS node diagram.

trajectory of robot 1 transporting the first block including the predefined construction strategies are plotted and compared with the ideal trajectory calculated using Eq. 4 as shown in Fig. 7. The fact that the ideal trajectory is the straight lines between each two points as the robot control system is designed to drive the robot into straight lines. The numbered arrows indicate the sequence for the robot following the construction strategies (Fig. 8).

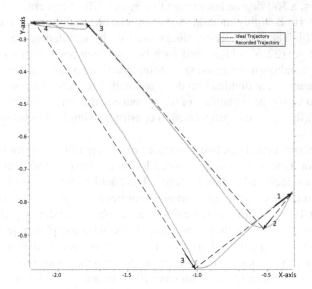

Fig. 8. Ideal trajectory versus the real trajectory plot.

The subsequent phase of the experiments involves validating the fault tolerance capability of the MURDOCH algorithm that has been integrated into our CRC system. In order to accomplish this, we conducted the third experimental set, which replicated the previous experiments, with the exception that removed one different robot in each trial to simulate a complete failure of a robot agent as recorded in this footage[2]. As planned, in the event of a robot failure, the auctioneer did not receive an acknowledgment message from the associated bidder, prompting the task monitor node to report the selected block that had not yet been transported and to initiate a new auction for that block until an available bidder responded. It is noted that the system temporarily halts until the block left by the failed robot is placed in the designated area. This is due to the fact that the construction process is sequential and a single failure can result in a cascade of failures throughout the entire structure

6 Conclusion

The prior advancements in collective robotics construction have encountered notable challenges that need to be addressed before these technologies can be widely implemented. These challenges primarily involve issues of scalability and reliability, which limit the number of robots that can be utilized and their effectiveness. Moreover, the communication and coordination among robots were highly dependent on one another, making them susceptible to communication failures and interference.

In response to the challenges faced by previous collective robotics construction, the present study proposes an adapted MURODCH MRTA architecture for the CRC system comprising multiple mobile robots and construction blocks. This architecture facilitates the transport of construction blocks to designated areas by allocating tasks for each block and implementing a construction strategy. The effectiveness of the proposed approach is demonstrated through a series of simulation scenarios on a group of Turtlebot3 robots, leading to the successful construction of 2D structures. The results indicate the expected scalability and fault tolerance and highlight the novelty of combining MRTA and construction rules in the CRC field.

Additionally, we aim to validate our system through hardware experiments. Furthermore, enhancing our CRC architecture and hardware components, such as introducing a scaffold manipulator, to extend our system to construct 3D structures. In the hardware experiments, it is planned to add a feature where, if the auctioneer fails, the available bidders can elect a new auctioneer.

Acknowledgement. This work was supported in part by the National Natural Science Foundation of China (Grant Nos. U19A20101 and 52105025). We would like to express our sincere gratitude and appreciation to the reviewers and editors for taking the time to review and provide feedback for this work.

References

1. United Nations, World's population increasingly urban with more than half living in urban areas, Department of Economic and Social Affairs (2014)
2. Petersen, K., Napp, N., Stuart-Smith, R., Rus, D., Kovac, M.: A review of collective robotic construction. Sci. Robot. **4**, 28 (2019). https://doi.org/10.1126/scirobotics.aau8479

---

[2] https://youtu.be/7Ag0mh-ERTQ.

3. Petersen, K., Nagpal, R., Werfel, J.: TERMES: an autonomous robotic system for three-dimensional collective construction. Robot. Sci. Syst. **7**, 257–264 (2012). https://doi.org/10.15607/rss.2011.vii.035

4. Lindsey, Q., Mellinger, D., Kumar, V.: Construction of cubic structures with quadrotor teams (2012). https://doi.org/10.15607/rss.2011.vii.025

5. Michael, N., Mellinger, D., Lindsey, Q., Kumar, V.: The GRASP multiple micro-UAV testbed. IEEE Robot. Autom. Mag. (2010). https://doi.org/10.1109/MRA.2010.937855

6. Gerkey, B., Matarić, M.J.: Sold!: auction methods for multirobot coordination. IEEE Trans. Robot. Autom. **18**(5), 758–768 (2002). https://doi.org/10.1109/TRA.2002.803462

7. Khamis, A., Hussein, A., Elmogy, A.: Multi-robot task allocation: a review of the state-of-the-art. Stud. Comput. Intell. **604**, 31–51 (2015). https://doi.org/10.1007/978-3-319-182 99-5_2

8. Allwright, M.: An Autonomous Multi-Robot System for Stigmergy-Based Construction (2017)

9. Werfel, J., Petersen, K., Nagpal, R.: Distributed multi-robot algorithms for the TERMES 3D collective construction system. In: Proceedings of Robotics: Science and Systems, (IROS 2011), pp. 1–6 (2011)

10. Werfel, J., Petersen, K., Nagpal, R.: Designing collective behavior in a termite-inspired robot construction team. Science (80-.) **343**(6172), 754–758 (2014)

11. Parker, L.: Alliance: an architecture for fault tolerant multirobot cooperation. IEEE Trans. Robot. Autom. **14**(2), 220–240 (1998). https://doi.org/10.1109/70.681242

12. Gerkey, B.P., Matarić, M.J.: Murdoch: publish/subscribe task allocation for heterogeneous agents. In: Proceedings of the Fourth International Conference on Autonomous agents, pp. 203–204 (2000)

13. Gerkey, B.: Pusher-watcher: An approach to fault-tolerant tightly-coupled robot coordination, p. 5 (2002)

14. Allwright, M., Zhu, W., Dorigo, M.: An open-source multi-robot construction system. HardwareX **5**, e00050 (2019). https://doi.org/10.1016/j.ohx.2018.e00050

15. Sugawara, K., Doi, Y.: Collective construction of dynamic structure initiated by semi-active blocks. In: 2015 IEEE/RSJ International Conference on Intelligent Robots and Systems (IROS), pp. 428–433. IEEE (2015). https://doi.org/10.1109/IROS.2015.7353408

16. https://docs.opencv.org/4.x/d5/dae/tutorial_aruco_detection.html OpenCV: Detection of ArUco Markers

17. Gerkey, B.P., Maja, J., Matari, C.: Principled communication for dynamic multi-robot task allocation. In: Sus, D., Singh, S., (eds.), Experirneiital Robotics VII, WIClS 271 (2001)

18. Guidotti, C., Baião, A., Bastos, G., Leite, A.: A murdoch-based ros package for multi-robot task allocation. In: 2018 Latin American Robotic Symposium, 2018 Brazilian Symposium on Robotics (SBR) and 2018 Workshop on Robotics in Education (WRE), pp. 58–64 (2018). https://doi.org/10.1109/LARS/SBR/WRE.2018.00019

19. Gazebo. https://staging.gazebosim.org/home

20. TurtleBot3. https://emanual.robotis.com/docs/en/platform/turtlebot3/overview/

21. Services - ROS Wiki. http://wiki.ros.org/Services

Performance Analysis and Configuration Optimization of a Hexapod Platform with Flexure Hinges

Xuewen Wang[1,2] ⓘ, Yang Yu[1,3(✉)], Zhenbang Xu[1,2,3(✉)], and Yu Zhang[1,2]

[1] Changchun Institute of Optics, Fine Mechanics and Physics, Chinese Academy of Sciences, Changchun 130033, China
{yuyang,xuzhenbang}@ciomp.ac.cn
[2] University of Chinese Academy of Sciences, Beijing 100049, China
[3] Laboratory of On-Orbit Manufacturing and Integration for Space Optics System, Chinese Academy of Science Key, Changchun 130033, China

Abstract. In order to improve the stability of the optical system, which is affected by the lateral compliance of the pointing mechanism, the compliance of the hexapod platform with flexure hinges is investigated in depth in this paper. Firstly, a hexapod platform with flexure hinges is presented. Secondly, the compliance model of the platform is established based on the virtual work theory and the superposition relationship of the deformation. Then, the compliance is analyzed based on the configuration parameters. The analysis results show that the lateral compliance has good consistency, and it is significantly higher than the axial compliance. Next, the compliance is subjected to multi-objective optimization, and the multi-objective function is established based on the configuration parameters. Finally, a rigid-flexible coupled multi-body simulation system is built to verify the correctness of the compliance and optimization. The simulation results show that the maximum relative error between the simulation results and the theoretical results does not exceed 10%, which can meet the requirements of engineering application. The findings provide a simple and effective method for determining the configuration parameters of the hexapod platform with flexure hinges in this paper.

Keywords: Flexure Hinge · Hexapod · Optimization · Rigid-flexible Coupling

1 Introduction

Compared to some conventional rotating joints, flexure hinges have the characteristics of non-backlash and non-assembly. Thus, flexure hinges are widely used as rotating joints in precision instruments, such as adjustment mechanisms [1], microgrippers [2], and bridge displacement amplifiers [3].

In recent years, a great number of investigations about flexure hinges have been done. Of course, the application of the flexure hinge is mainly in micro-positioning

© The Author(s), under exclusive license to Springer Nature Singapore Pte Ltd. 2023
H. Yang et al. (Eds.): ICIRA 2023, LNAI 14273, pp. 379–389, 2023.
https://doi.org/10.1007/978-981-99-6498-7_33

[4, 5] and active vibration isolation [6]. Chen et al. [7] have proposed a 6-DOF high-precision positioning system for spatial optics with flexure hinges, which is capable of a resolution of 9.5 nm. Du et al. [8] have proposed a high-precision pointing system using flexure hinges as passive joints, and its resolution can reach the sub-milliradian level. Lin et al. [9] have proposed a six-degree-of-freedom (6-DOF) micro-positioner based on compliant mechanisms and piezoelectric actuators (PZT). Lu et al. [10] have constructed a novel parallel precision positioning stage with the cylindrical flexure hinges, which can achieve high resolution and a large working range. Neill and Sneed et al. [11–13] have designed a hexapod platform with tons of load capacity, but the investigations associated with the platform have only focused on experimental testing. Yun et al. [14, 15] have proposed a two-stage vibration suppression and precision pointing platform with flexure hinges. In addition, Yang et al. [16] have proposed a hexapod platform for the secondary mirror with flexure hinges.

It is important to be noted that most of these investigations have focused on the design and performance testing of the platform, and few investigations have been able to determine the configuration parameters based on the requirements. Moreover, if the structure of the flexure hinge is complex, then its compliance is difficult to be calculated. Therefore, the compliance of hexapod platforms with flexure hinges is also difficult to be calculated and verified.

The main contribution of this paper is to develop a compliance model for hexapod platforms with flexure hinges, and an optimization method is proposed to determine the configuration parameters. The structure and compliance model of the hexapod platform is described in Sect. 2. The effect of configuration parameters on the compliance model is analyzed in Sect. 3. A multi-objective optimization method is proposed to determine the configuration parameters in Sect. 4. A rigid-flexible multi-body simulation system is built to verify the compliance and optimization method in Sect. 5. Some conclusions are presented in Sect. 6.

2 Compliance Model

Fig. 1. Schematic diagram of the structure of the hexapod platform.

As shown in Fig. 1, the hexapod platform consists mainly of a moving platform, a fixed base, flexure hinges and actuators. The actuator mostly includes an incremental encoder, a brushless torque motor, a harmonic drive, and a planetary roller screw.

In order to facilitate the modeling and analysis of the compliance of the hexapod platform, flexible and rigid bodies need to be clearly distinguished. It is worth noting that the compliance of the platform depends mainly on the flexure hinges. Therefore, all flexure hinges need to be considered as flexible bodies, and the other components are considered as rigid bodies.

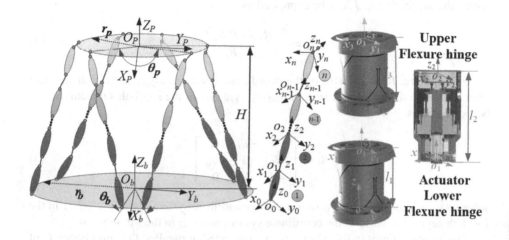

Fig. 2. The compliance model for the hexapod platform.

As shown in Fig. 2, the configuration of the hexapod platform is simplified. r_p and θ_p are the radius of the moving platform and the angle of the upper hinge distribution, respectively. Then, r_b and θ_b are the radius of the fixed base and the angle of the lower hinge distribution, respectively. l_1, l_2, and l_3 are the lengths of the upper hinge, the actuator, and the lower hinge, respectively. It is to be noted that $l_1 = l_3$. And H is the height of the hinge attachment point to the moving platform and the attachment point to the fixed base.

In order to investigate the compliance of the hexapod platform with flexure hinges, the compliance is modeled based on the virtual work theory and the superposition relationship of the deformation. It is assumed that each limb consists of n segments, and the compliance of the i-th segment in the m-th limb is $C_{m,i}$. The compliance $C_{m,i}$ can be expressed as

$$C_{m,i} = \begin{bmatrix} C_{\Delta x}^{Fx} & 0 & 0 & 0 & C_{\theta y}^{Fx} & 0 \\ 0 & C_{\Delta y}^{Fy} & 0 & C_{\theta x}^{Fy} & 0 & 0 \\ 0 & 0 & C_{\Delta z}^{Fz} & 0 & 0 & 0 \\ 0 & C_{\Delta y}^{Mx} & 0 & C_{\theta x}^{Mx} & 0 & 0 \\ C_{\Delta x}^{My} & 0 & 0 & 0 & C_{\theta y}^{My} & 0 \\ 0 & 0 & 0 & 0 & 0 & C_{\theta z}^{Mz} \end{bmatrix} = \begin{bmatrix} C_m^{11} & 0 & 0 & 0 & C_m^{15} & 0 \\ 0 & C_m^{22} & 0 & C_m^{24} & 0 & 0 \\ 0 & 0 & C_m^{33} & 0 & 0 & 0 \\ 0 & C_m^{42} & 0 & C_m^{44} & 0 & 0 \\ C_m^{51} & 0 & 0 & 0 & C_m^{55} & 0 \\ 0 & 0 & 0 & 0 & 0 & C_m^{66} \end{bmatrix} \quad (1)$$

Since the n segments of each limb are connected in series, the compliance C_m of the m-th limb can be expressed as

$$C_m = \sum_{i=1}^{n} J_i C_{m,i} J_i^T \tag{2}$$

where the Jacobi matrix J_i can be expressed as

$$J_i = \begin{bmatrix} R_i & -R_i S_i \\ 0_{3\times3} & R_i \end{bmatrix} \tag{3}$$

Furthermore, R_i is the pose of the coordinate system o_i-$x_i y_i z_i$ in the i-th segment with respect to the coordinate system o_{i+1}-$x_{i+1} y_{i+1} z_{i+1}$ in the $i+1$-th segment. S_i can be expressed as

$$S_i = \begin{bmatrix} 0 & -d_{iz} & d_{iy} \\ d_{iz} & 0 & -d_{ix} \\ -d_{iy} & d_{ix} & 0 \end{bmatrix} \tag{4}$$

where $d_i = [d_{ix}, d_{iy}, d_{iz}]$ is the position of the coordinate system o_{i+1}-$x_{i+1} y_{i+1} z_{i+1}$ in the $i+1$-th segment relative to the coordinate system o_i-$x_i y_i z_i$ in the i-th segment.

Since the six limbs in this platform are connected in parallel, the compliance C of the hexapod platform can be expressed as

$$C = \left(\sum_{m=1}^{6} \left(J_m C_m J_m^T \right)^{-1} \right)^{-1} \tag{5}$$

where the Jacobi matrix J_m can be expressed as

$$J_m = \begin{bmatrix} R_m & -R_m S_m \\ 0_{3\times3} & R_m \end{bmatrix} \tag{6}$$

It should be noted that R_m denotes the pose of the coordinate system o_n-$x_n y_n z_n$ in the m-th limb with respect to the coordinate system O_P-$X_P Y_P Z_P$ in the moving platform. And S_m can be expressed as

$$S_m = \begin{bmatrix} 0 & -d_{mz} & d_{my} \\ d_{mz} & 0 & -d_{mx} \\ -d_{my} & d_{mx} & 0 \end{bmatrix} \tag{7}$$

where $d_m = [d_{mx}, d_{my}, d_{mz}]$ is the position of the coordinate system O_P-$X_P Y_P Z_P$ in the moving platform relative to the coordinate system o_n-$x_n y_n z_n$ in the m-th limb.

To better describe the compliance of the platform, the compliance matrix C can be expressed as

$$
C = \begin{bmatrix}
C_{\Delta x-Fx} & 0 & 0 & 0 & C_{\theta y-Fx} & 0 \\
0 & C_{\Delta y-Fy} & 0 & C_{\theta x-Fy} & 0 & 0 \\
0 & 0 & C_{\Delta z-Fz} & 0 & 0 & 0 \\
0 & C_{\Delta y-Mx} & 0 & C_{\theta x-Mx} & 0 & 0 \\
C_{\Delta x-My} & 0 & 0 & 0 & C_{\theta y-My} & 0 \\
0 & 0 & 0 & 0 & 0 & C_{\theta z-Mz}
\end{bmatrix} \tag{8}
$$

Based on the above-mentioned analysis, the limb is divided into three segments (an upper hinge, an actuator, and a lower hinge), as shown in Fig. 2. The compliances of the three segments are $C_{m,1}$, $C_{m,2}$ and $C_{m,3}$ respectively. In addition, the deformation of the actuator needs to be neglected because its compliance is much smaller than that of the flexure hinge. Therefore $C_{m,2} \approx 0_{3 \times 3}$.

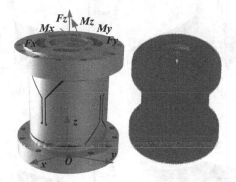

Fig. 3. Finite element model of the flexure hinge.

In addition, the structural peculiarities of the flexure hinge make it difficult to obtain the theoretical compliance matrix $C_{m,1}$ or $C_{m,3}$. Therefore, the compliance matrices $C_{m,1}$ and $C_{m,3}$ need to be obtained by using PATRAN and NASTRAN, as shown in Fig. 3. According to the simulation analysis, the compliance matrices $C_{m,1}$ and $C_{m,3}$ can be expressed as

$$
C_{m,1(3)} = \begin{bmatrix}
C_{\Delta x}^{Fx} & 0 & 0 & 0 & C_{\theta y}^{Fx} & 0 \\
0 & C_{\Delta y}^{Fy} & 0 & C_{\theta x}^{Fy} & 0 & 0 \\
0 & 0 & C_{\Delta z}^{Fz} & 0 & 0 & 0 \\
0 & C_{\Delta y}^{Mx} & 0 & C_{\theta x}^{Mx} & 0 & 0 \\
C_{\Delta x}^{My} & 0 & 0 & 0 & C_{\theta y}^{My} & 0 \\
0 & 0 & 0 & 0 & 0 & C_{\theta z}^{Mz}
\end{bmatrix} = \begin{bmatrix}
C_f^{11} & 0 & 0 & 0 & C_f^{15} & 0 \\
0 & C_f^{22} & 0 & C_f^{24} & 0 & 0 \\
0 & 0 & C_f^{33} & 0 & 0 & 0 \\
0 & C_f^{42} & 0 & C_f^{44} & 0 & 0 \\
C_f^{15} & 0 & 0 & 0 & C_f^{55} & 0 \\
0 & 0 & 0 & 0 & 0 & C_f^{66}
\end{bmatrix} \tag{9}
$$

where $C^{11}{}_f = 3.78 \times 10^{-3}$ mm/N, $C^{15}{}_f = 5.49 \times 10^{-5}$ rad/N, $C^{22}{}_f = 3.78 \times 10^{-3}$ mm/N, $C^{24}{}_f = -5.50 \times 10^{-5}$ rad/N, $C^{33}{}_f = 3.17 \times 10^{-6}$ mm/N, $C^{42}{}_f = -5.76 \times 10^{-5}$ mm/N·mm, $C^{44}{}_f = 8.58 \times 10^{-7}$ rad/N·mm, $C^{51}{}_f = 5.75 \times 10^{-5}$ mm/N·mm, $C^{55}{}_f = 8.57 \times 10^{-7}$ rad/N·mm, $C^{66}{}_f = 1.89 \times 10^{-7}$ rad/N·mm.

3 Parametric Sensitivity Analysis of Compliance

Since the structure of the optical load and fixed truss is fixed in the application, the radius of the moving platform and fixed base are fixed to $r_p = 383.97$ mm and $r_b = 444.13$ mm, respectively. At this moment, the configuration parameters affecting the compliance are mainly l_1, l_2, l_3, θ_p, and θ_b, and H. It should be noted that the initial length of the limb has been determined at the beginning of the structure design. As follows: $l_1 = l_3 = 128.20$ mm and $l_2 = 299.68$ mm. Therefore, the compliance of the platform needs to be investigated based on the configuration parameters θ_p, θ_b, and H.

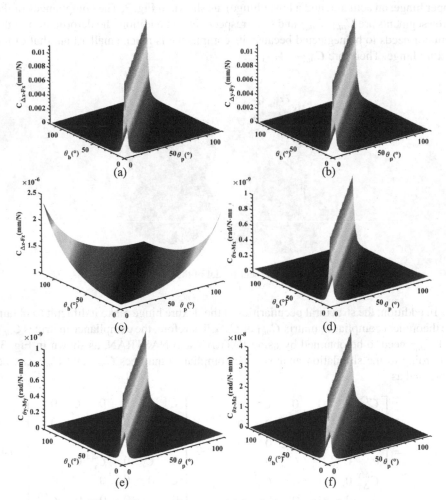

Fig. 4. The compliance model for the hexapod platform.

As shown in Fig. 4, the lateral compliance ($C_{\Delta x\text{-}Fx}$, $C_{\Delta y\text{-}Fy}$, $C_{\theta x\text{-}Mx}$, $C_{\theta y\text{-}My}$) along the x and y directions is always equal with the variation of θ_p and θ_b, and it has good consistency. Moreover, as the difference between θ_p and θ_b becomes larger, the lateral compliance and torsional compliance ($C_{\theta z\text{-}Mz}$) is smaller and the axial compliance ($C_{\Delta z\text{-}Fz}$) is larger. It is important to note that when $\theta_p = \theta_b$, the axial compliance is the lowest and the lateral compliance is the highest. However, higher lateral compliance can have a significant impact on the imaging quality of the optical load. Of course, if the load capacity of the hexapod platform can be satisfied, the lateral compliance needs to be reduced as much as possible in order to make it have a higher imaging stability. In addition, H is also an important configuration parameter. If the height H is neglected, then the configuration parameters that meet the engineering requirements can be easily obtained based on the analysis. However, with the variation of θ_p and θ_b, the actual height H varies very much, as shown in Fig. 5. Therefore, the desired configuration parameters need to be obtained by optimization to reduce the lateral compliance while satisfying the axial compliance.

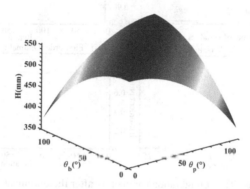

Fig. 5. The variation trend of height H.

4 Multi-objective Optimization Based on Configuration

Based on the mentioned analysis, the lateral compliance needs to be reduced as much as possible under the premise of satisfying the load capacity. Thus, the optimization objective function can be expressed as

$$\min f = \frac{C_{\Delta x\text{-}Fx} + C_{\Delta y\text{-}Fy} + C_{\theta x\text{-}Mx} + C_{\theta y\text{-}My}}{C_{\Delta x\text{-}Fx} + C_{\Delta y\text{-}Fy} + C_{\Delta z\text{-}Fz} + C_{\theta x\text{-}Mx} + C_{\theta y\text{-}My} + C_{\theta z\text{-}Mz}} \quad (10)$$

The constraints associated with the configuration parameters can be expressed as

$$\begin{cases} 100° \leq \theta_p \leq 108° \\ 15° \leq \theta_b \leq 20° \\ 465\,\text{mm} \leq H \leq 475\,\text{mm} \end{cases} \quad (11)$$

Then, the constraints associated with lateral compliance and axial compliance can be expressed as

$$\begin{cases} C_{\Delta y\text{-}Fy}(or C_{\Delta x\text{-}Fx}) \leq 7.5 \times 10^{-6}\text{mm/N} \\ C_{\Delta z\text{-}Fz} \leq 1.5 \times 10^{-6}\text{mm/N} \end{cases} \quad (12)$$

The initial configuration parameters are set to $[\theta_p, H, \theta_b] = [100°, 468$ mm, $18°]$. Then, the optimization is performed using *fmincon* (A constrained nonlinear minimization algorithm). As shown in Fig. 6, the results show that the optimized parameters are $[\theta_p, H, \theta_b] = [102.27°, 466.71$ mm, $18.18°]$. The compliances of the platform in all directions are $C_{\Delta x\text{-}Fx} = C_{\Delta y\text{-}Fy} \approx 7.38 \times 10^{-6}$ mm/N, $C_{\Delta z\text{-}Fz} \approx 1.50 \times 10^{-6}$ mm/N, $C_{\theta x\text{-}Mx} = C_{\theta y\text{-}My} \approx 2.10 \times 10^{-11}$ rad/N·mm, and $C_{\theta z\text{-}Mz} \approx 2.50 \times 10^{-11}$ rad/N·mm, which can meet the requirements of the application.

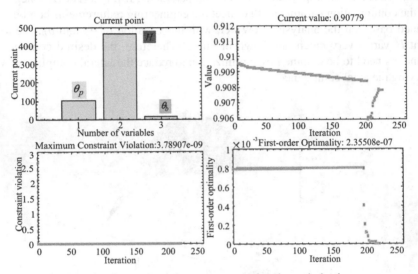

Fig. 6. The configuration parameters after the optimization.

5   Rigid-Flexible Coupling Multi-body Simulation

In order to verify the above optimization results and the correctness of the compliance model, a rigid-flexible coupling multi-body simulation system is built, as shown in Fig. 7.

First, a 3D model of the hexapod platform is built using UG; Then, the MNF modal neutral files of the flexure hinge supported by ADAMS are exported using PATRAN and NASTRAN; Next, the 3D model of the platform is imported into ADAMS, and the flexure hinge is replaced with the modal neutral files; Finally, after adding the corresponding kinematic pair, the rigid-flexible multi-body simulation system is finished.

The six operating conditions are set as $[F_x, 0, 0, 0, 0, 0]$, $[0, F_y, 0, 0, 0, 0]$, $[0, 0, F_z, 0, 0, 0]$, $[0, 0, 0, M_x, 0, 0]$, $[0, 0, 0, 0, M_y, 0]$ and $[0, 0, 0, 0, 0, M_z]$, respectively. As shown in Table 1, the simulation results show that the lateral compliance is in good consistency. And the relative error between simulation and theoretical results does not exceed 10%, which meets the application requirements.

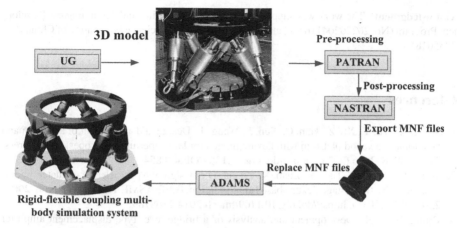

3D model

UG

Pre-processing

PATRAN

Post-processing

NASTRAN

Export MNF files

Replace MNF files

ADAMS

Rigid-flexible coupling multi-body simulation system

Fig. 7. The rigid-flexible coupling multi-body simulation system.

Table 1. The compliance based on the rigid-flexible coupling multi-body simulation system.

Items	Theoretical value	Simulation value	Error
$C_{\Delta x\text{-}Fx}$	7.38×10^{-6} mm/N	6.84×10^{-6} mm/N	7.31%
$C_{\Delta y\text{-}Fy}$	7.38×10^{-6} mm/N	6.84×10^{-6} mm/N	7.31%
$C_{\Delta z\text{-}Fz}$	1.50×10^{-6} mm/N	1.38×10^{-6} mm/N	8.00%
$C_{\theta x\text{-}Mx}$	2.10×10^{-11} rad/N·mm	1.93×10^{-11} rad/N·mm	8.00%
$C_{\theta y\text{-}My}$	2.10×10^{-11} rad/N·mm	1.93×10^{-11} rad/N·mm	8.09%
$C_{\theta z\text{-}Mz}$	2.50×10^{-11} rad/N·mm	2.32×10^{-11} rad/N·mm	7.20%

6 Conclusion

In this paper, a hexapod platform with flexure hinges is proposed, and its compliance model is established based on the virtual work theory and the superposition relationship of the deformation.

Then, the compliance matrix of the flexure hinge is obtained by finite element analysis, and the compliance of the hexapod platform is analyzed based on the configuration parameters. The analysis results show that the platform has a good consistency of lateral compliance along the x-axis and lateral compliance along the y-axis. In addition, the lateral compliance has an opposite trend to the axial compliance with respect to the hinge distribution angle. Then, in order to reduce the lateral compliance, a multi-objective optimal design is carried out using the constrained nonlinear minimization algorithm.

Finally, a rigid-flexible coupled multi-body simulation system is built to verify the optimization and the compliance model. The simulation results show that the maximum relative error between the optimized results and the theoretical results does not exceed 10%. The investigation shows the accuracy of the theory and the reliability of the optimization in the paper.

Acknowledgment. The work was supported by the Jilin Scientific and Technological Development Program (No. 20220204116YY) and the National Natural Science Foundation of China (No. 62235018).

References

1. Wang, X., Yu, Y., Xu, Z., Han, C., Sun, J., Wang, J.: Design and assessment of a micro-nano positioning hexapod platform with flexure hinges for large aperture telescopes. Opt Express. **31** (3), 3908–3926 (2023). https://doi.org/10.1364/OE.476854
2. Wang, F., Liang, C., Tian, Y., Zhao, X., Zhang, D.: Design of a piezoelectric-actuated micro-gripper with a three-stage flexure-based amplification. IEEE/ASME Trans. Mechatron. **20**(5), 2205–2213 (2015). https://doi.org/10.1109/tmech.2014.2368789
3. Dong, W., et al.: Development and analysis of a bridge-lever-type displacement amplifier based on hybrid flexure hinges. Precis. Eng. **54**, 171–181 (2018). https://doi.org/10.1016/j.precisioneng.2018.04.017
4. Yun, Y., Li, Y.: Design and analysis of a novel 6-DOF redundant actuated parallel robot with compliant hinges for high precision positioning. Nonlinear Dyn. **61**(4), 829–845 (2010). https://doi.org/10.1007/s11071-010-9690-x
5. Zhang, D., Li, P., Zhang, J., Chen, H., Guo, K., Ni, M.: Design and assessment of a 6-DOF micro/nanopositioning system. IEEE/ASME Trans. Mechatron. **24**(5), 2097–2107 (2019). https://doi.org/10.1109/tmech.2019.2931619
6. Yun, Y.L.Y.: Modeling and control analysis of a 3-PUPU Dual compliant parallel manipulator for micro positioning and active vibration isolation. J. Dyn. Sys. Meas. Control. **134**(2), 021001 (2012). https://doi.org/10.1115/1.4005036
7. Chen, F., Dong, W., Yang, M., Sun, L., Du, Z.: A PZT Actuated 6-DOF positioning system for space optics alignment. IEEE/ASME Trans. Mechatron. **24**(6), 2827–2838 (2019). https://doi.org/10.1109/TMECH.2019.2942645
8. Du, Z., Shi, R., Dong, W.: A piezo-actuated high-precision flexible parallel pointing mechanism: conceptual design, development, and experiments. IEEE Trans. Robot. **30**(1), 131–137 (2014). https://doi.org/10.1109/tro.2013.2288800
9. Lin, C., Zheng, S., Li, P., Shen, Z., Wang, S.: Positioning error analysis and control of a piezo-driven 6-DOF micro-positioner. Micromachines (Basel). **10**(8), 542 (2019). https://doi.org/10.3390/mi10080542
10. Lu, Q., Chen, X., Zheng, L., Xu, N.: A novel parallel precision stage with large working range based on structural parameters of flexible hinges. Int. J. Precis. Eng. Manuf. **21** (3), 483–490 (2019). https://doi.org/10.1007/s12541-019-00270-2
11. Neill, D., Sneed, R., Dawson, J., Sebag, J., Gressler, W.: Baseline design of the LSST hexapods and rotator. In: Proceedings of SPIE, Montréal, Quebec, CA (2014). https://doi.org/10.1117/12.2056799
12. Sneed, R., Neill, D., Caldwell, B., Walter, B., Sundararaman, H., Warner, M.: Testing and status of the LSST hexapods and rotator. In: Proceedings of SPIE, Austin, Texas, USA (2018). https://doi.org/10.1117/12.2311500
13. Sneed, R., et al.: Final design of the LSST hexapods and rotator. In: Proceedings of SPIE, Edinburgh, UK (2016). https://doi.org/10.1117/12.2231327
14. Yun, H., Liu, L., Li, Q., Li, W., Tang, L.: Development of an isotropic Stewart platform for telescope secondary mirror. Mech. Syst. Signal Process. **127**(1), 328–344 (2019). https://doi.org/10.1016/j.ymssp.2019.03.001

15. Yun, H., Liu, L., Li, Q., Yang, H.: Investigation on two-stage vibration suppression and precision pointing for space optical payloads. Aerosp. Sci. Technol. **96**(1), 105543 (2020). https://doi.org/10.1016/j.ast.2019.105543

16. Yang, D.-H., Cheng, Y., Wu, C.C., Fei, F., Jin, Z.Y.: A novel hexapod and its prototype for secondary mirror alignment in telescopes. Res. Astron. Astrophys. **18**(9), 115 (2018). https://doi.org/10.1088/1674-4527/18/9/115

Dynamic Modeling and Control of Winch-Integrated Cable-Driven Parallel Robots Using Singular Perturbation Method

Dongxing Li[1] , Senhao Hou[1], Yuheng Wang[1], and Xiaoqiang Tang[1,2(✉)]

[1] State Key Laboratory of Tribology, Department of Mechanical Engineering,
Tsinghua University, Beijing 100084, China
tang-xq@mail.tsinghua.edu.cn
[2] Beijing Key Laboratory of Tribology, Department of Mechanical Engineering,
Tsinghua University, Beijing 100084, China

Abstract. A winch-integrated cable-driven parallel robot (WICDPR) is a cable robot with winches mounted on the mobile platform. Such configuration leads to dynamic coupling effects between the winches and the mobile platform. The coupling effects, along with the elasticity of the cables, can cause unexpected vibrations in robot motion. In this paper, a controller design method for the WICDPRs considering cable elasticity and dynamic coupling effects is proposed based on the singular perturbation theory. Firstly, the elastic dynamic model of the WICD-PRs is established by considering the cable as an axial spring. Using the singular perturbation method, the elastic system is decomposed into two subsystems: a reduced-order system and a boundary layer system, achieving decoupling between rigid dynamics and elastic behavior. Then, the stability conditions of the overall closed-loop system are given by using the Tikhonov's theorem, and a composite controller comprising a rigid controller and an auxiliary controller is designed based on the stability conditions. Finally, the effectiveness of the proposed control scheme is verified through simulations.

Keywords: Dynamics control · Cable elasticity · Winch-integrated · Cable-driven parallel robots · Singular perturbation

1 Introduction

Cable-driven parallel robots (CDPRs) are a special type of parallel robot with advantages such as large workspace, outstanding dynamic performance, and high load capacity [1]. These unique advantages have led to the widespread application of CDPRs in many fields, such as radio telescopes [2], medical instruments [3],

Supported by the National Natural Science Foundation of China (Grant No. 51975044 and No. 51975307).

H. Yang et al. (Eds.): ICIRA 2023, LNAI 14273, pp. 390–401, 2023.
https://doi.org/10.1007/978-981-99-6498-7_34

manufacturing [4] and construction [5]. Typically, a CDPR consists of a mobile platform, a fixed frame, a driving system, a control system, and cables. In most applications, the driving system is installed on the fixed frame (see Fig. 1(a)) to achieve better dynamic performance and load capacity. However, changing the workspace of a cable-driven parallel robot is relatively difficult, as it requires the reinstallation of the driving system [6]. This makes traditional CDPRs inconvenient for use in some complex environments, such as outdoor and space environments.

To improve the flexibility, reconfigurability, and ease of installation of CDPRs, integrating the driving system and other components onto the moving platform is a feasible option (see Fig. 1(b)). Some existing studies have adopted this design. The Charlotte robot [7], for example, was developed to perform tedious and routine tasks in place of astronauts. The winches and control system are all contained within the robot's work envelope, and a video subsystem with two cameras is integrated inside it. The robot unit weighs less than 20 kg. Another example is the SpiderBot, an underconstrained cable-suspended mobile robot [8,9], where the actuation system of the robot is mounted on the motion platform. By changing its internal configuration, the SpiderBot can perform stable motion. Other cases of winch-integrated CDPRs (WICDPRs) are presented in [6,10].

However, the integrated design brings challenges to the motion control of the robot, especially when considering the elasticity of the cables. When considering the elasticity of cables, actuator position is not directly related to the mobile platform position. As a result, the motor acceleration cannot be directly calculated, making it hard to solve the inverse dynamics of the system. This increases the difficulty of the control system design and stability analysis for CDPRs. For distributed CDPRs whose winches are mounted on the fixed frame, the dynamic equations of the system have a chain integral form, and a cascade control scheme is suitable for such system. The singular perturbation theory can be used for stability analysis of the cascaded control scheme [11–13]. For WICDPRs, both cable elasticity and dynamic coupling effects can cause undesired vibrations. To achieve smooth robot motion, it is necessary to reduce the undesired vibrations. However, for WICDPRs, due to the dynamic couplings between the winches and the mobile platform, it is not allowing to directly design their cascade control scheme.

To address the abovementioned issues, this paper proposes a controller design method for WICDPRs based on singular perturbation theory, considering dynamic coupling effects and cable elasticity. By analyzing the elastic dynamic model in separate time scales, the elastic system can be decomposed into two subsystems: the fast system and the slow system. The slow subsystem (or reduced-order subsystem) is exactly the rigid dynamic model of WICDPRs and the cable elasticity is reflected in the fast subsystem (or boundary-layer subsystem), which achieves decoupling of elasticity and rigidity. Then, a controller can be separately designed for each model.

This article is organized as follows. The elastic dynamic model of WICDPRs is presented in the second section. The singular perturbation model is established in the third section. Then, the controller design processes is introduced in the fourth section and the simulation results is presented in the fifth section. Finally, the conclusions is discussed in the sixth section.

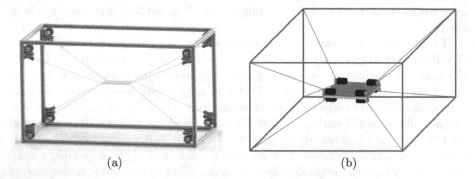

Fig. 1. (a): A CDPR with winches located on the fixed frame. (b): A CDPR with winches located on the mobile platform

2   Dynamic Model

This section presents the dynamic model of an ICDPR considering the cable elasticity. The end-effector pose is given by vector containing both the plat-form position vector $P = [x, y, z]^T$ and orientation vector $\psi = [\alpha, \beta, \gamma]^T$. The orientation vector is defined by Euler angles. The winch angular positions are denoted by vector $\theta = [\theta_1, \theta_2, \cdots, \theta_m]^T$. Let $L_1 = [l_{11}, l_{12}, \cdots, l_{1m}]^T$ denotes the lengths of the cables under tension. $L_2 = [l_{21}, l_{22}, \cdots, l_{2m}]^T$ denotes the lengths of the cables when cable tensions are zero, which can be calculated by the winch angular positions θ:

$$L_2 = L_0 - r\theta, \tag{1}$$

where L_0 is free lengths of the cables corresponding to pose $X = 0$ and r is the identical radii of winches. The cables are modeled as massless axial spring and assumed to be linear within nominal tension bounds. The stiffness of each cable is given by

$$k_i = \frac{ES}{l_{1i}}, i = 1, 2, \cdots, m, \tag{2}$$

where E is the Young's modulus of cables and S is the cross section of cables. Then, the dynamic model of ICDPRs with elastic cables can be written as

$$\begin{bmatrix} M(x) & S(x) \\ S^T(x) & I_w \end{bmatrix} \begin{bmatrix} \dot{t} \\ \ddot{\theta} \end{bmatrix} + \begin{bmatrix} C(x, \dot{x}) & C_w(x, \dot{x}) \\ 0_{m \times 6} & 0_{m \times m} \end{bmatrix} \begin{bmatrix} t \\ \dot{\theta} \end{bmatrix}$$
$$= \begin{bmatrix} A^T K(L_1(x) - L_2(\theta)) + W \\ T - rK(L_1(x) - L_2(\theta)) \end{bmatrix}, \tag{3}$$

where $M(x)$ is the 6×6 inertia matrix, I_w is the diagonal stiffness matrix of winch moment of inertia, $t = [\dot{p}^T, \omega^T]^T$ is the twist of the mobile platform, $S(x) \in \mathbb{R}^{6 \times m}$ and $C_w(x, \dot{x}) \in \mathbb{R}^{6 \times m}$ are the dynamic coupling terms, $C(x, \dot{x}) \in \mathbb{R}^{6 \times 6}$ denotes the Coriolis and centripetal terms, $K = \text{diag}[k_1, k_2, \cdots, k_m]$ is the stiffness matrix of cables, W represents the external wrenches including gravity, $T = [T_1, T_2, \cdots, T_m]^T$ is the vector of output torques of winches, and A is the Jacobian matrix of robot such that $\dot{L}_1 = A\dot{x}$. The first 6 equations and the last m equations in Eq. (3) represents the dynamics of the mobile platform and actuators, respectively.

Since the angular velocity ω is not equal to the derivative of the angular coordinates ψ, the following relation need to be introduce

$$t = Q\dot{x}, \tag{4}$$

$$\dot{t} = Q\ddot{x} + \dot{Q}\dot{x}. \tag{5}$$

Using (4) and (5) in (3) yields

$$\begin{bmatrix} MQ & S \\ S^T Q & B \end{bmatrix} \begin{bmatrix} \ddot{x} \\ \ddot{\theta} \end{bmatrix} + \begin{bmatrix} CQ + M\dot{Q}(x, \dot{x}) & C_w \\ S^T \dot{Q} & 0_{m \times m} \end{bmatrix} \begin{bmatrix} \dot{x} \\ \dot{\theta} \end{bmatrix} = \begin{bmatrix} A^T K (L_1 - L_2) + W \\ T - rK(L_1 - L_2) \end{bmatrix}. \tag{6}$$

3   Singular Perturbation Model

To apply the singular perturbation theory to the elastic system (3), the fast variable is defined as $z = K(L_1 - L_2)$. The diagonal stiffness matrix is assumed to have relatively large and similar elements, then a common scalar factor can be extracted as

$$K = \frac{\hat{K}}{\epsilon^2} = \frac{1}{\epsilon^2} \text{diag}\left[\hat{K}_1, \hat{K}_2, ..., \hat{K}_m\right], \hat{K}_i = O(1). \tag{7}$$

Replace the variable θ with the fast variable z, system (6) can be written as

$$\begin{bmatrix} MQ + r^{-1}SAQ & r^{-1}S\hat{K}^{-1} \\ S^T Q + r^{-1}I_w AQ & r^{-1}I_w \hat{K}^{-1} \end{bmatrix} \begin{bmatrix} \ddot{x} \\ \epsilon^2 \ddot{z} \end{bmatrix} +$$
$$\begin{bmatrix} CQ + M\dot{Q} + r^{-1}SA\dot{Q} + r^{-1}S\dot{A}Q + r^{-1}C_w AQ & r^{-1}C_w \hat{K}^{-1} \\ S^T \dot{Q} + r^{-1}I_w A\dot{Q} + r^{-1}I_w \dot{A}Q & 0_{m \times m} \end{bmatrix} \begin{bmatrix} \dot{x} \\ \epsilon^2 \dot{z} \end{bmatrix} \tag{8}$$
$$= \begin{bmatrix} A^T z + W \\ T - rz \end{bmatrix}.$$

When ϵ is set to zero, the dynamic equations of actuators reduce to algebraic equations. Then the quasi-steady state of z can be obtained as

$$\bar{z} = r^{-1}T - r^{-1}\left(S^T Q + r^{-1}I_w AQ\right)\ddot{x} - r^{-1}\left(S^T \dot{Q} + r^{-1}BA\dot{Q} + r^{-1}B\dot{A}Q\right)\dot{x}. \tag{9}$$

Substituting (9) to the dynamic equations of mobile platform yields the slow system

$$(M + r^{-1}SA + r^{-1}A^{T}S^{T} + r^{-2}A^{T}BA)Q\ddot{x} + [(r^{-1}S\dot{A} + C + r^{-1}C_{w}A$$
$$+ r^{-2}A^{T}B\dot{A})Q + (M + r^{-1}SA + r^{-1}A^{T}S^{T} + r^{-2}A^{T}BA)\dot{Q}]\dot{x}$$
$$= A^{T}r^{-1}T\mid_{\epsilon=0} + W.$$

(10)

System (10) is exactly the rigid model of WICDPRs. It can be abbreviated as

$$M_{eq}\ddot{x} + C_{eq}\dot{x} = A^{T}r^{-1}T_{S} + W,$$

(11)

where $T_{s} = T\mid_{\epsilon=0}$.

The fast system can be obtained by analyzing system (5) in the fast time scale $\tau = t/\epsilon$. The first step is to arrange Eq. (8) into the standard singular perturbation form as follows

$$\begin{aligned}\dot{X} &= f(t, X, Z, \epsilon)\\ \epsilon\dot{Z} &= g(t, X, Z, \epsilon)\end{aligned},$$

(12)

in which

$$X = \begin{bmatrix} x_1 \\ x_2 \end{bmatrix} = \begin{bmatrix} x \\ \dot{x} \end{bmatrix}$$

(13)

and

$$Z = \begin{bmatrix} z_1 \\ z_2 \end{bmatrix} = \begin{bmatrix} K(L_1 - L_2) \\ \epsilon K(\dot{L}_1 - \dot{L}_2) \end{bmatrix}.$$

(14)

The inverse of the block matrix

$$\begin{bmatrix} MQ + r^{-1}S_1AQ & r^{-1}S\hat{K}^{-1} \\ S^{T}Q + r^{-1}I_{w}AQ & r^{-1}I_{w}\hat{K}^{-1} \end{bmatrix}$$

(15)

can be abbreviated as

$$H = \begin{bmatrix} MQ + r^{-1}S_1AQ & r^{-1}S\hat{K}^{-1} \\ S^{T}Q + r^{-1}I_{w}AQ & r^{-1}I_{w}\hat{K}^{-1} \end{bmatrix}^{-1} = \begin{bmatrix} H_{11} & H_{12} \\ H_{21} & H_{22} \end{bmatrix}.$$

(16)

Let

$$\begin{bmatrix} C_{11} & C_{12} \\ C_{21} & C_{22} \end{bmatrix} = \begin{bmatrix} CQ + M\dot{Q} + r^{-1}SA\dot{Q} + r^{-1}S\dot{A}Q + r^{-1}C_{w}AQ & r^{-1}C_{w}\hat{K}^{-1} \\ S^{T}\dot{Q} + r^{-1}I_{w}A\dot{Q} + r^{-1}I_{w}\dot{A}Q & 0_{m\times m} \end{bmatrix}.$$

(17)

Then Eq. (8) can be written as

$$\begin{bmatrix} \ddot{x} \\ \epsilon^2\ddot{z} \end{bmatrix} + \begin{bmatrix} H_{11} & H_{12} \\ H_{21} & H_{22} \end{bmatrix}\begin{bmatrix} C_{11} & C_{12} \\ C_{21} & 0_{m\times m} \end{bmatrix}\begin{bmatrix} \dot{x} \\ \epsilon^2\dot{z} \end{bmatrix} = \begin{bmatrix} H_{11} & H_{12} \\ H_{21} & H_{22} \end{bmatrix}\begin{bmatrix} A^{T}z + W \\ T - rz \end{bmatrix}.$$

(18)

Substituting Eq. (13) and Eq. (14) into Eq. (18), the state space form of the system can be obtained as

$$
\dot{\boldsymbol{X}} = \begin{bmatrix} \dot{\boldsymbol{x}}_1 \\ \dot{\boldsymbol{x}}_2 \end{bmatrix}
$$

$$
= \begin{bmatrix} \boldsymbol{x}_2 \\ [-\left(\boldsymbol{H}_{11}\boldsymbol{C}_{11} + \boldsymbol{H}_{12}\boldsymbol{C}_{21}\right)\boldsymbol{x}_2 - \epsilon\boldsymbol{H}_{11}\boldsymbol{C}_{12}\boldsymbol{z}_2+ \\ \left(\boldsymbol{H}_{11}\boldsymbol{A}^{\mathrm{T}} - r\boldsymbol{H}_{12}\right)\boldsymbol{z}_1 + \boldsymbol{H}_{11}\boldsymbol{W} + \boldsymbol{H}_{12}\boldsymbol{T}] \end{bmatrix}, \tag{19}
$$

$$
\epsilon\dot{\boldsymbol{Z}} = \begin{bmatrix} \epsilon\dot{\boldsymbol{z}}_1 \\ \epsilon\dot{\boldsymbol{z}}_2 \end{bmatrix}
$$

$$
= \begin{bmatrix} \boldsymbol{z}_2 \\ [-\left(\boldsymbol{H}_{21}\boldsymbol{C}_{11} + \boldsymbol{H}_{22}\boldsymbol{C}_{21}\right)\boldsymbol{x}_2 - \epsilon\boldsymbol{H}_{21}\boldsymbol{C}_{12}\boldsymbol{z}_2+ \\ \left(\boldsymbol{H}_{21}\boldsymbol{A}^{\mathrm{T}} - r\boldsymbol{H}_{22}\right)\boldsymbol{z}_1 + \boldsymbol{H}_{21}\boldsymbol{W} + \boldsymbol{H}_{22}\boldsymbol{T}] \end{bmatrix}. \tag{20}
$$

If ϵ is set to zero, an alternative expression for the slow subsystem can be obtained, and another expression of the quasi-steady state of $\boldsymbol{z}$ can be obtained as

$$
\bar{\boldsymbol{z}}_1 = h\left(t, \boldsymbol{X}\right)
$$

$$
= \left(\boldsymbol{H}_{21}\boldsymbol{A}^{\mathrm{T}} - r\boldsymbol{H}_{22}\right)^{-1}\left(\left(\boldsymbol{H}_{21}\boldsymbol{C}_{11} + \boldsymbol{H}_{22}\boldsymbol{C}_{21}\right)\boldsymbol{x}_2 - \boldsymbol{H}_{21}\boldsymbol{W} - \boldsymbol{H}_{22}\boldsymbol{T}_S\right). \tag{21}
$$

In the fast time scale, system (19) and (20 becomes

$$
\frac{\mathrm{d}\boldsymbol{X}}{\mathrm{d}\tau} = \begin{bmatrix} \frac{\mathrm{d}\boldsymbol{x}_1}{\mathrm{d}\tau} \\ \frac{\mathrm{d}\boldsymbol{x}_2}{\mathrm{d}\tau} \end{bmatrix}
$$

$$
= \begin{bmatrix} \epsilon\boldsymbol{x}_2 \\ \epsilon[-\left(\boldsymbol{H}_{11}\boldsymbol{C}_{11} + \boldsymbol{H}_{12}\boldsymbol{C}_{21}\right)\boldsymbol{x}_2 - \epsilon\boldsymbol{H}_{11}\boldsymbol{C}_{12}\boldsymbol{z}_2 \\ + \left(\boldsymbol{H}_{11}\boldsymbol{A}^{\mathrm{T}} - r\boldsymbol{H}_{12}\right)\boldsymbol{z}_1 + \boldsymbol{H}_{11}\boldsymbol{W} + \boldsymbol{H}_{12}\boldsymbol{T}] \end{bmatrix}, \tag{22}
$$

$$
\frac{\mathrm{d}\boldsymbol{y}}{\mathrm{d}\tau} = \begin{bmatrix} \frac{\mathrm{d}\boldsymbol{y}_1}{\mathrm{d}\tau} \\ \frac{\mathrm{d}\boldsymbol{y}_2}{\mathrm{d}\tau} \end{bmatrix}
$$

$$
= \begin{bmatrix} \boldsymbol{y}_2 - \frac{\mathrm{d}\bar{\boldsymbol{z}}}{\mathrm{d}\tau} \\ [-\left(\boldsymbol{H}_{21}\boldsymbol{C}_{11} + \boldsymbol{H}_{22}\boldsymbol{C}_{21}\right)\boldsymbol{x}_2 - \epsilon\boldsymbol{H}_{21}\boldsymbol{C}_{12}\boldsymbol{y}_2 \\ + \left(\boldsymbol{H}_{21}\boldsymbol{A}^{\mathrm{T}} - r\boldsymbol{H}_{22}\right)\left(\boldsymbol{y}_1 + \bar{\boldsymbol{z}}\right) + \boldsymbol{H}_{21}\boldsymbol{W} + \boldsymbol{H}_{22}\boldsymbol{T}] \end{bmatrix}, \tag{23}
$$

where $\boldsymbol{y}_1 = \boldsymbol{z}_1 - \bar{\boldsymbol{z}}$, and $\boldsymbol{y}_2 = \boldsymbol{z}_2$. The purpose of the variable transformation is to move the equilibrium point of the fast subsystem to the origin. Setting $\epsilon = 0$ in (22) and yields $\frac{\mathrm{d}\boldsymbol{X}}{\mathrm{d}\tau} = 0$. Thus, $\bar{\boldsymbol{z}} = h\left(t, \boldsymbol{X}\right)$ can be regarded as a constant in the fast time scale. Using (21), the fast system can be obtained as

$$
\frac{\mathrm{d}\boldsymbol{y}}{\mathrm{d}\tau} = \begin{bmatrix} \boldsymbol{y}_2 \\ \left(\boldsymbol{H}_{21}\boldsymbol{A}^{\mathrm{T}} - r\boldsymbol{H}_{22}\right)\boldsymbol{y}_1 + \boldsymbol{H}_{22}\boldsymbol{T}_f] \end{bmatrix}, \tag{24}
$$

where $\boldsymbol{T}_f = \boldsymbol{T} - \boldsymbol{T}_s$.

By analyzing the singular perturbation system at slow and fast time scales separately, the overall elastic dynamics model is decomposed into slow subsystems (11) and fast subsystems (24). This decomposition achieves the decoupling of platform dynamics and cable dynamics. In the next section, the design of control strategy based on the Tikhonov's theorem.

4   Controller Design

The Tikhonov's theorem specifies the conditions that must be satisfied for the solutions of subsystems (11) and (24) to approximate the entire system (8). Moreover, the theorem can provide guidance for the design of control schemes for the system.

Theorem 1. *If the following conditions are satisfied for all $[t, \boldsymbol{X}, \boldsymbol{y}, \epsilon] \in [0, \infty) \times D_{\boldsymbol{X}} \times D_{\boldsymbol{y}} \times [0, \epsilon_0]$:*

1) on any compact subset of $D_{\boldsymbol{X}} \times D_{\boldsymbol{y}}$ including the origin, the functions f, g, their first partial derivatives with respect to $(\boldsymbol{X}, \boldsymbol{Z}, \epsilon)$, and the first partial derivative of g with respect to t are continuous and bounded, $h(t, \boldsymbol{X})$ and $[\partial g(t, \boldsymbol{X}, \boldsymbol{Z}, 0)/\partial \boldsymbol{Z}]$ have bounded first partial derivatives with respect to their arguments, and $[\partial f(t, \boldsymbol{X}, h(t, \boldsymbol{X}), 0)/\partial \boldsymbol{X}]$ is Lipschitz in $\boldsymbol{X}$, uniformly in t; the initial data are smooth functions of ϵ.

2) the origin is an exponentially stable equilibrium point of the reduced system (8).

3) the origin is an exponentially stable equilibrium point of the boundary-layer model uniformly in $(t, \boldsymbol{X})$.

Then, there is a positive constant ϵ^* such that for all $t \geqslant t_0 > 0$ and $0 < \epsilon < \epsilon^*$, the singular perturbation problem of (13) and (14) has a unique solution $\boldsymbol{X}(t, \epsilon)$, $\boldsymbol{Z}(t, \epsilon)$ on $[t_0, \infty)$, and

$$\boldsymbol{X}(t, \epsilon) - \bar{\boldsymbol{X}}(t) = O(\epsilon), \tag{25}$$

$$\boldsymbol{Z}(t, \epsilon) - h\left(t, \bar{\boldsymbol{X}}(t)\right) - \hat{\boldsymbol{y}}(\tau) = O(\epsilon), \tag{26}$$

in which $\bar{\boldsymbol{X}}(t)$ is the solution of the reduced model (11) and $\hat{\boldsymbol{y}}(\tau)$ is the solution of the boundary layer (24).

The first condition is automatically satisfied if the control input $\boldsymbol{T}$ is continuous and bounded, and the CDPR is within the feasible workspace. To satisfy the second and third conditions, we need to design the control inputs $\boldsymbol{T}_s$ and $\boldsymbol{T}_f$ for the two subsystems respectively. To achieve exponential stability at zero for the slow subsystem, we apply a classical feedback linearization control law to the slow subsystem (11):

$$\boldsymbol{T}_S = r\boldsymbol{A}^{\mathrm{T}\dagger}\left(\boldsymbol{M}_{eq}\left(\ddot{\boldsymbol{x}}^* + \boldsymbol{K}_v\left(\dot{\boldsymbol{x}}^* - \dot{\boldsymbol{x}}\right) + \boldsymbol{K}_p\left(\boldsymbol{x}^* - \boldsymbol{x}\right)\right) + \boldsymbol{C}_{eq}\dot{\boldsymbol{x}} - \boldsymbol{W}\right) + \boldsymbol{T}_{\mathrm{null}}. \tag{27}$$

Defining the tracking error as $e = x^* - x$, the closed-loop system becomes

$$\begin{bmatrix} \dot{e} \\ \ddot{e} \end{bmatrix} = \begin{bmatrix} 0 & I \\ -K_p & -K_v \end{bmatrix} \begin{bmatrix} e \\ \dot{e} \end{bmatrix}. \tag{28}$$

Obviously, the origin is an exponentially stable equilibrium point of the reduced system if $K_v > 0$ and $K_p > 0$. Similarly, the following feedback linearization control law is used for the fast subsystem

$$T_f = -H_{22}^{-1} K_{pf} y_1 - H_{22}^{-1} \left(H_{21} A^T - r H_{22} \right) y_1 - H_{22}^{-1} K_{vf} y_2, \tag{29}$$

where K_{pf} and K_{vf} are diagonal gain matrices. Substituting (29) into the fast system (24) yields the closed-loop system as

$$\frac{dy}{d\tau} = \begin{bmatrix} 0 & I \\ -K_{pf} & -K_{vf} \end{bmatrix} \begin{bmatrix} y_1 \\ y_2 \end{bmatrix}. \tag{30}$$

The origin is an exponentially stable equilibrium point of the boundary-layer system if $K_{vf} > 0$ and $K_{vf} > 0$. Finally, the composite controller $T = T_s + T_f$ is obtained.

5 Case Study

In order to validate the effectiveness of the proposed control scheme, a simulation study was conducted on a six-degree-of-freedom WICDPR with eight cables. The parametric values in SI units used in the simulations are listed in Table 1. The gains of the slow control law (27) are setting as $K_p = \text{diag}\,(5,5,5,10,10,10)$ and $K_v = \text{diag}\,(0.4,0.4,0.4,0.8,0.8,0.8)$ The gains of the fast control law (29) is setting as $K_{pf} = 0.7 I_{8\times 8}$ and $K_{vf} = 0.3 I_{8\times 8}$.

Table 1. Parameter values for the simulations

Parameter	Value	Unit
Size of the fixed frame	$3 \times 3 \times 2$	m
Size of the mobile platform	$0.6 \times 0.4 \times 0.15$	m
Mass of the mobile platform	12	kg
Inertia tensor of the mobile platform	$\text{diag}\,(0.31, 0.3, 0.47)$	$\text{kg} \cdot \text{m}^2$
Range of the drive torque	0.1 to 6	Nm
Drum radius	0.02	m
Winch moment of inertia	1.5×10^{-3}	$\text{kg} \cdot \text{m}^2$

Initially, the step response of the system was examined from $x = 0$ to $x = 0.15$. Figure 2 illustrates the output response when only rigid control T_s is applied to the system. Figure 3 presents the response of the robot system under composite control $T = T_s + T_f$. It can be observed that the system exhibits much more stable motion under composite control. Figure 4 illustrates the variations of tension forces in two ropes under different control schemes. The red and blue curves depict the results of the composite controller. It can be observed that when employing the composite controller, the tension in the cables stabilizes rapidly. Conversely, the green and cyan curves, representing the results of the rigid controller, exhibit slower stabilization of cable tensions. This observation highlights the effectiveness of the composite control scheme in achieving quick and stable tension control in the ropes.

During the initial stages of motion, the composite control scheme displays larger cable tension oscillations. This is primarily because the auxiliary controller T_f primarily operates in the early stages of motion to facilitate rapid convergence of the cable tensions to the desired values. Once the cable tensions stabilize, the output of the auxiliary controller becomes very small, and the rigid controller T_s takes over. Moreover, the dynamic performance metrics of the system, such as rise time and peak time, show negligible differences between the two control schemes. This implies that the inclusion of the auxiliary controller has virtually no impact on the dynamic performance of the system, while significantly improving the stability of the system's motion, which is an almost perfect outcome.

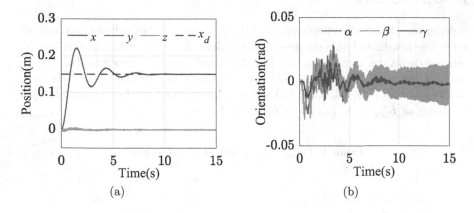

(a)   (b)

Fig. 2. Simulation results of the rigid control

In order to enhance the dynamic performance of the system, the speed feedback gain is increased to $K_v = \mathrm{diag}\,(2, 2, 2, 4, 4, 4)$ in the subsequent simulation. However, the system output under rigid control becomes unstable with this set of parameters. The system output of the composite control scheme, as depicted in Fig. 5, exhibits a noticeable improvement in the stability time of the system.

In order to validate the tracking performance of the closed-loop system for continuous trajectories, the following reference trajectory was used for simulation:

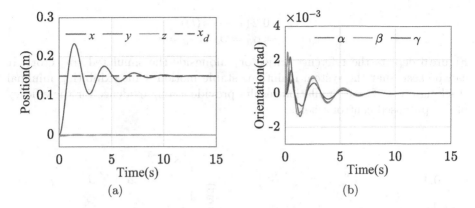

Fig. 3. Simulation results of the composite control

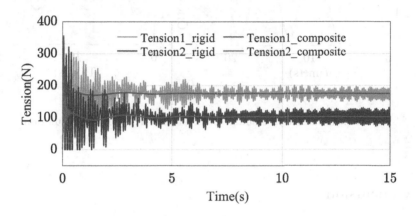

Fig. 4. Variation of tension in two cables under different control schemes.

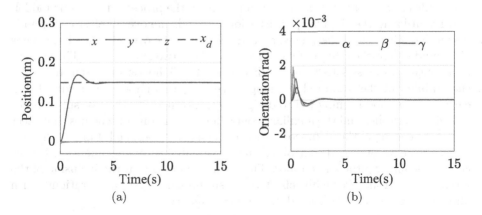

Fig. 5. Simulation results of the composite with larger feedback gains.

$$x_d = 0.2\left(1 - \cos\left(t\right)\right),$$
$$y_d = z_d = \alpha_d = \beta_d = \gamma_d = 0. \tag{31}$$

Figure 6 depicts the reference trajectory alongside the simulated trajectory. It can be seen that the system maintains stable motion while exhibiting minimal tracking error. These simulation results provide strong evidence for the efficacy of the proposed control scheme.

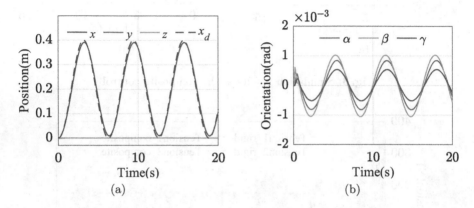

Fig. 6. (a): Simulation results. (b): Tracking errors of the simulation

6   Conclusion

This paper presents a control scheme for winch-integrated cable-driven parallel robots based on the singular perturbation method. The dynamic coupling effect and cable elasticity are taken into account during the process of dynamic modeling. By utilizing the singular perturbation method, the overall elastic system is decomposed into two subsystems, and the design of the overall control scheme is also divided into the design of controllers for these two subsystems. The subsystem controllers must satisfy the conditions of the Tikhonov's theorem to ensure the stability of the overall closed-loop system. In this paper, the feedback linearization method is employed to design the controllers for the two subsystems: the rigid controller and the auxiliary controller. Other control schemes that meet the requirements of the Tikhonov's theorem can also be applied. Finally, the performance of the proposed control scheme is evaluated through simulation studies conducted on a spatial cable robot. The results indicate that the inclusion of the auxiliary controller is highly effective in suppressing system vibrations, with almost no loss in the system's dynamic performance.

References

1. Pott, A.: Cable-Driven Parallel Robots: Theory and Application, Springer Tracts in Advanced Robotics, vol. 120. Springer, Cham (2018). https://doi.org/10.1007/978-3-319-76138-1
2. Yao, R., Tang, X., Wang, J., Huang, P.: Dimensional optimization design of the four-cable-driven parallel manipulator in FAST. IEEE/ASME Trans. Mechatron. **15**(6), 932–941 (2010). https://doi.org/10.1109/TMECH.2009.2035922
3. Li, C., et al.: Reconfigurable cable-driven parallel robot with adjustable workspace towards positioning in neurosurgery: a preliminary design. In: 2021 IEEE International Conference on Real-time Computing and Robotics (RCAR), pp. 51–56. IEEE, Xining, China, July 2021. https://doi.org/10.1109/RCAR52367.2021.9517400
4. Gueners, D., Chanal, H., Bouzgarrou, B.C.: Design and implementation of a cable-driven parallel robot for additive manufacturing applications. Mechatronics **86**, 102874 (2022). https://doi.org/10.1016/j.mechatronics.2022.102874
5. Bruckmann, T., Boumann, R.: Simulation and optimization of automated masonry construction using cable robots. Adv. Eng. Inform. **50**, 101388 (2021). https://doi.org/10.1016/j.aei.2021.101388
6. An, H., Liu, H., Liu, X., Yuan, H.: An all-in-one cable-driven parallel robot with flexible workspace and its auto-calibration method. In: 2022 IEEE/RSJ International Conference on Intelligent Robots and Systems (IROS), pp. 7345–7351. IEEE, Kyoto, Japan, October 2022. https://doi.org/10.1109/IROS47612.2022.9982214
7. Perry D., C., Patrick L., S., Clark J., T.: Charlotte^{TM} robot technology for space and terrestrial applications. In: International Conference on Environmental Systems, vol. SAE Technical Paper 951520. SAE, United States, July 1995
8. Capua, A., Shapiro, A., Shoval, S.: Motion analysis of an underconstrained cable suspended mobile robot. In: 2009 IEEE International Conference on Robotics and Biomimetics (ROBIO), pp. 788–793. IEEE, Guilin, China, December 2009. https://doi.org/10.1109/ROBIO.2009.5420574
9. Capua, A., Shapiro, A., Shoval, S.: Motion planning algorithm for a mobile robot suspended by seven cables. In: 2010 IEEE Conference on Robotics, Automation and Mechatronics, pp. 504–509. IEEE, Singapore (Jun 2010). https://doi.org/10.1109/RAMECH.2010.5513143
10. Wang, D., et al.: Winch-integrated mobile end-effector for a cable-driven parallel robot with auto-installation. Int. J. Control Autom. Syst. **15**(5), 2355–2363 (2017). https://doi.org/10.1007/s12555-016-0398-7
11. Babaghasabha, R., Khosravi, M.A., Taghirad, H.D.: Adaptive robust control of fully constrained cable robots: Singular perturbation approach. Nonlinear Dyn. **85**(1), 607–620 (2016). https://doi.org/10.1007/s11071-016-2710-8
12. Begey, J., Cuvillon, L., Lesellier, M., Gouttefarde, M., Gangloff, J.: Dynamic control of parallel robots driven by flexible cables and actuated by position-controlled winches. IEEE Trans. Rob. **35**(1), 286–293 (2019). https://doi.org/10.1109/TRO.2018.2875415
13. Khosravi, M.A., Taghirad, H.D.: Dynamic modeling and control of parallel robots with elastic cables: singular perturbation approach. IEEE Trans. Rob. **30**(3), 694–704 (2014). https://doi.org/10.1109/TRO.2014.2298057

Multi-input Multi-output Sliding Mode Control with High Precision and Robustness for a 6-PSU Parallel Robot

Xin Liu, Jianfeng Lin, Dongjin Li, Chenkun Qi$^{(\boxtimes)}$, and Feng Gao

State Key Laboratory of Mechanical System and Vibration, School of Mechanical Engineering, Shanghai Jiao Tong University, Shanghai 200240, China
chenkqi@sjtu.edu.cn

Abstract. In high precision tasks, the parallel robot is a good choice due to their advantages of no cumulative errors and high stiffness. The six-degree-of-freedom (six-DOF) 6-PSU parallel robot has a much lower inertia, but is a multi-input multi-output (MIMO) system with complex non-linear dynamics. Currently, there are rare studies on high-precision robust control methods for 6-PSU parallel robots. In this paper, a simplified dynamics model of the robot is presented first. We distribute the mass of the connecting rod on the two end joints, and then establish a general second-order system model to characterize the dynamic characteristics of the system at a minimum cost. By introducing the sliding mode, a six-DOF sliding mode controller (6PSU-SMC) is developed, which can effectively suppress the internal model error disturbance and external disturbance. The results show that the developed controller perfectly solves the dynamics control problem and achieve a high precision and robustness tracking task.

Keywords: Parallel robot · Sliding mode control · Dynamics modeling

1 Introduction

Robots are often used in applications that require high precision and reliability. These require the system to have high motion control accuracy and robustness to cope with disturbances [1,2]. Parallel robots have many unique advantages that are different from traditional robots, such as small inertia, no cumulative error of chains, and high stiffness [3]. However, the closed-chain characteristics of parallel robots lead to the complexity of the model, which is reflected in the complexity of kinematics and dynamics modeling [4].

Six-DOF parallel robots can be used in more scenarios due to its complete DOF. In the field of six-DOF parallel robots, most researchers focus on traditional configurations, such as the 6-SPS Stewart platform [5]. However, the actuation parts of most of them move relative to the base, which has large inertia and the small working range. Our study is based on a 6-PSU parallel robot.

The motors of it are fixed on one side of the frame and do not follow the platform, so it has the characteristics of low inertia and high frequency response.

At present, researchers have developed many control schemes for parallel robots, such as computed torque control [6–8] and PID control [9,10]. However, most traditional controllers have poor performance in addressing issues of model inaccuracy and unmodeled errors. Computed torque control is very effective when modeling is completely accurate, but it is difficult to achieve for parallel robots because simplification and parameter errors lead to model errors [11]. PID control is a typical model independent control method, but it is suitable for single-input single-output systems. For complex multi-input multi-output systems, tedious decoupling and pairing operations are required, and the sensitivity of parameters cannot effectively suppress external disturbances [12].

Sliding mode control is characterized by variable structure, which can treat unmodeled disturbances and external disturbances as lumped disturbances and suppress them [13,14]. However, the problem with sliding mode controllers lies in the occurrence of chattering. The fundamental cause of the chattering problem lies in the mutation of the linear sliding membrane switching control law. Currently, many researchers have solved the buffeting problem through various methods [15,16]. Sliding mode controllers have been successfully applied in systems with high nonlinearity and strong hysteresis such as piezoelectric ceramic actuators. Researchers have achieved nanoscale tracking accuracy and solved hysteresis effects [17]. There are many similarities between piezoelectric actuators and parallel robots due to their highly nonlinear characteristics and difficulties in modeling. However, the 6-PSU parallel robot is a MIMO system, and its control is relatively more complex. Therefore, it is appropriate to apply sliding mode control technology to solve the high precision and high robustness control problem of the 6-PSU parallel robot.

In this paper, an effective sliding mode controller is designed for the tracking control of the six-DOF 6-PSU parallel robot to address model inaccuracy and anti-interference issues. Improving robustness while completing precise tracking is beneficial for achieving accurate operation tasks [18]. In addition, on the modeling of parallel robots, the clever simplification of the model makes the modeling process easier, but increases the problem of model uncertainty, which is perfectly solved by the robustness advantage of sliding mode control.

The following parts of the paper are organized as follows. Section 2 completes the kinematics and simplified dynamics modeling for the 6-PSU parallel robot. The sliding mode controller (6PSU-SMC) for the 6-PSU parallel robot is designed in Sect. 3. Section 4 completes the simulation to verify the effectiveness of the sliding mode controller. Conclusion is summarized in Sect. 5.

2   Modeling of the 6-PSU Parallel Robot

2.1   Kinematics Modeling

Figure 1 shows the 3D model of the 6-PSU parallel robot. It consists of a hexagonal prism base, an end-effector, and six PSU kinematic chains. The six prismatic joints (P-joints) are respectively driven by six motors and screw nuts. The spherical joints (S-joints) are connected to the sliders of the P-joints. On the prism side of the base, there are six parallel moving guides arranged, facilitating the movement of sliders driven by screw nuts along these guides to form a mobile P-joint. Subsequently, following the P-joint, an equivalent S-joint is constructed, consisting of three interconnected rotating R-joints with intersecting axes. In the initial configuration of the robot, the geometric centers of the six S-joints are theoretically positioned in a coplanar arrangement, distributed symmetrically along the vertices of a hexagonal shape. Additionally, the axis of the R-joint nearest to the P-joint side is perpendicular to the plane of the guide rail. The second R-joint axis is parallel to the plane of the mobile rail and perpendicular to the axis of the first R-joint. The third R-joint axis is intentionally aligned with the axis of the link.

Figure 2 annotates a PSU closed-loop chain. Define the base coordinate system as $\{O\}$ and the connected coordinate system as $\{O'\}$. The connected coordinate system is fixed on the end-effector. Define the centers S_i and U_i $(i = 1, 2, \ldots, 6)$ of the S-joints and U-joints. h_i represents the vector O pointing to S_i under $\{O\}$ at the initial position. u_i represents the vector O_1 pointing to U_i under $\{O\}$ at the initial position. l_i represents the link vector between S_i and U_i. e_i represents the movement direction vector of the slider. q_i is the displacement of the actuation. The displacement and angular displacement of the end-effector under $\{O\}$ are $p = [x, y, z]^T$ and $\theta = [\alpha, \beta, \gamma]^T$.

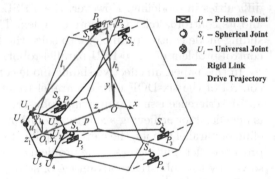

Fig. 1. 6-PSU parallel robot   Fig. 2. The robot mechanism diagram

According to $O - S_i - U_i - O_1$, the vector equation can be written as

$$p + u_i = h_i + q_i e_i + l_i. \tag{1}$$

The length of the link is L_i. Let $\xi_i = p + u_i - h_i$ and

$$L_i^2 = \|\xi_i - q_i e_i\|^2 = \xi_i^T \xi_i - 2\xi_i^T \cdot q_i e_i + q_i^2. \tag{2}$$

Separate the q_i and we can obtain the kinematics model:

$$q_i = \xi_i{}^T e_i - \sqrt{\left(\xi_i{}^T e_i\right)^2 - \xi_i{}^T \xi_i + L_i{}^2}. \tag{3}$$

2.2 Dynamics Modeling

To simplify the dynamics modeling, we divide the mass of the link equally at the joints. In fact, the mass of the lightweight link is much smaller than the mass of other parts, and this simplification is reasonable. Therefore, the mass of the equivalent P-joint and the equivalent end-effector are $m_{qi} = m_{si} + \frac{1}{2}m_{li}$ and $m_{dp} = m_p + 3m_{li}$ respectively. m_{si}, m_{li} and m_p are the mass of the slider, the link and the end-effector.

We establish the Newton-Euler equation for the moving parts. F and M are the external forces and moments to the end-effector respectively. $\dot{p}_c$ and $\ddot{p}_c$ under the $\{O'_c\}$ have changed due to the offset of the centroid:

$$\dot{p}_c = \dot{p} + \dot{\theta} \times r_{cmp}, \tag{4}$$

$$\ddot{p}_c = \ddot{p} + \ddot{\theta} \times r_{cmp} + \dot{\theta} \times \left(\dot{\theta} \times r_{cmp}\right), \tag{5}$$

where $r_{cmp} = Rr'_{cmp}$. R is the rotation matrix, and r'_{cmp} is the end-effector centroid position under $\{O'\}$. List the Newton and Euler equations for the equivalent end-effector:

$$F + \sum_{i=1}^{6} F_{lui} + m_{dp}g = m_{dp}\ddot{p}_c, \tag{6}$$

$$M + \sum_{i=1}^{6} \left(R\left(a'_i - r'_{cmp}\right) \times F_{lui}\right) = I_{dpo}\ddot{\theta} + \dot{\theta} \times \left(I_{dpo}\dot{\theta}\right), \tag{7}$$

where F_{lui} represents the restraining force of the link at the U-joint, a'_i is the U-joint position under $\{O'\}$, and I_{dpo} is the inertial tensor matrix of the equivalent end-effector for $\{O'_c\}$ under $\{O\}$.

For the equivalent link, it can be considered as a two-force link:

$$F_{lui} = -F_{lsi}, \tag{8}$$

where F_{lsi} represents the restraining force of the link at the S-joint.

u_i is the actuation force to the slider. The Newton equation for the slider is

$$u_i + m_{qi}g \cdot e_i + F_{lsi} \cdot e_i = m_{qi}\ddot{q}_i, \tag{9}$$

Then the single limb is extended to six limbs and organized into a matrix form:

$$u = M_q\ddot{q} + F_c, \tag{10}$$

where $u = \begin{bmatrix} u_1 & u_2 & \cdots & u_6 \end{bmatrix}^T$, $M_q = diag\left(m_{q1} \ m_{q2} \ \cdots \ m_{q6}\right)$, $\ddot{q} = \begin{bmatrix} \ddot{q}_1 & \ddot{q}_2 & \cdots & \ddot{q}_6 \end{bmatrix}^T$, and $F_c = \begin{bmatrix} F_{lu1} \cdot e_1 & F_{lu2} \cdot e_2 & \cdots & F_{lu6} \cdot e_6 \end{bmatrix}^T$.

The force analysis of the end-effector is based on $\{O'_c\}$, so the Jacobian matrix is

$$
G_c = \left[R(a'_1 - r'_{cmp}) \times \frac{l_1}{l_1 e_1} \quad R(a'_2 - r'_{cmp}) \times \frac{l_2}{l_2 e_2} \quad \cdots \quad R(a'_6 - r'_{cmp}) \times \frac{l_6}{l_6 e_6} \right].
$$
$$\frac{l_1}{l_1 e_1} \quad \frac{l_2}{l_2 e_2} \quad \cdots \quad \frac{l_6}{l_6 e_6}$$
(11)

Consider (5), (6), (7), (10), (11), and replace $\ddot{p}_c$ to get

$$
u = M_q \ddot{q} + G_c^{-1} M_{dp} \ddot{X} + G_c^{-1} \left[\begin{matrix} m_{dp}\left(\ddot{\theta} \times r_{cmp} + \dot{\theta} \times \left(\dot{\theta} \times r_{cmp}\right)\right) \\ I_{dpo}\ddot{\theta} + \dot{\theta} \times \left(I_{dpo}\dot{\theta}\right) \end{matrix} \right]
$$
$$
+ G_c^{-1} \left[\begin{matrix} -m_{dp}g \\ 0 \end{matrix} \right] + G_c^{-1} \left[\begin{matrix} -F \\ -M \end{matrix} \right],
$$
(12)

where $M_{dp} = \left[m_{dp}\mathbf{I} \; I_{dpo}^T \right]^T$, $\ddot{X} = \left[\ddot{p}^T \; \ddot{\theta}^T \right]^T$. And based on the kinematics, we can obtain

$$
u = \left(M_q + G_c^{-1} M_{dp}(G^T)^{-1} \right) \ddot{q} + G_c^{-1} M_{dp} \frac{d}{dt}(G^T)^{-1} \dot{q}
$$
$$
+ G_c^{-1} \left[\begin{matrix} m_{dp}\left(\ddot{\theta} \times r_{cmp} + \dot{\theta} \times \left(\dot{\theta} \times r_{cmp}\right)\right) \\ I_{dpo}\ddot{\theta} + \dot{\theta} \times \left(I_{dpo}\dot{\theta}\right) \end{matrix} \right] + G_c^{-1} \left[\begin{matrix} -m_{dp}g - F \\ -M \end{matrix} \right].
$$
(13)

Finally, it is sorted out as the general equivalent dynamics equation:

$$
M(q(t))\ddot{q}(t) + C(q(t), \dot{q}(t))\dot{q}(t) + G(q(t)) + \Gamma(t) = u(t),
$$
(14)

where q is the output of six actuation sliders, M is the generalized mass matrix, C is the Coriolis and centripetal term, G is the gravity term, and Γ is the external force on the system.

3   Design of the Sliding Mode Controller

3.1   Controlled System Model

By considering the dynamics without loads, we can obtain

$$
M(q(t))\ddot{q}(t) + C(q(t), \dot{q}(t))\dot{q}(t) + G(q(t)) = u(t) + d(t),
$$
(15)

where d is lumped disturbance including system unmodeled errors and external disturbances. For clarity, the following expressions omit time t.

3.2   Disturbance Estimation

According to (15), the disturbance can be solved by

$$
d = M\ddot{q} + C\dot{q} + G - u.
$$
(16)

However, the above equation cannot be implemented due to the algebraic ring. Therefore, d is estimated through the perturbation estimation technique [19]:

$$\bar{d} = M\ddot{q} + C\dot{q} + G - u\,(t - T)\,, \tag{17}$$

where T is the sampling time interval. Then the system (15) can be rewritten as

$$M\ddot{q} + C\dot{q} + G = u + \bar{d} + \tilde{d}, \tag{18}$$

where $\tilde{d} = d - \bar{d}$. Here, it is assumed that each element in the disturbance estimation and its rate of change are bounded, i.e. $\left|\tilde{d}\right| \leq \delta_1$ and $\left|\dot{\tilde{d}}\right| \leq \delta_2$. Where δ_1 and δ_2 are two specific constants and they represent the upper limits of disturbance estimation and its rate of change. The absolute value symbol here represents the absolute value of each element in the vector.

3.3 Design of the Sliding Mode Controller (6PSU-SMC)

Define the actuation tracking error vector as

$$e = q - q_d, \tag{19}$$

where q_d is the theoretical actuation calculated through the inverse kinematics according to the planned trajectory. We define a PD sliding mode function as

$$s = \dot{e} + ce, \tag{20}$$

where c is the positive definite diagonal constant gain matrix.

Then we take the derivative on both sides of equation (20) to obtain

$$\dot{s} = \ddot{e} + c\dot{e} = \ddot{q} - \ddot{q}_d + c\,(\dot{q} - \dot{q}_d)\,. \tag{21}$$

By substituting (18) into (21) and considering (17), the equivalent control law u_{eq} can be obtained.

$$u_{eq} = M \cdot [\ddot{q}_d - \ddot{q} - c\dot{e}] + u\,(t - T)\,. \tag{22}$$

The boundary layer technology is commonly used to alleviate the chattering problem [20]. The signum function is replaced by the smooth saturation function. We give a switch control law with boundary layer:

$$u_{sw} = -M\eta \cdot sat\,(s)\,, \tag{23}$$

$$sat\,(s\,(i)) = \begin{cases} \frac{s(i)}{\varepsilon(i)} & if\ \ |s\,(i)| \leq \varepsilon\,(i) \\ sign\,(s\,(i)) & if\ \ |s\,(i)| > \varepsilon\,(i) \end{cases}, \tag{24}$$

where η is the switch control gain coefficient. When the robot is affected by disturbance, it can be forced to move back to the sliding surface.

Then the sliding mode control law can be obtained as follows:

$$u = u_{eq} + u_{sw}. \tag{25}$$

And the sliding dynamics of the system is

$$\dot{s} = -\eta \cdot sat\,(s) + M^{-1}\tilde{d}. \tag{26}$$

According to (26), because M^{-1} and $\tilde{d}$ are bounded, $s = 0$ can be implemented in finite time [21]. Then, according to (20), it can be seen that $e = 0$ and $\dot{e} = 0$ can be implemented in finite time. An overview of our method is given in Fig. 3.

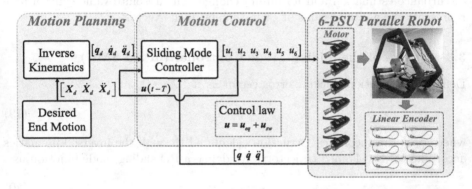

Fig. 3. The control method for the 6-PSU parallel robot

Table 1. Parameters of the 6-PSU parallel robot

Robot Parameters	Value
End-effector mass	2.172 kg
Link mass	0.0551 kg
Slider mass	0.613 kg
Initial position parameter of S-joint $\|h\|$	0.246 m
U-joint position parameter $\|u'\|$	0.082 m
Link length $\|l\|$	0.26 m
End-effector centroid offset (under $\{O'\}$)	$\begin{bmatrix} 0 & 0 & 0.02714 \end{bmatrix}^T$
End-effector inertia tensor matrix (under $\{O'_c\}$)	$diag\left(0.00732,\ 0.00732,\ 0.01286 \right)$

Table 2. Sliding mode controller parameters

Controller Parameters	Value
c	$diag\left(\ 35,\ 35,\ 35,\ 35,\ 35,\ 35\ \right)$
η	$diag\left(\ 1,\ 1,\ 1,\ 1,\ 1,\ 1\ \right)$
ε	$\left[\ 0.02\ 0.02\ 0.02\ 0.02\ 0.02\ 0.02\ \right]^{T}$

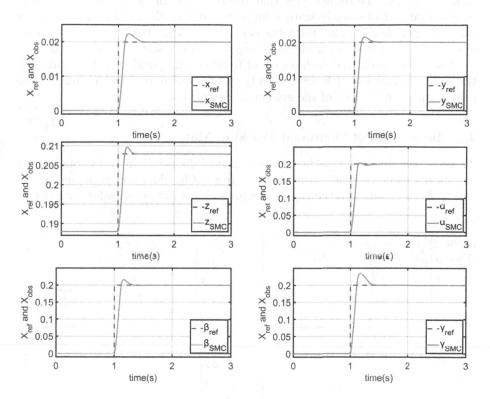

Fig. 4. Step response of the 6-PSU robot

Table 3. RMS at steady state of step response

DOF	$x\ (m)$	$y\ (m)$	$z\ (m)$	$\alpha\ (rad)$	$\beta\ (rad)$	$\gamma\ (rad)$
RMS	4.512988e-6	1.981510e-6	9.663002e-7	4.273362e-5	3.326828e-5	8.433375e-6

4 Simulation Results

The robot parameter values are shown in Table 1. The inputs of the physical system are the six actuation forces generated by the controller, and the outputs of the system are position, velocity, and acceleration of the end-effector.

4.1   Step Response Result

In this paper, step response is performed on each output to verify the effectiveness of the controller. By adjusting the controller parameters with a trial-and-error method, the rise time and overshoot are balanced. The parameters of the sliding mode controller are shown in Table 2. The sampling interval is T=0.001 s.

After simulation, the step response results of each degree of freedom are shown in Fig. 4. The results show that the rise time for each degree of freedom to reach 90% of the steady-state value is approximately 0.104 s. Finally, under the sliding mode controller, the robot can achieve target tracking. And the RMS of each degree of freedom in the step response steady state is shown in Table 3.

The results show that each degree of freedom can quickly track step instructions. The magnitude of RMS at steady state is about 10^{-6}, which reflects the zero-static characteristic of the system at steady state.

4.2   Simulation of Sinusoidal Tracking Motion

To verify the dynamic tracking performance of the 6-PSU parallel robot under the sliding mode controller, the all six degrees of freedom are given sine trajectories. After simulation, the tracking results of sine trajectories for each degree

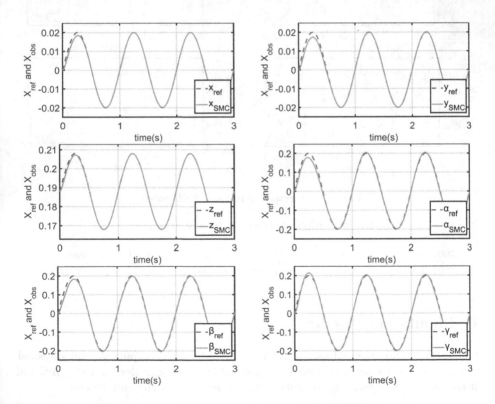

Fig. 5. Sinusoidal Motion Tracking of the 6-PSU robot

of freedom are shown in Fig. 5. And the RMS of each degree of freedom reaching steady-state is shown in the first row of the Table 4.

The results show that in sinusoidal dynamic trajectory, the system has an excellent tracking performance. The magnitude of RMS is about 10^{-5} in linear displacements and 10^{-3} in angular displacements. The results show that the trajectory can be tracked with very small errors when entering the stable tracking phase.

4.3   Robust Performance Test

In fact, the robot has model mismatch problems with inaccurate parameters, which are considered the internal disturbance. Moreover, the robot is simplified as a second-order system, which results in unmodeled errors. Nevertheless, the robot can still achieve great response, which has confirmed the robustness to some extent.

We further verify the robustness to deal with load disturbances by adjusting the end-effector mass. The load was ignored when designing the controller, in other words, the real model deviates from the actual model. In this case, the system is required to track the same sinusoidal trajectory, and the controller

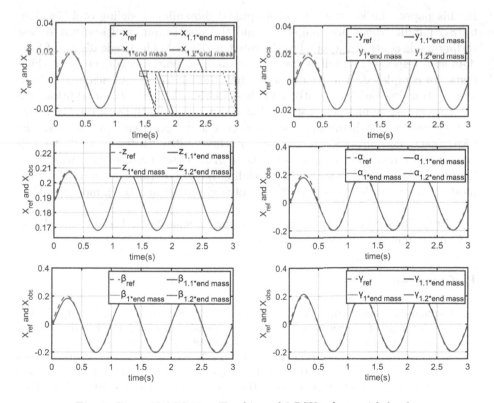

Fig. 6. Sinusoidal Motion Tracking of 6-PSU robots with loads

parameters are still set as shown in Table 1. The experimental results are shown in Fig. 6. The RMS is shown in Table 4.

Table 4. RMS at steady state of sinusoidal motion tracking

DOF	$x\,(m)$	$y\,(m)$	$z\,(m)$	$\alpha\,(rad)$	$\beta\,(rad)$	$\gamma\,(rad)$
$RMS_{1*endmass}$	8.51645e-5	7.87925e-5	2.50421e-5	4.56492e-3	4.35494e-3	4.37837e-3
$RMS_{1.1*endmass}$	8.24308e-5	8.18597e-5	2.11519e-5	4.59633e-3	4.35091e-3	4.38921e-3
$RMS_{1.2*endmass}$	8.20069e-5	8.19921e-5	2.11464e-5	4.59952e-3	4.34736e-3	4.38914e-3

The results show that after applying a reasonable load, the robot can still accurately track the planned trajectory. Importantly, even with load disturbances, there is no significant change in the steady-state RMS when the controller parameters remain unchanged. Overall, the experiments with load show that the controller has strong robustness.

5   Conclusion

In this paper, the kinematics and simplified dynamics modeling of a six-DOF 6-PSU parallel robot are completed, and the multi-input multi-output robust sliding mode controller applied to the robot is studied. The single degree of freedom step response and full degree of freedom sine synthesis trajectory tracking tests are completed. The results show that the controller can achieve the trajectory tracking task excellently, and there is almost no errors. In addition, the robustness test results demonstrate that the robot can still track the given trajectory even under disturbance, which is crucial for practical applications. The SMC mentioned above guarantee asymptotic stability. In future work, we will attempt to study sliding mode controllers with better performance, which can be designed as higher order nonlinear sliding mode functions or terminal sliding mode to improve the robot's ability to solve vibration and track more quickly.

Funding. The work is partially supported by the National Natural Science Foundation of China (Grant No. 51975351, 51927809).

References

1. Ibrahim, K., Ramadan, A., Fanni, M., Kobayashi, Y., Abo-Ismail, A., Fujie, M.G.: Development of a new 4-DOF endoscopic parallel manipulator based on screw theory for laparoscopic surgery. Mechatronics **28**, 4–7 (2015)
2. Ramadan, A.A., Takubo, T., Mae, Y., Oohara, K., Arai, T.: Developmental process of a chopstick-like hybrid-structure two-fingered micromanipulator hand for 3-D manipulation of microscopic objects. IEEE Trans. Ind. Electron. **56**(4), 1121–1135 (2009)

3. Terrier, M., Dugas, A., Hascoët, J.: Qualification of parallel kinematics machines in high-speed milling on free form surfaces. Int. J. Mach. Tool Manu 44(7), 865–877 (2004)
4. Dumlu, A., Erentürk, K., Kaleli, A., Koray, K.: Ayten: a comparative study of two model-based control techniques for the industrial manipulator. Robotica 35(10), 2036–2055 (2017)
5. Chen, S.-H., Fu, L.-C.: Observer-based backstepping control of a 6-dof parallel hydraulic manipulator. Control. Eng. Pract. 36, 100–112 (2015)
6. Liu, K., Xu, J., Ge, Z., Wang, Y., Zhao, D., Lu, Y.: Robust control of 3-DOF parallel robot driven by PMAs based on nominal stiffness model. Adv. Robot. 31(10), 531–543 (2017)
7. Zubizarreta, A., Marcos, M., Cabanes, I., Pinto, C.: A procedure to evaluate extended computed torque control configurations in the Stewart-Gough platform. Robot. Auton. Syst. 59(10), 770–781 (2011)
8. Wu, G., Lin, Z.: On the dynamics and computed torque control of an asymmetric four-limb parallel schoenflies motion generator. J. Robot. Autom. 4(1), 168–178 (2020)
9. Choubey, C., Ohri, J.: Tuning of LQR-PID controller to control parallel manipulator. Neural Comput. Appl. 34(4), 3283–3297 (2022)
10. Khosravi, M.A., Taghirad, H.D.: Robust PID control of fully-constrained cable driven parallel robots. Mechatronics (Oxford) 24(2), 87–97 (2014)
11. Zhang, X., Sørensen, R., Iversen, M.R., Li, H.: Computationally efficient dynamics modeling of robot manipulators with multiple flexible-links using acceleration-based discrete time transfer matrix method. Robot. Comput. Integr. Manuf. 49, 181–193 (2018)
12. Su, Y., Sun, D., Ren, L., Mills, J.K.: Integration of saturated PI synchronous control and PD feedback for control of parallel manipulators. IEEE Trans. Robot. 22(1), 202–207 (2006)
13. Wu, G., Zhang, X., Zhu, L., Lin, Z., Liu, J.: Fuzzy sliding mode variable structure control of a high-speed parallel PnP robot. Mech. Mach. Theory 162, 1043–1049 (2021)
14. Ding, S., Levant, A., Li, S.: Simple Homogeneous Sliding-mode Controller. Automatica (Oxford) 67, 22–32 (2016)
15. Sarkar, M.K., Dev, A., Asthana, P., Narzary, D.: Chattering free robust adaptive integral higher order sliding mode control for load frequency problems in multi-area power systems. IET Control Theory Appl. 12(9), 1216–1227 (2018)
16. Baek, S., Baek, J., Han, S.: An adaptive sliding mode control with effective switching gain tuning near the sliding surface. IEEE Access 7, 15563–15572 (2019)
17. Xu, Q.: Adaptive integral terminal third-order finite-time sliding-mode strategy for robust nanopositioning control. IEEE Trans. Ind. Electron. 68(7), 6161–6170 (2021)
18. Jia, H., Shang, W., Xie, F., Zhang, B., Cong, S.: Second-order sliding-mode-based synchronization control of cable-driven parallel robots. IEEE/ASME Trans. Mechatron. 25(1), 383–394 (2020)
19. Elmali, H., Olgac, N.: Implementation of sliding mode control with perturbation estimation (SMCPE). IEEE Trans. Control Syst. Technol. 4(1), 79–85 (1996)
20. Xu, Q.: Piezoelectric nanopositioning control using second-order discrete-time terminal sliding-mode strategy. IEEE Trans. Ind. Electron. 62(12), 7738–7748 (2015)
21. Levant, A.: Homogeneity approach to high-order sliding mode design. Automatica 41(5), 823–830 (2005)

Efficient Trajectory Planning for Coordinated Arrival of Fixed-Wing UAV Swarm

Yuhang Zhong[1,2], Yangxiu Hu[3], Yang Chen[3], Ningyu He[3], Guangtong Xu[1(✉)], Chao Xu[1,4], and Fei Gao[1,4]

[1] Huzhou Institute, Zhejiang University, Huzhou 313000, China
guangtong_xu@163.com
[2] College of Artificial Intelligence, Nankai University, Tianjin 300350, China
[3] Shanghai Aerospace Control Technology Institute, Shanghai 201109, China
[4] State Key Laboratory of Industrial Control Technology, College of Control Science and Engineering, Zhejiang University, Hangzhou 310027, China

Abstract. This paper proposes an efficient centralized trajectory planning algorithm for fixed-wing swarms to address the problem of coordinated arrival. A Dubins-based initial path sampling method is designed in the front end to provide a good initial guess considering kinodynamic feasibility. Then a joint optimization approach is carried out in the back end where constraints are formulated as a penalty in the cost function. Moreover, a well-formed trajectory representation is utilized to realize spatial-temporal optimization with few variables, leading to the high computational efficiency. A replanning strategy is also introduced to handle the situation when the target trajectory changes. Numerous simulation results demonstrate the efficiency and feasibility of the algorithm.

Keywords: Fixed-wing swarm · Coordinated arrival · Trajectory generation

1 Introduction

Fixed-wing swarm coordination is a popular issue in recent years due to its potential applications in various fields, such as surveillance, search and rescue, and collaborative terrain mapping. However, conducting a real-time planning for the coordinated arrival task still remains an open challenge. In this task, the fixed-wing unmanned aerial vehicles (UAVs) are requested to simultaneously arrive at a terminal with the expected angle while ensuring the safety. And the task becomes more challenging when the terminal state is constrained on the trajectory of the specific target, such as an interception mission. Besides, the simultaneous arrival, collision avoidance, and nonlinear kinodynamic constraints

Supported by the National Natural Science Foundation of China under Grants 62003299, 62088101, and 62203256.

increase the computational complexity. To execute the task, the robust swarm planning framework and the efficient trajectory generation method are required.

The swarm trajectory planning can be divided into centralized method and decentralized method according to the deployment on computation and communication resources. The centralized method sets a coordinator to solve the planning problem and allocates the planned trajectories to each one. Park et al. [6] use this framework to generate feasible trajectories for a quadrotor swarm, and the convex property is exploited to guarantee the safety and feasibility. Hönig et al. [4] construct the planning algorithm with the Enhanced Conflict-Based Search (ECBS) and optimization-based trajectory refinement, but the method plans the trajectory in known environment offline. These centralized methods suffer from the huge computational consumption when applied to large-scale swarms. Decentralized method alleviates the computational burden by distributing workload among the agents. Zhou et al. [10] propose a leader-follower swarm planning method, and each UAV computes the trajectory after receiving the trajectory information from other UAVs. Tordesillas and How [8] propose an asynchronous method which provides a check procedure to guarantee the safety between UAVs. For the coordinated arrival task, the decentralized method may result in poor optimality due to the communication latency, and have poor convergence due to the simultaneous arrival constraint. Moreover, since the swarm scale in the coordinated arrival task is small (less than 10) in this paper, the computation complexity of the centralized method is acceptable. Therefore, the centralized planning framework is preferred.

For the trajectory generation of fixed-wing UAVs, extensive works have investigated on it. Lugo-Cárdenas et al. [5] propose a Dubins-based path generation method for fixed-wing UAVs, which constrains the path curvature. Bry et al. [2] use the polynomial to correct the discontinuity in the second order curvature of Dubins, realizing a better flight performance. However, these methods lack the temporal information about path, which makes them hard to deploy on coordinated arrival task. Basescu et al. [1] use the nonlinear model predictive control method to generate trajectory directly on the full state of fixed-wing UAVs and realize the sharp turn maneuver in narrow corridor, but this method suffers from large computational burden. Bulka et al. [3] store various motion primitives in a library, and choose the best primitive during flight. In [7], the simplified aerodynamic model is used to explore the differential flatness of fixed-wing, thus the trajectory can be generated only on the flat space, improving the computational efficiency dramatically. However, these above mentioned methods all lack the ability to efficiently optimize the spatial and temporal property of the trajectory simultaneously, which is essential for the coordinated arrival task.

In this paper, we propose an efficient trajectory planning method to tackle the coordinated arrival problem of fixed-wing swarms. First, a complete and robust centralized planning framework is established, which fits the characteristic of the coordinated arrival task. A replanning strategy is designed to handle the situation when the target trajectory is varying. Once the initial states of UAVs are determined, a novel Dubins-based path sampling method is presented to get a rough initial guess. Then, a joint optimization is followed to refine the trajectories subject to the kinodynamic of fixed-wing UAVs and coordination constraints. In order to improve the efficiency of the solution, MINCO, a spatial-temporal parameterized trajectory representation is used to significantly reduce the number of variables required for optimization while ensuring the trajectory quality. Numerous simulations are performed to verify the efficiency and robustness of the method. The contributions of this work are summarized below:

1. A complete centralized planning framework that solves coordinated arrival problem for fixed-wing UAVs.
2. A novel Dubins-based path sampling method that provides reasonable initial guess for the later optimization.
3. A joint trajectory optimization approach that takes kinodynamics and coordinated arrival constraints into account.

2   Preliminary

2.1   Assumption

In this paper, the trajectory of the moving target is assumed to be known, thus the prediction for the trajectory of targets is beyond the scope of this paper.

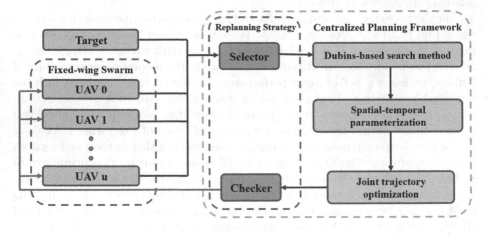

Fig. 1. Centralized planning framework.

2.2   Framework Overview

The whole framework is illustrated in Fig. 1, and all the computation runs on one coordinator which can be a UAV or a ground station. The centralized planning framework takes in the current states of all UAVs and the trajectory of the moving target. Inside, the replanning strategy contains two parts, where the Selector is used to select a good initial planning states and the Checker decides whether the planned trajectories are allowed to be published. The Dubins-based search method is operated to find initial paths. Then, the paths are transformed to a spatial-temporal trajectory presentation, which allows optimizing the time and shape of trajectory at the same time. Finally, the joint trajectory optimization is conducted to compute coordinated arrival trajectories.

2.3 Replanning Strategy

The replanning strategy ensures the robustness of trajectory generation method, especially facing the situation when the target trajectory changes. In the Selector, the initial planning states are carefully determined, since it should provide enough time for later trajectory generation. We use a heuristic way to decide the computation time, by which the time cost approximation δ_k for trajectory generation is calculated based on the last iteration:

$$\delta_k = \alpha \Delta_{k-1} \tag{1}$$

where Δ_{k-1} is the trajectory planning time in $k-1$th iteration, and $\alpha > 1$ is a scalar to determine the aggressiveness of estimation. The Checker mainly guarantees the feasibility of trajectory. If the trajectory generation time exceeds δ_k, the swarm will discard the new trajectory and execute the previous one.

3 Dubins-Based Path Sampling

Directly trajectory optimization without a good initial guess may result in a poor convergence, as the coordinate arrival mission involves both the time and space constraints. Unlike the normal kinodynamic search method for a single UAV, the coordinated arrival requests the time cooperation, which induces the high complexity to the search process. Thus, a novel front end is proposed to explore an approximate solution that is beneficial for the later optimization. We utilize the Dubins path to satisfy the kinodynamic of fixed-wing UAVs, and sample the potential terminal positions in sequence to find an approximate solution.

The method receives the initial states of fixed-wing UAVs $x_{0_{init}}, ..., x_{u_{init}}$ and target trajectory $\varphi(t)$, where $x = (p, v, a, \cdots)^{\top}$ and u is the number of UAVs in the swarm. Then it aims to find a path set P with the fixed arrival angle θ_{des}^u. The algorithm 1 gives the pseudocode. In the initialization process, the initial sample time T_s is calculated directly from the euclidean distance between the UAV and the target with the max speed assumption. Then, T_s is sampled in an increasing sequence. In each T_s loop, **GetDubinsPath** function first calculates a Dubins path in XY planar for each UAV, since the change of altitude is much smaller than the lateral in normal flight scenes. Then the

GetTimeError function is used to evaluate the metric of the current path:

$$g_{\text{tmp}} = \sum_{i=0}^{u} \left\| \frac{l(\boldsymbol{P}_c^i)}{v_{\max}} - T_s \right\|^2 \tag{2}$$

where $l(\boldsymbol{P}_c^u)$ denotes the Dubins path length of the uth UAV. In the lines 5–11, a Dubins set with a lower cost is stored, and if the cost of current paths is lower than a predefined threshold, the loop will terminate prematurely. After the best set of Dubins paths is chosen, the **3DConstruct** adds the z-axis value according to the difference in the altitude by linear interpolation.

Algorithm 1: Dubins-based multi-path sampling

Input: $x_0 \cdots x_u, \varphi(t), \theta_{des}^0 \cdots \theta_{des}^u$
Output: P
1   $T_s \leftarrow$ **initialization**
2 **while** T_s *not exceed limit* **do**
3     $P_c \leftarrow$ **GetDubinsPath**$(T_s, x_0 \cdots x_u, \theta_{des}^0 \cdots \theta_{des}^u, \varphi(t))$
4     $g_{\text{tmp}} \leftarrow$ **GetTimeError**(P_c)
5   **if** $g_{\text{tmp}} < g_c$ **then**
6        $P \leftarrow P_c$
7        $g_c \leftarrow g_{\text{tmp}}$
8   **if** $g_c <$ *Threshold* **then**
9   break ;
10   **end**
11   **end**
12   increase T_s ;
13 **end**
14 $P \leftarrow$ **3DConstruct**(P) ;

---

4 Spatial-Temporal Trajectory Optimization

4.1 Uniform MINCO Trajectory Representation

MINCO [9] is a minimum control effort polynomial trajectory class with M pieces, its coefficient $c = (c_1^\top, ..., c_M^\top)$ can be parameterized from a set of waypoints $q = (q_1^\top, ..., q_{M-1}^\top)$ and time vector $T = (T_1^\top, ..., T_M^\top)$ via a linear-complexity formulation:

$$c = \mathcal{M}(q, T) \tag{3}$$

which means the q and T directly determine the final trajectory. Here we construct a uniformed MINCO by modifying the T to be as $T = \tau \cdot \mathbf{1}$, where τ is the segment time and $\mathbf{1}$ denotes a vector with all component as 1. This modification improves the efficiency of trajectory optimization, at the cost of sacrificing temporal flexibility. Moreover, since coordinated arrival forces the trajectory executing time of each UAV to be the same, only one variable is needed to present time information of all UAVs.

4.2 Kinodynamic Constraints

Unlike quadrotors, there are stricter limitations on maneuverability of fixed-wing UAVs due to their unique aerodynamic structure. Since the lift used to balance the gravity is closely related to the flight speed, the lower bounds $v_{\min}$ and upper bounds $v_{\max}$ should be imposed to constrain the flight speed. In order to transform the constraint to be convex, it can be written as:

$$\mathcal{G}_v = \left(\|v\|^2 - v_{\text{mean}}^2 \right)^2 - v_{\text{gap}}^4 \le 0 \tag{4}$$

where $v_{\text{mean}} = (v_{\min} + v_{\max})/2$ and $v_{\text{gap}} = (v_{\max} - v_{\min})/2$. In the normal scenes, the fixed-wing UAV can only accelerate and decelerate in the velocity direction due to the aerodynamic characteristics, so the acceleration constraint is expressed as:

$$\mathcal{G}_a = \left(\frac{v^\top}{\|v\|} \cdot a - a_{\text{mean}} \right)^2 - a_{\text{gap}}^2 \le 0 \tag{5}$$

where $a_{\text{mean}} = (a_{\min} + a_{\max})/2$ and $a_{\text{gap}} = (a_{\max} - a_{\min})/2$. $a_{\min}$ and $a_{\max}$ denote the maximum and minimum values of acceleration in the velocity direction, respectively.

When turning, aerodynamic limitations make fixed-wing UAVs safe only within a certain range of curvature, otherwise too large curvature will result in post-stall or getting out of control. Therefore, a carefully designed curvature constraint is needed:

$$\mathcal{G}_c - \frac{\|v \times a\|}{\|a\|} - C_{\max} \le 0 \tag{6}$$

where $C_{\max}$ presents the maximum curvature.

4.3 Coordinated Constraints

In each replanning loop, the initial state for optimization is determined by:

$$x_i(0) = x_{i_{init}}, \ i = 0, \cdots, u \tag{7}$$

To achieve the requirement of simultaneous arrival at a fixed angle, the constraints are imposed on terminal states. τ is used to present uniform time step, and the total trajectory executing time can be calculate as $T = M \cdot \tau$. The terminal position of all UAVs is located on the trajectory of target, and the direction of velocity is constrained to be aligned with the fixed arrival angle:

$$p_0(T) = \cdots = p_u(T) = \varphi(T) \tag{8}$$

$$v_i(T) = v_i \cdot \theta_{des}^i, \ i = 0, \cdots, u \tag{9}$$

where v_i is a scalar variable denoting the magnitude of velocity for ith UAVs.

Collision avoidance between UAVs is another important cooperation requirement. This constraint is guaranteed by forcing the distance between UAVs greater than a safe clearance C_w at the same global timestamps. $\mathcal{G}_w(u,t)$ is designed to evaluate the constraint for the uth UAV at discrete timestamp t:

$$\mathcal{G}_w(u,t) = (\cdots, \mathcal{G}_{w_k}(u,t), \cdots)^\top \tag{10}$$

$$\mathcal{G}_{w_k}(u,t) = \begin{cases} C_w^2 - \|p_u(t) - p_k(t)\|^2, & k \neq u \\ 0 & k = u \end{cases} \tag{11}$$

Since the trajectories are optimized simultaneously in our framework, the coordinated constraints can be easily deployed in the optimization problem without considering the extra latency such as the communication delay.

4.4   Optimization Problem

With aforementioned constraints, we aims to generate smooth and fast trajectories for UAVs. The cost function is designed to trade off between control effort and time consumption:

$$\min_{q,\tau} \mathcal{J} = \sum_{i=0}^{u} \int_0^T p_i^{(s)}(t)^\top p_i^{(s)}(t)dt + \rho T \tag{12}$$

The optimization problem optimizes trajectory parameters q and τ to minimize the cost function, subject to the constraints (4–11). And s is set as 4 to minimize the snap of the whole trajectory.

To solve this problem efficiently, the penalty method is used to transport it to an unconstrained optimization problem. The kinodynamic constraints (4–6) and collision avoidance (10, 11) are transformed into the time integral penalties. For the numerical optimization, the penalty terms are written in the discrete formation:

$$\mathcal{J}_i^\star(c_i, \tau) = \rho_\star \frac{\tau}{\kappa_i} \sum_{j=0}^{\kappa_i} \bar{w}_k \max\left[\mathcal{G}_\star\left(c_i, \tau, \frac{j}{\kappa_i}\right), 0 \right]^3, \quad \star = v, a, c, w \tag{13}$$

where
$\rho_\star$ denotes the weight of the corresponding penalty and $[\bar{w}_0, \bar{w}_1, \cdots \bar{w}_{\kappa-1}, \bar{w}_\kappa]$ $= [1/2, 1, \cdots, 1, 1/2]$ are the discrete parameters in the trapezoidal rule. Note that the collision avoidance is not constrained in the vicinity of the terminal state, since it conflicts with simultaneous arrival requirement.

To relax the time constraint $\tau > 0$, a simple exponential function is used:

$$\tau = e^{\tau_{\mathrm{un}}} \tag{14}$$

where $\tau_{\mathrm{un}} \in \mathbb{R}$ is the new unconstrained variable. Substituting (14) into (12), τ_{un} replaces τ as the decision variable in the optimization process.

5 Simulations

The numerous simulations are conducted in this section. All the simulations run on a desktop with a GTX 1660 Ti graphics card and an i7-9750H processor. All code is written in C++ and implemented under ROS. To solve the formulated unconstrained optimization problem in the back end, the limited-memory BFGS (L-BFGS) method is used.

5.1 Evaluation of the Dubins-Based Sampling

To evaluate the performance of the Dubins-based sampling, we compare it with a method that calculates arrival time by directly measuring the euclidean distance between the UAV and the target. The evaluation result is shown in Table 1. Although the computation time of Dubins-based method in front end is slightly longer, the back-end optimization is much more efficient than that without Dubins. This is because the initial guess provided by Dubins-based method satisfies the kinodynamic feasibility constraints, resulting the reduction of optimization iterations. Another interesting insight is that the computational time of the method without Dubins maintains the same in the front end, but significantly increases in the back end as the number of fixed-wing UAVs increases. The reason could be that without the feasibility consideration, sampling may trigger the early termination with a poor approximation, providing a bad initial guess for the later optimization.

Table 1. Comparison between the method with the front-end based on Dubins and without Dubins.

Number of fixed-wing UAVs	Dubins-based		without Dubins	
	front-end sampling/ms	back-end optimization/ms	front-end sampling/ms	back-end optimization/ms
1	0.38	12.38	0.02	28.04
2	0.43	45.71	0.02	107.89
3	0.56	53.35	0.02	232.53

5.2 Trajectory Analysis

A coordinated arrival mission is designed with 3 fixed-wing UAVs, and the initial deployment is illustrated on Table 2. To simulate realistic fixed-wing UAV flight scenarios, the allowed acceleration is set much smaller than the velocity, and the curvature is also limited within a reasonable range. This scenario presents a significant challenge for the swarm to achieve coordinated arrival. The results

Table 2. Initial deployment for the coordinated arrival mission

Fixed-wing swarm		
	Initial states	Expected arriving angle
UAV0	$p_0 = (-1000, 0, 500)^\top, v_0 = (150, 0, 0)^\top$	$\theta_{des}^0 = (1, 0, 0)^\top$
UAV1	$p_1 = (-1000, 300, 500)^\top, v_1 = (150, 0, 0)^\top$	$\theta_{des}^1 = (0.707, -0.707, 0)^\top$
UAV2	$p_2 = (-1000, -500, 500)^\top, v_2 = (150, 0, 0)^\top$	$\theta_{des}^2 = (0.707, 0.707, 0)^\top$
Moving trajectory of target		
$\varphi(t) = \begin{bmatrix} 100t + 500 \\ -t^2 + 20t + 300 \\ t + 500 \end{bmatrix}$		
Constraints		
$v_{max} = 170, \ v_{min} = 130, \ a_{max} = 10, \ a_{min} = -2, \ C_{max} = 0.0023, \ C_w = 200$		

are shown in Fig. 2. It is notable in Fig. 2a that the velocity of UAV1 exceeds the upper bound slightly in some timestamp, since the optimization problem is solved by a soft constrained method. Moreover, the velocity of UAVs tends to the upper bound in the process, reflecting the requirement of minimizing the arrival time in the cost function. Figures 2b and 2c show that the acceleration and curvature of the UAVs are well constrained in the bound, and Fig. 2d demonstrates the terminal states of the UAVs and the target. Since the hard constraint is imposed on the terminal, the arrival angles of UAVs are consistent with the expected values.

To show the swarm reciprocal avoidance sufficiently, the expected arrival angles of UAV1 and UAV2 are exchanged to force a crossing maneuver. The whole trajectories and key shots are illustrated in Fig. 3, showing an inevitable cross in XY planar. As demonstrated in Figs. 3b and 3c, the swarm accomplishes reciprocal collision avoidance in 16.1 s with the difference on altitude. In Fig. 3d, the minimum distance is guaranteed to be larger than C_w, and decreases in the vicinity of terminal due to the coordinated arrival requirement.

5.3   Replanning Evaluation

To verify the feasibility of the proposed replanning strategy, the trajectory of the target changes at a specific timestamp. As Fig. 4a shows, the swarm replans the feasible trajectories successfully. The performance of the Selector is further evaluated, and the result is depicted in Fig. 4b. The computing time in each replanning step is shown as the blue curve, and the approximated planning time is expressed as the green column. The replanning is performed at a fixed frequency of 0.5 Hz. In each replanning step, the approximated planning time is larger than the real one, guaranteeing the feasibility of the replanned trajectories.

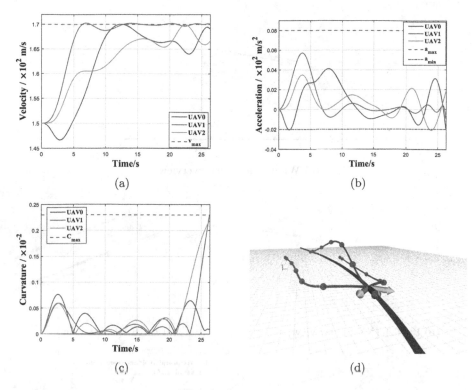

Fig. 2. Performance of the generated trajectories. (a)–(c) show the variation of the velocity, acceleration, and curvature, respectively. The dashed lines are corresponding constraints. (d) presents the terminal states of the swarm. The green and red arrows indicate the direction of the UAVs and the target in the terminal, respectively. The black and blue curves are the trajectories of the target and UAVs, and the red balls on the blue curves indicate the waypoints. (Color figure online)

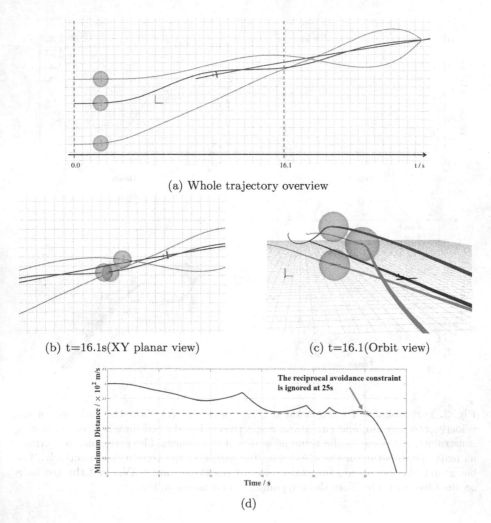

(a) Whole trajectory overview

(b) t=16.1s(XY planar view)   (c) t=16.1(Orbit view)

(d)

Fig. 3. Display of the generated trajectories. (a) shows the trajectories in the XY planar view, (b) and (c) demonstrate the key frame shot in the process. The green balls indicate the safety region of the corresponding grey UAVs, and the target UAV is colored red. (d) shows the minimum distance between UAVs in the swarm, and the dashed line denotes C_w. The reciprocal avoidance is ignored at 25 s to realize the simultaneous arrival. (Color figure online)

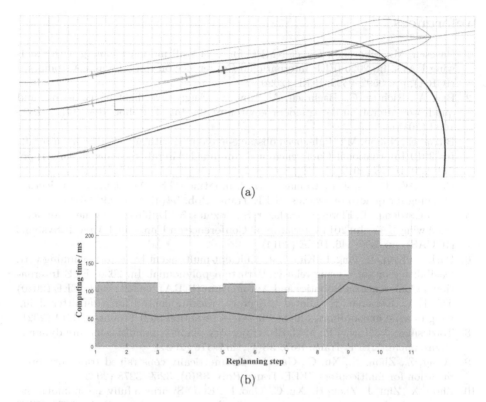

(a)

(b)

Fig. 4. Performance of the replanning strategy. (a) shows the situation that the trajectory of target changes, the solid trajectories are the current replanning result, and the transparent one is the last result. In (b), the blue curve and the green columns demonstrate the real planning time Δ_k and the approximated planning time δ_k in each replanning step, respectively. (Color figure online)

6   Conclusion

In this paper, an efficient trajectory planning algorithm is proposed for the fixed-wing swarm in the coordinated arrival mission. The key property of this method is that it uses a Dubins-based sampling method as the front end to provide a good initial guess, and utilizes the spatial-temporal trajectory presentation to reduce optimization complexity, leading to a quick convergence and low computing time. The replanning strategy is designed to improve the robustness of the planning framework. The simulations reveal the superiority of the trajectory planning method and demonstrate the potential for real-world applications. The future work will focus on combining the control and perception into the system to realize the real world implementation.

426   Y. Zhong et al.

References

1. Basescu, M., Moore, J.: Direct NMPC for post-stall motion planning with fixed-wing UAVs. In: 2020 IEEE International Conference on Robotics and Automation (ICRA), pp. 9592–9598. IEEE (2020)
2. Bry, A., Richter, C., Bachrach, A., Roy, N.: Aggressive flight of fixed-wing and quadrotor aircraft in dense indoor environments. Int. J. Robot. Res. **34**(7), 969–1002 (2015)
3. Bulka, E., Nahon, M.: High-speed obstacle-avoidance with agile fixed-wing aircraft. In: 2019 International Conference on Unmanned Aircraft Systems (ICUAS), pp. 971–980. IEEE (2019)
4. Hönig, W., Preiss, J.A., Kumar, T.S., Sukhatme, G.S., Ayanian, N.: Trajectory planning for quadrotor swarms. IEEE Trans. Rob. **34**(4), 856–869 (2018)
5. Lugo-Cárdenas, I., Flores, G., Salazar, S., Lozano, R.: Dubins path generation for a fixed wing UAV. In: 2014 International Conference on Unmanned Aircraft Systems (ICUAS), pp. 339–346. IEEE (2014)
6. Park, J., Kim, J., Jang, I., Kim, H.J.: Efficient multi-agent trajectory planning with feasibility guarantee using relative Bernstein polynomial. In: 2020 IEEE International Conference on Robotics and Automation (ICRA), pp. 434–440. IEEE (2020)
7. Tal, E.A., Karaman, S.: Global trajectory-tracking control for a tailsitter flying wing in agile uncoordinated flight. In: AIAA Aviation 2021 Forum, p. 3214 (2021)
8. Tordesillas, J., How, J.P.: MADER: trajectory planner in multiagent and dynamic environments. IEEE Trans. Rob. **38**(1), 463–476 (2021)
9. Wang, Z., Zhou, X., Xu, C., Gao, F.: Geometrically constrained trajectory optimization for multicopters. IEEE Trans. Rob. **38**(5), 3259–3278 (2022)
10. Zhou, X., Zhu, J., Zhou, H., Xu, C., Gao, F.: EGO-Swarm: a fully autonomous and decentralized quadrotor swarm system in cluttered environments. In: 2021 IEEE International Conference on Robotics and Automation (ICRA), pp. 4101–4107. IEEE (2021)

Spontaneous Emergence of Multitasking in Minimal Robotic Systems

Ji Zhang[1,2](✉) (iD), Han Li[1], Haoyuan Du[1,2], Yiming Liang[1,2], Wei Song[1,2] (iD), and Tiefeng Li[3] (iD)

[1] Zhejiang Lab, Hangzhou 311100, China
[2] Zhejiang Engineering Research Center for Intelligent Robotics, Hangzhou 311100, China
zhangji@zhejianglab.com
[3] State Key Laboratory of Fluid Power and Mechatronic Systems, Zhejiang University, Hangzhou 310027, China
litiefeng@zju.edu.cn

Abstract. This study investigates the behavior of a system of identical robots modeled as self-propelled particles using the Vicsek model. The focus is on understanding the emergence of a chimera state, which represents the spontaneous emergence of multitasking capabilities in the robot swarm. The study considers scenarios with limited communication in a minimal system of 3 identical robots. Numerical simulations and stability analysis are conducted to analyze the system's characteristics and motion patterns. The research aims to provide insights into the underlying mechanisms and develop a comprehensive framework for controlling and understanding the emergence of the chimera state in robot swarm systems. Additionally, the study examines the influence of coupling strength and phase lag on the occurrence of chimera states through direct numerical simulations and theoretical analysis. The results reveal the relationship between system structure and the manifestation of chimera states, providing valuable insights for further research in this field.

Keywords: robot swarm · complex task · chimera state · discrete-time Kuramoto-Sakaguchi model

1 Introduction

A promising approach to replacing a single, expensive and complex robot is the utilization of many low-cost small robots in a swarm system [1,2]. These robot swarms have the ability to form highly robust systems, capable of tackling challenging tasks. They have found extensive applications in various fields such

This work was supported by China Postdoctoral Science Foundation (Grant No. 2022M712927), Zhejiang Lab Open Research Project (No. K2022NB0AB01), and Key Research Project of Zhejiang Lab (No. G2021NB0AL03).

as logistics, warehousing [3,4], ocean monitoring [5,6], meteorological observation [7–9], and more.

Compared to centralized control multi-robot systems, swarm systems with distributed autonomous cooperation significantly reduce the need for hardware requirements such as communication networks and computational speed. As a result, these systems hold advantages in performing complex tasks in extreme environments, which has attracted the attention of numerous researchers. The scope of research encompasses unmanned aerial vehicle swarms [10–12], unmanned surface vehicle swarms [13,14], and autonomous underwater vehicle swarms [15–17].

For example, the BlueSwarm project has successfully developed a group of bionic robots functioning as autonomous underwater vehicles [18]. These robots utilize vision to perceive their surroundings and can autonomously switch between different control programs to complete tasks like evasion, pursuit, formation movement, and target search. Additionally, Harvard's Kilobot project achieved groundbreaking control over a swarm of thousands of tiny robots, enabling them to form intricate patterns through simple interactions [19]. Recently, Gao et al. introduced a swarm of small unmanned aerial vehicles, each equipped with sensing, positioning, and control capabilities [20]. Their system employs a spatiotemporal joint optimization-based approach to enable swarm navigation and autonomous formation in complex, cluttered environments. These examples highlight the capability of accomplishing complex tasks without a centralized controller, using large numbers of small robots in swarms.

Simultaneously, researchers have employed statistical physics methods to comprehend the self-organizing tendencies of decentralized clusters of robots. From a statistical physics standpoint, robotic swarms can be represented as intricate networks with loosely interconnected interactions, where network connections symbolize individual interactions. Taking inspiration from cellular organization, Li et al. conducted a study utilizing a single-degree-of-freedom particle robot as an example to examine the emergence mechanism and robustness of macroscopic swarm phenomena [21]. By regulating the motion cycle of each robot, they achieved various complex motions such as translation, rotation, and carrying. Similarly, Liu et al. devised a robotic swarm capable of dynamically evolving based on the external environment, revealing that interactions with the environment can give rise to complex behaviors in robotic swarms [22].

However, in the aforementioned research, realizing the diverse functionalities of the swarm necessitates actively or passively altering the robot's control strategy to accomplish complex tasks. Establishing a distributed collaborative system among robot clusters, enabling multitasking through a simple coupling method, still poses significant challenges. In a recent publication, Kruk et al. presented the discovery of the chimera state in a self-propelled particle system, offering a promising avenue for the spontaneous emergence of multitasking robotic swarms [23]. The concept of the chimera state has a relatively brief research history. It was initially observed in 2002 and subsequently named by Abrams and Strogatz in 2004 [24,25]. The chimera state represents a stable condition found in complex networks comprising identical units, characterized by the coexistence of coherent and incoherent components [25, 26].

When a robot swarm system exhibits a chimera state, it spontaneously segregates into two or more distinct parts, each demonstrating different motion behaviors, thereby enabling the simultaneous execution of multiple tasks [27]. Consequently, the objective of this study is to explore the underlying mechanisms responsible for this phenomenon's emergence and to provide a comprehensive framework for controlling and understanding this emergence phenomenon.

2   Setup and Method

This study centers around the spontaneous emergence of multitasking capabilities in a system of identical robots and aims to unravel the underlying mechanism. To facilitate our investigation, we adopt the concept of each robot being represented as a self-propelled particle, which can be modeled using the Vicsek model [28, 29]. The self-propelled particle model is widely employed in nonequilibrium statistical physics to capture the behavior of autonomous agents. Originally, this model was introduced to describe the collective motion observed in natural swarms such as fish, birds, and bacteria. Over time, it has been extended to encompass artificial agents like robotic systems.

In our study, we construct a physical model based on several assumptions and simplifications. Firstly, we focus on a two-dimensional system where robots move within a boundary-less plane. We assume that all robots maintain a constant speed of unity, denoted as $v = 1$, throughout their motion. Consequently, although each robot possesses three degrees of freedom encompassing its two-dimensional location r and spin φ, the multitasking capabilities can be effectively described by the intricate motion patterns exhibited by the robotic system, which are entirely determined by the spins of the robots. Therefore, the emergence of complex motion patterns, resulting from the breaking of symmetry, serves as the physical manifestation of a multitasking robotic system.

Furthermore, the real world often presents situations where communication is intermittent. For instance, in complex environments like jungles, signal transmission can be obstructed by obstacles such as trees, making continuous communication unreliable. Additionally, in long-term deployments of robots in the field, adopting periodic interval communication can help reduce communication costs and conserve energy. Consequently, this study focuses on scenarios with limited communication.

To capture the restricted communication dynamics, a discrete-time version of the Vicsek model is employed to describe the motion of the robotic system. At each time step, each robot adjusts its direction, denoted as φ, based on the strength parameter σ and by exchanging information with other robots. Building upon previous research, a Kuramoto-Sakaguchi interaction with a phase lag of α is utilized to model this information exchange. Thus, the Kinematics equations of the ith robot reads

$$\varphi_i^{t+1} = \varphi_i^t + \frac{\sigma}{N-1} \sum_{j \neq i} \sin\left(\varphi_j - \varphi_i - \alpha\right) . \tag{1}$$

The system under investigation in this paper exhibits two distinct characteristics, differentiating it from other systems in the field. Firstly, although the Kuramoto-Sakaguchi model has been extensively studied, with notable contributions found in research such as Gong et al. [30] and Mihara et al. [31], and the collective behavior can be effectively described by the Fokker-Planck equation [32], these approaches become inadequate for systems with a small number of robots, such as $N = 3$. In such cases, the time-discrete Kuramoto-Sakaguchi (DTKS) model cannot be accurately described using standard statistical physical approach, and conventional tools like the Fokker-Planck equation and Ito's lemma fail to provide accurate insights.

The numerical simulations of the DTKS model are performed using the standard first-order forward Euler scheme. The implementation of the code is done utilizing PETSc [33,34], and we conduct 64 independent simulations with random initial conditions for each parameter configuration to ensure the stability and reliability of the obtained results. Finally, due to the symmetry of equation Eq. 1, the influence of the phase lag α and its opposite $-\alpha$ on the DTKS model is identical. Therefore, our investigation primarily concentrates on small phase lags within the region $\alpha \in (0, 0.5\pi)$.

3   Results and Discussion

In our study, we conducted both direct numerical simulations and theoretical analysis to investigate the system's behavior. Our primary focus was to understand how the phenomenon evolves with variations in the coupling strength σ, as well as the phase lag α.

Previous research has indicated that larger systems tend to exhibit the chimera state [35]. This observation suggests that the emergence of chimera states in small-scale systems is more challenging to achieve. In the case of a Kuramoto model with globally coupled phase oscillators, Ashwin and Burylko found that the occurrence of a chimera state requires a minimum of four oscillators with two or more different types of coupling within the network [36]. This result implies that a certain level of complexity in the system structure is necessary for chimera states to arise. More recently, Burylko et al. analyzed the symmetry properties of the Kuramoto model and concluded that weak chimera states cannot exist in fully symmetric systems [37]. This finding suggests that the presence of symmetry-breaking mechanisms or structural asymmetry is crucial for the emergence of chimera states.

Subsequently, we delved into studying the mechanisms underlying the emergence of the chimera state. We specifically examined how changes in the system's coupling strength σ and phase lag α affect the occurrence of the chimera state. This investigation allowed us to gain insights into the relationship between system structure and the manifestation of chimera states.

3.1 Dependence of System Spin Pattern to Coupling Strength

In this subsection, we examine the influence of coupling strength on the angular patterns exhibited by the robot system, considering a constant phase lag ($\alpha = 0.9870$). Figure 1 illustrates the spatiotemporal evaluations of the DTKS model with different coupling strengths (σ).

As a consequence of the discrete-time nature of the model, even for the smallest system size of $N = 3$, the DTKS model exhibits complex phenomena that vary with the coupling strength σ. The upper and lower rows in the figure respectively display the temporal evolution of the robot's angle increment and phase angle. The indices of the robots in each panel are sorted based on their average phase angle.

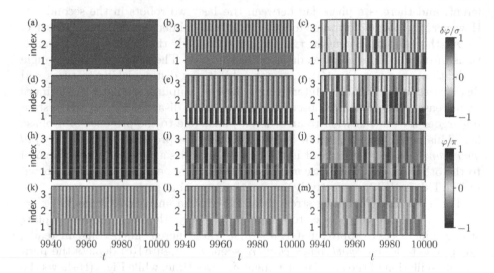

Fig. 1. Spatiotemporal evaluation of the DTKS model with three robots. Panels (a) to (f) illustrate the normalized angular increment $\delta\varphi$ per step, normalized by the coupling strength σ. Panels (h) to (m) display the normalized phase angle φ/π as a function of time. The indices of the robots in each panel are sorted based on their average phase angle. Panels (a) and (h) depict full synchronization for $\sigma = 2$, Panels (b) and (i) display an antiphase chimera state for $\sigma = 3$, Panels (c) and (j) exhibit chaotic behavior chaotic for $\sigma = 4$, Panels (d) and (k) illustrate a full synchronized chimera state full synchronize chimera for $\sigma = 5$, Panels (e) and (l) show a synchronized chimera state synchronize chimera for $\sigma = 5.35$, Panels (f) and (m) represent chaotic behavior chaotic for $\sigma = 6$. Each simulation begins with a random initial state and a constant phase lag of $\alpha = 0.9870$. The first 9940 time steps are ignored, and the subsequent 60 time steps displayed in the panels, providing a snapshot of the system's behavior.

The spatiotemporal evaluation of the DTKS model, as depicted in Fig. 1, reveals the transition from order to disorder with increasing coupling strength

σ. Initially, at very small coupling strengths, the DTKS model exhibits synchro-nization, as shown in Fig. 1(a). In this case, the phase angles of the robots exhibit periodic motion due to the system's symmetry, as illustrated in Fig. 1(h).

However, as the coupling strength σ increases, the DTKS model loses its sym-metry and new patterns emerge. For $\sigma = 2$, a distinct pattern appears, charac-terized by the spontaneous formation of two sets of robots. Figure 1(b) illustrates this pattern, known as an *antiphase chimera*. In the antiphase chimera, one robot in the first set maintains a constant angular increment per time step, while the other two robots in the secondary set exhibit an antisymmetric behavior differ-ent from the first set. It is noteworthy that this antiphase chimera state does not exist in the continuous model and is nontrivial for the minimal system with $N = 3$ robots. Figure 1(i) provides the phase angle evaluation of the antiphase chimera state, showing that the robot spin frequencies in the two sets are dif-ferent, and there is a phase lag between the last two robots in the second set. However, the parameter range for this antiphase chimera state is not extensive.

As the coupling strength σ is further increased, the DTKS model transi-tions into a chaotic regime, as depicted in Fig. 1(c). The associated phase angle evaluation, shown in Fig. 1(j), does not exhibit any distinguishing features and displays chaotic dynamics. Interestingly, as the coupling strength σ continues to increase, the previously observed chimera state disappears, and the system undergoes a new transition to an ordered phase due to the presence of a phase lag. This new chimera pattern is distinct from the previous ones. In this *full synchronize chimera*, the robot in the first set exhibits a different spin compared to the other robots. The phase angles and their increment per time step, shown in Fig. 1(d) and (k), respectively, are consistent within each set.

For a moderate coupling strength of $\sigma = 5$, the angular increments $\delta\varphi^t (= \varphi^{t+1} - \varphi^t)$ of the two sets of robots remain steady. However, as the coupling strength increases to approximately $\sigma = 5.35$, these increments become unsteady, giving rise to a new *synchronize chimera* scenario. Figure 1(e) depicts the peri-odical oscillation of the angular increment $\delta\varphi$ over time, while Fig. 1(l) shows the associated phase angle φ exhibiting nonlinear periodic behavior in this region. Continuing to increase the coupling strength σ, this oscillation becomes unstable, and the system transitions back into a chaotic regime, as illustrated in Fig. 1(f) and (m).

3.2   Bifurcation Phenomenon

To gain a deeper understanding of the DTKS model, we employ a commonly used definition from previous studies [2,38,39] and describe the global behavior by introducing the order parameter magnitude $R = \left| 1/N \sum_{j=1}^{N} \exp(i\phi_i) \right|$.

Indeed, a larger value of R indicates a higher degree of synchronization in the the DTKS model system. The bifurcation diagram in Fig. 2 illustrates the relationship between the order parameter R and the coupling strength σ for a constant phase lag $\alpha = 0.9870$. The specific parameters used to calculate the order parameter during the simulations are described in the figure's caption.

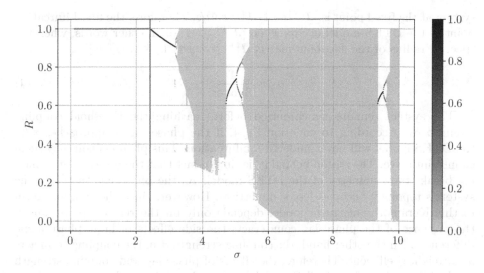

Fig. 2. Bifurcation diagram of order parameter R as function of coupling strength σ with a constant phase lag $\alpha = 0.9870$. The coupling strength σ is incremented from 0.1 to 10 in steps of 0.01, and for each value of σ, 64 independent simulations with random initial conditions are conducted. The first 30000 time steps are disregarded, and the order parameter R is recorded during the subsequent 10000 time steps to determine its probability. The color scale in the diagram represents the probability of the order parameter R for each coupling strength σ. The vertical blue line indicate the theoretical predictions of the first bifurcation $\sigma_1 = 2.4188$. (Color figure online)

Upon closer examination of Eq. 1 it becomes apparent that the evaluation of the phase angle φ in the DTKS model is solely dependent on its relative angle and does not rely on the phase angle φ itself. As a result, by defining the relative angle as $\eta_{2,3}^t = \varphi_{2,3}^t - \varphi_1^t$ for a minimal system $N = 3$, we can establish an equivalent two-dimensional reduced model for the DTKS model, given by the following expression:

$$\eta_{2,3}^{t+1} = \eta_{2,3}^t - \frac{\sigma}{2} \left(\begin{array}{c} \sin(\eta_{2,3}^t - \eta_{3,2}^t + \alpha) + \sin(\eta_{2,3}^t + \alpha) \\ + \sin(\eta_{2,3}^t - \alpha) + \sin(\eta_{3,2}^t - \alpha) \end{array} \right). \tag{2}$$

At low coupling strengths, the order parameter R is equal to 1, indicating a state of synchronization. In this regime, the relative angles η_2 and η_3 can be simplified by utilizing the symmetry $\eta_2 = \eta_3 = \tilde{\eta}$, leading to the reduced equation:

$$\tilde{\eta}^{t+1} = \tilde{\eta}^t - \frac{\sigma}{2} \left(\sin\alpha + \sin(\tilde{\eta}^t + \alpha) + 2\sin(\tilde{\eta}^t - \alpha) \right). \tag{3}$$

For arbitrary phase lag, the stable fixed point of the DTKS model remains at $\tilde{\eta}^{t+1} = \tilde{\eta}^t = \tilde{\eta}$. As a result, it can be shown that the only stable fixed point of the DTKS model is $\tilde{\eta} = 0$. Furthermore, the Jacobian matrix of this reduced system at the fixed point is: $J^{t+1} = 1 - (3\sigma\cos\alpha)/2$. Therefore, the first bifurcation point of the DTKS model occurs when $|J^{t+1}| > 1$, or in other words, when the spectral radius of the Jacobian matrix J^{t+1} exceeds 1

$$\sigma_1 = \frac{4}{3\cos\alpha}. \tag{4}$$

The system remains synchronized before reaching the threshold coupling strength σ_1. According to equation Eq. 4, if the phase lag α approaches $\pi/2$, the DTKS model will never undergo a bifurcation. This phenomenon may seem counterintuitive. The reason behind it lies in the fact that the presence of a phase lag breaks the symmetry of the DTKS model. As the phase lag increases, the system's topology becomes less symmetrical. However, since the coupling term in this Kuramoto-Sakaguchi model depends only on the relative phase angle, the presence of the phase lag counteracts the side effects of large phase angle differences. On the other hand, the coupling strength σ in the coupling term acts as a weight coefficient. Therefore, the effects of phase lag and coupling strength on the bifurcation of the DTKS model are opposite. A large phase angle reduces the side effects caused by the coupling strength, thereby stabilizing the DTKS model even for large values of σ.

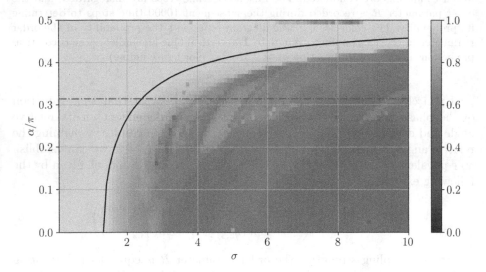

Fig. 3. Phase map of order parameter R as functions of coupling strength σ and phase lag α. The coupling strength σ is increased from 0.1 to 10 stepped by 0.1, and the phase lag $\alpha \in (0, \pi/2)$ is divided into 51 parts. We ignore the first 30000 time steps and calculate the order parameter R during the next 10000 time steps, and the color scale indicates the mean value of R for 64 independent simulations with random initial condition. The black solid line shown the theoretical result (see Eq. 4) of the first bifurcation σ_1. The red horizon line corresponding to phase lag $\alpha = 0.9870$. (Color figure online)

To gain a deeper understanding of the phenomenon, we conducted extensive calculations to generate the phase map of the order parameter R as a function of the coupling strength σ and phase lag α, as shown in Fig. 3. We exclude the first 30000 time steps and compute the order parameter R over the subsequent 10000 time steps to generate this phase map. The color scale represents the mean value of R obtained from 64 independent simulations with random initial conditions. We vary the coupling strength σ from 0.1 to 10 in increments of 0.1, and the phase lag α ranges from 0 to $\pi/2$ divided into 51 equal parts. Thus, a total of 326400 simulations were performed to ensure reliable statistical results.

Overall, the trend observed in the phase map is a decrease in the order parameter R from the upper left corner to the lower right corner, regardless of the phase lag α. In the region of small coupling strength, the DTKS model exhibits full synchronization, indicated by a unity order parameter $R = 1$. The black solid line in the figure represents the theoretical formulation of the first bifurcation point Eq. 4. As discussed earlier, this line separates the figure into two regions. The upper left region corresponds to full synchronization, while crossing this line triggers a second-order phase transition resulting in a decrease in the order parameter. Eventually, the DTKS model enters a chaotic region, represented by the dark green color in the figure. We should note that due to numerical uncertainties, some cases with a phase lag of $\alpha = 0.5\pi$ exhibit reduced synchronization, leading to an order parameter $R < 1$ in those instances.

The red line in the figure corresponds to cases with a phase lag of $\alpha = 0.9870$, which is associated with the parameter space discussed in Fig. 1 to Fig. 2. Remarkably, two uncommon ordered patterns, known as the synchronized chimera pattern, disappear with an increasing coupling strength σ. In Fig. 2, these patterns are observed around $\sigma = 4.6817$ and $\sigma = 9.3635$. In contrast to the previous antiphase chimera, the order parameter R strictly monotonically increases with the coupling strength σ in these regions. Furthermore, the repetition period doubles after each bifurcation, resulting in more complex patterns. For example, the angular increment $\delta\varphi$ of the synchronized chimera in Fig. 1e repeats itself every 4 time steps.

In Fig. 3, it is evident that the synchronized chimera pattern does not exist in the small phase lag region. Therefore, the synchronized chimera phenomenon is a result of the combined effect of the coupling strength σ and the phase lag α. The existence of the phase lag provides new opportunities to control the dynamics of the DTKS model in the large coupling region, potentially enabling the achievement of complex tasks.

4   Conclusion

This study specifically focuses on the spontaneous emergence of multitasking capabilities in a minimal system of 3 identical robots. By modeling the robots as self-propelled particles using the Vicsek model, the study captures the intricate motion patterns that describe the multitasking capabilities of the robotic system. The study investigates scenarios with limited communication and adopts a discrete-time version of the Vicsek model to account for the restricted communication dynamics. Through extensive numerical simulations and stability analysis, the study provides insights into the behavior of a minimal system with three robots and explores the influence of small phase lags on the emergence of complex motion patterns, known as chimera states.

Furthermore, the study examines the dependence of the system's spin pattern on the coupling strength and reveals a transition from order to disorder as the coupling strength increases. Different patterns, including synchronization, antiphase chimera, full synchronize chimera, and chaotic behavior, are observed as the coupling strength varies. The dynamics of the system are also investigated using an equivalent two-dimensional reduced model, which confirms the behavior observed in the original model. The reduced model highlights the role of the relative angle between robots in determining the system's behavior.

Additionally, the study explores the bifurcation phenomena in the DTKS model as the coupling strength is varied. Bifurcation analysis reveals the occurrence of transitions between synchronized states and different synchronized states, as well as the eventual transition to a chaotic regime. The bifurcation diagram and phase map provide valuable insights into the relationship between the order parameter, coupling strength, and phase lag, shedding light on the behavior of the DTKS model.

Overall, this study contributes to the understanding of swarm systems and their potential for multitasking capabilities. The findings enhance our knowledge of the underlying mechanisms and provide a comprehensive framework for controlling and comprehending the emergence of chimera states in robot swarm systems. The research contributes to the broader field of swarm technology, offering valuable insights for the development and application of swarm systems in various domains.

References

1. Dorigo, M., Theraulaz, G., Trianni, V.: Reflections on the future of swarm robotics. Sci. Robot. 5(49), eabe4385 (2020)
2. Nedjah, N., Junior, L.S.: Review of methodologies and tasks in swarm robotics towards standardization. Swarm Evol. Comput. 50, 100565 (2019)
3. Wen, J., He, L., Zhu, F.: Swarm robotics control and communications: imminent challenges for next generation smart logistics. IEEE Commun. Mag. 56(7), 102–107 (2018)
4. Li, Z., Barenji, A.V., Jiang, J., Zhong, R.Y., Xu, G.: A mechanism for scheduling multi robot intelligent warehouse system face with dynamic demand. J. Intell. Manuf. 31(2), 469–480 (2020)
5. Kouzehgar, M., Meghjani, M., Bouffanais, R.: Multi-agent reinforcement learning for dynamic ocean monitoring by a swarm of buoys. In: Global Oceans,: Singapore-US Gulf Coast. IEEE 2020, 1–8 (2020)
6. Agarwala, N.: Monitoring the ocean environment using robotic systems: advancements, trends, and challenges. Mar. Technol. Soc. J. 54(5), 42–60 (2020)
7. Schranz, M., Umlauft, M., Sende, M., Elmenreich, W.: Swarm robotic behaviors and current applications. Front. Robot. AI 7, 36 (2020)

8. Kim, K., Kim, H., Myung, H.: Bio-inspired robot swarm control algorithm for dynamic environment monitoring. Adv. Robot. Res. **2**(1), 1 (2018)
9. Ji, K., Zhang, Q., Yuan, Z., Cheng, H., Yu, D.: A virtual force interaction scheme for multi-robot environment monitoring. Robot. Auton. Syst. **149**, 103967 (2022)
10. Zheng, J., Yang, T., Liu, H., Su, T., Wan, L.: Accurate detection and localization of unmanned aerial vehicle swarms-enabled mobile edge computing system. IEEE Trans. Industr. Inf. **17**(7), 5059–5067 (2020)
11. Zhou, W., Liu, Z., Li, J., Xu, X., Shen, L.: Multi-target tracking for unmanned aerial vehicle swarms using deep reinforcement learning. Neurocomputing **466**, 285–297 (2021)
12. Tahir, A., Böling, J., Haghbayan, M.-H., Toivonen, H.T., Plosila, J.: Swarms of unmanned aerial vehicles-a survey. J. Ind. Inf. Integr. **16**, 100106 (2019)
13. Zhou, C., et al.: The review unmanned surface vehicle path planning: based on multi-modality constraint. Ocean Eng. **200**, 107043 (2020)
14. Sauter, J.A., Bixler, K.: Design of unmanned swarm tactics for an urban mission," in Unmanned Systems Technology XXI, vol. 11021. SPIE, pp. 124–139 (2019)
15. Che, G., Liu, L., Yu, Z.: An improved ant colony optimization algorithm based on particle swarm optimization algorithm for path planning of autonomous underwater vehicle. J. Ambient. Intell. Humaniz. Comput. **11**(8), 3349–3354 (2020)
16. Herlambang, T., Rahmalia, D., Yulianto, T.: Particle swarm optimization (pso) and ant colony optimization (aco) for optimizing pid parameters on autonomous underwater vehicle (auv) control system. J. Phys. Conf. Ser. **1211**(1). IOP Publishing, 2019, p. 012039
17. Vedachalam, N., Ramesh, R., Jyothi, V.B.N., Prakash, D., Ramadass, G.: Autonomous underwater vehicles-challenging developments and technological maturity towards strategic swarm robotics systems. Marine Georesources Geotechnol. **37**(5), 525–538 (2019)
18. Berlinger, F., Gauci, M., Nagpal, R.: Implicit coordination for 3d underwater collective behaviors in a fish-inspired robot swarm. Sci. Robot. **6**(50), eabd8668 (2021)
19. Rubenstein, M., Cornejo, A., Nagpal, R.: Programmable self-assembly in a thousand-robot swarm. Science **345**(6198), 795–799 (2014)
20. Zhou, X., et al.: Swarm of micro flying robots in the wild. Sci. Robot. **7**(66), eabm5954 (2022)
21. Li, S., et al.: Particle robotics based on statistical mechanics of loosely coupled components. Nature **567**(7748), 361–365 (2019)
22. Wang, G., et al.: Emergent field-driven robot swarm states. Phys. Rev. Lett. **126**(10), 108002 (2021)
23. Kruk, N., Maistrenko, Y., Koeppl, H.: Self-propelled chimeras. Phys. Rev. E **98**(3), 032219 (2018)
24. Kuramoto, Y., Battogtokh, D.: Coexistence of coherence and incoherence in nonlocally coupled phase oscillators, arXiv preprint cond-mat/0210694 (2002)
25. Abrams, D.M., Strogatz, S.H.: Chimera states for coupled oscillators. Phys. Rev. Lett. **93**(17), 174102 (2004)
26. Parastesh, F., et al.: Chimeras. Phys. Rep. **898**, 1–114 (2021)
27. Zhang, J., et al.: Spontaneous emergence of multitasking robotic swarms. In: 2022 IEEE International Conference on Robotics and Biomimetics (ROBIO). IEEE, pp. 184–188 (2022)
28. Chaté, H., Ginelli, F., Grégoire, G., Peruani, F., Raynaud, F.: Modeling collective motion: variations on the vicsek model. Eur. Phys. J. B **64**(3), 451–456 (2008)
29. Ginelli, F.: The physics of the vicsek model. Eur. Phys. J. Special Top. **225**(11), 2099–2117 (2016)

30. Gong, C.C., Zheng, C., Toenjes, R., Pikovsky, A.: Repulsively coupled kuramoto-sakaguchi phase oscillators ensemble subject to common noise. Chaos Interdisciplinary J. Nonlinear Sci. **29**(3), 033127 (2019)
31. Mihara, A., Medrano-T, R.O.: Stability in the kuramoto-sakaguchi model for finite networks of identical oscillators. Nonlinear Dyn. **98**(1), 539–550 (2019)
32. Ha, S.-Y., Xiao, Q.: Nonlinear instability of the incoherent state for the kuramoto-sakaguchi-fokker-plank equation. J. Stat. Phys. **160**, 477–496 (2015)
33. Abhyankar, S., et al.: Petsc/ts: A modern scalable ode/dae solver library. arXiv preprint arXiv:1806.01437 (2018)
34. Zhang, H., Constantinescu, E.M., Smith, B.F.: Petsc tsadjoint: a discrete adjoint ode solver for first-order and second-order sensitivity analysis. arXiv preprint arXiv:1912.07696 (2019)
35. Zhang, Y., Motter, A.E.: Mechanism for strong chimeras. Phys. Rev. Lett. **126**(9), 094101 (2021)
36. Ashwin, P., Burylko, O.: Weak chimeras in minimal networks of coupled phase oscillators. Chaos Interdisciplinary J. Nonlinear Sci. **25**(1), 013106 (2015)
37. Burylko, O., Martens, E.A., Bick, C.: Symmetry breaking yields chimeras in two small populations of kuramoto-type oscillators. Chaos Interdisciplinary J. Nonlinear Sci. **32**(9), 093109 (2022)
38. Kotwal, T., Jiang, X., Abrams, D.M.: Connecting the kuramoto model and the chimera state. Phys. Rev. Lett. **119**(26), 264101 (2017)
39. Kohar, V., Ji, P., Choudhary, A., Sinha, S., Kurths, J.: Synchronization in time-varying networks. Phys. Rev. E **90**(2), 022812 (2014)

Cooperative Control of Dual-Manipulator System with Unknown Dynamic Parameters

Yuanyuan Li[1,2,3] (ID), Guilin Yang[3] (ID), Wenjing Wu[1,2], and Wenjie Chen[1,2](✉) (ID)

[1] Blue-Orange Lab, Midea Group, Foshan, China
[2] Midea Corporate Research Center, Midea Group, Foshan, China
chenwj42@midea.com
[3] Ningbo Institute of Materials Technology and Engineering, Chinese Academy of Sciences, Ningbo, China

Abstract. The precise control of the cooperative operation for dual-manipulator system has high requirements for the dynamic controller. In this paper, the cooperative control method of dual-manipulator system with unknown dynamic parameters and time-varying task space constraints is studied. Firstly, the dynamic model of manipulator in the task space coordinate system is established. Then, the radial basis function (RBF) neural networks are employed to construct the dynamic controller of dual-manipulator system with unknown model parameters for cooperative operation under relative trajectory constraints in task space. The simulation results verify the effectiveness of the controller.

Keywords: Adaptive dynamic control · Trajectory constraints in task space · Radial basis function neural network

1 Introduction

With the emerging advanced application of robot system, the complex operation process often requires two manipulators to cooperate. For example, in hazardous environments such as nuclear environment, due to the inaccessibility of personnel, the workpiece operation often needs the cooperation of two manipulators (as shown in Fig. 1), such as one manipulator clamping the workpiece, another manipulator cutting, polishing, decontamination, bolt disassembly or doing other operations. For cooperative operation, many processes have strict restrictions on space constraints. For example, in order to avoid affecting the adjacent operation, operations such as grinding, cutting and so on with high accuracy requirements often need to limit the trajectory error to a certain range, and the error limit is often asymmetric, or even changes with the position. In addition, the dynamic parameters of the manipulator are often inaccurate or unknown, which makes it difficult to build the accurate dynamic model of the manipulator, thus affecting

Supported by organization Midea Group.

the accuracy of the controller. Therefore, the problems of task space constraints and unknown dynamic parameters for dual manipulator cooperative operation need to be studied.

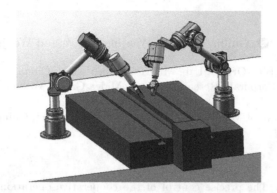

Fig. 1. Dual-manipulator cooperative operation

In the field of multi-manipulator cooperative control, a master-slave servo manipulator system is developed in reference [1]. The system consists of a driven dual manipulator module, an active dual manipulator operation module and a control system, which is controlled by a PD controller and a position based force feedback controller to realize the end effector force feedback without force sensor. In reference [2], a cooperative controller of dual-manipulator system is constructed by using Lyapunov method and adaptive neural network, which realizes the dynamic control of two manipulators under the condition of output hysteresis and unknown dynamic parameters of the manipulator. In reference [3], an adaptive controller for manipulator system operating the objects with uncertain pose is proposed. The controller can accurately control the trajectory of manipulator to grasp the uncertain pose target, and does not need the contact force sensor or calibrating by high-precision sensing device. In reference [4], a remote manipulator control system is proposed for the manual remote operation of two manipulators. The system combines the visual servo system and the bidirectional hybrid dynamic control method, and realizes the joint motion control process in the space motion through the damped least square method. In reference [5], the traditional non flutter sliding mode controller (SMC) is optimized by adding multi-input and multi-output fuzzy algorithm and optimizing the gain logic unit, resulting in enhanced tracking control effect of the controller. In reference [6], a control method is proposed for the dual-manipulator system mounted on the mobile platform, where the enhanced dynamic motion chain is established by combining the dual-manipulator model with the operation target model. In reference [7], the kinematic characteristics of a free floating space dual-manipulator system in closed-loop configuration are studied, and the dynamic model of the dual-manipulator system is established, and then a coordinated operation dynamic controller based on computational torque method and PI control method is proposed. In reference [8], a 3-DOF light compliant manipulator is designed, and a compliant control scheme is proposed to ensure the safety of the robot when interacting with the environment.

However, there is no research on adaptive control method of multi-manipulator cooperative operation system with unknown dynamic parameters and task space time-varying trajectory constraints in the above literatures.

This paper studies on the dynamic control problem of dual-manipulator system with unknown dynamic parameters for cooperative operation under time-varying constraints in task space. Firstly, the dynamic model of the manipulator in the task space coordinate system is established. Then, based on barrier Lyapunov method, the dynamic controller of dual-manipulator system with unknown model for cooperative operation under time-varying trajectory constraints in task space is constructed using adaptive neural networks (NNs), and the stability of the system is verified by Lyapunov method. Finally, the effectiveness of the dynamic controller is verified by simulation.

2 Problem Formulation

Considering the system friction and external force, the Lagrange dynamics model of a series manipulator based on the joint space coordinate is established as follows:

$$M(q)\ddot{q} + C(q,\dot{q})\dot{q} + F(q,\dot{q}) + G(q) = \tau - J^T(q)f \quad (1)$$

where, $q = [q(1), q(2), \cdots, q(i), \cdots, q(n)] \in \mathbb{R}^n$ is the joint space trajectory vector of serial manipulator; $q(i), i \in 1 \cdots n$ is the trajectory of the ith joint; $\tau \in \mathbb{R}^n$ is the input torque vector; $M(q) \in \mathbb{R}^{n \times n}$ is the inertia matrix which is symmetric and positive definite; $C(q,\dot{q})\dot{q} \in \mathbb{R}^n$ is the Centripetal and Coriolis torques vector; $G(q) \in \mathbb{R}^n$ is the gravitational force vector; $F(q,\dot{q}) \in \mathbb{R}^n$ is the friction vector of the system; $J^T(q)f \in \mathbb{R}^n$ is the torque vector in manipulator joint space caused by external force on the end of manipulator, where f is the external force in the task space coordinate system, and $J^T(q)$ is the Jacobian matrix of the velocity of the manipulator.

Let $x = [x(1), x(2), \cdots, x(n)] \in \mathbb{R}^n$ denote the trajectory vector of the manipulator in the task space coordinate, that is, the position and attitude trajectory of the manipulator end effector in Cartesian coordinate. Then the dynamic equation of the serial manipulator based on the task space can be obtained as follows:

$$M(x,q)\ddot{x} + C(x,\dot{x},q,\dot{q})\dot{x} + F_x(q,\dot{q}) + G_x(q) = \tau_x - f \quad (2)$$

where, $M(x,q), C(x,\dot{x},q,\dot{q}), F_x(q,\dot{q})$, and $G_x(q)$ are the matrices of serial manipulator dynamic equation corresponding to task space; τ_x is the virtual driving force vector of the manipulator in task space, which has no actual physical meaning and needs to be converted into the driving force in the joint space when controlling. $M(x,q), C(x,\dot{x},q,\dot{q}), F_x(q,\dot{q}), G_x(q)$ and τ_x are shown as Eq. 3–7.

$$M(x,q) = J^{-T}(q)M(q)J^{-1}(q) \quad (3)$$

$$C(x, \dot{x}, q, \dot{q}) = J^{-T} M(q) \frac{d}{dt} J^{-1}(q) + J^{-T} C(q, \dot{q}) J^{-1}(q) \qquad (4)$$

$$F_x(q, \dot{q}) = J^{-T} F(q, \dot{q}) \qquad (5)$$

$$G_x(q) = J^{-T} G(q) \qquad (6)$$

$$\tau_x = J^{-T} \tau \qquad (7)$$

For the dual-manipulator system of cooperative operation, the dynamic models of the two manipulators are established as below:

$$\tau_{x1} - f_1 = M_1(x_1, q_1)\ddot{x} + C_1(x_1, \dot{x}_1, q_1, \dot{q}_1)\dot{x}_1 + F_{x1}(q_1, \dot{q}_1) + G_{x1}(q_1) \qquad (8)$$

$$\tau_{x2} - f_2 = M_2(x_2, q_2)\ddot{x}_2 + C_2(x_2, \dot{x}_2, q_2, \dot{q}_2)\dot{x}_2 + F_{x2}(q_2, \dot{q}_2) + G_{x2}(q_2) \qquad (9)$$

Among them, vectors q_1, q_2, x_1 and x_2 represent the position trajectory vectors of manipulator 1 and 2 in joint space coordinate and task space coordinate respectively.

In order to ensure that the actual relative trajectories of the two manipulators is within the limited area of the operation space, the relative position trajectories of manipulator 1 and manipulator 2 are constrained, and $\underline{k}_c(t)$ and $\overline{k}_c(t)$ are respectively the upper and lower bounds of the relative trajectory of manipulator 1 relative to manipulator 2. The schematic diagram of time-varying trajectory constraints in task space is shown in Fig. 2.

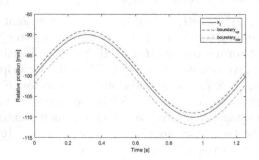

Fig. 2. Sketch of time-varying trajectories constraints in task space

3   Control Design

In this section, the adaptive NNs are employed to fit the dynamic parameters of the manipulators, and the Barrier Lyapunov function is employed to limit the system output to the required time-varying constraints. In addition, an auxiliary variable is created to help constructing the Barrier Lyapunov function. The strategy for the control method is shown as Fig. 3.

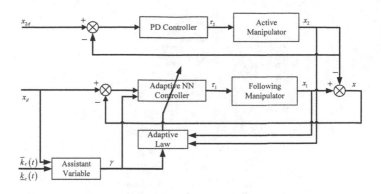

Fig. 3. Adaptive NN Control Strategy

As active manipulator, the manipulator 2 is controlled separately, which can use common PD control method. The manipulator 1 cooperates with manipulator 2 to realize the relative trajectory in task space. The actual relative trajectories vector of manipulator 1 relative to manipulator 2 in task space is expressed as follows:

$$x = x_1 - x_2 \tag{10}$$

Let x_d represent the expected relative trajectories vector of coordinate manipulator 1 relative to manipulator 2 in task space. The relative trajectories error between the actual trajectories and the expected trajectories is as follows:

$$e_1 = x - x_d = x_1 - x_2 - x_d \tag{11}$$

For a system with unknown dynamic parameters, the adaptive NNs $W_i^T S(Z)$ based on radial basis function (RBF) are employed to fit the unknown parts of the dynamic equation, which are shown as Fig. 4. The adaptive NNs are defined as Eq. 12.

$$\begin{aligned}
W^{*T} S(Z) = & f_1 + C_1 \left(x_1, \dot{x}_1, q_1, \dot{q}_1 \right) \gamma + M_1 \left(x_1, q_1 \right) \dot{\gamma} + F_{x1} \left(q_1, \dot{q}_1 \right) + \\
& G_{x1} \left(q_1 \right) + C_1 \left(x_1, \dot{x}_1, q_1, \dot{q}_1 \right) \dot{x}_2 + M_1 \left(x_1, q_1 \right) \ddot{x}_2 - \epsilon(Z)
\end{aligned} \tag{12}$$

where, $S(Z) = [S_1(Z), S_2(Z), \cdots, S_l(Z)]^T$ is vector of radial basis functions; $l > 1$ is the NNs nodes number; $Z = \left[x_1^T, \dot{x}_1^T, \ddot{x}_1^T, x_2^T, \dot{x}_2^T, \ddot{x}_2^T, \gamma, \dot{\gamma} \right]$ is the input vector of NNs; W^* is the expected weight value of adaptive NNs; $\epsilon(Z) \in \mathbb{R}^n$ is the estimation error of adaptive NNs. $\gamma(t)$ is a variable designed as below:

$$\gamma(t) = [\gamma_1(t), \gamma_1(t), \cdots, \gamma_n(t)] \tag{13}$$

$$\gamma_i(t) = x_{di} - k_{1i} * e_{1i} - k_{2i} * e_{1i} \tag{14}$$

where k_{1i} is a positive constant, and k_{2i} is shown in Eq. 15:

$$k_{2i} = \sqrt{\beta + \left(\frac{\dot{k}_{bi}}{k_{bi}} \right)^2 + \left(\frac{\dot{k}_{ai}}{k_{ai}} \right)^2} \tag{15}$$

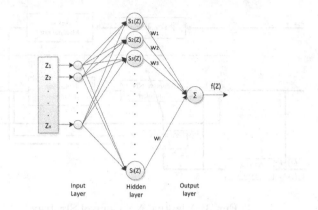

Fig. 4. Structure of RBF neural networks

where, β is a small positive number, which can ensure the system stability when $\dot{k}_{ai}$ and $\dot{k}_{bi}$ are both zero.

$$k_a(t) = x_d(t) - \underline{k}_c(t) \tag{16}$$

$$k_b(t) = \overline{k}_c(t) - x_d(t) \tag{17}$$

Let $\hat{W}$ represent the weight estimation value, and define the weight estimation error of the adaptive NNs as Eq. 18:

$$\tilde{W} = \hat{W} - W^* \tag{18}$$

The controller is designed as follows:

$$\tau_{x1} = -K_2 e_2 - (e_2^T)^{-1} \sum_{i=1}^{n} \varnothing_i e_{1i} e_{2i} + \hat{W}^T S(Z) \tag{19}$$

Design the following Barrier Lyapunov function:

$$V_1 = \sum_{i=1}^{n} \frac{1}{2} In \frac{1}{1-\varepsilon_i^2} + \frac{1}{2} e_2^T M_1(x_1, q_1) e_2 \tag{20}$$

where,

$$\varepsilon_i = h(i)\varepsilon_{bi} + (1 - h(i))\varepsilon_{ai} \tag{21}$$

$$\begin{cases} \varepsilon_{ai} = \frac{e_{1i}}{k_{ai}} \\ \varepsilon_{bi} = \frac{e_{1i}}{k_{bi}} \end{cases} \tag{22}$$

$$h(i) = \begin{cases} 0, e_{1i} \leq 0 \\ 1, e_{1i} > 0 \end{cases}, i = 1, 2, \cdots, n \tag{23}$$

$$e_2 = \dot{x} - \gamma(t) \tag{24}$$

The Barrier Lyapunov function is further designed as shown in Eq. 25.

$$V_3 = V_2 + \frac{1}{2}\sum_{i=1}^{n}\widetilde{W}_i^T \Gamma_i^{-1}\widetilde{W}_i \tag{25}$$

Deriving the Eq. 25 by t, Eq. 26 can be obtained. Due to space limitations, the derivation process is omitted.

$$\dot{V}_3 = \dot{V}_2 + \sum_{i=1}^{n}\widetilde{W}^T \Gamma_i^{-1}\dot{\widetilde{W}}$$

$$\leq -\sum_{i=1}^{n}\left(k_{1i}\frac{\varepsilon_i^2}{(1-\varepsilon_i^2)}\right) + \sum_{i=1}^{n}\widetilde{W}^T \Gamma_i^{-1}\dot{\widetilde{W}} + \tag{26}$$

$$e_2^T\left(-K_2 e_2 + \widetilde{W}^T S(Z) + \epsilon(Z)\right)$$

The adaptive law of NNs is designed as follows:

$$\dot{\widehat{W}}_i = -\Gamma_i\left(S(Z)e_{2i} + \delta_i\widehat{W}_i\right) \tag{27}$$

where, $i = 1, 2, \cdots, n$; Γ_i is a diagonal matrix of order l with positive constant elements; δ_i is a tiny positive constant, which can reduce the adverse impact of interferences on the system.

By substituting Eq. 27 into Eq. 26, Eq. 28 can be obtained. The proof process is omitted.

$$\dot{V}_3 \leq -\sum_{i=1}^{n}\frac{k_{1i}e_{1i}^2}{k_i^2 - e_{1i}^2} - e_2^T K_2 e_2 - e_2^T \epsilon(Z) - e_2^T f_1 - \sum_{i=1}^{n}\widetilde{W}^T \Gamma_i^{-1}\delta_i\widehat{W} \tag{28}$$

$$\leq -\rho V_3 + C$$

where,

$$\rho = \min\left\{\min_{i=1,2,\cdots,n}\left(2k_{1i}, \frac{2\lambda_{min}(K_2 - I)}{\lambda_{max}(M_1(x_1, q_1))}, \frac{\delta_i}{\lambda_{max}(\Gamma_i^{-1})}\right)\right\} \tag{29}$$

$$C = \frac{1}{2}\|\epsilon(Z)\|^2 + \frac{1}{2}\|f_{max}\|^2 + \sum_{i=1}^{n}\frac{\delta_i}{2}\|W_i^*\|^2 \tag{30}$$

It can be proved that the tracking trajectory of the cooperative manipulator relative to the active manipulator can asymptotic stably approach the input trajectory, that is, when $t \to \infty$, $x(t) \to x_d(t)$. The tracking trajectory error of the cooperative manipulator relative to the active manipulator meets the requirements of space constraints, that is, $\forall \underline{k}_c(t) \leq x_i(t) \leq \overline{k}_c(t), e_1 \in \Omega_{e1}$, where Ω_{e1} is defined as follows:

$$\Omega_{e1} = \left\{e_1 \in \mathbb{R}^n \mid -\sqrt{k_{ai}^2(1 - e^{-D})} \leq e_{1i} \leq \sqrt{k_{bi}^2(1 - e^{-D})}\right\} \tag{31}$$

where, $D = V_3(0) + C/\rho$; C and ρ are all positive, which are defined as Eqs. 29 and 30. The proof process is omitted.

4   Simulation

In this section, the control process of dual-manipulator system is simulated to verify the effectiveness of the controller 19. The dual-manipulator system is shown in Fig. 5. Both the active manipulator 2 and the cooperative manipulator 1 have two degrees of freedom in pitch. The base coordinate system origin for manipulator 2 coincides with the world coordinate system origin, and the base coordinate system origin of manipulator 1 coincides with the X axis of the world coordinate system, with the distance $d = 500mm$ from the origin of manipulator 2 to that of manipulator 1.

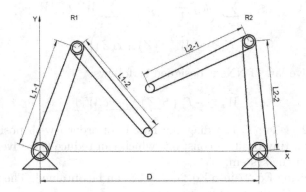

Fig. 5. Model of dual-manipulator system

To simplify the calculation, the arms of the manipulator are simplified as connecting rods, and the centroid of each arm is assumed to be on the center of the rod. The parameters for this dual-manipulator system are shown as below.

$$L_{11} = 500mm, L_{12} = 500mm, L_{21} = 500mm, L_{22} = 500mm$$
$$m_{11} = 50kg, m_{12} = 30kg, m_{21} = 50kg, m_{22} = 30kg \tag{32}$$

The two manipulators work cooperatively. The expected operation path of the active manipulator 2 is a sinusoidal curve; the cooperative manipulator 1 swings up and down in the vertical direction relative to the active manipulator, that is, the trajectory of the cooperative manipulator 1 is consistent with that of the active manipulator 2 in the x-axis direction, and is a sinusoidal curve relative to the active manipulator 2 in the y-direction.

Assume the expected trajectory of the active manipulator 2 is as follows.

$$\begin{cases} x_{2ed} = 250 + 20 * t \\ y_{2ed} = 400 + 50 * sin(t) \end{cases} \tag{33}$$

The trajectory of the cooperative manipulator 1 relative to the active manipulator 2 is as follows.

$$\begin{cases} x = 0 \\ y = -100 + 10 * sin(5 * t) \end{cases} \tag{34}$$

The goal of the controller is to make the actual trajectories of cooperative manipulator 1 relative to active manipulator 2 track the expected trajectories in the task space as precisely as possible, while meeting the following workspace constraints:

$$\begin{cases} kc_{xmin} < x < kc_{xmax} \\ kc_{ymin} < y < kc_{ymax} \end{cases} \tag{35}$$

where, $kc_{min} = -2$, $kc_{max=1}$, $kc_{ymin} = 10 * sin(5 * t) - 2$, $kc_{ymax} = 10 * sin(5 * t) + 1$.

The expected trajectories of the active manipulator 2 are shown in Fig. 6; the expected trajectories and constraints boundaries of the cooperative manipulator 1 relative to the active manipulator 2 are shown in Fig. 7.

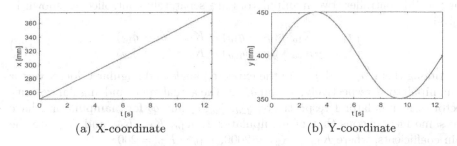

(a) X-coordinate   (b) Y-coordinate

Fig. 6. Expected trajectory of active manipulator 2

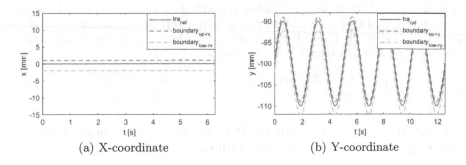

(a) X-coordinate   (b) Y-coordinate

Fig. 7. Expected trajectory of manipulator 1 relative to manipulator 2

The simulation is carried out by adaptive NNs controller proposed in this paper. The PD and model-based controllers are also simulated for this dual-manipulator system, so as to compare the effectiveness with the controller proposed in this paper.

4.1   Adaptive NNs Control

According to the controller constructed in this paper, a NNs structure $W^{*T}S(Z)$ is proposed to fit the unknown terms in the dynamic equation. The input variables of the NNs are the variables related to the unknown terms fitted, that is, $Z = [x_1; dx_1; dx_2; ddx_2; \gamma_1; d\gamma_1]$, which are 12 independent input variables. The hidden layer are set to have 4096 nodes, and the centers of basis functions are evenly distributed in the state space of input variables. The initial weights of NNs are all set to 0. The gain coefficients are set to $K_1 = diag[10, 10]$, $K_2 = diag[1, 1]$. Other parameters of the NNs are set to $\delta_1 = \delta_2 = 0.01$, $\Gamma_1 = \Gamma_2 = 0.001$.

4.2   PD Control

For the Pd controller, two manipulators are separately controlled as shown in Eq. 36.

$$\begin{cases} \tau_1 = -K_{1a} * (q_1 - q_{1d}) - K_{1b} * (\dot{q}_1 - \dot{q}_{1d}) \\ \tau_2 = -K_{2a} * (q_2 - q_{2d}) - K_{2b} * (\dot{q}_2 - \dot{q}_{2d}) \end{cases} \tag{36}$$

Among them, q_{1d} and $\dot{q}_{1d}$ are the expected angle and angular velocity vector of manipulator 1 respectively; q_1 and $\dot{q}_1$ are the actual angle and angular velocity vector of manipulator 1 respectively; q_{2d}, $\dot{q}_{2d}$, q_2 and $\dot{q}_2$ for manipulator 2 have the same meanings as that of manipulator 1. K_{1a}, K_{1b}, K_{2a} and K_{2b} are the gain coefficients, where $K_{1a} = K_{2a} = 2000$, $K_{1b} = K_{2b} = 200$.

4.3   Model-Based Control

Because the purpose of model-based control is to approach the expected trajectory as closely as possible, not only the follower manipulator but also the active manipulator need to employ model-based method to avoid excessive deviation from the expected trajectory. Thus, two manipulators are separately controlled by model-based method, and PD controllers are also employed to eliminate initial errors and external interference, as shown in Eq. 37.

$$\begin{cases} \tau_1 = \tau_{1pd} + M_1(q_1) \times \ddot{q}_{1d} + C_1(q_1, \dot{q}_1) \times \dot{q}_{1d} + G_1(q_1) \\ \tau_2 = \tau_{2pd} + M_2(q_2) \times \ddot{q}_{2d} + C_2(q_2, \dot{q}_2) \times \dot{q}_{2d} + G_2(q_2) \end{cases} \tag{37}$$

Among them, τ_{1pd} and τ_{2pd} are the PD controller as the same as Eq. 36, and $M(q)$, $C(q, \dot{q})$ and $G(q)$ are consistent with the annotations in Eq. 1.

4.4   Analysis of Simulation Results

The relative trajectories of simulation results and constraints boundaries under above three control methods are shown in Fig. 8. The figure shows that there is a certain error between the actual motion trajectory and expected trajectory of manipulator 1 under PD controller, and the trajectory exceeds the constraint boundaries many times; the relative error under model-based controller is small

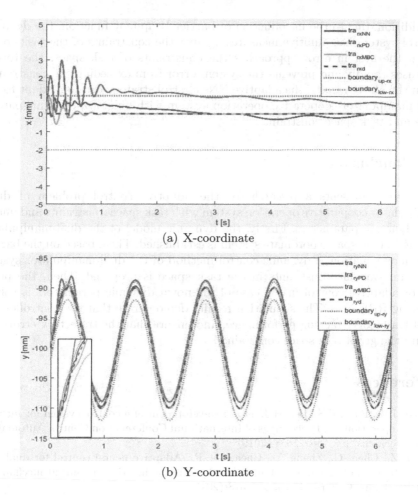

(a) X-coordinate

(b) Y-coordinate

Fig. 8. Comparison of relative trajectories under three control methods

and can converge to zero soon, but still slightly exceeds the constraints boundaries at initial stage; relatively, the motion trajectory under NNs controller can track the expected trajectory well, and it is strictly controlled within the constraints boundaries.

The simulation results show that the performance of the traditional PD controller is not good in the dynamic control of the dual manipulator cooperative operation system with unknown dynamic parameters and task space constraints. The model-based controller can track the relative trajectory good, but it's hard to obtain the accurate dynamic parameters of dual-manipulator system, especially when the payload changes frequently.

In contrast, the adaptive NNs controller proposed in 19 can effectively realize the learning and approximation of robot dynamic parameters, and make the dynamic control errors decrease step by step with the increase of running time.

In addition, due to the introduction of barrier Lyapunov function, the dynamic control system has punitive measures against the constraints of the task space. When the system error approaches the constraints of task space, the torque increases rapidly and prevents the system error from exceeding the constraints. From the above results, the adaptive NNs control strategy can well adapt to the dual-manipulator cooperative operation system with unknown dynamic parameters and task space constraints.

5   Conclusion

This paper presents a research for the adaptive control problem of dual-manipulator cooperative operation system with task space constraints and uncertain dynamic parameters. Firstly, the dynamic model of the dual-manipulator system in task space coordinate system is established. Then, based on the barrier Lyapunov equation, a dynamic control method of the dual manipulator system with time-varying constraints in the task space is proposed. Then, the problem of adaptive control in the case of unknown dynamic parameters is solved by using RBF NNs. The simulation results demonstrate that the controller has good trajectory tracking performance, and ensure that the trajectory errors are within the given task space constraints.

References

1. Lee, J.K., Park, B.S., Lee, H.J., et al.: Development of a control system for master-slave operation. In: Proceedings of International Conference on Control Automation and Systems, pp. 1851–1854 (2010)
2. Liu, Z., Chen, C., Zhang, Y., Chen, C.L.P.: Adaptive neural control for dual-arm coordination of humanoid robot with unknown nonlinearities in output mechanism. IEEE Trans. Cybern. **45**(3), 507–518 (2015)
3. Aghili, F.: Adaptive control of manipulators forming closed kinematic chain with inaccurate kinematic model. IEEE/ASME Trans. Mechatron. **18**(5), 1544–1554 (2012)
4. Kruse, D., Wen, J.T., Radke, R.J.: A sensor-based dual-arm tele-robotic system. IEEE Trans. Autom. Sci. Eng. **12**(1), 4–18 (2014)
5. Hacioglu, Y., Arslan, Y.Z., Yagiz, N.: MIMO fuzzy sliding mode controlled dual arm robot in load transportation. J. Franklin Inst. **348**(8), 1886–1902 (2011)
6. Likar, N., Nemec, B., Žlajpah, L.: Mechanism approach for dual-arm manipulation. Robotica **32**(6), 321–326 (2014)
7. Shi, Z.K.: Research on Dynamics Control of Dual-arm Free-floating Space Robotic System. Nanjing University of Aeronautics and Astronautics, Nanjing (2005)
8. Zhao, H.F.: Study on Structure Design and Control of Light Compliant Robotic Arm for Human-robot Cooperation. Beijing Jiaotong University, Beijing (2017)

Disturbance Rejection Fixed Point Control of DELTA Parallel Manipulator Mounted on Autonomous Underwater Vehicle

Yuantao Li, Shaowen Yang, Yihang Xu, and Jian Liu[✉]

School of Automation, Southeast University, Nanjing 210018,
People's Republic of China
yuantao_li@seu.edu.com, bkliujian@163.com

Abstract. This paper studied the fixed point control task of a DELTA parallel manipulator mounted on an autonomous underwater vehicle. Such a system features complex dynamics and susceptibility to disturbances due to its parallel structure and floating base. The main disturbances of the fixed point control task are the coupling reaction between the vehicle and the manipulator and the position error of the end-effector caused by the fluctuation of the underwater vehicle. We proposed a method to achieve better performance in aspects of accuracy and stability for the DELTA manipulator used in the underwater vehicle manipulator system (UVMS). First, we introduce the mechanical structure of the UVMS studied in this paper. Second, we derive the coupling relationship between the manipulator and the underwater vehicle and then feed it to the controller of the vehicle. Third, the vehicle's velocity and position changes are obtained through the acceleration data of the vehicle under a hovering state. Then the changes are compensated by the controller of the DELTA manipulator, which adjusts the trajectory in joint space. Finally, simulation results are presented to verify the feasibility of our method.

Keywords: Underwater vehicle manipulator system · DELTA parallel manipulator · Fixed point control

1 Introduction

Autonomous underwater vehicle (AUV) has undoubtedly become a promising platform in the field of ocean exploration and marine resource utilization. Underwater manipulators also have enormous potential in these fields. In order to

This work was supported in part by the Natural Science Foundation of Jiangsu Province of China under Grant BK20210214, the Fundamental Research Funds for the Central Universities, and the "Zhishan" Scholars Programs of Southeast University.

H. Yang et al. (Eds.): ICIRA 2023, LNAI 14273, pp. 451–463, 2023.
https://doi.org/10.1007/978-981-99-6498-7_39

fully develop the functionality of underwater manipulators, the underwater vehicle manipulator system (UVMS) that combines manipulators with underwater vehicles has received attention from researchers [1–4].

In current research on UVMS, underwater robots with a serial manipulator as the operating arm are the mainstream [5–8]. In [9], researchers established a hydrodynamic model of a UVMS equipped with a Reach5 Mini manipulator using Morrison's formula to approximate the hydrodynamic forces. The primary reason for utilizing a serial manipulator rather than a parallel manipulator is that the modeling of serial manipulators is simple, and there are mature control and design solutions. At the same time, the workspace of serial manipulators is also large, and the motion is relatively flexible. However, there are also obvious flaws in the use of serial manipulators. For instance, the inertia is greater for the reason that each link of serial manipulators is heavier as the driving motor fixed on it and that the moving range of each link is larger when operating. On the contrary, although the dynamic model of a parallel manipulator is relatively complex and the workspace is more limited, its servo motors are mounted at the static base, and the material of the connecting rods is lighter, which declines the inertia of the motion mechanism. Besides, compared to serial manipulators whose motion error is accumulated by each joint, the motion error of parallel manipulators is averaged by each joint, resulting in higher motion accuracy. Therefore, parallel manipulators can complete actions more precisely and smoothly and introduce less interference to the base. Moreover, due to their slender and lighter linkages, parallel manipulators can reduce the influence of drag forces and restoring forces when operating in water. Simoni R, Rodríguez P R, Cieálak P, et al. proposed a 6-DOF DELTA manipulator which can be folded and deployed under different circumstances and utilized it for a UVMS, which was modeled and analyzed then [10].

Two issues cannot be ignored when considering the operations of UVMS in the underwater environment. For one thing, coupling forces and torques exist between the manipulator and the floating base AUV, which can cause unexpected movements and tilts. For another thing, the turbulent flow of seawater generates a propulsive effect on the AUV, causing a deviation from the pre-specified position, and thus the end-effector of the manipulator drifts away from the target point. Research aimed at addressing these two problems is primarily focused on UVMS armed with serial manipulators, and the degrees of freedom of these manipulators are typically low [11–14]. In [15], Brian Lynch and Alex Ellery studied the reaction between the vehicle and the manipulator and computed the forces and torques needed to maintain both vehicle stability and barycenter stability (which demands the attitude of the vehicle staying unchanged) by introducing compensation into the vehicle controller. In addition to model-based methods, observer-based methods are also a research focus, as they can bypass the complexity of the model and unmodeled errors. Yong Dai, Shuanghe Yu, et al. conducted research on the trajectory tracking mission carried by UVMS under the influence of unmodeled uncertainties, noises in sensor data, and time-varying external disturbances [16,17]. They addressed the sensor measurement error by using an extended Kalman filter (EKF) and removed the constraint of the previous works that the reference trajectory must be known precisely at the same time. And a robust fast tube model predictive controller is presented in their papers to overcome the uncertainties and disturbances. Most research mentioned above, which aims at eliminating the external disturbance of fluctuating water, compensates for the position error by adjusting the input of the controller of the AUV instead of that of the manipulator. In [18], Hildebrandt M, Christensen L, Kerdels J, et al. brought up a compensation algorithm utilizing not AUV movements but manipulator movements. Compares and combinations with conventional station-keeping methods are presented. As substantial conclusions on UVMS armed with serial manipulators as drawn by researchers, researches on those with DELTA manipulator are relatively limited but undoubtedly valuable considering the conveniences brought by the features mentioned before.

This paper aims to achieve the fixed point control task of a UVMS composed of an AUV and a DELTA manipulator. A control method is proposed to compensate for the coupling reaction between the AUV and the DELTA manipulator and to eliminate the position error of the end-effector caused by the seawater current interference. This paper makes the following contribution:

- Formulation of a method for compensating coupling reaction between the AUV and the DELTA manipulator using the manipulator's dynamic model of;
- Development of an approach for fixed point control of the end-effector in the underwater environment with flow disturbance;
- Simulated results showing significant reduction in attitude error of AUV and position error of end-effector.

The remainder of the paper is structured as follows. Section 2 elucidates the composition, structure, and establishment of coordinate systems of the UVMS. Furthermore, the dynamic model of the DELTA manipulator is also obtained for usage in the latter sections. Section 3 delineates the controllers of thrusters of the AUV and actuators of the DELTA manipulator. Section 4 exhibits simulation results, and Sect. 5 draws a conclusion for this paper.

2   Overview and Dynamics of UVMS

2.1   Overview of the UVMS

The robot platform used in this paper is a UVMS consisting of an AUV and a DELTA parallel manipulator. The motion of the vehicle is achieved through the propeller thrust of eight thrusters, which are distributed symmetrically, as shown in Fig. 1. The four vertically-oriented thrusters account for the underwater vehicle's vertical motion, roll, and pitch. And the four horizontally-oriented thrusters are responsible for horizontal translation and yaw rotation. The attitude of the AUV is obtained by the IMU located on its body, while the relative position between the grasping target and the vehicle can be obtained by the stereo cameras located in the front. The DELTA manipulator is a parallel configuration with three identical kinematic chains. Each chain includes an active revolve joint mounted on the static platform which is fixed to the bottom part of the underwater vehicle frame, an upper arm driven by the actuator as an active arm, and a lower arm as a passive arm connecting the active arm and the motion platform. Due to this structural feature, the motion platform and the static platform of the DELTA manipulator remain parallel to each other, which means the motion platform cannot rotate. Thus, the manipulator has only three degrees of freedom.

The frames defined for the description of motion states of the UVMS are depicted in Fig. 1. The frame $\{W\}$ is an arbitrarily placed inertial frame with the Z-axis aligned in the opposite direction of the gravity vector. $\{B\}$ is the frame attached to the center of mass of the AUV with the X-axis pointing its heading direction. Frame $\{S\}$ is rigidly attached to the static platform of the DELTA manipulator at its center of gravity, and frame $\{D\}$ is rigidly attached to the motion platform in the same way. The X-Y planes of frame $\{S\}$ and $\{D\}$ coincide with the planes formed by three connecting joints, and the X-axis passes through one of the joints for the convenience of kinematics analysis.

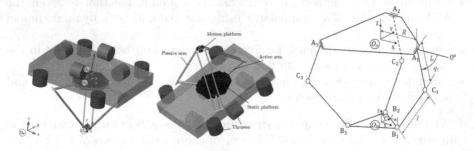

Fig. 1. Defined frames of the UVMS model and geometry structure of the DELTA parallel manipulator.

The simplified geometry structure of the DELTA parallel manipulator is also shown in Fig. 1. A_1, A_2, A_3 represent the locations where the actuators are mounted on the static platform, and the plane $A_1A_2A_3$ represents the static platform. C_1, C_2, C_3 represent the connection joints between active arms and passive arms, B_1, B_2, B_3 represent the revolve joints where the slave arms are joined with the motion platform, and the plane $B_1B_2B_3$ represents the motion platform. The angle between each active arm and the static platform is represented by $q_i(i = 1, 2, 3)$, and the positive direction of rotation is indicated in the figure.

2.2   Dynamics of the DELTA Manipulator

In order to compensate for the coupling forces generated by the DELTA manipulator action and exerted on the underwater vehicle, it is necessary to obtain each active joint's output torque for the following action of the manipulator. The research and application of dynamic modeling methods for manipulators have become relatively mature. Given the complexity brought about by the high coupling structure, the Lagrange method and the virtual work principle method are usually chosen by researchers for the dynamic modeling of the DELTA manipulator [20]. In this paper, the virtual work principle method was used. The hydrodynamic effects on the arms of the DELTA manipulator are disregarded, owing to their lightweight and slender nature.

According to the virtual work principle, for a system composed of n rigid bodies, the dynamic equation can be written in the following form:

$$\sum_{i=1}^{n}[(m_i\ddot{\boldsymbol{x}}_i - \boldsymbol{F}_i)\cdot\delta\boldsymbol{x}_i + (\boldsymbol{I}_i\dot{\boldsymbol{\omega}}_i + \boldsymbol{\omega}_i \times \boldsymbol{I}_i\boldsymbol{\omega}_i - \boldsymbol{T}_i)\cdot\delta\boldsymbol{\varphi}_i] = 0 \tag{1}$$

where m_i and $\boldsymbol{I}_i$ denote the mass and inertia of the i-th rigid respectively, $\boldsymbol{F}_i$ and $\boldsymbol{T}_i$ denote the external force and moment applied to the i-th rigid respectively, $\ddot{\boldsymbol{x}}_i$ is the acceleration of the i-th rigid's center of mass, $\boldsymbol{\omega}_i$ is the angular rate of the i-th rigid and $\dot{\boldsymbol{\omega}}_i$ is its angular acceleration, $\delta\boldsymbol{x}_i$ and $\delta\boldsymbol{\varphi}_i$ denote the virtual linear displacement and virtual angular displacement of the i-th rigid respectively.

For the DELTA manipulator, the motion analysis is divided into three parts: the active arms, the passive arms, and the motion platform. According to equation (1), the dynamic equation of the DELTA manipulator can be written as (2):

$$\boldsymbol{\tau}_n + \sum_{i=1}^{3}\boldsymbol{\tau}_{a,i} + \sum_{i-1}^{3}\boldsymbol{\tau}_{p,i} - \boldsymbol{0} \tag{2}$$

where $\boldsymbol{\tau}_n$ is the component standing for the moment produced by the motion platform, $\boldsymbol{\tau}_{a,i}$ is the component standing for the moment produced by each active arm, and $\boldsymbol{\tau}_{p,i}$ is the component produced by each passive arm.

The component of the motion platform must include gravity and inertial force, but there is no moment generated by the rotation of the motion platform, for it is always parallel to the static platform. So the formula can be derived as follows:

$$\boldsymbol{\tau}_n = \boldsymbol{J}^T(m_n\ddot{\boldsymbol{x}}_n - \boldsymbol{G}_n) \tag{3}$$

where $\boldsymbol{J}$ is the Jacobian matrix which represents the transformation from the angular velocity vector of actuators to the velocity vector of the motion platform. m_n and $\ddot{\boldsymbol{x}}_n$ denote the mass, acceleration, and gravity of the motion platform, respectively. $\boldsymbol{G}_n = m_n[0\ 0\ -g]^T$ is the gravity of the motion platform and g is the gravitational acceleration.

The relationship between the angle and angular velocity of active joints and the position and velocity of the DELTA manipulator can be obtained from relevant geometric constraints. The details of the derivation process will not be elaborated on, and the Jacobian matrix $\boldsymbol{J}$ can be derived as follows:

$$\boldsymbol{J} = -\begin{bmatrix} \boldsymbol{s}_1^T \\ \boldsymbol{s}_2^T \\ \boldsymbol{s}_3^T \end{bmatrix}^{-1}\begin{bmatrix} \boldsymbol{s}_1^T\boldsymbol{b}_1 & 0 & 0 \\ 0 & \boldsymbol{s}_2^T\boldsymbol{b}_2 & 0 \\ 0 & 0 & \boldsymbol{s}_3^T\boldsymbol{b}_3 \end{bmatrix} \tag{4}$$

where $s_i = \overrightarrow{B_iC_i}$, and b_i is given as follows:

$$b_i = R_i^S \begin{bmatrix} L\sin q_i \\ 0 \\ L\cos q_i \end{bmatrix} \qquad i = 1, 2, 3. \tag{5}$$

where R_i^S presents the rotation matrix of the i-th actuator with respect to the static platform frame. L is the length of the active arm.

For the active arms which only rotate around three driving joints, the driving torques output by the actuators must be accounted:

$$\tau_a = I_a \ddot{q} - T_{Ga} - \tau \tag{6}$$

where τ_a represents the sum of vector $\tau_{a,i}(i = 1, 2, 3)$ mentioned in equation (2). $\tau \in \mathbb{R}^3$ is the vector of torques produced by the actuators. $I_a = \text{diag}(I_{a1}, I_{a2}, I_{a3})$ is the inertia matrix of three active arms. T_{Ga} denotes the torque produced by the gravity of three active arms and is given as:

$$T_{Ga} = \frac{1}{2}m_a Lg[\cos q_1 \; \cos q_2 \; \cos q_3]^\top \tag{7}$$

where m_a is the mass of each active arm.

For the passive arms, the contribution of inertial forces is computed using the accelerations at both ends of the arms and the corresponding Jacobian matrices. And the torques exerted during their rotation can be neglected since the rotational angles are relatively small. So the expression of the torque contribution is obtained as follows:

$$\tau_{p,i} = \frac{1}{3}m_p \left[J^\top \left(\ddot{x}_n + \frac{1}{2}a_{u,i} \right) + J_{u,i}^\top \left(\frac{1}{2}\ddot{x}_n + a_{u,i} \right) \right]$$
$$- \frac{1}{2}(J + J_{u,i})^\top m_p \begin{bmatrix} 0 \\ 0 \\ -g \end{bmatrix} \tag{8}$$

where m_p is the mass of each passive arm. $a_{u,i}$ is the acceleration of the upper end of each passive arm, which is marked using point $C_i(i = 1, 2, 3)$ in Fig. 2. $J_{u,i}$ denotes the Jacobian matrix which relates angular velocity vector $\dot{q}$ and the velocity vector of upper ends of passive arms $v_{u,i}$. Specifically, $J_{u,1} = [-b_1 \; 0 \; 0]$, $J_{u,2} = [0 \; -b_2 \; 0]$, and $J_{u,3} = [0 \; 0 \; -b_3]$. The acceleration of the upper end of each passive arm can be obtained using the following equation:

$$a_{u,i} = -R_i^S \left(\begin{bmatrix} L\sin q_i \\ 0 \\ L\cos q_i \end{bmatrix} \ddot{q}_i + \begin{bmatrix} L\cos q_i \\ 0 \\ -L\sin q_i \end{bmatrix} \dot{q}_i^2 \right) \tag{9}$$

Finally, by substituting Eqs. (3) (6) (8) into formula (2) and transposing terms in the result, the expression of output torques of three actuators can be obtained as follows:

$$\boldsymbol{\tau} = \boldsymbol{I}_a \ddot{\boldsymbol{q}} + \boldsymbol{J}^\top m_n \ddot{\boldsymbol{x}}_n - \boldsymbol{G}_a - \boldsymbol{J}^\top \boldsymbol{G}_n + \sum_{i=1}^{3} \boldsymbol{\tau}_{p,i} \tag{10}$$

For the purpose of counteracting the coupling reaction introduced by the manipulator, transformation to the X-Y plane of the AUV is then done by projecting each actuator torque into the X-Z and Y-Z planes following the topology of the actuators' location. The coupling torques vector expressed in base frame $\hat{\boldsymbol{\tau}}$ is computed as follows:

$$\hat{\boldsymbol{\tau}} = \sum_{i=1}^{3} \begin{bmatrix} \tau_{ix} \\ \tau_{iy} \\ \tau_{iz} \end{bmatrix} = \sum_{i=1}^{3} \tau_i \begin{bmatrix} R^{-1} & 0 & 0 \\ 0 & R^{-1} & 0 \\ 0 & 0 & 1 \end{bmatrix} \boldsymbol{R}_i^B \begin{bmatrix} 0 \\ 0 \\ 1 \end{bmatrix} \tag{11}$$

where $\boldsymbol{R}_i^B$ is the rotation matrix of the i-th joint frame with respect to the vehicle base frame.

3 Control Framework Design

In this section, the design of the control scheme is discussed. We consider designing control signals from two aspects, as shown in Fig. 2. The AUV is assumed to be hovering at the target position. The command attitude φ_B^{des} of the AUV is fed to the AUV controller, and the desired coordinate position x_{ee}^{des} and velocity $\dot{x}_{ee}^{des}$ of the DELTA manipulator are transformed to the joint-space trajectory q_{ee}^{des} and $\dot{q}_{ee}^{des}$ which are fed to the actuator controller of the manipulator. First, considering AUV attitude stability, the coupling reaction generated by the dynamics of the DELTA manipulator acts on the AUV while the torque compensation algorithm using the dynamic model established in section 2 generates a control signal u_{comp} to counteract this force. Second, considering manipulator fixed point control, the deviation of position x_B and speed $\dot{x}_B$ of the AUV caused by flow disturbance in the underwater environments are utilized to correct the target trajectory of the manipulator. From the perspective of disturbance rejection of the DELTA manipulator, this paper considered the coupling interaction between the manipulator and the vehicle as internal disturbances of the UVMS, while the influences of seawater currents on the UVMS are considered external disturbances. In summary, the control objectives are to maintain the ideal attitude of the AUV in the presence of the coupling interaction and to hold the target position of the end-effector of the DELTA manipulator under wave disturbances.

3.1 Baseline Controller

In the fixed point control of the DELTA manipulator end-effector, the AUV should be relatively stable in position and attitude, for their deviation from the pre-specified pose will introduce a decrease in posture accuracy. The feedback data for the position and attitude loop is obtained by the IMU which can sense the acceleration and angular velocity of the AUV. And the input signals for the thrusters are computed using a PD controller.

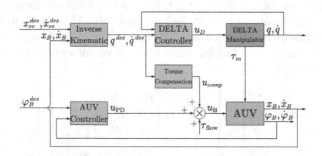

Fig. 2. General control scheme

To diminish the coupling effect on the AUV, we use feedforward compensation to address the interaction forces caused by the motion of the DELTA manipulator. The control input u_B can be designed as follows:

$$u_B = u_{PD} + u_{comp} \tag{12}$$

where u_{PD} is the output of the PD controller for thrusters. u_{comp} is the compensation item computed according to the forces and torques calculated using the dynamic model mentioned earlier in this paper and can be expressed as:

$$u_{comp} = -K_{comp}\hat{\tau} \tag{13}$$

where K_{comp} is constant coefficient.

3.2   Manipulator Controller

Considering the interference of waves while working in shallow nearshore water, the DELTA manipulator controller is designed to take the AUV's acceleration into account. The acceleration is obtained through the IMU data, and the velocity and position deviations of the AUV are estimated using the acceleration data. In ideal conditions, the velocity and position changes can be obtained from its acceleration data using an integrator. However, in practical applications, the accelerometer data unavoidably contains noises. Besides, the integrator also leads to drifting errors. This paper focus on the correction method for position error of the end-effector under flow disturbance rather than data procession.

The motion control of the end-effector of the DELTA manipulator is investigated from two perspectives, as shown in Fig. 3. In one approach, the joint controller of the manipulator aims to control three joint angles directly using a cascaded PID structure. In another approach, the joint controller aims to directly control the joint velocities by utilizing the joint angle error as an adding correction term. In the figure, $\boldsymbol{x}_{ee}^{des}$ and $\dot{\boldsymbol{x}}_{ee}^{des}$ represent the desired position and velocity of the end-effector. $\boldsymbol{x}_B^{est}$ and $\dot{\boldsymbol{x}}_B^{est}$ represent the estimated position and velocity changes of the AUV. And the block "IK" means inverse kinematics of the DELTA manipulator.

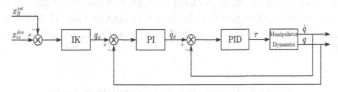

(a) Block diagram of the cascaded PID method

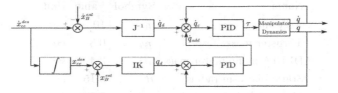

(b) Block diagram of the velocity tracking method

Fig. 3. Block diagram of the DELTA manipulator controller.

The control input of the velocity tracking method can be obtained as shown below:

$$ \boldsymbol{u} = k_{\text{P1}} \left(\dot{\boldsymbol{q}}_d - \dot{\boldsymbol{q}} \right) + k_{\text{I1}} \int_0^T \left(\dot{\boldsymbol{q}}_d - \dot{\boldsymbol{q}} \right) \mathrm{d}t + k_{\text{D1}} \ddot{\boldsymbol{q}} \tag{14} $$

where

$$ \dot{\boldsymbol{q}}_d = \boldsymbol{J}^{-1} \left(\dot{\boldsymbol{x}}_{ee}^{des} - \dot{\boldsymbol{x}}_B^{est} \right) + k_{\text{P2}} \left(\boldsymbol{q}_d - \boldsymbol{q} \right) + k_{\text{I2}} \int_0^T \left(\boldsymbol{q}_d - \boldsymbol{q} \right) \mathrm{d}t + k_{\text{D2}} \dot{\boldsymbol{q}} \tag{15} $$

$$ \boldsymbol{q}_d = \boldsymbol{q}_{plan} + \boldsymbol{q}_{comp} \tag{16} $$

where $\boldsymbol{q}_{plan}$ and $\boldsymbol{q}_{comp}$ denote the target joint angle output by the trajectory planner and the estimated compensation joint position, respectively. $\boldsymbol{q}_d, \dot{\boldsymbol{q}}_d, \boldsymbol{q}, \dot{\boldsymbol{q}}, \ddot{\boldsymbol{q}} \in \mathbb{R}^3$ are the active joints' desired angular position, velocity, and actual angular position, velocity, and acceleration respectively. $k_{\text{P1}}, k_{\text{I1}}, k_{\text{D1}}, k_{\text{P2}}, k_{\text{I2}}, k_{\text{D2}} \in \mathbb{R}^3$ are the manually tuned control gains.

4   Simulation Results

This section simulates the fixed points control performance of a UVMS consisting of an AUV and a DELTA parallel manipulator using SIMULINK and SIMSCAPE. The simplified model is built up in Solidworks and imported to SIMSCAPE, and the controllers for the AUV and the manipulator are established using the method described earlier in this paper. The simulation scenario involves the UVMS hovering at a specified underwater location in a nearshore area while the end-effector of the DELTA manipulator moves along the trajectory generated by the trajectory planner and arrives at then maintains the target position. This simulation applied a simplified model of wave disturbances. It assumes that wave disturbances result in a change in the relative velocity between the AUV and the fluid, thereby affecting the hydrodynamic terms associated with the relative velocity and causing an impact on the AUV's acceleration. The premise of the proposed simplification method is that the size of the AUV is much smaller than the wavelength of the waves, which aligns with the conditions investigated in this study.

Table 1. Parameters of the simulation model

Name	Symbol	Value	Unit
AUV mass	m_A	10	kg
Thruster mass	m_T	0.5	kg
DELTA manipulator mass	m_D	3.4	kg
Static platform radius	R	0.15	m
Motion platform radius	r	0.03	m
Active arm length	L	0.2	m
Passive arm length	l	0.5	m

The parameters of the simulation model are listed in Table 1. Assuming the mass distribution of components is uniform. The vector of adding pushing forces from the waves is set as $f_{add} = [28cos(1.75\pi t)\ 20cos(1.75\pi t)\ 23cos(1.75\pi t)]N$. The simulation results are illustrated using Fig. 4 and Fig. 5. Figure 4 shows the position error of the end-effector of the DELTA manipulator in fixed point control. It's obvious that both methods with joint trajectory correction significantly reduce the position error. Besides, the velocity tracking method gets the target position faster and has smaller errors in the first four seconds, which can meet the requirements of short-term tasks, including grasping. After four seconds, the reduction of position error is limited by the disturbance observer, which can be a key problem to be solved in future works. Figure 5 shows the attitude deviation of the AUV caused by the motion of the DELTA manipulator when tracking a spiral trajectory. It manifests that the AUV controller with torque compensation can achieve better attitude stabilization.

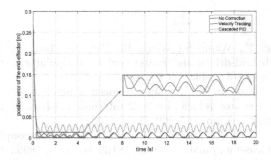

Fig. 4. Position error of the end-effector of the DELTA manipulator.

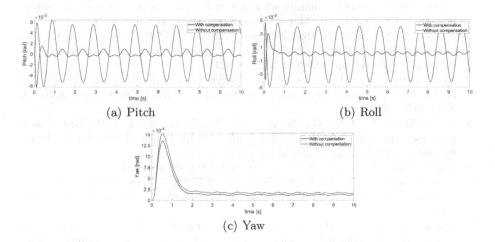

Fig. 5. Attitude errors of the AUV.

5   Conclusion

This paper investigated the fixed point control task carried out by a UVMS in an underwater environment. A method for mitigating the effects of disturbances during the task was proposed. The coupling reaction was compensated by the torque compensation algorithm using the dynamic model of the DELTA manipulator, and the deviation of the AUV was taken into account to correct the coordinate trajectory of the manipulator for fixed point control of the end-effector. Besides, to enhance fixed point control performance, a velocity tracking method was proposed and compared with the cascaded PID method. The simulation results verified the advantages of the proposed method. Future work aims to make use of the period flow disturbance knowledge to investigate the multi-task trajectory planning of UVMS. Further work aims for hardware implementation in a real underwater environment with flow disturbances.

References

1. Cai, M., Wang, Y., Wang, S., Wang, R., Ren, Y., Tan, M.: Grasping marine products with hybrid-driven underwater vehicle-manipulator system. IEEE Trans. Autom. Sci. Eng. **17**(3), 1443–1454 (2020)
2. Konoplin, A., Krasavin, N.: Automatic speed control system for manipulator mounted on underwater vehicle. In: 2022 International Russian Automation Conference (RusAutoCon), pp. 205–209. IEEE (2022)
3. Han, H., Wei, Y., Ye, X., Liu, W.: Modeling and fuzzy decoupling control of an underwater vehicle-manipulator system. IEEE Access **8**, 18962–18983 (2020)
4. Liu, J., Zhang, Y., Yu, Y., Sun, C.: Fixed-time event-triggered consensus for nonlinear multiagent systems without continuous communications. IEEE Trans. Syst. Man Cybern. Syst. **49**(11), 2221–2229 (2019)
5. Cai, M., Wang, S., Wang, Y., Wang, R., Tan, M.: Coordinated control of underwater biomimetic vehicle-manipulator system for free floating autonomous manipulation. IEEE Trans. Syst. Man Cybern. Syst. **51**(8), 4793–4803 (2019)
6. Zhekov, Z., Atanasov, N.: Modelling and Control of 2-DOF underwater manipulator in presence of disturbances. In: 2021 International Conference Automatics and Informatics (ICAI), pp. 333–336. IEEE (2021)
7. Liu, J., Yu, Y., He, H., Sun, C.: Team-triggered practical fixed-time consensus of double-integrator agents with uncertain disturbance. IEEE Trans. Cybern. **51**(6), 3263–3272 (2021)
8. Lv, J., Wang, Y., Tang, C., Wang, S., Xu, W., Wang, R., Tan, M.: Disturbance rejection control for underwater free-floating manipulation. IEEE/ASME Trans. Mechatron. **27**(5), 3742–3750 (2021)
9. Gao, L., Song, Y., Gao, J., Chen, Y.: Dynamic modeling and simulation an underwater vehicle manipulator system. In: 2022 IEEE 9th International Conference on Underwater System Technology: Theory and Applications(USYS), pp. 1–6. IEEE (2022)
10. Simoni, R., Rodriguez, P.R., Cieslak, P., Weihmann, L., Carboni, A.P.: Design and kinematic analysis of a 6-DOF foldable/deployable Delta parallel manipulator with spherical wrist for an I-AUV. In: OCEANS 2019-Marseille, pp. 1–10. IEEE (2019)
11. Zohedi, F.N., Aras, M.S.M., Kasdirin, H.A., Bahar, M.B., Aripin, M.K., Azis, F.A.: Modelling and controlling of Underwater Remotely Operated Vehicle vertical trajectory using Gradient Descent Algorithm Single Input Fuzzy Logic Controller and Fuzzy Logic Controller. In: 2022 IEEE 9th International Conference on Underwater System Technology: Theory and Applications(USYS), pp. 1–6. IEEE (2022)
12. Periasamy, T., Asokan, T., Singaperumal, M.: Controller design for manipulator trajectory control of an AUV-manipulator system. In: 2008 IEEE Region 10 and the Third international Conference on Industrial and Information Systems, pp. 1–6. IEEE (2008)
13. De Wit, C.C., Diaz, O.O., Perrier, M.: Nonlinear control of an underwater vehicle/manipulator with composite dynamics. IEEE Trans. Control Syst. Technol. **8**(6), 948–960 (2000)
14. Sakagami, N.: Precise control of underwater vehicle manipulator systems using iterative learning control. In: 2009 ICCAS-SICE, pp. 3089–3093. IEEE (2009)
15. Lynch, B., Ellery, A.: Efficient control of an AUV-manipulator system: an application for the exploration of Europa. IEEE J. Oceanic Eng. **39**(3), 552–570 (2013)
16. Dai, Y., Yu, S., Yan, Y.: An adaptive EKF-FMPC for the trajectory tracking of UVMS. IEEE J. Oceanic Eng. **45**(3), 699–713 (2019)

17. Dai, Y., Yu, S., Yan, Y., Yu, X.: An EKF-based fast tube MPC scheme for moving target tracking of a redundant underwater vehicle-manipulator system. IEEE/ASME Trans. Mechatron. **24**(6), 2803–2814 (2019)
18. Hildebrandt, M., Christensen, L., Kerdels, J., Albiez, J., Kirchner, F.: Realtime motion compensation for ROV-based tele-operated underwater manipulators. In: OCEANS 2009-EUROPE, pp. 1–6. IEEE (2009)
19. Cai, M., Wang, Y., Wang, S., Wang, R., Tan, M.: Autonomous manipulation of an underwater vehicle-manipulator system by a composite control scheme with disturbance estimation. IEEE Trans. Autom. Sci. Eng. (2023)
20. Featherstone, R.: Rigid body dynamics algorithms. Springer (2014)

Efficient Autonomous Exploration of Unknown Environment Using Regions Segmentation and VRP

Chaoyu Xue[1], Tianhao Zhao[2], Anhuan Xie[3], Qiuguo Zhu[1,2,4](✉), Jun Wu[1,4], and Rong Xiong[1,4]

[1] College of Control Science and Engineering, Zhejiang University, Hangzhou, China

[2] Polytechnic Institute, Zhejiang University, Hangzhou, China
[3] Zhejiang Lab, Hangzhou, China
[4] State Key Laboratory of Industrial Control and Technology, Zhejiang University, Hangzhou, China
qgzhu@zju.edu.cn

Abstract. Autonomous exploration of unknown environments is a critical application scenario in robotics. However, existing studies have strived to generate an efficient tour plan that enables the robots to fully explore the environment. This is due to the greedy strategies and the lack of utilizing the information of the unexplored area. To address the above issues, we propose a new exploration strategy. Our approach involves partitioning the unexplored area into distinct regions and utilizing their estimated workload and spatial structure to construct a region graph. Subsequently, a VRP (Vehicle Routing Problem) planner allocates regions to robots and generates a global tour for each robot in a coordinated manner, which is then refined and provided to the robot's navigation module. Experimental results demonstrate that that our method outperforms existing approaches in terms of exploration speed, total distance, and overlap ratio.

Keywords: Exploration · unknown environment · multi-robot coordination · region segmentation · vehicle routing problem

1 Introduction

Exploration of unknown environments is an important application scenario for unmanned robots. There are many real-life scenarios that require rapid and thor-

This work was supported by the National Key R&D Program of China (Grant No. 2022YFB4701502), the "Leading Goose" R&D Program of Zhejiang (Grant No. 2023C01177), the Key Research Project of Zhejiang Lab (Grant No. 2021NB0AL03), and the Key R&D Project on Agriculture and Social Development in Hangzhou City (Asian Games) (Grant No. 20230701A05).

H. Yang et al. (Eds.): ICIRA 2023, LNAI 14273, pp. 464–476, 2023.
https://doi.org/10.1007/978-981-99-6498-7_40

ough exploration of the unknown environment, such as environment reconstruction, wilderness rescue, space exploration, and more. Compared to the single-robot system, a multi-robot system offers significant advantages such as higher efficiency and greater robustness.

Existing studies on multi-robot exploration of unknown environments often employs a greedy strategy, where robots prioritize the selection of the closest goal that provides the most information. However, the greedy manner neglects the overall structure of the environment. While it maximizes the rate of information acquisition, it can lead to backtracking. Furthermore, most of the studies only focus on the information directly available from the explored area, overlooking the potential of estimating the information of the unexplored space. The explored space only provides information about the distance between the robots and the targets, but information about the unexplored space, such as workload, spatial structure, etc., is equally important for task assignment.

To address these issues, we proposed a novel exploration method. We introduced a new modeling approach that partitions the unexplored space into distinct regions and constructs a region graph. This model allows the estimation of the spatial structure and the required workload of the unexplored space, which can guide the task assignment step. Based on this model, we designed a TSP/VRP-based planner to obtain the optimal sequence of visiting all regions, thereby avoiding backtracking. In addition, we presented a path refinement method that uses the information obtained from the regions to smooth the final paths executed by the robot's navigation module.

This article will be presented as follows: Sect. 2 summarizes the previous related work; Sect. 3 introduces the overall structure of our method, followed by Sects. 4 and 5, which describe the two main modules: the task generation module and the route planning module. The experiment results are displayed in Sect. 6, and finally Sect. 7 concludes this article and discusses possible improvements in future work.

2   Related Works

The problem of exploring unknown environments with robots has been widely studied. We divided the previous contributions into three parts: task generation, goal selection, and multi-robot collaboration.

2.1   Task Generation

Nearly all studies used target points as tasks for planning. There are two primary methods for generating target points: frontier-based and sampling-based. Yamauchi [20] pioneered the frontier-based method in 1997. Robots continuously move towards the boundary of known and unknown space to advance the exploration process. [2,13,16,21] also employed a similar approach.

Literature [3] is a typical example of sampling-based approaches. It is based on a Rapid-exploring Random Tree (RRT) that grows from the robot's current location and expands to the entire explored space. The nodes with high information gain will be used for candidate goals. There are many studies that have improved the RRT-based method, such as [17], which combined a real-time local RRT and an incrementally updated global RRT, enabling fast exploration and complete coverage at the same time. Literature [6] introduced RRG, where a graph replaces the tree structure, and the outermost nodes are selected as target points; local RRG is also used to construct a global RRG for global planning. Our work combines the frontier-based method and the sampling-based method, and introduces the concept of regions.

2.2   Goal Selection

There are two mainstream strategies for goal selection: greedy algorithms and the Traveling Salesman Problem (TSP).

Many studies employed a greedy strategy to select goals for robots. These studies use a utility function to evaluate the quality of assigning a robot to a given goal. The simplest utility function is the opposite of the distance a robot must travel to reach the goal, as in [13,19,20,24]. In [16], Burgard et al. introduce the information gain into the utility function, which represents the number of unknown grid cells that can be explored near a target point. The concept of information gain is widely adopted by many studies, such as [3,6,12,22]. Some methods considered not only the information gain at the goal, but also along the way from the robot to the goal, such as [1,11].

TSP-based approaches consider assigning a sequence of goals to the robots, optimizing the total distance from a long-term perspective, thus avoiding the short-sightedness of greedy algorithms. In [23], TSP was used to compute the visit sequence of all frontiers. [22] proposed a hierarchical design using a greedy planner for local exploration and a TSP planner for global exploration. In [5], the TSP planning was used for both local and global routes, differing only in the granularity of the local and global tasks.

2.3   Multi-robot Collaboration

In a single-robot scenario, the next target could be obtained by greedily selecting the goal with the highest utility or by solving a TSP to visit all goals. In a multi-robot scenario, however, it is necessary to consider the task distribution among the robots. Several classical algorithms have been used for multi-robot task assignment, such as the greedy algorithm employed in [4], the Hungarian algorithm employed in [19], and the linear programming employed in [15]. Another commonly used method is market-based auctions [18,25].

Assignment after clustering the target points is also a commonly used approach. In [19], a Voronoi diagram was constructed by utilizing distance fields to partition different regions, and then regions were assigned to robots accordingly. In [10], Voronoi partitions were computed by using the robots' location as the origin of each partition, and then each robot selects only the goals in the partition that belong to it. [8] applied the K-Means algorithm to cluster candidate goals and assigned clusters to robots.

The TSP-based task assignment algorithms are more sophisticated because the TSP itself is an NP-hard problem, which is complex and computationally intensive, especially for multi-robot scenarios. Therefore, a combination of the TSP-based method and other methods is often used as a compromise. In [9], a greedy algorithm is used, but the distance cost part in the utility function is calculated by solving a TSP. In [8], after clustering the goals, each robot independently solves the TSP to compute its own order of visiting each goal. In [7], an approximate solution to TSP is obtained by summing the"distance from the robot to the center of the goals" and the "distance from the center of the goals to each goal", which is then used for task assignment.

Our work employs a VRP-based planner to implement both the goal selection part and the multi-robot collaboration part. However, instead of planning the shortest route through all frontiers, which limits the route to the explored area, we plan the shortest route through all unexplored regions by estimating their workload and spatial structure.

3   System Overview

The proposed method consists of two modules: a task generation module and a route planning module, as shown in Fig. 1. The task generation module detects frontiers from the occupancy grid, partitions the unexplored space into multiple regions and estimates their workload. The route planning module constructs a region graph and uses a VRP solver to calculate the order in which the robots should visit each region, then optimizes the path, and finally sends it to the navigation server.

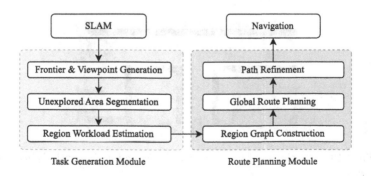

Fig. 1. An overview of the proposed exploration method

4   Task Generation

4.1   Frontiers and Viewpoints

The concept of frontiers is also used in this paper. After the raw frontier cells are detected from the map, we cluster them according to the sensor radius of the robot to ensure that no frontier cluster is larger than the observable range of a robot. This also means that it only requires one robot to observe a frontier. It is therefore inefficient to assign more than one robot to a frontier.

The center of a frontier cluster is not suitable as a viewpoint because it may be too close to the obstacles and may be in the unexplored space. We use a RRG (Rapid-exploring Random Graph) to represent the known feasible space, and we search the vertices of the RRG near the frontier cluster to find the viewpoint that provides the most information gain.

It is difficult to determine the exact information gain of a viewpoint. The environment behind the frontier is unknown. The ray tracing needed to calculate the information gain is also too computationally intensive. We choose the field-of-view angle when observing the frontier cluster from a vertex as the approximation of its information gain. Let G be the RRG and $\mathcal{F}: \{F_1, F_2, \ldots, F_{N_F}\}$ be the set of frontier clusters. The best viewpoint vp_i of F_i is solved by:

$$\arg\max_{vp \in G} fov(vp, F_i),$$
$$s.t. fov(vp, F_i) > fov_{min}, \tag{1}$$
$$d(vp, F_i) < d_{max}$$

If no viewpoint satisfies the constraints, the frontier F_i will be considered as unobservable and will be discarded. A result of frontiers detection and viewpoints selection is illustrated in Fig. 2.

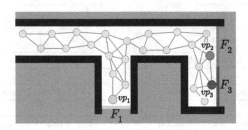

Fig. 2. The RRG, the clustered frontiers F_1, F_2, F_3 and each frontier's best viewpoint vp_1, vp_2, vp_3

Note that the best viewpoint selected in this step may not be used as the final navigation goal due to the path refinement, as detailed in Sect. 6.3.

4.2 Unexplored Space Segmentation

We do not use frontiers or their viewpoints as tasks directly. We only take them as entrances of unexplored regions. It is the unexplored regions behind those frontiers that are really used as tasks in the subsequent allocation process.

The unexplored areas are partitioned into smaller pieces that at the same time represent the spatial structure. We use a method inspired by the Voronoi tessellation algorithm. Let $\mathcal{S} = \{s_k\}$ be the segmented unexplored regions. Let $M_{unexplored}$ be the unexplored space of the environment. Let c be a cell of the occupancy grid and C_k be the set of cells that belong to s_k, then:

$$C_i = \{c \in M_{unexplored} \mid d(c, vp_i) \leq d(c, vp_j), \forall j \neq i\} \qquad (2)$$

where $d(c, vp)$ is the distance between cell c and viewpoint vp computed using the RRG. A segmentation result is shown in Fig. 3.

Fig. 3. Frontiers detection (left), unexplored space segmentation (center), and the region graph (right).

With this segmentation method, the unexplored areas with multiple entrances will be divided into multiple regions with only one entrance. How these regions are formed into a region graph to represent the spatial structure will be described later in Sect. 6.1.

4.3 Regions' Workload

In order to reasonably decide which regions each robot should visit, we estimate the amount of work required for each region. We choose the "distance to be travelled to explore the region" to describe the workload of a region.

It is not possible to evaluate the exact workload of an unknown region as the exact environment within it is unknown. We use the size of a region to roughly estimate its workload. Let $\hat{w}_i$ be the estimated workload of region s_i, and let $|C_i|$ be the size of region s_i, then:

$$\hat{w}_i = k \cdot |C_i| \qquad (3)$$

where k is a variable meaning "on average, a robot need to travel km to explore $1m^2$ of unexplored area". Obviously, the value of k depends on the specific characteristics of the environment. The spatial topology of the free space, the density of obstacles, etc. will all affect the value of k. It is therefore obviously not possible to set its value manually before starting the exploration. We use a simple adaptive method to calculate k:

$$k = \frac{\sum_{i=1}^{N_R} d_i}{|M_{explored}|} \qquad (4)$$

where d_i is the distance travelled by robot r_i, and $|M_{explored}|$ is the size of the explored area.

5 Route Planning

5.1 Region Graph

To describe the spatial structure among regions, and for later use in providing the cost matrix to the VRP solver, a weighted graph is constructed, where the nodes represent unexplored regions, and the edges represent the connection between two regions. The algorithm for constructing the region graph is depicted in Algorithm 1.

Algorithm 1. Build Region Graph

---
for s_i in S **do**
$\quad v_i \leftarrow G$.add_vertex $(\hat{w}_i)$
end for
for s_i, s_j in S **do**
$\quad$ **if** $adj(s_i, s_j)$ **then**
$\quad\quad G$.add_edge $(v_i, v_j, 0)$
$\quad$ **else**
$\quad\quad G$.add_edge $(v_i, v_j, dist (vp_i, vp_j))$
$\quad$ **end if**
end for

A constructed region graph is shown in Fig. 3. If two regions are directly adjacent, the weight of the edge connecting them is 0 because a robot can go directly to the other after exploring one. If the two regions are not directly adjacent, the weight of the edge connecting them is equal to the distance travelled on the feasible space from the viewpoint of one to the viewpoint of the other. This does not mean that the movement between two non-adjacent regions has to be achieved through explored feasible space. A robot can do this by moving through other unexplored regions. Thus, it requires further processing to generate the cost matrix used by the VRP solver.

5.2   Global Route Planning

The standard VRP does not consider the cost of each node. It only requires a matrix describing the cost of travelling between any two nodes. We design the engaged cost matrix from the region graph in three steps.

Firstly, we transform the weights of the nodes into the weights of the edges connected to them. In this way when a robot enters a node and then leaves it, the weight of the route is equivalent to the case before the transformation.

$$w_{ij}^{\star} = \frac{1}{2}\left(\hat{w}_i + \hat{w}_j\right) + w_{ij} \tag{5}$$

Secondly, we use an all-pairs shortest path algorithm, such as Johnson's algorithm, to compute the distance matrix of all regions.

Finally, we add robots to the cost matrix. The cost from a robot to a region is equal to the distance from the robot to the region's viewpoint on the feasible space. Since the robot doesn't need to return to its starting point, the cost from any region to a robot will be 0.

Now we have the complete cost matrix. By solving a TSP for a single robot or a VRP for multiple robots, an optimal sequence for visiting each region can be found. Then each robot will navigate to the viewpoint of the first region on the robot's visiting sequence.

5.3   Path Refinement

The viewpoint selected for a frontier in Sect. 5.2 has the best view of the unexplored area behind the frontier and can obtain the most information. However, this also means that it is often very close to the frontier, which will make robot's path rather twisted. If a region can be observed in one go, there is no need for a robot to go to the optimal viewpoint.

Thanks to the concept of "region", we can get the exact shape and size of an unexplored region and therefore have the ability to find all the viewpoints that can observe the entire region. Figure 4 illustrates the process of the path refinement. To simplify the notation, suppose that $s_i, 1 \leq i < N_{rf}$ are the regions considered for path refinement for robot r_k. For each s_i, let $\mathcal{VP}'_i$ be the viewpoints that can observe the entire region. We use the Dijkstra algorithm to find a path $\varepsilon = \left\{\xi_k, x_1, x_2, \ldots, x_{N_{rf}-1}, vp_{N_{rf}}\right\}$ where $x_i \in \mathcal{VP}'_i, 1 \leq i < N_{rf}$ that minimizes the overall distance cost:

$$J = |x_1 - \xi_k| + \sum_{i=1}^{N_{rf}-2} |x_{i+1} - x_i| + |vp_{N_{rf}} - x_{N_{rf}-1}| \tag{6}$$

6   Experiments

We compared the proposed method with two other methods. The first one is a greedy method. It chooses the robot-frontier pair with the largest utility, and

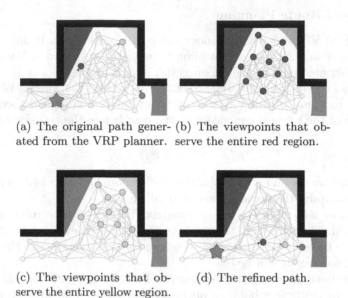

(a) The original path gener- (b) The viewpoints that ob-
ated from the VRP planner.   serve the entire red region.

(c) The viewpoints that ob-   (d) The refined path.
serve the entire yellow region.

Fig. 4. Path refinement process.

then adjusts the information gain of the frontiers around, and so on iteratively. The second one is a TSP-based method. It groups the frontiers using a Voronoi method, then assigns them to robots, and finally calculates the visiting sequence for each robot using a TSP solver. We have evaluated the three methods in three types of environments: a grid-like one, a campus-like one, and one with random obstacles, illustrated in Fig. 5. All three maps have a size of $30 \times 50 \text{m}^2$. Furthermore, to evaluate the scalability of the proposed method, we performed experiments with groups of 1, 2 and 4 robots.

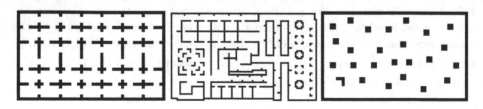

Fig. 5. The environments used for the experiments: a grid (left), a campus (center), and a random one (right).

The simulation was implemented in a ROS2-Gazebo framework. All scenarios were performed within the same computational environment. All robots have the same configuration: each robot is equipped with a LIDAR with a sensing radius of 12m and is capable of omnidirectional movement at a speed of 0.5m/s. Each scenario has been run 10 times to reduce the impact of randomness.

We use the OR-Tools [14] to solve the VRP. However, we find that the solution is not stable, causing robots moving back and forth. To get more stable solution, we have to allow the solver to take longer time to solve the problem. We allow the solver to take up to 3 s to find a solution each time.

The exploration task discussed in this paper requires robots to fully explore the designated environment in the least amount of time. We use the following three metrics to evaluate the performance of the methods:

1. Average Exploration Time (AET): The time it takes the robots to finish the exploration. It measures the general efficiency of the exploration algorithm. It is further divided into two metrics: average movement time (AMT) and average computation time (ACT).
2. Average Travel Distance (ATD): The total distance travelled by all robots from the start to the end of the exploration. It measures the energy consumed by the robots during the exploration.
3. Average Overlap Ratio (AOR): The ratio of the sum of the area explored by each robot to the total area explored. It measures the level of coordination between multiple robots.

The results of our experiments are listed in Table 1, 2 and 3. As can be seen from the statistics, in most of the scenarios, our method outperformed other methods in all three aspects of movement time, travel distance, and overlay ratio.

Table 1. Performance of the methods in the grid environment

Robots	1 robot			2 robots			4 robots		
Method	Ours	Greedy	mTSP	Ours	Greedy	mTSP	Ours	Greedy	mTSP
ATD [m]	**219.15**	251.44	233.97	**256.63**	268.10	267.63	**251.26**	311.64	273.84
AET [s]	552.82	449.74	**409.62**	369.68	**239.48**	260.52	228.91	**142.75**	175.79
AMT [s]	**380.56**	446.77	406.97	**221.20**	236.99	258.01	**117.90**	140.81	173.59
ACT [s]	172.26	2.97	**2.65**	148.48	**2.49**	2.52	111.01	**1.94**	2.20
AOR [100%]				**1.45**	1.51	1.53	**1.95**	2.28	1.96

The total distance and movement time in the same scenario are not always positively correlated, because there are times when some robots are not assigned goals and therefore stay in place. In the campus environment, the mTSP method sometimes resulted in less total travel distance but more exploration time, while our method assigns tasks to each robot more evenly.

The exploration progress illustrated in Fig. 6 shows that our method was not necessarily faster than other methods in the early stages of exploration. But in the later stages, when other methods cause the robots to backtrack, our method was able to maintain the high speed and complete the exploration sooner.

Table 2. Performance of the methods in the campus environment

Robots	1 robot			2 robots			4 robots		
Method	Ours	Greedy	mTSP	Ours	Greedy	mTSP	Ours	Greedy	mTSP
ATD [m]	**461.94**	464.07	472.50	512.22	507.80	**451.52**	522.98	539.82	**416.03**
AET [s]	1179.91	**835.08**	859.39	888.79	**449.61**	478.85	501.49	**257.34**	275.87
AMT [s]	**799.94**	831.17	855.76	548.99	**446.35**	474.33	**246.67**	254.55	273.00
ACT [s]	379.96	3.91	**3.63**	339.80	**3.25**	4.52	254.82	**2.79**	2.87
AOR [100%]				**1.21**	1.51	1.21	1.73	1.84	**1.51**

Table 3. Performance of the methods in the random environment

Robots	1 robot			2 robots			4 robots		
Method	Ours	Greedy	mTSP	Ours	Greedy	mTSP	Ours	Greedy	mTSP
ATD [m]	**214.80**	240.93	256.68	**235.68**	269.93	274.25	**250.48**	296.67	282.50
AET [s]	542.91	**437.52**	455.25	323.50	**253.94**	258.34	221.92	**135.35**	197.39
AMT [s]	**374.37**	434.00	451.47	**201.80**	250.86	255.78	**121.93**	133.20	194.99
ACT [s]	168.54	**3.52**	3.78	121.70	3.08	**2.56**	100.00	**2.16**	2.40
AOR [100%]				**1.32**	1.61	1.70	**1.95**	2.43	2.05

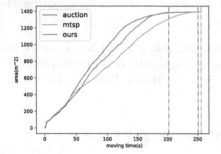 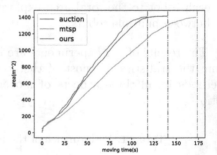

Fig. 6. The exploration progress of three methods in the random environment with 2 robots (left) and in the grid environment with 4 robots (right)

Our method shows different performance in different types of environments. The performance advantage is greater in the grid-like environment and in the random environment. This is because our method assumes that adjacent unexplored regions are in fact also connected, while the large number of rooms and corridors in the campus-like environment does not fit this assumption.

7 Conclusion and Discussion

In this paper, we proposed a new approach for single or multiple robots to explore unknown environments. We partitioned the unexplored space into multiple regions and took use of the additional information provided by the regions - their size and spatial structure - to make an estimate of the unknown space and thus get a better plan. A VRP-based planner has been proposed to assign regions to robots. Our method has been implemented and evaluated in simulation. The experiments show that our method is able to reduce the exploration execution time and the overlap ratio compared to existing methods.

The total exploration time in the multi-robot experiments failed to outperform the existing methods because the VRP is strongly NP-hard and time-consuming to find the solution. We plan to try some approximation algorithm to reduce the computation time. We also plan to design a hierarchical method to reduce the number of times the central node computes the VRP, to mitigate the back and forth movement of the robots due to the non-optimal solutions.

The universality of our method also needs further improvement. We need a more accurate estimation of the unexplored area, considering not only the size of the region, but also the characteristics of the environment, such as the density of obstacles or the spatial topology. Some AI-driven environment prediction method may could help.

References

1. Akbari, A., Bernardini, S.: Informed autonomous exploration of subterranean environments. IEEE Robot. Autom. Lett. **6**(4), 7957–7964 (2021)
2. Bautin, A., Simonin, O., Charpillet, F.: MinPos?: a novel frontier allocation algorithm for multi-robot exploration. In: Su, C.Y., Rakheja, S., Liu, H. (eds.) Intell. Robot. Appl., pp. 496–508. Lecture Notes in Computer Science, Springer, Berlin, Heidelberg (2012). https://doi.org/10.1007/978-3-642-33515-0_49
3. Bircher, A., Kamel, M., Alexis, K., Oleynikova, H., Siegwart, R.: Receding horizon next best view planner for 3D exploration. In: 2016 IEEE International Conference on Robotics and Automation (ICRA), pp. 1462–1468 (2016)
4. Burgard, W., Moors, M., Stachniss, C., Schneider, F.: Coordinated multi-robot exploration. IEEE Trans. Rob. **21**(3), 376–386 (2005)
5. Cao, C., Zhu, H., Choset, H., Zhang, J.: TARE: a hierarchical framework for efficiently exploring complex 3D environments. Robot.: Sci. Syst. 5 (2021)
6. Dang, T., Tranzatto, M., Khattak, S., Mascarich, F., Alexis, K., Hutter, M.: Graph-based subterranean exploration path planning using aerial and legged robots. J. Field Robot. (2020)
7. Dong, S., et al.: Multi-robot collaborative dense scene reconstruction. Acm Trans. Graph. **38**(4), 84 (2019)
8. Faigl, J., Kulich, M., Preucil, L.: Goal assignment using distance cost in multi-robot exploration. In: 2012 IEEE/RSJ International Conference on Intelligent Robots and Systems (IROS), pp. 3741–3746 (2012)
9. Hardouin, G., Moras, J., Morbidi, F., Marzat, J., Mouaddib, E.M.: Next-Best-View planning for surface reconstruction of large-scale 3D environments with multiple UAVs. In: 2020 IEEE/RSJ International Conference on Intelligent Robots and Systems (IROS), pp. 1567–1574. IEEE, New York (2020)
10. Hu, J., Niu, H., Carrasco, J., Lennox, B., Arvin, F.: Voronoi-based multi-robot autonomous exploration in unknown environments via deep reinforcement learning. IEEE Trans. Veh. Technol. **69**(12), 14413–14423 (2020)
11. Lindqvist, B., Agha-Mohammadi, A.A., Nikolakopoulos, G.: Exploration-RRT: a multi-objective path planning and exploration framework for unknown and unstructured environments. In: 2021 IEEE/RSJ International Conference on Intelligent Robots and Systems (IROS), pp. 3429–3435 (2021)

12. Mannucci, A., Nardi, S., Pallottino, L.: Autonomous 3D exploration of large areas: a cooperative frontier-based approach. In: Mazal, J. (ed.) Model. Simul. Auton. Syst. Lecture Notes in Computer Science, pp. 18–39. Springer International Publishing, Cham (2018). https://doi.org/10.1007/978-3-319-76072-8_2
13. Nieto-Granda, C., Rogers, J.G., Christensen, H.I.: Coordination strategies for multi-robot exploration and mapping. Int. J. Robot. Res. **33**(4), 519–533 (2014)
14. Perron, L., Furnon, V.: OR-Tools (2023)
15. Puig, D., Garcia, M.A., Wu, L.: A new global optimization strategy for coordinated multi-robot exploration: development and comparative evaluation. Robot. Auton. Syst. **59**(9), 635–653 (2011)
16. Simmons, R., et al.: Coordination for multi-robot exploration and mapping. In: AAAI/IAAI, pp. 852–858 (2000)
17. Umari, H., Mukhopadhyay, S.: Autonomous robotic exploration based on multiple rapidly-exploring randomized trees. In: 2017 IEEE/RSJ International Conference on Intelligent Robots and Systems (IROS), pp. 1396–1402 (Sep 2017)
18. Wei, C., Hindriks, K.V., Jonker, C.M.: Dynamic task allocation for multi-robot search and retrieval tasks. Appl. Intell. **45**(2), 383–401 (2016)
19. Wurm, K.M., Stachniss, C., Burgard, W.: Coordinated multi-robot exploration using a segmentation of the environment. In: 2008 IEEE/RSJ International Conference on Intelligent Robots and Systems (IROS), pp. 1160–1165 (2008)
20. Yamauchi, B.: A frontier-based approach for autonomous exploration. In: 1997 IEEE International Symposium on Computational Intelligence in Robotics and Automation (CIRA), pp. 146–151 (1997)
21. Yu, J., et al.: SMMR-Explore: SubMap-based multi-robot exploration system with multi-robot multi-target potential field exploration method. In: 2021 IEEE International Conference on Robotics and Automation (ICRA), pp. 8779–8785 (2021)
22. Zheng, Z., Cao, C., Pan, J.: A hierarchical approach for mobile robot exploration in pedestrian crowd. IEEE Robot. Autom. Lett. **7**(1), 175–182 (2022)
23. Zhou, B., Zhang, Y., Chen, X., Shen, S.: FUEL: fast UAV exploration using incremental frontier structure and hierarchical planning. IEEE Robot. Autom. Lett. **6**(2), 779–786 (2021)
24. Zhu, H., Cao, C., Xia, Y., Scherer, S., Zhang, J., Wang, W.: DSVP: Dual-Stage viewpoint planner for rapid exploration by dynamic expansion. In: 2021 IEEE/RSJ International Conference on Intelligent Robots and Systems (IROS), pp. 7623–7630 (2021)
25. Zlot, R., Stentz, A., Dias, M., Thayer, S.: Multi-robot exploration controlled by a market economy. In: 2002 IEEE International Conference on Robotics and Automation (ICRA), vol. 3, pp. 3016–3023 (2002)

Modeling of the Electromagnetic Launching Process for a Tethered-Net Capturing System

Zongming Zhu, Weihao Luo, Junxin Huang, Yuzhe Kang, Zongjing Lin, Maoying Zhou[✉], Ban Wang, Zhenlong Xu, Juyong Zhang, and Huawei Qin

School of Mechanical Engineering, Hangzhou Dianzi University, Hangzhou 310018, Zhejiang, China
myzhou@hdu.edu.cn

Abstract. In modern high-altitude rescuing work, the traditional rescuing methods have problems of low safety and reliability. To solve this problem, a tethered-net rescuing method based on electromagnetic launching is proposed in this paper. The method launches four ferromagnetic mass blocks through the reluctance coil launchers and uses the kinetic energy of the mass blocks to drive the tethered net to fly out. Finally, the object will be trapped and the rescuing task will then be completed as long as the tethered net can be restored along with the trapped object. On this basis, the structural design of the reluctance coil launching unit is presented with its mathematical model established. The correctness of the model is verified by experiments. The exit velocity of the projectile is measured and agreed with the numerical results. The current investigation provides an important theoretical basis for the tethered-net capturing to perform high-altitude rescues.

Keywords: Electromagnetic launching · Modeling of the reluctance coil launcher · Rescuing robot

1 Introduction

In recent years, high-altitude accidents occur frequently, which has caused a bad impact on social security. Due to the general high-altitude accident strong suddenness and rescuing work is extremely difficult, rescuers are not well prepared to face such incidents, and even cause the rescue mission failure. At present, manual rescue is an important and most widely used rescue method for high-altitude accidents. Under normal circumstances, people involved in accidents are usually so nervous that they cannot respond well to the rescuers. The manual rescue will relieve the psychological pressure of the trapped object. However, this kind of rescuing method has uncertain factors, which pose high requirements to the rescuer. Once the rescuer does not respond properly, it will cause bad consequences. In addition, deploying air cushions is also a common rescuing method [1]. However, this method is inefficient in the face of urgent situations. Because of

H. Yang et al. (Eds.): ICIRA 2023, LNAI 14273, pp. 477–488, 2023.
https://doi.org/10.1007/978-981-99-6498-7_41

the shortcomings of the above existing methods, a flexible tethered-net capture rescuing method based on electromagnetic launching is proposed in this paper, which can meet the characteristics of high safety and good fault tolerance of high-altitude rescue.

At present, the launching methods of the tethered net mainly include gunpowder [2], compressed gas [3], compression spring [4], and electromagnetic motor [5]. However, these methods suffer from low energy efficiency and low launching controllability. As a new launching technology, electromagnetic launching has been utilized in military applications due to its high launch efficiency and high launching speed [6–8]. Therefore, this paper uses the electromagnetic launching method to replace the traditional launching method.

According to the different structures and working principles, electromagnetic launching devices are mainly divided into the following three types: rail launcher [9], coil launcher [10], and reconnection launcher [11]. The rail launcher accelerates the sliding armature mainly through the Lorentz force [12]. Although this launching mode has a relatively simple structure, the armature will produce serious structural ablation due to the contact between the rails and the armature maintained during the launching process, leading to its shorter life. According to the main driving force of the projectile inside the coil, the coil launcher can be divided into the reluctance coil launcher [13] and the inductance coil launcher [14]. In both cases, the projectile is launched by a Lorentz force created by applying an electric current to the coil. Besides, there is no contact between the projectile and the coil during the launching process. However, the hollow metal projectile is typically used in the inductance coil launcher. And the projectile is pushed from the center to the exit of the solenoid [15]. Different from this, the reluctance coil launcher utilizes ferromagnetic material as the projectile. When the coil launcher working, the magnetized thrust will pull the projectile towards the coil center. In a fundamental sense, the reconnection launcher is a special coil launcher. What makes it different from the coil launcher is the number of driving coils involved and the orientation of the established magnetic field [16]. However, due to the simple structure and fabrication and the ease of control and actuation, the development of reconnection is relatively immature.

Through the analysis of the above three electromagnetic launching modes, the reluctance coil launcher has attracted our attention successfully by the simple structure and its compatibility with the tethered-net launching device. In this paper, the tethered-net launching prototype is built based on the reluctance launcher. Then, the electromagnetic and dynamics model of the reluctance launcher is established by combining numerical calculation with finite element simulation. The effectiveness of the model is verified by experiments. On this basis, the calculated values of projectile exit velocity are consistent with the experimental values under the different initial voltages.

2   Design of the Tethered-Net Launcher

The process of the tethered-net capturing rescuing method based on electromagnetic launching is shown in Fig. 1. Firstly, a square tethered net connected with four mass blocks is put into the tethered-net storage, and then ferromagnetic mass blocks are launched through the reluctance launching units. When the four mass blocks are launched, they will pull the tethered net in the central storage forward until they fall onto the ground or get into contact with the object. Finally, the object is successfully captured and rescued.

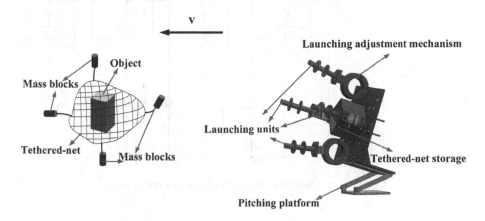

Fig. 1. The schematic diagram of the tethered-net capturing and rescuing method.

The tethered-net launcher is mainly composed of mechanical parts and electrical parts. The mechanical part includes the pitching platform, four reluctance launching units, a tethered-net storage, and the launching adjustment mechanism, as shown in Fig. 1. To control the time when the tethered net is expanded to the maximum area, the launching adjustment mechanism is used to adjust the angle between the axis of the launching unit and the central axis of the tethered-net storage. The pitching adjustment mechanism is used to adjust the angle between the bottom coil and the horizontal plane. No matter how much the launching angle is, the bottom coil is always parallel to the horizontal plane. The electrical part is mainly divided into two parts, the charging circuit, and the discharge circuit, as shown in Fig. 2. The first step is to press switch 1. 12 V lithium battery pack charges the four capacitors through the ZVS booster module. To prevent interference between the four capacitors during the charging process, four diodes(6A10) are put into the circuit respectively. After charging, switch 1 is off and press switch 2, four SCR(70TPS16) are triggered simultaneously to activate the discharge circuit. At this time, the capacitor and the coil form a simple RCL circuit. To protect the SCR and capacitor from damage, a freewheel diode(Fr607) is connected in parallel with the coil. When the current flows through the coil, the magnetic field is created around the coil and magnetizes the ferromagnetic projectiles. Eventually, projectiles are pulled toward the center of the coil and launched successfully.

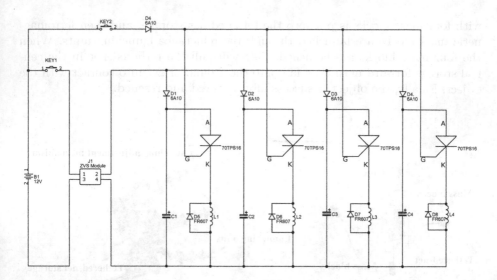

Fig. 2. The schematic diagram of the electrical part.

3   The Theoretical Model of the Reluctance Coil Launcher

When the reluctance coil launcher is working, the ferromagnetic projectile and the coil form a magnetic circuit. According to the principle of reluctance coil launcher, the magnetic flux always tends to pass through the path with minimum reluctance [17]. The reluctance is minimum when the center of the projectile coincides with the center of the coil, so the ferromagnetic projectile is always attracted to move toward the center of the coil. When the center of the projectile passes through the center of the coil, the projectile will be pulled back [18]. The entire circuit can be simplified to the RCL circuit as shown in Fig. 3.

In Fig. 3, $u(t)$ is the voltage across the capacitor at time t, R is the resistance of the coil, C is the capacitance value of the capacitor, and $i(t)$ is the current value flowing through the coil at time t. Unlike the general RCL circuits, the equivalent inductance in the coil is affected by the motion of the projectile because the projectile is in constant motion during capacitor discharge. Therefore, $L(x)$ is defined here as the equivalent inductance of the coil. The value of $L(x)$ is related to the position of the projectile [20]. The equation of the entire circuit can be expressed as:

$$u(t) = R \cdot i(t) + \frac{d[L(x) \cdot i(t)]}{dt} \tag{1}$$

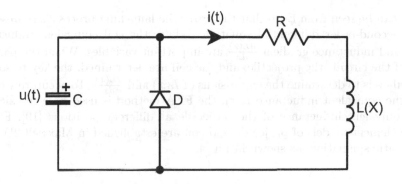

Fig. 3. Equivalent circuit diagram of reluctance coil launcher.

Here, substitute $\frac{d[L(x)\cdot i(t)]}{dt} = L(x)\frac{di(t)}{dt} + i(t)\frac{dL(x)}{dt}$ and $i(t) = -C\frac{du(t)}{dt}$ into Eq. 1, we can get:

$$u(t) + C \cdot L(x) \cdot \frac{d^2 u(t)}{dt^2} + C \cdot \left(R + \frac{dL(x)}{dx} \cdot \frac{dx}{dt}\right) \cdot \frac{du(t)}{dt} = 0 \qquad (2)$$

As for the energy stored in the capacitor, assuming that no magnetic leakage phenomenon occurs, it will be stored in the form of magnetic energy in the coil:

$$W = \frac{1}{2}L(x) \cdot i^2(t) \qquad (3)$$

where W is the magnetic energy stored in the coil during time 0-t, $L(x)$ is the equivalent inductance, and $i(t)$ is the current in the coil at time t. Assuming that the projectile moves a small displacement x within $0 - t$, the electromagnetic force applied on the projectile can be calculated:

$$F_w = \frac{dw}{dx} = \frac{1}{2}i^2(t)\frac{dL(x)}{dx} \qquad (4)$$

The projectile is subjected to the initial friction force and electromagnetic force in the acceleration process, ignoring the air drag. According to the kinematic law, it can be obtained:

$$\frac{1}{2}i^2(t)\frac{dL(x)}{dx} - \mu mg = m\frac{d^2x}{dt^2} \qquad (5)$$

where μ is the friction coefficient between the projectile and the launching tube, and m is the mass of the projectile

At this point, the electromagnetic and dynamic equation of the whole launching system can be obtained by combining Eq. 2 and Eq. 5:

$$u(t) + C \cdot L(x) \cdot \frac{d^2 u(t)}{dt^2} + C \cdot (R + \frac{dL(x)}{dx} \cdot \frac{dx}{dt}) \cdot \frac{du(t)}{dt} = 0$$

$$\frac{1}{2}i^2(t)\frac{dL(x)}{dx} - \mu mg - m\frac{d^2x}{dt^2} = 0 \qquad (6)$$

It can be seen from Eq. 6 that the projectile launching process is represented by a second-order differential equation. Where the coil equivalent inductance L(x) and inductance gradient $\frac{dL(x)}{dx}$ are important variables. When the parameters of the circuit, the projectile, and the coil are determined, the key to solving formula 6 is to determine the expressions of $L(x)$ and $\frac{dL(x)}{dx}$. To accurately calculate the equivalent inductance $L(x)$, the FEA method is used here to calculate the equivalent inductance of the projectile at different positions [19]. Firstly, finite element models of projectile and coil are established in Maxwell 2D magnetostatic simulation, as shown in Fig. 4.

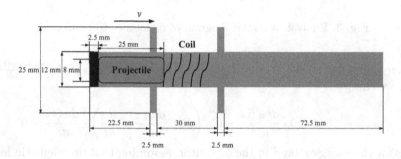

Fig. 4. FEA model of reluctance coil launching unit.

In the simulation, the projectile is used of ferromagnetic material 8 g and the relative permeability is 1000. The coil is used of copper. The eddy current loss is not considered in the simulation. Select 20 points from the initial position of the projectile to the exit position. Put a 30 A current load on the coil and place the central position of the projectile on the positions of 20 points respectively to simulate the inductance calculation. Then fit the expression of equivalent inductance $L(x)$ and inductance gradient $\frac{dL(x)}{dx}$ according to the following equation [20]:

$$L(x) = a + be^{-\frac{1}{2}\left(\frac{x-x_0}{c}\right)^2}$$
$$\frac{dL(x)}{dx} = -b \cdot \frac{(x-x_0)}{c^2} \cdot e^{-\frac{1}{2}\left(\frac{x-x_0}{c}\right)^2} \tag{7}$$

After simulating the equivalent inductance of the projectile at different positions, the waveform of equivalent inductance $L(x)$ is fitted by Eq. 7, as shown in Fig. 5. The fitting calculation results of the three coefficients are respectively $1.188 \cdot 10^{-3}, b = 2.2491 \cdot 10^{-3}, c = 0.011$.

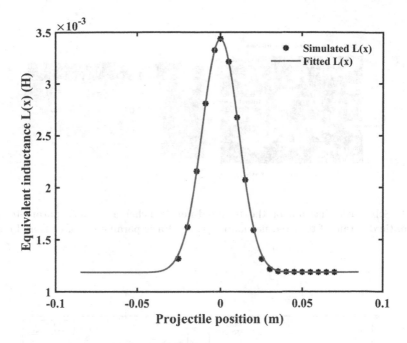

Fig. 5. Simulation and fitting of equivalent inductance.

4   Experiments and Discussions

The tethered-net launcher is shown in Fig. 6 (a). To verify the reluctance launching model established in the previous section, we first measured the basic parameters of the four coils and capacitors, and the results are shown in Fig. 6 (b). Since the parameters of the four coils are the same, coil No. 1 is selected for subsequent experimental analysis.

Then the initial voltage u_0 of the capacitor is adjusted, and the current in the coil during the launching process is measured using a current probe (Tektronix-TCP2020). Initial capacitance-voltage $u_0 = 100/110/120/130$, initial coil current $i_0 = 0$, initial position of projectile $x = 0$, initial velocity of projectile $v = 0$. Basic parameters such as coil, projectile, and capacitance are substituted into Eq. 6. The numerical calculation results and experimental measurement results are obtained as shown in Fig. 7. It can be seen from the results that the numerical results are consistent with the curve of current change measured by the experiment, but This proves that the electromagnetic and dynamics model of the reluctance coil launcher proposed in the previous section is correct. However, due to the existence of a freewheel diode in the circuit, the current change curve measured in the experiment does not oscillate after 2 ms. Besides, the eddy current loss of the projectile is not taken into account when calculating the equivalent inductance, so there is a little bit of error.

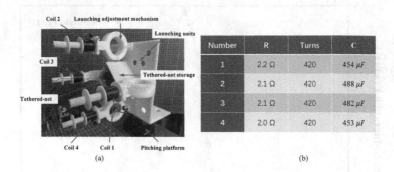

Number	R	Turns	C
1	2.2 Ω	420	454 μF
2	2.1 Ω	420	488 μF
3	2.1 Ω	420	482 μF
4	2.0 Ω	420	453 μF

(a)   (b)

Fig. 6. Schematic diagram of the tethered-net launcher and basic parameters. (a) Schematic diagram of tethered-net launcher, (b) Basic parameters of coils and capacitors.

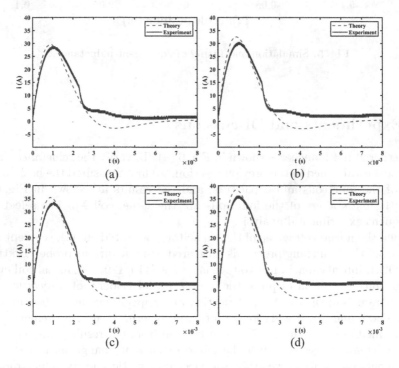

Fig. 7. The current curve in coil 1 is compared with the numerical calculation results under different initial voltages. (a) under 100 V charged voltage; (b) under 110 V charged voltage; (c) under 120 V charged voltage; (d) under 130 V charged voltage.

After verifying the correctness of the model proposed in this paper, the velocity changes of the projectile under different initial voltages are obtained as shown in Fig. 8.

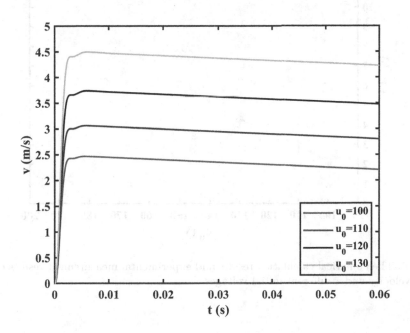

Fig. 8. The velocity changes of the projectile under different initial voltages.

In order to determine the exit velocity of the projectile, a tachymeter is installed at the exit of the launching unit to measure the exit velocity of the projectile under different initial voltages. By substituting the exit position $x = 0.115$ into Eq. 6, the numerical calculation results and experimental measurement results are obtained as shown in Fig. 9. It can be seen that the experimental results are consistent with the calculated results, but there is also a small error. After analysis, the main reason for the error is that the eddy current loss of the projectile is not taken into account when calculating the equivalent inductance, which results in a small error between the calculated results and the experimental value.

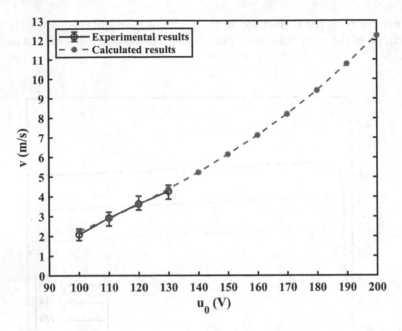

Fig. 9. The numerical calculation results and experimental measurement results of the exit velocity under different initial voltages.

5   Conclusion

Aiming at the problems existing in high-altitude rescue, a tethered-net capturing rescuing method based on electromagnetic launching is proposed in this paper. According to the proposed method, a kind of tethered-net launcher based on electromagnetic launching is designed. The launching principle of the reluctance coil launching unit is analyzed emphatically. The electromagnetic and kinematics model of the launching system is constructed according to the reluctance coil launching principle. The correctness of the proposed model is verified in the current measurement experiment. The time and the velocity of the projectile arriving at the exit are calculated by using the proposed model, which is consistent with the experimental measurement results. The above work provides some theoretical support for the follow-up research.

In the follow-up work, we will upgrade the whole launching mechanism and improve the projectile exit speed to complete the capture of the object by the tethered net. Some algorithms are to be used to detect, target, and lock the object. Recovering mechanisms are to be included to pull back the tethered net after the object is captured. If possible, the object-capturing module is to be optimized and with the tethered-net launcher to form a multi-robot rescue system. It is believed that based on this study, can provide a new way of thinking for high-altitude rescue.

ACKNOWLEDGEMENTS. The authors would like to thank the financial support from the Zhejiang Provincial Natural Science Foundation of China under contract number LY22E050013, the China Postdoctoral Science Foundation funded project under contract number 2021M690545, and the National Natural Science Foundation of China (NSFC) under contract number 51805124.

References

1. Faraj, R., Popławski, B., Gabryel, D., Kowalski, T., Hinc, K.: Adaptive airbag system for increased evacuation safety. Eng. Struct. **270**, 114853 (2022)
2. Yiming, L., Ziming, X., Xi, C., Sidong, Z., Derong, W.: Simulation and experimental study of the traction and deployment of an interceptive space net wih anti-UAV. Acta Armamentarii **43**(9), 2048 (2022)
3. Yu, D., Judasz, A., Zheng, M., Botta, E.M.: Design and testing of a net-launch device for drone capture. In: AIAA SCITECH 2022 Forum, p. 0273 (2022)
4. Carlson, E., et al.: Final design of a space debris removal system. Tech. Rep. **92**, 25832 (1990)
5. Sinn, T.: Lessons learned from REXUS12'S Suaineadh experiment: spinning deployment of a space web in milli gravity. In: 21st ESA Symposium on European Rocket and Balloon Programmes and Related Research (2013)
6. Ma, W., Junyong, L.: Thinking and study of electromagnetic launch technology. IEEE Trans. Plasma Sci. **45**(7), 1071–1077 (2017)
7. Ma, W., Junyong, L., Liu, Y.: Research progress of electromagnetic launch technology. IEEE Trans. Plasma Sci. **47**(5), 2197–2205 (2019)
8. Fair, H.D.: Guest editorial the past, present, and future of electromagnetic launch technology and the IEEE international EML symposia. IEEE Trans. Plasma Sci. **43**(5), 1112–1116 (2015)
9. McNab, I.R.: Launch to space with an electromagnetic railgun. IEEE Trans. Magn. **39**(1), 295–304 (2003)
10. Kaye, R.J.: Operational requirements and issues for coilgun EM launchers. In: 2004 12th Symposium on Electromagnetic Launch Technology, pp. 59–64. IEEE (2004)
11. Brown, M.R., et al.: Energetic particles from three-dimensional magnetic reconnection events in the Swarthmore Spheromak experiment. Phys. Plasmas **9**(5), 2077–2084 (2002)
12. Nechitailo, N.V., Lewis, K.B.: Critical velocity for rails in hypervelocity launchers. Int. J. Impact Eng **33**(1–12), 485–495 (2006)
13. Zizhou, S., et al.: Investigation of armature capture effect on synchronous induction coilgun. IEEE Trans. Plasma Sci. **43**(5), 1215–1219 (2015)
14. Slade, G.W.: A simple unified physical model for a reluctance accelerator. IEEE Trans. Magn. **41**(11), 4270–4276 (2005)
15. Orbach, Y., Oren, M., Einat, M.: 75 m/s simulation and experiment of two-stage reluctance coilgun. J. Mech. Sci. Technol. **36**(3), 1123–1130 (2022). https://doi.org/10.1007/s12206-022-0205-8
16. Cowan, M., Cnare, E., Duggin, B., Kaye, R., Tucker, T.: The reconnection gun. IEEE Trans. Magn. **22**(6), 1429–1434 (1986)
17. Bresie, D.A., Andrews, J.A.: Design of a reluctance accelerator. IEEE Trans. Magn. **27**(1), 623–627 (1991)
18. Hou, Y., Liu, Z., Ouyang, J-M., Yang, D.: Parameter settings of the projectile of the coil electromagnetic launcher. In: 2012 16th International Symposium on Electromagnetic Launch Technology, pp. 1–4. IEEE (2012)

19. Zhu, B., Junyong, L., Wang, J., Xiong, S.: A compulsator driven reluctance coilgun-type electromagnetic launcher. IEEE Trans. Plasma Sci. **45**(9), 2511–2518 (2017)
20. Mengkun, L., Zhang, J., Yi, X., Zhuang, Z.: Advanced mathematical calculation model of single-stage RCG. IEEE Trans. Plasma Sci. **50**(4), 1026–1031 (2022)

Neural Network-Based Formation Control of Autonomous Underwater Vehicles Under Disturbance in 3D Space

Wen Pang, Daqi Zhu$^{(\boxtimes)}$, and Mingzhi Chen

School of Mechanical Engineering, University of Shanghai for Science and Technology, Shanghai 200093, China
zdq367@aliyun.com

Abstract. This paper addresses the decentralized formation control problem of multiple autonomous underwater vehicles (AUVs) in three-dimensional (3D) space. To achieve formation control, we formulate a control framework for the multiple AUVs. The upper layer is a formation algorithm based on a novel leader-follower control law. The bottom layer is a nonlinear component that is dependent on the closed-loop error dynamics plus a neural net component that is linear in the output weights (a one tunable layer neural net is used). The stability and convergence properties of the proposed distance-based control strategy have been analyzed using the Lyapunov stability method and shows that neural net weights remain bounded. Numerical simulations are carried out to demonstrate the performance of the proposed formation control and validate the control framework.

Keywords: Autonomous underwater vehicle control · Formation control · Lyapunov stability · neural networks

1 Introduction

Rapid advances in sensing, computing, and communication technologies have led to the development of autonomous underwater vehicles (AUVs). In many applications, a given task is too complex to be achieved by a single AUV alone [1]. As a result, multi-AUV systems working cooperatively are required to complete the task [2]. A multi-AUV system is more robust than single AUV system because a team of AUVs can provide certain amount of redundancy which is useful in the case that an AUV malfunctions [3,4]. Therefore, in recent years, cooperative control of multi-AUV systems has received considerable attentions, a considerable amount of research effort [5–7] has been devoted to the study of multiple AUV systems due to its potential applications in areas such as environmental surveying, ocean exploration, underwater pipeline or cable inspection/maintenance. Among various cooperative control techniques, the formation control problem is one of the most important research topics in multi-AUV systems [8].

© The Author(s), under exclusive license to Springer Nature Singapore Pte Ltd. 2023
H. Yang et al. (Eds.): ICIRA 2023, LNAI 14273, pp. 489–500, 2023.
https://doi.org/10.1007/978-981-99-6498-7_42

The primary objective of formation control is to construct, maintain, and switch certain formation pattern while moving along the desired trajectory. There are numerous results on formation control of multi-AUV systems [9–11]. Formation control is generally classified into six major approaches, namely behavior-based formation control [12], leader-following strategy [13], artificial potential field approach [14], virtual structure method [15], consensus-based approach [16], and graph theory approach [17]. Each strategy has its own strengths and weaknesses. Among these formation control types, the leader-follower formation strategy has been widely considered by many researchs, because of its advantages such as simplicity and scalability, and they can easily expand the number of swarm AUVs [18].

The main difficulties of the AUV formation control lie in that the parameters of the AUV motion mathematical model are hard to determine precisely; AUVs are inevitably exposed to unpredictable and unknown time-varying ocean environments; AUVs need to exchange the state information from each other through underwater acoustic communication with high propagation delay, thus, there evidently exist communication delays among AUVs [19]. Another important performance index of the control strategy is the convergence speed. Most of the existing literature only guarantee asymptotic convergence of the tracking errors, which means the formation task can only be achieved as time approaches infinity [20,21]. Clearly, it would be a great advance if AUVs can construct a given configuration in finite time.

To solve the challenge of uncertain dynamics and unknown time-varying ocean environment disturbances, many researchers have employed the adaptive control technique [22], neural networks (NNs) [23], and the disturbance observer-based control method [24] to develop the robust formation control laws of AUVs. Considering unknown constant disturbances, Wang et al. [22] designed a 2-D formation adaptive control scheme of fully-actuated AUVs employing the backstepping design tool, where the adaptive technique was used to estimate the constant disturbances. Considering uncertain dynamics, the authors in [23] developed the 2-D and 3-D formation control schemes of fully-actuated and underactuated AUVs combining NNs with the backstepping design tool, respectively, where the uncertain dynamics of AUVs were approximated using NNs. In the simultaneous presence of uncertain dynamics and time-varying disturbances, the authors in [24] proposed the finite-time disturbance observer to handle the lumped disturbances consisting of unknown dynamics and disturbances of AUVs.

Motivated by those observations, this paper focuses on developing a new control design for the stabilization of AUVs modeled by an undirected graph. As in [25], we address the distance-based formation control of multi-AUV systems and use a double integrator model for the AUVs motion proposes a formation control scheme by utilizing backstepping and adaptive neural network (NN) techniques. The following advantages of this approach are highlighted: 1) The presented formation controller only needs the distance measurements between adjacent AUVs, no other information about the AUVs are required, which demands less information than the previous controllers; 3) the proposed controller does not rely on any prior knowledge about hydrodynamic damping and external disturbances, which is easily implemented in practice. The proposed formation control strategy ensures AUVs to maintain the desired 3-D formation pattern, while achieving the fast stability with respect to formation errors and satisfying the performance constraints simultaneously. Simulation studies on a group of AUVs demonstrate the remarkable performance of our developed formation control law.

The remaining parts of the paper are organized as follows. Section 2 gives some basic concepts of rigid graph theory and Neural Network (NN) topology are described. The formation control problem formulation is introduced in Sect. 3. The main results and stability analysis are presented in Sect. 4. Section 5 provides the full numerical simulations to verify the effectiveness of the proposed method. Finally, some concluding remarks are drawn in Sect. 6.

2 Preliminaries

2.1 Multi-AUV Formation and Graph Rigidity

Graph theory is a natural tool for analyzing the multi-AUV formation shape and describing the information architecture of the system [26]. In this paper, the formation shape of a multi-AUV system is represented by an undirected graph $\mathcal{G} = (\mathcal{V}, \mathcal{E}, \mathcal{A})$, where $\mathcal{V} = \{1, 2, ..., n\}$ is the vertex set of this graph that represents the AUVs and $\mathcal{E} \subseteq \mathcal{V} \times \mathcal{V}$ is the edge set that represents the communication links between the AUVs. Define $\mathcal{A} = [a_{ij}] \in \mathbb{R}^{n \times n}$ as the adjacency matrix of the graph $\mathcal{G}$, where $a_{ij} = 1$ if $(i, j) \in \mathcal{E}$ exist, otherwise, $a_{ij} = 0$. The number of vertices and edges of $\mathcal{G}$ are denoted by m and l, respectively.

A framework is a realization of a graph at given points in $\mathbb{R}^3$. A 3-dimensional framework $\mathcal{F}$ is a pair $(\mathcal{G}, p)$ where $p = (p_1, p_2, ..., p_n) \in \mathbb{R}^{3n}$ and $p_i \in \mathbb{R}^3$ is the coordinate of AUV i. Given an arbitrary ordering of the edges of $\mathcal{G}$, an edge function $f_{\mathcal{G}} : \mathbb{R}^{3n} \in \mathcal{R}^l$ associated with $(\mathcal{G}, p)$ is given by

$$f_{\mathcal{G}}(p) = (..., \|p_i - p_j\|^2, ...), (i, j) \in \mathcal{E} \tag{1}$$

where $\|\cdot\|$ denotes the Euclidean norm. The rigidity matrix $R(p) : \mathbb{R}^{23n} \to \mathbb{R}^{l \times 3n}$ of $(\mathcal{G}, p)$ is defined as:

$$R(p) = \frac{1}{2} \frac{\partial f_{\mathcal{G}}(p)}{\partial p} \tag{2}$$

A graph is minimally rigid if it is rigid and if no single edge can be removed from the graph without causing the graph to lose its rigidity. A graph $\mathcal{G} = (\mathcal{V}, \mathcal{E}, \mathcal{A})$ is minimally rigid in three dimensions if and only if $l = 3n - 6$ [26].

Lemma 1 ([27]): If the framework $\mathcal{F} = (\mathcal{G}, p)$ is infinitesimally and minimally rigid in three dimensions, then $R(p)R^T(p)$ is invertible.

2.2   Neural Network Topology

Artificial NNs, which are based on biological neuronal structures of intercon-nected nodes, have properties such as learning and adaptation, function approx-imation, classification, generalization, etc. A two-layer NN (Fig. 1) is commonly used for closed-loop control purposes. This NN consists of a hidden layer with nodes and an output layer with c nodes. We denote the first-to-second-layer interconnections weights as v_{jk} and the second to-third-layer interconnection weights by w_{ij}. The NN inputs are $x_1(t), x_2(t), ..., x_k(t)$. By collecting all the neural network weights v_{jk}, w_{ij} into matrices of weights V^T, W^T, the output $y(t)$ can be written in terms of vectors as:

$$y = W^T \sigma(V^T x) \tag{3}$$

where $\sigma(\cdot)$ is an activation function. In this paper, the sigmoid (logistic) function was selected as the activation function.

The function approximation property of NNs plays an important role in control applications. The basic approximation result states that any smooth function $f(x)$ can be approximated arbitrarily closely over a compact set $\Omega \in \mathbb{R}^k$. That is, for a positive constant ε_N, there exists a two layer NN with an ideal weight matrix W and a number of hidden layer nodes L such that:

$$f(x) = W^T \sigma(V^T x) + \varepsilon \tag{4}$$

where ε is the NN function approximation error and satisfies $\|\varepsilon\| < \varepsilon_N$. If the first layer weights and biases V are fixed, the NN is Linear-in-the-Parameter (LIP) and the approximation property can be satisfied by tuning the second layer weights and biases W. The first layer weights V are selected randomly and are not tuned. The second layer weights are tunable. The approximation holds [28] for such NN, with approximation error convergence to zero of order $O(C/\sqrt{L})$, where C is independent of L. It is assumed that the approximating weights W are bounded such that $\|W\|_F < W_m$, where $\|W\|_F$ is the Frobenius

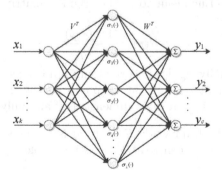

Fig. 1. Two Layer feedforward Neural Network.

norm. Given a matrix $A = [a_{ij}]$, the Frobenius norm is defined by:

$$\|A\|_F^2 = \sum a_{ij}^2 = tr(A^T A) \qquad (5)$$

with $tr()$ being the trace.

3 Problem Formulation

As regards the AUVs dynamics, a variety of models have been proposed in the literature, including the single integrator, the double integrator or Newtonian particle model and linear models in state space representation. This paper uses the double integrator model, consider a system of n AUVs in 3D space modeled by the double integrator:

$$\dot{p} = v_i \qquad (6a)$$

$$\dot{v}_i = u_i + d_i, i = 1, 2, ..., n \qquad (6b)$$

where $p_i = (x_i, y_i, z_i) \in \mathbb{R}^3$ for $i = 1, 2, ..., n$ is the position of the i-th AUV, $v_i = (v_{xi}, v_{yi}, v_{zi}) \in \mathbb{R}^3$ is the i-th AUV velocity and $u_i = (u_{xi}, u_{yi}, u_{zi}) \in \mathbb{R}^3$ is the acceleration-level control input, d_i is the bounded time-varying disturbance signal.

Let the desired formation for the agents be represented by an infinitesimally and minimally rigid framework $\mathcal{F}^* = (\mathcal{G}^*, p^*)$, where $\mathcal{G}^* = (\mathcal{V}^*, \mathcal{E}^*)$ and $p^* = (p_1^*, p_2^*, ..., p_n^*)$. Given the actual formation $\mathcal{F}(t) = (\mathcal{G}^*, p(t))$, where $p = (p_1, p_2, ..., p_n)$ and assuming that at $t = 0$, $\|p_i(0) - p_j(0)\| \neq d_{ij}$ for $(i, j) \subset \mathcal{E}$, where $d_{ij} = \|p_i^* - p_j^*\| > 0$ is the constant desired distance between AUVs i and j in the formation, the control objective is to design the control input u_i such that the distance error:

$$e_{ij} = \|p_i(t) - p_j(t)\| - d_{ij}(t), (i, j) \in \mathcal{E}^* \qquad (7)$$

is uniformly ultimately bounded. That is, after transition period, the distance error remains within a small neighborhood of zero.

4 Control Algorithms

Define the relative position of two AUVs as:

$$\tilde{p}_{ij} = p_i - p_j, \ (i, j) \in \mathcal{E}^* \qquad (8)$$

The distance error dynamics for the group of n AUVs is given by:

$$\dot{e}_{ij} = (\tilde{p}_{ij}^T \tilde{p}_{ij})^{-\frac{1}{2}} \tilde{p}_{ij}^T (v_i - v_j) = \frac{\tilde{p}_{ij}^T (v_i - v_j)}{e_{ij} + d_{ij}} \qquad (9)$$

To simplify the subsequent control design and stability analysis, we introduce the following alternative error variable:

$$z_{ij} = \|\tilde{p}_{ij}\|^2 - d_{ij}^2 = e_{ij}(e_{ij} + 2d_{ij}) \qquad (10)$$

using (7). Given that $\|\tilde{p}_{ij}\| \geq 0$, it is not difficult to check that $z_{ij} = 0$ if and only if $e_{ij} = 0$. Now, define the following Lyapunov function candidate:

$$W_{ij}(e_{ij}) = \frac{1}{4}z_{ij}^2 \qquad (11)$$

and note that it is positive definite and radially unbounded. We now define the following function:

$$M_{(e)} = \sum_{(i,j) \in \mathcal{E}^*} M_{ij}(e_{ij}) \qquad (12)$$

The time derivative of (12) along (9) is given by:

$$\dot{M} = \sum_{(i,j) \in \mathcal{E}^*} e_{ij}(e_{ij} + 2d_{ij})\tilde{p}_{ij}^T(v_i - v_j) \qquad (13)$$

It follows from (2) and (10) that (13) can be rewritten as:

$$\dot{M} = z^T R(p)v \qquad (14)$$

where $v = (v_1, v_2, ..., v_n) \in \mathbb{R}^{3n}$, $z = (..., z_{ij}, ...) \in \mathbb{R}^l, (i, j) \in \mathcal{E}^*$.

Using the backstepping method [16], we introduce the variable:

$$s = v - v_f \qquad (15)$$

where $v_f \in \mathbb{R}^{3n}$ denotes the fictitious velocity input. For control algorithm development and stability analysis, we also introduce the function:

$$M_d(e, s, \tilde{W}) = M(e) + \frac{1}{2}s^T s + \frac{1}{2}tr(\tilde{W}^T S\tilde{W}) \qquad (16)$$

where S is symmetric positive definite and $\tilde{W}$ is the weight estimation error matrix and is defined as $\tilde{W} = W - \hat{W}$ with $\hat{W}$ being the actual weight matrix. After taking the time derivative of (16), we obtain:

$$\dot{M}_d = \dot{M} + s^T \dot{s} + tr(\tilde{W}^T S\dot{\tilde{W}}) = z^T R(p)v_f + s^T[u + R^T(p)z - \dot{v}_f] + tr(\tilde{W}^T S\dot{\tilde{W}}) \qquad (17)$$

where (14), (6b), and (15) were used, and $u = (u_1, u_2, ..., u_n) \in \mathbb{R}^{3n}$.

The following theorem gives the control and NN tuning laws for the formation control problem.

Theorem 1: Let $\mathcal{F}(t) = (\mathcal{G}, p(t))$ in $\mathbb{R}^3$ be the formation of a group of n AUVs. Select the control input as:

$$u = -k_a s + \dot{v}_f - R^T(p)z \qquad (18a)$$

$$v_f = R^+(p)(-k_v z + \tilde{W}^T \sigma(V^T \boldsymbol{x}) \qquad (18b)$$

where $R^+(p) = R^T(p)[R(p)R(p)^T]^{-1}$ is the Moore-Penrose Pseudo inverse of $R(p)$, k_a and k_v are positive constants and x is the relative position p_{ij} of the AUVs. Let the estimated NN weights be given by the NN tuning algorithm.

$$\dot{\hat{W}} = S^{-1}\sigma(V^T x)z^T - k_c\|z\|S^{-1}\hat{W} \tag{19}$$

where k_c is a user selected constant. Then, by properly selecting the control gain and the design parameters, the distance error e and the NN weights $\hat{W}$ are uniformly ultimately bounded.

Proof: Substituting (18a) and (18b) into (17) yields:

$$\dot{M}_d = z^T R(p)R^+(p)[-k_v z + \tilde{W}^T\sigma(V^T x)] - k_a s^T s + tr(\tilde{W}^T S\dot{\hat{W}}) \tag{20}$$

Choose $\dot{\tilde{W}}$ (or equivalently $\dot{\hat{W}}$) such that $\dot{M}_d$ is negative definite outside of a compact set around the origin. From Lemma (1), we can state that $R(p)R^T(p)$ is invertible in the compact set. Then, the previous equation is equivalent to

$$\dot{M}_d = -k_v z^T z + z^T(W^T - \tilde{W}^T)\sigma(V^T x) - k_a s^T s + tr(\tilde{W}^T S\dot{\hat{W}}) \tag{21}$$

$$\dot{M}_d = -k_v z^T z - k_a s^T s + z^T W^T\sigma(V^T x) - z^T\tilde{W}^T\sigma(V^T x) + tr(\tilde{W}^T S\dot{\hat{W}}) \tag{22}$$

$$\dot{M}_d = -k_v z^T z - k_a s^T s + z^T W^T\sigma(V^T x) + tr[\tilde{W}^T(S\dot{\hat{W}} - \sigma(V^T x)z^T)] \tag{23}$$

Using the tuning law (19), we have

$$\dot{M}_d = -k_v z^T z - k_a s^T s + z^T W^T\sigma(V^T x) + k_c\|z\|tr(\tilde{W}^T\hat{W}) \tag{24}$$

From the Cauchy-Schwarts inequality we know that

$$z^T W^T\sigma(V^T x) \leq \|z\|\|W^T\sigma(V^T x)\| \leq \|z\|W_m L \tag{25}$$

It can be shown, from the definitions of trace and the Frobenius norm, that for any two matrices X and Y the following inequality holds:

$$tr[X(Y - X)] \leq \|X\|_F\|Y\|_F - \|z\|_F^2 \tag{26}$$

Therefore one has,

$$\dot{M}_d = -k_v z^T z - k_a s^T s + z^T W^T\sigma(V^T x) + k_c\|e\|tr(\tilde{W}^T\hat{W}) \leq -k_v\|e\|^2 - k_a\|s\|^2$$
$$+ \|z\|W_m L + k_c\|z\|(\|\tilde{W}\|_F\|W\|_F - \|\tilde{W}\|_F^2) \leq -\|z\|(k_v\|z\| + k_c\|\tilde{W}\|_F^2$$
$$- W_m L - k_c\|\tilde{W}\|_F W_m) - k_a\|s\|^2 = -\|z\|(k_v\|z\| + k_c(\|\tilde{W}\|_F - \frac{1}{2}W_m)^2$$
$$- W_m L - \frac{k_c}{4}W_m^2) - k_a\|s\|^2$$

$$\tag{27}$$

It follows that $\dot{M}_d < 0$ if either of the following is true:

$$\|z\| > \frac{N}{k_v} \tag{28}$$

$$\|\tilde{W}\|_F > \sqrt{\frac{N}{k_c}} + \frac{1}{2}W_m \tag{29}$$

where

$$N = \frac{k_c}{4}W_m^2 + W_m L \tag{30}$$

This shows that $\dot{M}_d$ is negative definite outside of a compact set, which can be reduced arbitrarily by increasing the gain k_v and k_a. Therefore, the distance error converges to the bounded neighborhood of zero.

Note that bounds in terms of the error e can be derived from (28):

$$e_{ij} > \frac{N}{k_v} \tag{31}$$

Furthermore, note that the bounds are functions of the number of hidden layer nodes L, which is to be expected.

5   Simulation Results Analysis

To validate the effectiveness of the proposed formation control law (18), simulation experiments are conducted, in which eight AUVs steered by their own onboard controllers are employed to forme a prescribed cube in 3D space. The desired formation was chosen as an infinitesimally and minimally rigid cube shape shown in Fig. 2. The edges of the desired framework are indexed by their vertices, and the side length of the cube is set to 1.

The initial conditions of AUVs were chosen as $p_i(0) = p_i^* + \alpha[I - 0.5], i = 1, 2, ..., n$, in which, α is the maximum offset which was set to 1 and I generates a random 3×1 vector whose elements are uniformly distributed on the interval $(0, 1)$. In the simulation, the value of k_p was set to 1 in (18), $L = 24$ was chosen as the number of hidden layer nodes, the entries of matrix V were random values, the weight matrix W was initiated at zero, S was an identity matrix, and k_c was set to 1 in (19).

5.1   Formation Acquisition Without Environment Disturbance

Figure 2 shows the trajectories of eight AUVs as they move from their initial position to the final position to form the desired cube formation without environment disturbance.

Figure 3 (a) demonstrates the distance errors e_{ij} between any of two AUVs approaching zero. The control input $u_i(t)$ for $i = 1, 2, ..., 8$ in the x, y and z directions are shown in Fig. 3 (b). Each of the neural network outputs and thus each column of W is associated with an edge. Elements of W plotted in Fig. 4 are chosen to correspond to the sampled errors in Fig. 3 (a) and are indexed in a similar manner.

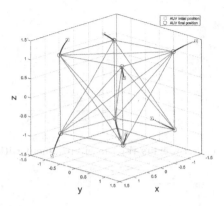

Fig. 2. AUV trajectories $p_i(t), i = 1, 2, ..., 8$ (blue dotted line) and desired formation (green solid line). (Color figure online)

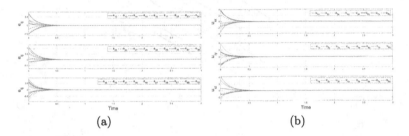

(a)   (b)

Fig. 3. (a) Inter-AUV distance errors $e_{ij}, i, j \in \mathcal{V}^*$, (b) Control inputs $u_i(t), i = 1, 2, ..., 8$ in three coordinate directions.

5.2   Formation Acquisition with Environment Disturbance

In this section, a scenario is simulated, that is, in the presence of random external environment disturbance, to verify that the designed formation controller can effectively reduce the influence of ocean current disturbance on the formation process, and improve the robustness and strong anti-interference ability of the system.

Figure 5 shows the trajectories of eight AUVs as they move from their initial position to the final position to form the desired cube formation with environment disturbance.

Figure 6 (a) demonstrates the distance errors e_{ij} between any of two AUVs approaching zero in the environment with disturbance. The control input $u_i(t)$ for $i = 1, 2, ..., 8$ in the x, y and z directions are shown in Fig. 6 (b). Sample of NN weights W_{1ij} are plotted in Fig. 7.

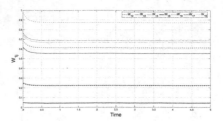

Fig. 4. Sample of NN weights W_{1ij} in environment with disturbance.

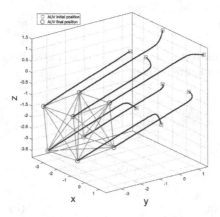

Fig. 5. Trajectory of AUV position in 3D environment with disturbance.

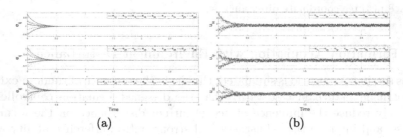

Fig. 6. (a) Inter-AUV distance errors $e_{ij}, i, j \in \mathcal{V}^*$, (b) Control inputs $u_i(t), i = 1, 2, ..., 8$ in three coordinate directions.

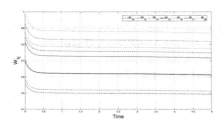

Fig. 7. Sample of NN weights W_{1ij} in environment with disturbance.

From the simulation results, one can conclude that multi-AUV systems with external disturbance can achieves the robust formation by the proposed formation control protocol (18).

6   Conclusion

We introduced a decentralized NN-based controller for multi-AUV system to stabilizing inter-AUV distances to desired values in a 3D space. Our method makes use of graph rigidity, and the nonlinear control law consists of a nonlinear component that depends on inter-AUV distances and a neural net component. Lyapunov analysis showed that the designed controller ensures the uniformly ultimately bounded stability of the infinitesimally and minimally rigid desired formation. The simulation of multi-AUV formation in undisturbed and disturbed 3D environments verifies the effectiveness of the designed controller. In the future, we will study formation maintenance and navigation obstacle avoidance in disturbed environments.

References

1. Hou, S.P., Cheah, C.C.: Can a simple control scheme work for a formation control of multiple autonomous underwater vehicles. IEEE Trans. Control Syst. Technol. **19**(5), 1090–1101 (2011)
2. Balch, T., Arkin, R.C.: Behavior-based formation control for multirobot teams. IEEE Trans. Robot. Automat. **14**(6), 926–939 (1998)
3. Lakhekar, G.V., Waghmare, L.M., Roy, R.G.: Disturbance observer based fuzzy adapted S-surface controller for spatial trajectory tracking of autonomous underwater vehicle. IEEE Trans. Intell. Veh. **4**(4), 622–636 (2019)
4. Wang, X.: Active fault tolerant control for unmanned underwater vehicle with actuator fault and guaranteed transient performance. IEEE Trans. Intell. Veh. **6**(3), 470–479 (2021)
5. Cui, R.X., Ge, S.S., How, B.V.E., Choo, Y.S.: Leader-follower formation control of underactuated autonomous underwater vehicles. Ocean Eng. **37**(17–18), 1491–1502 (2010)
6. Skjetne, R., Moi, S., Fossen, T.I.: Nonlinear formation control of marine craft. In: Proceedings of 41st IEEE Conference Decision Control, Las Vegas, NV, USA, pp. 1699–1704 (2002)
7. Stilwell, D.J., Bishop, B.E.: Platoons of underwater vehicles. IEEE Control. Syst. **20**(6), 45–52 (2000)
8. Fiorelli, E., Leonard, N.E., Bhatta, P., Paley, D.A., Bachmayer, R., Fratantoni, D.M.: Multi-AUV control and adaptive sampling in Monterey Bay. IEEE J. Ocean. Eng. **31**(4), 935–948 (2006)
9. Wynn, R.B., et al.: Autonomous underwater vehicles (AUVs): their past, present and future contributions to the advancement of marine geoscience. Mar. Geol. **352**(1), 451–468 (2014)
10. Zereika, E., Bibuli, M., Miskovic, N., Ridao, P., Pascoal, A.: Challenges and future trends in marine robotics. Annu. Rev. Control. **46**, 350–368 (2018)

11. Hu, Z.L., Ma, C., Zhang, L.X., Halme, A., Hayat, T., Ahmad, B.: Formation control of impulsive networked autonomous underwater vehicles under fixed and switching topologies. Neurocomputing **147**, 291–298 (2015)
12. Balch, T., Arkin, R.C.: Behavior-based formation control for multirobot teams. IEEE Trans. Robot. Autom. **14**(6), 926–939 (1998)
13. Droge, G.: Distributed virtual leader moving formation control using behavior-based MPC. In: 2015 American Control Conference (ACC), Chicago, IL, USA, pp. 2323–2328 (2015)
14. Tingbin, C., Qisong, Z.: Robot motion planning based on improved artificial potential field. In: Proceedings of 2013 3rd International Conference on Computer Science and Network Technology, Dalian, China, p. 1208C1211 (2013)
15. Ren, W., Beard, R.W.: A decentralized scheme for spacecraft formation flying via the virtual structure approach. In: Proceedings of the 2003 American Control Conference, Denver, CO, USA, pp. 1746–1751 (2003)
16. Mei, J., Ren, W., Ma, G.: Distributed coordinated tracking with a dynamic leader for multiple Euler-Lagrange systems. IEEE Trans. Autom. Control **56**(6), 1415–1421 (2011)
17. Pang, W., Zhu, D., Chu, Z., Chen, Q.: Distributed adaptive formation reconfiguration control for multiple AUVs based on affine transformation in three-dimensional ocean environments. IEEE Trans. Veh. Technol. **72**(6), 7338–7350 (2023)
18. Pang, W., Zhu, D., Liu, C., Wang, L.: The multi-AUV time-varying formation reconfiguration control based on rigid-graph theory and affine transformation. Ocean Eng. **27**, 113521 (2023)
19. Wang, L., Zhu, D., Pang, W., Luo, C.: A novel obstacle avoidance consensus control for multi-AUV formation system. IEEE/CAA J. Autom. Sinica. **10**(5), 1304–1318 (2023)
20. Park, B.S.: Adaptive formation control of underactuated autonomous underwater vehicles. Ocean Eng. **96**, 1–7 (2015)
21. Li, H.P., Xie, P., Yan, W.S.: Receding horizon formation tracking control of constrained underactuated autonomous underwater vehicles. IEEE Trans. Ind. Electron. **64**(6), 5004–5013 (2017)
22. Wang, Y., Yan, W., Li, J.: Passivity-based formation control of autonomous underwater vehicles. IET Control Theory Appl. **6**(4), 518–525 (2012)
23. Wang, J.Q., Wang, C., Wei, Y.J., Zhang, C.J.: Neuroadaptive sliding mode formation control of autonomous underwater vehicles with uncertain dynamics. IEEE Syst. J. **14**(3), 3325–3333 (2020)
24. Gao, Z.Y., Guo, G.: Fixed-time sliding mode formation control of AUVs based on a disturbance observer. IEEE-CAA J. Automatica Sinica. **7**(2), 539–545 (2020)
25. Oh, K.-K., Ahn, H.-S.: Formation control of mobile agents based on inter-agent distance dynamics. Automatica **47**(10), 2306–2312 (2011)
26. Anderson, B.D.O., Yu, C., Fidan, B., Hendrickx, J.: Rigid graph control architectures for autonomous formations. IEEE Control. Syst. **28**(6), 48–63 (2008)
27. Ramazani, S,. Selmic, R,. de Queiroz, M.: Non-planar multiagent formation control using coning graphs. In: Proceedings of IEEE International Conference on Systems, Man and Cybernetics (SMC), San Diego, CA, USA, pp. 3091–3096 (2014)
28. Igelnik, B., Pao, Y.-H.: Stochastic choice of basis functions in adaptive function approximation and the functional-link net. IEEE Trans. Neural Networks **6**(6), 1320–1329 (1995)

Event-Triggered Model Predictive Mean-Field Control for Stabilizing Robotic Swarm

Di Cui[1], Huiping Li[1(✉)] ⓘ, and Panfeng Huang[2]

[1] School of Marine Science and Technology, Northwestern Polytechnical University,
Xi'an, China
dicui@mail.nwpu.edu.cn, lihuiping@nwpu.edu.cn
[2] School of Astronautics, Northwestern Polytechnical University, Xi'an, China
pfhuang@nwpu.edu.cn

Abstract. This paper investigates the resource-aware density regulation problem for a large-scale robotic swarm. A perturbed mean-field model(MFM) is first developed to describe the evolution process of the swarm's actual density distribution (ADD) in a macroscopic manner, thus endowing the control algorithm with scalability property. A novel event-triggered (ET) model predictive mean-field control (MFC) algorithm is proposed to reduce the computation and communication burdens of agents while providing high control performance. Finally, by means of the numerical example, we verify the effectiveness of this algorithm.

Keywords: Large-scale swarm · Mean-filed model · Event-triggered · Model predictive control

1 Introduction

With the extraordinary flexibility and adaptability properties, robotic swarm is capable to collaboratively perform various complex tasks. Potential applications of the swarm are broadening, ranging from the combat support for military to traffic monitoring for civilian applications [1,2]. However, when referring to the collaborative control for a large-scale robotic swarm, the implementation of the control algorithm suffers from the non-negligible heavy computation and communication burdens. It becomes significant importance to explicitly handle the resource constraints in the controller design. Indeed, the resource limitation primarily raised by the increasing state space and periodically updating the control law. Hence, improving the algorithm scalability with the population size and reducing the frequency to calculate the control law are of primary importance.

This work was supported in part by the National Natural Science Foundation of China (NSFC) under Grant U22B2039, 62273281; in part by Aoxiang Youth Scholar Program under Grant.

Motivated by the above statements, in this paper, we are interested in developing resource-aware density regulation strategies for a large-scale robotic swarm. It should be noted that directly implementing the control algorithms for multi-agent systems is not practicable here. Since the majority of existing works on the collaborative control of multi-agent systems use an individual-agent-based Lagrangian framework that describes the swarm state as a collection of the agents' local state, the computation cost becomes prohibitively expensive [3,4]. In addition, such bottom-up controller design philosophy places more emphasis on the individual agent. In a swarm, individuals are not the primary focus, and achieving the whole control object from the macroscopic perspective is all that matters.

Controller designed by the top-down strategy recently gives an inspiring solution to avoid the aforementioned resource consumption [5]. The core idea behind this strategy is to combine the Eulerian framework, which uses mean-field model (MFM) to describe the spatio-temporal evolution of the probability density distribution (PDD) of the agent. In this case, each individual's behavior is captured by identical finite-state Markov chains and each state is associated with different behavior for agent to perform. The actual density distribution of the swarm tends to the PDD as population size increases. As a result, the swarm's collective behavior could be approximated by a single agent, and the state space simply relates to the number of alternative behaviors, endowing the controller scalability. For more details, readers are referred to [6], and the references therein.

MFM based swarm density regulation methods mainly falls into two categories: using time-invariant transition probabilities [7–9] and time-varying one [10–13]. In the former, each agent evolves in a homogenous Markov chain (HMC). To obtain Markov matrix stabilizing the swarm to a strictly elementwise positive target distribution, an iterative function was designed in [7]. Açikmeşe et al. further extended the results to nonnegative case by proposing a spectral radius condition [8]. In [9], a Monte Carlo sampling method, Metropolis-Hastings algorithm, was used for constructing Markov matrix with a given steady-state distribution. However, a major drawback of these HMC-based algorithms is that the agent still stochastically transits its behavior at equilibrium, that is, the swarm only stays at the macroscopic equilibrium while the individual is not in microscopic equilibrium, leading to unnecessary resource usage. Therefore, inhomogenous Markov chain (IMC) is employed. In this framework, time-varying Markov matrices relating to the swarm state were designed in [10] and [11]. The work in [12] presented an optimal transport (OT) algorithm to update the Markov matrix at each sampling instant. A distributed density regulation algorithm is proposed in [13] to periodically optimize the current transition probabilities.

Although HMC-based algorithms avoid the state transition at equilibrium, the controllers only give feasible solutions [10,11] or optimized solutions in one time step [12,13], which cannot help to further enhance the control performance in the long term. Model predictive control (MPC), as one of the most widely used optimization-based control techniques, provides a promising solution [14–16], which calculates an optimal control input sequence by optimizing a constrained finite-horizon cost function and only implements the first one. Nevertheless, it is worthwhile to remark that implementing such algorithms requires periodically measuring the swarm state and calculating a new Markov matrix, which is both computation and communication inefficient.

Therefore, in this paper, we propose a novel event-triggered (ET) model predictive mean-field control (MFC) algorithm. In this algorithm, the resource consumption is reduced from two aspect. First, in order to guarantee that the computation burden is free from the population size, we develop a perturbed MFM to describe the evolution process of the swarm's actual density distribution (ADD) in a macroscopic manner, where the disturbance term comes from the fact that the actual density distribution cannot equals to PDD in practical robotic swarm. We then combine event-triggered mechanism into the MPC controller design, which updates the control input only when a specific condition is verified to be true [17–19].

The rest of this paper is organized as follows. Section 2 gives the preliminaries of the swarm description and problem formulation. In Sect. 3, a novel ET model predictive MFC algorithm is designed. Then, numerical example is given in Sect. 4. Finally, Sect. 5 makes the conclusion.

Notations: Let $\mathbb{N}_{\geq 0}$ and $\mathbb{R}$ denote the non-negative integers and real number, respectively. $\boldsymbol{v} \in \mathbb{R}^n$ represents a n-dimensional column vector, and $\boldsymbol{v}_i$ is the ith element of the vector. $\forall \boldsymbol{x} \in \mathbb{P}^n$ indicates a $n \times 1$ column-stochastic vector, which satisfies $\boldsymbol{x}^T \cdot \mathbf{1} = 1$ and $\boldsymbol{x}_i \geq 0, \forall i = 1, \cdots, n$. For two nonempty sets A and B, $A/B = \{x | x \in A, x \notin B\}$. $\chi_x(y) : \mathbb{N}_{\geq 0} \to \{0, 1\}$ is the indicator function of y, and $\chi_x(y) = 1$ only if $x = y$. $\mathbb{R}_{(a,b)}$ and $\mathbb{I}_{[a,b]}$ denote the set $\{x \in \mathbb{R} | a < x < b\}$ and the integer set $\{x \in \mathbb{N}_{\geq 0} | a \leq x \leq b\}$, respectively.

2 Preliminaries and Problem Formulation

2.1 Preliminaries

This subsection presents some necessary definitions and assumptions to facilitate formulating the density regulation problem.

Definition 1 *(Bins) The physical space over which the swarms with N agents are distributed is divided into n_v disjoint bins $\mathcal{P}_j, j \in \{1, 2, \cdots, n_v\}$ and satisfies $\mathcal{P}_j \cap \mathcal{P}_l = \emptyset, \forall j \neq l$. Borrowing the concepts from graph theory, we denote the set of all bins by the vertex set $\mathcal{V} = \{1, 2, \cdots, n_v\}$.*

In this paper, The state evolution of agent $i, \forall i \in \mathbb{I}_{[1,N]}$ on the finite state space $\mathcal{V}$ is a stochastic process $X_i(k)$. We capture this process by identical finite-state Markov chains, where the state transition is governed by a Markov matrix $\boldsymbol{M}^i(k)$ with the element defined by the following conditional probability:

$$M_{jl}^i(k) = \mathbb{P}(X_i(k+1) = l | X_i(k) = j) = \begin{cases} r_{jl}^i(k) & j \neq l, \\ 1 - \sum_{l=1, l \neq j}^{n_v} r_{jl}^i(k) & j = l. \end{cases} \quad (1)$$

Here, $j, l \in \mathcal{V}$, $\boldsymbol{M}^i(k)$ is row stochastic, $r_{jl}^i(k)$ is the detailed transition rate for agent i from bin $\mathcal{P}_j$ to $\mathcal{P}_l$.

Note that we define the bin by local physical space in the density regulation problem. However, the definition of bin can be further extended into the detailed task in task allocation problem and behavior in self-organization. Hence, with a slight modification of the problem setting, our control scheme has great potential to settle multiple issues in robotic swarms.

Using the vertex defined in Definition 1, the underlying relations among the vertices are represented by a directed graph $\mathcal{G} = (\mathcal{V}, \mathcal{E})$ with $\mathcal{E} \subseteq \mathcal{V} \times \mathcal{V}$. The edge $e = (j, l) \in \mathcal{E}$ denotes that bin $\mathcal{P}_l$ can be directly visited by any agent in bin $\mathcal{P}_j$, with j and l are the source and target vertices of the edge e, respectively. Under this circumstances, the transition rate of agent i satisfies $r_e^i(k) = r_{jl}^i(k) \geqslant 0, \forall e \in \mathcal{E}$, and $r_{jl} = 0$ if there exists motion constraints between the bins $\mathcal{P}_j$ and $\mathcal{P}_l$. Then, we make the following standard assumption:

Assumption 1 *(Connectivity)* $\mathcal{G}$ *is strongly connected and the set* $\hat{\mathcal{E}} = \{(j,j)|j \in \mathcal{V}\}$ *belongs to* $\mathcal{E}$, *which indicates that the Markov matrix* $\boldsymbol{M}^i(k)$ *is irreducible.*

Definition 2 *(Actual swarm distribution) At time instant k, the actual population fraction of the robotic swarms at vertex j is denoted as:*

$$\boldsymbol{x}_j(k) = \frac{1}{N}\sum_{i=1}^{N}\chi_j(X_i(k)), \tag{2}$$

where $j \in \mathcal{V}$, $i \in \mathbb{I}_{[1,N]}$. Then, the column-stochastic actual swarm distribution $\boldsymbol{x}(k) = [\boldsymbol{x}_1(k), \cdots, \boldsymbol{x}_{n_v}(k)]^T$.

Definition 3 *(Target swarm distribution) The target swarm distribution $\boldsymbol{\theta} = [\boldsymbol{\theta}_1, \cdots, \boldsymbol{\theta}_{n_v}]^T$ is a column-stochastic vector, where the element $\boldsymbol{\theta}_j$ represents the desired population fraction of the robotic swarms at vertex j (the desired swarm density in bin $\mathcal{P}_i$).*

In terms of actual implementation, we also assume that the agent can recognize the vertex at which it stays. Furthermore, the target swarm distribution $\boldsymbol{\theta}$ is received in advance.

2.2 Problem Formulation

In this subsection, system dynamics of the probability density distribution for each agent is provided first, followed by establishing the evolution process of the swarm density distribution. Then, ET model predictive MFC strategy is designed.

Let the vector $\bar{\boldsymbol{x}}^i(k)$ represent the probability density distribution function (PDDF) of agent i over n_v bins at time instant k, i.e., $\bar{\boldsymbol{x}}_j^i(k) = \mathbb{P}(X_i(k) = j), j \in \mathcal{V}$, $i \in \mathbb{I}_{[1,N]}$. Using the transition rate defined in (1), the probability density distribution $\bar{\boldsymbol{x}}^i(k)$ evolves according to the discrete-time Kolmogorov Forward Equation (mean-filed model) as follows:

$$\bar{\boldsymbol{x}}^i(k+1) = \bar{\boldsymbol{x}}^i(k) + \sum_{e \in \mathcal{E}} r_e^i(k)\boldsymbol{B}_e\bar{\boldsymbol{x}}^i(k) \tag{3}$$

with $\bar{x}^i(0)$ is a n_v-dimensional column-stochastic vector. The entries in matrix $\boldsymbol{B}_e \in \mathbb{R}^{n_v \times n_v}$ are detailed as:

$$\boldsymbol{B}_e[j,l] = \begin{cases} 1 & j = T(e), l = S(e), \\ -1 & j = l = S(e), \\ 0 & otherwise. \end{cases} \tag{4}$$

Here, $S(e)$ and $T(e)$ are the source and target vertices of e, respectively.

According to the definition of $\boldsymbol{B}_e$, the transition rate r_e^i only changes the probability density of agent i at vertices $S(e)$ and $T(e)$. Furthermore, $\boldsymbol{B}_e$ also ensures that $\bar{x}^i(k)$ is a column-stochastic vector. Let $r_e^i(k)\bar{x}_{S(e)}^i(k)$ be the flux from $S(e)$ to $T(e)$ at time instant k. The second term on the right side of the model in (3) quantifies the overall difference between the influx and outflux of the probability density at each vertex.

Combining with the Markov matrix in (1), the compact form of the system dynamics in (3) is:

$$\bar{x}^i(k+1) = \boldsymbol{M}^{i^T}(k)\bar{x}^i(k), \tag{5}$$

where $\boldsymbol{M}^{i^T}(k)$ denotes the transpose of $\boldsymbol{M}^i$.

It should be noted that the robotic swarm's actual density distribution $x(k)$ is the main focus to be stabilized in this paper. To facilitate the controller design, the evolution process of the swarm distribution must be determined. However, due to the stochastic characteristic of the agent here, establishing such a model is extremely difficult. To address this issue, the system dynamics of the probability density distribution $\bar{x}^i(k)$ originating from $x(0)$ is firstly taken as the nominal model:

$$\bar{x}^i(k+1) = \boldsymbol{M}^{i^T}(k)\bar{x}^i(k), \quad \bar{x}^i(0) = x(0). \tag{6}$$

On the basis of the dynamic law of large numbers, $x(k)$ converges to $\bar{x}^i(k)$ when $N \to \infty$. Because that practical robotic swarms only consists of limited agents, there always admits a disturbance term $\omega^i \in \mathcal{W} \subset \mathbb{R}^{n_v}$, which describes the discrepancy between $x(k)$ and $\bar{x}^i(k)$. Then, taking $x(k)$ as the actual value of the nominal state $\bar{x}^i(k)$, agent i estimates the detailed evolution process of $x(k)$ as the following perturbed system dynamics:

$$x(k+1) = \boldsymbol{M}^{i^T}(k)x(k) + \omega^i(k) \tag{7}$$

Here, $\omega^i(k)$ is assumed to be bounded by $\tau_i \triangleq \sup_{\omega^i(k) \in \mathcal{W}} \|\omega^i(k)\|$.

As a result of the above modeling process, each agent has a direct access to the macroscopic behavior, which regulates the actual density distribution by determining a series of inhomogenous Markov Matrices $\boldsymbol{M}^i(k), k = 0, 1, 2 \cdots$. Because that the dimension of the state space is uniquely specified by the number of bins, increasing the population size of the swarm has no influence on the computation complexity to calculate $\boldsymbol{M}^i(k)$, ensuring the control algorithm's scalability.

To facilitate the ET model predictive MFC design, the following assumption is made for the nominal model in (6):

Assumption 2 *There always exsists a a local Markov matrix $M(\bar{x}(k); \theta)$ for all $\bar{x}(k; k) \in \Omega(\theta, \varepsilon)$ such that*

$$V_f(\bar{x}(k+1); \theta) - V_f(\bar{x}(k); \theta) \leqslant -F(\bar{x}(k), M(\bar{x}(k); \theta); \theta) \qquad (8)$$

holds, where $\varepsilon > 0$ is a given constant, $\Omega(\theta, \varepsilon) \triangleq \{\bar{x} \in \mathbb{R}^{n_v} : V_f(\bar{x}; \theta) \leqslant \varepsilon^2\}$ is the terminal region, $V_f(\bar{x}; \theta(k)) \triangleq \|\bar{x}(k) - \theta\|_P^2$ and $F(\bar{x}(k), M(\bar{x}(k); \theta); \theta) \triangleq \|\bar{x}(k) - \theta\|_Q^2 + r \sum_{e \in \mathcal{E}} r_e^2(\bar{x}(k); \theta).$

Assumption 2 is a standard condition in model predictive control (MPC) literature. Moreover, many approaches for calculating the local control law have been developed, e.g., [14,15].

3   ET Model Predictive MFC Strategy

In this section, in order to reduce the computation load and overcome the performance degradation raised by the existence of the disturbance term $\omega^i(k)$, an optimization-based ET strategy for swarm systems is first presented, then the detailed robust ET model predictive MFC algorithm is provided.

3.1   ET in Optimzation

Let the sequence $\{k_0^i, k_1^i, \cdots, k_j^i, \cdots\}, j = 0, 1, \cdots$ be the time steps at which the swarm distribution is measured by agent i, $i \in \mathbb{I}_{[1,N]}$, where $k_0^i = 0$. A finite horizon optimal control problem (OCP) to be solved by the agent at the time steps for triggering is:

Problem $\mathcal{Q}_i$:

$$\hat{M}^{i*}(k_j^i) = \arg \min_{\hat{M}^{i*}(h; k_j^i)} J(\hat{M}^i(k_j^i); \hat{x}^i(k_j^i), \theta) \qquad (9)$$

$$s.t. \ \hat{x}^i(h+1; k_j^i) = \hat{M}^{iT}(h; k_j^i)\hat{x}^i(h; k_j^i), \qquad (10)$$

$$\sum_{e \in \mathcal{E}} r_e^i(h; k_j^i) B_e \theta = 0, \qquad (11)$$

$$\hat{x}^i(k_j^i + H; k_j^i) \in \Omega(\theta, \alpha_i \varepsilon_i), \qquad (12)$$

where $h \in \mathbb{I}_{k_j^i, k_j^i + H - 1}$, H is the prediction horizon. $\hat{M}^i(k_j^i) = \{\hat{M}^i(k_j^i; k_j^i), \cdots, \hat{M}^i(k_j^i + H - 1; k_j^i)\}$ denotes the feasible Markov matrix sequence predicted at time step k_j. $\hat{x}^i(k_j^i) = \{\hat{x}^i(k_j^i; k_j^i), \cdots, \hat{x}^i(k_j^i + H; k_j^i)\}$ is the corresponding feasible state sequence emanating from $\hat{x}^i(k_j^i; k_j^i) = x(k_j^i)$ and subjecting to the nominal model in (6), $\alpha_i \in (0, 1)$. The cost function is formulated by

$$J(\hat{\boldsymbol{M}}^i(k_j^i); \hat{\boldsymbol{x}}^i(k_j^i), \boldsymbol{\theta})$$

$$\triangleq \sum_{h=k_j^i}^{k_j^i+H-1} F(\hat{\boldsymbol{x}}^i(h; k_j^i), \hat{\boldsymbol{M}}^i(h; k_j^i); \boldsymbol{\theta}) + V_f(\hat{\boldsymbol{x}}^i(k_j^i + H; k_j^i); \boldsymbol{\theta}) \tag{13}$$

$$= \sum_{h=k_j^i}^{k_j^i+H-1} [\|\hat{\boldsymbol{x}}^i(h; k_j^i) - \boldsymbol{\theta}\|_{Q_i}^2 + r_i \sum_{e \in \mathcal{E}} \hat{r}_e^{i2}(h; k_j^i)] + \|\hat{\boldsymbol{x}}^i(k_j^i + H; k_j^i) - \boldsymbol{\theta}\|_{P_i}^2,$$

where Q_i, and P_i are positive definite weighting matrices, and $r_i > 0$.

Because of the positive definite quadratic form, both the stage cost $F(\hat{\boldsymbol{x}}^i(h; k_j^i), \hat{\boldsymbol{M}}^i(h; k_j); \boldsymbol{\theta})$ and the terminal cost $V_f(\hat{\boldsymbol{x}}^i(k_j^i + H; k_j^i); \boldsymbol{\theta})$ are locally Lipschitz continuous in $\hat{\boldsymbol{x}}^i$ over the stability region with Lipschitz constants L_{F_i} and $L_{V_{f_i}}$, respectively. For more details, the readers are referred to [20].

In problem $\mathcal{Q}_i$, $\hat{\boldsymbol{M}}^{i*}(k_j^i)$ has the following properties:

1) According to the expanded form of MFM in (3), the hard constraint in (11) guarantees that $\hat{\boldsymbol{M}}^{i*}(h, k_j^i)$ takes $\boldsymbol{\theta}$ as its stationary distribution, that is:

$$\boldsymbol{\theta} = \hat{\boldsymbol{M}}^{iT}(h, k_j^i)\boldsymbol{\theta}. \tag{14}$$

2) Different from the IMC strategy, $\hat{\boldsymbol{M}}^{i*}(h, k_j^i)$ in this paper is time-varying and tends to identical matrix while $\hat{\boldsymbol{x}}^i(k_j^i; k_j^i)$ converges to $\boldsymbol{\theta}$ as $k_j \to \infty$, indicating that both the macroscopic equilibrium of the swarm and microscopic equilibrium of the agent can be realized. Moreover, this mechanism removes the additional constraint imposed on the diagonal element of $\hat{\boldsymbol{M}}^i(h, k_j^i)$ in [13], hence reducing the calculation cost.

For Problem $\mathcal{P}_i$, it should also be noticed that the equation in (14) should also hold for the controller in the terminal region. Therefore, we propose a candidate local controller $\bar{\boldsymbol{M}}^i(\hat{\boldsymbol{x}}^i(k); \boldsymbol{\theta})$ with the element designed by:

$$\bar{\boldsymbol{M}}_{jl}^i(\hat{\boldsymbol{x}}^i(k); \boldsymbol{\theta})) = \begin{cases} \gamma\theta_l\|\hat{\boldsymbol{x}}^i(k) - \boldsymbol{\theta}\| & j \neq l, \\ 1 - \sum_{l=1, l \neq j}^{n_v} \bar{\boldsymbol{M}}_{jl}^i(\hat{\boldsymbol{x}}^i(k); \boldsymbol{\theta})) & j = l, \end{cases} \tag{15}$$

where γ is a constant value. Then, the condition in (14) holds because that:

$$\sum_{j=1}^{n_v} \bar{\boldsymbol{M}}_{jl}^i)(\hat{\boldsymbol{x}}^i(k); \boldsymbol{\theta}))\theta_j = \sum_{j=1}^{n_v} \bar{\boldsymbol{M}}_{lj}^i(\hat{\boldsymbol{x}}^i(k); \boldsymbol{\theta})\theta_l = \theta_l \sum_{j=1}^{n_v} \bar{\boldsymbol{M}}_{lj}^i(\hat{\boldsymbol{x}}^i(k); \boldsymbol{\theta}) = \hat{\Theta}_l. \tag{16}$$

In the event-triggered framework, the triggering time step is determined by verifying a predefined triggering condition. Due to the existence of the disturbance term, the actual swarm distribution $x(h)$ is not consistent with the optimal state $\hat{\boldsymbol{x}}^{i*}(h; k_j^i)$. Then, the triggering condition in this paper is designed by:

$$\hat{k}_{j+1}^i = \min\{k_1, k_2\}, \tag{17}$$

where

$$k_1 = \inf\{h \in \mathbb{N}_{\geq 0} | h > k_j^i \wedge \|\boldsymbol{x}(h) - \hat{\boldsymbol{x}}^{i*}(h; k_j^i)\| \geqslant (1 - \alpha_i)\varepsilon_i/\bar{\lambda}(P_i)\sqrt{n_v}\} \quad (18)$$

$$k_2 = \inf\{h \in \mathbb{N}_{\geq 0} | h > k_j^i \wedge \|\boldsymbol{x}(h) - \hat{\boldsymbol{x}}^{i*}(h; k_j^i)\| \geqslant \\ \|\boldsymbol{x}(k_j^i) - \boldsymbol{\theta}\|_{Q_i}^2/(L_{F_i}(H-2) + L_{V_{f_i}})\sqrt{n_v}\}. \quad (19)$$

Considering the finite prediction horizon, the triggering time step k_{j+1}^i is:

$$k_{j+1}^i = \min\{\hat{k}_{j+1}^i, k_j^i + H\}. \quad (20)$$

3.2   ET Model Predictive MFC Algorithm

We use dual-mode control strategy to further reduce the computation load [17]. In this control paradigm, the control law is determined by solving Problem $\mathcal{Q}_i$ when $\boldsymbol{x}(k_j^i) \notin \Omega(\boldsymbol{\theta}, \varepsilon)$, and switches to the local Markov matrix $\bar{M}(\boldsymbol{x}(k_j^i); \boldsymbol{\theta})$ in (15) when $\boldsymbol{x}(k_j^i) \in \Omega(\boldsymbol{\theta}, \varepsilon)$. The ET model predictive MFC strategy for each agent i is detailed in Algorithm 1.

Algorithm 1 ET Model Predictive MFC Algorithm

Require: initial state $\boldsymbol{x}(0)$, target density distribution $\boldsymbol{\theta}$, and set $k_j^i = 0$.
1: **while** $\boldsymbol{x}(k_j^i) \notin \Omega(\boldsymbol{\theta}, \varepsilon_i)$ **do**
2:    Generate the optimal Markov matrix sequence $\hat{M}^{i*}(k_j^i)$ and the optimal state sequence $\hat{\boldsymbol{x}}^{i*}(s; k_j^i)$ by solving Problem $\mathcal{Q}_i$;
3:    $\hat{k}_{j+1}^i = k_j^i$, $h = 0$;
4:    **while** (18) or (19) not holds at $\hat{k}_{j+1}^i$ and $h \leqslant H$ **do**
5:       Apply the optimal Markov matrix $\hat{M}^{i*}(k_j^i + h; k_j^i)$;
6:       $h = h + 1$, $\hat{k}_{j+1}^i = k_j^i + h$;
7:    **end while**
8:    Let $k_{j+1}^i = \min\{\hat{k}_{j+1}^i, k_j^i + H\}$;
9:    Set $\boldsymbol{x}(k_j^i) \leftarrow \boldsymbol{x}(k_{j+1}^i)$ and update $k_j^i \leftarrow k_{j+1}^i$;
10: **end while**
11: Apply the local Markov matrix $\bar{M}(\boldsymbol{x}(k); \boldsymbol{\theta})$.

In lines 5 and 11, inverse transform sampling is used to implement a Markov matrix $M(k)$. First, a random number n from the uniform distribution in range $\mathbb{R}_{0,1}$ is sampled. Assume that agent i remains in bin $\mathcal{P}_j$ at time step k. The j row of Markov matrix is then represented as a cumulative distribution function (CDF). Finally, the next bin $\mathcal{P}_j$ that agent i will transit into is uniquely determined by checking the following inequalities:

$$\sum_{e=1}^{l-1} M_{je}(k) \leqslant z < \sum_{e=1}^{l} M_{je}(k) \quad (21)$$

4   Numerical Example

Consider an example of the swarm density regulation in a physical space divided by four disjoint bins. Fig. 1 shows the underlying connected graph among bins.

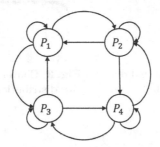

Fig. 1. The underlying connected graph among the bins.

The initial swarm distribution and the target one are $x(0) = [0.4, 0.1, 0.1, 0.4]^T$ and $\theta = [0.1, 0.4, 0.4, 0.1]^T$, respectively. The weight matrices are chosen as $Q_i = diag(1,1,1,1)$ and $P_i = diag(1,1,1,1)$; the weight parameter $r_i = 20$; the horizon H is chosen to be 10; the Lipschitz constants $L_{F_i} = \sqrt{2}$ and $L_{V_{f_i}} = 0.2$; the parameters ε_i and α_i are set as 0.1 and 0.2, respectively.

We conduct the simulation by MATLAB, and use *fmincon* function to solve optimization problem. To compare the control performance on different swarm size, the algorithm is performed on four groups of swarm, with $N = 10, 10^2, 10^3$ and 10^4, respectively. It should be noticed that the variation of N has no influence on the calculation complexity of Problem $\mathcal{Q}_i$. Furthermore, in the proposed algorithm, the calculated Markov matrix only provides the transition probabilities for a agent from the current bin to the others. Each agent moves in a random way. Therefore, we run the algorithm 50 times for different N, and reflect the control performance by statistic. Figs. 2, 3, 4 and 5 show the evolution process of the actual density distribution. The solid lines represent the mean value of the actual density distribution at each bins, and the shaded regions are the range of standard deviation about the mean value. We can see that all the mean values reach the target value in 20 time step. Note that the actual density distribution has stronger fluctuation and larger value of standard deviation for a smaller population size. Since that the difference between actual density distribution and PDD increases with the decrease of N, leading to a larger disturbance term, and therefore harder to be stabilized. This results can also be verified by Figs. 6, 7, 8 and 9, which show the detailed average triggering intervals in 10 step. With the increase of swarm size, a longer triggering interval is realized, and hence the control law only need to be updated at fewer time step, which can release the computation and communication burden.

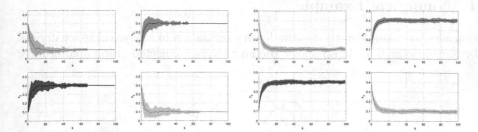

Fig. 2. Convergence of the actual density distribution with $N = 10$.

Fig. 3. Convergence of the actual density distribution with $N = 10^2$.

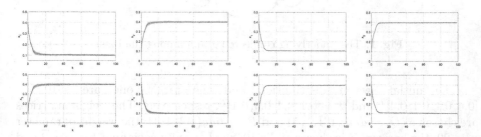

Fig. 4. Convergence of the actual density distribution with $N = 10^3$.

Fig. 5. Convergence of the actual density distribution with $N = 10^4$.

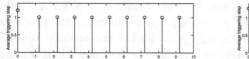

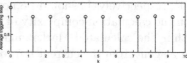

Fig. 6. Average triggering interval at each triggering instant with $N = 10$ under 50 realizations.

Fig. 7. Average triggering interval at each triggering instant with $N = 10^2$ under 50 realizations.

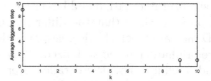

Fig. 8. Average triggering interval at each triggering instant with $N = 10^3$ under 50 realizations.

Fig. 9. Average triggering interval at each triggering instant with $N = 10^4$ under 50 realizations.

5   Conclusions

In this paper, we have proposed an event-triggered (ET) model predictive mean-field control (MFC) algorithm that enables the density regulation of a large-scale robotic swarm under limited resource. We have established a perturbed MFM to macroscopically approximate the evolution process of the actual density distribution, showing scalability with the population size. Combination of the even-triggered mechanism and MPC has also been designed to synthesis the optimized control law in an aperiodic way. Finally, The simulation study has also been carried out to verify the algorithm.

References

1. Elamvazhuthi, K., Kakish, Z., Shirsat, A., et al.: Controllability and stabilization for herding a robotic swarm using a leader: a mean-field approach. IEEE Trans. Rob. **37**(2), 418–432 (2021)
2. Bono, A., Fedele, G., Franze, G.: A swarm-based distributed model predictive control scheme for autonomous vehicle formations in uncertain environments. IEEE Trans. Cybern. (2021). https://doi.org/10.1109/TCYB.2021.3070461
3. La, H., Nguyen, T., Le, T., Jafari, M.: Formation control and obstacle avoidance of multiple rectangular agents with limited communication ranges. IEEE Trans. Control Netw. Syst. **4**(4), 680–691 (2017)
4. Peng, Z., Wang, J., Wang, D.: Distributed maneuvering of autonomous surface vehicles based on neurodynamic optimization and fuzzy approximation. IEEE Trans. Control Syst. Technol. **26**(3), 1083–1090 (2018)
5. Bandyopadhyay, S., Chung, S., Hadaegh, F.Y.: Probabilistic and distributed control of a large-scale swarm of autonomous agents. IEEE Trans. Robot. **33**(5), 3896–3901 (2009)
6. Elamvazhuthi, K., Berman, S.: Mean-field models in swarm robotics: a survey. Bioinspiration Biomimetics **15**(1), 015001 (2019)
7. Chattopadhyay, I., Ray, A.: Supervised self-organization of homogeneous swarms using ergodic projections of Markov chains. IEEE Trans. Syst. Man, Cybern. Part B (Cybernetics) **39**(6), 1505–1515 (2009)
8. Açikmeşe, B., Bayard, D.S.: A Markov chain approach to probabilistic swarm guidance. In: 2012 American Control Conference (ACC), pp. 6300–6307. IEEE, Canada (2012)
9. Billera, L.J., Diaconis, P.: A geometric interpretation of the Metropolis-Hastings algorithm. Stat. Sci. **16**(4), 335–339 (2001)
10. Hsieh, M.A., Halasz, A., Berman, S., Kumar, V.: Biologically inspired redistribution of a swarm of robots among multiple sites. Swarm Intell. **2**, 121–141 (2008)
11. Zheng, T., Han, Q., Lin, H.: Transporting robotic swarms via mean-field feedback control. IEEE Trans. Autom. Control **67**(8), 4170–4177 (2022)
12. Bandyopadhyay, S., Chung, S.-J., Hadaegh, F.Y.: Probabilistic swarm guidance using optimal transport. In: 2014 IEEE Conference on Control Applications (CCA), pp. 498–505. IEEE, France (2014)
13. Bandyopadhyay, S., Chung, S.-J., Hadaegh, F.Y.: Probabilistic and distributed control of a large-scale swarm of autonomous agents. IEEE Trans. Rob. **33**(5), 1103–1123 (2017)

14. Chen, H., Allgöwer, F.: A quasi-infinite horizon nonlinear model predictive control scheme with guaranteed stability. Automatica **34**(10), 1205–1217 (1998)
15. Zhu, Y., Ozguner, U.: Robustness analysis on constrained model predictive control for nonholonomic vehicle regulation. In: Proceedings of American Control Conference, pp. 1103-1123. IEEE, USA (2009)
16. Michalska, H., Mayne, D.Q.: Robust recedindg horizon control of constrained nonlinear systems. IEEE Trans. Autom. Control **38**(11), 1623–1633 (1993)
17. Zou, Y., Su, X., Li, S., Niu, Y., Li, D.: Event-triggered distributed predictive control for asynchronous coordination of multi-agent systems. Automatica **99**, 92–98 (2019)
18. Li, H., Yan, W., Shi, Y., Wang, Y.: Periodic event-triggering in distributed receding horizon control of nonlinear systems. Syst. Control Lett. **86**, 16–23 (2015)
19. Cui, D., Li, H.: Dual self-triggered model-predictive control for nonlinear cyberphysical systems. IEEE Trans. Syst. Man, Cybern.: Syst. **52**(6), 3442–3452 (2022)
20. Eqtami, A., Heshmati-alamdari, S., Dimarogonas, D.V., Kyriakopoulos, K.J.: Self-triggered model predictive control for nonholonomic systems. In: Proceedings of the European Control Conference, pp. 638–643. IEEE, Switzerland (2013)

Risk-Aware Motion Planning for Very-Large-Scale Robotics Systems Using Conditional Value-at-Risk

Xuru Yang[1], Han Gao[1], Pingping Zhu[2], and Chang Liu[1(✉)]

[1] Department of Advanced Manufacturing and Robotics, College of Engineering,
Peking University, Beijing 100871, China
xuru.yang@stu.pku.edu.cn {hangaocoe,changliucoe}@pku.edu.cn
[2] Department of Computer Sciences and Electrical Engineering (CSEE), Marshall
University, Huntington, WV 25755, USA
zhup@marshall.edu

Abstract. The field of Very-Large-Scale Robotics (VLSR) has garnered significant attention due to its ability to tackle complex and coordinated tasks. However, current motion planning methods for VLSR face challenges related to scalability and ensuring safety. To address these limitations, we propose a novel risk-aware motion planning framework for VLSR. Our approach formulates a finite-time optimal control (FTOC) problem based on the macroscopic state of VLSR and incorporates conditional value-at-risk (CVaR) to avoid collision. We present a systematic approach that leverages the linearized Signed Distance Function to efficiently compute the CVaR of the distance between VLSR and obstacles. Subsequently, we develop an approximation approach to reformulate the nonlinear FTOC as a linear programming problem using the discretized workspace, resulting in computationally efficient online motion planning. Simulations on VLSR consisting of five hundred robots demonstrate the effectiveness of the proposed approach in both computational efficiency and risk mitigation.

Keywords: Very-Large-Scale Robotics Systems · Conditional Value-at-Risk · Optimal Control · Motion Planning · Gaussian Mixture Model

1 Introduction

Very-Large-Scale Robotics (VLSR) systems comprised of hundreds of autonomous and interacting robots are becoming an increasingly important research area. Robot swarms have the potential to achieve complex and coordinated tasks such as military operations, delivery and search and rescue [1].

This work is sponsored by Beijing Nova Program (20220484056) and the National Natural Science Foundation of China (62203018). It is also partially supported by the NASA Established Program to Stimulate Competitive Research, Grant # 80NSSC22M0027. All correspondences should be sent to Chang Liu.

H. Yang et al. (Eds.): ICIRA 2023, LNAI 14273, pp. 513–525, 2023.
https://doi.org/10.1007/978-981-99-6498-7_44

Scalability poses a significant challenge for VLSR and hinders the wide applications of VLSR . Traditional works have developed microscopic control laws that consider each robot as an individual and analyze the interactions both among robots and between the individual robots and the environment [2,3]. Despite the achievements in controlling small and medium-scale robot swarms, these methods fail to scale to VLSR due to high computational overhead. Macroscopic approaches enhance the scalability of VLSR by treating the swarm as an entity while ignoring the microscopic state in the motion planning level. One widely used idea to model the macroscopic state is based on the mean-field theory [4,5], which assumes that the dynamics and rewards of each robot are only affected by the average behavior of the entire swarm. This treatment requires coupling between microscopic and macroscopic state of the robot swarm.

Another popular approach, namely the distributed optimal control (DOC) [6,7], models the macroscopic state by the time-varying probability density function (PDF) of robots, which is independent of the microscopic state of each individual robot. Recently, Zhu, Liu and Ferrari proposed a computationally efficient Adaptive DOC approach [8], in which collision avoidance is incorporated as a penalty term in the objective function. Due to this soft constraint of collision avoidance, the generated PDF trajectories can be overly close to obstacles, thus requiring the underlying microscopic control to take large efforts to avoid collision and leading to unsteady motion of robots.

Chance constraint based methods have been a popular tool for risk-aware motion planning [9,10], which constrains the collision probability under a user-defined threshold. A related measurement of risk to chance constraints is value-at-risk (VaR), which represents the maximum amount of risk that could occur with a given probability. Taking the tail risk into consideration, conditional value-at-risk (CVaR) measures the average amount of loss that would occur beyond the VaR level. CVaR has gained increasingly research interests in motion planning in the past few years. For instance, Fan et al. proposed a risk-aware planning framework incorporating CVaR that modifies different sources of traversability risk and solved non-convex risk-constrained optimal control problems in MPC architecture [11]. Hakobyan et al. adopted CVaR constraints in a linearly constrained mixed-integer convex program to limit the safety risk in an uncertain environment [12]. Despite the progresses made, these works focus on either single or small-scale robotic systems due to high computational expenses.

To bridge the gap, we propose a risk-aware motion planner using CVaR for VLSR. The primary contributions can be summarized as follows:

- We propose a novel motion planning framework for VLSR that integrates CVaR for risk-aware collision avoidance constraints. Instead of considering motion planning on the individual robot level, we present a finite-time optimal control (FTOC) formulation for the macroscopic state of VLSR, represented as Gaussian Mixture Models (GMMs), to generate collision-free trajectories in cluttered environments.
- We develop a systematic approach to evaluate the CVaR between the GMM macroscopic state and obstacles. The linearized Signed Distance Function

(SDF) is leveraged to approximate the distance distribution between the swarm and obstacles, which is then utilized to efficiently approximate CVaR.
- We reformulate the computationally expensive FTOC problem into lightweight linear programming (LP) by discretizing the workspace and computing CVaR and Wasserstein metric offline. This efficient computational strategy enables online motion planning of VLSR, as validated in simulations.

2 Background

2.1 Wasserstein Metric

The Wasserstein metric measures the distance between two probability distributions on a given metric space, and is widely used in the optimal transport problems [13]. Let $\wp_1, \wp_2 \in \mathcal{P}(\Omega)$ denote two PDFs defined on Ω, where $\mathcal{P}$ and Ω refer to a set of all probability distributions and the sample space, respectively. Let $\Pi(\wp_1, \wp_2) \subset \mathcal{P}(\Omega \times \Omega)$ be the set of all joint PDFs $\pi \in \mathcal{P}(\Omega \times \Omega)$, where the marginal PDFs along the two coordinates are $\wp_1$ and $\wp_2$, respectively, i.e.,

$$\Pi(\wp_1, \wp_2) \triangleq \left\{ \pi \in \mathcal{P}(\Omega \times \Omega) \mid \int_{x_2 \in \Omega} \pi(\cdot, x_2) dx_2 = \wp_1, \int_{x_1 \in \Omega} \pi(x_1, \cdot) dx_1 = \wp_2 \right\}, \quad (1)$$

where $\times$ denotes the Cartesian product. Then the Wasserstein metric $W_2(\wp_1, \wp_2)$ is defined by

$$W_2(\wp_1, \wp_2) \triangleq \inf_{\pi \in \Pi(\wp_1, \wp_2)} \left[\int_{\Omega \times \Omega} \|x_1 - x_2\|^2 d\pi(x_1, x_2) \right]^{1/2}, \quad (2)$$

where $\| \cdot \|$ indicates the Euclidean distance.

Though Wasserstein metric for general distributions does not have an analytical expression, for two Gaussian PDFs denoted by $g_1 = \mathcal{N}(\mu_1, \Sigma_1)$ and $g_2 = \mathcal{N}(\mu_2, \Sigma_2)$, their Wasserstein metric can be efficiently calculated as follows [14]:

$$W_2(g_1, g_2) = \left\{ \|\mu_1 - \mu_2\|^2 + tr \left[\Sigma_1 + \Sigma_2 - 2 \left(\Sigma_1^{1/2} \Sigma_2 \Sigma_1^{1/2} \right)^{1/2} \right] \right\}^{1/2}, \quad (3)$$

where $tr(\cdot)$ indicates the trace operator. Further, the Wasserstein metric of two GMMs can be approximated utilizing Eq. (3) [14]. Specifically, consider two GMMs with N_1 and N_2 Gaussian components denoted by $\wp_1 = \sum_{i=1}^{N_1} \omega_1^i g_1^i$, $\sum_{i=1}^{N_1} \omega_1^i = 1$ and $\wp_2 = \sum_{j=1}^{N_2} \omega_2^j g_2^j$, $\sum_{j=1}^{N_2} \omega_2^j = 1$, where g_1^i, g_2^j denote the i_{th} and j_{th} Gaussian components of $\wp_1$ and $\wp_2$, respectively, and ω_1^i, ω_2^j denote their corresponding weight. The approximated Wasserstein metric $W_2(\wp_1, \wp_2)$ can be formulated as:

$$W_2(\wp_1, \wp_2) \triangleq \left\{ \min_{\pi \in \Pi(\omega_1, \omega_2)} \sum_{i=1}^{N_1} \sum_{j=1}^{N_2} [W_2(g_1^i, g_2^j)]^2 \pi(i, j) \right\}^{1/2}. \quad (4)$$

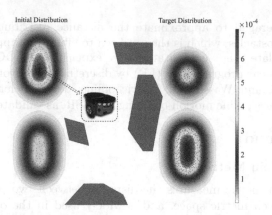

Fig. 1. The VLSR needs to plan a trajectory in the 2 dimentional workspace to move from the initial distribution on the left side of the diagram to the target distribution on the right side in a cluttered environment.

where $\boldsymbol{\omega}_1 = [\omega_1^1, \cdots, \omega_1^{N_1}], \boldsymbol{\omega}_2 = [\omega_2^1, \cdots, \omega_2^{N_2}]$, and $\pi(i,j)$ is the joint probability distribution between the i_{th} Gaussian component weight in $\wp_1$ and the j_{th} Gaussian component weight in $\wp_2$.

2.2 VaR and CVaR

The VaR represents the minimum possible value of risk that can be achieved given a specific risk tolerance level. Specifically, the VaR of a random variable ζ under risk tolerance level $\alpha \in (0,1]$ is defined as

$$VaR_\alpha(\zeta) = \min\{z | Pr(\zeta \leqslant z) \geqslant 1 - \alpha\}, \qquad (5)$$

where $Pr(\cdot)$ denotes the probability. For a random variable ζ with a continuous distribution, the relationship between VaR and CVaR can be expressed by $CVaR_\alpha(\zeta) = \mathbb{E}[\zeta | \zeta \geq VaR_\alpha(\zeta)]$.

Let $\phi(\cdot)$ and $\Phi(\cdot)$ denote the PDF and the cumulative distribution function of a standard normal distribution, respectively. The CVaR of a Gaussian random variable $\zeta \sim \mathcal{N}(\mu, \sigma^2)$ has the following closed-form expression [15]

$$CVaR_\alpha(\zeta) = \mu + \sigma \frac{\phi(\Phi^{-1}(1-\alpha))}{\alpha}. \qquad (6)$$

3   Problem Formulation

Consider the workspace $\mathcal{W} \subset \mathbb{R}^2$ that contains a robot swarm consisting of N_r robots and N_o static obstacles $\mathcal{O}_i \subset \mathcal{W}, i = 1, 2, \cdots, N_o$ (Fig. 1). Let $\mathcal{O} = \bigcup\limits_{i=1}^{N_o} \mathcal{O}_i$

represent the union of all obstacles. For simplicity, $\mathcal{O}_i$ is assumed to be a convex obstacle or the convex-hull of a concave obstacle.

The macroscopic state of the swarm is represented as a random variable $X(k) \in \mathbb{R}^2$ such that the position of every single robot $x_i(k), i = 1, 2, \cdots, N_r$, can be treated as a random sample from $X(k)$. Given the universal approxima-tion property of Gaussian Mixture Models (GMMs), we assume $X(k) \sim \wp_k$, where $\wp_k$ is a GMM in the GMM distribution space $\mathcal{G}(\mathcal{W})$, formulated as $\wp_k = \sum_{j=1}^{N} \omega_j g_j$. Here N denotes the number of GMM distributions, and g_j is the j_{th} Gaussian distribution with mean value μ_j, covariance matrix Σ_j and weight $\omega_j \geq 0$, $\sum_{j=1}^{N} \omega_j = 1$. For simplicity, we define $\omega = [\omega_1, \omega_2, \cdots, \omega_N]$, $g = [g_1, g_2, \cdots, g_N]$.

The motion model of the swarm can be described by

$$X(k+1) = f(X(k), u(k)) + W(k), k = 0, 1, \cdots, T_f, W(k) \sim \mathcal{N}(0, \Sigma_0), \quad (7)$$

where $u(k)$, $W(k)$ and T_f denote system control input, white Gaussian process noise, and the terminal time step, respectively.

The motion planning of the swarm takes a hierarchical strategy that com-prises the macroscopic planning stage and the microscopic control stage. The macroscopic planning stage generates optimal trajectory of swarm PDF, and in the microscopic control stage, individual robots generate control inputs to keep track of the swarm PDF.

The motion planning of swarm PDF is formulated as a finite-time optimal control (FTOC) problem to drive the swarm move from an initial distribution $\wp_0 \in \mathcal{G}(\mathcal{W})$ to a target distribution $\wp_{targ} \in \mathcal{G}(\mathcal{W})$ while minimizing the total transport distance and transport risks while satisfying a risk-aware collision avoidance constraint. In particular, the FTOC at time step k is formulated as

$$\min_{\wp_{k+1}, \dots, \wp_{T_f}} J \triangleq \sum_{t=k}^{T_f - 1} \lambda_{t+1} \mathcal{L} \left[\mathcal{D}(\wp_t, \wp_{t+1}), F_\alpha(\varphi_t, \varphi_{t+1}) \right]$$

$$s.t. \quad CVaR_\alpha(\varphi_{k+1}) < \epsilon, \quad (8)$$

where $\lambda_{t+1} > 0$ and $\epsilon \in \mathbb{R}$ represent the weight and the collision risk bound, respectively, and φ_t is a random variable representing the distance between swarm PDF and obstacles. The cost term $\mathcal{L}(\cdot)$ represents the transport cost between two consecutive time steps, consisting of a distance term $\mathcal{D}(\cdot)$ adopting Wasserstein metric and the risk term $F_\alpha(\cdot)$ utilizing $CVaR_\alpha(\cdot)$. Detailed formu-lation of the objective function and the constraint will be discussed in Secs. 5.1 and 5.2, respectively. Note that the constraint is only applied to the next step, not steps afterward.

In the microscopic control stage, individual robots use the artificial potential field method to generate motion control inputs to follow the swarm PDF and avoid collision with static obstacles and other robots. The microscopic control is out of the scope of this work. Interested readers can refer to [8] for details.

4   Computation of CVaR for VLSR

4.1   Signed Distance Function

The SDF measures the signed distance between two sets. In particular, the SDF between a point $p \in W$ and the obstacle $\mathcal{O}_i$ can be calculated as follows

$$sd(p, \mathcal{O}_i) = \begin{cases} -d(p, \partial\mathcal{O}_i) \text{ if } p \in \mathcal{O}_i \\ d(p, \partial\mathcal{O}_i) \text{ if } p \notin \mathcal{O}_i \end{cases}, \tag{9}$$

where $\partial\mathcal{O}_i$ is the boundary of $\mathcal{O}_i$ and $d(p, \partial\mathcal{O}_i) = \min_{o_i \in \partial\mathcal{O}_i} \|p - o_i\|_2$. The closest point to p on $\partial\mathcal{O}_i$ is denoted as o_i^*, i.e., $o_i^* = \arg\min_{o_i \in \partial\mathcal{O}_i} \|p - o_i\|_2$, and the normal vector along the SDF direction is given by $n = sgn(sd(p, \mathcal{O}_i)) \cdot (p - o_i^*)/\|p - o_i^*\|$, where $sgn(\cdot)$ is the sign function.

The calculation of SDF and its corresponding normal vector n can be performed with either of the two popular algorithms: Gilbert-Johnson-Keerthi (GJK) algorithm [16] for minimum distance between two non-overlapping sets, and Expanding Polytope Algorithm (EPA) [17] for penetration depth between two overlapping sets.

4.2   Calculation of SDF Under Gaussian Uncertainty

SDF is a commonly used metric in collision avoidance tasks. To account for the stochastic SDF when calculating the probabilistic collision loss, we first derive the SDF expression under Gaussian uncertainty.

For every Gaussian distribution g_j, we first utilize the GJK algorithm or EPA to calculate the SDF between the mean μ_j and the obstacle $\mathcal{O}_i$, denoted by $sd(\mu_j, \mathcal{O}_i)$, and the corresponding normal vector n_j. Inspired by [18], we assume that the point o_i^* and normal vector n_j remain unchanged in the neighborhood of μ_j when calculating $sd(X^j, \mathcal{O}_i)$, where $X^j \sim \mathcal{N}(\mu_j, \Sigma_j)$. The SDF between the random variable X^j and the obstacle $\mathcal{O}_i$ can be subsequently approximated by the first-order Taylor expansion as follows,

$$sd(X^j, \mathcal{O}_i) \approx sd(\mu_j, \mathcal{O}_i) + \nabla sd(X^j, \mathcal{O}_i)|_{X^j = \mu_j}(X^j - \mu_j), \tag{10}$$

where $\nabla sd(X^j, \mathcal{O}_i)|_{X^j = \mu_j} = n_j^T$. Hence, $sd(X^j, \mathcal{O}_i)$ is a Gaussian random variable as a result of the linear transformation of a Gaussian random variable X^j, i.e.,

$$sd(X^j, \mathcal{O}_i) \sim \mathcal{N}(sd(\mu_j, \mathcal{O}_i), n_j^T \Sigma_j n_j). \tag{11}$$

4.3   Calculation of CVaR Under GMM Uncertainty

To calculate the CVaR of a collision risk, we calculate the CVaR under the condition of a negative SDF between the swarm PDF and the obstacle, i.e. $sd(X, \mathcal{O}_i) \leqslant 0$. To adhere to the definition of CVaR, we transform the condition into $-sd(X, \mathcal{O}_i) \geqslant 0$.

Notice that the probability distribution of $-sd(\boldsymbol{X}, \mathcal{O}_i)$ is hard to obtain. For computational convenience, we use $\sum_{j=1}^{N} \omega_j p(-sd(\boldsymbol{X}^j, \mathcal{O}_i))$ as an approximation of $p(-sd(\boldsymbol{X}, \mathcal{O}_i))$, where $p(\cdot)$ denotes the PDF of a random variable.

We now derive the upper bound of $CVaR(-sd(\boldsymbol{X}, \mathcal{O}_i))$. For clarity, we define two random variables $Y = -sd(\boldsymbol{X}, \mathcal{O}_i)$ and $Y^j = -sd(\boldsymbol{X}^j, \mathcal{O}_i)$.

$$CVaR_\alpha(Y) = \mathbb{E}[Y | Y \geqslant VaR_\alpha(Y)] \tag{12a}$$

$$= \frac{\int_{VaR_\alpha(Y)}^{+\infty} y \sum_{j=1}^{N} \omega_j p(Y^j) dy}{Pr(Y \geqslant VaR_\alpha(Y))} \tag{12b}$$

$$\leqslant \frac{1}{\alpha} \sum_{j=1}^{N} \omega_j CVaR_{\alpha^*}(Y^j). \tag{12c}$$

where $\alpha_j = \int_{VaR_\alpha(Y)}^{+\infty} p(Y^j) dy$ and $\alpha^* = \min\{\alpha_1, \cdots, \alpha_N\}$. Equations (12a) and (12b) are derived by the definition of CVaR and conditional expectation, respectively. Then, Eq. (12c) is obtained using the fact that $\alpha_j \in (0, 1]$ and $CVaR_{\alpha^*}(Y^j) \geqslant CVaR_{\alpha^j}(Y^j)$.

Since $CVaR_{\alpha^*}(Y^j)$ can be obtained by solving Eq. (6), the derived upper bound of $CVaR(-sd(\boldsymbol{X}, \mathcal{O}_i))$ can be computed.

5   Optimal Control for VLSR

5.1   Objective Function

We define a risk metric $R_\alpha(\cdot)$ that adopts the CVaR of the SDF between the swarm PDF and the closest obstacle, i.e.,

$$R_\alpha(-sd(\boldsymbol{X}, \mathcal{O})) = \max\{CVaR_\alpha(-sd(\boldsymbol{X}, \mathcal{O}_i)), i = 1, 2, \cdots, N_o\}. \tag{13}$$

Then the risk term $F_\alpha(\cdot, \cdot)$ of two random variable ρ_1 and ρ_2 in Eq. (8) is defined as the arithmetic mean of $R_\alpha(-sd(\rho_1, \mathcal{O}))$ and $R_\alpha(-sd(\rho_2, \mathcal{O}))$, i.e.,

$$F_\alpha(\rho_1, \rho_2) = \frac{R_\alpha(-sd(\rho_1, \mathcal{O})) + R_\alpha(-sd(\rho_2, \mathcal{O}))}{2}. \tag{14}$$

We approximate the transport distance using the square of Wasserstein metric, and employ γ as a weight coefficient between the transport distance and the transport risk under risk acceptance leval α'. Then the objective function in Eq. (8) can be expressed by

$$J \triangleq \sum_{t=k}^{T_f-1} \lambda_{t+1} \left\{ [W_2(\wp_t, \wp_{t+1})]^2 + \gamma F_{\alpha'}(\boldsymbol{X}(t), \boldsymbol{X}(t+1)) \right\}, \tag{15}$$

which consists of the cost of motion from time k to $k+1$, denoted as the *stage cost*, and that from time $k+1$ to T_f, denoted as the *terminal cost*.

We explicitly express and calculate the stage cost by obtaining Wasserstein metric between two GMMs as defined in Eq. (4) and representing the risk term between two GMMs with risk term of their corresponding Gaussian distributions. Thus, the objective function can be written as

$$J \triangleq \sum_{i=1}^{N_k} \sum_{j=1}^{N_{k+1}} \lambda_{k+1}\pi(i,j) \left\{ [W_2(g_i,g_j)]^2 + \gamma F_{\alpha'}(g_i,g_j) \right\}$$

$$+ \sum_{t=k+1}^{T_f-1} \lambda_{t+1} \left\{ [W_2(\wp_t,\wp_{t+1})]^2 + \gamma F_{\alpha'}(\boldsymbol{X}(t),\boldsymbol{X}(t+1)) \right\}, \qquad (16)$$

where $\pi(i,j)$ represents the joint probability satisfying the constraints $\boldsymbol{\omega}_{k+1} = \sum_{i=1}^{N_k} \pi(i,j)$ and $\boldsymbol{\omega}_k = \sum_{j=1}^{N_{k+1}} \pi(i,j)$.

The terminal cost will be described in Sect. 5.3. As the distributions of the robotic swarm are all GMMs, the distribution at time step $t = k+1$ can be characterized by a parameter tuple $\Theta_{k+1} = (\boldsymbol{g}_{k+1}, N_{k+1}, \pi(i,j))$. The optimal PDF of the next time step $k+1$ can be given by $\Theta_{k+1}^* = \arg\min_{\Theta_{k+1}} J$.

5.2   CVaR Constraint

The PDF collision avoidance constraints in Eq. (8) at time step $k+1$ with SDF as a distance metric can be written as

$$CVaR_\alpha(-sd(\boldsymbol{X},\mathcal{O}_i)) \leqslant \epsilon, i = 1,2,\cdots,N_o. \qquad (17)$$

According to Eq. (12), this collision avoidance constraint can be approximated with the upper bound of $CVaR_\alpha(-sd(\boldsymbol{X},\mathcal{O}_i))$, written as

$$\sum_{j=1}^{N_{k+1}} \omega_j CVaR_{\alpha^*}(-sd(\boldsymbol{X}^j,\mathcal{O}_i)) \leqslant \alpha\epsilon, \sum_{j=1}^{N_{k+1}} \omega_j = 1, i = 1,2,\cdots,N_o. \qquad (18)$$

Although this constraint is stronger than the original one, it still cannot directly control the distance between every Gaussian component and an obstacle, which may result in some Gaussian components being too close to obstacles. Therefore, we again strengthen the constraint Eq. (18) into a more risk-averse one, i.e.

$$CVaR_{\alpha^*}(-sd(\boldsymbol{X}^j,\mathcal{O}_i)) \leqslant \alpha\epsilon, j = 1,2,\cdots,N_{k+1}, i = 1,2,\cdots,N_o. \qquad (19)$$

5.3   Approximation to Linear Programming

It is computationally infeasible to iteratively compute the optimal control law based on the current distribution to obtain the distributions at every future time step, as well as the corresponding transport distance and CVaR value. Therefore, we assume that from time step $k+1$ to T_f-1, the Gaussian components of the robot swarm GMM only bypass the obstacles towards the target distribution and do not spilt or merge, i.e. maintaining the same covariance matrices, weights and the number of Gaussian components as time step $k+1$. From time step $T_f - 1$ to T_f, the robot distribution is transformed to the target distribution to complete the transport task. Thus, there are $N_{k+1} \cdot N_{targ}$ trajectories from time step $k+1$ to T_f, denoted by $\mathcal{T} = \{\mathcal{T}_{j,\iota} | j = 1, 2, \cdots, N_{k+1}, \iota = 1, 2, \cdots, N_{targ}\}$.

Like the stage cost, the corresponding cost for each trajectory $\mathcal{T}_{j,\iota}$ can be represented by

$$\mathcal{Q}_{j,\iota} = (W_2^{j,\iota})^2 + \gamma F_{\alpha'}^{j,\iota}, j = 1, 2, \cdots, N_{k+1}, \iota = 1, 2, \cdots, N_{targ}, \qquad (20)$$

where $(W_2^{j,\iota})^2$ and $F_{\alpha'}^{j,\iota}$ denote the sum of the square of Wasserstein metrics and the risk terms along the trajectory $\mathcal{T}_{j,\iota}$. Thus, the terminal cost in Eq. (16) can be denoted by

$$\sum_{j=1}^{N_{k+1}} \sum_{\iota=1}^{N_{targ}} \lambda_{T_f} \mathcal{Q}_{j,\iota} \pi(j, \iota). \qquad (21)$$

Solving the nonlinear optimization problem Eq. (8) is computationally burdensome. To enable online motion planning, we present an approximation solution by assuming that the number of Gaussian components in the next time step $k+1$ is fixed and the Gaussian components can only be chosen from a predefined set $\mathcal{C}$ containing N_c Gaussian components. For simplicity, we assume N_{k+1} to be equal to N_c. The predefined Gaussian component set is denoted by $\mathcal{C} = \{g_c | g_c = \mathcal{N}(\boldsymbol{\mu}_c, \boldsymbol{\Sigma}_c), c = 1, 2, \cdots, N_c\}$, where the means $\boldsymbol{\mu}_c$ are uniformly deployed on $\mathcal{W}$ with same spacial intervals and the covariance matrices $\boldsymbol{\Sigma}_c$ are the same.

For the time step $k+1$ to T_f, the nonlinear computation of Wasserstein metric and CVaR in $\mathcal{Q}$ can be executed beforehand with known Gaussian components at both time steps. Let $\mathcal{V} = \mathcal{C} \cup \{g_\iota | \iota = 1, 2, \cdots, N_{targ}\}$ denote a set of vertices and $\mathcal{E} = \{\mathcal{Q}_{j,\iota} | j = 1, 2, \cdots, N_{k+1}, \iota = 1, 2, \cdots, N_{targ}\}$ represent a set of edges. Then a shortest-path-planning algorithm can be implemented on the directed graph $\mathcal{DG} = (\mathcal{V}, \mathcal{E})$ to find the minimum of the terminal cost.

With these manipulations, the original FTOC is reformulated into an LP problem as follows

$$\pi^*(i, j) = \arg \min_{\pi(i,j)} \left\{ \sum_{j=1}^{N_c} \left[\sum_{i=1}^{N_k} \lambda_{k+1} \mathcal{Q}_{i,j} \pi(i, j) + \sum_{\iota=1}^{N_{targ}} \lambda_{T_f} \mathcal{Q}_{j,\iota} \pi(j, \iota) \right] \right\}$$

$$s.t. \quad \boldsymbol{\omega}_k = \sum_{j=1}^{N_c} \pi(i, j), \boldsymbol{\omega}_{k+1} = \sum_{i=1}^{N_k} \pi(i, j) = \sum_{\iota=1}^{N_{targ}} \pi(j, \iota), \boldsymbol{\omega}_{targ} = \sum_{j=1}^{N_c} \pi(j, \iota),$$

$$CVaR_{\alpha^*}(-sd(\boldsymbol{X}^j, \mathcal{O}_i)) \leqslant \alpha \epsilon, i = 1, 2, \cdots, N_o, j = 1, 2, \cdots, N_c. \qquad (22)$$

The optimal PDF of robot swarm at $k+1$ time step can be obtained by

$$\wp_{k+1}^* = \sum_{j=1}^{N_c} \sum_{i=1}^{N_k} \pi^*(i, j) g_j, g_j = g_c \in \mathcal{C}. \qquad (23)$$

6   Simulation and Results

6.1   Simulation Setup

The proposed CVaR-based optimal control (OC-CVaR) method is evaluated in a swarm motion planning task simulated in MATLAB. The VLSR in simulation consists of five hundred robots. The workspace $\mathcal{W}$ with four obstacles is $[0, 20] \times [0, 16] km^2$ in size. The initial swarm distribution consists of four Gaussian components with the same covariance matrix $\Sigma = I_2$, where I_2 denotes 2×2 identity matrix. Other parameters are $\mu_1 = [3, 13], \omega_1 = 0.25, \mu_2 = [2.5, 11], \omega_2 = 0.375, \mu_3 = [4, 4], \omega_3 = 0.1875, \mu_4 = [2.5, 2.5], \omega_4 = 0.1875$. The target distribution is composed of three Gaussian components with parameters $\mu_1 = [17.5, 12], \omega_1 = 0.25, \mu_2 = [17.5, 6], \omega_2 = 0.375, \mu_3 = [17.5, 4], \omega_3 = 0.375$ and an identical covariance matrix $\Sigma = I_2$. The discretization time interval Δt is 0.01 hr. The simulation is run on a desktop (13th Intel(R) i7 CPU@2.10GHz) and LP is solved using the "linprog" solver with the dual-simplex algorithm in MATLAB.

We designed the set of Gaussian components $\mathcal{C}$ setting the mean of each Gaussian on fixed grids, where the X coordinates range from 0.5 to 19.5 and the Y coordinates range from 0.5 to 15.5, with a discretization interval of 1. Consequently, the set $\mathcal{C}$ comprises a total of $20 \times 16 = 320$ Gaussian components, each with the same covariance matrix $\Sigma_c = diag(0.5, 0.5)$.

When formulating the constraints, α^* and ϵ are set to 0.1 and 0 respectively. When establishing the objective function, α' is set to 0.1, and the negative CVaR values are uniformly set to 0 to ensure that the directed graph $\mathcal{DG}$ used in shortest-path-planning algorithm does not contain any negative cycle. We set the relative weight γ to 3, λ_{T_f} to 2 and λ_{k+1} to 1.

6.2   Comparison with Other Approaches

We compared the performance of the proposed OC-CVaR method with three other state-of-art approaches including PDF-based artificial potential field approach (PDF-APF), sampling-based artificial potential field approach (SAPF), and sampling-based path-planning approach (SPP).

The PDF-APF approach adopts the same microstate control law as our proposed method, with the only difference being that the optimal control PDF in the attractive potential at each time step is set to the target PDF. The SAPF approach involves sampling N_r points from the target PDF, which serve as attractive points generating attractive potential to each robot if these points have not been occupied by any robot. The SPP approach also requires N_r samples from the target PDF as target points, and matches each robot with a target position based on their relative distance. A shortest-path-planning algorithm is then employed in a graph composed of N_r target points and N_c mean points of Gaussian components selected as described in Sect. 6.1.

The three benchmark approaches and our proposed method adopt the same parameters in microscopic control. Additionally, since the required time steps

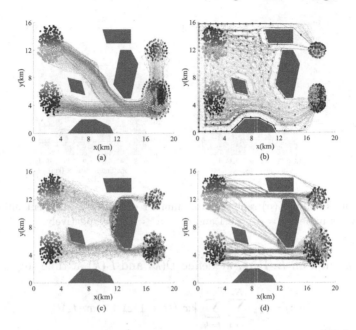

Fig. 2. Figure (a)-(d) show the trajectories generated by OC-CVaR, PDF-APF, SAPF, SPP, respectively. Initial positions of robots are denoted by circles, while their corresponding final positions are highlighted by diamonds. The gray polygons represent static obstacles in the workspace. (Color figure online)

Table 1. Numerical Comparision of the Approaches

Approach	T_f	t(min)	$\bar{D}(0)$(km)	$\bar{E}(T_f)$(J/kg)
OC-CVaR	490	4.2833	20.992	410.30
PDF-APF	2000	65.313	100.00	1929.0
SAPF	2000	2.9565	90.401	3358.3
SPP	790	109.75	43.741	477.36

to complete the task cannot be predetermined, a maximum terminal time step $T_f^{max} = 2000$ was imposed on all four methods. In the case that the task cannot be completed within 2000 steps, it is considered a failure.

The generated robot trajectories are presented in Fig. 2. Only OC-CVaR and SPP can successfully transport the robot swarm to target locations within 2000 time steps. Some robots faced difficulty in circumventing obstacles under SAPF approach. The PDF-APF method resulted in some robots being evenly scattered at equilibrium positions in the artificial potential field and make no further progress towards the target location.

A numerical comparison of four approaches is presented in Table 1 from the aspect of required time steps T_f, run time t, average distance to go $\bar{D}$ and average

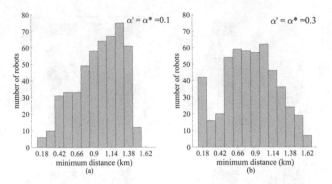

Fig. 3. Figures (a) and (b) represent the number of robots in different minimum distance intervals under $\alpha' = \alpha^* = 0.1$ and $\alpha' = \alpha^* = 0.3$, respectively.

energy consumption $\bar{E}$. Here, we define $\bar{D}(k)$ and $\bar{E}(k)$ at time step k as

$$\bar{D}(k) = \frac{1}{N_r} \sum_{i=1}^{N_r} \sum_{t=k}^{T_f-1} \|x_i((t+1)\Delta t) - x_i(t\Delta t)\|, \qquad (24)$$

$$\bar{E}(k) = \frac{\vartheta}{2N_r} \sum_{i=1}^{N_r} \sum_{t=0}^{k} \left[\frac{\|x_i((t+1)\Delta t) - x_i(t\Delta t)\|}{\Delta t} \right]^2, \qquad (25)$$

where $\vartheta = (\frac{1000}{3600})^2$ is a constant used for unit conversions.

OC-CVaR can complete the transport task with only 490 time steps and is computationally efficient compared to SPP. Our method also outperforms other methods in terms of average transport distance and average energy consumption.

6.3 Comparison Between Different Risk Levels

In order to evaluate the risk control ability of OC-CVaR, which cannot be achieved by other state-of-the-art approaches mentioned above, we conduct the following comparative experiment. We set the α^* and α' to 0.3 in comparison with $\alpha' = \alpha^* = 0.1$ in Sect. 6.1 and calculated the minimum distance between each robot and obstacles in the whole trajectory for both cases. The frequency distribution histograms of minimum ditance are presented in Fig. 3 and they clearly show that, with different risk acceptance levels, we can regulate the proximity of the robot swarm to obstacles. Smaller α''s and α^*'s result in more risk-averse trajectories, leading to the robots being further away from the obstacles.

7 Conclusion

We propose a risk-aware motion planning framework that incorporates CVaR-based collision avoidance constraints for VLSR to safely navigate in cluttered environments. Simulation results show that the proposed approach outperforms state-of-the-art methods in both computational efficiency and risk mitigation. Future work includes developing formal quantification of CVaR associated with trajectories and evaluation of the proposed motion planning framework in physical experiments.

References

1. Bevacqua, G., Cacace, J., Finzi, A., Lippiello, V.: Mixed-initiative planning and execution for multiple drones in search and rescue missions. Proc. Int. Conf. Autom. Planning Sched. **25**, 315–323 (2015)
2. Cortes, J., Martinez, S., Karatas, T., Bullo, F.: Coverage control for mobile sensing networks. IEEE Trans. Robot. Autom. **20**(2), 243–255 (2004)
3. Prorok, A., Correll, N., Martinoli, A.: Multi-level spatial modeling for stochastic distributed robotic systems. Int. J. Rob. Res. (IJRR) **30**, 574–589 (2011)
4. Elamvazhuthi, K., Berman, S.: Mean-field models in swarm robotics: a survey. Bioinspiration Biomimetics **15**(1), 015001 (2019)
5. Crespi, V., Galstyan, A., Lerman, K.: Top-down vs bottom-up methodologies in multi-agent system design. Auton. Robot. **24**, 303–313 (2008)
6. Foderaro, G., Zhu, P., Wei, H., Wettergren, T.A., Ferrari, S.: Distributed optimal control of sensor networks for dynamic target tracking. IEEE Trans. Control Netw. Syst. **5**(1), 142–153 (2016)
7. Rudd, K., Foderaro, G., Zhu, P., Ferrari, S.: A generalized reduced gradient method for the optimal control of very-large-scale robotic systems. IEEE Trans. Rob. **33**(5), 1226–1232 (2017)
8. Zhu, P., Liu, C., Ferrari, S.: Adaptive online distributed optimal control of very large-scale robotic systems. IEEE Trans. Control Netw. Syst. **8**(2), 678–689 (2021)
9. Ono, M., Pavone, M., Kuwata, Y., Balaram, J.: Chance-constrained dynamic programming with application to risk-aware robotic space exploration. Auton. Robot. **39**, 555–571 (2015)
10. Wang, A., Jasour, A., Williams, B.C.: Non-gaussian chance-constrained trajectory planning for autonomous vehicles under agent uncertainty. IEEE Robot. Autom. Lett. **5**(4), 6041–6048 (2020)
11. Fan, D.D., Otsu, K., Kubo, Y., Dixit, A., Burdick, J., Agha-Mohammadi, AA.: Step: stochastic traversability evaluation and planning for risk-aware off-road navigation. Robot.: Sci. Syst., 1–21, RSS Foundation (2021)
12. Hakobyan, A., Kim, G.C., Yang, I.: Risk-aware motion planning and control using cVaR-constrained optimization. IEEE Robot. Autom. Lett. **4**(4), 3924–3931 (2019)
13. Villani, C.: Topics in optimal transportation. Am. Math. Soc. **58** (2021)
14. Chen, Y., Georgiou, T.T., Tannenbaum, A.: Optimal transport for gaussian mixture models. IEEE Access **7**, 6269–6278 (2018)
15. Norton, M., Khokhlov, V., Uryasev, S.: Calculating CVaR and bPOE for common probability distributions with application to portfolio optimization and density estimation. Ann. Oper. Res. **299**, 1281–1315 (2021)
16. Gilbert, E.G., Johnson, D.W., Keerthi, S.S.: A fast procedure for computing the distance between complex objects in three-dimensional space. IEEE J. Robot. Autom. **4**(2), 193–203 (1988)
17. Van Den Bergen, G.: Proximity queries and penetration depth computation on 3D game objects. In: Game Developers Conference, vol. 170 (2001)
18. Gao, H., et al.: Probabilistic visibility-aware trajectory planning for target tracking in cluttered environments. ArXiv Preprint ArXiv:2306.06363 (2023)

Physical and Neurological Human-Robot Interaction

An Adaptive Impedance Control Method for Human-Robot Interaction

Yanjiang Huang[1,2], Haoyang Chen[1,2], Zhaoyu Cui[3], and Xianmin Zhang[1,2(✉)]

[1] School of Mechanical and Automotive Engineering, South China University of Technology, Guangzhou 510640, China
zhangxm@scut.edu.cn
[2] Guangdong Province Key Laboratory of Precision Equipment and Manufacturing Technology, South China University of Technology, Guangzhou 510640, Guangdong, People's Republic of China
[3] Key Laboratory of Safety of Intelligent Robots for State Market Regulation, Guangdong Testing Institute of Product Quality Supervision, Guangzhou 510670, People's Republic of China

Abstract. In human-robot collaborative grinding tasks, the compliance of the robot to the operator is required, while the robot end effector is limited to a certain space to avoid danger. Therefore, an adaptive impedance control method, in which the stiffness coefficient changes with the position of the robot end effector, is proposed in this paper. Based on the Lyapunov method, the stability of the adaptive impedance controller is demonstrated. The results of simulation and experiments show that, with the method proposed in this paper, the operating space of the robot is limited to a certain range, and its compliance to the operator is good.

Keywords: Impedance control · Self-adaption · Human-robot interaction

1 Introduction

With the development of robotics, position control can no longer meet the requirement of all tasks. Robots are required to interact with operators and environment. Therefore, control methods based on external force have attracted the interest of many researchers.

In 1985, Hogan proposed impedance control, which is the theoretical basis of human-robot interaction [1]. The coefficients of traditional impedance controller are constant, and it cannot be applied to some tasks. Therefore, researchers proposed adaptive impedance control. With adaptive control law, the coefficients of the controller can be adjusted in real time for better performance [2–5]. Theories from many fields have been applied to adaptive impedance control such as sliding mode control [6], fuzzy mathematics [7–13], neural networks [7] and reinforcement learning [14]. Now, robots with adaptive impedance controller have been used in a variety of tasks including rehabilitation [7, 12, 13], manufacturing [3–5, 8, 9] and space operations [14, 15].

For some grinding tasks, where the variety of workpieces is large and the number of workpieces is small, robots cannot be applied. In many cases, the laborer works alone to complete the grinding task. In order to reduce the workload of labor and improve production efficiency, human-robot collaborative grinding is proposed. In this case, the robot supports the gravitational force of the grinder, and the grinding force, and the laborer drags or pushes the robot end effector to move the grinder with relatively little force. This paper proposes an adaptive impedance control method for human-robot collaborative grinding tasks. In those cases, good compliance and limited operating space of the robot are both required. With the method proposed in this paper, the operating space of the robot is limited to a certain range, and its compliance to the operator is good.

The rest of this paper is organized as follows: Sect. 2 introduces the overall framework of the adaptive impedance control method. The adaptive impedance controller is introduced in detail and the stability is demonstrated based on the Lyapunov method. Section 3 analyses the simulation and experiment, which show that compared with traditional impedance controllers, the controller proposed in this paper has better performance in human-robot interaction. Section 4 summarizes the full paper.

2   Adaptive Impedance Control Method

2.1   Overall Control Framework

Figure 1 shows the overall control framework of the method proposed in this paper.

When an external force is applied on the robot end effector, the impedance controller will adjust the expected position and posture. Through the inverse kinematics of the robot, the adjusted expected position and posture are converted into the expected angle of the joint motors. The trapezoidal speed curve makes the change of the expected angles smoother. The PID controller makes the robot joint motors track the expected angles. With the actual angles of the joint motors, the actual position and posture of the robot end effector can be obtained through robot inverse kinematics.

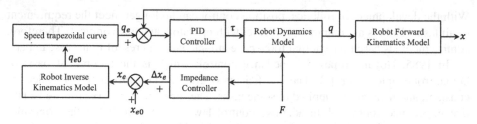

Fig. 1. The overall control framework

The robot dynamics model can be written as:

$$D(q)\ddot{q} + C(q,\dot{q})\dot{q} + G(q) = \tau + J^T(q)F \qquad (1)$$

where $q \in \mathbb{R}^n$ is the actual joint position, and n is the degrees of freedom of the robot. $\tau \in \mathbb{R}^n$ is the torque of joint motors. $F \in \mathbb{R}^6$ is the external force on the robot end effector in the Cartesian coordinates. $D(q) \in \mathbb{R}^{n \times 6}$, $C(q, \dot{q}) \in \mathbb{R}^{n \times 6}$ and $G(q) \in \mathbb{R}^6$ are the inertia matrix, the Coriolis matrix and the gravity vector, respectively. $J(q) \in \mathbb{R}^{n \times 6}$ is the Jacobian matrix of the robot.

If the expected angle of a joint motor changes rapidly, the driving torque of the motor is large, and accordingly, the actual angle also changes rapidly. To make the joint motor rotate smoothly, the trapezoidal speed curve is adopted. The process of the motor rotating from one angle to another is divided into three stages: acceleration, constant speed, and deceleration. Two important coefficient α_0, $\omega_{max} \in \mathbb{R}$ are the given angular acceleration and maximum angular velocity, which are preset.

PID controller can be written as:

$$\tau = K_p(q_e - q) + K_d(\dot{q}_e - \dot{q}) + K_i \int_0^t (q_e - q)dt \tag{2}$$

where $K_p \in \mathbb{R}$, $K_d \in \mathbb{R}$, $K_i \in \mathbb{R}$ are the proportional matrix, differential matrix and integral matrix, which are diagonal.

2.2 Adaptive Impedance Controller

To make the robot compliant to the operator, the impedance controller adjusts the expected position and posture according to the external force, which can be written as:

$$F = M(\ddot{x}_e - \ddot{x}_{e0}) + B(\dot{x}_e - \dot{x}_{e0}) + K(x_e - x_{e0}) \tag{3}$$

where $x_{e0} \in \mathbb{R}^6$, $x_e \in \mathbb{R}^6$ are the original expected position and posture, and the adjusted expected position and posture of the robot. $M \in \mathbb{R}^{6 \times 6}$, $B \in \mathbb{R}^{6 \times 6}$, $K \in \mathbb{R}^{6 \times 6}$ are the inertia coefficient matrix, damping coefficient matrix, stiffness coefficient matrix, which are generally diagonal matrices to avoid coupling.

For simple expression, let

$$\Delta x_e = x_e - x_{e0} \tag{4}$$

so that (3) can be written as:

$$F = M\Delta\ddot{x}_e + B\Delta\dot{x}_e + K\Delta x_e \tag{5}$$

To simplify the analysis, limit the movement of the robot end effector into one direction. Then (5) can be written as:

$$f = m\Delta\ddot{x}_e + b\Delta\dot{x}_e + k\Delta x_e \tag{6}$$

where $m \in \mathbb{R}$, $b \in \mathbb{R}$, $k \in \mathbb{R}$ are the inertia coefficient, damping coefficient, stiffness coefficient.

In some tasks such as human-robot collaborative surgery and assembly, the operating space of the robot needs to be limited within a certain range, and the robot should be compliant to the operator for better human-robot interaction performance. In this paper, an adaptive impedance controller is proposed. By changing the stiffness coefficient k in real time according to the position of the robot end effector, the robot operating space is limited, and the compliance of the robot is good.

For the given stiffness coefficients k_l and k_h ($k_h > k_l$), the weight function $\omega(\cdot)$ is adopted, and the stiffness coefficient k can be described as:

$$k = \omega k_h + (1 - \omega)k_l \tag{7}$$

When the robot end effector is moved away from the original expected position, ω should increase, causing the weight of k_h to increase, and k increases accordingly. In this case, the farther the robot end effector is moved, the much larger the external force required, limiting the operating space of the robot. On the other side, as the robot end effector gets close to the original expected position, k decreases. In this case, it is easy to move the robot, which means better compliance. To meet the above requirements, based on the *sigmoid* function, ω can be described as:

$$\omega(\Delta x_e) = \frac{1}{1 + e^{-a(|\Delta x_e| - b)}} \tag{8}$$

where a and b are the preset coefficient.

Substitute (8) into (7), k can be written as:

$$k(\Delta x_e) = k_l + (k_h - k_l)\frac{1}{1 + e^{-a(|\Delta x_e| - b)}} \tag{9}$$

Therefore, substitute (9) into (6), the adaptive impedance controller can be written as:

$$f = m\Delta \ddot{x}_e + b\Delta \dot{x}_e + \left[k_l + (k_h - k_l)\frac{1}{1 + e^{-a(|\Delta x_e| - b)}} \right]\Delta x_e \tag{10}$$

The stability of the adaptive impedance controller is demonstrated as followed. The state equation of the controller can be written as:

$$\begin{cases} \Delta \dot{v}_e = -\frac{k(\Delta x_e)}{m}\Delta x_e - \frac{b}{m}\Delta v_e \\ \Delta \dot{x}_e = \Delta v_e \end{cases} \tag{11}$$

To demonstrate the stability, a Lyapunov-like function is proposed as:

$$V(\Delta x_e, \Delta v_e) = [\Delta x_e \Delta v_e]P\begin{bmatrix} \Delta x_e \\ \Delta v_e \end{bmatrix} + b\int_0^{\Delta x_e} k(\Delta x_e)\Delta x_e d\Delta x_e \tag{12}$$

where

$$P = \begin{bmatrix} P_{11} & P_{12} \\ P_{21} & P_{22} \end{bmatrix} = \begin{bmatrix} b/m & 1/2 \\ 1/2 & 2m/b \end{bmatrix} \tag{13}$$

Since P is a symmetric matrix and $P_{11} > 0$, $P_{11}P_{22} - P_{12}^2 > 0$, $[\Delta x_e \; \Delta v_e]P[\Delta x_e \; \Delta v_e]^T$ is positive definite. Meanwhiles,

$$\begin{cases} \int_0^{\Delta x_e} k(\Delta x_e)\Delta x_e d\Delta x_e > 0, \Delta x_e > 0 \\ \int_{\Delta x_e}^0 k(\Delta x_e)(-\Delta x_e)d\Delta x_e > 0, \Delta x_e < 0 \\ \int_0^{\Delta x_e} k(\Delta x_e)\Delta x_e d\Delta x_e = 0, \Delta x_e = 0 \end{cases} \tag{14}$$

so the above formula is also positive definite. Finally, $V(\Delta x_e, \Delta v_e)$ is positive definite. Differentiating (12) with respect to time yields and simplifying it:

$$\dot{V}(\Delta x_e, \Delta v_e) = -2\Delta v_e{}^2 - \frac{2k(\Delta x_e)}{m}\Delta x_e{}^2 \le 0 \tag{15}$$

Obviously, $\dot{V}(\Delta x_e, \Delta v_e)$ is negative definite. In summary, $V(\Delta x_e, \Delta v_e)$ is positive definite and $\dot{V}(\Delta x_e, \Delta v_e)$ is negative definite, which demonstrates that the adaptive impedance controller is asymptotically stable.

3   Simulation and Experiment Analysis

3.1   Simulation Analysis

The adaptive impedance control method is simulated in MATLAB/Simulink. As shown in Fig. 4, for simple calculation, a three degrees-of-freedom robot is analyzed.

In the simulation, a Cartesian coordinate system is established whose origin is in the robot base. The length of each link is $l_1 = 301$ mm, $l_2 = 299$ mm, $l_3 = 84$ mm. The angle of each joint can be expressed as $\theta_1, \theta_2, \theta_3$ respectively. The position and posture of the robot end effector can be expressed as (p_x, p_y, p_θ). The external force on the robot end effector can be expressed as $(F_x F_y \tau_z)$. Let $F_x = 0$N, $\tau_z = 0$ Nm. Therefore, the robot end effector moves linearly along the x-axis.

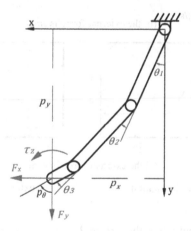

Fig. 4. Schematic diagram of the simulation model

With the trapezoidal speed curve, the adjusted expected angle changes smoothly. Therefore, it can be considered that the PID controller has no tracking error, which means $q_e = q$.

The parameters of trapezoidal velocity curve and adaptive impedance controller are set as follows: $\alpha_0 = 54°/s^2$, $\omega_{max} = 108°/s$; $k_h = 0.4$ $k_l = 0.1$, $a = 0.1$, $b = 120$, $\boldsymbol{m} = 0$, $\boldsymbol{b} = 0.01$.

The original expected position and posture of the robot end effector are set to (350 mm, 500 mm, 90°). Without external force, the robot does not move.

The following part discusses the movement of the robot with different impedance controllers under different external force. The low stiffness impedance controller ($k = k_l$), the high stiffness impedance controller ($k = k_h$) and the adaptive impedance controller ($k = k(\Delta x_e)$) are included.

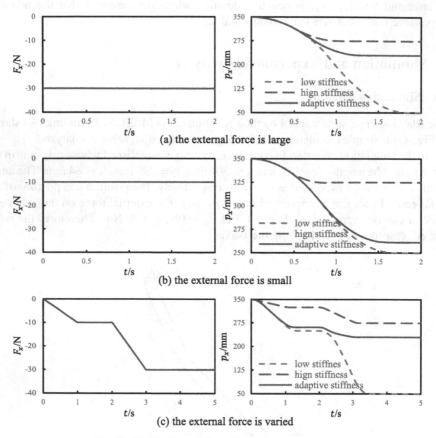

Fig. 5. Simulation results with varied external force

Figure 5 (a) shows that when the external force is large ($F_x = -30N$), compared with the low stiffness impedance controller, the adaptive impedance controller makes the movement of the robot smaller. However, Fig. 5 (b) shows that when the external force is small ($F_x = -10N$), compared with the high stiffness impedance controller, the adaptive impedance controller moves the robot farther away from original expected position. In Fig. 5 (c), when close to original expected position, the robot with the adaptive impedance controller is moved easily as same as that with the low stiffness impedance controller. While getting far away from original expected position, the external force required to move the robot farther become greatly large, like the high stiffness impedance controller.

3.2 Experiment Analysis

The experiment is carried out on the self-built robot experimental platform as shown in Fig. 6 to verify the actual performance of the method proposed in this paper. In the platform, MINTASCA modular motors are used to be the joint motors, which can realize the control and feedback of current, velocity, and angle. The computer is responsible for complex calculations. The MCU (STM32) is connected to the computer through the RS232 serial port, and is connected to the robot through the CAN bus to realize the control of the robot by the upper computer. The force sensor is installed at the end of the robot to measure the external force. The MCU reads the output voltage of the sensor through ADC to obtain the external force value, and feeds back to the computer.

Fig. 6. The robot experimental platform

As shown in Fig. 7, the experiment is designed as follows: Three joint motors are activated, so that the robot obtains three degrees of freedom in the vertical plane. The operator pushes the robot end effector, and the robot moves horizontally accordingly. The original expected position and coefficient of the controllers are the same as those in the simulation above.

With the three impedance controller (k_l, k_h, $k(\Delta x_e)$), the operator pushes the robot with large force. Figure 8 (a) shows the external force and actual position of the robot end effector over time. Comparing the peak of external force and the position in the figure, it can be seen that when the operator pushes the robot with large force, the movement of the robot with the adaptive impedance controller is much smaller than that with the low stiffness impedance controller.

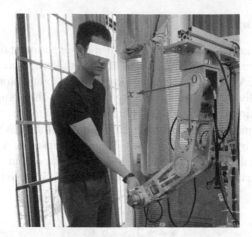

Fig. 7. Schematic diagram of the experimental process

On the other hand, as shown in Fig. 8 (b), when the external force is small, the movement of robot with the adaptive impedance controller is farther than that with the high stiffness impedance controller.

The simulation and experiment results show that with the adaptive impedance controller, when the robot gets far away from the original expected position, the external force required to move the robot outward greatly increases, which limits the robot within the expected operating space. Meanwhiles, when closed to the original expected position, it is easy to move the robot, which has good compliance. In summary, with the adaptive impedance controller, the operating space of the robot is limited to a certain range, and its compliance to the operator is good.

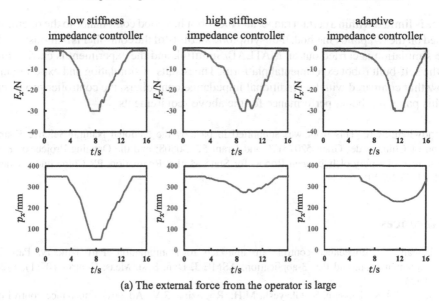

(a) The external force from the operator is large

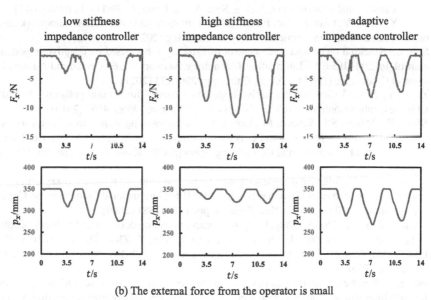

(b) The external force from the operator is small

Fig. 8. The experimental results under different external force from the operator. Left column: low stiffness k_l; middle column: high stiffness k_h; right column: variable stiffness $k(\Delta x_e)$

4 Conclusion

In this paper, an adaptive impedance controller is designed. It can adjust the stiffness coefficient in real time according to the position and posture of the robot end effector. With this controller, in human-robot collaborative grinding tasks, the robot's operating space is limited within a certain range, and the robot has good compliance to the operator. Based on the Lyapunov method, the asymptotic stability of the controller is demonstrated. The simulation is carried out on MATLAB/Simulink and the experiment is carried out on the self-built robot experimental platform. The results of simulation and experiments show that compared with the traditional impedance controllers, the controller proposed in this paper has better performance for the above requirements.

Acknowledgment. This work was supported in part by the National Natural Science Foundation of China under Grant 52075178 and Grant 52130508; and the Opening Project of Key Laboratory of Safety of Intelligent Robots for State Market Regulation, PR China under Grant GOI-KFKT202201.

References

1. Hogan, N.: Impedance control: an approach to manipulation: Part 1-theory, Part 2-implementation, and Part 3-application. ASME J. Dyn. Syst. Meas. Control **107**(1), 1–24 (1985)
2. Jamwal, P.K., Hussain, S., Ghayesh, M.H., Rogozina, S.V.: Adaptive impedance control of parallel ankle rehabilitation robot. J. Dyn. Syst. Meas. Control **139**(11), 111006 (2017)
3. Zhao, X., Chen, Y., Qian, L., Tao, B., Ding, H.: Human–robot collaboration framework based on impedance control in robotic assembly. Engineering (2023)
4. Sun, L.: Research on contact force control of grinding robot based on adaptive impedance control. In: 2021 IEEE 5th Information Technology, Networking, Electronic and Automation Control Conference (ITNEC), Xi'an, China, pp. 290–293 (2021)
5. Zhou, Y., et al.: Vision-based adaptive impedance control for robotic polishing. In: 2019 Chinese Control Conference (CCC), Guangzhou, China, pp. 4560–4564 (2019)
6. Khan, H., Abbasi, S.J., Salman, M., Lee, M.C.: Super twisting sliding mode control-based impedance control for robot arm end-effector force tracking. In: 2022 61st Annual Conference of the Society of Instrument and Control Engineers (SICE), Kumamoto, Japan, pp. 158–162 (2022)
7. Xu, G., Song, A.: Adaptive impedance control based on dynamic recurrent fuzzy neural network for upper-limb rehabilitation robot. In: 2009 IEEE International Conference on Control and Automation, Christchurch, New Zealand, pp. 1376–1381 (2009)
8. Chen, P., Zhao, H., Yan, X., Ding, H.: Force control polishing device based on fuzzy adaptive impedance control. In: Yu, H., Liu, J., Liu, L., Ju, Z., Liu, Y., Zhou, D. (eds.) ICIRA 2019. LNCS, Part IV, vol. 11743, pp. 181–194. Springer, Cham (2019). https://doi.org/10.1007/978-3-030-27538-9_16
9. Wang, X.: Force estimation based position impedance control for robotic machining process. In: 2010 International Conference on Mechanic Automation and Control Engineering, Wuhan, China, pp. 5814–5817 (2010)
10. Qu, Z., et al.: Research on fuzzy adaptive impedance control of lower extremity exoskeleton. In: 2019 IEEE International Conference on Mechatronics and Automation (ICMA), Tianjin, China, pp. 939–944 (2019)
11. Jing-Zheng, L., Jia, L., Sheng-Qiang, Y., Jing-Jing, Z., Zhi-Jie, Q.: Fuzzy impedance control for robot impact force. In: 2021 33rd Chinese Control and Decision Conference (CCDC), Kunming, China, pp. 340–344 (2021)
12. Sun, H., Zhang, L., Hu, X., Tian, L.: Experiment study of fuzzy impedance control on horizontal lower limbs rehabilitation robot. In: 2011 International Conference on Electronics, Communications and Control (ICECC), Ningbo, China, pp. 2640–2643 (2011)

13. Kalani, H., Akbarzadeh, A., Mousavi, A.: Fuzzy impedance control strategy for jaw rehabilitation using 6-UPS Stewart robot. In: 2015 3rd RSI International Conference on Robotics and Mechatronics (ICROM), Tehran, Iran, pp. 645–650 (2015)
14. Sun, Y., Cao, H., Ma, R., Wang, G., Ma, G., Xia, H.: Impedance control of space manipulator based on deep reinforcement learning. In: 2022 41st Chinese Control Conference (CCC), Hefei, China, pp. 3609–3614 (2022)
15. Dongming, G.E., Guanghui, S., Yuanjie, Z., Jixin, S.: Impedance control of multi-arm space robot for the capture of non-cooperative targets. J. Syst. Eng. Electron. **31**(5), 1051–1061 (2020)

Design of A Lower Limb Rehabilitation Training Robot Based on A Double Four-Bar Synchronous Motion Mechanism

Xiankun Qu[1], Hao Chu[2,3], and Wenrui Liu[2,3](✉)

[1] School of Mechanical and Electrical Engineering, Changchun University of Technology, Changchun 130012, China

[2] School of Mechanical Engineering, Hubei University of Arts and Sciences, Xiangyang 441053, China
lwr@hbuas.edu.cn

[3] Xiangyang Key Laboratory of Rehabilitation Medicine and Rehabilitation Engineering Technology, Hubei University of Arts and Science, Xiangyang 441053, China

Abstract. For patients with lower limb dysfunction who need to complete gait rehabilitation training, a new single-degree-of-freedom human lower limb rehabilitation training robot was designed, and a mechanism dimensional synthesis method was proposed. In order to realize the motion trajectory of the foot, a single-degree-of-freedom planar four-bar mechanism is selected as the mechanism unit, and the functional relationship between the input and output of the planar four-bar mechanism is analyzed and established, and a double four-bar synchronous motion mechanism is used to realize the relative motion of the heel and toe joint. Then, a Watt II six-link mechanism and a deflation mechanism are used to realize the motion trajectory of the toes. By acquiring the human gait trajectory through the Xsens MVN Analyze, thus giving the rigid-body line of desired according to the motion trajectory. The desired rigid-body line is processed by the non-equal interval normalization method, and the mechanism is designed by the numerical atlas method and the approximate synthesis method. The results show that the designed single-degree-of-freedom mechanism can simulate the motion of normal human gait motion trajectory, and the effectiveness of the design method is verified by experiments.

Keywords: Lower limb rehabilitation training robot · Dimensional synthesis · Planar four-bar mechanism · Gait trajectory · Single-degree-of-freedom

1 Introduction

At present, lower limb rehabilitation robots can be divided into exoskeleton type and end-driven type according to the driving method [1]. The execution structure of a lower limb exoskeleton rehabilitation robot is based on the human joint movement and typically consists of two exoskeleton legs that follow the same construction principles as human lower limbs. During the rehabilitation training, the exoskeleton legs are connected side

© The Author(s), under exclusive license to Springer Nature Singapore Pte Ltd. 2023
H. Yang et al. (Eds.): ICIRA 2023, LNAI 14273, pp. 540–551, 2023.
https://doi.org/10.1007/978-981-99-6498-7_46

by side with the thighs and calves of the patient, which directly exerts physical effects on each joint of the patient, and then drives the lower limbs to complete the gait training movements, and finally achieves the effect of rehabilitation training. Many research institutions have designed and developed exoskeleton type robots, for example the Lokomat [2] designed by Swiss Hocoma Company, Nature-gaits [3] proposed by Nanyang Technological University in Singapore, the robot suit HAL was researched by Tsukuba University in Japan [4], and the four-degree-of-freedom gait rehabilitation exoskeleton robot proposed by Zhejiang University in China [5]. The end-driven rehabilitation device is fitted in such a way that it makes contact with the human lower limb through the end of the limb. As a power source, the lower limb rehabilitation robot guides the end of the limb to move according to a certain trajectory. Most of them are connected to the human foot through the pedal, which in turn drives the lower limbs of the human body to complete the gait action, so as to achieve the effect of rehabilitation training. For example, Tianjin University of China [6] proposed a gait rehabilitation robot based on cam linkage mechanism, Haptic Walker designed by Free University of Berlin in Germany [7], and a six-degree-of-freedom lower limb rehabilitation robot proposed by Gyeongsang University in South Korea [8].

The above mentioned multi-degree-of-freedom rehabilitation robots are capable of human lower limb rehabilitation training and can be programmed to generate different gait trajectories and applied to a variety of rehabilitation training environments. However, their complicated structural design and a large number of actuation units greatly increase the control difficulty and lead to high production and fabrication costs, and there are still a large number of patients with lower limb dysfunction facing the problem of inadequate rehabilitation training [9]. Therefore, it is important to design a lower limb rehabilitation robot with simple control and structure as well as low production cost. Alves et al. [10] proposed a four-link mechanism, Li et al. [11] invented a single-degree-of-freedom six-bar mechanism to achieve gait trajectory, and motors were used to control the mechanism. Ji et al. [12] designed a crank rocker lower limb rehabilitation robot mechanism. The Free University of Berlin designed a lower limb rehabilitation robot based on a planetary wheel system planar four-bar combination mechanism for lower limb rehabilitation robot [13]. Negrello et al. [14] arranged the knee drive motor of the WALK-MAN robot near the hip and the ankle front joint motor at the knee position to transfer the motion to the ankle through a four-link mechanism. Lohmeier et al. [15] designed a bipedal robot LOLA, in order to reduce the inertia of the leg, the drive motor of the knee joint was arranged between the knee and hip joints, near the hip side, and the knee motion was realized through a crank slider mechanism.

Human walking is a complex process, including two main phases, called "stance phase" and "swing phase". When a new gait period starts, one foot touches the ground with the heel. At the end of the standing phase, the toe of the standing foot leaves the ground [16]. In addition to the relative motion of the toes, researchers generally do not consider the foot posture, i.e., researchers usually use a mechanism to output one position rather than the posture, which generally requires the output of at least two positions and requires consideration of the relative motion of the toe joint and the heel. Therefore, the foot function of the robot has a lot of space for improvement [17]. Kouchaki et al. [18] studied the effect of toe joint bending on the performance of bipedal animals. The

WABIAN-2R robot designed by Waseda University, which has a foot of the same size as a normal human body and actively moving toes, walks first with its heel on the ground and finally with its toes off the ground like a human gait to improve its stability [19].

In this paper, a single-degree-of-freedom double four-bar human lower limb rehabilitation training robot capable of realizing human gait motion trajectory is designed, and the base unit of the execution structure is planar four-bar mechanism. A dimensional synthesis method is proposed based on the non-equal time interval normalized. Taking the motion trajectory of the foot and toes as the design requirement, a double four-bar mechanism was designed to be able to realize the posture of the foot according to the design requirement, and then a Watt II six-bar mechanism was designed to realize the toe trajectory based on the relative motion of the foot and toes. The designed mechanism can greatly approximate the human gait trajectory. In addition, the new lower limb rehabilitation robot is composed of a double four-bar synchronous motion mechanism, and only one motor is sufficient to control the mechanism, which greatly simplifies the robot control system design.

The paper is organized as follows: in Sect. 2, introduces the method of obtaining the gait trajectory of the desired objective. In Sect. 3, the conceptual design of the lower limb rehabilitation mechanism is briefly described. Then, Sect. 4 researches the dimensional synthesis of the mechanism and proposes a non-equal time interval normalized characteristic processing method based on the principle of Fourier series and least squares fitting. Section 5 describes the steps of mechanism path synthesis and function synthesis, and illustrates the feasibility of the method based on the given arithmetic examples. Finally, conclusions are drawn in Sect. 6.

2   Gait Acquisition

The purpose of designing a human lower limb rehabilitation training robot is to assist the lower limbs of patient to complete the walking movement, thereby helping the patient to regain walking ability. Therefore, the similarity between the gait trajectory of the rehabilitation training robot and the normal human gait directly affects the effect of lower limb rehabilitation training [20]. Normal adult males were used as experimental subjects. The height of the experimenter was 1820 mm and the foot length was 253 mm. With the help of Xsens MVN Analyze, a complete gait period is captured from the motion trajectory of the experimental object. The normal human gait phase is shown in Fig. 1. Because the joint position data of Xsens MVN Analyze usually have certain errors, it needs to be corrected according to the length of the limb itself, i.e., the distance from the hip joint to the knee joint is always equal to the length of the thigh, the distance from the knee joint to the ankle joint is always equal to the length of the calf, and the distance from the ankle joint to the heel is always equal to the length of the instep.

Firstly, according to the various positions of the lower limb joints, the hip joint angle, knee joint angle, ankle joint angle and the angle between the foot and the ground normal vector are calculated inversely, so as to obtain the sequence of each joint angle, and the Gaussian filter is used to process it. Secondly, human walking is actually a three-dimensional movement on the sagittal, coronal and horizontal planes. Compared with the coronal and horizontal planes, the sagittal plane has a very large range of motion [21].

Therefore, the three-dimensional motion trajectory of the lower limb joints is projected onto the sagittal plane to obtain pre-processed two-dimensional trajectory data, which is used as a reference gait for the design of the lower limb rehabilitation robot mechanism.

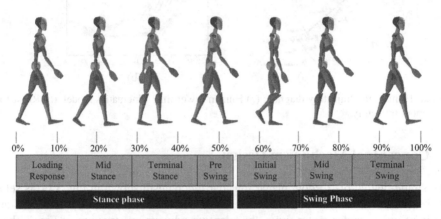

Fig. 1. Timing of gait phases

The Xsens MVN Analyze consists of an infrared signal receiver and 17 sensors attached to the whole body of the experimenter. The sampling frequency of the capture system is 60 Hz, and human lower limb kinematics model is shown in Fig. 2 (a). During the capture process, the experimenter walks normally on the ground, and the motion trajectory of the human right heel and right toe joint in one gait period can be obtained as shown in Fig. 2 (b). In order to obtain the required human gait trajectory, a human lower limb kinematic model was generated using the hip angle θ_{hip} and knee angle θ_{knee} obtained from the Clinical Gait Analysis Normative Gait Database, and a simplified mathematical model of lower limb kinematics is developed as follows:

$$\begin{bmatrix} x_{heel} \\ y_{heel} \end{bmatrix} = \begin{bmatrix} -\sin\theta_{hip} & \sin(\theta_{knee}-\theta_{hip}) & \sin\theta_{ankle} \\ -\cos\theta_{hip} & -\cos(\theta_{knee}-\theta_{hip}) & -\cos\theta_{ankle} \end{bmatrix} \begin{bmatrix} L_{instep} \\ L_{thigh} \\ L_{shank} \end{bmatrix} + \begin{bmatrix} x_{hip} \\ y_{hip} \end{bmatrix} \quad (1)$$

$$\begin{bmatrix} x_{toejoint} \\ y_{toejoint} \end{bmatrix} = \begin{bmatrix} -\sin\theta_{angle}L_{sole} + x_{heel} \\ -\cos\theta_{angle}L_{sole} + y_{heel} \end{bmatrix} \quad (2)$$

where, (x_{heel}, y_{heel}) is the heel position coordinates, $(x_{toe\,joint}, y_{toe\,joint})$ is the toe joint position coordinates, $L_{thigh}, L_{shank}, L_{instep}$ and L_{sole} are the length of thigh, shank, instep and sole respectively, and the $\theta_{hip}, \theta_{knee}, \theta_{ankle}$ and θ_{angle} are the hip angle, knee angle, ankle angle and the angle between the sole and the ground normal vector, respectively.

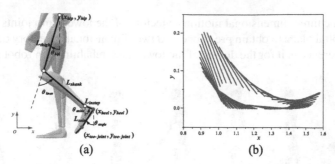

(a)   (b)

Fig. 2. Human gait trajectory diagram: (a) Human lower limb kinematics model. (b) Right foot movement trajectory.

3   Conceptual Mechanism Design

The single-degree-of-freedom planar four-bar mechanism shown in Fig. 3 (a) is set as the basic mechanism. In order to realize the accurate path synthesis of the heel and toe joint points under motor drive, the adaptive adjustment structure of Fig. 3 (b) is designed, and the motion trajectory of the mechanism is obtained by kinematics. Because in the actual design process, there is a certain error in the results of the mechanism dimensional synthesis, which makes it have a dead point. In order to ensure that the designed mechanism can move smoothly and satisfy the desired trajectory, a slider needs to be added to a four-bar mechanism to make it an adaptive adjustment mechanism, and the designed double four-bar mechanism is connected with a synchronous belt to ensure the synchronous operation of the mechanism. In order to satisfy the motion trajectory requirements of the toe, and then bring in the Watt II six-link mechanism and deflation mechanism, the actuator of lower limb rehabilitation robot mechanism can be designed (Fig. 3 (c)).

In this paper, we use the path synthesis method to synthesize the position of the toe joint, and then synthesize the heel position according to the prescribed timing, so as to achieve the final foot posture with one input driving two outputs. On the basis of this, we use Watt II six-bar mechanism for its function synthesis, so that the angle between the mechanism crank and connecting rod is the input angle, and the mechanism is synthesized and designed. Note that the function synthesis method mentioned in this paper is not affected by the output function according to a certain proportion of deflation, so the

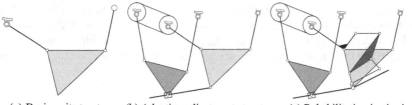

(a) Basic unit structure   (b) Adaptive adjustment structure   (c) Rehabilitation institution

Fig. 3. Lower limb rehabilitation training robot mechanism concept design

function is possible to use an deflation mechanism mechanism to amplify the output angle, which can improve the synthesis accuracy.

4 Dimensional Synthesis

4.1 Kinematics Model

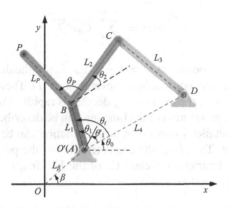

Fig. 4. Kinematic model of planar four-bar mechanism

The planar four-bar mechanism in a general installation position is shown in Fig. 4, the length of bars AB, BC, CD, AD and BP are $L_1, L_2, L_3, L_4, L_\beta$ and L_P, respectively. P is any point on the linkage bar, θ_P is the angle between BP and linkage bar BC; θ_0 is the angle between frame AD and x axis; θ_1 is the input angle. θ_2 is the coupler angle; Let Oxy is the complex plane, where x is the real axis, y is the imaginary axis, and i is an imaginary unit. On the complex plane, when the input component starts at θ_1' and the ω is uniformly rotated at angular velocity, the coordinates of any point P on the linkage bar of the planar four-bar mechanism in general installation position can be expressed as:

$$P(\theta_1) = L_\beta e^{i\beta} + L_1 e^{i(\theta_0+\theta_1'+\theta_1)} + L_p e^{i(\theta_0+\theta_2+\theta_P)} \tag{3}$$

where $\theta_1 = \omega t$, according to the geometric relationship, the coupler angle θ_2 can be expressed as:

$$\theta_2 = \arctan\left[\frac{(a+b\cos\theta_t)\sin\theta_t + c(L_4 - L_1\cos\theta_t)}{d + e\cos\theta_t + b\cos^2\theta_t + cL_1\sin\theta_t}\right] \tag{4}$$

where,

$$a = -L_1(L_1^2 + L_2^2 - L_3^2 + L_4^2)$$
$$b = 2L_1^2 L_4$$
$$c = [4L_2^2(L_1^2 + L_4^2) - (L_1^2 + L_2^2 - L_3^2 + L_4^2)^2 - [8L_1 L_2^2 L_4 - 4L_1 L_4$$
$$\quad (L_1^2 + L_2^2 - L_3^2 + L_4^2)] \times \cos\theta_t - 4L_1^2 L_4^2 \cos^2\theta_t]^{1/2}$$
$$d = L_4(L_1^2 + L_2^2 - L_3^2 + L_4^2)$$
$$e = -L_1(L_1^2 + L_2^2 - L_3^2 + L_4^2) - 2L_1 L_4^2$$

4.2 Non-equal Time Interval Normalized Method

4.2.1 Fourier Series Description of Complex Functions

For a periodic complex function $Y(t) = x(t) + iy(t)$, where i is an imaginary unit ($i^2 = -1$), let the period of $Y(t)$ be $2L$. Then, according to the Fourier series theory, the Fourier series of $Y(t)$ can be expressed as:

$$S(t) = \sum_{n=-\infty}^{+\infty} C_n e^{i\frac{n\pi t}{L}} \tag{5}$$

where C_n is the Fourier coefficient ($n = 0, \pm1, \pm2, \ldots$). If the derivative of $Y(t)$ satisfies the piecewise continuity condition, $S(t)$ converges to $Y(t)$. Therefore, with the increase of the absolute value of n, the mode of C_n decreases rapidly. According to Eq. (5), the approximate contour information of the function can be described by the low-frequency component and the detailed information of the function can be described by the high-frequency component. Therefore, the characteristics of the periodic complex function are expressed by the Fourier coefficient C_n of the low-frequency component, and the equation of C_n is expressed as:

$$C_n = \frac{1}{2L} \int_{-l}^{l} Y(t)e^{-i\frac{n\pi t}{L}} dt \tag{6}$$

The N equally time interval sampling points of the periodic complex function are represented by the sequence (t_k, y_k), i.e., $t_k = kT/N$, $k = 0, 1, \ldots, N-1$, where T is the function period. According to the theory of discrete Fourier series, the expression for the discrete C_n is given by:

$$C_n = \frac{1}{N} \sum_{k=0}^{N-1} Y_k e^{-i\frac{nk2\pi}{N}} \tag{7}$$

According to Eq. (7), $Y(t)$ can be approximated by the following reduction:

$$\tilde{Y}(t) = \sum_{n=-\text{order}}^{\text{order}} C_n e^{i\frac{n2\pi t}{T}} \tag{8}$$

where order is the order-number of the equation and takes values in the range $[1, N/2]$. The above equation shows that the complex trigonometric polynomial summation of order can be used to approximately describe the trajectory of N points on the complex plane, providing a theoretical basis for the design requirements of non-equal time interval positions. The frequency of this term is higher when the absolute value of n is larger; the frequency of this term is lower when the absolute value of n is smaller; the general term is a constant term when $n = 0$. The accuracy of the fit can be controlled by adjusting the value of order to keep the low-frequency term and remove the high-frequency term. When order $<N/2$, the curve fitting approximates the given point. When order $= N/2$, the curve passes precisely through the given N points.

4.2.2 Non-equal Time Interval Position Design Requirements

According to Eq. (3), it can be obtained that Y and t constitute a periodic complex function. And by the smoothness of the motion trajectory of the planar four-bar mechanism, it is shown that the derivatives of Y are continuous and satisfy the Fourier series convergence condition, so the characteristics of the trajectory curve can be expressed by the Fourier coefficient Cn. It is assumed that the given design requirement is a sequence $\{(t_k, y_k)\}$, which contains N sampling points; however, t_k is usually non-equal interval between them, so the value of Cn cannot be directly obtained by Eq. (7). To address this problem, based on the Fourier series and least squares theory, the least squares method is applied to the complex function to approximate the Fourier coefficients of a non-equally interval input sequence.

According to Eq. (8), the fitted approximation curve can be expressed as:

$$\tilde{Y}(t) = C_0 + C_1 e^{i\frac{1\times 2\pi t}{T}} + C_{-1} e^{i\frac{-1\times 2\pi t}{T}} + \ldots + C_{\text{order}} e^{i\frac{\text{order}\times 2\pi t}{T}} + \cdots C_{-\text{order}} e^{i\frac{-\text{order}\times 2\pi t}{T}}$$

$$(9)$$

Substituting each (t_k, Y_k) into Eq. (9), it is obtained that

$$\begin{cases} Y_0 = C_0 + C_1 X_{0,1} + C_{-1} X_{0,-1} + \ldots + C_{\text{order}} X_{0,\text{order}} + C_{-\text{order}} X_{0,-\text{order}} \\ Y_1 = C_0 + C_1 X_{1,1} + C_{-1} X_{1,-1} + \ldots + C_{\text{order}} X_{1,\text{order}} + C_{-\text{order}} X_{1,-\text{order}} \\ \vdots \\ Y_{N-1} = C_0 + C_1 X_{N-1,1} + C_{-1} X_{N-1,-1} + \ldots + C_{\text{order}} X_{N-1,\text{order}} + C_{-\text{order}} X_{N-1,-\text{order}} \end{cases}$$

$$(10)$$

where, $X_{k,n} = e^{i\frac{t_k n 2\pi}{T}}$, for any given k and n, $X_{k,n}$ have unique values and C_n is calculated using the least squares method to obtain:

$$C = (\overline{X}^T X)^{-1} \overline{X}^T Y$$

$$(11)$$

where,

$$C = [C_0, C_1, \cdots, C_{-\text{order}}]^T$$
$$Y = [Y_0, Y_1, \cdots, Y_{N-1}]^T$$
$$X = \begin{bmatrix} 1 & X_{0,1} & \cdots & X_{0,-\text{order}} \\ 1 & X_{1,1} & \cdots & X_{1,-\text{order}} \\ \vdots & \vdots & \ddots & \vdots \\ 1 & X_{N-1,1} & \cdots & X_{N-1,-\text{order}} \end{bmatrix}$$

where, $\overline{X}^T$ represents the conjugate transpose matrix of X The Eq. (11) is the least squares equation in the complex field. Compared with the least squares equation in the real field, the matrix X increases the conjugate operation. By substituting the C_n obtained above into Eq. (7), the equal time interval discrete points can be obtained, so as to realize the discrete sampling of non-equal time intervals.

5 Analysis and Discussion

Based on the non-equal time interval normalized characteristic processing method proposed in this paper, the mechanism output characteristic parameters are processed, and
the numerical atlas method is combined with the approximate synthesis method to dimensional synthesis of the planar linkage mechanism, so as to realize the solution of the
planar linkage mechanism path synthesis problem with non-equal time interval position
design requirements. Figure 4 is the structure diagram of planar four-bar mechanism
with general installation position on the complex plane. According to the characteristic
that the change of structural parameters does not affect the Fourier harmonic characteristic parameters of the output trajectory of the four-bar mechanism, a database of
harmonic characteristic parameters of the output trajectory of the four-bar mechanism is
established in this paper. The database contains only the basic dimensional type of the
four-bar mechanism and the corresponding harmonic characteristic parameters. Using
the non-equal time interval normalized characteristic processing method proposed in
Sect. 4, the sampling is discretized for any given design condition, and the sampled
points are subjected to a two-dimensional Fourier transform.

Using the pre-established numerical atlas database, according to the similarity
between the harmonic characteristic parameters of the given design conditions and the
harmonic characteristic parameters of the basic size type stored in the database, the basic
size types and structural parameters of the target mechanism are matched and identified
respectively. Combined with genetic algorithm, the mechanism parameters obtained by
matching identification are optimized to obtain the target mechanism parameters. On
this basis, the actual size and installation position parameters of the mechanism can
be solved according to the difference between the harmonic components of the given
curve and the harmonic components of the corresponding basic size type linkage corner
operator, thus realizing the solution of the comprehensive problem of the trajectory of a
planar four-bar mechanism satisfying the design requirements of non-equal time interval
positions. Then, according to the position of the toe relative to the foot, the function synthesis is used to find the parameters of the Watt II mechanism. The theoretical calculation
equation is as follows:

$$\theta_1' = \frac{1}{n+1}(\zeta_n - \zeta_{-1} - \varphi_n + \varphi_{-1}), (n \neq 0, 1, -1) \tag{12}$$

Terminal guidance length:

$$L_p = D_{-1}/c_{-1} \tag{13}$$

Frame deflection angle and linkage and terminal guide angle:

$$\theta_0 + \theta_p = \zeta_{-1} - \varphi_{-1} + \theta_1' \tag{14}$$

Frame installation position:

$$L_\beta e^{i\theta_\beta} + L_p c_0 e^{i(\theta_0 + \theta_p + \varphi_0)} = D_0 e^{i\zeta_0} \tag{15}$$

Actual bar length of the mechanism:

$$L_1 e^{i(\theta_1' + \theta_0)} + L_p c_1 e^{i(\theta_0 + \theta_p + \varphi_1 + \theta_1')} = D_1 e^{i\zeta_1} \tag{16}$$

where D_n and ζ_n represent the nth term amplitude and phase of the generated curve for a given design condition, respectively; c_n and φ_n represent the nth term amplitude and phase of the generated trajectory curve for the basic size type, respectively.

The lower limb rehabilitation robot system consists of two sets of robot mechanisms arranged left and right, during the lower limb rehabilitation training, the mechanism generates human gait trajectory under motor drive, and drives the foot of patient movement through the pedal, so as to realize the rehabilitation training. The lower limb rehabilitation training robot designed in this paper has the advantages of high trajectory reproduction and simple control compared with the existing rehabilitation robots.

This example takes the sampling points given in Fig. 2 (b) as the design requirements, and uses the method proposed in this paper to synthesize the path of the design requirements. The comprehensive results are listed in Table 1, and the fitting curve is shown in Fig. 5.

Table 1. Actual dimensions and installation positions of the resulting synthesis

Dimensional type	L_1^1	L_2^1	L_3^1	L_4^1	L_β^1	β^1	θ_0^1	L_p^1	θ_p^1
Value	0.2224	0.5854	0.7504	1.0452	0.8555	5.8534	−1.1145	0.6652	1.0250
Dimensional type	L_1^2	L_2^2	L_3^2	L_4^2	L_β^2	β^2	θ_0^2	L_p^2	θ_p^2
Value	0.0993	0.2947	0.1703	0.3515	1.3529	0.5475	-0.5621	0.6520	4.8037

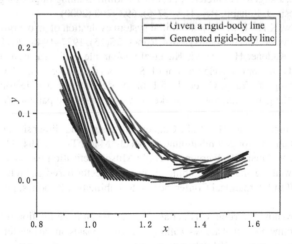

Fig. 5. Comparison of the trajectory generated by the rehabilitation training mechanism with the desired trajectory

6 Conclusion

The paper proposes a new single-degree-of-freedom lower limb rehabilitation training robot mechanism. The required data is obtained through a Xsens MVN Analyze, the normal gait trajectory of the human body is used as the objective, and the required mechanism is obtained by dimensional synthesis and optimization. The designed mechanism can pass any point on the normal gait trajectory, and only one motor is needed to accurately complete the speed control of the rehabilitation training robot, which greatly simplifies the control system of the robot and its operation.

The structure design and optimization method proposed in this paper is not only applicable to the gait trajectory shown in Fig. 2 (b), but also to the specific gait patterns of patients, which can obtain a new set of rehabilitation training models and thus help patients with lower limb dysfunction to complete gait rehabilitation training. The proposed dimensional synthesis method can theoretically achieve path synthesis for any given number of positions, avoiding the solution of a nonlinear system of equations and making up for the shortcomings of the existing numerical atlas method of path synthesis.

Acknowledgments. This project was supported by the Science and Technology Research Project of the Jilin Provincial Department of Education [grant no. JJKH20220672KJ], Projects of Hubei Science and Technology Department [grant no. 2022CFC035], and Scientific Research Project of Education Department of Hubei Province under [grant no. D20222603].

References

1. Díaz, I., Gil, J.J., Sánchez, E.: Lower-limb robotic rehabilitation: literature review and challenges. J. Robot., 759–764 (2011)
2. Colombo, G., Joerg, M., Schreier, R., et al.: Treadmill training of paraplegic patients using a robotic orthosis. J. Rehabil. Res. Dev. 37(6), 693–700 (2000)
3. Wang, P., Low, K.H., Tow, A., et al.: Initial system evaluation of an overground rehabilitation gait training robot (NaTUre-gaits). Adv. Robot. 25(15), 1927–1948 (2011)
4. Hassan, M., Kadone, H., Suzuki, K., et al.: Wearable gait measurement system with an instrumented cane for exoskeleton control. Sensors 14(1), 1705–1722 (2014)
5. Zhang, J., Dong, Y., Yang, C., et al.: 5-Link model based gait trajectory adaption control strategies of the gait rehabilitation exoskeleton for post-stroke patients. Mechatronics 20(3), 368–376 (2010)
6. Shao, Y., Xiang, Z., Liu, H., et al.: Conceptual design and dimensional synthesis of cam-linkage mechanisms for gait rehabilitation. Mech. Mach. Theory 104, 31–42 (2016)
7. Schmidt, H., Volkmar, M., Werner, C., et al.: Muscle activation patterns of healthy subjects during floor walking and stair climbing on an end-effector-based gait rehabilitation robot. In: 2007 IEEE 10th International Conference on Rehabilitation Robotics, pp. 1077–1084. IEEE (2007)
8. Yoon, J., Novandy, B., Yoon, C.H., et al.: A 6-DOF gait rehabilitation robot with upper and lower limb connections that allows walking velocity updates on various terrains. IEEE/ASME Trans. Mechatron. 15(2), 201–215 (2010)
9. Song, W., Zhao, P., Li, X., et al.: Data-driven design of a six-bar lower-limb rehabilitation mechanism based on gait trajectory prediction. In: IEEE Transactions on Neural Systems and Rehabilitation Engineering, pp. 109–118 (2022)
10. Li, M., Yan, J., Zhao, H., et al.: Mechanically assisted neurorehabilitation: a novel six-bar linkage mechanism for gait rehabilitation. IEEE Trans. Neural Syst. Rehabil. Eng. 29, 985–992 (2021)
11. Goncalves, R.S., Soares, G., Carvalho, J.C.: Conceptual design of a rehabilitation device based on cam-follower and crank-rocker mechanisms hand actioned. J. Braz. Soc. Mech. Sci. Eng. 41, 1–12 (2019)

12. Ji, Z., Manna, Y.: Synthesis of a pattern generation mechanism for gait rehabilitation. J. Med. Devices **2**(3), 031004 (2008)
13. Hesse, S., Uhlenbrock, D., Werner, C., et al.: A mechanized gait trainer for restoring gait in nonambulatory subjects. Arch. Phys. Med. Rehabil. **81**(9), 1158–1161 (2000)
14. Negrello, F., Garabini, M., Catalano, M.G., et al.: A modular compliant actuator for emerging high performance and fall-resilient humanoids. In: 2015 IEEE-RAS 15th International Conference on Humanoid Robots (Humanoids), pp. 414–420. IEEE (2015)
15. Lohmeier, S., Buschmann, T., Ulbrich, H., et al.: Modular joint design for performance enhanced humanoid robot LOLA. In: Proceedings 2006 IEEE International Conference on Robotics and Automation, 2006. ICRA 2006, pp. 88–93. IEEE (2006)
16. Nguyen, V.T., Kiuchi, D., Hasegawa, H.: Development of foot structure for humanoid robot using topology optimization. Adv. Eng. Forum **29**, 34–45 (2018)
17. Nerakae, K., Hasegawa, H.: Bigtoe sizing design of small biped robot by using gait generation method. Appl. Mech. Mater. **541**, 1079–1086 (2014)
18. Kouchaki, E., Sadigh, M.J.: Effect of toe-joint bending on biped gait performance. In: 2010 IEEE International Conference on Robotics and Biomimetics, pp. 697–702. IEEE (2010)
19. Narang, G., Kong, W., Xu, P., et al.: Comparison of bipedal humanoid walking with human being using inertial measurement units and force-torque sensors. In: Proceedings of the 2013 IEEE/SICE International Symposium on System Integration, pp. 198–203. IEEE (2013)
20. Yang, W., Zhang, X., Yang, C., et al.: Design of a lower extremity exoskeleton based on 5-bar human machine model. J. Zhejiang Univ. (Eng. Sci.) **48**(3), 430–435 (2014)
21. Jiang, L., Wang, L., Wang, Y., Chen, J.: Mechanism design and analysis of a hybrid-input parallel rehabilitation robot with humanoid gaits. Robot **38**(4), 495–503 (2016)

Upper Limb Motion Rehabilitation Training Robot Based on a Spatial RRSS Rigid-Body Guidance Mechanism

Yi Zhao[1], Ge Xu[2,3], and Wenrui Liu[2,3]([✉])

[1] School of Mechanical and Electrical Engineering, Changchun University of Technology, Changchun 130012, China

[2] School of Mechanical Engineering, Hubei University of Arts and Sciences, Xiangyang 441053, China
lwr@hbuas.edu.cn

[3] Xiangyang Key Laboratory of Rehabilitation Medicine and Rehabilitation Engineering Technology, Hubei University of Arts and Science, Xiangyang 441053, China

Abstract. In this paper, a spatial RRSS rigid-body guidance mechanism is taken as the human upper limb rehabilitation training robot actuator to realize human upper limb rehabilitation movement training. First, a mathematical model of the rigid-body posture output of a spatial RRSS mechanism is established. Second, a parametric description of the characteristic of the rigid-body guidance-line of the spatial RRSS mechanism is proposed. Third, the wavelet feature parameter method is used to extract the characteristics of rigid-body poses. Based on the relationship of the wavelet coefficients between the centrifugal angle obtained from rigid-body guidance-line and the coupler angles of mechanism generated by dimensional parameters, the other geometric parameters can be obtained. Finally, the installation parameters, dimensional parameters and input angles of a spatial RRSS rigid-body guidance mechanism are designed, and the single-degree-of-freedom spatial linkage mechanism as an actuator is used to replace a multi-degree-of-freedom robot realizing the rehabilitation exercise for the patient. The rationality of the spatial linkage mechanism is verified by experiments, and its potential in medical treatment and rehabilitation work is illustrated to a certain extent.

Keywords: Rehabilitation robot · Mechanism design · Rigid-body guidance synthesis · Spatial RRSS mechanism

1 Introduction

The mechanism is the core of robots and mechanical devices. At this stage, upper limb rehabilitation robots can be divided into exoskeleton type rehabilitation robots and end-guidance rehabilitation robots according to the robot structure [1]. The former is bound to the upper limb and the rehabilitation is accomplished through coordinated movements between the rod systems, and the latter has the body structure placed on a separate bracket

© The Author(s), under exclusive license to Springer Nature Singapore Pte Ltd. 2023
H. Yang et al. (Eds.): ICIRA 2023, LNAI 14273, pp. 552–564, 2023.
https://doi.org/10.1007/978-981-99-6498-7_47

and then uses the end-effector to control the movement of the upper limb according to the planned trajectory [2, 3]. The representative exoskeleton upper limb rehabilitation robots include the ARMin [4], developed by ETH Zurich and the Catholic University of America. It has six degrees of freedom and at least six motors. It can provide targeted rehabilitation for patients. The BONES, designed by the University of California, Irvine [5]. It has three degrees of freedom and all of three motors. The device can be driven by air and employs a parallel structure of mechanical ground brakes. The NeReBot [6], a rope-based exoskeleton upper limb rehabilitation robot researched at the University of Padova, Italy. It has 3 degrees of freedom and leastways three motors, with low cost, high acceptance, portability and good space performance. The representative end-guidance upper limb rehabilitation robots include the MIME developed by Stanford University, USA [7–9]. The MIME robot has an intuitive interface which be capable to connect motion therapy with virtual reality games. Developed by the University of Genoa, Italy, Braccio di Ferro [10], Braccio di Ferro's modular design allows for improved flexibility in exercise instruction and task-specific rehabilitation exercises. GENTLE/S invented by the University of Reading, UK [11, 12]. GENTLE/S can provide patients with more personalized rehabilitation through adaptive assistance and its own user feedback mechanism.

The characteristics of multi-degree of freedom robots are high precision and complex motion control capabilities, which make them to complete a various of operational tasks. However, the multi-degree of freedom robot has the disadvantages of high costs, large sizes, high maintenance costs and complex operation procedures, which need to be overcome. In the study, it is found that the linkage structure not only overcomes the above shortcomings, but has the advantages of good stability, strong flexibility, wide adaptability, etc., which is the ideal for upper limb rehabilitation robots. The Massachusetts Institute of Technology (MIT) has designed the first upper limb rehabilitation robot, the MIT-MANUS7 [13, 14]. MIT-MANUS7 uses a five-link mechanism to achieve upper limb rehabilitation exercise. The device manipulates motors and sensors to control and monitor movement, and force sensors can help experimenters monitor patients' movements while recording their rehabilitation process. The representative one in China is the UECM developed by Tsinghua University [15]. The UECM contains a two-link mechanism with 2 degrees of freedom. The device can complete passive motion training, active training and resistance training for specific trajectories. In terms of man-machine information interaction, UECM adopts dual video feedback system. Through the hand-eye coordination training, the training operation is more consistent with the daily behavior of patients.

Currently, most of the end-guidance rehabilitation machines on the market can assist patients in completing rehabilitation training on a specific trajectory in the horizontal plane. However, since the movement of the human body is on the three-dimensional spatial dimensions, the range of motion and trajectory provided by the planar linkage mechanism may differ from the patient's daily behavioral movement pattern. Spatial linkage mechanism has the advantages of compact structure, strong load-bearing capacity, rich and diverse motion output, and the mechanism can generate complex spatial motion. In order to make the spatial linkage mechanism more flexible to be applied in various modern high-end machinery and equipment motion actuator, in this paper, a design method of spatial RRSS (revolute-revolute-spherical-spherical) mechanism is proposed, and an actuator of upper limb motion rehabilitation training robot is designed by using the proposed method. The upper limb swimming movement acquired by the motion capture experiment is used as the desired poses, the proposed dimensional synthesis method for motion generation is used to design geometric parameters of the spatial RRSS mechanism, rigid-body guidance synthesis of the mechanism geometric parameters. The results show that the robot mechanism can approximately realize the desired poses and only needs one driver.

2 Swim Acquisition

A healthy adult male with a height of 1800 mm, an upper arm length of 328 mm and a forearm length of 252 mm, who had learned the standard swimming stroke, was used as the experimental subject, acquisition of normal human swimming posture (As shown in Fig. 1) with Xsens 3D motion capture and analysis system, to use this as a reference swimming posture for the design of upper limb rehabilitation robot mechanism. To ensure the reliability and stability of the experimental data, prior to data acquisition, subjects were preadapted for two minutes, wait for its swimming posture to stabilize before data acquisition. During the capture, the right heel of the experimental subject is used as the coordinate origin, Acquisition of right forearm motion trajectory, the motion trajectory of the rigid-body poses in one swimming cycle can be obtained as shown in Fig. 2 (b).

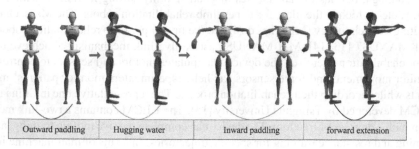

| Outward paddling | Hugging water | Inward paddling | forward extension |

Fig. 1. Swim step-by-step flow chart

As shown in Fig. 2 (a), the sampled human upper limb movement is used as the target rigid-body guidance-line, and a spatial RRSS mechanism is designed with a rod cemented above the linkage, and the wrist and elbow are fixed on the rod respectively, to realize the target motion on the generate space by a driver driving the mechanism movement, the core is the design of the rod length dimensions and mounting position parameters of the mechanism. The device has the characteristics of simple structure, low cost, and can realize movement on complex three-dimensional space, which provides more scientific and effective rehabilitation training paths for patients and has certain practicality.

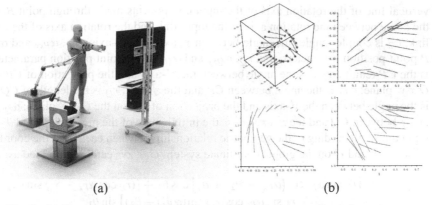

(a)   (b)

Fig. 2. (a) Human upper limb kinematics model. (b) Swim sampling schematic.

3 Mathematical Model of Spatial RRSS Rigid-Body Guidance Mechanism

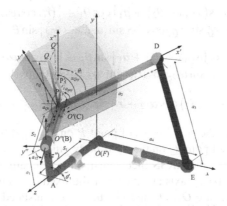

Fig. 3. Spatial RRSS rigid guidance mechanism in standard installation position

As shown in Fig. 3, the spatial RRSS mechanism in the standard installation position. AB is the inputlink, CD is the coupler link, DE is the driven link, EF is the frame. $O - xyz$ is a fixed coordinate system, where the coordinate origin O coincides with the point of the rack F, z-axis coincides with the rotation axis of the input rod, the x-axis coincides with the vertical lines of z-axis made through the center E of the Ball vice. The lengths of each component of the RRSS mechanism AB, CD, DE, EF, FA and BC are a_1, a_2, a_3, a_4, S_1, and S_2). Two local coordinate system, $O' - x'y'z'$ and $O'' - x''y''z''$, are respectively attached to the input link and coupler link, the origin O' of the coordinate system $O' - x'y'z'$ coincides with the point C, the x' axis coincides with the axis $O'D$ which passes through the spherical sub-center D, the z'-axis coincides with the x'-axis vertical line made through point B; the origin O'' of the coordinate system $O'' - x''y''z''$ coincides with the point B, z''-axis coincides with z'-axis, the x''-axis coincides with the vertical line of the rotation axis of the input components made through point B. α_{12} is the angle between the rotation axis of the input link and the rotation axis of the coupler link. θ_2 is coupler angle (the angle between x'-axis and x''-axis). r_P, α_{Pxy} and α_{Pz} are P point position parameters, and r_Q, α_{Qxy} and α_{Qz} are Q point position parameters. r_P is the CP length; α_{Pxy} is the angle between the x'-axis and the projection of CP on the $O'x'y'$ plane; α_{Pz} is the angle between CP and the z'-axis; r_Q is the length of CQ; α_{Qxy} is the angle between the x'-axis and the projection of CQ on the $O'x'y'$ plane; α_{Qz} is the angle between CQ and the z'-axis. θ_1' is the initial angle of the mechanism and θ_1 is the input angle. According to the geometric relationship between each link, the coordinates of points P and Q on the global coordinate system $O - xyz$ can be expressed as:

$$x_P = \left[r_P \sin \alpha_{Pz} \cos(\alpha_{Pxy} - \theta_2) + a_1 \right] \cos \theta_1 + \left[(r_P \cos \alpha_{Pz} - S_2) \sin \alpha_{12} \right.$$
$$\left. - r_P \sin \alpha_{Pz} \cos \alpha_{12} \sin(\alpha_{Pxy} - \theta_2) \right] \sin \theta_1 \tag{1}$$

$$y_P = \left[r_P \sin \alpha_{Pz} \cos(\alpha_{Pxy} - \theta_2) + a_1 \right] \sin \theta_1 - \left[(r_P \cos \alpha_{Pz} - S_2) \sin \alpha_{12} \right.$$
$$\left. - r_P \sin \alpha_{Pz} \cos \alpha_{12} \sin(\alpha_{Pxy} - \theta_2) \right] \cos \theta_1 \tag{2}$$

$$z_P = (r_P \cos \alpha_{Pz} - S_2) \cos \alpha_{12} + r_P \sin \alpha_{Pz} \sin(\alpha_{Pxy} - \theta_2) \sin \alpha_{12} + S_1 \tag{3}$$

$$x_Q = \left[r_Q \sin \alpha_{Qz} \cos(\alpha_{Qxy} - \theta_2) + a_1 \right] \cos \theta_1 + \left[(r_Q \cos \alpha_{Qz} - S_2) \sin \alpha_{12} \right.$$
$$\left. - r_Q \sin \alpha_{Qz} \cos \alpha_{12} \sin(\alpha_{Qxy} - \theta_2) \right] \sin \theta_1 \tag{4}$$

$$y_Q = \left[r_Q \sin \alpha_{Qz} \cos(\alpha_{Qxy} - \theta_2) + a_1 \right] \sin \theta_1 - \left[(r_Q \cos \alpha_{Qz} - S_2) \sin \alpha_{12} \right.$$
$$\left. - r_Q \sin \alpha_{Qz} \cos \alpha_{12} \sin(\alpha_{Qxy} - \theta_2) \right] \cos \theta_1 \tag{5}$$

$$z_Q = (r_Q \cos \alpha_{Qz} - S_2) \cos \alpha_{12} + r_Q \sin \alpha_{Qz} \sin(\alpha_{Qxy} - \theta_2) \sin \alpha_{12} + S_1 \tag{6}$$

where x_p, y_p and z_p are the coordinates of point P on the rigid-body poses; x_Q, y_Q and z_Q are the coordinates of point Q on the rigid-body guidance-line; $\theta_A = \theta_1' + \theta_1$.

As shown in Fig. 4, the RRSS mechanism in a standard installation position is translated along the x-axis, y-axis and z-axis of the fixed coordinate system O-xyz, and the translation amounts are O_x, O_y and O_z, then the translated mechanism is rotated around the x-axis, y-axis and z-axis by θ_x, θ_y and θ_z, respectively, to obtain the spatial RRSS mechanism in a general installation position.

For a general installation position mechanism, the rigid-body poses can be expressed by θ_A, the geometric parameters of the mechanism a_1, a_2, a_3, a_4, S_1, S_2, r_P, α_{12}, α_{xy}, α_z r_Q, α_{Qxy} and α_{Qz}, the frame installation position parameters O_x, O_y and O_z, and the frame installation angle parameters θ_x, θ_y and θ_z as:

$$x_p'' = (x_p + O_x) \cos \theta_y \cos \theta_z + (y_p + O_y)(\sin \theta_x \sin \theta_y \cos \theta_z - \cos \theta_x \sin \theta_z)$$
$$+ (z_p + O_z)(\cos \theta_x \sin \theta_y \cos \theta_z + \sin \theta_x \sin \theta_z) \tag{7}$$

$$y_p'' = (x_p + O_x) \cos \theta_y \sin \theta_z + (y_p + O_y)(\sin \theta_x \sin \theta_y \sin \theta_z + \cos \theta_x \cos \theta_z)$$
$$+ (z_p + O_z)(\cos \theta_x \sin \theta_y \sin \theta_z - \sin \theta_x \cos \theta_z) \tag{8}$$

$$z_p'' = -(x_p + O_x) \sin \theta_y + (y_p + O_y) \sin \theta_x \cos \theta_y + (z_p + O_z) \cos \theta_x \cos \theta_y \tag{9}$$

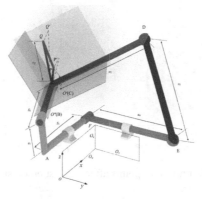

Fig. 4. Spatial RRSS rigid guidance mechanism in general installation position

$$x''_Q = (x_Q + O_x)\cos\theta_y\cos\theta_z + (y_Q + O_y)(\sin\theta_x\sin\theta_y\cos\theta_z - \cos\theta_x\sin\theta_z) \\ + (z_Q + O_z)(\cos\theta_x\sin\theta_y\cos\theta_z + \sin\theta_x\sin\theta_z) \tag{10}$$

$$y''_Q = (x_Q + O_x)\cos\theta_y\sin\theta_z + (y_Q + O_y)(\sin\theta_x\sin\theta_y\sin\theta_z + \cos\theta_x\cos\theta_z) \\ + (z_Q + O_z)(\cos\theta_x\sin\theta_y\sin\theta_z - \sin\theta_x\cos\theta_z) \tag{11}$$

$$z''_Q = -(x_Q + O_x)\sin\theta_y + (y_Q + O_y)\sin\theta_x\cos\theta_y + (z_Q + O_z)\cos\theta_x\cos\theta_y \tag{12}$$

4 Feature Extraction Method for Spatial RRSS Mechanism Rigid-Body Guidance-Line

In our previous study, we found that the coupler angle is only relate to the basic dimensional types a_1, a_2, a_3, a_4, S_1, S_2 and α_{12}. In order to extract the coupler angle from prescribed poses, we take two-step processing to the rigid-body poses of the RRSS mechanism in the standard installation position. In the first processing, the rigid-body guidance-line are rotated clockwise around the z-axis, rotation angle is corresponding θ_A. After the first step processing, the coordinates of the projection of points P and Q on the xOy plane are:

$$x''_P(\theta_A^n) = r_P\sin\alpha_{P_z}\cos(\alpha_{Pxy} - \theta_2^n) + a_1 \tag{13}$$

$$y''_P(\theta_A^n) = r_P\sin\alpha_{P_z}\cos\alpha_{12}\sin(\alpha_{P_{xy}} - \theta_2^n) - (r_P\cos\alpha_{P_z} - S_2)\sin\alpha_{12} \tag{14}$$

$$x''_Q(\theta_A^n) = r_Q\sin\alpha_{Q_z}\cos(\alpha_{Qxy} - \theta_2^n) + a_1 \tag{15}$$

$$y''_Q(\theta_A^n) = r_Q\sin\alpha_{Q_z}\cos\alpha_{12}\sin(\alpha_{Qxy} - \theta_2^n) - (r_Q\cos\alpha_{Q_z} - S_2)\sin\alpha_{12} \tag{16}$$

Figure 5 shows the projection point P_{xy} and Q_{xy} of the nth P and Q sampling points on the rigid-body poses in the xOy plane after the first step processing.

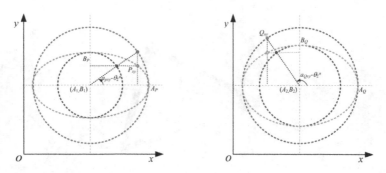

Fig. 5. Projection points after the first processing step

According to Eqs. (13) to (16), it can be found that the projection points after the first step processing form an ellipse, the length of the long semi-axis of the ellipse are respectively $A_P = r_P \sin \alpha_z$ and $A_Q = r_Q \sin \alpha_{Qz}$; short half shaft length are respectively $B_P = r_P \sin \alpha_z \cos \alpha_{12}$ and $B_Q = r_Q \sin \alpha_{Qz} \cos \alpha_{12}$; the center coordinates are respectively $(A_1, B_1) = (a_1, -r_P \cos \alpha_z \sin \alpha_{12} + S_2 \sin \alpha_{12})$ and $(A_2, B_2) = (a_1, -r_Q \cos \alpha_{Qz} \sin \alpha_{12} + S_2 \sin \alpha_{12})$; the centrifugal angle of the projection point after preprocessing are respectively $\theta_P = a_{Pxy} - \theta_2^n$ and $\theta_Q = a_{Qxy} - \theta_2^n$

Further processing of the rigid-body guidance-line after the first step, the rigid-body poses rotated counterclockwise around the x-axis, and the rotation angle is the angle between the rotation axis of the input link and the coupler link of the mechanism ($\alpha 12$), at this time, the projection on the Oxy plane (as shown in Fig. 6) can be expressed as follows:

$$x_p'(\theta_A^n) = r_{Pz} \sin \alpha_{Pz} \cos(\alpha_{Pxy} - \theta_2^n) + a_1 \tag{17}$$

$$y_p'(\theta_A^n) = r_{Pz} \sin \alpha_{Pz} \sin(\alpha_{Pxy} - \theta_2^n) + S_1 \sin \alpha_{12} \tag{18}$$

$$x_Q'(\theta_A^n) = r_{Qz} \sin \alpha_{Qz} \cos(\alpha_{Qxy} - \theta_2^n) + a_1 \tag{19}$$

$$y_Q'(\theta_A^n) = r_{Qz} \sin \alpha_{Qz} \sin(\alpha_{Qxy} - \theta_2^n) + S_1 \sin \alpha_{12} \tag{20}$$

Based on the Eqs. (17) to (20), it can be found that the two sets of points P and Q on the rigid-body guidance-line lie on two circles in the Oxy plane, and since the circle center coordinates are only related to the linakge length of the mechanism AB (a_1), the linakge length of AF (S_1), and the angle between the rotation axis of the input link and the coupler link of the linkage (α_{12}), these two circles form two concentric circles. The center coordinates are $(A_3, B_3) = (a_1, S_1 \sin \alpha_{12})$; the radius are respectively $R_P = r_P \sin \alpha_{pz}$ and $R_Q = r_Q \sin \alpha_{Qz}$; centrifugal angle are respectively $\theta_P = a_{Pxy} - \theta_2^n$ and $\theta_Q = a_{Qxy} - \theta_2^n$. Based on this, if we know the installation position parameters (O_x, O_y and O_z) and the installation angle parameters (θ_x, θ_y and θ_z), then the P and Q points can be restored back to the standard installation position, thus forming two concentric circles.

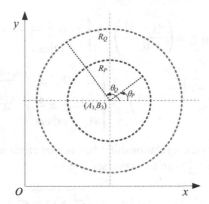

Fig. 6. Projection points after the second processing step

Therefore, we can create a database of installation angle parameters and a database of installation position parameters, based on the above findings, the prescribed rigid-body poses can be rotated and translated to a special position. In that position, the rigid-body guidance-line can generate two concentric circles after two step processing. The special position is the installation position and the frame installation position parameters (O_x, O_y, O_z) and frame installation angle parameters $(\theta_x, \theta_y, \theta_z)$ can be obtained. And the relative coupler angle of the mechanism is obtained. The error function as follows:

$$\delta_1 = \sqrt{(A_{3P} - A_{3Q})^2 + (B_{3P} - B_{3Q})^2} \tag{21}$$

Discrete sampling of the objective function rigid-body lines according to the given design conditions of the RRSS mechanism, combined with the "RRSS mechanism characteristic elliptic structure parameter extraction method" proposed in the literature [16], the angle between the rotation axis of the input components of the mechanism and the rotation axis of the linkage (α_{12}), the centrifugal angle of the projection point on the characteristic elliptic curve of the target mechanism $(\alpha_{xy} - \theta_2)$, the length of the long half-axis (A_0), the length of the short half-axis (B_0), and the coordinates of the center of the characteristic ellipse (A_1, B_1) can be obtained. In this paper, we define the above parameters as the mechanism characteristic parameters.

The wavelet transform is applied to the centrifugal angle of the sampled points on the target rigid-body poses, and the j-level wavelet expansion of the centrifugal angle can be expressed as:

$$f(\alpha_{xy} - \theta_2) = a_{(j,1)}\phi_{(j,1)} + \sum_{J=1}^{j}\sum_{l=1}^{2^{j-J}}\left[d_{(J,l)}\psi_{(J,l)}\right] \tag{22}$$

$$a_{(j,1)} = \frac{(\alpha_{xy} - \theta_2^1) + \cdots + (\alpha_{xy} - \theta_2^{2^j})}{2^j} \tag{23}$$

$$d_{(J,l)} = \frac{\left[(\alpha_{xy} - \theta_2^{2^J l - 2^J + 1}) + \cdots + (\alpha_{xy} - \theta_2^{2^J l - 2^{J-1}})\right] - \left[(\alpha_{xy} - \theta_2^{2^J l - 2^{J-1} + 1}) + \cdots + (\alpha_{xy} - \theta_2^{2^J l})\right]}{2^J}$$

$$\tag{24}$$

$$\phi_{(j,1)} = \phi\left(\frac{\theta_A - \theta_A^1}{\theta_s}\right) = \begin{cases} 1, \ 0 \leq \frac{\theta_A - \theta_A^1}{\theta_s} < 1 \\ 0, \ \text{others} \end{cases} \tag{25}$$

$$\psi_{(J,l)} = \psi\left(2^{j-J}\frac{\theta_A - \theta_A^1}{\theta_s} - l + 1\right) = \begin{cases} 1, \quad 0 \leq 2^{j-J}\frac{\theta_A - \theta_A^1}{\theta_s} - l + 1 < \frac{1}{2} \\ -1, \ \frac{1}{2} \leq 2^{j-J}\frac{\theta_A - \theta_A^1}{\theta_s} - l + 1 < 1 \\ 0, \quad \text{others} \end{cases} \tag{26}$$

According to the geometric relationship, the coupler angle at the nth sampling point of the RRSS mechanism (θ_2^n) can be expressed as:

$$\theta_2^n = 2 \arctan\left(\frac{e_1 - \sqrt{e_1^2 + e_2^2 - e_3^2}}{e_3 - e_2}\right) \tag{27}$$

where

$$e_1 = \cos\alpha_{12}\sin\theta_A^n + S_1\sin\alpha_{12}/a_4$$

$$e_2 = \cos\theta_A^n + \alpha_1/a_4$$

$$e_3 = (a_1^2 + a_2^2 - a_3^2 + a_4^2 + S_1^2 + S_2^2 - 2S_1S_2\cos\alpha_{12})/(2a_2a_4) + (S_2\sin\alpha_{12}\sin\theta_A^n - a_1\cos\theta_A^n)/a_2$$

According to Eq. (27), the coupler angle of the RRSS mechanism is only related to seven characteristic dimensional types ($a_1, a_2, a_3, a_4, S_1, S_2$, and α_{12}) and θ_A. According to the wavelet decomposition method, the wavelet transform is performed on the coupler angle to obtain the j-level wavelet expansion formula of the coupler angle:

$$f(\theta_2) = a'_{(j,1)}\phi_{(j,1)} + \sum_{J=1}^{j}\sum_{l=1}^{2^{j-J}}\left[d'_{(J,l)}\psi_{(J,l)}\right] \tag{28}$$

$$a'_{(j,1)} = \frac{\theta_2^1 \cdots + \theta_2^{2^j}}{2^j} \tag{29}$$

$$d'_{(J,l)} = \frac{\left[\theta_2^{2^J l - 2^J + 1} + \cdots + \theta_2^{2^J l - 2^{J-1}}\right] - \left[\theta_2^{2^J l - 2^{J-1} + 1} + \cdots + \theta_2^{2^J l}\right]}{2^J} \tag{30}$$

Comparing Eqs. (24) and (30), it can be seen that the centrifugal angle at the sampling point on the characteristic elliptic curve of the mechanism and the wavelet detail coefficients of the corresponding coupler angle are opposite to each other. Based on this finding, this paper builds a dynamic adaptive numerical atlas database of the last 3 levels of wavelet detail coefficients of the RRSS mechanism coupler angle. The numerical atlas database consists of RRSS mechanism feature size types and corresponding output wavelet feature parameters. Determine the eigensize of the target mechanism by calculating the error between the output wavelet characteristic parameters for a given centrifugal angle of the rigid-body guidance-line and the opposite number of output wavelet characteristic parameters stored in the numerical atlas database. The error function can be expressed as:

$$\delta_2 = \sum_{J=j-2}^{j} \sum_{l=1}^{2^{j-J}} \left| d_{(J,l)} - \left(-d'_{(J,l)} \right) \right| \tag{31}$$

where $(d_{(J,l)})$ is the output wavelet characteristic parameter of the centrifugal angle in the characteristic parameter of the prescribed rigid-body poses and $(d'_{(J,l)})$ is the output wavelet characteristic parameter of the coupler angle of the characteristic dimension type generating mechanism stored in the database.

5 Spatial RRSS Mechanism Rigid-Body Guidance Synthesis Step

5.1 Spatial RRSS Mechanism Rigid-Body Guidance Synthesis Step

(1) Establish a database of mounting angle parameters and a database of mounting position parameters: The installation angle parameters include θx, θy, and θz, given that the starting angle is $0°$ and the ending angles are $179°$, $359°$, and $359°$, respectively, and a database with a total inventory of 864,000 in $3°$ intervals is created; The installation position parameters include Ox, Oy and Oz, given that the starting position is -1500 and the ending position is 1500, and a database with a total inventory of 337,5000 in 20 intervals is created.

(2) After the rotation and translation of the prescribed poses by the installation angle database and the installation position database, the frame installation angle and the frame installation position of the target mechanism can be determined by calculating the concentric circle center error. And according to the "RRSS mechanism characteristic ellipse structure parameter extraction method", the mechanism starting angle and mechanism characteristic parameters of the target mechanism are determined.

(3) The wavelet transform is applied to the centrifugal angle of the sampled points on the characteristic elliptic curve of the target mechanism obtained in Step (2) to extract the wavelet feature parameters.

(4) A database of RRSS mechanism characteristic dimensional types is established. Based on the initial angle of the desired mechanism and the angle between the rotation axis of the input components and the rotation axis of the linkage obtained in Step (2), extract the characteristic dimensional type of each group in the database to generate the coupler angle of the mechanism.

(5) According to wavelet theory, wavelet transform is performed on each group of the coupler angle obtained from Step (4), and the wavelet feature parameters are extracted to establish a dynamic adaptive numerical atlas database of the spatial RRSS mechanism rigid-body guidance-line.

(6) Based on the error between the output wavelet characteristic parameters of the centrifugal angle of the target mechanism and the output wavelet characteristic parameters stored in the numerical atlas database, Output multiple sets of feature size type with minimum error.

(7) Based on the given target rigid-body poses, the actual rod length dimensions of the target mechanism and the position parameters of the two points P and Q on the rigid-body guidance-line are solved by combining the mechanism start angle, mechanism characteristic parameters and characteristic dimension type of the target mechanism obtained from the above steps. The specific theoretical equations are as follows:

The angle $(\alpha_{Pxy}, \alpha_{Qxy})$ between the x' axis of the target mechanism and the projection of CP and CQ on the $O'x'y'$ plane:

$$\alpha_{Pxy} = a_{P(j,1)} + a'_{P(j,1)} \tag{32}$$

$$\alpha_{Qxy} = a_{Q(j,1)} + a'_{Q(j,1)} \tag{33}$$

where $(a_{P(j,1)}, a_{Q(j,1)})$ are the wavelet approximation coefficients of the centrifugal angle of a given rigid-body poses and $(a'_{P(j,1)}, a'_{Q(j,1)})$ are the wavelet approximation coefficients of the linkage angle of the resulting dimensional parameter generating mechanism.

Ratio of the actual rod length dimension of the target mechanism to the obtained characteristic dimension type k:

$$k = A'_1/a_1 \tag{34}$$

where, (A'_1) is the x-coordinate of the target mechanism characteristic ellipse center; (a_1) is the AB rod length of the input components in the characteristic dimension type.

Lengths of target mechanism CP, CQ and angles of CP, CQ with z'-axis:

$$r_P = \sqrt{A_P'^2 + \left(-B'_1/\sin\alpha_{12} + kS_2\right)^2} \tag{35}$$

$$\alpha_{Pz} = \arctan\left[A'_P/\left(-B'_1/\sin\alpha_{12} + kS_2\right)\right] \tag{36}$$

$$r_Q = \sqrt{A_Q'^2 + \left(-B'_2/\sin\alpha_{12} + kS_2\right)^2} \tag{37}$$

$$\alpha_{Qz} = \arctan\left[A'_Q/\left(-B'_2/\sin\alpha_{12} + kS_2\right)\right] \tag{38}$$

where, (A'_P, A'_Q) are the lengths of the long semi-axis of the characteristic ellipse of the target mechanism; (B'_1, B'_2) are the y-coordinates of the characteristic ellipse center; (S_2) is the length of the BC rod of the linkage in the characteristic dimensional type.

According to Eqs. (32) to (38), the actual rod length dimensions of the target mechanism and the position parameters of the P and Q points on the linkage can be obtained.

5.2 Design Results and Simulation

In this example, the actual rigid body guide line obtained from swimming pose acquisition in Fig. 2 is used as the design requirement, and the method proposed in this paper is used for dimensional synthesis of the target rigid body pose, and the design results obtained are shown in Table 1, the corresponding model diagrams, rigid body guide line fitting results and error diagrams are shown in Fig. 7.

Table 1. Actual dimensions and installation locations of the resulting synthesis results

Dimensional type	$a_1(mm)$	$a_2(mm)$	$a_3(mm)$	$a_4(mm)$	$S_1(mm)$	$S_2(mm)$	$r_P(mm)$	$r_Q(mm)$	$\alpha_{12}(°)$	$\theta'_1(°)$
Value	161.4	948.2	1069.5	965.0	789.6	109.4	481.6	430.1	336.84	344.95
Dimensional type	$\theta_x(°)$	$\theta_y(°)$	$\theta_z(°)$	$O_x(mm)$	$O_y(mm)$	$O_z(mm)$	$\alpha_{Pxy}(°)$	$\alpha_{Qxy}(°)$	$\alpha_{Pz}(°)$	$\alpha_{Qz}(°)$
Value	218.85	144.12	81.41	−862.7	−1218.6	−170.2	206.20	185.31	120.91	94.73

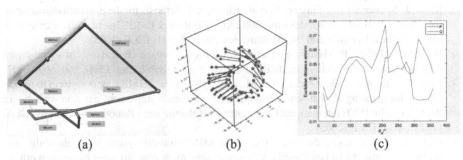

Fig. 7. (a) Model picture. (b) Fitted graph. (c) Error chart.

6 Conclusion

This paper proposes an actuator for upper limb motion rehabilitation training that utilizes a single-degree-of-freedom spatial linkage mechanism to drive the small arm and achieve the required training motions. To achieve this, we present a dimensional synthesis method for motion generation, which utilizes actual data from standard swimming training as input samples. Using the proposed method, we design a spatial linkage mechanism that meets the requirements for upper limb rehabilitation training. Experimental results show that the designed mechanism can effectively assist patients in completing the corresponding swimming training exercises, thus demonstrating the validity and practicality of the proposed method. The successful implementation of our approach provides valuable insights for the innovative design of upper limb rehabilitation robots, which has significant implications for enhancing patient outcomes and improving clinical practice, promoting the development of emerging technologies in medical rehabilitation.

Acknowledgments. This project was supported by the Science and Technology Research Project of the Jilin Provincial Department of Education [grant no. JJKH20220672KJ], Projects of Hubei Science and Technology Department [grant no. 2022CFC035], and Scientific Research Project of Education Department of Hubei Province under [grant no. D20222603].

564   Y. Zhao et al.

References

1. Qassim, H.M., Wan Hasan, W.Z.: A review on upper limb rehabilitation robots. Appl. Sci. **10**(19), 6976 (2020)
2. Colombo, G., Joerg, M., Schreier, R., et al.: Treadmill training of paraplegic patients using a robotic orthosis. J. Rehabil. Res. Dev. **37**(6), 693–700 (2000)
3. Shao, Y., Xiang, Z., Liu, H., et al.: Conceptual design and dimensional synthesis of cam-linkage mechanisms for gait rehabilitation. Mech. Mach. Theory **104**, 31–42 (2016)
4. Nef, T., Mihelj, M., Riener, R.: ARMin: a robot for patient-cooperative arm therapy. Med. Biol. Eng. Comput. **45**(9), 887–900 (2007)
5. Klein, J., Spencer, S.J., Allington, J., et al.: Biomimetic orthosis for the neurorehabilitation of the elbow and shoulder (BONES). In: 2008 2nd IEEE RAS & EMBS International Conference on Biomedical Robotics and Biomechatronics, pp. 535–541. IEEE (2008)
6. Rosati, G., Gallina, P., Masiero, S.: Design, implementation and clinical tests of a wire-based robot for neurorehabilitation. IEEE Trans. Neural Sys. Rehabil. Eng. **15**(4), 560–569 (2007)
7. Lum, P.S., Burgar, C.G., van der Loos, M., et al.: Use of the MIME robotic system to retrain multi-joint reaching in post-stroke hemiparesis: why some movement patterns work better than others. In: IEEE International Conference on Rehabilitation Robotics. Piscataway, USA, pp. 511–514. IEEE (2005)
8. Lum, P.S., Burga, C.G., Shor, P.C.: Use of the MIME robotic system to retrain multi-joint reaching in post-stroke hemiparesis: why some movement patterns work better than others. In: Annual International Conference of the IEEE Engineering in Medicine and Biology, Piscataway, USA, pp. 1475–1478. IEEE (2003)
9. Burgar, C.G., Lum, P.S., Shor, P.C., et al.: Development of robots for rehabilitation therapy: the Palo Alto VA/Stanford experience. J. Rehabil. Res. Dev. **37**(6), 663–673 (2000)
10. Casadio, M., Morasso, P., Noriaki Ide, A., et al.: Measuring functional recovery of hemiparetic subjects during gentle robot therapy. Measurement **42**(8), 11761187 (2009)
11. Amirabdollahian, F., Gradwell, E., Loureiro, R., et al.: Effects of the GENTLE/S robot mediated therapy on the outcome of upper limb rehabilitation post-stroke: analysis of the battle hospital data. In: 8th International Conference on Rehabilitation Robotics, pp. 55–58 (2003)
12. Harwin, W., Loureiro, R., Amirabdollahian, F., et al.: The GENTLE/S project: a new method of delivering neurorehabilitation. In: 6th European Conference for the Advancement of Assistive Technology, Amsterdam, Netherlands, pp. 36–41. IOS Press (2001)
13. Krebs, H.I., Hogan, N., Aisen, M.I., et al.: Robot-aided neurorehabilitation. IEEE Trans. Rehabil. Eng. **6**(1), 75–87 (1998)
14. Volpe, B.T., Krebs, H.I., Hogan, N.: A novel approach to stroke rehabilitation. Robot-aided sensorimotor stimulation. Neurology, **54**(10), 1938–1944 (2000)
15. Hu, Y., Ji, L.: A Multriple-motion rehabilitation training robot for hemiplegia upper limbs. Mach. Des. Manuf. **6**, 47–49 (2004)
16. Liu, W., Zhao, Y., Qin, T., et al.: Optimal synthesis of a spatial RRSS mechanism for path generation. Meccanica **58**(1), 255–285 (2023)

Mask-RCNN with Attention Mechanism for Detection and Segmentation

Xuejing Han, Yongxu Li, Chengyi Duan, Ruixue He, and Hui Jin[✉]

Chongqing University of Technology, Chongqing 400054, China
jinhui1861@126.com

Abstract. In many existing hospitals and pharmacies, check medicine is done manually which is a time-consuming process. In addition, simple repetitive tasks can lead to eye fatigue and improper drug tests can lead to medical accidents. For the sake of solve this problem, this paper proposes a object detection and semantic segmentation algorithm based on improved Mask R-CNN. We use a new feature extraction network ResNeXt to improve the generalization ability of the feature extraction network. Moreover, the Coordinate Attention mechanism is added to the feature extraction network to increase the attention to location information and improve the performance of the network. Experiments show that the proposed method is superior to the previous methods in object detection and instance segmentation.

Keywords: Mask R-CNN · Pill detection · Attention mechanism · Transfer learning

1 Introduction

Dispensing and checking drugs in pharmacy is an important work in hospital. Whether it can be completed quickly and accurately is of great significance to the improvement of work efficiency. At present, the automatic dispensing technology has been widely used [1,14], but the check medicine work is still done manually, which inevitably leads to the occurrence of wrong dispensing problems and greatly improves the risk of patients.

Visual inspection using machines has been widely used in various fields and has become a mature method for detection and recognition tasks. Yao et al.[7] realized real-time detection of tablets by using traditional machine vision to extract image features and using SVM classifier for recognition. Nevertheless, there are problems such as low accuracy and long time consumption, therefore traditional machine vision cannot solve the problem well. Deep learning is one of the most cutting-edge technologies at present. It can realize tasks such as object detection and instance segmentation through images according to data learning features. Because deep learning demands a mass of data, a method for expanding the amount of data for effective data of a single pill is proposed in [9], which improves the accuracy of the network. Nevertheless, there is no

H. Yang et al. (Eds.): ICIRA 2023, LNAI 14273, pp. 565–574, 2023.
https://doi.org/10.1007/978-981-99-6498-7_48

improvement to the algorithm itself. Li et al.[8] proposed a tablet positioning recognition method based on improved MobilenetV3-Small network structure. After the image is preprocessed, the pill detection is realized in the MobilenetV3-Small network after changing the feature layer. Dong et al.[3] realized the one-stage detection of the original image capsule by using the YOLO algorithm in deep learning. Although the accuracy rate has been greatly improved compared with the traditional image processing method, the accuracy rate is still lower than the better method.

In this paper, we propose a method based on improved Mask R-CNN [4] to improve the generalization ability and accuracy of the network by replacing ResNet with a more advanced and excellent ResNeXt [15] network. we also add CA (Coordinate Attention)[6] to the feature extraction network to enhance the feature extraction ability of the feature network. Our method is expected to improve the performance of automation equipment (such as automatic dispensing equipment) and minimize the probability of problems.

2   Mask R-CNN

Mask R-CNN is a network developed on fast / faster R-CNN [2,13], using full convolutional network (FCN) [10] for mask prediction, box regression and classification. The feature pyramid network(FPN) [11] is used to improve the performance of the feature extraction network. ROIpool [5] is replaced by ROIAlign, which does not smoothly transform the features in ROI into fixed-size feature vectors. The overall framework is shown in Fig. 1:

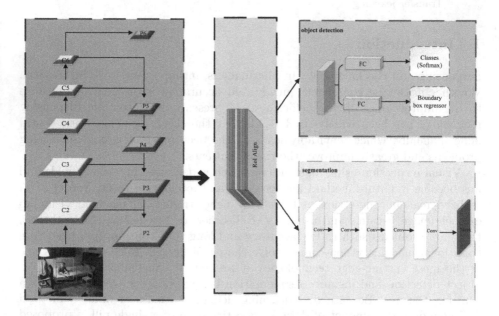

Fig. 1. Mask R-CNN network structure framework

Steps of Mask R-CNN algorithm:

- Enter the picture into the network to obtain the corresponding feature map;
- Set a ROI (region of interest) for each point in the feature map to obtain multiple candidate ROIs;
- These candidate ROIs are sent into the RPN network for binary classification (foreground or background) and regression, and some candidate ROIs are removed;
- The ROI Align operation is performed on these remaining ROIs (that is, the pixel of the original image and the feature map is first matched, and then the feature map and the fixed feature are matched);
- These ROIs are classified (multi-classification), regression (BB) and MASK generation (FCN operation in each ROI).

3 Improved Mask R-CNN Pill Detection Algorithm

We propose a network based on improved Mask R-CNN to improve the accuracy of pill detection. We introduce a new feature extraction network ResNeXt, which makes the parameters of the network less, reduces the amount of calculation, and strengthens the generalization ability of the network. The CA attention mechanism is added to the feature extraction network to improve the feature extraction ability of the network. The following will elaborate on the two improvements.

3.1 Improvement of the Feature Extraction Network Structure

In order to improve the accuracy of target detection, it is usually achieved by increasing the number of network layers. However, the method of increasing the number of layers will lead to the increase of hyperparameters and the increase of calculation, which makes the model training difficult. A new method ResNeXt is proposed to solve this problem perfectly, which improves the accuracy without increasing the number of parameters. Its advantages are as follows:

(1) The structure is simple, flexible and requires less parameters.

Fig 2 is the structural comparison between ResNet and ResNeXt. On the basis of ResNet, ResNeXt is improved by combining the stacking idea of VGG network and the splitting-conversion-merging idea of Inception network. The generalization ability of the network is improved without increasing the number of parameters.

(2) The performance of ResNeXt-50 is better than ResNet-50.

Table 1 lists the internal structure of ResNet-50 and ResNeXt-50. It can be found that the total number of channels in ResNeXt in each Conv is more than that in ResNet, but their parameters are the same. The last two rows in the table show that the number of parameters of ResNeXt is small, and the number of floating-point operations is not much different.

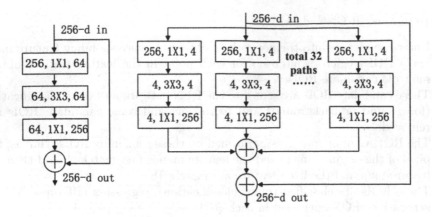

Fig. 2. The comparison structure of ResNet (left) and ResNeXt (right) network blocks.

Table 1. Parameter tables of ResNet-50 and ResNeXt-50.

Stage	Output	ResNet-50	ResNeXt-50
Conv1	112×112	7×7, 64, stride2, 3×3, max pool, stride2	7×7, 64, stride2, 3×3, max pool, stride2
Conv2	56×56	[1 × 1, 64; 3 × 3, 64; 1 × 1, 256] × 3	[1 × 1, 128; 3 × 3, 128; 1 × 1, 256; C = 32] × 3
Conv3	28×28	[1 × 1, 128; 3 × 3, 128; 1 × 1, 512] × 3	[1 × 1, 256; 3 × 3, 256; 1 × 1, 512; C = 32] × 3
Conv4	14×14	[1 × 1, 256; 3 × 3, 256; 1 × 1, 1024] × 3	[1 × 1, 512; 3 × 3, 512; 1 × 1, 1024; C = 32] × 3
Conv5	7×7	[1 × 1, 512; 3 × 3, 512; 1 × 1, 2048] × 3	[1 × 1, 1024; 3 × 3, 1024; 1 × 1, 2048; C = 32] × 3
	1×1	Global average pool, 1000-d fc, softmax	Global average pool, 1000-d fc, softmax
# params		25.5×10^6	25.0×10^6
# FLOPs		4.1×10^9	4.2×10^9

3.2   Attention Mechanism

As everyone knows, attention awareness is an important role in human perception. Human vision does not dispose all scenes at once, but selectively concentrates on the parts that attract attention to better capture the visual structure [12]. Attention mechanisms have been certified to be a very effective method to enhance deep neural networks. We add CA attention Mechanism to the feature extraction network, for the sake of improve the feature extraction ability of the network.

CA is proposed for mobile networks by embedding location information into channel attention. For the sake of solve the problem that pooling will lead to the loss of location information, CA divides channel attention into two parallel one-dimensional coding processes to achieve the purpose of adding location information to the attention map. Specifically, CA collects features along two spatial directions, capturing remote dependencies in one direction and retaining accurate location information in the other direction. The feature maps generated in two directions are encoded into attention maps, and then the attention map is applied to the input feature map by multiplication to realize the attention mechanism.

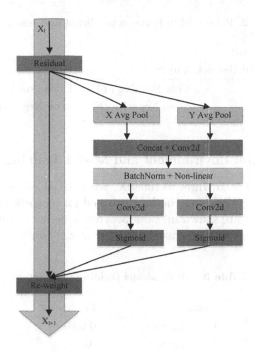

Fig. 3. Coordinate Attention Block

4   Experiment and Analysis

For the sake of estimating the performance of our method, we compare it with other advanced networks. This section will introduce data set acquisition and experimental environment configuration and evaluation results.

4.1   Dataset and Evaluation Indicators

In this paper, 54 original images are collected by mobile phone camera. The size is 4000×3000, the format is jpg format, and finally the size is 800×600. Labelme software is used to label and convert to coco format.

To improve the training model, we enhance the image data by blurring, zooming in and out, randomly cutting the side length ratio, changing the brightness, adding clouds, snow, and learning points. These enhancement methods were randomly combined to generate images, thus expanding the data set to 324, including 261 training sets, 33 test sets, and 30 validation sets.

The standard evaluation metrics we follow are as follows: AP, AP_{50}, AP_{75}.The meaning of precision and recall is shown in Table 2:

Table 2. Relationship between predicted and real results.

Real Result		
Predicted Results	hands	Others
hands	True Positive (TP)	False Positive (FP)
Others	False Negative (FN)	True Negative (TN)

4.2 Experimental Environment and Model Training

The processor used is an Intel i9-10940X, with 64GB of internal memory and an NVIDIA 2080Ti GPU. Our method is based on tensorflow2 framework. The training parameters are shown in Table 3. After a definite number of iterations, the learning rate decreases to ensure that the model converges slowly.

Table 3. APNS Model training parameters

Name	Parameter
Learning rate	0.0001
Momentum	0.9
Batch size	2
Epoch	200
Steps-per-epoch	770
Optimistic algorithm	Adam

4.3 Experiment Results and Analysis

As shown in Fig. 4 and Fig. 5, our algorithm can accurately detect a single type of single pill, and can also accurately detect and segment multiple types of multiple pills.

Table 4 and Table 5, demonstrate the performance comparison of our method, Mask R-CNN, and YOLACT on different feature extraction networks. As you can see from the tables that our method has higher AP in object detection and instance segmentation than Mask R-CNN and YOLACT, with improvements of 5.1%, 7.8%, 3.8% and 7.0% respectively. These results show that our method is better than previous methods in generalization ability, terms of robustness and accuracy.

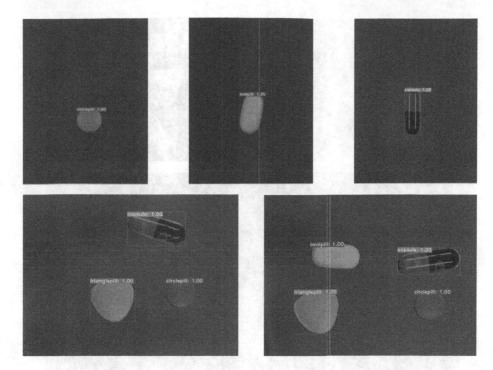

Fig. 4. Experimental results from single category to multi-category.

Table 4. Comparison of detection accuracy between our method and other algorithms

Method	AP	AP_{50}	AP_{75}	Backbone
YOLACT	88.9%	93.9%	95.9%	ResNet-100
Mask R-CNN	91.6%	94.2%	96.3%	ResNet-50
Mask R-CNN	94.2%	95.8%	96.8%	ResNet-101
Our method	**96.7%**	**97.5 %**	**98.1%**	ResNeXt-50

Table 5. Comparison of segmentation accuracy between our method and other algorithms

Method	AP	AP_{50}	AP_{75}	Backbone
YOLACT	89.7%	95.9%	95.9%	ResNet-100
Mask R-CNN	92.5%	95.4%	96.5%	ResNet-50
Mask R-CNN	94.0%	95.8%	95.8%	ResNet-101
Our method	**96.7%**	**96.1 %**	**97.9%**	ResNeXt-50

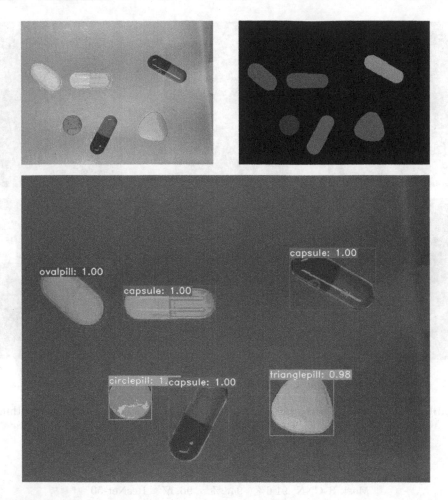

Fig. 5. The original image (upper left), Mask (upper right), experimental results (lower).

5   Conclusion

In this paper, an improved algorithm based on Mask R-CNN is proposed to solve the problem of time-consuming, laborious and error-prone check medicine process. We propose to use ResNeXt to replace the original feature extraction network ResNet to improve the generalization ability of the network. At the same time, the CA attention mechanism is added to the feature extraction network to help the feature network extract features better. Through comparative experiments on the self-made pill data set, it is proved that our method has high accuracy and good performance.Our next work plan is to extend our method to RGBD data and apply it to more areas.

Acknowledgments. Research supported by Science and Technology Research Youth Project of Chongqing Municipal Education Commission(No. KJQN202001132); General Program of Chongqing Science and Technology Commission (2023NSCQ-MSX1478).

Informed Consent Statement. The authors declared that they have no conflicts of interest to this work. We declare that we do not have any commercial or associative interest that represents a conflict of interest in connection with the work submitted.

References

1. Craswell, A., Bennett, K., Hanson, J., Dalgliesh, B., Wallis, M.: Implementation of distributed automated medication dispensing units in a new hospital: nursing and pharmacy experience. J. Clin. Nurs. **30**(19–20), 2863–2872 (2021)
2. Girshick, R.: Fast R-CNN. In: Proceedings of the IEEE International Conference on Computer Vision, pp. 1440–1448 (2015)
3. Hao, D., Shaobo, L., Jing, Y., Jun, W.: Surface defect detectionmethod of medicinal hollow capsule based on YOLOv4 algorithm. Packag. Eng. **43**(7), 254–261 (2022). (In Chinese)
4. He, K., Gkioxari, G., Dollár, P., Girshick, R.: Mask R-CNN. In: Proceedings of the IEEE International Conference on Computer Vision, pp. 2961–2969 (2017)
5. He, K., Zhang, X., Ren, S., Sun, J.: Spatial pyramid pooling in deep convolutional networks for visual recognition. IEEE Trans. Pattern Anal. Mach. Intell. **37**(9), 1904–1916 (2015)
6. Hou, Q., Zhou, D., Feng, J.: Coordinate attention for efficient mobile network design. In: Proceedings of the IEEE/CVF Conference on Computer Vision and Pattern Recognition, pp. 13713–13722 (2021)
7. Jiangtao, Y.: Research of tablet detection and recognition algorithm based on machine vision. Master's thesis, Harbin Instituteof Technology, Shenzhen (2018). (In Chinese)
8. Jinqiao, L., Wenyun, W., Kaikai, X., Caijiang, W.: Improved tablet positioning and recognition method based on mobilenetv3-small network structure. Optical Technol. **49**(01), 6 (2023). (In Chinese)
9. Kwon, H.J., Kim, H.G., Lee, S.H.: Pill detection model for medicine inspection based on deep learning. Chemosensors **10**(1), 4 (2022)
10. Lin, T.Y., Dollár, P., Girshick, R., He, K., Hariharan, B., Belongie, S.: Feature pyramid networks for object detection. In: Proceedings of the IEEE Conference on Computer Vision and Pattern Recognition, pp. 2117–2125 (2017)
11. Long, J., Shelhamer, E., Darrell, T.: Fully convolutional networks for semantic segmentation. In: Proceedings of the IEEE Conference on Computer Vision and Pattern Recognition, pp. 3431–3440 (2015)
12. O Pinheiro, P.O., Collobert, R., Dollár, P.: Learning to segment object candidates. In: Advances in Neural Information Processing Systems 28 (2015)
13. Ren, S., He, K., Girshick, R., Sun, J.: Faster R-CNN: towards real-time object detection with region proposal networks. In: Advances in Neural Information Processing Systems 28 (2015)

14. Shumin, Z.: Safety hazard analysis and preventive measures of intravenous drug dispensing center. J. Clin. Ra-tional Use **13**(23), 3 (2020). (In Chinese)
15. Xie, S., Girshick, R., Dollár, P., Tu, Z., He, K.: Aggregated residual transformations for deep neural networks. In: Proceedings of the IEEE Conference on Computer Vision and Pattern Recognition, pp. 1492–1500 (2017)

Design and Variable Parameter Control Strategy of Weight Support Gait Training Robot

Xin Li[1], Wenbo Zhang[1], Xifang Liu[2], Peng Zhang[3], and Wendong Wang[1(✉)]

[1] School of Mechanical and Electrical Engineering, Northwestern Polytechnical University, Xi'an 710072, China
wdwang@nwpu.edu.cn
[2] Department of Rehabilitation, Xi'an Honghui Hospital, Xi'an Jiaotong University, Xi'an, Shaanxi, China
[3] Training Center for Engineering Practices, Northwestern Polytechnical University, Xi'an 710072, China

Abstract. The body weight support walking training robot is a rehabilitation device used to improve the basic walking ability of the lower limbs of patients with movement disorders. In this paper, a BWS (Body weight support) system based on the principle of a series elastic actuator is designed to achieve structural passive compliance. Then the overall model and dynamic equation of the system are established. Aiming at the precision error caused by instability of weight reduction control, aging of elastomer, and various damping friction, this paper proposes a variable parameter class admittance control strategy based on the BWS system model to realize dynamic weight reduction and compensation weight reduction control effect. Finally, based on the established mathematical model, the simulation is carried out in Simulink. The maximum error of walking weight reduction is less than 5 N, which proves the effectiveness of the control strategy. At present, a preliminary experimental platform has been built, which can provide a convenient and efficient rehabilitation training method for patients with lower limb movement disorders in the future.

Keywords: Body-weight support training system · Variable parameter control · Dynamic weight support

1 Introduction

A large number of elderly people in China have cerebrovascular diseases or neurological diseases, which leads to a large number of patients with lower limb motor dysfunction [1]. The body weight support gait training system reduces the load of the patient's weight on the affected limb through the weight support device and performs walking training to improve the basic walking ability of the lower limbs [2]. It can not only provide patients with scientific and reasonable rehabilitation training but also liberate the hands of medical staff, and alleviate the shortage of medical resources. Compared with the traditional method, its advantage lies in allowing patients to actively integrate into training and improve their initiative [3]. At present, the device has become an important part of the field of clinical rehabilitation.

H. Yang et al. (Eds.): ICIRA 2023, LNAI 14273, pp. 575–587, 2023.
https://doi.org/10.1007/978-981-99-6498-7_49

In the 1980s, Finch and Barbeau proposed the weight support system, and then the weight support system developed rapidly [4]. As a reliable flexible transmission medium, the rope has small vibration and low motion inertia, so it has good human-computer interaction [5]. Therefore, the driving method based on rope traction is widely used in weight support rehabilitation robots. For example, the LOKOMAT series launched by the Swiss Federal Institute of Technology in Zurich, the National Rehabilitation Hospital of the United States has developed a single rope suspension ZeroG active weight support walking rehabilitation training system [6]. According to the different principles of weight support, the rope weight support robot is divided into two categories: passive and active weight support systems [7]. The passive system adopts a counterweight block to reduce weight, and the weight reduction fluctuation is large, so it has been gradually eliminated. Active weight reduction technology uses controllable driving sources such as motors to provide weight reduction and realizes closed-loop feedback control by obtaining actual weight reduction, to achieve relatively high weight reduction control accuracy. The Active weight support is divided into weight unloading and virtual mass unloading [8]. During the training process, the patient's center of gravity has an acceleration and deceleration in the vertical direction. Weight unloading does not consider the inertial force that must be applied to achieve walking. In the virtual mass unloading system, on the contrary, these inertial forces are considered to be the product of the main body acceleration and the expected unloading mass, and compensation control is needed [9].

At present, most of the rope-driven BWS systems use flexible bodies as buffers, but the control does not consider the aging of the flexible body and the inaccurate coefficient, resulting in low weight support accuracy. At the same time, only simple force single-loop control is carried out, and the speed is not coordinated. Control, there will be a more obvious shock problem, affecting the rehabilitation effect.

Based on the above analysis of the development status and existing problems of the weight support system, this paper designs a weight support walking training system based on rope transmission and designs the corresponding admittance variable parameter control strategy which can realize the two functions of dynamic weight support and compensation weight support to overcome the above problems. The feasibility of the scheme is verified by Simulink simulation.

2   Mechanical Structure Design of BWS System

In this paper, the weight support robot is refined into two basic functions: adaptive follow-up in the horizontal direction and multiple ways of weight support in the vertical direction. The concept diagram of the weight support system shown in Fig. 1 is proposed. The system is mainly composed of a horizontal moving unit and a vertical weight reduction unit. The vertical weight support unit follows the patient's vertical movement and provides gravity support to offset some or all of the patient's gravity. The overhead moving unit makes the vertical tension unit follow the patient's horizontal movement so that the tension of the sling is always in the opposite direction of gravity and vertically upward.

Combined with the specific rehabilitation needs, the specific weight support structure principle is designed as shown in Fig. 2.

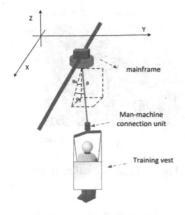

Fig. 1. Conceptual design

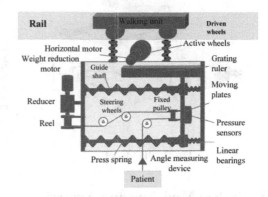

Fig. 2. BWS system structure principle.

The controller controls the weight-reducing servo motor to drive the weight-reducing rope through the drum to lift and reduce the weight of the human body. The force on the rope is indirectly collected through the spoke pressure sensor, and the closed-loop control is until the collected actual pressure reaches the weight-reducing target. At the same time, the force on the weight-reducing rope will continuously pull the plate compression spring, thus effectively preventing the sudden change of the weight-reducing rope tension caused by the fluctuation of the patient's training center of gravity, forming the passive flexibility of the structure, leaving time for the controller to respond to the correction error in time and increasing the robustness of the system. To restrain the oscillation problem in the process of moving, it is necessary to detect the speed of the moving plate. This paper chooses the grating ruler sensor to realize.

During the gait training of the patient, the weight support device needs to follow the patient and keep it above the patient at all times to prevent the force on the sling from producing a horizontal traction effect on the human body. In this paper, the corresponding horizontal mobile unit is designed to be embedded in the weight support unit in the sky rail for movement. Therefore, the swing angle measurement mechanism is designed, and the angle between the rope and the vertical direction is detected by the magnetic angle sensor as the feedback signal. With the angle as the 0-bit control target, the effect of the adaptive following can be achieved. In addition to the functional structure, the corresponding protection mechanism is designed. According to the structural principle of the design, the corresponding three-dimensional model is established and the primary experimental prototype is built as shown in Fig. 4. The controller selects the STM32 microcontroller (Fig. 3).

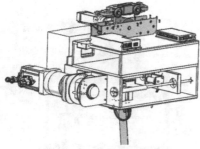

Fig. 3. 3D Model.

Fig. 4. Experimental platform.

3 System Modeling and Analysis

Figure 5 is the overall mathematical model of the system. The system has two controllers C_1 and C_2. C_1 acts on the mobile unit through the servo motor, and the mobile unit generates displacement x under the combined action of the servo motor and the horizontal component of the rope tension F_{rx}, thereby following the human body movement. The difference between the horizontal position of the mobile unit and the patient is converted into the deflection angle of the rope through the calculation of the function to simulate the angle sensor. The controller C_2 controls the force used to reduce weight in the vertical direction. The patient's movement in the vertical direction and the rotation of the rope reeling motor affect the pressure spring together so that the deformation Δs and the rope tension form a force balance.

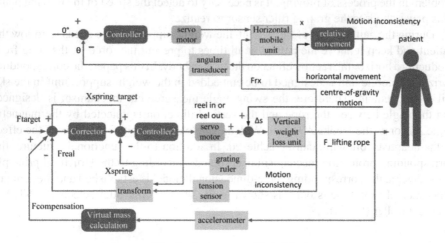

Fig. 5. System overall model.

The analysis shows that the system has strong coupling. The tension of the rope is coupled with the spring compression. At first, to control the weight reduction to achieve the goal, the motor needs to roll the lifting rope to compress the spring to the corresponding position. In the subsequent dynamic weight support, it is assumed that the patient moves downward. To maintain the weight support force unchanged, the motor needs to put the rope to make up for the human body movement distance to maintain the spring compression unchanged. Therefore, while reducing gravity, it also achieves adaptive up-and-down following of the human body.

However, if force is taken as the direct control target, it is difficult to establish the corresponding transfer function and state space equation in principle. In this paper, the idea of transforming force control into position control in admittance control is used. At the same time, based on the mathematical relationship between spring force and displacement on the structure, the control target is transformed into spring compression so that the corresponding state space equation can be established for subsequent control. In addition, the speed state of the moving plate cannot be controlled only by force, and there will be jitter problems in the control process and the target point. Therefore, speed control should also be considered in the control. In summary, this paper transforms the control objectives in the subsequent control system design.

The rope tension is also coupled with the deflection angle of the rope. The horizontal component of the rope tension will affect the displacement of the moving unit, which in turn affects the deflection angle of the rope. At the same time, the existence of the rope deflection angle will change the tension in the vertical direction of the rope in real-time. The strength of its coupling depends on the size of the rope deflection angle.

According to the structural principle and coupling analysis of the designed system, the dynamic differential equation of the weight reduction unit is established. The weight reduction unit includes a weight reduction servo motor, a reducer, a roller, and a moving plate, as shown in Figs. 6 and 7. Firstly, the rotation equation of the weight reduction motor is established.

$$T_q - T_f = J_m \ddot{\theta}_m + B_m \dot{\theta}_m \tag{1}$$

In the formula, T_q is the electromagnetic torque of the drive motor; T_f is the motor resistance torque; B_m is the viscous friction coefficient of the weight support motor; J_m is the moment of inertia of the weight reduction motor.

The rotation equation of the drum is

$$T_f i - F_r \eta R = J_b \ddot{\theta}_b + B_b \dot{\theta}_b \tag{2}$$

Taking the moving plate as the analysis object, the force analysis is carried out, as shown in Fig. 7.

$$2F_r - 2K\ddot{x} \pm f = m_l \ddot{x} \tag{3}$$

where

$$\ddot{x} = \frac{\theta_b R}{2}, \theta_m = \theta_b i \tag{4}$$

In the formula, f is the resistance of the moving plate during the movement; m_l is the quality of the hanger; $\ddot{x}$ is the displacement of the moving plate; R is the radius of the drum; i is the deceleration ratio; η is the transmission efficiency of the mobile motor.

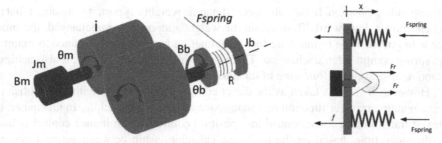

Fig. 6. Force analysis of motor module.   **Fig. 7.** Force analysis of moving plate module

For the subsequent control needs, the mathematical model of the weight reduction unit needs to be transformed into a state space equation. The speed and displacement of the moving plate are selected as the state variables, and the input is the motor torque. The following formula is obtained.

$$\dot{x} = \dot{x} \tag{5}$$

$$\ddot{x} = Ax + B\dot{x} + CT_q \tag{6}$$

where

$$A = \frac{-kR^2}{2\eta i^2 den}, B = \frac{-(B_m + B_b/\eta i^2)}{den}, C = \frac{R}{2iden} \tag{7}$$

Then the state space equation of the weight reduction unit is obtained as follows

$$\begin{bmatrix} \dot{x} \\ \ddot{x} \end{bmatrix} = \begin{bmatrix} 0 & 1 \\ A & B \end{bmatrix} \begin{bmatrix} x \\ \dot{x} \end{bmatrix} + \begin{bmatrix} 0 \\ C \end{bmatrix} T_q \tag{8}$$

Because of the discreteness of the actual system, it needs to be transformed into a discrete state. Then, to be used for embedded control, the error deformation is carried out, let $e = x_d - x$.

$$\begin{bmatrix} e(k+1) \\ \dot{x}(k+1) \end{bmatrix} = \begin{bmatrix} 1 & -\Delta t \\ -A\Delta t & 1 - B\Delta t \end{bmatrix} \begin{bmatrix} e(k) \\ \dot{x}(k) \end{bmatrix} + \begin{bmatrix} 0 \\ A\Delta tx_d \end{bmatrix} + \begin{bmatrix} 0 \\ C\Delta t \end{bmatrix} T_{q2} \tag{9}$$

To simulate the real motion of the system, the selected servo motor is modeled for subsequent simulation. The motor used in this paper is a servo motor based on a permanent magnet synchronous motor. The built-in three-loop PID algorithm controls the angular displacement, angular velocity, and current of the motor. Create a model as shown in Fig. 8.

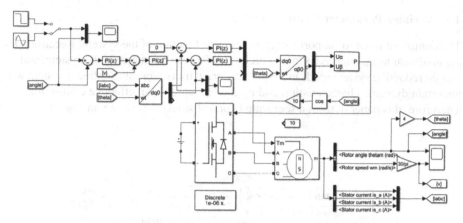

Fig. 8. Permanent magnet synchronous motor model.

4 Control Strategy

The control objectives of the system include maintaining the component of the rope tension in the vertical direction at a given value and controlling the rope to be vertical at the same time.

4.1 Follow Control Strategy

After analysis, the automatic following of the patient's movement can be transformed into a stabilization problem that makes the angle between the rope and the vertical direction 0°. Therefore, this paper designs a series PID double-loop control model, which is shown in Fig. 9.

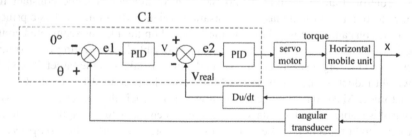

Fig. 9. Following controller.

With the angle of 0° as the control target, the rope deflection angle is measured by the angle sensor and fed back, which is input into the PID controller and output as the target electromagnetic torque of the drive motor.

582   X. Li et al.

4.2   Variable Parameter Control Strategy

The control of force to support weight is the core function of the system. Because there are nonlinear terms such as spring elasticity and friction resistance in the system, and the weight reduction system needs to adapt to different users. For this nonlinear system with uncertain dynamic characteristics, sliding mode control is an effective control method. Therefore, this paper designs a segmented control strategy as shown in Fig. 10.

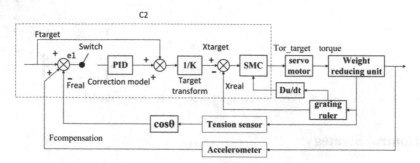

Fig. 10. Force of weight support controller.

In the system analysis section, it can be seen that the control target needs to be transformed into the spring compression distance, but this mathematical transformation is inevitably affected by factors such as stiffness error, which makes the transformed control target error. Therefore, it is necessary to collect forces for weight support to form the outer loop feedback for error compensation, that is, the PID compensator is designed, and the integral term is used to accumulate the cumulative error to modify the initial control target to eliminate the error. This is the significance of variable parameter control.

The control strategy is divided into two control modes: dynamic constant force weight reduction and virtual mass compensation weight reduction. The basic principle of dynamic constant force weight reduction is based on the idea of segmented control. At the initial stage of control, the compensator is disabled. The grating ruler signal is collected, and the target spring compression distance is taken as the target. The sliding film weight reduction algorithm is used for closed-loop control to output the motor control torque. Make the motor compression spring reach the target position. When the control is stable in the later stage, the gap between the actual weight reduction and the target weight reduction exceeds the set reasonable error range, the compensator is started. The compensator calculates the deviation between the actual and the target force for weight support, outputs the corrected spring compression target after the integral action, and then performs the position control with the front.

The virtual mass mode introduces the acceleration feedback in the vertical direction of the center of gravity of the human body based on dynamic constant weight support, calculates the virtual gravity generated during the movement, and corrects the control target. When the squat is down, the weight reduction is reduced, so that the downward acceleration is generated when the leg muscle load is constant; when standing, the same.

The design process of a discrete synovial controller is as follows. First, select the design synovial surface and synovial approach rate.

$$S(k + 1) = Pe(k + 1) + \dot{x}(k + 1) \tag{10}$$

$$\frac{S(k + 1) - S(k)}{\Delta t} = -\varepsilon \cdot sgn(S(k)) - qS(k) \tag{11}$$

In the formula, P, ε and q are the three parameters of the synovial membrane controller; sgn is a sign function.

Combining (10) and (11), we obtain

$$Pe(k + 1) + \dot{x}(k + 1) = -\varepsilon sgn(S(k))\Delta t + (1 - q\Delta t)S(k) \tag{12}$$

Substitute it into (9) to solve T. To prove the stability of the designed synovial control algorithm, the Lyapunov function is set

$$v(s) = \frac{1}{2}s^2 \tag{13}$$

Derivate it and we obtain

$$\dot{v}(s) = s \cdot \dot{s} = -\varepsilon \cdot s \cdot sgn(s) - qs^2 \tag{14}$$

By Lyapunov's second stability theorem, because v(s) > 0, < $\dot{v}$(s) 0, the system is stable.

5 Simulation Experiments and Results

5.1 Experimental Design

According to the above system mathematical model and control model, the simulation model of the BWS system is built on the Simulink platform, and the performance of the controller is tested by simulation experiments. To improve the authenticity of the simulation model, the simulation model uses the real parameters of the built physical prototype, including the structural and the parameters of the selected servo motor, as shown in Table 1.

To simulate the actual use of the weight support system, this paper uses the step signal to test the static weight support performance. A single-peak sinusoidal signal is used to simulate the squatting action, which avoids the acceleration distortion of the slope signal. By consulting the data, it is found that the normal human body's horizontal movement speed roughly satisfies the law of $v = 0.819 + 0.23sin(\frac{\pi}{0.325} t)$, and the fluctuation of the center of gravity conforms to the trend of the sine curve. Therefore, the sine curve is used to simulate the speed of the movement and the fluctuation speed of the center of gravity when the human body walks. Take these curves as the input of the model (Figs. 11 and 12).

Table 1. Simulation model system parameters.

Physical quantity	Value	Servomotor parameters	Value
Spring stiffness K	13475 N/m	Maximum torque	0.5 and 5 N/m
System quality M	40 kg	Maximum acceleration	$\pm 5 \times 10^4$ rad/s^2
Moving plate quality m	3 kg	Top speed	3000 r/min
Roller radius r	0.0355 m	Moment of inertia	1.65/0.046 kg·m^2·10^{-4}
Roller radius R	0.045 m		

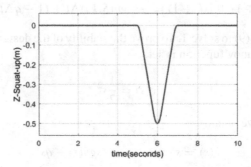

Fig. 11. The vertical position of the subject when crouching and standing up

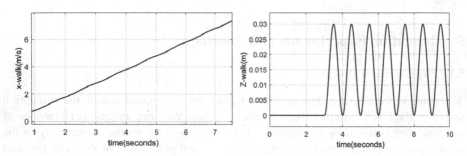

Fig. 12. The horizontal and vertical position of the subject during ground walking

5.2 Simulation Result

Figure 13 shows the control effect of the system on the deflection angle of the rope. It can be seen from the figure that during the patient's walking process, the system always controls the rope deflection angle within 4° through the designed controller. This angle error will not have a substantial impact on the training, and the adaptive tracking function is realized.

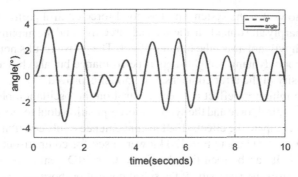

Fig. 13. The deviation angle during ground walking.

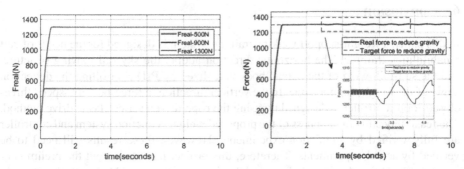

Fig. 14. The cable forces of different targets.　**Fig. 15.** The cable force during a walking Signal.

It can be seen from Fig. 14 that using three different numerical weight reduction targets to test the static weight support function, the rope tension will quickly reach the target value, and the static weight reduction steady-state error is less than 5N. Figure 15 shows that the system can provide stable and accurate weight reduction when the patient is walking, and the error does not exceed 5N.

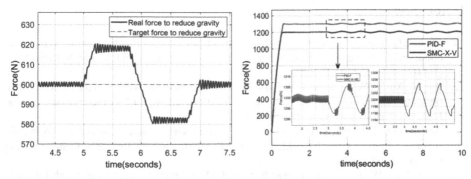

Fig. 16. The cable force in the squatting state.　　**Fig. 17.** PID and SMC

Figure 16 shows that the system still has good force control performance when the patient moves sharply and quickly in the vertical direction, and the maximum error is less than 20 N, which will not affect the training effect. The above results not only show that the system has good dynamic weight support performance but also has a small absolute error. The necessity of the error compensation model is proved.

To prove the inhibitory effect of speed control on the oscillation phenomenon, the PID single-loop control force and the synovial force-position double closed-loop control force are used to compare the effects. For the convenience of observation, similar weight support targets $F = 130$ kg and $F = 120$ kg were used for comparison. The results are shown in Fig. 17. It can be seen that the single-loop PID control oscillation is more serious, which proves the necessity of the speed control proposed above.

6 Conclusion

In this paper, a weight-support walking training system is designed for the needs of gait rehabilitation training. The horizontal direction adopts the sky rail moving structure, and the self-following of the human body is realized by PID controlling the deflection angle of the weight support rope. In the vertical direction, a force-position-speed three-closed-loop controller is designed by using the rope-driven series elastic drive method. The feasibility and effectiveness of the proposed weight reduction system and controller are fully verified by simulation experiments. However, these results still need to be verified by actual experiments. Therefore, this project has carried out the preliminary construction of the physical platform and the design of the embedded control system. In the future, the control algorithm of this paper will be applied to the experimental platform to verify the actual performance of the system and carry out clinical application research.

Acknowledgment. This work was supported by the Science and technology plan project of Xi'an city (Grant no. 21XJZZ0079) and the Innovation and Entrepreneurship Foundation of Northwestern Polytechnical University Party Committee Student Work Department (Grant No. 2023-cxcy-021).

References

1. Chen, Z.Q., Juan, H., Zhang, Y., et al.: The effect of Lokohelp robotic training on the reha-bilitation of lower extremity motor function of stroke patients. Chin. Manip. Rehabil. Med. (2016)
2. Wu, X., Xu, Z., Wang, J., et al.: An adaptive control approach of body weight support system for lower limb exoskeleton based on trajectory feedforward. In: IEEE Conference on Industrial Electronics and Applications. IEEE (2021)
3. Wei, C., Qin, T., Meng, X., et al.: Design and position servo control of an active body-weight support training system. In: IEEE International Conference on Real-time Computing and Robotics. IEEE (2021)
4. Xiao, Z., Li, W., Li, J., et al.: Research of the BWS system for lower extremity rehabilitation robot. In: International Conference on Rehabilitation Robotics, pp. 240–245. IEEE (2017)

5. Yu, N., Yang, Z., Sun, Y., Zou, W., Wang, Z.: A single rope suspension master and control method for gait and balance rehabilitation training. Acta Automatica Sinica **42**(12), 1819–1831 (2016)
6. Vallery, H, et al.: Multidirectional transparent support for overground gait training. In: Proceedings of the 2013 IEEE International Conference on Rehabilitation Robotics (ICORR), Seattle, WA, pp. 1−7. IEEE (2013)
7. Mirzaee, A., Moghadam, M.M., Saba, A.M.: Conceptual design of an active body weight support system using a linear series elastic actuator. In: 2019 7th International Conference on Robotics and Mechatronics (ICRoM) (2019)
8. Lu, Q., Liang, J., Qiao, B., et al.: A new active body weight support system capable of virtually offloading partial body mass. IEEE/ASME Trans. Mechatron. **18**(1), 11–20 (2013)
9. Sun, Y., Zhang, P., Yu, N.: A novel double-rope BWS system for locomotion training of hemiplegic patients. In: 2018 IEEE 8th Annual International Conference on CYBER Technology in Automation, Control, and Intelligent Systems (CYBER). IEEE (2018)
10. Rad, M.H., Behzadipour. S.: Design and implementation of a new body weight support (BWS) system. In: 2017 5th RSI International Conference on Robotics and Mechatronics (ICRoM) (2017)

CMM-Based Cooperative Control Strategy of Supernumerary Robotic Limbs for Human Motion

QiAo Zhan[1], Yinzhen Peng[1], Junwen Cui[1], Qingyun Xia[1], Hongqing Xie[1],
Hong Cheng[1], Hangyu Zou[2], and Jing Qiu[1]($\boxtimes$)

[1] University of Electronic Science and Technology of China,
Chengdu 611713, People's Republic of China
qiujing@uestc.edu.cn

[2] Buffalo Robotics Technology Co., Ltd., Chengdu, China

Abstract. The Supernumerary Robotic Limbs (SRL) have been proven to cooperate with the wearer to perform tasks in manufacturing domains such as aircraft assembly, mainly by providing support to the wearer through physical contact with the environment, thus reducing human energy consumption. However, current SRL control strategies cannot provide synchronous motion with the wearer's motion, which causes interference and requires the wearer to expend more energy to maintain the human-SRL system balance. Therefore, in order to meet the demand for synchronized human and SRL motion, this study proposes a centroid-momentum-matrix (CMM)-based SRL control strategy to effectively reduce the human energy consumption caused by the non-cooperative motion of the SRL with the human motion. The method indirectly controls the interaction forces and moments between the SRL and the wearer by solving a quadratic programming problem to control the rate of change of the linear and angular momentum of the SRL. Finally, experiments on the bending motion of the human trunk were conducted to validate the proposed control method by measuring the interaction forces and moments as well as the surface electromyography of the erector spinae muscles, which demonstrating the effectiveness of the proposed control method.

Keywords: Supernumerary Robotic Limbs ·
centroid-momentum-matrix-based · forces · energy consumption

1 Introduction

Neuroscientific research has demonstrated the possibility for humans to have additional limbs, thereby augmenting their operational capabilities [1, 2]. The need for strong support in labor-intensive industries, such as aircraft manufacturing, has led to the development of a wearable robot SRL as an additional limb to extend and enhance human physical capabilities. In traditional industrial settings, the SRLs can aid wearers in completing various tasks, including fixing screws [3], grabbing tools, holding wooden boards [4], thus improving work efficiency and optimizing performance [5, 6]. As the key technologies of the SRLs are gradually developed, current SRLs are able to assist wearers in completing specific tasks [3, 7].

However, it should be noted that the SRLs inevitably disturb their wearers because of their weight and non-cooperative motion while cooperating with the wearers in completing tasks. Thus, maintaining balance of the human-SRL system can result in increasing energy consumption and fatigue for the wears. Therefore, reducing the energy consumption caused by the characteristics and motion of SRL in order to enhance wearer comfort is one of the challenges faced by the current SRLs.

Researchers have investigated different motion strategies to support humans in performing tasks. Parietti and colleagues designed a bilateral SRL specifically for aircraft assembly. This device supports the human body by analyzing statics and inverse dynamics of the robot joint torque, thereby reducing the force on the human body [3]. Davenport and co-authors proposed and analyzed a biomechanical model of coupling between the wearer and a six-degree-of-freedom SRL to assist in gripping tools. This model reduces energy consumption during static load tasks [8]. Parietti et al. designed an SRL with two extra legs that provide self-balancing support to the wearer. Unlike crutches or walkers, this device enhances balance and anti-interference ability during standing and walking by using real-time kinematic and static models [9]. Kurek and Asada developed an SRL support robot for ground work specifically designed to support the wearer during this activity [10]. Parietti also investigated reducing human energy consumption by minimizing the torque required for joints during uncomfortable postures or static loads while wearing an SRL [11]. Currently, the focus of the previous studies is whether SRL can effectively complete a particular task when assisting wearers in grasping or gripping, or other tasks. However, during the performance of tasks by operators and SRLs, there may be times when SRLs are not performing a task. In the current strategy, when in task-free mode, the SRLs remain stationary relative to the human body until the next task begins. This approach fails to reduce SRLs disturbance to the human body and decrease energy consumption. Previous studies have mostly concentrated on keeping the human torso stationary with respect to the environment [3, 8] and reducing the force on the human body through the interaction of the SRL and the environment to generate a reaction force. However, few studies have addressed reducing the disturbance exerted by dynamic movement of the SRL on the human body.

Hence, in order to reduce the forces exerted on the human body by the SRL because of the motion of the wearer's torso and to increase the stability of the human-SRL system. a momentum control method based on the Centroidal Momentum Matrix (CMM) of the SRL is proposed.

This manuscript is organized as follows: Sect. 2 introduces the momentum control method based on CMM used to reduce the interference of the external limb on the human body in the task-free mode. Section 3 presents the experimental data and results obtained on both the Mujoco simulation platform and the SRL platform. Finally, Sect. 4 summarizes the entire article and proposes suggestions for future work.

2 Method

This study proposed the use of a CMM-based control strategy framework as shown in Fig. 1 to decrease the energy consumption needed to maintain balance in the human-machine system during the motion of the SRL. The framework comprises three primary components. The first is the control system for the SRL. The second is the decision-making module that executes the corresponding task control algorithm when the SRL is assigned a task and applies a momentum-based control algorithm when the SRL is in a task-free mode. Finally, the momentum-based control algorithm aims to perform adaptive motion for human motion during the task-free mode. In this algorithm, the forward kinematics of the SRL were calculated based on the joint angle, angular velocity, and torque data from the SRL joint motor, as well as the angle, angular velocity, and angular acceleration of the human torso, which were collected in real-time by an IMU. The previous algorithms from [12–14] were used to obtain the CMM and its first derivative with respect to time. The ideal joint angle acceleration was then determined through linear and nonlinear quadratic optimization to meet user-defined criteria. Finally, the joint angle, joint angular velocity, joint angle acceleration, and related information were input into the inverse dynamics calculation module, which computed the joint torque (u) by using Inverse Dynamics. This torque (u) was then utilized to control the adaptive motion of the SRL system.

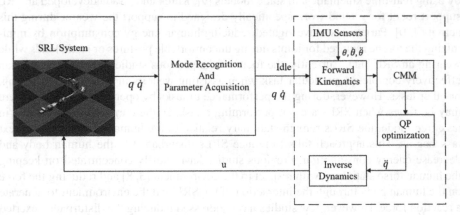

Fig. 1. SRL control based on Centroidal Momentum Matrix

The dynamic analysis of the SRL is shown in Eq. (1) below:

$$f = mg - ma \tag{1}$$

where f is the force exerted by the human torso, g is the acceleration from gravity, m is the SRL's total mass, and a is the combined external limb acceleration. With no external forces, the SRL's linear and angular momentum (L and H) are conserved. Hence, the forces and torques applied to the SRL can be approximated as generalized changes in momentum (linear and angular). Therefore, when there are no external disturbances, the SRL's momentum changes only due to the combination of human forces and gravity. To that end, the momentum balance equations for the SRL are given by Eqs. (2) and (3):

$$\dot{L} = mg + f \tag{2}$$

$$\dot{H} = s \times f \tag{3}$$

where L is the rate of change of linear momentum of the SRL, while H is the rate of change of angular momentum of the SRL, m is the mass of the SRL, s is the distance from the Center of Mass (COM) to the Center of Press (COP).

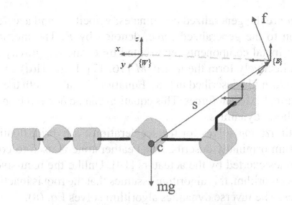

Fig. 2. The linkage diagram of the SRL.

Figure 2 illustrates the simulation model of the SRL. The COM of the SRL is denoted by c and the center of the external force applied by the human body on the SRL is denoted by p. Hence, the vector distance from p to c is denoted by s. For the ith rigid body, the linear momentum, L_i, is defined as $L_i = m_i v_i$, where m_i is the mass of that rigid body. The total momentum of the articulated body, L, is calculated as the summation of the momentum of each individual object, i.e., $L = \sum_{i=1}^{n} m_i v_i$ and its derivative. Alternatively, L can also be defined as $L = m\dot{c}$ and $L = m\ddot{c}$, where m represents the summation of all the masses of the individual objects. Therefore, controlling the derivative of the linear momentum can be equated with controlling the COM acceleration [15]. Furthermore, Eq. 2 explains that if there is no force acting on the SRL other than f, the control of $\dot{L}$ can be equated with the control of f, which represents the external force applied by the human body on the SRL, taking into account the current state of the SRL (i.e., identifying the point "c"). Equation 3 establishes that it is possible to achieve both angular and linear momentum control through the manipulation of COM and the COP, as well as torque.

The centroidal momentum matrix, Ag, which is also referred to as the CMM, can be calculated as shown in Eqs. (4) and (5):

$$hg = Ag\,\dot{q} \tag{4}$$

$$\dot{hg} = \dot{Ag} * \dot{q} + Ag * \ddot{q} \tag{5}$$

where, $hg = [LH]^T$ represents the centroidal spatial momentum of the SRL, and $\dot{q}$ and $\ddot{q}$ are the joint velocity and acceleration, respectively. From Eqs. (1), (2), (3), (4), and (5), we can derive Eq. (6):

$$\begin{bmatrix} f \\ \dot{H} \end{bmatrix} = \begin{bmatrix} \dot{L} - mg \\ k \end{bmatrix} = [Ag\ Ag] \begin{bmatrix} \dot{q} \\ \ddot{q} \end{bmatrix} - mg \tag{6}$$

The equation representing the motion of the SRL in matrix form is displayed as Eq. (7):

$$F = M(\theta)\ddot{\theta} + C(\theta, \dot{\theta}) + G(\theta) \tag{7}$$

where θ, $\dot{\theta}$, and $\ddot{\theta}$ are the generalized coordinates, velocities, and accelerations, respectively, in addition to the generalized force, denoted by F. The inertia matrix M, the Coriolis and centripetal components represented by C and the gravity component represented by G collectively form the matrix M [16, 17]. Here, H(q) and C(q, $\dot{q}$) can be calculated via the formula described in [18]. Equation (7) takes both the u and f input, as well as any additional external forces. This equation can be derived from the Lagrangian formula of rigid body dynamics.

Once the optimization solves for the accelerations, a hybrid, floating-base inverse dynamics algorithm originally described by Featherstone is used to convert the accelerations into torques exerted by the actuators [19]. Unlike the recursive Newton-Euler inverse dynamics algorithm, this algorithm assumes that the root is inactive and produces consistent torques. The inverse dynamics algorithm solves Eq. (8):

$$u = M(\theta)\ddot{\theta} + C(\theta, \dot{\theta}) + G(\theta) + J^T f \tag{8}$$

The internal joint torque, denoted by u, is affected only by the force vector of the trunk (f) acting on the SRL. Therefore, no other external forces are considered. Additionally, the Jacobian matrix's transpose (J^T) is used, $J(\theta) = [\frac{\partial \theta}{\partial \hat{x}}]$.

The control laws used in this study are expressed as quadratic optimization.

$$\min_{X} \|AX - mg + CX\|$$
$$subject\ to\ lb \leq X \leq ub$$
$$0 \leqslant J\dot{q} \leqslant 0.2 \tag{9}$$

where, $A = (\dot{A}g\ Ag)$ and $X = (\dot{q}\ddot{q})^T$. Here C is the weighting matrix used to adjust the weight of linear and angular momentum rate in the quadratic optimization. Equation (9) shows the Jacobian matrix used to calculate the end-effector spatial velocity of the SRL and constrain its velocity. The range of X is determined based on the constraints of our actual SRL system to ensure consistency with the real-world.

3 Experiments and Discussion

3.1 Simulations

The aim of this experiment was to validate the proposed algorithm's effectiveness by optimizing the overall momentum, which included angular momentum and linear momentum of the SRL, and to reduce the interaction forces and torques between the SRL and the wearer. A simulation model of the SRL was built using the open-source physics engine Mujoco, and the motion data of human trunk were used to create a simulated environment that mimics human movement. To validate the algorithm's performance, the interaction forces and torques between the wearer and the SRL were analyzed in this study.

1) Experimental Setup

A simulation model was developed using Mujoco by that involved a three-dimensional representation of the SRL and a URDF file, illustrated in Fig. 3(a). The simulation SRL model consisted of six rotational joints, six degrees of freedom, and weight approximately 5.2 kg, as show in Fig. 3(b).

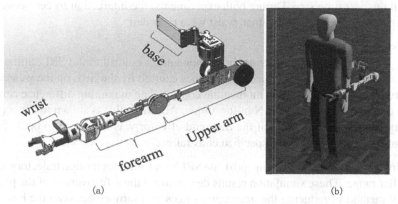

(a)   (b)

Fig. 3. (a) The three-dimensional representation of the SRL; (b) Simulation model of the SRL

The Xsens MTw Awinda series IMU sensors, demonstrated in Fig. 4(a), were utilized to mimic human movement in the simulated environment by detecting the motion state of the human body. To measure the bending angle, angular velocity, and angular acceleration of the trunk, the IMU sensors were fastened to the L5 spinal area of the body, as shown in Fig. 4(b).

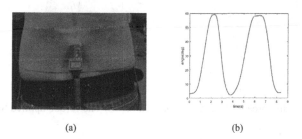

(a)   (b)

Fig. 4. (a) IMU wearing; (b) Trunk bending angle

The experimental procedure of the participant was as follows: Initially, the participant started in a stationary standing position. Once the experiment began, their upper body tilted forward as the right hand reaches out to grab a screwdriver from a table in front. Afterward, the participant returned to the stationary standing position. The process was repeated twice. The collected trajectory of the human trunk motion served as the input for the base end of the external limb system so that the motion trajectory of the SRL's base's end aligned with that of the human trunk.

The simulation verification was performed through two sets of experiments. In the first set, the SRL remained stationary with respect to the upper body of the human. In the second set, the motion planning algorithm presented in this paper was implemented on the SRL. At each time step of the simulation, the CMM was calculated, and the desired joint angular accelerations of the SRL were determined. These values were then used in inverse dynamic calculations to compute the required joint torques for the joints of the SRL in the next time step. During both experiments, the interaction forces between the base end of the SRL and the human waist were recorded.

2) Results and Discussion

As shown in Fig. 5, after applying momentum control to the SRL, utilizing this method reduced both the forces and torques exerted by the SRL on the wearer compared with the case without momentum control. The maximum difference can reach up to 2 N for force and 1.5 N·m for torque. Additionally, as shown in Fig. 6(a), the maximum spatial velocity of the SRL end-effector was measured to be 0.153 m/s, complying with within the specified constraints.

Moreover, as illustrated in Fig. 6(b), the SRL's end-effector motion trajectory showed a smaller range. These simulation results demonstrate the effectiveness of the proposed control method in reducing the interaction forces and torques between the base of the SRL and the wearer, indicating the reduction in disturbance caused by the SRL on the human body.

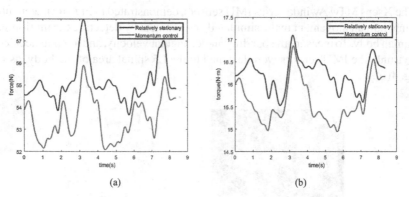

(a)   (b)

Fig. 5. (a) The force of the SRL on the wearer; (b) The torque applied to the SRL

3.2 Experiments on the SLR System

1) Experimental Setup:

The SRL system, used in this study, consists of the SRL structure, a control unit, and several communication lines. The control unit employed an Intel NUC11TNKi5 computer with a 2.4 GHz processor to meet the necessary performance requirements for SRL system control. The SRL comprised six rotational degrees of freedom, three at the base end and three at the end effector, as shown in Fig. 7.

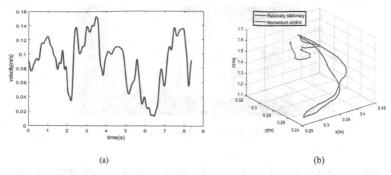

(a)   (b)

Fig. 6. (a) Speed at the end of the SRL; (b) Spatial trajectory of the end of the SRL

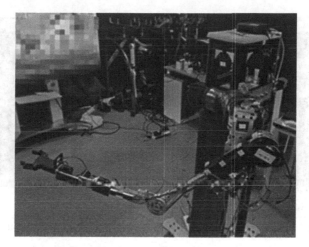

Fig. 7. The SRL system.

The angle, angular velocity, and angular acceleration of the human L5 spine were measured, using IMU sensors, as in the simulation experiments and taken as input for the SRL's base. Nonetheless, measuring the interaction forces between the wearer and the SRL accurately posed certain inherent limitations. Hence, this verification experiment, as demonstrated in Fig. 8, employed surface electromyography (sEMG) using Noraxon's muscle activity monitoring system to assess the magnitude of forces and torques exerted by the SRL on the human body.

Two sets of tests were performed to experimentally verify the effectiveness of the proposed control method on the SRL, one with the SRL stationary relative to the trunk and the other with the SRL being controlled based on momentum. The interval between the two sets of tests was 30 min to confirm that the wearer's muscles were in a normal non-fatigued state. In both cases, the wearer started by standing still after wearing the SRL. When the experiment began, the individual tilted their upper body and reached out their right hand to pick up a screwdriver from the table shown in front of them. Afterward, the wearer resumed the stationary standing position as shown in Fig. 9.

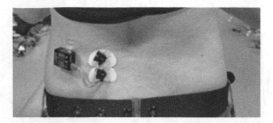

Fig. 8. The EMGs wearing

The electromyographic signals generated by the wearer's erector spinae muscles were recorded throughout the tests.

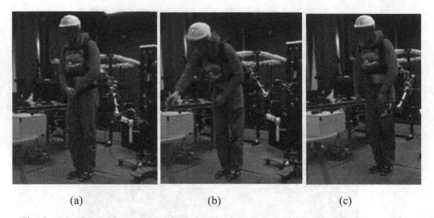

| (a) | (b) | (c) |

Fig. 9. (a) The stationary position; (b) Tilt forward; (c) back to stationary position

The sEMG signal is a bioelectric signal which is recorded from the surface of muscles with the help of electrodes. It reflects the neuromuscular activity and is correlated to varying degrees with the activity state of muscles. The sEMG signal was processed by first applying denoising techniques to eliminate noise introduced by the surrounding electronic devices and other sources. The next step involved a full-wave rectification technique applied to obtain the absolute value of the sEMG signal. Finally, a linear envelope extraction was performed on the rectified sEMG signal to enable subsequent processing for feature extraction. The root mean square (RMS) value of the sEMG signal was directly proportional to the energy of the surface electromyographic signal which can indicate changes in the signal's amplitude. A higher RMS value of the sEMG signal indicates greater muscle force. The RMS value is calculated using the following formula:

$$RMS = \sqrt{\frac{\sum_{i=0}^{N} Data[i]^2}{N}} \tag{10}$$

2) Results and Discussion

The experimental results, as shown in Fig. 10, demonstrate that the use of the momentum-based control strategy for the SRL leaded to a decrease in overall muscle strength of the erector spinae muscles compared to when the SRL was stationary relative to the body. In addition, the RMS value of the sEMG signal was also smaller. These findings indicate that the proposed control method can generate coordinated movements between the SRL and the human body, thus decreasing the disturbance imposed on the human body by the SRL while also reducing the wearer's energy expenditure.

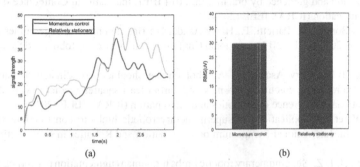

(a)   (b)

Fig. 10. (a) sEMG of the erector spinalis muscle; (b) RMS value of the sEMG

The results of both simulation experiments and physical experiments indicate the effectiveness of the proposed control strategy in reducing the disruption caused by the SRL to the human body. This was achieved by measuring the interaction forces between the SRL base and the wearer, as well as the surface electromyographic signals of the wearer's erector spinae muscles. The findings provide empirical support for the feasibility of the strategy in mitigating the impact of the SRL on the wearer.

4   Conclusion and Future Work

In this paper, a momentum-based control method was proposed to minimize the disturbance of the SRL to the human body when it is driven by the motion of the human torso in task-free situations. This approach provides a basis for minimizing human disturbance caused by the SRL during motion. Future studies should explore integrating the proposed method into the expected trajectory of the SRL during task performance to minimize its disturbance to the human body.

Acknowledgments. This work was supported in part by Sichuan key research and development program (No. 2021YFS0016), in part by the National Key Research and Development Program of China (No. 2018AAA010 2504), in part by the National Natural Science Foundation of China (NSFC) (No. 62003073, No. 62203089), in part by the Sichuan Science and Technology Program (No. 2021ZDYF3828, No. 2022NSFSC0890, No. 2021YFS0016), in part by the Fundamental Research Funds for the Central Universities (ZYGX2022YGRH003, ZY GX2021YGLH003), and in part by the China Postdoctoral Science Foundation (No. 2021M700695).

References

1. Guterstam, A., Petkova, V.I., Henrik Ehrsson, H.: The illusion of owning a third arm. PLoS ONE **6**(2), e17208 (2011)
2. Botvinick, M., Cohen, J.: Rubber hands 'feel' touch that eyes see. Nature **391**(6669), 756 (1998)
3. Parietti, F., Harry Asada, H.: Supernumerary robotic limbs for aircraft fuselage assembly: body stabilization and guidance by bracing. In: 2014 IEEE International Conference on Robotics and Automation (ICRA). IEEE (2014)
4. Llorens-Bonilla, B., Parietti, F., Harry Asada, H.: Based control of supernumerary robotic limbs. In: 2012 IEEE/RSJ International Conference on Intelligent Robots and Systems. IEEE (2012)
5. Bonilla, B.L., Harry Asada, H.: A robot on the shoulder: coordinated human-wearable robot control using coloured petri nets and partial least squares predictions In: 2014 IEEE International Conference on Robotics and Automation (ICRA). IEEE (2014)
6. Seo, W., et al.: Applications of supernumerary robotic limbs to construction works: case studies. In: International Symposium on Automation and Robotics in Construction, vol. 33 (2016)
7. 7. Bright, L.L.Z.: Supernumerary robotic limbs for human augmentation in overhead assembly tasks. Diss. Massachusetts Institute of Technology (2017)
8. Davenport, C., Parietti, F., Harry Asada, H.: Design and biomechanical analysis of supernumerary robotic limbs. In: Dynamic Systems and Control Conference, vol. 45295. American Society of Mechanical Engineers (2012)
9. Parietti, F., et al.: Design and control of supernumerary robotic limbs for balance augmentation. In: 2015 IEEE International Conference on Robotics and Automation (ICRA). IEEE (2015)
10. Kurek, D.A., Harry Asada, H.: The MantisBot: design and impedance control of supernumerary robotic limbs for near-ground work. In: 2017 IEEE International Conference on Robotics and Automation (ICRA). IEEE (2017)
11. Parietti, F., Asada, H.: Supernumerary robotic limbs for human body support. IEEE Trans. Robot. **32**(2), 301–311 (2016)
12. Orin, D.E., Goswami, A., Lee, S.-H.: Centroidal dynamics of a humanoid robot. Auton. Robot. **35**, 161–176 (2013)
13. Orin, D.E., Goswami, A.: Centroidal momentum matrix of a humanoid robot: Structure and properties. In: 2008 IEEE/RSJ International Conference on Intelligent Robots and Systems. IEEE (2008)
14. Wensing, P.M., Orin, D.E.: Improved computation of the humanoid centroidal dynamics and application for whole-body control. Int. J. Humanoid Robot. **13**(01), 1550039 (2016)
15. Macchietto, A., Zordan, V., Shelton, C.R.: Momentum control for balance. In: ACM SIGGRAPH 2009 Papers, pp. 1–8 (2009)
16. Featherstone, R.: Rigid Body Dynamics Algorithms. Springer, New York (2014)
17. Featherstone, R., Orin, D.: Robot dynamics: equations and algorithms. In: Proceedings 2000 ICRA. Millennium Conference. IEEE International Conference on Robotics and Automation. Symposia Proceedings (Cat. No. 00CH37065), vol. 1. IEEE (2000)
18. Siciliano, B., Khatib, O., Kröger, T. (eds.) Springer Handbook of Robotics, vol. 200. Springer, Berlin (2008). https://doi.org/10.1007/978-3-540-30301-5
19. Featherstone, R.: Robot Dynamics Algorithms. Kluwer Academic Publishers, Boston (1987)

Author Index

H. Yang et al. (Eds.): ICIRA 2023, LNAI 14273, pp. 599–601, 2023.
https://doi.org/10.1007/978-981-99-6498-7

Printed in the United States
by Baker & Taylor Publisher Services